Windows NT™
Resource Guide

D1318574

Microsoft® WINDOWS NT
RESOURCE KIT

*For Windows NT Workstation and
Windows NT Server Version 3.5*

PUBLISHED BY
Microsoft Press
A Division of Microsoft Corporation
One Microsoft Way
Redmond, Washington 98052-6399

Library of Congress Cataloging-in-Publication Data pending.
Printed and bound in the United States of America.

1 2 3 4 5 6 7 8 9   QMQM   0 9 8 7 6 5

Distributed to the book trade in Canada by Macmillan of Canada, a division of Canada Publishing
Corporation.

A CIP catalogue record for this book is available from the British Library.

Microsoft Press books are available through booksellers and distributors worldwide. For further
information about international editions, contact your local Microsoft Corporation office. Or
contact Microsoft Press International directly at fax (206) 936-7329.

3Com, EtherLink, and EtherLink II are registered trademarks of 3Com Corporation. Adaptec is a trademark
of Adaptec Inc. Adobe, Adobe Type Manager, ATM, and PostScript are registered trademarks of Adobe
Systems, Inc. ALR is a registered trademark of Advanced Logic Research, Inc. Matrix is a registered
trademark and Type Director is a trademark of Agfa Corporation. Aldus and PageMaker are registered
trademarks of Aldus Corporation. AT&T is a registered trademark of American Telephone & Telegraph
Company. Apple, AppleShare, AppleTalk, LaserWriter, LocalTalk, Macintosh, and TrueType are registered
trademarks of Apple Computer, Inc. Archive is a registered trademark of Archive Corporation. AST is a
registered trademark of AST Research, Inc. Banyan and VINES are registered trademarks of Banyan
Systems, Inc. Lucida is a registered trademark of Bigelow & Holmes. Bitstream and Facelift are registered
trademarks and Fontware is a trademark of Bitstream, Inc. The Fontware mark is licensed to Bitstream, Inc.,
in the U.K., France, and Germany by Electronic Print Systems Ltd. ObjectVision and Quattro are registered
trademarks of Borland International, Inc. Brother is a registered trademark of Brother Industries, Ltd. C. Itoh
is a registered trademark of C. Itoh & Co. Canon is a registered trademark of Canon USA, Inc. Porta-Drive
is a trademark of C D Technology. Chinon is a registered trademark of Chinon Industries, Inc. COMPAQ,
DESKPRO, and SystemPro are registered trademarks and NetFlex is a trademark of COMPAQ Computer
Corporation. CompuAdd is a registered trademark of CompuAdd Corporation. CompuServe is a registered
trademark of CompuServe, Inc. Sound Blaster is a trademark of Creative Labs, Inc. Data General is a
registered trademark of Data General Corporation. ArcNet is a registered trademark of Datapoint Corporation. DCA is a trademark of Digital Communications Associates, Inc. Dell is a registered trademark of Dell
Computer Corporation. Digiboard is a registered trademark of Digi International, Inc. DEC and VMS are
registered trademarks and Alpha AXP, DECnet, Pathworks, and VT 100 are trademarks of Digital Equipment Corporation. Truespeech is a trademark of DSP Group, Inc. Kodak is a registered trademark of
Eastman Kodak Company. Everex is a trademark of Everex Systems, Inc. Fujitsu is a registered trademark
of Fujitsu Limited. Future Domain is a registered trademark of Future Domain Corporation. Gateway 2000 is
a registered trademark of Gateway 2000, Inc. GRiD is a registered trademark of GRiD Systems. SQLBase is
a registered trademark of Gupta Technologies, Inc. Hayes is a registered trademark of Hayes Microcomputer

continued on page 846

This book is dedicated to all the hardworking Windows NT writers, editors, reviewers, and numerous production staff people at Microsoft that make books like this possible. Thank you!

Contributors to this book include the following:

Technical Writers:
Greg Bailey, David Collins, Chris Dragich, Peggy Etchevers, Jim Groves, John Jacobs, Sharon Kay, Gary McGinnis, Sonia Marie Moore, Doralee Moynihan, Annie Pearson, Jim Purcell, Laura Sheppard

Technical Consultants:
Ty Carlson, Glen Clark, Ray Cort, Tom Hazel, Caribe Malo (the Windows NT Corporate Technology Team), Keith Moore, and numerous Windows NT Developers and Product Support Specialists

Technical Editor:
Sonia Marie Moore

Project Lead:
Peggy Etchevers

Indexer:
Jane Dow

Production Team:
Karye Cattrell, Yong Ok Chung, and Cathy Pfarr

Graphic Designer:
Sue Wyble

Graphic Artists:
Gwen Grey, Elizabeth Read, and Stephen Winard

Contents

PART I   About Windows NT

PART II   Setting up Windows NT

PART IV   Windows NT Registry

PART V   Migration and Compatibility

PART VI Troubleshooting

PART VII Appendixes

Figures and Tables

Figures

Tables

Introduction

Welcome to the *Microsoft Windows NT Resource Kit Volume 1: Windows NT Resource Guide.*

The *Windows NT Resource Kit* also includes the following volumes:

- *Volume 2: Windows NT Networking Guide*, which provides more specific information on Windows NT networking, TCP/IP, and the Internet.
- *Volume 3: Windows NT Messages*, which provides information on local and remote debugging and on interpreting error messages.
- *Volume 4: Optimizing Windows NT*, which provides a step-by-step approach to understanding all the basic performance management techniques.

The *Windows NT Resource Guide* is designed for people who are, or who want to become, expert users of Microsoft® Windows NT™ Workstation and Microsoft Windows NT Server. The book presents detailed, easy-to-read technical information to help you better manage how Windows NT is used at your site. It contains specific information for system administrators who are responsible for installing, managing, and integrating Windows NT in a network or multiuser environment.

The *Windows NT Resource Guide* is a technical supplement to the documentation included as part of the Windows NT product and does not replace that information as the source for learning how to use Windows NT features and utilities.

This introduction includes three kinds of information you can use to get started:

- The first section outlines the contents of this book, so that you can quickly find technical details about specific elements of Windows NT.
- The second section introduces the *Windows NT Resource Kit* CD and disks.
- The third section describes the conventions used to present information in this book.

About the Resource Guide

This guide includes the following chapters. Additional tables of contents are included in each part to help you quickly find the information you want.

Part I, About Windows NT

Chapter 1, "Windows NT Architecture," describes the architecture of Windows NT and discusses the components of its modular design.

Chapter 2, "Windows NT Security Model," describes in detail the security architecture for Windows NT. This security architecture is pervasive throughout the entire operating system, from logon security to access control for files, directories, printers, and other resources on the system.

Part II, Setting Up Windows NT

Chapter 3, "Customizing Windows NT Setup," contains a technical discussion of the Windows NT Setup program, details about setting up Windows NT on a network, and instructions for creating a custom installation and for using automated setup.

Chapter 4, "Windows NT Files," describes the purpose of each file in the Windows NT directory structure. It also provides tips for freeing hard disk space and memory by deleting components that are not essential to the operation of Windows NT.

Part III, Using Windows NT

Chapter 5, "Windows NT File Systems and Advanced Disk Management," describes the three main file systems supported by Windows NT—the file allocation table (FAT), the high-performance file system (HPFS), and the Windows NT file system (NTFS). This chapter also describes how to organize and safeguard data on disk using Windows NT disk-management techniques.

Chapter 6, "Printing," presents the components of the Windows NT printing model and describes some advanced printing features you can use.

Chapter 7, "Fonts," examines technical issues related to fonts, focusing on TrueType, the font technology available in Windows NT. This chapter also presents details about using printer fonts with specific types of printers, and using Adobe Type 1 fonts.

Chapter 8, "Microsoft Mail," presents information about the Microsoft Mail application provided with Windows NT. This chapter describes the architecture of Mail and tips for customizing Mail.

Chapter 9, "Microsoft Schedule+," presents information about the Microsoft Schedule+ application provided with Windows NT, including architecture and key features of interest to system administrators.

Part IV, Windows NT Registry

Chapter 10, "Overview of the Windows NT Registry," describes the Windows NT Registry, which replaces the configuration files used with MS-DOS® and the .INI files used with Microsoft Windows® for MS-DOS.

Chapter 11, "Registry Editor and Registry Administration," describes what Registry Editor is and how to use it, with an emphasis on protecting the Registry contents and using Registry Editor to monitor and maintain the system configuration on remote computers.

Chapter 12, "Configuration Management and the Registry," provides some examples of problem-solving tasks that involve changes made to the Registry using Registry Editor.

Chapter 13, "Initialization Files and the Registry," describes how .INI files and other configuration files are used under Windows NT and how these values are stored in the Registry.

Chapter 14, "Registry Value Entries," identifies the Registry entries that you can add or change using the Registry Editor to configure system startup, network adapter cards, device drivers, services, Mail and Schedule+, user preferences, fonts and printing, and the Windows NT subsystems.

Part V, Migration and Compatibility

Chapter 15, "Windows 3.x Compatibility," presents issues for running versions of Microsoft Windows for MS-DOS under Windows NT and describes how that subsystem is implemented.

Chapter 16, "OS/2 Compatibility," describes how to run Microsoft OS/2 1.*x* applications under Windows NT and also presents the related application programming interface (API) and implementation of the OS/2® subsystem.

Chapter 17, "POSIX Compatibility," describes how to run POSIX applications and also presents information about POSIX conformance and the implementation of this subsystem under Windows NT.

Part VI, Troubleshooting

Chapter 18, "Troubleshooting," provides specific information for trouble-shooting problems, showing the key steps for isolating and solving common problems with software and hardware under Windows NT.

Part VII, Appendixes

Appendix A, "Windows NT Resource Directory," provides a list of resources for product support, training, and consulting for Windows NT, plus information about related Microsoft Press books and the Windows NT Driver Library.

Appendix B, "Windows NT User Rights," describes the advanced user rights defined by Windows NT.

Appendix C, "International Considerations," describes Unicode™ support in Windows NT, plus information about supported locales, code pages, and national language support (NLS) information for the subsystems.

Appendix D, "Hardware Compatibility List," presents a list of the tested hardware that is compatible with Windows NT, including microprocessors, small computer system interface (SCSI) adapters and drives, disk controllers, video displays, network adapters, audio adapters, modems, pointing devices, uninterruptible power supplies, keyboards, and printers.

The **Glossary** presents a rich set of definitions for the technical terms that appear in the *Windows NT Resource Guide* and the *Windows NT Networking Guide*.

Resource Kit Compact Disc

The compact disc (CD) that accompanies the *Windows NT Resource Kit* is bound into the back cover of the *Windows NT Resource Guide*, but contains utilities that also apply to information in the *Windows NT Networking Guide*. This CD includes a collection of information resources, tools, and utilities that can make networking and working with Windows NT even easier. 3.5-inch floppy disks are also available upon request. See the final page of the *Windows NT Resource Guide* for a coupon explaining how to obtain them from MS-Press.

The Windows NT Messages database and the utilities for *Optimizing Windows NT* are included on both the *Windows NT Resource Kit* CD and on 3.5-inch floppy disks bound into the back covers of their respective books.

The *Windows NT Resource Kit* CD includes the following kinds of tools. A complete list of all the tools in the *Windows NT Resource Kit* is available on the CD in the README.WRI file with instructions on how to use them in the RKTOOLS.HLP file.

Administrative Tools

- Windows NT Domain Planner (OLPG.EXE) is a Wizard that helps you plan and implement the most effective domain model for your networked organization. The Wizard prompts you for information about the resources on your network and how you want to manage them. It then recommends a domain model and provides a printed report with instructions on how to implement this domain model. It does not help plan your network topology, nor can it replace an experienced network administrator or consultant.

- DNS Service provides a static DNS server and a dynamic DNS to WINS (and vice versa) service.

- EMWAC Internet utilities, including WWW, GOPHER, WAIS servers, and WAIS tool.

- Net Watcher (NETWATCH.EXE) shows who is connected to shared directories.

- PERMS.EXE displays a user's access permissions to a specified file or set of files.

- POSIX utilities, including CAT.EXE, CHMOD.EXE, GREP.EXE, VI.EXE, and others.

- Command Scheduler (WINAT.EXE) enables you to schedule commands and programs easily to run at a specified time and date.

- REMOTECMD Service enables you to start and control command-line programs remotely and with Windows NT authentification.

Desktop Tools

- Animated Cursor Editor (ANIEDIT.EXE) creates animated cursors.

- Access Pack provides accessibility tools for people with disabilities.

- TopDesk (TOPDESK.EXE) provides a powerful virtual desktop that allows for switching between and organizing applications while conserving screen space.

- Image Editor (IMAGEDIT.EXE) enables you to edit or create cursor and icon images.

File System Tools

- DIRUSE.EXE shows disk space usage.

- SCOPY.EXE copies files and directories with their security intact.

- WINDIFF.EXE graphically shows the difference between two files or directories.

Performance and System Monitoring Tools

- Performance Monitor Service enables Performance Monitor to run without requiring a logon.

- Browser Monitor (BROWMON.EXE) enables you to check the status of browsers on selected domains.

- Domain Monitor (DOMMON.EXE) enables you to check the status of servers in a domain.

- Process Viewer (PVIEWER.EXE) displays everything you want to know about running processes.

- QuickSlice (QSLICE.EXE) shows the total CPU used by each process in the system.

- SMBTRACE.EXE, a network diagnostic tool that traces Server Message Blocks (SMBs) sent and received by the server and redirector.

Registry Tools

- REGBACK.EXE and REGREST.EXE, used to back up and restore Registry hives without the use of a tape drive.

- REGENTRY.HLP, a database of Registry entries. Use this Help file while working in Registry Editor to find ranges, minimum-maximum values, and instructions for setting specific values in the Registry. This file may also contain entries that did not make it into the printed version in the *Windows NT Resource Guide* due to publication deadlines.

- Registry Settings (REGKEY.EXE) provides a graphical way to set several of the new Registry settings without actually editing the Registry. Its main focus is on logon settings and turning long filename support off and on in FAT.

Setup and Troubleshooting Tools

- Computer Profile Setup for easy installation of Windows NT on multiple computers that are all configured the same.

- SETUPAPP.EXE creates a response file for customized versions of Windows NT Setup.

- NTCARD.HLP assists you in the Setup of adapter cards for Windows NT.

How To Find and Use These Tools and Utilities

The following procedures help you to find and use these items:

▶ **To see a list of the files and installation instructions**

- See the README.WRI file on the CD or first floppy disk.

▶ **To find out how to use a tool or utility**

- See the RKTOOLS.HLP file on the CD or first floppy disk.

Conventions in This Manual

This document assumes that you have read the Windows NT documentation set and that you are familiar with using menus, dialog boxes, and other features of the Windows operating system family of products. It also assumes that you have installed Windows NT on your system and that you are using a mouse. For keyboard equivalents to menu and mouse actions, see the Microsoft Windows NT online Help.

This document uses several conventions to help you identify information. The following table describes the typographical conventions used in the *Windows NT Resource Guide*.

Convention	Used for
bold	MS-DOS–style command and utility names such as **copy** or **ping** and switches such as **/?** or **-h**. Also used for Registry value names, such as **IniFileMapping** and OS/2 application programming interfaces (APIs).
italic	Parameters for which you can supply specific values. For example, the Windows NT root directory appears in a path name as *systemroot*\SYSTEM32, where *systemroot* can be C:\WINNT35 or some other value.
ALL CAPITALS	Directory names, filenames, and acronyms. For example, DLC stands for Data Link Control; C:\PAGEFILE.SYS is a file in the boot sector.
Monospace	Sample text from batch and .INI files, Registry paths, and screen text in non-Windows–based applications.

Other conventions in this document include the following:

- "MS-DOS" refers to Microsoft MS-DOS version 3.3 or later.

- "Windows-based application" is used as a shorthand term to refer to an application that is designed to run with 16-bit Windows and does not run without Windows. All 16-bit and 32-bit Windows applications follow similar conventions for the arrangement of menus, dialog box styles, and keyboard and mouse use.

- "MS-DOS–based application" is used as a shorthand term to refer to an application that is designed to run with MS-DOS but not specifically with Windows or Windows NT and is not able to take full advantage of their graphical or memory management features.

- "Command prompt" refers to the command line where you type MS-DOS–style commands. Typically, you see characters such as C:\> to show the location of the command prompt on your screen. In Windows NT, you can double-click the MS-DOS Prompt icon in Program Manager to use the command prompt.

- An instruction to "type" any information means to press a key or a sequence of keys, and then press the ENTER key.

- Mouse instructions in this document, such as "Click the OK button" or "Drag an icon in File Manager," use the same meanings as the descriptions of mouse actions in the *Windows NT System Guide* and the Windows online tutorial.

P A R T I

About Windows NT

Part One provides an overview of the software components that make up Windows NT and its security subsystem. This part contains more theory and less practice but provides a foundation that helps you understand the technical details you'll find while reading this *Resource Guide* and while working with Windows NT.

C H A P T E R 1

Windows NT Architecture

When users first look at Microsoft® Windows NT™, they notice the familiar Windows 3.*x* interface. But what is visible to users is only a small part of Windows NT—a host of powerful features lie beneath the surface.

Windows NT is a preemptive, multitasking operating system based on a 32-bit design. It includes security and networking services as fundamental components of the base operating system. Windows NT also provides compatibility with many other operating systems, file systems, and networks. This operating system runs on both complex instruction set computing (CISC) and reduced instruction set computing (RISC) processors. Windows NT also supports high-performance computing by providing kernel support for computers that have symmetric multiprocessor configurations.

Windows NT only looks familiar. This chapter describes the powerful features under the graphical user interface. It provides an overview by introducing the Windows NT components and showing how they interrelate. Other chapters in this book provide the details, explaining more about particular components such as the Windows NT security model, integrated networking features and connectivity options, Windows NT file systems, the printing system, and the Registry.

Windows NT Design Goals

Windows NT was not designed as an upgraded version of an earlier product. Its architects began with a clean sheet of paper and this list of goals for a new operating system:

- In making this operating system *compatible*, the designers included the well-received Windows interface and provided support for existing file systems (such as FAT) and applications (including those written for MS-DOS, OS/2 1.*x*, Windows 3.*x*, and POSIX). The designers also provided network connectivity to several existing networking environments.

- *Portability* means that Windows NT runs on both CISC and RISC processors. CISC includes computers running with Intel® 80386 or higher processors. RISC includes computers with MIPS® R4000™ or Digital Alpha AXP™ processors.

- *Scalability* means that Windows NT is not bound to single-processor architectures but takes full advantage of symmetric multiprocessing hardware. Today, Windows NT can run on computers with from 1 to 32 processors. Windows NT allows you to add bigger and faster workstations and servers to your corporate network as your business requirements grow. And, it gives you the advantage of having the same development environment for both workstations and servers.

- Windows NT includes a uniform *security* architecture that meets the requirements for a U.S. government rating. For the corporate environment, it provides a safe environment to run mission-critical applications.

- *Distributed processing* means that Windows NT is designed with networking built into the base operating system. Windows NT also allows for connectivity to a variety of host environments through its support of multiple transport protocols and high-level client-server facilities including named pipes, remote procedure calls (RPCs), and Windows Sockets.

- *Reliability and robustness* refer to an architecture that protects applications from damaging each other and the operating system. Windows NT employs the robustness of structured exception handling throughout its entire architecture. It includes a recoverable file system, NTFS, and provides protection through its built-in security and advanced memory management techniques.

- *Localization* means that Windows NT will be offered in many countries around the world, in local languages, and that it supports the International Organization for Standardization (ISO) Unicode standard.

- *Extensibility* points to the modular design of Windows NT, which, as described in the next section, provides for the flexibility of adding future modules at several levels within the operating system.

Windows NT Architectural Modules

As Figure 1.1 shows, Windows NT is a modular (rather than monolithic) operating system composed of several relatively simple modules. From the lowest level to the top of the architecture, the Windows NT modules are the: Hardware Abstraction Layer, the Kernel, the Executive, the protected subsystems (included as part of the security model), and the environment subsystems.

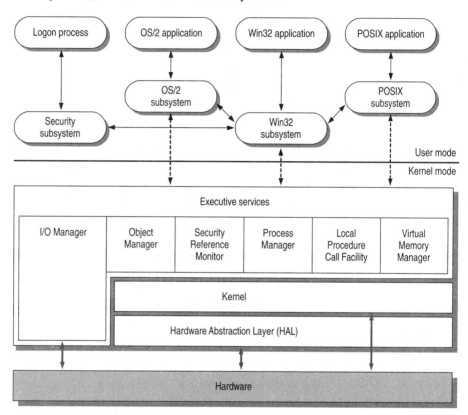

Figure 1.1   Windows NT Modular Architecture

The modular architecture of Windows NT is briefly described in the following paragraphs. The remainder of this chapter describes in detail these architectural components, beginning with the Hardware Abstraction Layer (HAL), the layer seated between the computer's hardware and the rest of the operating system.

- The *Hardware Abstraction Layer* virtualizes hardware interfaces, making the hardware dependencies transparent to the rest of the operating system. This allows Windows NT to be portable from one hardware platform to another.

- The *Kernel* is at the core of this layered architecture and manages the most basic operations of Windows NT. This component is designed to be small and efficient. The Kernel is responsible for thread dispatching, multiprocessor synchronization and hardware exception handling.

- The *Executive* is a collection of kernel-mode modules that provide basic operating system services to the environment subsystems. It includes several components; each manages a particular set of system services. One component, the Security Reference Monitor, works together with the protected subsystems to provide a pervasive security model for the system.

- *Environment subsystems* are user-mode protected servers that run and support applications native to different operating systems environments. Examples of these subsystems are the Win32® subsystem and the OS/2 subsystem.

Hardware Abstraction Layer

The Hardware Abstraction Layer (HAL) is a thin layer of software provided by the hardware manufacturer that hides, or *abstracts*, hardware differences from higher layers of the operating system. Thus, through the filter provided by HAL, different types of hardware all look alike to the operating system, removing the need to specifically tailor the operating system to the hardware with which it communicates.

The goal for HAL was to provide routines that allow a single device driver to support the same device on all platforms. HAL allows a large number of variations in hardware platforms for a single processor architecture without requiring a separate version of the operating system for each one.

HAL routines are called from both the base operating system (including the Kernel component) and from device drivers. For drivers, HAL provides the ability to support a wide variety of input/output (I/O) architectures, instead of either being restricted to a single hardware model or needing extensive adaptation for each new hardware platform.

HAL is also responsible for hiding the details of symmetric multiprocessing hardware from the rest of the operating system.

Kernel

Working very closely with the HAL is the Kernel, the heart of Windows NT. It schedules activities for the computer processor to perform. If the computer has multiple processors, the Kernel synchronizes activity among the processors to optimize performance.

The activities the Kernel schedules are called *threads*, the most basic entity in the system that can be scheduled. Threads are defined in the context of a process, (described more fully later in "Process Manager") which represents an address space, a set of *objects* visible to the process, and a set of threads that runs in the context of the process. Objects are resources that can be manipulated by the operating system. (These are discussed more fully in the "Object Manager" section.)

The Kernel dispatches threads in a way that ensures that the system's processors are always as busy as possible, processing the highest-priority threads first. (There are 32 priorities distributed across two priority classes—real-time and variable.) This helps make the operating system as efficient as possible.

Subcomponents at the Executive level, such as the I/O Manager and the Process Manager, use the Kernel to synchronize activities. They also rely on the Kernel for higher levels of abstraction, called *Kernel objects*, some of which are exported within user-level application programming interface (API) calls.

The Kernel manages two types of objects:

- *Dispatcher objects* have a signal state (either signaled or nonsignaled) and control the dispatching and synchronization of system operations. Dispatcher objects include the following: events, mutants, mutexes, semaphores, threads, and timers.

- *Control objects* are used to control the operation of the Kernel but do not affect dispatching. *Control objects* include the following: asynchronous procedure calls, interrupts, processes, and profiles.

Table 1.1 describes how the Executive uses each type of dispatcher object.

Table 1.1   Dispatcher Objects

Object type	Description
Event	Used to record the occurrence of an event and synchronize it with some action that is to be performed.
Mutant	One of two objects that the Kernel provides for controlling mutually exclusive access to a resource. This type of object is intended for use in providing a user-mode mutual exclusion mechanism that has ownership semantics. It can also be used in Kernel mode.
Mutex	The other of two objects that the Kernel provides for controlling mutually exclusive access to a resource. This type of object can only be used in Kernel mode and is intended to provide a deadlock-free mutual exclusion mechanism with ownership and other special system semantics.
Semaphore	Used to control access to a resource, but not necessarily in a mutually exclusive fashion. A semaphore object acts as a gate through which a variable number of threads may pass concurrently, up to a specified limit. The gate is open (signaled state) as long as there are resources available. When the number of resources specified by the limit are concurrently in use, the gate is closed (nonsignaled state).
Thread	The agent that runs program code and is dispatched to be run by the Kernel. Each thread is associated with a process object, which specifies the virtual address space mapping for the thread and accumulates thread run time. Several thread objects can be associated with a single process object, which enables the concurrent execution of multiple threads in a single address space (possibly simultaneous execution in a multiprocessor system).
Timer	Used to record the passage of time and to time out operations

Table 1.2 describes how the Executive uses each type of control object.

Table 1.2   Control Objects

Object type	Description
Asynchronous Procedure Call	Used to break into the execution of a specified thread and cause a procedure to be called in a specified processor mode.
Interrupt	Used to connect an interrupt source to an interrupt service routine via an entry in an Interrupt Dispatch Table (IDT). Each processor has an IDT that is used to dispatch interrupts that occur on that processor.
Process	Used to represent the virtual address space and control information necessary for the execution of a set of thread objects. A process object contains a pointer to an address map, a list of ready threads containing thread objects while the process is not in the balance set, a list of threads that belong to the process, the total accumulated time for all threads executing within the process, a base priority, and a default thread affinity. A process object must be initialized before any thread objects that specify the process as their parent can be initialized.
Profile	Used to measure the distribution of run time within a block of code. Both user and system code may be profiled.

Generally, the Kernel does not implement any policy since this is the responsibility of the Executive. However, the Kernel does make policy decisions about when it is appropriate to remove processes from memory.

The Kernel runs entirely in kernel mode and is nonpageable. Software within the Kernel is not preemptible and therefore cannot be context-switched, whereas much software outside the Kernel is almost always preemptible and can be context-switched.

The Kernel can run simultaneously on all processors in a multiprocessor configuration, synchronizing access to critical regions as appropriate.

The third and most intricate module that runs in Kernel mode is the Executive. The next several pages describe the functions of the Executive and its components.

Windows NT Executive

The Executive, which includes the Kernel and HAL, provides a set of common services that all environment subsystems can use. Each group of services is managed by one of these separate components of the Executive:

- Object Manager
- Virtual Memory Manager
- Process Manager
- Local Procedure Call Facility
- I/O Manager
- Security Reference Monitor, which along with the Logon and Security protected subsystems, makes up the Windows NT security model

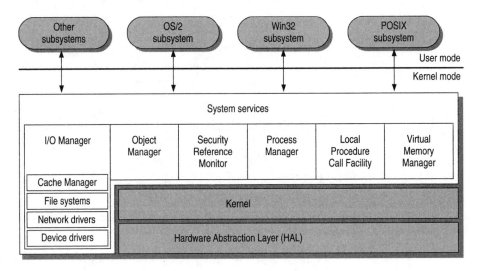

Figure 1.2   Windows NT Executive and its Components

A thin top layer of the Executive is called the *System Services*. The System Services shown in Figure 1.2 are the interface between user-mode environment subsystems and kernel mode. The following sections describe the role of each Executive component.

Object Manager

Objects are run-time instances of a particular object type that can be manipulated by an operating system process. An *object type* includes a system-defined data type, a list of operations that can be performed upon it (such as wait, create, or cancel), and a set of object attributes. *Object Manager* is the part of the Windows NT Executive that provides uniform rules for retention, naming, and security of objects.

Before a process can manipulate a Windows NT object, it must first acquire a handle to the object. An *object handle* includes access control information and a pointer to the object itself. All object handles are created through the Object Manager.

Note   Thus, the same routines that are used to create a file handle can be used to create an object handle.

Like other Windows NT components, the Object Manager is extensible so that new object types can be defined as technology grows and changes.

In addition, the Object Manager manages the global *namespace* for Windows NT and tracks the creation and use of objects by any process. This namespace is used to access all named objects that are contained in the local computer environment. Some of the objects that can have names include the following:

- Directory objects
- Object type objects
- Symbolic link objects
- Semaphore and event objects

- Process and thread objects
- Section and segment objects
- Port objects
- File objects

The object name space is modeled after a hierarchical file system, where directory names in a path are separated by a backslash (\). You can see object names in this form, for example, when you double-click entries in the Event Viewer log, as shown in the following illustration.

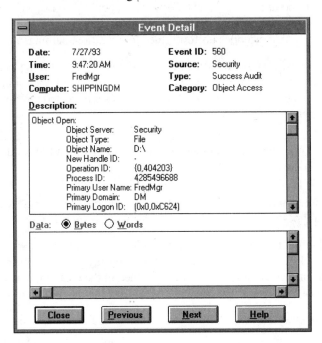

Process Manager

The *Process Manager* is the component that tracks two types of objects—process objects and thread objects. A *process* is defined as an address space, a set of objects (resources) visible to the process, and a set of threads that run in the context of the process. A *thread* is most the basic schedulable entity in the system. It has its own set of registers, its own Kernel stack, a thread environment block, and user stack in the address space of its process.

The Process Manager is the Windows NT component that manages the creation and deletion of processes. It provides a standard set of services for creating and using threads and processes in the context of a particular subsystem environment. Beyond that, the Process Manager does little to dictate rules about threads and processes. Instead, the Windows NT design allows for robust environment subsystems that can define specific rules about threads and processes.

The Process Manager does not impose any hierarchy or grouping rules for processes, nor does it enforce any parent/child relationships.

The Windows NT process model works in conjunction with the security model and the Virtual Memory Manager to provide interprocess protection. Each process is assigned a *security access token*, called the primary token of the process. This token is used by the Windows NT access-validation routines when threads in the process reference protected objects. For more information about how Windows NT uses security access tokens, see Chapter 2, "Windows NT Security Model."

Virtual Memory Manager

The memory architecture for Windows NT is a demand-paged virtual memory system. It is based on a flat, linear address space accessed via 32-bit addresses.

Virtual memory refers to the fact that the operating system can actually allocate more memory than the computer physically contains. Each process is allocated a unique virtual address space, which is a set of addresses available for the process's threads to use. This virtual address space is divided into equal blocks, or *pages*. Every process is allocated its own virtual address space, which appears to be 4 gigabytes (GB) in size—2 GB reserved for program storage and 2 GB reserved for system storage. Windows NT can see up to 4 GB of physical memory, if the computer hardware can provide it. Few operating systems can see this much memory. MS OS/2 version 1.3, for example, can only see 16 MB of physical memory.

Demand paging refers to a method by which data is moved in pages from physical memory to a temporary paging file on disk. As the data is needed by a process, it is paged back into physical memory.

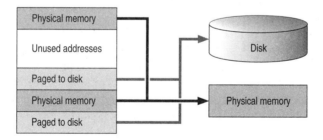

Figure 1.3   Conceptual View of Virtual Memory

The *Virtual Memory Manager* maps virtual addresses in the process's address space to physical pages in the computer's memory. In doing so, it hides the physical organization of memory from the process's threads. This ensures that the thread can access its process's memory as needed, but not the memory of other processes. Therefore, as illustrated by Figure 1.4, a thread's view of its process's virtual memory is much simpler than the real arrangement of pages in physical memory.

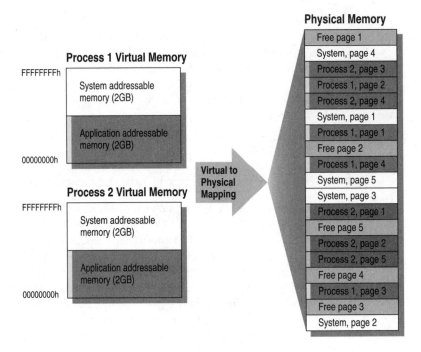

Figure 1.4   Protecting Processes' Memory

Because each process has a separate address space, a thread in one process cannot view or modify the memory of another process without authorization.

Local Procedure Call Facility

Applications and environment subsystems have a client-server relationship. That is, the client (an application) makes calls to the environment server (a subsystem) to satisfy a request for some type of system services. To allow for a client-server relationship between applications and environment subsystems, Windows NT provides a communication mechanism between them. The Executive implements a message-passing facility called a *Local Procedure Call* (LPC) facility. It works very much like the Remote Procedure Call (RPC) facility used for networked processing (described in Chapter 1, "Windows NT Networking Architecture," in the *Networking Guide*). However, the LPC facility is optimized for two processes running on the same computer.

Applications communicate with environment subsystems by passing messages via the LPC facility. The message-passing process is hidden from the client applications by function *stubs* (nonexecutable placeholders used by calls from the server environment) provided in the form of special dynamic-link libraries (DLLs), as illustrated by Figure 1.5.

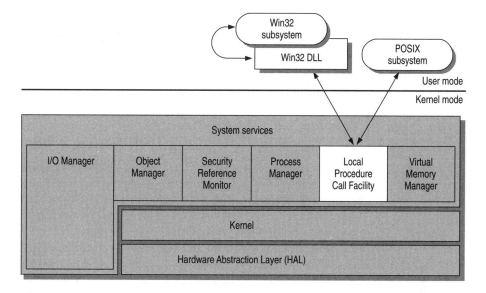

Figure 1.5   Interaction with the Local Procedure Call Facility

When an application makes an application program interface (API) call to an environment subsystem, the stub in the client (application) process packages the parameters for the call and sends them to a server (subsystem) process that implements the call. It is the LPC facility that allows the stub procedure to pass the data to the server process and wait for a response.

For example, consider how this process works in the Win32 subsystem. When a Win32 application is loaded to run, it is linked to a DLL that contains stubs for all of the functions in Win32 API. When the application calls a Win32 function (in this example, the **CreateWindow** Win32 function) the call is processed as follows:

1. The **CreateWindow()** stub function in the DLL is called by the client Win32 application.
2. The stub function constructs a message that contains all of the data needed to create a window and sends the message to the Win32 server process (that is, the Win32 subsystem).
3. The Win32 subsystem receives the message and calls the real **CreateWindow()** function. The window is created.
4. The Win32 subsystem sends a message containing the results of the **CreateWindow()** function back to the stub function in the DLL.
5. The stub function unpacks the server message from the subsystem and returns the results to the client Win32 application.

From the application's perspective, the **CreateWindow**() function in the DLL created the window. The application does not know that the work was actually performed by the Win32 server process (the Win32 subsystem), that a message was sent to make it happen, or even that the Win32 server process exists. It does not know that the subsystem called one or more Executive system servers to support its call to **CreateWindow**.

I/O Manager

The I/O Manager is the part of the Windows NT Executive that manages all input and output for the operating system. A large part of the I/O Manager's role is to manage communications between drivers. The I/O Manager supports all file system drivers, hardware device drivers, and network drivers and provides a heterogeneous environment for them. It provides a formal interface that all drivers can call. This uniform interface allows the I/O Manager to communicate with all drivers in the same way, without any knowledge of how the devices they control actually work. The I/O Manager also includes driver support routines specifically designed for file system drivers, for hardware device drivers, and for network drivers.

The Windows NT I/O model uses a layered architecture that allows separate drivers to implement each logically distinct layer of I/O processing. For example, drivers in the lowest layer manipulate the computer's physical devices (called *device drivers*). Other drivers are then layered on top of the device drivers, as shown in Figure 1.6. These higher-level drivers do not know any details about the physical devices. With the help of the I/O Manager, higher-level drivers simply pass logical I/O requests down to the device drivers, which access the physical devices on their behalf. The Windows NT installable file systems and network redirectors are examples of high-level drivers that work in this way.

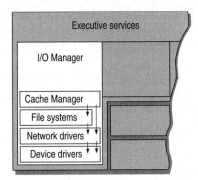

Figure 1.6   Layered Device Drivers

This scheme allows easy replacement of file system drivers and device drivers. It allows multiple file systems and devices to be active at the same time while being addressed through a formal interface.

Drivers communicate with each other using data structures called *I/O request packets*. The drivers pass I/O request packets to each other via the I/O Manager, which delivers the packets to the appropriate target drivers using the drivers' standard services. The simplest way to perform an I/O operation is to synchronize the execution of applications with completion of the I/O operations that they request. (This is known as *synchronous I/O*.) When such an application performs an I/O operation, the application's processing is blocked. When the I/O operation is complete, the application is allowed to continue processing.

One way that applications can optimize their performance is to perform *asynchronous I/O*, a method employed by many of the processes in Windows NT. When an application initiates an I/O operation, the I/O Manager accepts the request but doesn't block the application's execution while the I/O operation is being performed. Instead, the application is allowed to continue doing work. Most I/O devices are very slow in comparison to a computer's processor, so an application can do a lot of work while waiting to be notified that an I/O operation is complete.

When an environment subsystem issues an asynchronous I/O request, the I/O Manager returns to the environment subsystem immediately after putting the request in a queue, without waiting for the device driver to complete its operations. Meanwhile, a separate thread from the I/O Manager runs requests from the queue in the most efficient order (not necessarily the order received).

When each I/O request is finished, the I/O Manager notifies the process that requested the I/O.

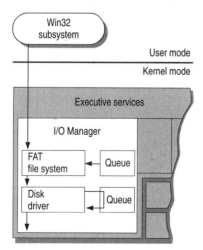

Figure 1.7   Queued I/O Requests

While asynchronous I/O permits an application to use the computer's processor during I/O operations, it also makes it harder for the application to determine when I/O operations have been completed. Some applications provide a callback function (APC) that is called when the asynchronous I/O operation is completed. Other applications use synchronization objects, such as an event or the file handle, that the I/O system sets to the signaled state when the I/O operation is complete.

Cache Manager

The I/O architecture includes a single *Cache Manager* that handles caching for the entire I/O system. *Caching* is a method used by a file system to improve performance. For example, instead of reading and writing directly to the disk, frequently used files are temporarily stored in a cache in memory, and reads and writes to those files are performed in memory. Reading and writing to memory is much faster than reading and writing to disk.

The Cache Manager uses a file-mapping model that is closely integrated with the Windows NT Virtual Memory Management. Cache Manager provides caching services to all file systems and network components under the control of the I/O Manager. Cache Manager can dynamically grow and shrink the size of the cache as the amount of available RAM varies. When a process opens a file that already resides in the cache, Cache Manager simply copies data from the cache to the process's virtual address space, and vice versa, as reads and writes are performed.

Cache Manager offers services such as *lazy write* and *lazy commit*, which can improve overall file system performance. Lazy write is the ability to record changes in the file structure cache, which is quicker than recording them on disk, and then later, when demand on the computer's central processing unit (CPU) is low, the Cache Manager writes the changes to the disk. Lazy commit is similar to lazy write. Instead of immediately marking a transaction as successfully completed, the committed information is cached and later written to the file system log as a background process.

For more information about how file systems interact with Cache Manager, see Chapter 5, "Windows NT File Systems and Advanced Disk Management."

File System Drivers

In the Windows NT I/O architecture, file system drivers are managed by the I/O Manager. Windows NT supports multiple active file systems, including existing file systems such as FAT. Windows NT supports FAT and HPFS file systems for backward compatibility with MS-DOS, Windows 3.x, and OS/2 1.x operating systems.

Windows NT also supports *NTFS*—a new file system designed for use with Windows NT. NTFS provides many features including file system security, Unicode support, recoverability, long filename support, and support for POSIX.

The Windows NT I/O architecture not only supports traditional file systems but has implemented its network redirector and server as file system drivers. From the perspective of I/O Manager, there is no difference between accessing files stored on a remote networked computer and accessing those stored locally on a hard disk. In addition, redirectors and servers can be loaded and unloaded dynamically, just like any other driver, and multiple redirectors and servers can coexist on the same computer.

For more information about supported file systems, see Chapter 5 "Windows NT File Systems and Advanced Disk Management." For more information about supported redirectors and servers, see Chapter 1, "Windows NT Networking Architecture," in the *Networking Guide*.

Hardware Device Drivers

Hardware device drivers are also components of the I/O architecture. All hardware device drivers (such as printer drivers, mouse drivers, and disk drivers) are written in the C programming language, are 32-bit addressable, and are multiprocessor-safe.

Device drivers access the hardware registers of the peripheral devices through support routines that are supplied by the Windows NT operating system. There is a set of these routines for every platform that Windows NT supports; since the routine names are the same for all platforms, device drivers for Windows NT are portable across different processor types.

Designers of device drivers are encouraged to create separate drivers for different devices, rather than monolithic drivers, and the design of I/O Manager makes it easy to do so. This allows more flexibility to customize device configurations on the computer and to layer device drivers and other drivers.

For example, the Intel 8042 processor is an interface device—the keyboard and mouse communicate with the i8042 driver as well as with their own respective drivers. Three separate drivers are used—for the i8042, for the keyboard, and for the mouse—rather than one large monolithic driver. This makes it easier to change one component (exchanging the mouse for a different pointing device, for example).

Network Drivers

A third type of driver implemented as a component in the I/O architecture is network device drivers. Windows NT includes integrated networking capabilities and support for distributed applications. As shown in Figure 1.8, networking is supported by a series of network drivers.

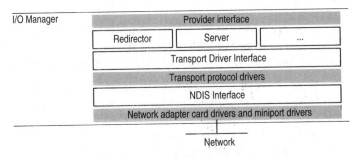

Figure 1.8   Networking Components in Windows NT

Redirectors and servers are implemented as file system drivers and run at or below a provider interface layer where NetBIOS and Windows Sockets reside.

Transport protocol drivers communicate with redirectors and servers through a layer called the *Transport Driver Interface* (TDI). Windows NT includes a number of transports:

- Transmission Control Protocol/Internet Protocol (TCP/IP), which provides a popular routable protocol for wide-area networks.
- NBF, a descendant of NetBIOS extended user interface (NetBEUI), which provides compatibility with existing LAN Manager, LAN Server, and MS-Net installations.
- Data Link Control (DLC), which provides an interface for access to mainframes and network-attached printers.
- NWLink, an implementation of IPX/SPX, which provides connectivity with Novell NetWare®.

At the bottom of the networking architecture is the network adapter card device driver. Windows NT currently supports device drivers written to the *Network Device Interface Specification* (NDIS) version 3.0. NDIS allows for a flexible environment of data exchange between transport protocols and network adapters. NDIS 3.0 allows a single computer to have several network adapter cards installed in it. In turn, each network adapter card can support multiple transport protocols for access to multiple types of network servers.

For more information about network device drivers, see Chapter 1, "Windows NT Networking Architecture," in the *Networking Guide*.

Windows NT Security Model

The *Security Reference Monitor* component plus two others—the *Logon Process* and *Security* protected subsystems—form the Windows NT security model. In a multitasking operating system such as Windows NT, applications share a variety of system resources including the computer's memory, I/O devices, files, and system processor(s). Windows NT includes a set of security components (shown in Figure 1.9) that ensure that applications cannot access these resources without authorization.

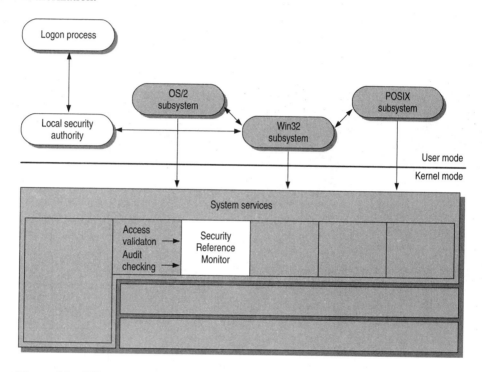

Figure 1.9   Windows NT Security Components

The Security Reference Monitor is responsible for enforcing the access-validation and audit-generation policy defined by the local Security subsystem. The Reference Monitor provides services to both kernel and user mode for validating access to objects, checking user privileges, and generating audit messages. The Reference Monitor, like other parts of the Executive, runs in kernel mode.

The user-mode Logon Process and Security protected subsystems are the other two components of the Windows NT security model. The Security subsystem is known as an *integral subsystem* rather than an environment subsystem because it affects the entire Windows NT operating system. (Environment subsystems are discussed later in this chapter.)

The Windows NT Kernel and Executive are based on an object-oriented model that allows for a consistent and uniform view of security, right down to the fundamental entities that make up the base operating system. This means that Windows NT uses the same routines for access validation and audit checks for all protected objects. That is, whether someone is trying to access a file on the disk or a process in memory, there is one component in the system that is required to perform access checks, regardless of the object type.

The Windows NT Logon Process provides for mandatory logon to identify users. Each user must have an account and must supply a password to access that account. Figure 1.10 illustrates the interaction among Windows NT components during logon.

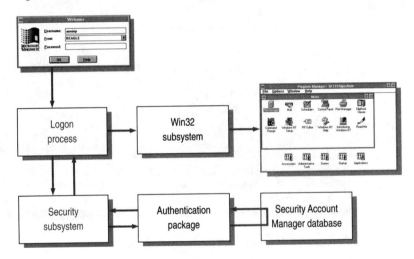

Figure 1.10   Logon Security Process

Before a user can access any resource on a Windows NT computer, they must logon through the Logon Process so that the Security subsystem can authenticate the person's username and password. After successful authentication, whenever the user tries to access a protected object, the Security Reference Monitor runs an access-validation routine against the user's security information to ensure the user has permission to access the object.

The security model also provides for discretionary access control so that the owner of a resource can specify which users or groups can access resources and what types of access they're allowed (such as read, write, and delete).

Resource protection is another feature provided by the security model. Tasks can't access each others' resources, such as memory, except through specific sharing mechanisms. This feature helps enforce object hiding.

Windows NT also provides for auditing so that administrators can keep an audit trail of which users perform what actions.

By providing these features, the Windows NT security model prevents applications from gaining unauthorized access to the resources of other applications or the operating system either intentionally or unintentionally.

For a complete description of how the security model works, see Chapter 2, "Windows NT Security Model."

In addition to the protected subsystems—Logon Process and Security—Windows NT includes a number of other user-mode components called environment subsystems. The next section describes each of the Windows NT environment subsystems.

Environment Subsystems

Windows NT was designed to allow many different types of applications to run seamlessly on the same graphical desktop. It runs applications written for existing operating systems such as MS-DOS, OS/2 1.*x*, and Windows 3.*x*. It also runs applications written for newer APIs such as POSIX and Win32.

Windows NT supports a variety of applications through the use of *environment subsystems*, which are Windows NT processes that emulate different operating system environments.

This chapter has discussed how the Windows NT Executive provides generic services that all environment subsystems can call to perform basic operating system functions. The subsystems build on the Executive's services to produce environments that meet the specific needs of their client applications. Figure 1.11 shows a simplified view of the Windows NT environmental subsystem design.

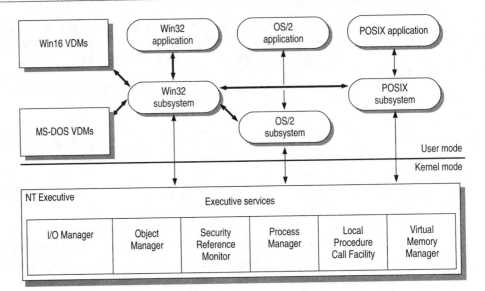

Figure 1.11   Conceptual View of Windows NT Environment Subsystems

As shown in this figure, each subsystem runs as a separate user-mode process. Failure in one won't cause another subsystem or the Executive to be disabled. Each subsystem is protected from errors in the others. (An exception to this is if the Win32 subsystem crashes, since it handles keyboard and mouse input and screen output for all subsystems.) Applications are also user-mode processes, so they can't hinder the subsystems or Executive.

Windows NT provides these protected environments subsystems and multiple Virtual DOS Machines (VDMs):

- MS-DOS VDM
- Win16 VDMs
- OS/2 subsystem
- POSIX subsystem
- Win32 subsystem

With the exception of the Win32 subsystem, each environment is optional and is loaded only when its services are needed by a client application.

MS-DOS Environment

When run on Windows NT, MS-DOS-based applications run within the context of a process called a *Virtual DOS Machine* (VDM). A *VDM* is a Win32 application that establishes a complete virtual *x*86 (that is, 80386 or higher) computer running MS-DOS. There is no limit on the number of VDMs that can be run. Each VDM runs in its own address space, which protects the applications from each other and the rest of the operating system from the VDMs.

When Windows NT is running on an *x*86 processor, a processor mode called *Virtual-86* mode is available. This mode allows direct execution of most instructions in an MS-DOS–based application. A few instructions, such as I/O instructions, must be emulated in order to virtualize the hardware. When Windows NT is running on a RISC processor, hardware support for executing *x*86 instructions is not available. In such an environment, it is necessary to emulate all of the *x*86 instructions in addition to providing a virtual hardware environment.

To run MS-DOS–based applications, the VDM creates a virtual computer that provides the following features:

- Support for processing *x*86 instructions, provided by the Instruction Execution Unit
- Support for read-only memory basic input and output (ROM BIOS) interrupt services, provided by the MS-DOS emulation module
- Support for MS-DOS Interrupt 21 services, provided by the MS-DOS emulation module
- Virtual hardware for devices such as the screen and keyboard, provided by Virtual Device Drivers (VDDs)

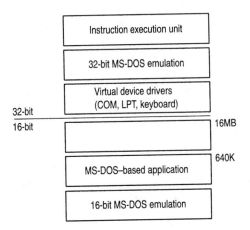

Figure 1.12   Structure of an MS-DOS VDM

On *x*86-based computers, character-based applications can run either in a window or in a full screen. Graphical applications can run only in full screen. If an application is in a window and then changes the video mode, it is automatically switched to full screen. On RISC-based computers, character-based and graphical applications run only in a window.

Windows 16-bit Environment

Windows NT uses a single multithreaded VDM support to run 16-bit Windows-based (Win16) applications. One of the main goals for Win16 support is to provide a seamless interface for running Win16 applications in the Windows NT environment.

The Win16 VDM (sometimes called *WOW* for Win16 on Win32) is preemptively multitasked with respect to other processes running on the system. However, each Win16 application is nonpreemptively multitasked with respect to each other. That is, only one Win16 application can run at a time while the others are blocked. If the Win16 VDM is preempted when the system returns, it always unblocks the Win16 application that was running before the Win16 VDM was preempted.

Additionally, the Win16 VDM provides stubs for Windows 3.1 Kernel, User, graphical device interface dynamic-link libraries (GDI DLLs), and it automatically handles translation of 16-bit Windows APIs and messages.

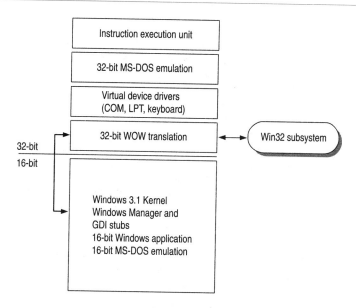

Figure 1.13   Structure of the Win16 VDM

For more information about using Windows 3.*x* applications on Windows NT, see Chapter 15, "Windows 3.*x* Compatibility."

OS/2 Subsystem

The OS/2 subsystem supports OS/2 1.*x* character-based applications on *x*86-based computers. This subsystem isn't supported on RISC-based computers; however, OS/2 real-mode applications can run on a RISC-based computer in the MS-DOS environment.

Bound applications, which are applications designed to run under either OS/2 or MS-DOS, will always run in the OS/2 subsystem if it is available.

For more information about using OS/2 1.*x* applications on Windows NT, see Chapter 16, "OS/2 Compatibility."

POSIX Subsystem

The Windows NT POSIX subsystem is designed to run POSIX applications and meets the requirements of POSIX.1.

POSIX (Portable Operating System Interface for Computing Environments) is a set of standards being drafted by the Institute of Electrical and Electronic Engineers (IEEE) that define various aspects of an operating system, including topics such as programming interface, security, networking, and graphical interface. So far, only one of these standards, POSIX.1 (also called IEEE Standard 1003.1-1990), has made the transition from draft to final form and gained a base of customer acceptance.

POSIX.1 defines C-language API calls between applications and the operating system. It is an API based on ideas drawn from the UNIX® file system and process model. Because POSIX.1 addresses only API-level issues, most applications written to the POSIX.1 API must rely on non-POSIX operating system extensions to provide services such as security and networking.

POSIX applications need certain file-system functionality, such as support for case-sensitive filenames and support for files with multiple names (or *hard links*). The new file system, NTFS, supports these POSIX requirements. Any POSIX application requiring access to file system resources must have access to an NTFS partition. POSIX applications that do not access file system resources can run on any of the supported file systems.

For more information about using POSIX applications on Windows NT, see Chapter 17, "POSIX Compatibility."

Win32 Subsystem

The main environment subsystem is the Win32 subsystem. In addition to being able to run Win32 applications, this subsystem manages keyboard and mouse input and screen output for all subsystems.

The Win32 subsystem is responsible for collecting all user input (or messages, in this message-driven environment) and delivering it to the appropriate applications. The Win32 input model is optimized to take advantage of the Windows NT preemptive multitasking capabilities. Figure 1.14 shows how the Win32 subsystem handles input for Win32 and 16-bit Windows-based applications.

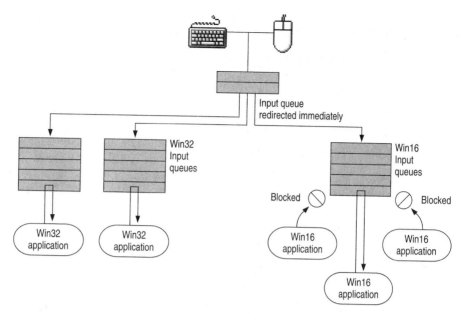

Figure 1.14   Win16 (Synchronized) and Win32 (Desynchronized) Input

Win32 uses a desynchronized input model for Win32 applications and the synchronized input for 16-bit Windows-based applications.

For example, when the Win32 subsystem receives a message for a Win32 application, it stores the message in a single raw input queue. As soon as it can, the Win32 subsystem transfers the message to the input queue thread for the appropriate Win32 application. If the input queue thread stops retrieving its messages, no other Win32 applications are affected.

By contrast, all input messages for 16-bit Windows-based applications sit in a common queue. At any point in time, all applications except the one retrieving messages from the input queue are blocked. However, as with Windows 3.1, if the executing application has some problem with retrieving messages from the queue, or it does it very slowly, the remaining applications stay blocked.

Application Types on Various Hardware Platforms

Windows NT runs on computers with Intel 80386 or higher processors, MIPS, or Digital Alpha AXP processors. The following table shows how Windows NT supports applications of various types on these different hardware platforms.

Table 1.3   Application Compatibility

Processor	Win32	MS-DOS and Windows 3.x	POSIX	OS/2 1.x
Intel x86	Source-compatible	Runs application in a VDM	Source-compatible	16-bit character-based only
Digital Alpha AXP	Source-compatible	Runs application in 286 emulation	Source-compatible	Not available; can run real-mode applications in MS-DOS subsystem
MIPS R4000	Source-compatible	Runs application in 286 emulation	Source-compatible	Not available; can run real-mode applications in MS-DOS subsystem

C H A P T E R   2

Windows NT Security Model

Security in Windows NT was included as part of the initial design specifications for Windows NT and is pervasive throughout the operating system. The security model includes components to control who accesses which objects (such as files and shared printers), which actions an individual can take on an object, and which events are audited.

This chapter provides an overview of the security model and describes the components that make up the model. It also explains how Windows NT tracks each user and each securable object. This overview helps you understand system messages and information found in the Event Viewer. This chapter also provides examples of Windows NT security, showing how Windows NT validates access requests and how it audits activities performed on protected objects.

The Security Model

Chapter 1, "Windows NT Architecture," describes the overall architecture of Windows NT. As shown in Figure 2.1, the Windows NT security model includes these components:

- *Logon processes*, which accept logon request from users. These include the initial interactive logon, which displays the initial logon dialog box to the user, and remote logon processes, which allow access by remote users to a Windows NT server process.

- *Local Security Authority*, which ensures that the user has permission to access the system.

  This component is the center of the Windows NT security subsystem. It generates access tokens (described later in this chapter), manages the local security policy, and provides interactive user authentication services. The Local Security Authority also controls audit policy and logs the audit messages generated by the Security Reference Monitor.

- *Security Account Manager (SAM)*, which maintains the user accounts database. This database contains information for all user and group accounts. SAM provides user validation services, which are used by the Local Security Authority.

- *Security Reference Monitor*, which checks to see if the user has permission to access an object and perform whatever action the user is attempting. This component enforces the access validation and audit generation policy defined by the Local Security Authority. It provides services to both kernel and user mode to ensure the users and processes attempting access to an object have the necessary permissions. This component also generates audit messages when appropriate.

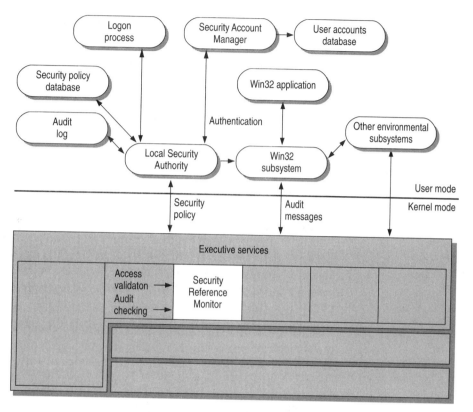

Figure 2.1   Windows NT Security Components

Together, these components are known as the security subsystem. This subsystem is known as an *integral subsystem* rather than an *environmental subsystem* because it affects the entire Windows NT operating system.

The Windows NT security model is designed for C2-level security as defined by the U.S. Department of Defense. Some of the most important requirements of C2-level security are the following:

- The owner of a resource (such as a file) must be able to control access to the resource.

- The operating system must protect objects so that they are not randomly reused by other processes. For example, the system protects memory so that its contents cannot be read after it is freed by a process. In addition, when a file is deleted, users must not be able to access the file's data.

- Each user must identify himself or herself by typing a unique logon name and password before being allowed access to the system. The system must be able to use this unique identification to track the activities of the user.

- System administrators must be able to audit security-related events. Access to this audit data must be limited to authorized administrators.

- The system must protect itself from external interference or tampering, such as modification of the running system or of system files stored on disk.

Users, Objects, and Permissions

The key objective of the Windows NT security model is to monitor and control who accesses which objects. The security model keeps security information for each user, group, and object. It can identify access attempts that are made directly by a user, and it can identify access attempts that are made indirectly by a program or other process running on a user's behalf. Windows NT also tracks and controls access to both objects that users can see in the user interface (such as files and printers) and objects that users can't see (such as processes and named pipes).

As mentioned before, the security model controls not only which users can access which objects; it also controls how they may be accessed. An administrator can assign *permissions* to users and groups to grant or deny access to particular objects.

For example, these permissions may be assigned to a user for a particular file:

Read	Execute
Delete	Take Ownership
Write	No access
Change Permission	

The ability to assign permissions at the discretion of the owner (or other person authorized to change permissions) is called *discretionary access control*. Administrators can assign permissions to individual users or groups. (For maintenance purposes, it's best to assign permissions to groups.) For example, an administrator can control access to the REPORTS directory by giving GROUP1 read permission and GROUP2 read, write, and execute permissions. (To do this, in File Manager, choose Permissions from the Security menu.)

Auditing Security Events in the Security Log

Windows NT auditing features can record events to show which users access which objects, what type of access is being attempted, and whether or not the access attempt was successful. You can view audited security events through Event Viewer by selecting Security from the Log menu. (For complete information about how to use Event Viewer, see the chapter on Event Viewer in either the *Microsoft Windows NT System Guide* or the *Microsoft Windows NT Advanced Server System Guide*.)

You can see detailed information about a particular audited event in the security log by double-clicking on that event.

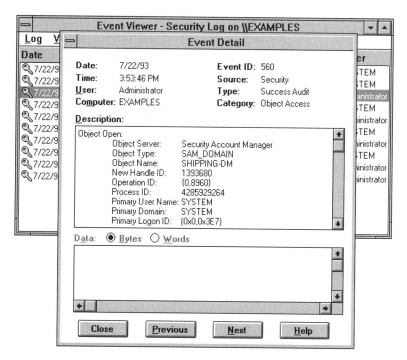

To set up auditing on your computer, use the Auditing and Security options in the User Manager, File Manager, Print Manager, and other tools. From these tools, you can specify the types of auditing events you want to include in the security log. For more information about setting auditing options within these tools, see the Windows NT documentation.

Note While Event Viewer is adequate for most requirements, the security model is defined so that developers can write their own custom security event viewer/monitor. For details on Windows NT security-related APIs, see the *Microsoft Win32 Software Development Kit.*

Security Information for Users

Users are identified to the system by a unique *security ID* (SID). Security IDs are unique across time and space, meaning that there is no possibility of having two identical security IDs. For example, suppose Sally, who has a Windows NT account, leaves her job at a company but later returns to a different job at the same company. When Sally leaves, the administrator deletes her account, and Windows NT no longer accepts her security ID as valid. When Sally returns, the administrator creates a new account, and Windows NT generates a new security ID for that account. The new security ID does not match the old one, so nothing from the old account is transferred to the new account.

When a user logs on, Windows NT creates a *security access token*. This includes a security ID for the user, other security IDs for the groups to which the user belongs, plus other information such as the user's name and the groups to which that user belongs. In addition, every process that runs on behalf of this user will have a copy of his or her access token. For example, when Sally starts Notepad, the Notepad process receives a copy of Sally's access token.

Figure 2.3 illustrates the contents of an access token.

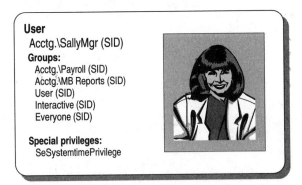

Figure 2.2   Access Token Contents

Windows NT refers to the security IDs within a user's access token when he or she tries to access an object. The security IDs are compared with the list of access permissions for the object to ensure that the user has sufficient permission to access the object.

How Windows NT Creates an Access Token

Before a user can do anything on a Windows NT system, he or she must log on to the system by supplying a username and password. Windows NT uses the username for identification and password for validation. The following procedure illustrates the interactive logon process for Windows NT.

The initial logon process for Windows NT is *interactive*, meaning that the user must type information at the keyboard in response to a dialog box the operating system displays on the screen. Windows NT grants or denies access based upon the information provided by the user.

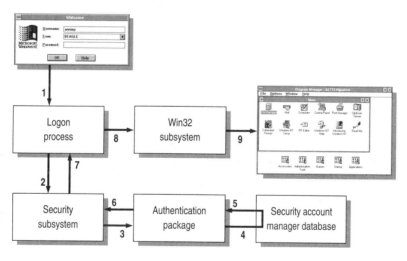

Figure 2.3   Windows NT Validation Process

The following list details the steps included in the interactive logon and validation process, as illustrated in Figure 2.4:

1. The user presses CTRL+ALT+DEL to gain the attention of Windows NT. This key combination before logon protects against Trojan Horse-type programs that impersonate the operating system and trick users into disclosing their username and password.

2. When the user provides a username and a password, the logon process calls the Local Security Authority.

3. The Local Security Authority runs the appropriate authentication package.

Note Windows NT has the ability to support multiple authentication packages that are implemented as DLLs. This flexibility allows third-party software vendors the opportunity to integrate their own custom authentication packages with Windows NT. For example, a network vendor might augment the standard Windows NT authentication package by adding one that allows users to log onto Windows NT and the vendor's network simultaneously.

---

4. The authentication package checks the user accounts database to see if the account is local. If it is, the username and password are verified against those held in the user accounts database. If not, the requested logon is forwarded to an alternate authentication package.

5. When the account is validated, the SAM (which owns the user accounts database) returns the user's security ID and the security IDs of any global groups to which the user belongs.

6. The authentication package creates a logon session and then passes the logon session and the security IDs associated with the user to the Local Security Authority.

7. If the logon is rejected, the logon session is deleted, and an error is returned to the logon process.

   Otherwise, an access token is created, containing the user's security ID and the security IDs of Everyone and other groups. It also contains user rights (described in the next section) assigned to the collected security IDs. This access token is returned to the logon process with a Success status.

8. The logon session calls the Win32 subsystem to create a process and attach the access token to the process, thus creating a *subject* for the user account. (Subjects are described in the section called "Subjects and Impersonation," later in this chapter.)

9. For an interactive Windows NT session, the Win32 subsystem starts Program Manager for the user.

After the validation process, a user's shell process (that is, the process in which Program Manager is started for the user) is given an access token. The information in this access token is reflected by anything the user does, or any process that runs on the user's behalf.

User Rights

Typically, access to an object is determined by comparing the user and group memberships in the user's access token with permissions for the object. However, some activities performed by users are not associated with a particular object.

For example, you may want certain individuals to be able to create regular backups for the server. These people should be able to do their job without regard to permissions that have been set on those files. In cases like this, an administrator could assign specific *user rights* (sometimes called privileges) to give users or groups access to services that normal discretionary access control does not provide. (You can use the dialog box shown below from the User Manager tool to assign user rights.)

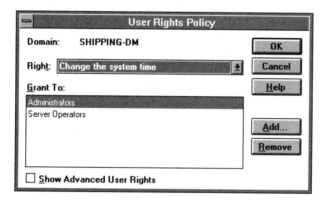

Backing up files and directories, shutting down the computer, logging on interactively, and changing the system times are all examples of user rights defined by Windows NT.

Note In the current release of Windows NT, the set of user rights is defined by the system and cannot be changed. Future versions of Windows NT may allow software developers to define new user rights appropriate to their application.

For more information about permissions and user rights, see the *Windows NT System Guide*. Details for administrators are also included in the *Windows NT Advanced Server Concepts and Planning Guide* and the *Windows NT Advanced Server System Guide*.

Subjects and Impersonation

One objective of the Windows NT security model is to ensure that the programs that a user runs have no more access to objects than the user does. That is, if a user is granted only read access to a file, then when he or she runs a program, that program cannot write to the file. The program, like the user, is granted only read permission.

A *subject* is the combination of the user's access token plus the program acting on the user's behalf. Windows NT uses subjects to track and manage permissions for the programs each user runs.

When a program or process runs on the user's behalf, it is said to be running in the *security context* of that user. The security context controls what access the subject has to objects or system services.

To accommodate the client-server model of Windows NT, there are two classes of subjects within the Windows NT security architecture:

- A *simple subject* is a process that was assigned a security context when the corresponding user logged on. It is not acting in the capacity of a protected server, which may have other subjects as clients.

- A *server subject* is a process implemented as a protected server (such as the Win32 subsystem), and it does have other subjects as clients. In this role, a server subject typically has the security context of those clients available for use when acting on their behalf.

In general, when a subject calls an object service through a protected subsystem, the subject's token is used within the service to determine who made the call and to decide whether the caller has sufficient access authority to perform the requested action.

Windows NT allows one process to take on the security attributes of another through a technique called *impersonation*. For example, a server process typically impersonates a client process to complete a task involving objects to which the server does not normally have access.

In the scenario shown in Figure 2.5, a client is accessing an object on a Windows NT server.

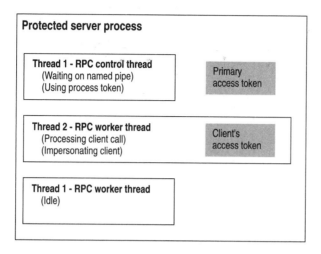

Figure 2.4   Server Subject Security Context

The first thread in the process is a control thread. It is waiting to receive RPC calls via a named pipe. This thread is not impersonating another process, so any access validation to which Thread 1 is subjected will be carried out against the process's primary token.

The second thread in the process is currently handling a call from a client. This thread handles the client's call by temporarily using the client's access token to run with that client's access permissions (that is, the client's security context). While impersonating the client, any access validation to which Thread 2 is subjected is carried out in the security context of the client.

The third thread in this scenario is an idle worker thread that is not impersonating any other process.

The following illustration shows an audited event in which impersonation was used. (Use the Event Viewer to see this type of information for your system.) Here, information for both the primary user and client user is recorded in the security log.

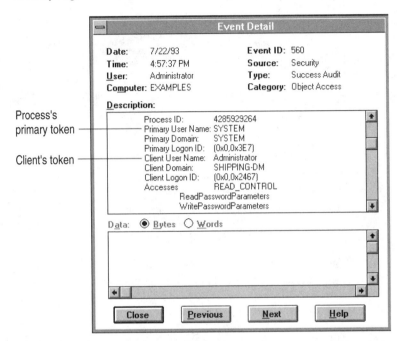

Security Information for Objects

All named objects in Windows NT, and some unnamed objects, can be secured. The security attributes for an object are described by a *security descriptor.* An object's security descriptor includes four parts (see Figure 2.6):

- An owner security ID, which indicates the user or group who owns the object. The owner of an object can change the access permissions for the object.

- A group security ID, which is used only by the POSIX subsystem and ignored by the rest of Windows NT.

- A discretionary *access control list* (ACL), which identifies which users and groups are granted or denied which access permissions. Discretionary ACLs are controlled by the owner of the object. (These are described later, in "Access Control Lists and Access Control Entries.")

- A system ACL, which controls which auditing messages the system will generate. (For more information about auditing objects, see "Auditing Security Events," later in this chapter.) System ACLs are controlled by the security administrators.

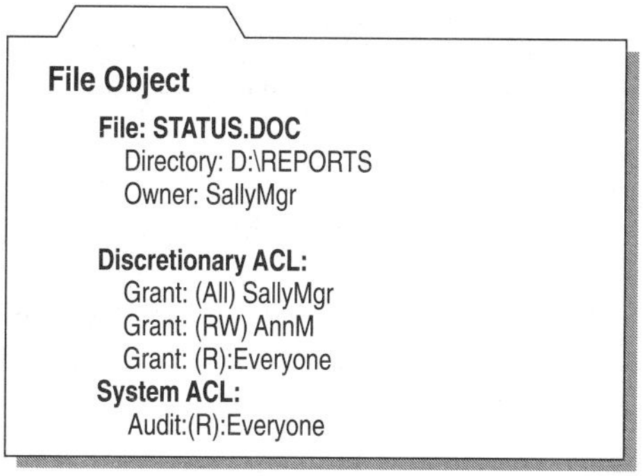

File Object

   File: STATUS.DOC
   Directory: D:\REPORTS
   Owner: SallyMgr

   Discretionary ACL:
   Grant: (All) SallyMgr
   Grant: (RW) AnnM
   Grant: (R):Everyone
   System ACL:
   Audit:(R):Everyone

Figure 2.5   Security Descriptor for a File Object

Types of Objects

The type of permissions that can be granted or denied for an object depends on the object's type. For example, you can specify permissions like Manage Documents and Print for a printer queue, while for a directory you can specify Read, Write, Execute, and so on.

Another quality that affects the permissions of an object is whether that object is a container object or a noncontainer object. A *container object* is one that logically contains other objects; *noncontainer* objects do not contain other objects. For example, a directory is a container object that logically contains files and other directories. Files are noncontainer objects. This distinction between container and noncontainer objects is important because objects within a container object can inherit certain permissions from the parent container. For more information, see "Access Control Inheritance," later in this chapter.

Note NTFS (described in Chapter 5, "Windows NT File Systems and Advanced Disk Management") supports the inheritance of ACLs from directory objects to file objects that are created within the directory.

Access Control Lists and Access Control Entries

Each ACL is made up of *access control entries* (ACEs), which specify access or auditing permissions to that object for one user or group. There are three ACE types—two for discretionary access control and one for system security.

The discretionary ACEs are AccessAllowed and AccessDenied. Respectively, these explicitly grant and deny access to a user or group of users.

Note There is an important distinction between a discretionary ACL that is empty (one that has no ACEs in it) and an object without any discretionary ACL. In the case of an empty discretionary ACL, no accesses are explicitly granted, so access is implicitly denied. For an object that has no ACL at all, there is no protection assigned to the object, so any access request is granted.

SystemAudit is a system security ACE which is used to keep a log of security events (such as who accesses which files) and to generate and log security audit messages.

Access Masks

Each ACE includes an *access mask*, which defines all possible actions for a particular object type. Permissions are granted or denied based on this access mask.

One way to think of an access mask is as a sort of menu from which granted and denied permissions are selected:

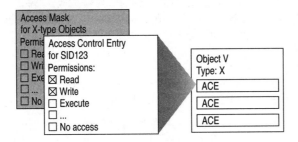

Figure 2.6   Access Control Mask

Specific types include access options that apply specifically to this object type. Each object type can have up to 16 specific access types. Collectively, the specific access types for a particular object type are called the *specific access mask*. (These are defined when the object type is defined.) For example, Windows NT files have the following specific access types:

ReadData	WriteEA (Extended Attribute)
WriteData	Execute
AppendData	ReadAttributes
ReadEA (Extended Attribute)	WriteAttributes

Standard types apply to all objects and consist of these access permissions:

- SYNCHRONIZE, which is used to synchronize access and to allow a process to wait for an object to enter the signaled state
- WRITE_OWNER, which is used to assign write owner
- WRITE_DAC, which is used to grant or deny write access to the discretionary ACL
- READ_CONTROL, which is used to grant or deny read access to the security descriptor and owner
- DELETE, which is used to grant or deny delete access

The following table shows the generic types that are mapped from specific and standard types.

Generic type	Mapped from these specific and standard types
FILE_GENERIC_READ	STANDARD_RIGHTS_READ FILE_READ_DATA FILE_READ_ATTRIBUTES FILE_READ_EA SYNCHRONIZE
FILE_GENERIC_WRITE	STANDARD_RIGHTS_WRITE FILE_WRITE_DATA FILE_WRITE_ATTRIBUTES FILE_WRITE_EA FILE_APPEND_DATA SYNCHRONIZE
FILE_GENERIC_EXECUTE	STANDARD_RIGHTS_EXECUTE FILE_READ_ATTRIBUTES FILE_EXECUTE SYNCHRONIZE

Specific and standard types appear in the details of the security log, as in the following display. Here, Administrator is accessing D:\ . The access types used are SYNCHRONIZE (a standard type) and ReadData/ListDirectory (a specific type for files and directories).

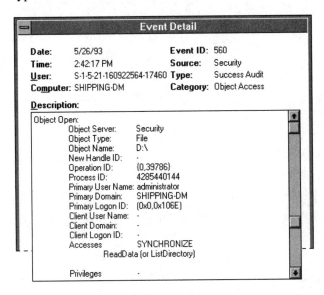

Note Generic types do not appear in the security log. Instead, the corresponding specific and standard types are listed.

Access Control Inheritance

Objects can be classified as either container objects or noncontainer objects. Container objects (such as a directory) can logically contain other objects; noncontainer objects (such as a file) can't.

By default, when you create new objects within a container object, the new objects inherit permissions from the *parent* object. For example, in the following dialog box, D:\REPORTS\ANNM inherited permissions from its parent directory, D:\REPORTS.

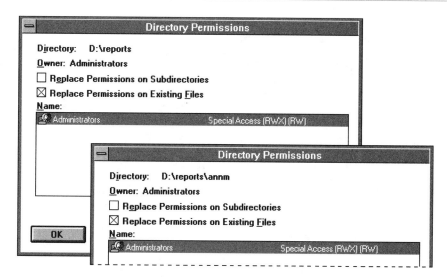

In the case of files and directories, when you change permissions on a directory, those changes affect that directory and its files but do not automatically apply to existing subdirectories and their contents. (They do, however, if you check the Replace Permissions On Existing Files check box.) You can apply the changed permissions to existing subdirectories and their files by selecting the Replace Permissions On Subdirectories check box.

The following dialog box shows the file permissions that are inherited from the parent directory by a file within that directory.

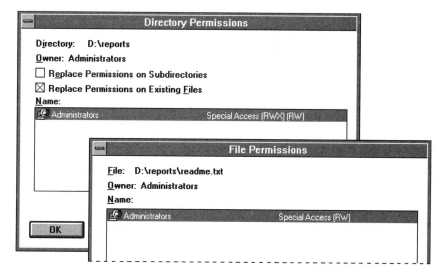

Access Validation

When a user tries to access an object, Windows NT compares security information in the user's access token with the security information in the object's security descriptor, as shown in Figure 2.10:

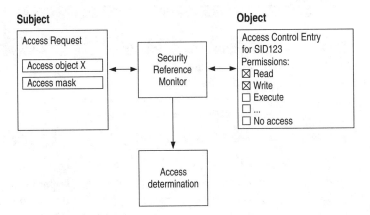

Figure 2.7   Access Validation

A *desired access mask* for the subject is created based on what type of access the user is attempting. This desired access mask, usually created by a program that the user is running, is compared with the object's ACL. (All generic access types in the ACL are mapped to standard and specific access types.)

Each ACE in the ACL is evaluated in this way:

1. The security ID in the ACE is compared with the set of security IDs in the user's access token. If a match is not found, the ACE is skipped.

    Further processing is based upon the type of the ACE. AccessDenied ACEs are ordered (and therefore processed) before AccessAllowed ACEs.

2. If access is denied, the system checks to see if the original desired access mask contained only a ReadControl and/or WRITE_DAC. If so, the system also checks to see if the requester is the owner of the object. In this case, access is granted.

3. For an AccessDenied ACE, the accesses in the ACE access mask are compared with the desired access mask. If there are any accesses in both masks, further processing is not necessary, and access is denied. Otherwise, processing continues with the next requested ACE.

4. For an AccessAllowed ACE, the accesses in the ACE are compared with those listed in the desired access mask. If all accesses in the desired access mask are matched by the ACE, no further processing is necessary, and access is granted. Otherwise, processing continues with the next ACE.

5. At the end of the ACL, if the contents of desired access mask are still not completely matched, access is implicitly denied.

Four examples of this access validation process are described next.

Example 1: Requesting Read and Write Access

A user whose user ID is FredMgr tries to gain Read and Write access to G:\FILE1.TXT, which has the discretionary ACL as shown in the next figure. The FredMgr access token indicates that he is a member of the groups Users, Mgrs, and Everyone.

Note The order in which permissions are listed by the File Permissions dialog box doesn't necessarily reflect the order in which ACEs are processed by Windows NT. It is important to note, however, that the Permissions Editor (controlled by means of this dialog box) orders all AccessDenied ACEs first so that they are the first to be processed within each ACL.

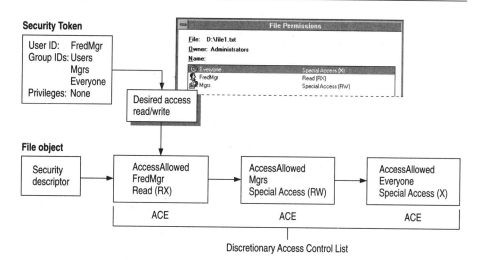

In this example, Windows NT evaluates the ACL by comparing the desired access mask with each ACE and processes the desired mask as follows:

1. Windows NT reads FredMgr's desired access mask to see that he is trying to gain Read and Write access.

2. Windows NT reads the AccessAllowed ACE for FredMgr and finds a match to the Read permission requested in the desired access mask.

3. Windows NT reads the AccessAllowed ACE for Mgrs and finds a match to the Write permission requested in desired access mask.

At this point, processing of the ACL stops even though there is another ACE in the ACL. Processing stops, and access is granted because Windows NT found matches for everything in the desired access mask.

Example 2: When Access Is Denied

In this example, FredMgr wants Read and Write access to the file whose discretionary ACL is shown next. FredMgr is a member of the Users and Mgrs groups.

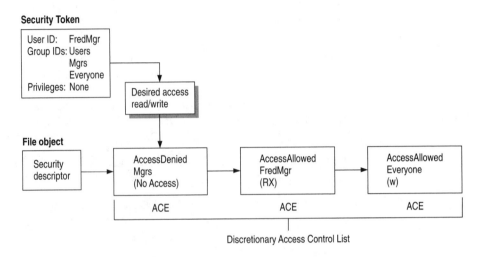

Note The File Manager Permissions Editor always orders AccessDenied ACEs first in the ACL.

In Example 2, the ACL is evaluated as follows:

1. Windows NT reads FredMgr's desired access mask to see that he is trying to gain Read and Write access.

2. Windows NT reads the AccessDenied ACE, which denies all access (No Access) to Mgrs.

At this point, processing of the ACL stops even though there are other ACEs in the ACL that grant permissions to FredMgr.

Example 3: Requesting Read and Write Access as Object Owner

In the example shown next, Windows NT knows by reading FredMgr's access token that he is a member of the Mgrs group. Processing of the ACL will stop as soon as Windows NT sees that NoAccess (None) is assigned to the Mgrs group, even though the other two ACEs allow Read, Write, and Execute access for FredMgr.

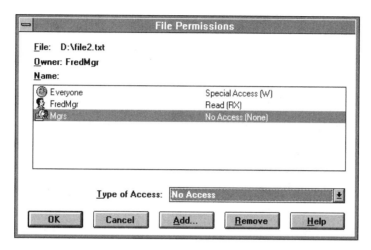

However, after failing to gain access via the discretionary ACL, Windows NT notices that FredMgr is the owner of the object. Because of this, he is granted ReadControl and WRITE_DAC automatically. Since this is all the access he is asking for, his request is granted.

If FredMgr had asked for any other access in addition to ReadControl and WRITE_DAC, the request would be denied even though Fred is the object's owner. In this case, FredMgr receives the following message:

```
G:\FILE2.TXT
You do not have permission to open this file.
See the owner of the file or an administrator to obtain permission.
```

In this case, because FredMgr is the owner, he can change his own permissions to grant himself appropriate access to the file.

Example 4: When a Custom Application Assigns Permissions

Important The three preceding examples demonstrate discretionary access
control for file and directory permissions that are applied through the
Windows NT Permissions Editor (found in File Manager) either directly or
by inheritance. If you use a custom application that sets and changes permissions
on files and directories, the Windows NT Permissions Editor may not be able to
handle the ACL that the custom application creates or modifies.

Even though the logic above still applies, there is no way of precisely
determining the access to the object. The following example illustrates this point.

The user BobMgr wants Read and Write access to the file object that has the
discretionary ACL shown next. The access token for BobMgr indicates that he is
a member of the groups Users, JnrMgrs, and Everyone.

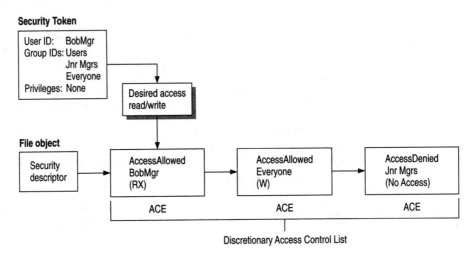

In this example, a custom application has been used to update the ACL for a file,
thus confusing the usual order in which the ACEs for this file are processed.
Normally, all AccessDenied ACEs are processed first.

Windows NT evaluates this ACL as follows:

1. Windows NT reads BobMgr's desired access mask to see that he is trying to gain Read and Write access.

2. Windows NT reads the AccessAllowed ACE for BobMgr and finds a match to the Read permission requested in the desired access mask.

3. Windows NT reads the AccessAllowed ACE for Everyone and finds a match to the Write permission requested in the desired access mask.

BobMgr is granted Read and Write access to the file object, even though the third ACE explicitly denies JnrMgrs access to the file object.

If the Windows NT Permissions Editor had been used to apply the same permissions to the file object, the AccessDenied ACE for JnrMgrs would have been ordered first in the ACL, and BobMgr would have been denied access to the file.

Auditing Security Events

Windows NT includes auditing features you can use to collect information about how your system is being used. These features also allow you to monitor events related to system security, to identify any security breaches, and to determine the extent and location of any damage. The level of audited events is adjustable to suit the needs of your organization. Some organizations need little auditing information, while others would be willing to trade some performance and disk space for detailed information they can use to analyze their system.

Note Remember that when you enable auditing, there is some small performance overhead for each audit check the system performs.

Windows NT can track events related to the operating system itself and to individual applications. Each application can define its own auditable events. Definitions of these events are added to the Registry when the application is installed on your Windows NT computer.

Audit events are identified to the system by the event source module name (which corresponds to a specific event type in the Registry) and an event ID.

In addition to listing events by event ID, the security log in Event Viewer lists them by category. The following categories of events are displayed in the Security Log. (Those in parentheses are found in the Audit Policy dialog box of User Manager.)

Category	Meaning
Account Management (User and Group Management)	These events describe high-level changes to the user accounts database, such as User Created or Group Membership Change. Potentially, a more detailed, object-level audit is also performed (see Object Access events).
Detailed Tracking (Process Tracking)	These events provide detailed subject-tracking information. This includes information such as program activation, handle duplication, and indirect object access.
Logon/Logoff (Logon and Logoff)	These events describe a single logon or logoff attempt, whether successful or unsuccessful. Included in each logon description is an indication of what type of logon was requested or performed (that is, interactive, network, or service).
Object Access (File and Object Access)	These events describe both successful and unsuccessful accesses to protected objects.
Policy Change (Security Policy Changes)	These events describe high-level changes to the security policy database, such as assignment of privileges or logon capabilities. Potentially, a more detailed, object-level audit is also performed (see Object Access events).
Privilege Use (Use of User Rights)	These events describe both successful and unsuccessful attempts to use privileges. It also includes information about when some special privileges are assigned. These special privileges are audited only at assignment time, not at time of use.
System Event (System)	These events indicate something affecting the security of the entire system or audit log occurred.

See "Security Event Examples" later in this chapter for examples of most of these event categories.

Process IDs and Handle IDs of Audit Events

One of the most important aspects of security is determining who is actually behind operations of security interest, such as file writes or security policy change. With the client-server model of Windows, user account identification can be rather tricky. Although a thread that requests access to a resource is identified by the user ID, the thread may be impersonating someone else. In this case, it would be misleading to log events by user ID and may not be very useful in finding the perpetrator in the case of a security breach.

To prevent this problem, there are two levels of subject identification used in Windows NT auditing and the security log—the user ID (also called the primary ID) and the impersonation ID (also called the client ID), as applicable. These two IDs show security administrators who are performing auditable actions.

In some cases, however, a security administrator wants to see what is happening with each process. To meet this need, auditing information also includes a subject's process ID where possible.

When process tracking is enabled (through the Audit Policy dialog box of User Manager), audit messages are generated each time a new process is created. This information can be correlated with specific audit messages to see not only which user account is being used to perform auditable actions, but also which program was run.

Many audit events also include a handle ID, enabling the event to be associated with future events. For example, when a file is opened, the audit information indicates the handle ID assigned. When the handle is closed, another audit event with the same handle ID is generated. With this information, you can determine exactly how long the file remained open. This could be useful, for example, when you want to assess damage following a security breach.

The following list shows some of the information that Windows NT tracks within a process's access token. This information also is used for auditing.

- The security ID of the user account used to log on
- The group security IDs and corresponding attributes of groups to which the user is assigned membership
- The names of the privileges assigned to and used by the user, and their corresponding attributes
- Authentication ID, assigned when the user logs on

Security Event Examples

As described earlier, you can track several categories of security events. This section provides examples for most of these categories. This set of examples does not constitute a strategy for using the auditing capabilities of Windows NT; they merely serve as an introduction to help you interpret these events when you enable auditing for your Windows NT system.

Example 1: Tracking File and Object Access

In this example, auditing is enabled as follows (assuming you are logged on as an administrator):

- From File Manager, select the .TXT file, and then choose Auditing from the Security menu. Assign Full Control permission to the user accessing the .TXT file and enable auditing for Success and Failure of Read and Write events.

- From User Manager, choose Audit from the Policies menu. Then enable auditing for Success and Failure of File and Object Access and Process Tracking.

From File Manager, the user double-clicks the .TXT file (which is associated with Notepad) and then writes some data to the file, saves it, and closes the file.

This results in audit events, as shown below:

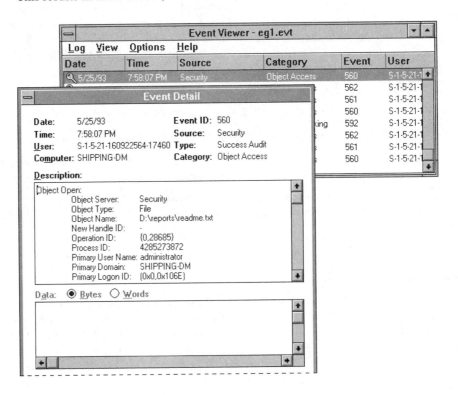

From this view of the security log, you get a quick summary of security-related events that occurred. Double-click the first event to examine the details. (For example, details of this first event are shown in the Event Detail box.)

The data that needs to be interpreted is listed in the Description list box. The following table summarizes the audited events for this example, in the order they occurred.

Table 2.1   Security Events for File Access Example

Event ID and description	Analysis
Event 560: Object Open Event 561: Handle Allocated Event 562: Handle Closed	In this sequence of events, Windows NT is doing some internal checks, such as checking to see if the file exists and checking to see that there is no sharing violation.
Event 592: A New Process Has Been Created Event 560: Object Open Event 561: Handle Allocated Event 562: Handle Closed	In this series of events, a new process is created for NOTEPAD.EXE. This process opens the .TXT file for reading. Next, the process allocates, then closes, a handle to the file. Note that from the security log it is clear that Notepad does not keep an open handle to the file; it simply keeps a copy of the file in memory.
Event 560: Object Open Event 561: Handle Allocated Event 562: Handle Closed	The process opens the file for reading and writing, and since the event is a successful audit, new data is written to the file. Next, the handle is allocated for the open file, then closed.
Event 593: A Process Has Exited	This event indicates that the process, whose process ID relates to NOTEPAD.EXE, has ended.

Example 2: Use of User Rights

In this example, auditing is enabled by using User Manager to enable auditing for Success and Failure of Use of User Rights.

When the user tries to change the system time, only one event is generated, as shown below.

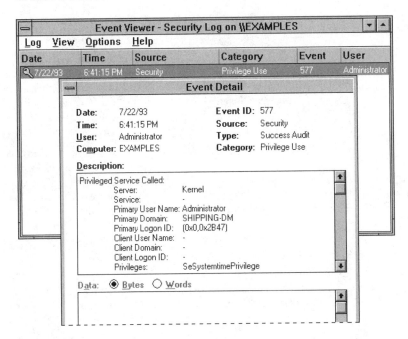

This event indicates that a privileged service was called and that a server component named Kernel has called an audit check on the primary username of the user. The audit type is a Success Audit, meaning that the user successfully exercised the right to use the SeSystemtimePrivilege (that is, the right to change the system time).

Example 3: User and Group Management

In this example, a new user account is added to the user accounts database. Auditing is enabled in User Manager by specifying both Success and Failure of User and Group Management. This generates four audit events, as shown below:

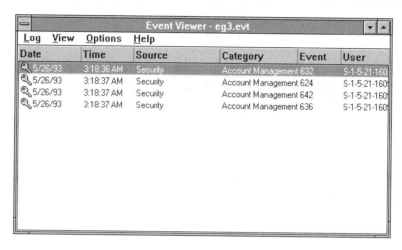

Table 2.2   **Security Events for Added User Account**

Event ID and description	Analysis
Event 632: Global Group Member Added Event 624: User Account Created	A new security ID (member) is created and added to the group represented by the target account ID. This is a default global group Domain Users. At this point, the security ID does not have a username allocated to it.
Event 642: User Account Changed	This event indicates that the account name of the security ID represented by the Target Account ID has been changed to the new user's.
Event 636: Local Group Member Added	This event indicates that the account represented by the new user's security ID is created. The new user is added to the local group represented the security ID under Target Account ID (Users).

Example 4: Restart, Shutdown and System

In this example, auditing is enabled in User Manager for both Success and Failure of Restart, Shutdown and System.

In this example, seven events were generated. Note, however, that the number of events generated is related to the number of trusted systems that you start when the system is restarted. This number may vary if you replicate this scenario on your own Windows NT computer.

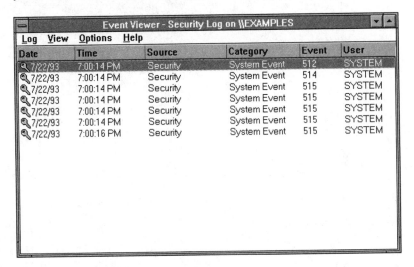

Table 2.3   Security Events for System Startup

Event ID and description	Analysis
Event 512: Windows NT is starting up.	Identifies the date and time the system started.
Event 514: Authentication package loaded	The description of this event says:
	An authentication package has been loaded by the Local Security Authority. This authentication package will be used to authenticate logon attempts. Authentication Package Name: msv 1_0
	This is the standard authentication package shipped with Windows NT.

Table 2.3   Security Events for System Startup *(continued)*

Event ID and description	Analysis
Events 515: Trusted logon process	The description for each of these events says:

(continued in right column:)

The description for each of these events says:

```
A trusted logon process has registered with the
Local Security Authority. This logon process
will be trusted to submit logon requests.
```

The logon process name is listed for each of these events, as follows:

Winlogon
Service Control Manager
LAN Manager Workstation Service
LAN Manager Server
LAN Manager Redirector

Each of these events is a successful audit in the category of system event. These events indicate that the respective logon processes have registered themselves with the Local Security Authority and are now trusted to submit logon requests.

Audit Determination

Windows NT has an audit determination process similar to its access determination process, described earlier in this chapter. Following access determination, Windows NT evaluates the following information for possible auditing:

- The subject attempting the access (that is, the set of identifiers representing the subject)

- The desired accesses with all generic access types mapped to standard and specific access types

- The final determination of whether access is granted or denied

- The audit ACL associated with the target object

Each ACE in the audit ACL is evaluated as follows:

1. Windows NT checks to see if the type is SystemAudit. If not, the ACE is skipped.

2. Windows NT compares the identifier in the ACE to the set of identifiers representing the subject. If no match is found, the ACE is skipped.

3. The desired accesses are compared to the access mask specified in the ACE.

4. If none of the accesses specified in the ACE's mask were requested, the ACE is skipped. The SUCCESSFUL_ACCESS_ACE_FLAG and FAILED_ACCESS_ACE_FLAG flags of the ACE are compared to the final determination of whether access was granted or denied.

5. If access was granted but the SUCCESSFUL_ACCESS_ACE_FLAG flag is not set, or if access was denied but the FAILED_ACCESS_ACE_FLAG flag is not set, the ACE is skipped.

If Windows NT performs all of these steps successfully, an audit message is generated.

The scenario shown below illustrates this process. In this scenario, a system access ACL is being evaluated. Here, Write access to the file object is granted, and the SUCCESSFUL_ACCESS_ACE_FLAG is set in each ACE.

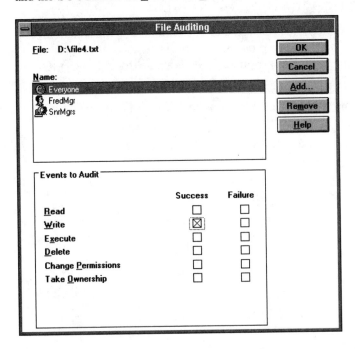

In this example, Windows NT evaluates the ACL by comparing the desired access mask with each ACE and processes the desired mask as follows:

1. Windows NT evaluates an ACE for SnrMgrs (of which FredMgr is a member). However, when the desired access is compared to the access mask of the ACE, no match is found, and the ACE is skipped.

2. Windows NT evaluates the ACE for FredMgr and finds a match.

3. Windows NT checks access flags and finds the SUCCESSFUL_ACCESS_ACE_FLAG is set. Processing stops, and an audit message is generated.

PART II

Setting Up Windows NT

Part Two discusses issues related to installing and starting Windows NT on your computer, including how to use computer profiles to set up multiple Windows NT computers. Chapter 4 also describes the files included on the Windows NT Setup disks.

C H A P T E R   3

Customizing Windows NT Setup

This chapter describes how an administrator can customize the Windows NT Setup program to meet the specific needs of an organization. Administrators can customize Setup, for example, by adding files and applications to Windows NT, or by excluding certain unused features, such as POSIX or OS/2 support, to reduce the amount of disk space needed to install Windows NT.

This chapter also explains how to use Computer Profile Setup (CPS), a utility that makes it easy to install Windows NT on multiple computers with identical configurations within your organization.

This chapter assumes that you are familiar with the Windows NT Setup procedures presented in the *Windows NT System Guide*, and with the material in the *Windows NT Installation Guide*.

You can customize Windows NT installation for your organization by using an unattended answer file for unattended setup, modifying TXTSETUP.SIF and selected .INF files, or by using Computer Profile Setup (CPS), or by using some combination of these three.

Using an unattended answer file for unattended setup is the simplest method. You can create an unattended answer file for each hardware configuration used in your organization (for example, where a large number of users have the same model of computer with the same adapter cards and video displays), or an unattended answer file for each division, or even an unattended answer file for each user. The granularity you choose depends on how much input you want to require from your users when they install or upgrade to Windows NT 3.5. For more information about unattended setup, see "Installing Without Bootable Floppy Disks" later in this chapter.

If you want to modify the normal Windows NT installation by adding or excluding files, you'll need to modify TXTSETUP.SIF and selected .INF files. These files control what files are copied, what changes are made to the Registry, and so on. For more information about unattended setup, see "Customizing Setup" later in this chapter.

If there is little or no variation in the hardware configurations used on your network, CPS is a convenient method of installation. CPS can be used to copy either a stock or a customized setup to large numbers of identical systems. This method is often used by hardware manufacturers to pre-load the operating system on the units they sell. If you have created a customized installation on your master system (by modifying the TXTSETUP.SIF and .INF files), then the customized version will be downloaded to all the target systems. For more information about unattended setup, see "Preinstalling Windows NT Using CPS" later in this chapter.

About Windows NT Information Files

To customize Windows NT Setup, you need a clear understanding of the Windows NT information (.INF) files and the TXTSETUP.SIF file, which control the Setup program. You modify these files to customize Windows NT Setup for your organization.

The .INF files are used by Windows NT Setup to install the operating system. The structure of the Windows NT .INF files is somewhat different than those used in Windows 3.x and Windows for Workgroups. One main difference is that Windows NT .INF files utilize a scripting language that allows the Setup program to perform various tasks.

The .INF files also contain lists of files that need to be copied to the target computer; for each file a disk number is specified to indicate where Setup can find the file. The location of the source file depends on the *source media* used—3.5-inch floppy disks or compact disk (CD). If you are setting up from a shared network directory, Setup ignores any source disk numbers it finds, assuming instead that all files are on that shared directory. The .INF files also list destinations for the files it copies.

A new feature in Windows NT 3.5 is the TXTSETUP.SIF file. This file controls the text mode portion of Setup, including changes to the Registry when you are upgrading from an earlier version of Windows NT. Because the TXTSETUP.SIF file lists all of the files supplied for a specific platform, it is used when you repair your system if it becomes damaged.

Key Information Files Used by Setup

Before customizing Setup for your organization, you need to become familiar with the following four files used by Setup. These files call the other .INF files and control the Setup process. For a complete list of the .INF files and what they do, see Chapter 4, "Windows NT Files." The four key files are described in the following table.

Filename	Controls this part of Setup
TXTSETUP.SIF	Text-mode installation of core Windows NT components. Used by Setup from CD or floppy disks, or via the **winnt** or **winnt32** utility (discussed later in this chapter).
INITIAL.INF	Graphical-mode installation of additional Windows NT components. Used by Setup via CD, floppy disks, or the **winnt** or **winnt32** utility.
PARTIAL.INF	Graphical-mode installation of optional Windows NT components and creation of Program Manager groups. Used by Setup via CD, floppy disks, or the **winnt** or **winnt32** utility.
DOSNET.INF	Contains the list of files copied to your local hard disk during **winnt** or **winnt32** Setup. Used by the MS-DOS portion of **winnt**, and by **winnt32** Setup.

This section explains how each of these files is used by Setup and how you might use them to customize your installation.

The TXTSETUP.SIF File

When you begin the Setup program from CD or floppy disks, Setup first prompts you where you want to install Windows NT and lets you reformat and repartition your hard disk. This stage uses text mode rather than Windows graphics mode. After the questions are answered, Setup copies the minimum set of files necessary for running Windows NT and completing the setup process.

During this text-mode phase of Setup, drivers for the keyboard, mouse, video, SCSI adapter, and the computer itself (the *hardware access layer*, or HAL) are installed. The TXTSETUP.SIF file provides the lists of choices for drivers for all of these components.

The TXTSETUP.SIF file is the file that specifies all the files to be copied during setup, and all the keys and values to be added or changed in the Registry during upgrades. Since this file is used at the very beginning of the text mode portion of setup, any changes made to it must be made on the first boot floppy disk itself or on the copy on the distribution share. Since this file is also used if a system needs to be repaired, any file that you add to your installation should also be added to the list at the end of this file.

The INITIAL.INF File

After the minimum set of files have been copied to your hard disk, Setup restarts the computer. The computer boots into the graphical Windows Setup. The INITIAL.INF file guides this next part of Setup.

The INITIAL.INF file causes Setup to install key components, including File Manager, Program Manager, fonts, and compatibility files for MS-DOS, Windows 16-bit, OS/2, and POSIX environments; but not optional components such as accessories.

The INITIAL.INF file initiates other parts of Setup, for example asking the user to choose optional components and install a printer.

You must change this file to change the fonts that are installed by Setup.

The PARTIAL.INF File

The PARTIAL.INF file contains the list of optional components, including screen savers, wallpapers, README files, and games. All optional components are automatically installed with Windows NT if you selected Express Setup. During Custom Setup, the user specifies which of the optional components are installed, choosing from the components listed in the PARTIAL.INF file.

The PARTIAL.INF file is also responsible for creating Program Manager groups and adding programs to those groups.

If you want to increase or restrict the set of optional components from which a user can choose, modify the PARTIAL.INF file. If you want new program groups to be added during installation, modify this file.

The DOSNET.INF File

The DOSNET.INF file is only used when setting up Windows NT across the network via the **winnt** or **winnt32** utility. These commands copy files from a distribution share or CD to the target computer. The distribution share includes the complete set of files from the Windows NT Setup CD or floppy disk set.

When you run the **winnt** or **winnt32** utility, all of the necessary files on the distribution share are copied to a temporary directory called WIN_NT.~LS on the hard disk of the target computer. The DOSNET.INF file defines which files are copied to this temporary directory. If you add files to the distribution share, you must add the filenames to the list in the DOSNET.INF file so that they will be copied. If you want to exclude files, you'll need to comment out the lines in the file list that refer to those files.

Once the files are copied to the temporary directory, the **winnt** or **winnt32** utility prompts you to restart the computer. From this point, Setup proceeds as though you were running Setup from a CD, except that files are copied from the WIN_NT.~LS directory rather than from the CD. At the end of Setup, the WIN_NT.~LS directory is deleted.

In addition, information from the DOSNET.INF file is used to create the boot floppy disks that are used to install Windows NT on x86 computers.

Important   Whenever you alter the DOSNET.INF file, you must alter the TXTSETUP.SIF file and at least one other .INF file (either the INITIAL.INF or PARTIAL.INF file).

For example, if you add a file to the INITIAL.INF, PARTIAL.INF, or TXTSETUP.SIF files, you must also add it to the DOSNET.INF file. Otherwise, Setup will not be able to find the file in the WIN_NT.~LS directory and generates an error when it tries to copy the file. Conversely, if you add a file to the DOSNET.INF file but do not add one to the TXTSETUP.SIF file or one of the other .INF files, then when you run the **winnt** or **winnt32** utility, the file will be copied to the WIN_NT.~LS directory but will not be installed on your computer.

Format of the INF Files

This chapter details several different scenarios for customizing Setup by altering the Windows NT .INF files. To best understand these scenarios, you need to understand how each of these four key .INF files are formatted.

Format of the INITIAL.INF and PARTIAL.INF Files

The INITIAL.INF and PARTIAL.INF files are text files that contain one or more sections. Each section begins with a section title in brackets (for example, "[Files-I386-nt-system32]"). Some sections contain lists of files to be installed by Setup. Other sections contain a Setup scripting language. The scripting language is not usually needed for customizing setup, and is beyond the scope of this chapter.

In the INITIAL.INF file, files are listed in the following format:

disk number, filename, SIZE=*file size*

where *disk number* is the number of the Setup floppy disk or CD on which the file exists. The following is an example of a typical section in the INITIAL.INF file.

```
[Files-i386-WindowsOptions]
1,256COLOR.BMP , SIZE=999
1,ARCADE.BMP , SIZE=999
```

In the PARTIAL.INF file, the name assigned to the option is also indicated. The format is as follows:

option name = disk number, filename, SIZE=*file size*

where *option name* is defined in the [Optional*TypeLanguage*] section.

For example, the options presented during Setup as "256-Color Wallpaper" and "Arcade Wallpaper" are defined in the following section of the PARTIAL.INF file:

```
[OptionalWallpapersENG]
    256ColorWallpaper = "256-Color Wallpaper"
    ArcadeWallpaper   = "Arcade Wallpaper"
...
```

The file used for this option is defined as shown in the following example from the PARTIAL.INF file:

```
[Files-i386-WindowsOptions]
256ColorWallpaper = 1,256COLOR.BMP , SIZE=999
ArcadeWallpaper = 1,ARCADE.BMP , SIZE=999
```

Each .INF file also contains a [Source Media Descriptions] section, which lists the Setup media. Usually, there will be only one entry for the CD. In this case, the section looks similar to the following:

```
[Source Media Descriptions]
    1  = "Windows NT Server CD-ROM"  , TAGFILE = cdrom.s
```

The number in the first column is the *disk number*, which is used in the file list described earlier. If you are using a floppy disk set, each disk in the set is listed, and the [Source Media Descriptions] sections looks similar to the following:

```
[Source Media Descriptions]
    1  = "Windows NT Setup Disk #1"  , TAGFILE = disk1
    2  = "Windows NT Setup Disk #2"  , TAGFILE = disk2
    3  = "Windows NT Setup Disk #3"  , TAGFILE = disk3
    ...
```

Note Lines in the files that begin with a semicolon (;) are treated as comments and are ignored by Setup. Including comments in these files is helpful, for example, when you want to document changes you are making to the file.

You can also use a semicolon for commenting out lines in the TXTSETUP.SIF file. In the DOSNET.INF file, use a pound sign (#) instead of a semicolon for commenting out lines.

Remember that you must use the correct symbol for the file you are modifying; otherwise, Setup fails.

Format of the DOSNET.INF File

The DOSNET.INF file is a text file composed of sections that contain no scripting language. Files are listed in the following format:

d1,*filename*

Note The **d1** value is not a disk number. This value, as defined in the [Directories] section of this file, indicates where the file exists relative to the directory in which the DOSNET.INF file is located on the distribution share. You can specify subdirectories, but not parent directories, of the directory in which the DOSNET.INF file is located.

Unlike the other .INF files, the DOSNET.INF file does not have a [Source Media Descriptions] section. In fact, no disk numbers are listed in it, because it is used for installing over the network or CD, rather than from floppy disks.

The following is an example of a typical section in the DOSNET.INF file:

```
[Files]
d1,256COLOR.BMP
d1,3DGARRO.CUR
d1,3DGMOVE.CUR
d1,3DGNESW.CUR
...
```

Format of the TXTSETUP.SIF File

Like the INITIAL.INF and PARTIAL.INF files, the TXTSETUP.SIF file is a text file containing sections marked by section titles in square brackets. The TXTSETUP.SIF file specifies what files are to be copied and what changes are to be made to an existing Registry during the initial, text mode, phase of Setup. The structure of this file allows conditional file copies.

For example, certain files might need to be copied only during an upgrade from an earlier version of Windows NT, and not during a fresh installation. Or, a file might need to be copied only if a version of the file already exists in the target directory. What Setup should do in each case is specified in the TXTSETUP.SIF file. In the case of an upgrade, sections in this file also specify changes to the existing Registry. In addition, the TXTSETUP.SIF file specifies supported hardware, files that should be deleted if found on the existing system, and options for booting.

The sections that you most likely need to modify in order to customize Setup are listed in the following table, in the order they are found in the TXTSETUP.SIF file.

Section	Specifies
[Files.DeleteOnUpgrade]	Files used in a previous version of Windows NT that are to be deleted before the new version is installed.
[Files.BackupOnUpgrade]	Files used in a previous version of Windows NT that are to be backed up before the new version is installed.
[Files.BackupOnOverwrite]	Files that are to be backed up (if they exist) before overwriting them during Setup. The files are only backed up if they are to be overwritten.
[Files.UpgradeWin31]	Files used with a Microsoft Windows 3.1 product (including Windows for Workgroups) that are also used by Windows NT. These files will not be replaced with Windows NT files by the same name during Setup if you are installing Windows NT into a Windows 3.1 directory.
[WinntDirectories]	Numbers assigned to each subdirectory of the Windows NT root directory. These numbers are used in other sections to locate the individual files.
[SetupData]	Required resources, such as available disk space; also options to be used during setup, such as debugging.
[Media]	Short name assigned to each floppy disk in the Windows NT installation disk set or to the Windows NT installation CD.
[Files]	All files in the installation set for this platform.

There are also sections for manipulating the Registry. Generally, it is best to make changes to the Registry only through graphical interfaces such as the Administrative tools and Control Panel icons, and avoid working with the Registry directly. However, if you routinely use Regedit32 to change Registry entries after installation, you can use these sections to incorporate the changes during Setup. For more information, see "Using the TXTSETUP.SIF File to Update the Registry," later in this chapter.

The [Files.DeleteOnUpgrade] Section

The [Files.DeleteOnUpgrade] section of the TXTSETUP.SIF file lists the files that you might have installed in a previous version of Windows NT that need to be deleted when you upgrade to the current version.

The format of this section is *file*, *dir* where *file* is the filename and *dir* is the subdirectory of the Windows NT root directory where the file will be found. The subdirectory is specified with a number, as defined in the [WinntDirectories] section.

The [Files.BackupOnUpgrade] Section

The [Files.BackupOnUpgrade] section of the TXTSETUP.SIF file lists the files that you might have installed in a previous version of Windows NT that need to be backed up before you upgrade to the current version.

The format of this section is *file*, *dir*, *newname* where *file* is the filename, *dir* is the subdirectory of the Windows NT root directory where the file will be found, and *newname* is the name you want to give the backup copy of the file. The subdirectory is specified with a number, as defined in the [WinntDirectories] section.

The [Files.BackupOnOverwrite] Section

The [Files.BackupOnOverwrite] section of the TXTSETUP.SIF file lists the files that you might have installed in a previous version of Windows NT that need to be backed up before they are overwritten during an upgrade to the current version of Windows NT. If the files are not overwritten during the upgrade process, they are not backed up.

The format of this section is *file*, *dir*, *newname* where *file* is the filename, *dir* is the subdirectory of the Windows NT root directory where the file will be found, and *newname* is the name you want to give the backup copy of the file. The subdirectory is specified with a number, as defined in the [WinntDirectories] section.

The [Files.UpgradeWin31] Section

The [Files.UpgradeWin31] section of the TXTSETUP.SIF file lists the files that might exist in an existing installation of Windows 3.1 or related operating system (such as Windows for Workgroups 3.1) that are also used by Windows NT. The files are listed in this section if they are not to be replaced with Windows NT files by the same filename during setup.

The format of this section is *file*, *dir* where *file* is the filename and *dir* is the subdirectory of the Windows NT root directory where the file will be found. The subdirectory is specified with a number, as defined in the [WinntDirectories] section.

The [WinntDirectories] Section

The [WinntDirectories] section of the TXTSETUP.SIF file assigns a number to the Windows NT root directory and each of its subdirectories. These numbers are used in other sections of the TXTSETUP.SIF file to specify the locations of files. If you want to add a subdirectory for files specific to your corporation, you can specify it in this section.

The format of this section is *n* = *directory*, where *n* is an integer and *directory* is the path, relative to the Windows NT root directory. The following is an example of a typical [WinntDirectories] section:

```
[WinntDirectories]
1  = \
2  = system32
3  = system32\config
4  = system32\drivers
```

The [SetupData] Section

The [SetupData] section of the TXTSETUP.SIF file supplies data used by Setup. This includes required resources, such as available disk space, and debugging options.

The following is an example of a typical [SetupData] section:

```
[SetupData]
ProductType = 0
MajorVersion = 3
MinorVersion = 50
FreeDiskSpace = 80000
FreeSysPartDiskSpace = 750
UpgradeFreeDiskSpace = 10000
UpgradeFreeSysPartDiskSpace = 500
DefaultPath=\WINNT35
LoadIdentifier  = "Windows NT Workstation Version 3.5"
BaseVideoLoadId = "Windows NT Workstation Version 3.5 [VGA mode]"
OsLoadOptions = "/nodebug"
AllowFloppySetup = 1
RequiredMemory = 7864320
```

The lines that you might need to modify in the [SetupData] section are as follows:

FreeDiskSpace

Specifies the amount of free disk space that must be available for a fresh installation of Windows NT. If you add files to your custom installation, increase this value by the number of bytes in the files you add. If you exclude files from your custom installation, decrease this value by the number of bytes in the files you exclude.

UpgradeFreeDiskSpace

Specifies the amount of free disk space that must be available for an upgrade from an earlier version of Windows NT. If you add files to your custom installation, increase this value by the number of bytes in the files you add. If you exclude files from your custom installation, decrease this value by the number of bytes in the files you exclude.

DefaultPath

Specifies the location of the system root directory of Windows NT relative to the drive the files are installed on. If you want your custom installation to be written to a directory other than \WINNT35, change the specification on this line.

LoadIdentifier

Specifies the text that appears during setup to identify the system that is being installed. You can change the text in quotes to describe your custom installation.

BaseVideoLoadId

Specifies the text that appears when the installation is using the /BASEVIDEO option. This applies only when installing on x86 computers.

OsLoadOptions

Specifies debugging options, which are enclosed in double quote marks. The options you specify here apply only to text mode setup. To have one or more of these options applied after text mode setup (that is, during Graphical mode setup and any other time the computer is started), add the line **OsLoadOptionsVar =** */option* [*/option*...]. For **OsLoadOptionsVar**, as for **OsLoadOptions**, the options you specify must be enclosed in double quote marks.

The options for OsLoadOptionsVAR are the same as those for OsLoadOptions and are listed in the following table:

Option	Description
/NODEBUG	The default; it means that no debugging information is collected or transmitted during installation.
/DEBUG	The customary switch to enable debugging. The last standard COM port found is used, unless a port is specified with the /DEBUGPORT=COMx switch.
/DEBUGPORT=COMx	Sends debug output to the specific COM port.
/BAUDRATE=nnnnn	Specifies the baud rate at which data is sent through the COM port for remote debugging using a modem. The default is 19200.
/NoSerialMice	Disables the serial mouse detection on certain COM ports. It is mostly used to exclude ports used by the uninterruptible power supply (UPS) system. The detection signal causes some UPS units to power down, thereby turning off the computer. If you need to use this switch, you might also want to add it to the BOOT.INI file, as described in Chapter 18, "Troubleshooting."
	You can use multiple **/NoSerialMice** switches. The format is as follows:
	/NoSerialMice=[COMx | COMx,COMy,COMz,...]
	If **/NoSerialMice** is specified without parameters, serial mouse detection is disabled on all the serial ports. If **/NoSerialMice=COMx** is specified, serial mouse detection is only disabled on COMx. If **/NoSerialMice=COMx,COMy,COMz ...** is specified, serial mouse detection is disabled on each of the specified ports.

AllowFloppySetup

Specifies whether the installation must be from a CD or whether floppy disk sets can be used. To prevent installations from being made using floppy disk sets, set this value to **0**.

The [Media] Section

The [Media] section of the TXTSETUP.SIF file is used to assign a code to each of the floppy disks in the Windows NT installation disk set and to assign the **dx** code to the Windows NT installation CD. If you add a disk to the installation disk set, add it to the end of this section. The code you assign to it can then be used in other sections of the TXTSETUP.SIF file to indicate to Setup where to find the files you have placed on this disk. Files that you add to a distribution share will all be identified as being on **dx**.

The [Files] Section

The [Files] section of the TXTSETUP.SIF file lists all the files for the platform. Each file in this section is listed in the following format:

filename = **dx**, *disk id*, [*boot floppy*], *install directory*, *conditions for upgrade* [*,conditions for fresh install*[*,new file name*]]

where the **dx** parameter is read when installing from the CD. It is defined in the [Media] section of this file, which immediately precedes the [Files] section. This parameter must always be present.

Disk id is used when installing from a set of floppy disks, and specifies the floppy disk on which the file is found. It also is defined in the [Media] section.

Boot floppy specifies the bootable floppy disk on which the file can be found. If the file is not on any bootable floppy disk, this field is blank. This parameter is primarily used to specify a SCSI miniport driver.

Install directory is the directory to which the file will be copied, as defined in the [WinntDirectories] section. All definitions in the [WinntDirectories] section are subdirectories of the Windows NT root directory. You are prompted for this directory during the text mode stage of Setup.

Conditions for upgrade is a single digit that specifies whether the file is to be copied during the text mode portion of setup when upgrading from an earlier version of Windows NT. The possible values for *conditions for upgrade* are listed in the following table:

Code	Action
0	Copy always
1	Copy only if the file exists in the install directory
2	Do not copy if the file exists in the install directory
3	Do not copy

Conditions for fresh install is a single digit that specifies whether the file is to be copied during the text mode portion of setup when installing on a computer that has no earlier version of Windows NT. This value is optional; if it is not included, the file is not copied. The possible values are the same as those for *conditions for upgrade*.

New file name is the name the file will be renamed to when it is copied. If this parameter is omitted, the file will not be renamed.

The following is an example of a typical line in the [Files] section of the TXTSETUP.SIF file:

```
ntkrnlmp.exe = dx,d4,_1,2,3
```

This line specifies that the file, NTKRNLMP.EXE, is found on the CD or on floppy disk **d4** (as defined in the [Media] section). It is also found on boot floppy disk **_1**, which is also defined in the [Media] section. It is to be installed in directory **2**, as defined in the [WinntDirectories] section. Since the line in the [WinntDirectories] section for directory 2 reads as **2 = system32**, the file is installed in the \SYSTEM32 subdirectory of the Windows NT root directory. The **3** at the end of the line means the file is not copied during text mode setup when upgrading from an earlier version of Windows NT. Since the last two parameters are missing, this line does not cause the file to be copied during text mode setup when installing on a computer that has no version of Windows NT installed, and the file is not renamed when copied.

Note Lines in the TXTSETUP.SIF file beginning with a semicolon (;) are comments and ignored by Setup. Remember that you must use the correct symbol for the file you are modifying; otherwise, Setup fails.

Creating a Distribution Share

In most cases, people who customize Windows NT Setup are doing so for a corporation whose users will run Setup from a distribution share. Therefore, the first step (after installing Windows NT on at least one computer) is to set up a distribution share for your corporation. You need separate shares for Windows NT workstation and Windows NT server. You will modify the files after they are in the shared directory.

This section explains some of the caveats to creating Setup shares along with a few preparatory steps you will need to take before modifying the files.

▶ **To create a distribution share**

1. Create a share for the installation files for Windows NT servers and a separate share for the installation files for Windows NT workstations.

2. Copy the installation files to the shares you have created.

   By copying the entire set of files you can reproduce the directory structure on the distribution media. As a result, your distribution share will have different subdirectories for the different platforms (x86, MIPS, and so on).

   Copy the files from the Windows NT Setup CD, using the following syntax for the **xcopy** command:

   xcopy *cd*:\ *share* /s

   where *cd* is the drive letter you have assigned to your CD-ROM drive. *Share* is the location of the distribution share you created. For example:

   ```
   xcopy f:\i386 \\winnt35_dist\x86
   ```

3. Share the destination directory, making it read-only.

From target computers, users can connect to the appropriate directory on the distribution share to install Windows NT. Users running MS-DOS, Microsoft Windows, or Windows NT can connect to the appropriate directory on the distribution share and run the **winnt** or **winnt32** utility to start the installation process. For more information, see the *Windows NT System Guide*.

These distribution shares are used primarily for installing Windows NT with the **winnt** or **winnt32** utility. They can also be used by a user who has installed Windows NT and wants to install additional files. For instance, a user who wants to install a printer driver can type in the path to the network distribution share when Setup prompts for the location of the printer driver.

Customizing Setup

This section discusses how to customize the setup files on a distribution share.

The files on the Windows NT installation CD cannot, of course, be altered because you would have to create a custom CD. Also, it is not recommended that you try to alter the files on the Windows NT installation disk set because the altered files might be larger than the original installation files; thus, reassigning disk numbers to numerous files can quickly become a daunting task.

It is recommended that you perform a plain installation on a new computer, and then use the network to upgrade to your custom installation. However, if you simply want to add a few files to a floppy disk installation set, you can put them in an additional disk, and specify the disk and the files in the [Media] and [Files] sections of the TXTSETUP.SIF file. Where the file is named in the [Files] section, specify that it be copied always, as described under "Format of the TXTSETUP.SIF File" earlier in this chapter.

Caution Be careful when making modifications to the .SIF and .INF files. Troubleshooting changes made to these files is quite difficult. Setup is unforgiving about incorrect syntax in its instructions. Never modify the original file; always make a backup copy. When you get part of your changes working, make a backup copy of the working file.

Making changes to these files is *not* supported by Microsoft Product Support Services. This information is only provided for your reference.

Adding a File to the Windows NT Installation

If you want to add files during the installation of Windows NT, but don't need the file added to a Program Manager group, you only need to put the files on the distribution share and modify the TXTSETUP.SIF and DOSNET.INF files.

For example, suppose an administrator at Terra Flora, Inc. wants to add an online help file that employees can use to help resolve common problems for Terra Flora's business. The administrator adds TERRA.HLP to the distribution share, then makes changes to the TXTSETUP.SIF and DOSNET.INF files as described in the following sections.

Note When you add files to Setup, be sure to change the minimum required disk space needed for installation. For more information, see "Changing Minimum Disk Space Requirements" later in this chapter.

The TXTSETUP.SIF File

After the file has been created and placed in the distribution share, it must be added to the [Files] section of the TXTSETUP.SIF file. If you want Setup to create a special subdirectory in the Windows NT root directory for this file, it should be specified in the [WinntDirectories] section. For example, you might add the following line to the [WinntDirectories] section:

```
[WinntDirectories]
...
19  = TerraFlora
```

This directory could then be specified when adding the Terra Flora help file, TERRA.HLP, to the end of the [Files] section, as follows:

```
[Files]
...
terra.hlp = dx,d33,,19,0,0
```

This causes the file to be copied to directory 19 (the \TERRAFLORA subdirectory of the Windows NT root directory); it will be copied whenever anyone upgrades or installs Windows NT for the first time from this distribution share.

For more information on the format of the [WinntDirectories] and [Files] sections, see "Format of the TXTSETUP.SIF" section earlier in this chapter.

The DOSNET.INF File

All files that need to be copied from the Setup share when a user runs the **winnt** or **winnt32** utility are listed in the [Files] section of the DOSNET.INF file, preceded by "**d1,**".

To add the TERRA.HLP file, the Terra Flora administrator adds a line specifying the file in the [Files] section of the DOSNET.INF file. In the following example, the line has been added at the end of the section:

```
[Files]
d1,256COLOR.BMP
d1,40291730.PPD
d1,40293930.PPD
d1,terra.hlp
```

Adding a New Program Manager Group

Windows NT Setup automatically creates the Main, Accessories, Administrative Tools, Games, and Startup groups in Program Manager. To have Windows NT create a new Program Manager group you need to modify the PARTIAL.INF file.

For example, the Terra Flora administrator creates a new program group called TerraFlora in which the TERRA.HLP file, Terra Flora Help, will be included. To do this, the administrator adds lines to the [ProgmanGroups] and [ProgmanGroupsDescriptionENG] sections of the PARTIAL.INF file. In the following example, the new lines are shown at the bottom of each section:

```
[ProgmanGroups]
    Main
    Accessories
    AdminTools
    Games
    Startup
    TerraFlora


[ProgmanGroupsDescriptionENG]
    Main           = "Main"
    Accessories    = "Accessories"
    Games          = "Games"
    Startup        = "Startup"
    AdminTools     = "Administrative Tools"
    TerraFlora     = "Terra Flora Help"
```

Adding File Manager and Other Programs to the Startup Group

You might want to add frequently-used programs to the Startup group so that they are automatically run after logon. To add a program to the Startup group, you need to modify the PARTIAL.INF file.

For example, to start File Manager automatically after the user logs on, you need to edit the PARTIAL.INF file. In the [InstallProgramGroups] section, change the "set StartupToInstall" line and add the [StartupItems] and [StartupItemsENG] sections with the necessary references to File Manager in those sections. For example, the resulting sections of the PARTIAL.INF file would look similar to the following:

```
[InstallProgramGroups]
    set Groups       = ^(ProgmanGroups, 1)
    set MainToInstall = ^(MainItems$(!STF_PRODUCT)$(!STF_PLATFORM), 1)
    set AdminToolsToInstall    = ^(AdminToolsItems$(!STF_PRODUCT), 1)
    set StartupToInstall    = ^(StartupItems,1)
; NOTE: Comment out the following line by prepending a semicolon.
;    set StartupToInstall       = {}
```

```
[PartialDestinationVars]
    AdminToolsDest    = $(!STF_WINDOWSSYSPATH)
    StartupDest       = $(!STF_WINDOWSSYSPATH)

[StartupItems]
    FileManager

[StartupItemsENG]
    FileManager = "File Manager", WINFILE.EXE , WINFILE.EXE , "" , 0
```

You can install other standard Windows NT programs in the Startup group
by adding to the items in the [StartupItems] and [StartupItemsENG] sections.
The following table shows what to type in these sections. The last item,
MiniUserManager, is part of Windows NT only. UserManager and ServerManager
are part of Windows NT server only.

[StartupItems]	[StartupItemsENG]
FileManager	FileManager = "File Manager", WINFILE.EXE , WINFILE.EXE , ""
Mail	Mail = "Mail", MSMAIL32.EXE , MSMAIL32.EXE , ""
SchedulePlus	SchedulePlus = "Schedule+", SCHDPL32.EXE , SCHDPL32.EXE , ""
ControlPanel	ControlPanel = "Control Panel", CONTROL.EXE , CONTROL.EXE , ""
PrintManager	PrintManager = "Print Manager", PRINTMAN.EXE , PRINTMAN.EXE , ""
Clipboard	Clipboard = "ClipBook Viewer", CLIPBRD.EXE , CLIPBRD.EXE , ""
Command	Command = "Command Prompt", CMD.EXE , CMD.EXE , "progman.exe",10
PerformanceMon	PerformanceMon = "Performance Monitor", PERFMON.EXE , PERFMON.EXE , "" , 0
Backup	Backup = "Backup", NTBACKUP.EXE , NTBACKUP.EXE , "" , 0
DiskManager	DiskManager = "Disk Administrator", WINDISK.EXE , WINDISK.EXE , "" , 0
EventViewer	EventViewer = "Event Viewer", EVENTVWR.EXE , EVENTVWR.EXE , "" , 0
UserManager	UserManager = "User Manager for Domains", USRMGR.EXE , USRMGR.EXE , "" , 0
ServerManager	ServerManager = "Server Manager", SRVMGR.EXE , SRVMGR.EXE , "" , 0
MiniUserManager	MiniUserManager = "User Manager", MUSRMGR.EXE , MUSRMGR.EXE , "" , 0

Adding Any Program to Any Program Manager Group

You can have Setup add items to any program group, not just the Startup group. This example shows how the Terra Flora administrator added the file, TERRA.HLP, (with the TERRA.ICO icon) to the Terra Flora Help Program group. The steps shown here can be used to add any program to any Program Manager group.

The first step in this process is to make sure the files are installed. In this case, the Terra Flora administrator adds the files TERRA.HLP and TERRA.ICO to Setup as described earlier in "Adding a File to the Windows NT Installation."

Next, if you are adding programs to a new program group, you must create that group, as described earlier in "Adding a New Program Manager Group."

Finally, you need to modify the PARTIAL.INF file. For example, the Terra Flora administrator makes a number of changes to the PARTIAL.INF file to ensure that TERRA.HLP is added to the Terra Flora Help program group.

The first change that the administrator makes is to the [PartialDestinationVars] section. In the following example, the new line is added to the end of the section:

```
[PartialDestinationVars]
    ReadmeDest            = $(!STF_WINDOWSPATH)
    AccessoriesDest       = $(!STF_WINDOWSSYSPATH)
    GamesDest             = $(!STF_WINDOWSSYSPATH)
    SaversDest            = $(!STF_WINDOWSSYSPATH)
    WallpapersDest        = $(!STF_WINDOWSPATH)
    MainDest              = $(!STF_WINDOWSSYSPATH)
    AdminToolsDest = $(!STF_WINDOWSSYSPATH)
    StartupDest = $(!STF_WINDOWSSYSPATH)
    TerraFloraDest  = $(!STF_WINDOWSSYSPATH)
```

The [PartialDestinationVars] section indicates where the files for the specific components will be installed in the system. $(!STF_WINDOWSPATH) means to install the files in the *SystemRoot* directory. $(!STF_WINDOWSSYSPATH) means to install the files in the *SystemRoot*\SYSTEM32 directory. The name in the left column matches the name of the group listed in the [ProgmanGroups] section, followed in the [ProgmanGroups] section by the text "Dest".

Next, the Terra Flora administrator adds a line to the [InstallProgramGroups] section. In the following example, the new line is added to the end of the section:

```
[InstallProgramGroups]
    set Groups = ^(ProgmanGroups, 1)
    set MainToInstall = ^(MainItems$(!STF_PRODUCT)$(!STF_PLATFORM), 1)
    set AdminToolsToInstall = ^(AdminToolsItems$(!STF_PRODUCT), 1)
    set TerraFloraToInstall    = ^(TerraFloraItems,1)
```

The [InstallProgramGroups] section specifies which group items will be installed in their respective groups. The item in the left column is the name of the group as mentioned in the [ProgmanGroups] section, followed in the [ProgmanGroups] section by the text "ToInstall". The text in the right column is the name of the section where the program items are listed.

The administrator adds a new section, [TerraFloraItems], to the PARTIAL.INF file to specify the new program group, with the new program item specified in that section. In the following example the new section appears after the [MainItemsWinntI386] section:

```
[MainItemsWinntI386]
    FileManager
    ControlPanel
    ...
    readme


[TerraFloraItems]
    TerraFloraHelp
```

The [TerraFloraItems] section lists the key names of the items that will be installed in the TerraFlora group.

Finally, the administrator creates the [TerraFloraItemsENG] section of the PARTIAL.INF file. In this section the name of the file that is represented by the name TerraFloraHelp is specified, using this format:

keyname = item description, command line, command line parameters, icon resource file, icon offset

The new section looks similar to the following:

```
[TerraFloraItemsENG]
    TerraFloraHelp = "Terra Flora Help",WINHLP32.EXE,"WINHLP32.EXE
"$(!STF_WINDOWSSYSPATH)"\TERAFLOR.HLP","TERAFLOR.ICO",0
```

Adding a New Optional Accessory

Setup gives the user the opportunity to choose what optional accessories to install and then creates a new program item for them in the Accessories Program Manager group. To add a new accessory, you must create the files, add the files to the distribution share, and then add the files to the [Files] section of the TXTSETUP.SIF file. Then you need to make modifications to the PARTIAL.INF and DOSNET.INF files.

For example, the Terra Flora administrator is adding a program called ORGCHART.EXE to the Accessories program group. To do this, the administrator first modifies the PARTIAL.INF file by adding "OrgChart" lines to the [Files-I386-WindowsOptions], [OptionalAccessoriesENG], and [AccessoriesItemsENG] sections, as shown in the following example:

```
[Files-I386-WindowsOptions]
Calculator = 2,CALC.EXE , SIZE=999
Cardfile = 2,CARDFILE.EXE , SIZE=999
OrgChart = 2,ORGCHART.EXE , SIZE=999
CDPlayer = 2,CDPLAYER.EXE , SIZE=999


[OptionalAccessoriesENG]
    Calculator   = "Calculator"
    Cardfile     = "Cardfile"
    OrgChart     = "Terra Flora Organizational Chart"
    Clock        = "Clock"


[AccessoriesItemsENG]
    Paintbrush = "Paintbrush", PBRUSH.EXE  , PBRUSH.EXE  , "" , 0
    Chat       = "Chat", WINCHAT.EXE  , WINCHAT.EXE  , "" , 0
    OrgChart   = "Org. Chart" , ORGCHART.EXE , ORGCHART.EXE , "" , 0
    Terminal   = "Terminal", TERMINAL.EXE , TERMINAL.EXE , "" , 0
```

Next, the administrator adds the line "d1,ORGCHART.EXE" to the DOSNET.INF file as shown in the following example:

```
[Files]
d1,256COLOR.BMP
d1,40291730.PPD
d1,40293930.PPD
d1,ORGCHART.EXE
...
```

Adding TrueType Fonts to Setup

If you have a license for the Microsoft Font Pack for Windows, you might want to have those fonts installed automatically by Setup. For each TrueType font there is a .TTF file and a .FOT file. The extension .TTF is given to the actual TrueType font file. The .FOT extension is used for the font header that points to the .TTF file.

Typically, during installation of the font pack or when installing a TrueType font from the Control Panel, the .FOT file is created and appropriate entries are made in the Windows NT Registry. To create the .FOT files that are installed on the Windows NT workstation, you first need to install the font pack on any computer, and then copy the .TTF and .FOT files to the Windows NT distribution share.

For the purpose of demonstration, we will install only four fonts—Arial® Narrow, Arial Narrow Bold, Arial Narrow Bold Italic, and Arial Narrow Italic. The files for these fonts are listed in the following table:

TrueType file	TrueType font header
ARIALN.TTF	ARIALN.FOT
ARIALNB.TTF	ARIALNB.FOT
ARIALNBI.TTF	ARIALNBI.FOT
ARIALNI.TTF	ARIALNI.FOT

Add these files to Setup, as described earlier in "Adding a File to the Windows NT Installation." Make sure to install the files into the *SystemRoot*\SYSTEM directory by including them in the [Files-I386-nt-system16always] section.

Next, add the fonts to the [FontList] section of the INITIAL.INF file, so that the fonts will be added to the Windows NT Registry. In the example that follows, the last four lines have been added.

```
INITIAL.INF

[FontList]
"Arial (TrueType)"                          = ARIAL.FOT
....
"Times New Roman Italic (TrueType)"         = TIMESI.FOT
"WingDings (TrueType)"                       = WINGDING.FOT
"Arial Narrow (TrueType)"                    = ARIALN.FOT
"Arial Narrow Bold (TrueType)"               = ARIALNB.FOT
"Arial Narrow Bold Italic (TrueType)"        = ARIALNBI.FOT
"Arial Narrow Italic (TrueType)"             = ARIALNI.FOT
```

Excluding Files from Windows NT

If you do not need to have all of the functionality that Windows NT provides, you can reduce the amount of disk space required for your installation of Windows NT by modifying the Setup script files so that supporting files for functionality you do not want are not installed. It is possible, for example, to save several megabytes of disk space by excluding help files, NTBACKUP.EXE (tape backup), Windows NT sequence files (.SEQ), and infrequently-used programs. However, it is important that you do not exclude files that are required for the functioning of Windows NT. Refer to Chapter 4, "Windows NT Files," for information on the files you are thinking about excluding. Chapter 4 describes the function of each file and helps to identify which ones you can safely exclude.

To exclude a file you must first comment out the filename in the DOSNET.INF file by prepending the appropriate line in the [Files] section with a pound sign (#). In the following example, EXE2BIN.EXE has been excluded:

```
[Files]
...
d1,EXEBYTE2.SYS
# d1,EXE2BIN.EXE
d1,EXPAND.EXE
```

Next, if the file is listed in the INITIAL.INF file, comment out all occurrences of the file by adding a semicolon (;) to the beginning of the appropriate line(s).

Note Some files are listed more than once in the INITIAL.INF file. To exclude these files you must comment out both occurrences. If you comment out only one of them, Setup displays an error message. Use the searching capability of your text editor to verify that you have commented out all occurrences of any file you want to exclude.

In the following example, the line "2,EXE2BIN.EXE , SIZE=8424" has been commented out in the INITIAL.INF file:

```
[Files-I386-nt-system]
...
2,EVENTVWR.EXE , SIZE=204676
;2,EXE2BIN.EXE , SIZE=8424
2,EXPAND.EXE , SIZE=39284
```

In the TXTSETUP.SIF file, comment out the file by inserting a semicolon (;) at the beginning of the appropriate line in the [Files] section. Four lines have been commented out in the following example:

```
[Files]
...
d2,MSMAIL32.HLP,2
d2,PERFMON.HLP,2
;d2,PIFEDIT.HLP,2
;d2,PRINTMAN.HLP,2
;d2,PROGMAN.HLP,2
d2,RASSETUP.HLP,2
;d2,REGEDT32.HLP,2
d2,SCHDPL32.HLP,2
```

Note The **findstr** command can help you find out which files contain the name of a file you want to exclude.

Excluding the OS/2 Subsystem

If you do not need support for OS/2 applications, you can exclude the files needed for OS/2 support by commenting them out in the .INF files that install them. If you do so and a user tries to start an OS/2 application, they will receive a message saying the executable file could not be located or that the subsystem is not available.

In the INITIAL.INF file, comment out the lines specifying the OS/2 files by prepending the lines with a semicolon (;), as shown in the following example:

```
[Files-I386-nt-system-os2-dll]
;2,DOSCALLS.DLL , SIZE=12341
[Files-I386-nt-system]
;2,NETAPI.DLL , SIZE=119808
;2,OS2.EXE , SIZE=53552
;2,OS2SRV.EXE , SIZE=206848
;2,OS2SS.EXE , SIZE=15360
```

In the DOSNET.INF file, comment out the lines specifying the OS/2 files by prepending the lines with a pound sign (#), as shown in the following example:

```
# d1,DOSCALLS.DLL
# d1,NETAPI.DLL
# d1,OS2.EXE
# d1,OS2SRV.EXE
# d1,OS2SS.EXE
```

In the TXTSETUP.SIF file, comment out the lines specifying the OS/2 files by prepending the lines with a semicolon (;).

If you are upgrading from an earlier version of Windows NT in which the OS/2 subsystem was used, list these same files in the [Files.DeleteOnUpgrade] section of the TXTSETUP.SIF file. Lines in this section use the following format:

file, dir

where *file* is the filename and *dir* is the code number that is assigned (in the [WinntDirectories] section) to the directory in which the file is found.

Excluding the POSIX Subsystem

To exclude the POSIX subsystem, comment out the lines specifying the following files in the TXTSETUP.SIF, INITIAL.INF and DOSNET.INF files:

- PSXDLL.DLL
- PAX.EXE
- POSIX.EXE
- PXSSS.EXE

If you are upgrading from an earlier version of Windows NT in which the POSIX subsystem was used, list these same files in the [Files.DeleteOnUpgrade] section of the TXTSETUP.SIF file. Lines in this section use the following format:

file, dir

where *file* is the filename and *dir* is the code number that is assigned (in the [WinntDirectories] section) to the directory in which the file is found.

Excluding Support for MS-DOS and Windows 16-bit Applications

To exclude the files needed to support for MS-DOS and Windows 16-bit applications, you must modify the INITIAL.INF file, commenting out the routine that modifies the Registry key for MS-DOS and Windows 16-bit support.If the supporting files are excluded but this routine is not commented out, Setup will report an error. Lines should be commented out using the semicolon (;) as shown in the following example:

```
;vdmconfig =+
;    shell "subroutn.inf" PushBillboard STATUSDLG $(Billboard5)
;    Debug-Output "SETUP.INF: Configuring the DOS Subsystem."
;    ifstr(i) $(!STF_WIN31UPGRADE) == NO
;        shell "registry.inf" AppendToSystemPath "%SystemRoot%"
;    endif
;    read-syms ConfigSysAppend
;    read-syms AutoexecBatAppend
;    LibraryProcedure STATUS,$(!LIBHANDLE),VdmFixup $(AddOnConfig)
$(AddOnBatch)
;    ifstr(i) $(STATUS) == ERROR
;        shell "subroutn.inf" PopBillboard
;        EndWait
;        read-syms NonFatalError2$(!STF_LANGUAGE)
;        shell "subroutn.inf" SetupMessage $(!STF_LANGUAGE) NONFATAL
$(NonFatal)
;        StartWait
;    endif
```

```
;       ifstr(i) $(!STF_PLATFORM) == $(!PlatformID_Mips)
;           set wowfile = krnl286
;       else
;           set wowfile = krnl386
;       endif
;       shell "registry.inf" MakeWOWEntry $(wowfile)
```

Next, comment out the following files from the TXTSETUP.SIF, INITIAL.INF and DOSNET.INF files so the files that support MS-DOS and Windows 16-bit applications will not be installed. If you are upgrading from an earlier version of Windows NT in which MS-DOS and Windows 16-bit applications were used, list these same files in the [Files.DeleteOnUpgrade] section of the TXTSETUP.SIF file. Lines in this section use the following format:

file, dir

where *file* is the filename and *dir* is the code number that is assigned (in the [WinntDirectories] section) to the directory in which the file is found.

_DEFAULT.PIF	ANSI.SYS	APP850.FON
APPEND.EXE	ATTRIB.EXE	AUTOEXEC.NT
BIOS1.ROM	BIOS2.ROM	BLACK16.SCR
CGA40850.FON	CGA40WOA.FON	CGA80850.FON
CGA80WOA.FON	CHCP.COM	CHKDSK.EXE
CMOS.RAM	COMM.DRV	COMMAND.COM
COMMDLG.DLL[1]	COMP.EXE	CONFIG.NT
COUNTRY.SYS	DDEML.DLL	DEBUG.EXE
DISKCOMP.COM	DISKCOPY.COM	DOSAPP.FON
DOSKEY.EXE	DOSX.EXE	DRWATSON.EXE
EDIT.COM	EDIT.HLP	EDLIN.EXE
EGA.CPI	EGA40850.FON	EGA40WOA.FON
EGA80850.FON	EGA80WOA.FON	EXE2BIN.EXE
EXPAND.EXE	FASTOPEN.EXE	FC.EXE
FIND.EXE	FINDSTR.EXE	FORCEDOS.EXE
FORMAT.COM	GDI.EXE	GRAFTABL.COM
GRAPHICS.COM	GRAPHICS.PRO	HELP.EXE
HIMEM.SYS	KB16.COM	KEYB.COM
KEYBOARD.DRV	KEYBOARD.SYS	KRNL386.EXE
LABEL.EXE	LANMAN.DRV	LOADFIX.COM
MAPI.DLL	MCIOLE16.DLL	MEM.EXE
MMSYSTEM.DLL[1]	MMTASK.TSK[1]	MODE.COM

MORE.COM	MOUSE.DRV	NTCMDS.HLP
NTCMDS.IND	NTDOS.SYS	NTIO.SYS
NTVDM.DLL	NTVDM.EXE	OLECLI.DLL
OLESVR.DLL[1]	PIFEDIT.EXE	QBASIC.EXE
RECOVER.EXE	REDIR.EXE	REGEDIT.EXE
REGEDIT.HLP	REMLINE.BAS	REPLACE.EXE
RESTORE.EXE	SETUP16.INF	SETVER.EXE
SHARE.EXE	SHELL.DLL[1]	SORT.EXE
SOUND.DRV	SUBST.EXE	SYSEDIT.EXE
SYSTEM.DRV	SYSTEM.INI	TOOLHELP.DLL
TREE.COM	V7VGA.ROM	VDMDBG.DLL
VDMREDIR.DLL	VER.DLL[1]	VGA.DRV
WFWNET.DRV	WIN.COM	WIN.INI
WIN87EM.DLL	WINFILE.INI	WINHELP.EXE
WOW32.DLL	WOWDEB.EXE	WOWEXEC.EXE
WRITE.EXE	XCOPY.EXE	

[1] These files are listed twice in the INITIAL.INF file. Be sure to remove both occurrences of each to avoid receiving an error message from Setup.

Bypassing Printer and Application Setup on Express Installation

To skip printer and application Setup when Express Setup is chosen, add the lines "set !DoPrinter = $(!NotChosen)" and "set !DoAppSetup = $(!NotChosen)" under the "ifstr(i) $(!STF_INSTALL_MODE) == EXPRESS" line in the [DoOption] section of the INITIAL.INF file as shown in the following example:

```
[DoOptions]
    set Status = STATUS_FAILED
options = +
    ifstr(i) $(!STF_PRODUCT) == Winnt
        set OptionsGreyed = {}
    else
        set OptionsGreyed = {3}
    endif
    ifstr(i) $(!STF_WIN31UPGRADE) == "YES"
        set !DoAppSetup = $(!NotChosen)
        set OptionsGreyed = >($(OptionsGreyed), 4)
    endif
    ifstr(i) $(!STF_INSTALL_MODE) == EXPRESS
        set !DoPrinter   = $(!NotChosen)
        set !DoAppSetup  = $(!NotChosen)
        set Status = STATUS_SUCCESSFUL
```

Skipping Installation of All Optional Components

In Express Setup, the Setup program automatically installs all optional components. To install none of the optional components in Express installation, comment out the lines in the PARTIAL.INF file that tell Windows NT Setup to install the components, as shown in the following example:

```
set_partial_components = +
    StartWait
    ForListDo $(ComponentList)
        set $($)ToInstall = $($($)Install)
        set $($)ToRemove  = {}
    EndForListDo
    set SrcDir = $(!STF_SRCDIR)
;   install Install-PartialFileCopy
....
[ConfigureProgman]
    set Status = STATUS_FAILED
    read-syms PartialDestinationVars
    set AccessoriesToInstall = {}
    set ReadmeToInstall    = {}
    set GamesToInstall     = {}
    set WallpapersToInstall = {}
    set SaversToInstall    = {}
;   ForListDo $($0)
;       set *($($), 1)ToInstall = *($($), 2)
;   EndForListDo
```

Changing Minimum Disk Space Requirements

If you change the files installed by Setup, it is a good idea to change the minimum disk space requirement as well. If the disk space requirement is too large, Setup will request more free disk space than necessary, and you might not be able to install on computers that really do have enough disk space. If the disk space requirement is too small, Setup may fail when trying to copy files to a full hard disk.

First, modify the DOSNET.INF file by changing the value for *NtDrive* in the [SpaceRequirements] section, as follows:

```
[SpaceRequirements]
BootDrive = 1048576
# NtDrive  = 89128960 NOTE: Commented out original disk space
requirement.
NtDrive  = 76000000
```

NtDrive specifies the number of bytes required on the drive where Windows NT is to be installed. Change this number as appropriate. For example, if you exclude 3 megabytes of files that were included in the original Windows NT installation, subtract 3 megabytes from the *NtDrive* number. If you add 3 megabytes of files to the Windows NT installation, add 3 megabytes to the *NtDrive* number. Do not change the value for *BootDrive*.

Also, change the values for FreeDiskSpace and UpgradeFreeDiskSpace in the [SetupData] section of the TXTSETUP.SIF file.

Updating the Registry During Setup

The following sections provide information on how to update the Registry while you are in the process of setting up.

Using Template Hives to Update the Registry

Three template hives are supplied with Windows NT 3.5. During a fresh installation, these hives are copied in their entirety to the new Registry. During an upgrade from an earlier version of Windows NT, portions of the template hives are copied to the existing Registry, as described in the text that follows.

If you are proficient with Regedit32, you can edit the template hives after you have copied them to your distribution share. This section explains how to specify that existing registry values be overwritten, and how to specify values in the template hives so that they do not overwrite existing information in the Registry. During a fresh installation, of course, the entire template hives are copied to the new Registry.

The following template hives are supplied:

- System
- Software
- Default

Normally, values in the Software and Default template hives, and in the "Current Control Set" key of the System template hive, are copied to an existing Registry only if the value is not found in the existing Registry -- existing values are not overwritten. However, values in other keys of the System template hive are normally copied even if it means overwriting existing values. You can alter any of this behavior through entries in the TXTSETUP.SIF file.

Using the TXTSETUP.SIF File to Update the Registry

You can specify that certain values or keys in the Software and Default template hives, and in the "Current Control Set" key of the System template hive, always be copied to an existing Registry (even if it means overwriting existing values) by specifying them in the [KeysToAdd] section of the TXTSETUP.SIF file.

In addition, you can use the [KeysToAdd] section together with the [Values.*section*] section to create new keys or values, or to change values, without editing the template hives directly.

The choice of whether to add a key or value by editing a hive or by adding to the TXTSETUP.SIF file depends on the extent of the changes you want to make, whether you want existing values to be overwritten, and often on personal preference. However, you should be comfortable with editing the Registry before you use either method. In either case, you are using Setup to change the Registry; both the Registry and the Setup files are unforgiving of errors. The Registry Editor does not understand or recognize errors in syntax or semantics.

The sections in the TXTSETUP.SIF file that you are most likely to change in order to have Setup change registry values are listed in the following table:

Section	Used to
[KeysToAdd]	Add or change keys, or add or change values under keys.
[Values.*section*]	Specify values for specific keys listed in the [KeysToAdd] section.

The [KeysToAdd] Section

The lines in the [KeysToAdd] section specify that a key, or one or more values in a key, be written to an existing Registry. If the key or value already exists, it will be overwritten. The keys and/or values can be read from a template hive, or from a [values.*section*] section in the TXTSETUP.SIF file if one is specified. The format for lines in this section is as follows:

hive, "*key*"[, values.*section*]

where h*ive* is the template hive from which the key should be copied. *Key* specifies the key in the specified hive. (It is enclosed in double-quotes.) Values.*Section* points to the section in the TXTSETUP.SIF file that lists the values to be added to this key. If you use this parameter, the information is taken from the TXTSETUP.SIF file rather than from the template hive. If you omit this parameter, Setup looks for the information in the template hive.

Examples

The following line specifies that everything in the PBrush32 key under Classes in the Software template hive be added to the registry:

```
Software, "Classes\PBrush32"
```

Normally, since this key is in the Software hive, it would be copied to an existing Registry only if the key did not already exist. By specifying it here, you ensure that the entire key and any subkeys will be written to the Registry, even if it involves overwriting an existing key by that name.

The following line, with the associated [Values.*section*] section, specifies a value (no wallpaper) for the Control Panel\Desktop key in the Default hive:

```
Default, "Control Panel\Desktop",  Values.Desktop


[Values.Desktop]
  Wallpaper,                       REG_SZ,    (None)
```

No other values in this key will be affected.

The [Values.*section*] Section

This section specifies the values assigned to a key that was specified in the [KeysToAdd] section. You can list as many values as you want. The format is as follows:

name[, *type*, *value*]

where *name* is the name of the key to which you want to add the value. If the key does not already exist in the Registry, it will be created. (The hive in which the key is placed is specified in the line in the [KeysToAdd] section that points to this [Value.*section*] section.) If only *name* is entered, that entire key, including any subkeys, will be copied to the existing Registry. If a key by that name already exists it will be overwritten. *Type* is the value type, and can be any of the following:

- REG_SZ
- REG_EXPAND_SZ
- REG_MULTI_SZ
- REG_BINARY
- REG_DWORD
- REG_BINARY_DWORD

Value is the value you want to assign to this entry. For types REG_SZ, REG_EXPAND_SZ, and REG_MULTI_SZ, the value is a string and must be enclosed in double quote marks.

Installing Without Bootable Floppy Disks

To install Windows NT on an x86-based computer, you normally need three bootable floppy disks, in addition to the distribution CD-ROM, distribution share, or distribution floppy set. When the **winnt** or **winnt32** command is used to install Windows NT over the network, these floppy disks are normally created by Setup.

If you don't need to reformat the file system on the boot drive (usually C:), you can dispense with the bootable floppy disks by using the **/b** switch with the **winnt** or **winnt32** command. You can reformat drives (other than the boot drive and the drive holding the temporary installation files) while installing without floppy disks.

Note In rare instances, you might be using a SCSI drive for which Windows NT does not have a driver. If this drive is the drive on which you want to install Windows NT, the **winnt /b** or **winnt32 /b** command will not work, because the target drive is not visible to the Setup program. Check the hardware compatibility list in your Windows NT documentation set to make sure the driver you need is included.

Unattended Installation

If people in your organization will be installing without bootable floppy disks, you might want them to perform an unattended setup as well. In an unattended setup, an unattended answer file is used to answer all of the questions that Setup asks. The Windows NT Setup Manager utility, included with this resource kit, makes it easy to create the unattended answer file. You can create as many different unattended answer files as needed to accommodate the various users in your organization.

The command to perform an unattended installation is **winnt /u[:***answer_file***]** or **winnt32 /u[:***answer_file***]**, where *answer_file* is the file name of the unattended answer file. The **/b** switch is always assumed when the **/u** switch is used with the **winnt** or **winnt32** command. If no unattended answer file is specified, the defaults will be used for all installation options (as though you pressed ENTER at every prompt in an attended installation). Since there is no default for the username or organization name, the user must be present to respond to prompt for these values if no unattended answer file is specified, or if the unattended answer file that is specified has no entries for these values. These prompts occur early in the graphical mode portion of Setup. Your users can enter the **winnt /u[:***answer_file***]** or **winnt32 /u[:***answer_file***]** command, wait long enough to answer the username and/or organization name prompt, and then leave the Setup program to continue unattended.

Creating an Unattended Answer File

You can create an unattended answer file for each user, to allow completely unattended installation, or you can create more general unattended answer files, in which case the user must provide user information interactively after entering the **winnt /u** [*answer_file*] or **winnt32 /u** [*answer_file*] command. Unattended answer files are easy to create with the Windows NT Setup Manager utility that is included with this resource kit. The help file included with the utility provides general information about unattended answer files and unattended setup, as well as specific help on the individual dialogs and on the values you are asked to supply.

Since Setup Manager allows you to edit existing unattended answer files, and to save your edits to a new unattended answer file, you might want to begin by making template unattended answer files for the various setup configurations used in your organization. For example, you might have many users in each of three different time zones. Or, some users might be participating in a workgroup only, while others are participating in a domain. Once you have created a template unattended answer file for a group of users, you can open the template, edit the user information to specify the user name and computer name, and save the file to a new name based on the user name. Each user can then specify his or her personal unattended answer file in the **winnt** or **winnt32** command.

▶ **To create or edit the unattended answer file**

1. Start the SETUPMGR.EXE program The Windows NT Setup Manager dialog appears.

2. If you want to edit an existing unattended answer file, choose the Open button.

3. Specify the settings that you want. The dialogs are described in Setup Manager Help.

4. Specify the filename for the script file, as described in Setup Manager Help.

5. Choose OK.

If you are using Microsoft Systems Management Server (SMS) to manage computer resources in your organization, you can use *package definition files* (PDFs) to install or upgrade Windows NT. See the Microsoft Systems Management Server documentation for information on using PDFs to install operating systems.

Importance of the SETUP.LOG File

Setup creates a hidden, system, read-only file called SETUP.LOG in your *SystemRoot*\REPAIR directory. This file becomes very important if you need to repair or reinstall Windows NT.

Caution   Do not delete the SETUP.LOG file.

To reinstall Windows NT, the Setup program must be started again. As it did in the initial installation, Setup inspects your system's configuration and determines whether your computer has the required free disk space to install Windows NT. It also detects existing versions of Windows NT.

If your computer does not have the required free disk space, Setup gives you the option to delete the previous versions. If you select Yes, Setup uses the SETUP.LOG file to determine which files it can delete to make space on your hard disk. If SETUP.LOG is missing, no files can be deleted and you might be forced to reformat your hard disk to reinstall.

Preinstalling Windows NT Using CPS

The Windows NT Computer Profile Setup (CPS) utility simplifies the process for preinstalling and configuring Windows NT workstation and Windows NT server on a large number of Intel-based computers. The CPS utility uploads a profile of a fully installed Windows NT or Windows NT server system from a master computer to a distribution server and then distributes the system to identically configured target computers. With the CPS utility, you can also distribute other directories containing application files to the target computers.

The CPS preinstallation process generally consists of the following steps:

- Creating a master system by installing Windows NT and other files and applications to be distributed on the master system computer.
- Uploading the master system to a distribution server.
- Copying the master system to the identically configured target computers.
- Testing duplicated systems.

The duplicated systems are then ready for use.

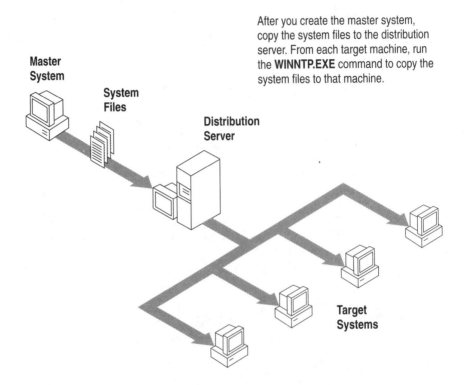

After you create the master system, copy the system files to the distribution server. From each target machine, run the **WINNTP.EXE** command to copy the system files to that machine.

Master System

System Files

Distribution Server

Target Systems

Installing the Master System

When you have decided on the configuration for the master system, which will be propagated exactly to all the target computers, install Windows NT on the master system computer. For detailed instructions on installing Windows NT, see the *Windows NT Installation Guide.*

If you are installing Windows NT on more than one hardware configuration, you should use the **winnt** or **winnt32** setup tool described in the Windows NT documentation. If you want to use the CPS utility for multiple hardware configurations, you must preinstall a separate master system for each hardware configuration.

Uploading the Master System to the Distribution Server

Once you have installed the master system, you can upload it and any additional directories you want to the distribution server.

During a normal Windows NT installation, the Setup program interactively requests information. Because the CPS utility installs Windows NT on identically configured computers at which users are not present, the requested information is provided in a file named PROFILE.INI. For information about editing PROFILE.INI, see the PROFILE.TXT file in the \I386\CPS directory on the Windows NT resource kit CD-ROM.

▶ **To upload the master system**

1. On the master system computer, create a directory to hold the CPS utility files, and then change the default to that directory.

2. With the Windows NT resource kit CD-ROM in the CD-ROM drive of the master system computer, copy the \I386\CPS directory from the CD-ROM to the directory you created in step 1. For example, if your CD-ROM drive is D:, type the following:

   xcopy d:\i386\cps

3. If you need to edit PROFILE.INI, edit the copy you made in step 2 using a text editor such as Windows Notepad.

4. On the distribution server, create the directory that is to receive the master system files, and share this directory.

5. On the master system computer, type the following:

   uplodprf -s:*master* **-i:profile.ini** [*dir1*] [*dir2*] [...]

   where *master* is the UNC name of the directory you created in step 4 (or the network path to that directory, if you have a network connection to it), and *dir1, dir2, ...* are the paths to additional directories on the master system computer that you want to preinstall on the target computers.

In addition to the Windows NT system files and any additional directories or files you specify, the **uplodprf** tool uploads the registry files from the master system and then removes user-specific information from the copy on the distribution server. For options available with the **uplodprf** tool, at the command prompt type **uplodprf /?**.

As a final step, review entries in the [DefaultValues] section of the DEFAULTS.INF file in the %systemroot%/system32 subdirectory of the shared directory you have created on the master system computer. Some of the values in this section, such as DefaultOrgName and DefaultTimeZone, will probably be the same for all the users who will use this profile, and can be set at this time.

You are now ready to distribute the master profile to the target computers.

Distributing the Master System to the Target Computers

The target computers must have the same hardware options, such as video card and bus type, as the master system computer. Target computers can, however, have more memory and a larger hard disk than the master system computer. You can choose from several duplication options, according to your manufacturing requirements. Some of the methods used for distributing the master profile include:

- Serial or parallel port file transfer using a parallel connector such as Xircom® Pocket Ethernet Adapter™

- Network adapter or interface

- Hard-disk duplication equipment

- Tape or disk backup-and-restore process

The duplication method you choose depends on the resources and needs of your organization. This list is not exhaustive but is intended to suggest some common approaches to duplicating the master system files.

▶ **To distribute the master system profile to target computers**

1. Create a bootable floppy disk that can access the network and/or a SCSI disk drive and copy the WINNTP.EXE utility from the resource kit to this floppy disk.

2. From the target computer, connect to the directory on the distribution server that contains the master system files.

3. Boot the computer off the floppy disk and establish a network connection to the distribution server and sharepoint.

4. At the command prompt, type the following:

   winntp /r /s:*server**share* /b

   where ***server**share*** is the network path to the master system files on the distribution server. The **/r** switch indicates that a profiled directory is being downloaded instead of a normal CD-ROM installation. For information on other **winntp** options, at the command prompt type **winntp /?**.

   The **winntp** tool copies the Windows NT profile to the local computer and starts Windows NT setup, prompting the user for local machine information (such as: User Name, Organization Name, Machine Name, and so forth). This information can also be provided on the command line, allowing unattended installation of the Windows NT Profiled setup.

5. When the system reboots after Setup is completed, Windows NT is completely installed and ready for use.

Merging Profiles for Similar Systems

If you have systems that are slightly different, you can merge profiles rather than dedicate space on master systems for a full profile for each of the similar systems. For example, suppose there are hundreds of computers in your organization that are identical in every respect except for the video cards — each computer has one of three different video cards. Despite the other similarities, these are three different configurations; they cannot all use the same CPS profile. However, you can make a master profile for one configuration (that is, for one of the video cards), and two other "difference" profiles for each of the other configurations, containing only the Registry and any additional files needed for the video cards used by these other configurations.

▶ **To create difference profiles**

1. On the distribution server, create the directory that is to receive the "difference" profile, and share this directory. This step is analogous to step 4 of the procedure "To upload the master system" that appeared earlier in this section.

2. After you have completed the steps under "To upload the master system" for the first system, reconfigure the master system for the alternate configuration. In this example, you would be configuring it for a different video setup by changing the video cards and the associated settings.

3. If you want, edit the PROFILE.INI file you have created, just as you would edit PROFILE.INI for the first configuration, using a text editor such as Windows Notepad. For example, to copy certain files (such as those used for a specific adapter driver) when uploading the profile with the "hives-only" parameter, you would list those files in the [HivesOnlyFilesToSubstitute] section of PROFILE.INI.

4. On the master system computer, type the following:

   uplodprf -h -s:_diff_1_ **-i:profile.ini** [_dir1_] [_dir2_] [...]

   where _diff_1_ is the UNC name of the directory you created in step 1 of this procedure (or the network path to that directory, if you have a network connection to it), and _dir1, dir2,_ ... are the paths to additional directories on the master system computer that you want to preinstall on the target computers. The **-h** parameter indicates that only the hive is to be copied to the PROFILE.INI file in the indicated subdirectory.

When downloading the profile to the target machine, the user specifies the master profile, and if that computer uses one of the alternate video cards also specifies the appropriate "difference" profile. That is, follow the directions in the procedure "To distribute the master system profile to target computers," but in step 4 use a command of the form

winntp /r /s:**_server_**_share,_****_server_****_share2_ **/b**

The first *\\server\share* after the **/s:** is the one with the base configuration. The subdirectory with the differences is specified in the second *\\server\share* entry, which is separated from the first with a comma and no spaces.

Adding a Processor

To take advantage of the multiprocessor capabilities in Windows NT, you might want to install an additional processor on a computer running Windows NT. The potentially difficult task of adjusting all the necessary settings so that Windows NT can take full advantage of the new processor is made simple with the **UpToMP** utility included with this resource kit.

To use the utility you must know:

- The drive your Windows NT installation software is on (this can be a distribution share, a CD-ROM drive, or a floppy drive).

- The type of processor you are installing (this information should be included with the processor.

Start UpToMP from the command line or by double-clicking the file in File Manager. Specify the drive that has the installation software in the text box provided, and choose your processor type (HAL) from the combo box. Then choose Continue.

C H A P T E R   4

Windows NT Files

This chapter describes the files included with Windows NT. It also provides tips for freeing hard disk space and memory by deleting components that are not essential to the operation of Windows NT.

Note Not all of these files may appear on your system, depending on your system hardware and applications and accessories you choose to install.

The following list identifies the table to which you can refer for more information on files with a particular filename extension.

Extension	See
.ANI	Table 4.1 Cursor (.ANI and .CUR) Files
.BAS	Table 4.16 Quick Basic (.BAS) Sample Files
.BMP	Table 4.23 Wallpaper (.BMP) Files
.COM	Table 4.5 Executable (.EXE and .COM) Files
.CPL	Table 4.2 Control Panel (.CPL) Tool Files
.CUR	Table 4.1 Cursor (.ANI and .CUR) Files
.DLL	Table 4.4 Dynamic Link Library (.DLL) Files
.DRV	Table 4.3 Driver (.DRV and .SYS) Files
.EXE	Table 4.5 Executable (.EXE and .COM) Files
.FNT and .FON	Table 4.6 Raster and Vector Font (.FON and .FNT) Files
.FOT	Table 4.7 TrueType Font and Font Header (.TTF and .FOT) Files
.HLP	Table 4.11 Online Help (.HLP) Files
.IND	Table 4.12 Full-Text Search Index (.IND) Files for Online Help

Extension	See
.INF	Table 4.18 Setup Script (.INF) Files and Table 4.19 OEM Setup Script (.INF) Files
.LEX	Table 4.21 Spelling Lexicon (.LEX) Files
.NLS	Table 4.10 National Language Support (.NLS) Files
.PCD	Table 4.13 Plotter (.PCD) Driver Files
.PPD	Table 4.14 Adobe® PostScript Printer Description (.PPD) Files
.SCR	Table 4.17 Screen Saver (.SCR) Files
.SEP	Table 4.15 Printer Separator (.SEP) Files
.SEQ	Table 4.8 Introducing Windows NT Sequence (.SEQ) Files
.SYS	Table 4.3 Driver (.DRV and .SYS) Files
.TTF	Table 4.7 TrueType Font and Font Header (.TTF and .FOT) Files
.TXT	Table 4.22 Text (.TXT and .WRI) Files
.WAV	Table 4.20 Sound Wave (.WAV) Files
.WRI	Table 4.22 Text (.TXT and .WRI) Files
Other	Table 4.9 Miscellaneous Files

Adding and Removing Windows NT Components

You can use the Windows NT Setup program to add and remove various components that are not essential to the operation of Windows NT. For example, you might want to remove some non-essential Windows files to free up space on your hard disk, or add components you previously removed or that you did not install during initial setup. You can decide at any time to add or remove all or part of components such as README files, accessories, games, screen savers, and wallpaper.

Note When you remove components, the files are deleted from your computer. If you want to add them later, you must supply the files from the Windows NT installation disks or from a source directory on your network.

For more information about adding or removing files or components, see "Adding and Removing Windows NT Components" in Chapter 12, "System Maintenance with Windows NT Setup," in the *Windows NT System Guide*.

Cursor Files

You can change the look of your cursor by choosing from the many static and animated cursors included with Windows NT. The default cursor scheme is Windows Default. To select a different cursor scheme or modify a scheme, use the Cursors icon in the Control Panel window.

To free hard disk space, you can remove the cursor schemes that don't intend to use. For information about removing cursor schemes, see "Changing the Cursor Appearance" in Chapter 5, "Control Panel," in the *Windows NT System Guide*.

Windows NT includes the following static and animated cursors.

Table 4.1   Cursor (.ANI and .CUR) Files

Filename	Description	Cursor Scheme
3DGARRO.CUR	Arrow	3D-Bronze
3DGMOVE.CUR	Move or size all	3D-Bronze, Old Fashioned
3DGNESW.CUR	Sizing arrow pointing northeast to southwest	3D-Bronze, Dinosaur, Old Fashioned
3DGNO.CUR	Universal "no" symbol	3D-Bronze
3DGNS.CUR	Sizing arrow pointing north to south	3D-Bronze, Old Fashioned
3DGNWSE.CUR	Sizing arrow pointing northwest to southeast	3D-Bronze, Old Fashioned
3DGWE.CUR	Sizing arrow pointing west to east	3D-Bronze, Dinosaur, Old Fashioned
3DSMOVE.CUR	Move or size all	Dinosaur
3DSNS.CUR	Sizing arrow pointing north to south	Dinosaur
3DSNWSE.CUR	Sizing arrow pointing northwest to southeast	Dinosaur
3DWARRO.CUR	Arrow	3D-White
3DWMOVE.CUR	Move or size all	3D-White
3DWNESW.CUR	Sizing arrow pointing northeast to southwest	3D-White
3DWNO.CUR	Universal "no" symbol	3D-White
3DWNS.CUR	Sizing arrow pointing north to south	3D-White
3DWNWSE.CUR	Sizing arrow pointing northwest to southeast	3D-White
3DWWE.CUR	Sizing arrow pointing west to east	3D-White

Table 4.1 Cursor (.ANI and .CUR) Files *(continued)*

Filename	Description	Cursor Scheme
APPSTAR2.ANI	Application starting	3D-Bronze
APPSTAR3.ANI	Application starting	3D-White
APPSTART.ANI	Application starting	Windows Animated
BANANA.ANI	No	Dinosaur
BARBER.ANI	Wait	Old Fashioned
COIN.ANI	No	Old Fashioned
COUNTER.ANI	Wait	Variations
CROSS.CUR	Cross hair	Dinosaur, Variations, Windows Animated
DINOSAU2.ANI	Wait	Dinosaur
DINOSAUR.ANI	Application starting	Dinosaur
DRUM.ANI	Application starting	Conductor
FILLITUP.ANI	Arrow	Variations
HAND.ANI	Wait	Hands 1
HANDAPST.ANI	Application starting	Hands 1, Hands 2
HANDNESW.ANI	Sizing from northeast to southwest	Hands 2
HANDNO.ANI	No	Hands 2
HANDNS.ANI	Sizing from north to south	Hands 2
HANDNWSE.ANI	Sizing from northwest to southeast	Hands 2
HANDWAIT.ANI	Wait	Hands 2
HANDWE.ANI	Sizing from west to east	Hands 2
HARROW.CUR	Arrow	Hands 1, Hands 2, Old Fashioned
HCROSS.CUR	Cross hair	Hands 1, Hands 2, Old Fashioned
HIBEAM.CUR	I-beam	Hands 1, Hands 2, Old Fashioned
HMOVE.CUR	Move or size all	Hands 1, Hands 2
HNESW.CUR	Sizing arrow northeast to southwest	Hands 1
HNODROP.CUR	Universal "no" symbol	Hands 1
HNS.CUR	Sizing arrow pointing north to south	Hands 1

Table 4.1   Cursor (.ANI and .CUR) Files *(continued)*

Filename	Description	Cursor Scheme
HNWSE.CUR	Sizing arrow pointing northwest to southeast	Hands 1
HORSE.ANI	Application starting	Old Fashioned
HOURGLA2.ANI	Wait	3D-Bronze
HOURGLA3.ANI	Wait	3D-White
HOURGLAS.ANI	Wait	Windows Animated
HWE.CUR	Wait	Hands 1
LAPPSTRT.CUR	Application starting	Magnified
LARROW.CUR	Arrow	Magnified
LCROSS.CUR	Cross hair	Magnified
LIBEAM.CUR	I-beam	Magnified
LMOVE.CUR	Move or size all	Magnified
LNESW.CUR	Sizing arrow pointing northeast to southwest	Magnified
LNODROP.CUR	Universal "no" symbol	Magnified
LNS.CUR	Sizing arrow pointing north to south	Magnified
LNWSE.CUR	Sizing arrow pointing northwest to southeast	Magnified
LWAIT.CUR	Wait	Magnified
LWE.CUR	Sizing arrow pointing west to east	Magnified
METRONOM.ANI	Wait	Conductor
PIANO.ANI	No	Conductor
RAINBOW.ANI	Arrow	Windows Animated
RAINDROP.ANI	Application starting	Variations
SIZENESW.ANI	Sizing arrow pointing northeast to southwest	Variations, Windows Animated
SIZENS.ANI	Sizing arrow pointing north to south	Variations, Windows Animated
SIZENWSE.ANI	Sizing arrow pointing northwest to southeast	Variations, Windows Animated
SIZEWE.ANI	Sizing arrow pointing west to east	Variations, Windows Animated
STOPWTCH.ANI	Stopwatch	N/A
VANISHER.ANI	Vanishing arrow	N/A
WAGTAIL.ANI	No	Variations

Control Panel Tool Files

Control Panel tools provide many options for customizing Windows NT so that it works and looks the way you want.

Windows NT includes the following control panel files.

Table 4.2   Control Panel (.CPL) Tool Files

Filename	Description
CURSORS.CPL	Control Panel tool used for customizing cursor schemes consisting of static and animated cursors
DISPLAY.CPL	Control Panel tool used for customizing the Display Settings option
FTPMGR.CPL	Control Panel tool used for customizing FTP Server options
MAIN.CPL	Control Panel tool used for customizing the following options: Color, Fonts, Ports, Mouse, Desktop, Keyboard, Printers, International, System, and Date/Time
MULTIMED.CPL	Control Panel tool used for customizing the following options: Sound, MIDI Mapper, and Drivers
NCPA.CPL	Control Panel tool used for customizing the Network Settings option
NWC.CPL	Control Panel tool used for customizing NWCS options
SFMMGR.CPL	Control Panel tool used for customizing Services for Macintosh options
SRVMGR.CPL	Control Panel tool used for customizing the following options: Server, Services, and Devices
UPS.CPL	Control Panel tool used for customizing the uninterruptible power supply (UPS) option

Driver Files

Drivers make device independence possible for Windows NT applications, providing the hardware-specific interface between physical devices and Windows NT. The Setup program can install several kinds of drivers for Windows NT, including the following:

Comm drivers	Display drivers	Keyboard drivers
Mouse drivers	Multimedia drivers	Network drivers
Printer drivers	Sound drivers	System drivers

Note Multimedia and printer drivers are optional.

Windows NT includes the following driver files.

Table 4.3   Driver (.DRV and .SYS) Files

Filename	Description
4MMDAT.SYS	4 mm DAT drive support; Archive® 4x20, WangDAT, HP® 35470a, HP 35480a, COMPAQ®
4MMSONY.SYS	Archive 4x20 Sony driver
8514A.SYS	Miniport driver
ABIOSDSK.SYS	MCA non-SCSI (WD1003 compatible controller); *x*86 only
AFD.SYS	Ancillary Function Driver that provides kernel-mode support for Windows Sockets transport interface by extending the functionality of TDI
AHA154X.SYS	Adaptec™ 154x SCSI driver
AHA174X.SYS	Adaptec 174x SCSI driver
AIC78XX.SYS	CSI miniport driver
ALWAYS.SYS	Always SCSI miniport
AM1500T.SYS	AMD AM2100, AM1500T, and PCnet driver support
AMI0NT.SYS	AMI series 44/48 SCSI controller driver
ANSI.SYS	MS-DOS utility
ARCHQIC.SYS	Tape driver support for Archive 2150s, 2525s, 2750
ARROW.SYS	SCSI miniport disk driver for Adaptec 2740/AIC 777x
ASYNCMAC.SYS	Remote Access Server Serial network driver
ATAPI.SYS	CD-ROM driver with non-SCSI interface
ATDISK.SYS	ISA/EISA non-SCSI (WD1003 compatible controller)
ATI.SYS	ATI video display driver (640 x 480 x 16 colors up to 1280 x 1024 x 16,777,216 colors)
BEEP.SYS	Speaker port driver (ISA, MCA, EISA)
BHNT.SYS	Network Monitor driver for capturing packets
BRHJ770.DLL	Network browser kernel component; redirector
BUSLOGIC.SYS	BusLogic family SCSI miniport
BUSMOUSE.SYS	Microsoft or Logitech bus mouse driver
CDAUDIO.SYS	CD Audio support, only for specific non-SCSI-2 CD-ROM drives
CDFS.SYS	CD-ROM file system driver
CDFS_REC.SYS	CD-ROM file system recognizer
CIRRUS.SYS	Cirrus Logic display driver (640 x 480 x 16 colors to 1024 x 768 x 256 colors)
COMM.DRV	Win16 communications driver

Table 4.3   Driver (.DRV and .SYS) Files *(continued)*

Filename	Description
COUNTRY.SYS	MS-DOS utility; supports international time, dates, currency, case conversions, and decimal separators
CPQARRAY.SYS	COMPAQ disk array driver
DAC960NT.SYS	Mylex DAC960 SCSI driver
DELL_DGX.SYS	Dell® DGX video display driver (640 x 480 x 256 colors to 1280 x 1024 x 256 colors; note: 1152 x 900 x 65536 color mode)
DELLDSA.SYS	Driver for Dell intelligent disk array controller (available on high-end server systems from Dell)
DIGIFEP5.SYS	Digiboard® FEP 5 adapter driver
DISKDUMP.SYS	Crash dump disk driver
DISKPERF.SYS	Disk performance statistics gatherer, collects simple statistics on the system disk performance; used in conjunction with the Performance Monitor
DLC.SYS	Data Link Control driver
DLTTAPE.SYS	Digital Equipment TZ86 and DLT2000 SCSI tape driver
DPTSCSI.SYS	EISA DPT controller
DTC329X.SYS	DTC329x SCSI miniport driver
EE16.SYS	Network NDIS driver: Intel EtherExpress® card
ELNK16.SYS	Network NDIS driver: 3Com Etherlink-16 card
ELNK3.SYS	Network NDIS driver: 3Com Etherlink-III card
ELNKII.SYS	Network NDIS driver: 3Com Etherlink-II card
ELNKMC.SYS	Network NDIS driver: 3Com Etherlink-MC card, 3Com® EtherLink® MCA driver
ET4000.SYS	Video driver for Tseng Labs ET-4000 video chipset
EXABYTE1.SYS	Tape driver for Exabyte 8200 series (SCSI-1)
EXABYTE2.SYS	Tape driver for Exabyte 8500 series (SCSI-2)
FASTFAT.SYS	File Allocation Table (FAT) file system driver
FAT_REC.SYS	FAT file system recognizer
FD16_700.SYS	SCSI miniport driver for Future Domain® 16*xx* series cards
FD7000EX.SYS	SCSI disk driver for Future Domain/Western Digital™ 7000EX controller (EISA)
FD8XX.SYS	SCSI disk driver for Future Domain 8*xx* controller
FLOPPY.SYS	Floppy disk driver (non-SCSI)
FS_REC.SYS	File system recognizer
FTDISK.SYS	Fault Tolerant volume management driver

Table 4.3   Driver (.DRV and .SYS) Files *(continued)*

Filename	Description
HIMEM.SYS	XMS driver for VDMs
HPFS_REC.SYS	High-performance file system recognizer driver
HPSCAN16.SYS	Scanner
I8042PRT.SYS	Keyboard and i8042 mouse port driver
IBMTOK.SYS	Network NDIS driver for IBM® Token Ring adapter and IBM Token Ring adapter/A
IBMTOK2I.SYS	IBM Token Ring 16/4 Adapter II ISA network driver
INPORT.SYS	Microsoft InPort mouse port driver
KBDCLASS.SYS	Keyboard class driver
KEYBOARD.DRV	Win16 keyboard driver
KEYBOARD.SYS	Command-line keyboard driver
LANCE.SYS	Network NDIS driver: DEC® Lance adapter driver
LANMAN.DRV	Win16 LAN Manager network driver
LOOP.SYS	Microsoft loop-back network NDIS driver
LT200.SYS	Software for Macintosh, Apple® LocalTalk® driver
MCIAVI.DRV	MCI driver for AVI
MCISEQ.DRV	MCI driver for MIDI sequencer
MCIWAVE.DRV	MCI driver for waveform audio
MINIQIC.SYS	Exabyte 2501 miniqic driver
MIPSSND.SYS	MIPS ARCSystem 100/150 sound
MITSUMI.SYS	Mitsumi non-SCSI CD-ROM driver
MKECR5XX.SYS	MKE CR-56X/CR-52X miniport driver
MOUCLASS.SYS	Mouse Class driver
MOUSE.DRV	Win16 mouse stub driver
MSACM32.DRV	Microsoft Audio Compression Manager driver
MSFS.SYS	Mailslot file system driver
MUP.SYS	Network Multiple UNC Provider (required)
MVAUDIO.SYS	Media Vision™ ProAudio Spectrum 16 driver
MVOPL3.SYS	Media Vision OPL3 FM Synthesizer driver
NBF.SYS	NetBEUI Frame (NBF) driver
NBT.SYS	NetBIOS for TCP/IP driver, used for Windows Networking (RFC1001/1002)
NCR53C9X.SYS	NCR® SCSI disk driver for MIPS-based computers
NCR77C22.SYS	Video driver for NCR 77C22 SVGA adapters

Table 4.3   Driver (.DRV and .SYS) Files *(continued)*

Filename	Description
NCRC700.SYS	SCSI disk driver for NCR 53c700 controller
NCRC710.SYS	SCSI disk driver for NCR 53c710 controller
NCRC810.SYS	NCR 53C810 SCSI driver
NDIS.SYS	NDIS wrapper driver; required for NDIS drivers
NDISTAPI.SYS	NDIS 3.0 connection wrapper driver
NDISWAN.SYS	Remote Access network driver
NE1000.SYS, NE2000.SYS, NE3200.SYS	Network NDIS drivers for Novell® NE1000, NE2000, and NE3200 adapters
NETBIOS.SYS	NetBIOS API driver; Microsoft NetBIOS Transport Interface
NETBT.SYS	Netbt driver
NETDTECT.SYS	Network card detection driver
NETFLX.SYS	Network NDIS driver for COMPAQ NetFlex/DualSpeed Token Ring adapter card
NETWARE.DRV	Netware driver
NPEISA.SYS	Network peripherals FDDI, EISA NDIS driver
NPFS.SYS	Named pipes file system driver
NPMCA.SYS	Network peripherals FDDI, MCA NDIS driver
NTCX.SYS	Network NDIS driver for Digiboard C/X adapter
NTDOS.SYS	Command-line emulation drive
NTEPC.SYS	Digi International EPC communications miniport driver
NTFS.SYS	Windows NT file system driver
NTFS_REC.SYS	Windows NT file system recognizer driver
NTIO.SYS	MS-DOS emulation BIOS driver
NTXALL.SYS	Network NDIS driver for Digiboard PC/Xi, PC/2e, PC/4e, PC/8e
NTXEM.SYS	Network NDIS driver for Digiboard PC/Xem
NULL.SYS	NULL device driver
NWLINK.SYS	NWLink library
NWLNKIPX.SYS	NWLINK2 IPX protocol driver
NWLNKNB.SYS	NWLINK2 IPX NetBIOS protocol driver
NWLNKRIP.SYS	NWLINK2 RIP protocol driver
NWLNKSPX.SYS	NWLINK2 SPX protocol driver
NWNBLINK.SYS	NetWare® NetBIOS Link (NWNBLink) network transport driver
NWRDR.SYS	NetWare redirector file system driver
OLISCSI.SYS	SCSI disk driver for Olivetti® ESC-1/ESC-2

Table 4.3   Driver (.DRV and .SYS) Files *(continued)*

Filename	Description
PARALLEL.SYS	Parallel port driver
PARPORT.SYS	Parallel port driver
PCIMAC.SYS	Network NDIS driver for Digiboard ISDN adapter
PINBALL.SYS	HPFS driver
PRONET16.SYS	Proteon ProNET4/16 Token Ring network driver
QIC117.SYS	Floppy tape driver for QIC 117 floppy/tape drive
QV.SYS	Video miniport driver for COMPAQ Qvision
RASARP.SYS	Remote Access IP ARP driver
RASHUB.SYS	RAS Hub driver
RDR.SYS	Network redirector driver
S3.SYS	Video driver library for S3 video chipsets (640 x 480 x 256 colors up to 1280 x 1024 x 256 colors)
SCSICDRM.SYS	SCSI CD-ROM class driver
SCSIDISK.SYS	SCSI disk class driver
SCSIFLOP.SYS	SCSI class floppy driver; not required for startup
SCSIPORT.SYS	SCSI port driver
SCSIPRNT.SYS	SCSI print class driver
SCSISCAN.SYS	SCSI scanner class driver
SERIAL.SYS	Serial port driver
SERMOUSE.SYS	Serial mouse driver
SETUPDD.SYS	Windows NT Setup (kernel mode portion of character-based phase)
SFMATALK.SYS	Services for Macintosh AppleTalk protocol driver
SFMSRV.SYS	Services for Macintosh file server driver
SLCD32.SYS	SLCD CD-ROM controller driver
SMBTRSUP.SYS	SMB trace support; required for RDR.SYS and SRV.SYS
SMC8000N.SYS	Network NDIS driver for SMC (Western Digital) network adapter cards
SNDBLST.SYS	Audio driver for Creative Labs Sound Blaster™, also the Media Vision Thunder Board
SNDSYS.SYS	Multimedia kernel driver
SONIC.SYS	Network NDIS driver for MIPS (built-in on Jazz computers)
SOUND.DRV	Win16 Sound driver
SPARROW.SYS	Adaptec 151*x* and 152*x* SCSI miniport driver
SPOCK.SYS	SCSI MCA SCSI driver

Table 4.3   Driver (.DRV and .SYS) Files *(continued)*

Filename	Description
SRV.SYS	Network Server driver
STREAMS.SYS	Streams driver; used by Streams-based protocols including TCP/IP and NWLink
SYNTH.SYS	Synthesizer driver
SYSTEM.DRV	Win16 system driver
T128.SYS	Trantor 128 SCSI miniport driver
T13B.SYS	Trantor 130b SCSI miniport driver
TANDQIC.SYS	Tape driver for Tandberg 3660, 3820, 4120, and 4220
TCARC.SYS	ARCNET network driver
TCPIP.SYS	TCP/IP driver; includes TCP/IP modules such as IP, UDP, TCP, and ARP
TDI.SYS	Network TDI wrapper (required)
TELNET.SYS	Telnet driver
TIMER.DRV	Timer driver for PC compatibles
TMV1.SYS	SCSI miniport driver for Trantor MediaVision
TRIDENT.SYS	Video driver for Trident display adapters (640 x 480 x 16 colors to 1024 x 768 x 256 colors)
UBNEI.SYS	Ungermann-Bass® network adapter driver
ULTRA124.SYS	SCSI disk driver for UltraStor 124f controller
ULTRA14F.SYS	SCSI disk driver for UltraStor 14f, 34f controller
ULTRA24F.SYS	SCSI disk driver for UltraStor 24f controller
V7VRAM.SYS	Video Seven VRAM driver
VGA.DRV	Windows-16 VGA stub driver
VGA.SYS	VGA class driver
VGA_ALT.SYS	VGA alternate video driver
VIDEOPRT.SYS	VGA video port driver
VIDEOSIM.SYS	Frame buffer simulator
WANGQIC.SYS	Tape driver for Wangtek 525, 250 tape drives
WD33C93.SYS	SCSI disk driver for Maynard/Western Digital 33c93 controller (ISA)
WDVGA.SYS	Video driver for Western Digital/Paradise display adapters (604 x 480 x 16 colors to 1024 x 768 x 256 colors)
WFWNET.DRV	Windows for Workgroups 16-bit network stub driver
WINSPOOL.DRV	Win32 print spooler interface that contains the print spooler API calls
XGA.SYS	XGA video driver

Dynamic Link Library Files

Windows NT includes the following dynamic link library files.

Table 4.4   Dynamic Link Library (.DLL) Files

Filename	Description
8514A.DLL	ATI 8514/A display driver
AB32.DLL	Microsoft Mail and Microsoft Schedule+ Address Book (32-bit) library
ACLEDIT.DLL	Access control list editor library
ADVAPI32.DLL	Advanced API Services library supporting numerous APIs including many security and Registry calls
ALRSVC.DLL	Alerter Service Library
AMDNCDET.DLL	Network Control Panel Tool detection library for AM1500T card
ATI.DLL	Driver support library for ATI video display driver
ATKCTRS.DLL	AppleTalk Performance Monitor counter
AVICAP32.DLL	Microsoft AVI capture window class
AVIFIL32.DLL	Microsoft AVI file support library
AVIFILE.DLL	Microsoft AVI file support library
BASESRV.DLL	Windows NT base services support
BHMON.DLL	Network Monitor component that provides network statistics to Performance Monitor
BHNETB.DLL	Network Monitoring NetBIOS remote protocol driver
BHSUPP.DLL	General support DLL for Network Monitor network drivers
BRHJ770.DLL	Brother® HJ-770 printer driver library
BROTHER9.DLL	Brother 9-pin dot-matrix driver (Brother M-1309, M-1809, M-1818, M-1909, M-1918)
BROTHR24.DLL	Brother 24-pin dot-matrix driver (Brother M-1324, M-1824L, M-1924L)
BROWSER.DLL	Network browser service
CANON330.DLL	Canon® Bubble-Jet driver (supports BJ models 10e, 10ex, 10sx, 130, 130e, 20, 200, 230, 300, 330); also supports Mannesmann Tally® MT 93, 94
CANON800.DLL	Canon Bubble-Jet BJC-800 driver
CANONLBP.DLL	Canon CapSL printer driver
CARDS.DLL	Playing cards library used by FREECELL.EXE

Table 4.4   Dynamic Link Library (.DLL) Files *(continued)*

Filename	Description
CIT24US.DLL	Citizen 24-pin dot-matrix printer driver; supports Citizen models 124D, 224, GSX models 130, 140, 140+, 145, 230, PN48, Prodot24, Swift models 200, 24, 24e, 24x
CIT9US.DLL	Citizen 9-pin dot-matrix printer driver, supports Citizen models 120D, 120D+, 180D, 200GX, 200GX/15 and HSP models 500, 550, Prodot 9, Prodot 9x, Swift 9 and Swift 9x
CITOH.DLL	C. Itoh® printer driver supports AT&T 470, 475 and C-Itoh 8510
CLB.DLL	Microsoft Diagnostics support library
COMCTL32.DLL	Windows NT common internal controls library
COMDLG32.DLL	Windows NT common dialog API library
COMMDLG.DLL	Win16 common dialog API library
COMPOBJ.DLL	OLE version 2.1 16/32 interoperability library
CRTDLL.DLL	C Run-time support library (not recommended to remove this file)
CSRRTL.DLL	Client-server run-time library
CSRSRV.DLL	Client-server run-time server
CUFAT.DLL	FAT to NTFS file system conversion library
CUHPFS.DLL	HPFS to NTFS file system conversion library
DDEML.DLL	DDE Manager library API library
DEC24PIN.DLL	Digital printer driver; supports the DECwriter 95, Digital LA models 324, 424, 75 Plus
DEC3200.DLL	Digital printer driver; supports the DEClaser 1100, 2100, 2200, 3200
DEC9PIN.DLL	Digital printer driver; supports the LA models 310, 70, 75
DECPSMON.DLL	Digital network printing SW
DEMIL32.DLL	Microsoft Workgroup Applications System Services layer
DGCONFIG.DLL	Network NDIS driver for Digiboard serial driver
DHCPCSVC.DLL	DHCP Client Service
DHCPMIB.DLL	DHCP SNMP agent
DHCPSAPI.DLL	DHCP Server API stub dynamic link library
DHCPSSVC.DLL	DHCP Server Service
DICONIX.DLL	Diconix 150 Plus
DIGIINST.DLL	Network NDIS driver for Digiboard ISDN
DLCAPI.DLL	Data Link Control API library
DOSCALLS.DLL	OS/2 subsystem thunk DLL

Table 4.4 Dynamic Link Library (.DLL) Files *(continued)*

Filename	Description
DRIVERS.DLL	Control Panel tool for installing drivers
Epson24.DLL	Printer driver for Epson® compatible 24-pin dot-matrix printers
Epson9.DLL	Printer driver for Epson compatible 9-pin dot-matrix printers
ESCP2E.DLL	Printer drive for Epson compatible scalable printers, Citizen GSX 240, Citizen Swift 240, and Epson AP models 3250, 5000, 5500, and Epson models LQ-100, LQ-1070, LQ-570, LQ-870, SQ-1170
ESCP2MS.DLL	ESC/P 2 printer driver
EVENTLOG.DLL	Eventlog Service
FMIFS.DLL	Mediator between the Installable File System utilities and File Manager
FRAME32.DLL	Microsoft Workgroup Applications Framework layer
FRAMEBUF.DLL	Display library to support the DELL DGX display driver
FTENG32.DLL	Full-text search engine library
FTPCTRS.DLL	FTP Service performance counters
FTPSMX.DLL	File Transfer Program (FTP) Server management extensions for Server Manager
FTPSVAPI.DLL	FTP Service Client API stubs
FTPSVC.DLL	FTP Server management API support for Control Panel
FTUI32.DLL	Full text search user interface library
FUJI24.DLL	Printer driver for Fujitsu® DL series of printers, including the 900, 1100, 1100 color, 1150, 1200, 1250, 2400, 2600, 3300, 3350, 3400, 3450, 3600, 4400, 4600, and 5600
FUJI9.DLL	Printer driver for Fujitsu DX series of printers, including the 2100, 2200, 2300, 2400
GDI32.DLL	Windows NT 32-bit Graphics Device Interface API library; core Windows NT component
GDIEXTS.DLL	GDI Symbolic debugger extensions
GLU32.DLL	Open GL utility library
HAL.DLL	Hardware Abstraction Layer (HAL) for Industry Standard Architecture (ISA) computers
HAL486C.DLL	HAL for COMPAQ 486C computers
HALAST.DLL	HAL for AST® computers
HALAVANT.DLL	HAL for Alpha Avanti systems
HALCBUS.DLL	HAL for Corollary Extended C-bus

Table 4.4   Dynamic Link Library (.DLL) Files *(continued)*

Filename	Description
HALDTI.DLL	HAL for Deskstation Arcstation I
HALDUOMP.DLL	HAL for duo MP computers
HALFXS.DLL	HAL for Jazz computers
HALFXSPC.DLL	HAL for R4600-based Jazz systems
HALMCA.DLL	HAL for MCA
HALMIKAS.DLL	HAL for Alpha server 1000 family
HALMPS.DLL	HAL for MPS 1.1 system
HALNCR.DLL	HAL for NCR
HALNECMP.DLL	HAL for NEC® R96 duo systems
HALOLI.DLL	HAL for Olivetti
HALSABMP.DLL	HAL for Sable systems
HALSABUP.DLL	HAL for Sable systems
HALSP.DLL	SystemPro version of HAL
HALTYNE.DLL	HAL for Desk station R4600 systems
HALWYSE7.DLL	HAL for Wyse®
HPDSKJET.DLL	Printer driver for HP DeskJet® and DeskJet models 500, 500C, 510, 550C, Plus, and Portable
HPMON.DLL	HP Monitor; HP LaserJet® IIIsi support library
HPMON.DLL	Hewlett-Packard network port monitor
HPPCL.DLL	HP Printer Control Language driver; used by many HPPCL compatible printers
HPPCL5MS.DLL	Microsoft implementation of the HPPCL 5.0 driver; used by various HPPCL5-compatible printers
HPSCAN32.DLL	SCSI scanner support dynamic link library
HTUI.DLL	User interface library provided for display or printer driver's halftone color adjustments
IBM238X.DLL	Printer driver for IBM 4216-020 version 47.0
IBM239X.DLL	Printer driver for IBM Personal Printer II models 2390, and 2391
IBM5204.DLL	Printer driver for IBM QuickWriter® 5204
IBMPORT.DLL	Printer driver for IBM Portable 5183
IBMPPDSL.DLL	IBM PPDS printer driver
ICCVID.DLL	Cinepak Codec driver
ICMP.DLL	ICMP helper DLL used by Ping

Table 4.4   Dynamic Link Library (.DLL) Files *(continued)*

Filename	Description
IFSUTIL.DLL	Startup **chkdsk** utility; can be omitted from a bare-bones startup system if all volumes used to startup are guaranteed not to be corrupt
IMAGEHLP.DLL	An API set for manipulating images
IMPEXP32.DLL	Microsoft Mail file import utility
INETMIB1.DLL	TCP/IP Management Information Base
IOLOGMSG.DLL	Contains message file for error log status codes
IPADRDLL.DLL	IP address custom control
IPXCFG.DLL	IPX configuration DLL
ISDN.DLL	Network NDIS driver for Digiboard ISDN
JET.DLL	JET engine DLL
JP350.DLL	Printer driver used by the Universal Printer Driver (RASDD.DLL) to support Olivetti JP 350, Olivetti JP 350S, Digital DECmultiJET 2000, Bull Compuprint PM 201, Fujitsu Breeze 200, Citizen PROjet, Olivetti JP 150, Digital DECmultiJET 1000, Fujitsu Breeze 100, Royal CJP 450, NEC Jetmate 400, NEC Jetmate 800
JZVXL484.DLL	Video driver
KBDBE.DLL	Belgian keyboard layout
KBDBR.DLL	Brazilian ABNT keyboard layout
KBDBU.DLL	Bulgarian keyboard layout
KBDCA.DLL	Canadian multilingual keyboard layout
KBDCR.DLL	Croatian keyboard layout
KBDCR.DLL	Slovenian keyboard layout
KBDCZ.DLL	Czech keyboard layout
KBDDA.DLL	Danish keyboard layout
KBDDV.DLL	U.S. English Dvorak keyboard layout
KBDES.DLL	Spanish (alternate) keyboard layout
KBDFC.DLL	French Canadian keyboard layout
KBDFI.DLL	Finnish keyboard layout
KBDFR.DLL	French keyboard layout
KBDGR.DLL	German keyboard layout
KBDHE.DLL	Hellenic Greek keyboard layout
KBDHU.DLL	Hungarian keyboard layout
KBDIC.DLL	Icelandic keyboard layout

Table 4.4   Dynamic Link Library (.DLL) Files *(continued)*

Filename	Description
KBDIT.DLL	Italian keyboard layout
KBDLA.DLL	Latin (Latin American Spanish) keyboard layout
KBDNE.DLL	Netherlands (Dutch) keyboard layout
KBDNO.DLL	Norwegian keyboard layout
KBDPL1.DLL	Polish Programmers' keyboard layout
KBDPO.DLL	Polish keyboard layout
KBDRO.DLL	Romanian keyboard layout
KBDRU.DLL	Russian keyboard layout
KBDSF.DLL	Swiss-French keyboard layout
KBDSG.DLL	Swiss-German keyboard layout
KBDSL.DLL	Slovak keyboard layout
KBDSP.DLL	Spanish keyboard layout
KBDSW.DLL	Swedish keyboard layout
KBDTUF.DLL	Turkish keyboard layout
KBDTUQ.DLL	Turkish keyboard layout
KBDUK.DLL	UK-English keyboard layout
KBDUS.DLL	U.S. keyboard layout
KBDUSX.DLL	U.S. English keyboard layout
KERNEL32.DLL	Windows NT 32-bit base API support; core Windows NT component
KYOCERA.DLL	Printer driver for Apricot Laser and Kyocera® F series printers
LMHSVC.DLL	NetBIOS over TCP/IP (NBT) LMHOSTS parsing support
LMMIB2.DLL	LAN Manager management information base
LMUICMN0.DLL	Network user interface DLLs
LMUICMN1.DLL	LAN Manager Common User Interface library
LOCALMON.DLL	Local Monitor; used to send a print job to a port
LOCALSPL.DLL	Local Spooling support for printing
LPDSVC.DLL	LPDSVC Service, the server side of TCP/IP printing for UNIX clients
LPRHELP.DLL	LPR Print Monitor
LPRMON.DLL	TCP/IP connectivity utility used to print a file to a host running an LPD server
LSASRV.DLL	Local Security Authority server process
LZ32.DLL	Windows NT 32-bit compression routines

Table 4.4   Dynamic Link Library (.DLL) Files *(continued)*

Filename	Description
LZEXPAND.DLL	Windows NT 32-bit expansion routines
MAILM32.DLL	Microsoft Mail Manager and support functions (32-bit)
MANTAL24.DLL	Printer driver for Mannesmann Tally 24-pin dot-matrix printers; supports MT series 82, 130/24, 131/24, 150/24, 230/24, 330, 350, 360
MANTAL90.DLL	Printer driver for Mannesmann Tally MT 90
MANTALBJ.DLL	Printer driver for Mannesmann Tally MT 92, 92C
MAPI.DLL	Microsoft Messaging API library (16-bit)
MAPI32.DLL	Microsoft Messaging API library (32-bit)
MAPIXX.DLL	Microsoft MAPI support routines for Microsoft Mail and Microsoft Schedule+; used by the MAPSRV.EXE process to service MAPI calls
MCIAVI32.DLL	Media Control Interface Audio Video Interleave API support library
MCICDA.DLL	Compact Disk Audio MCI library
MCIOLE16.DLL	MCI Object Linking and Embedding (OLE) library, 16-bit
MCIOLE32.DLL	MCI OLE library, 32-bit
MCISEQ.DLL	Music Instrument Digital Interface Sequencer MCI layer
MCIWAVE.DLL	MCI Wave output library
MF3216.DLL	Converts Win32 metafiles to Win16 metafiles
MGMTAPI.DLL	SNMP component; Management API library
MIDIMAP.DLL	Control Panel tool library
MMDRV.DLL	Multimedia API library
MMSNDSRV.DLL	Multimedia sound server library
MMSYSTEM.DLL	16-bit entry point to multimedia applications
MORICONS.DLL	More Icons, a resource library of icons
MPR.DLL	Multiple Provider Router library; takes Win32 networking APIs and passes the call to the correct network provider (should not be required for startup, except that Program Manager calls restore connections)
MPRUI.DLL	Multiple Provider user interface, helper library for MPR.DLL
MSACM.DLL	Microsoft Audio Compression Manager
MSACM32.DLL	Microsoft Audio Compression Manager
MSAUDITE.DLL	Message library used by the Audit Event Viewer
MSGSVC.DLL	Windows NT Messenger Service
MSNCDET.DLL	Network card detection library

Table 4.4   Dynamic Link Library (.DLL) Files *(continued)*

Filename	Description
MSOBJS.DLL	Auditing support
MSPELF32.DLL	Finnish language spell checker help
MSPELL32.DLL	Spell checker help for all languages except Finnish
MSPRIVS.DLL	Microsoft privilege name strings library
MSRLE32.DLL	Microsoft RLE compressor
MSSCHD32.DLL	Microsoft Schedule+
MSSFS32.DLL	Microsoft Shared File System Transport library (32-bit)
MSV1_0.DLL	LAN Manager logon library
MSVFW32.DLL	Microsoft Video for Windows 32-bit driver
MSVIDC32.DLL	Microsoft video 1 compressor
MSVIDC32.DLL	Supporting library for Microsoft Video for Windows driver
MSVIDEO.DLL	Microsoft video for Windows DLL
MT735.DLL	Printer driver for Mannesmann Tally MT 730/735
MT99.DLL	Printer driver for Mannesmann Tally MT 98/99
MVAPI32.DLL	Full text search
MVAUDIO.DLL	Media Vision ProAudio Spectrum 16 driver library
MVFS32.DLL	Microsoft Viewer File System; Microsoft multimedia-specific installable file system support for Windows multimedia applications
MVOPL3.DLL	Media Vision OPL3 FM Synthesizer driver library
NAL.DLL	Network Abstraction Layer used to communicate with NDIS30.DLL
NBTSVC.DLL	NetBIOS over TCP/IP (NBT) service
NDDEAPI.DLL	Network DDE API library
NDDENB32.DLL	Network DDE NetBIOS interface
NDIS30.DLL	Used to communicate with the BHNT.SYS file, the network driver used to capture packets
NEC24PIN.DLL	Printer driver for NEC Pinwriter models CP6, CP7, P20, P2200, P2plus, P30, P3200, P3300, P5200, P5300, P5XL, P6, P60, P6200, P6300, P6plus, P7, P70, P7plus, P90, P9300, and P9XL
NETAPI.DLL	OS/2 subsystem thunk DLLs
NETAPI32.DLL	Windows NT 32-bit Network API library
NETBIOS.DLL	Network DDE
NETDTECT.DLL	Network card auto-detection library

Table 4.4   Dynamic Link Library (.DLL) Files *(continued)*

Filename	Description
NETEVENT.DLL	Network components error messages library
NETFLX.DLL	NET NDIS driver: COMPAQ detection DLL
NETH.DLL	Help messages for NETCMD (network command-line interface) and network services; needed even without a network adapter card to start and stop services and to add users to groups at the command line
NETLOGON.DLL	Network logon library
NETMSG.DLL	LAN Manager network error messages library
NETRAP.DLL	Routines library used for talking to or from downlevel systems; support routines for Rpcxlate and Xactsrv
NETUI0.DLL	Windows NT LM user interface common code (GUI classes)
NETUI1.DLL	Windows NT LM user interface common code (GUI classes)
NETUI2.DLL	Windows NT LM user interface common code (GUI classes)
NPINCDET.DLL	Network peripherals detection driver (EISA)
NTDLL.DLL	Windows NT API library; core Windows NT component
NTLANMAN.DLL	Windows NT LAN Manager provider for MPR
NTLANUI.DLL	LAN Manager control DLL
NTLMSSPS.DLL	Security Support Provider Service
NTLSAPI.DLL	Licensing API
NTSDEXTS.DLL	Symbolic debugger extensions
NTVDM.DLL	Windows NT Virtual DOS Machine (VDM) support library
NWAPI16.DLL	NW Windows/DOS API
NWAPI32.DLL	NW Win32 API
NWCFG.DLL	NWC configuration DLL
NWEVENT.DLL	Event messages for Client Service for NetWare
NWLNKCFG.DLL	NWLink configuration library
NWLNKMSG.DLL	NWLink message library
NWNBLINK.DLL	NetWare NetBIOS Link (NWNBLink); Novell NetWare NetBIOS compatible network transport library
NWPROVAU.DLL	Client Service for NetWare Provider and authentication package DLL
NWSAP.DLL	NW SAP agent DLL
NWWKS.DLL	Client Service for NetWare
OKI24.DLL	Printer driver for Okidata® ML Plus and Elite models 380, 390, 391, 393, 393C, 590, and 591

Table 4.4   Dynamic Link Library (.DLL) Files *(continued)*

Filename	Description
OKI9.DLL	Printer driver for Okidata ML models 192, 192 Plus, 193, 193 Plus, 320, and 321
OKI9IBM.DLL	Printer driver for Okidata ML (Elite and IBM) models 92, 93, 182, 192, 193, 280, 320, 321, 3410, also the AT&T® 473/478, and the Generic IBM 9-pin graphics printers
OLE2.DLL	OLE version 2.1 16/32 interoperability library
OLE2DISP.DLL	OLE version 2.1 16/32 interoperability library
OLE2NLS.DLL	OLE version 2.1 16/32 interoperability library
OLE32.DLL	OLE version 2.1 for Windows NT
OLEAUT32.DLL	OLE version 2.1 for Windows NT
OLECLI.DLL	OLE client API library (16-bit)
OLECLI32.DLL	OLE client API library (32-bit)
OLECNV32.DLL	OLE version 2.1 for Windows NT
OLEPRX32.DLL	OLE version 2.1 for Windows NT
OLESVR.DLL	OLE server API library (16-bit)
OLESVR32.DLL	OLE server API library (32-bit)
OLETHK32.DLL	OLE version 2.1 for Windows NT
OLIDM24.DLL	Printer driver for Olivetti DM series 124 C, 124L, 124, 324, 324L, 324S, 324SL, 600, 600S, and 624
OLIDM9.DLL	Printer driver for Olivetti DM series 109,309, 309 L, 309 S, and 309 SL
OPENGL32.DLL	OpenGL client DLL
PABNSP32.DLL	Library used by Microsoft Mail
PAINTJET.DLL	Printer driver for HP PaintJet® and HP PaintJet XL
PANSON24.DLL	Printer driver for Panasonic® KX series models P1123, P1124, P1124i, P1624, P2123, P2124, and P2624
PANSON9.DLL	Printer driver for Panasonic KX series models P1081, P1180, P1695, and P2180
PERFCTRS.DLL	Performance Monitor counter library
PERFNW.DLL	NWCS file
PLOTTER.DLL	Raster/pen plotter driver
PLOTUI.DLL	Raster/pen plotter driver user interface
PMSPL.DLL	Print Manger spooler library
PROPRINT.DLL	Printer driver for IBM Proprinter® II, Proprinter III, Proprinter XL, Proprinter XL II, Proprinter XL III and the IBM Proprinter
PROPRN24.DLL	Printer driver for IBM Proprinter X24, X24e, XL24, and XL24e

Table 4.4   Dynamic Link Library (.DLL) Files *(continued)*

Filename	Description
PS1.DLL	Printer driver for IBM PS/1 2205
PSCRIPT.DLL	PostScript® printer driver
PSCRPTUI.DLL	PostScript print driver user interface
PSXDLL.DLL	Provides core POSIX API support
QUIETJET.DLL	Printer driver for HP QuietJet® and QuietJet Plus
QWIII.DLL	Printer driver for IBM QuietWriter III
RASADMIN.DLL	Remote Access Server Administrator library
RASAPI16.DLL	Remote Access 16/32 API thunks
RASAPI32.DLL	Remote Access Server API library
RASCAUTH.DLL	Remote Access Server Client authority library
RASCBCP.DLL	Remote Access Server callback control protocol. Negotiates callback information with the remote client.
RASCCP.DLL	Remote Access PPP compression control protocol
RASCFG.DLL	Remote Access Server configuration library
RASCHAP.DLL	Remote Access Server Crypto-Handshake Authentication Protocol
RASCTRS.DLL	Remote Access Performance Monitor counters
RASDD.DLL	Raster printer device driver library
RASDDUI.DLL	Raster printer device driver user interface library
RASFIL32.DLL	Remote Access Server filter library
RASGPRXY.DLL	Remote Access Server NetBIOS gateway proxy
RASGTWY.DLL	Remote Access Server gateway library
RASIPCP.DLL	Remote Access PPP Internet protocol control protocol
RASIPHLP.DLL	Remote Access IP configuration helper
RASIPXCP.DLL	Remote Access PPP Internet protocol control protocol
RASMAN.DLL	Remote Access Server Manager library
RASMSG.DLL	Remote Access Server message library
RASMXS.DLL	Library used by Remote Access
RASNBFCP.DLL	Remote Access NBF control protocol
RASNBIPC.DLL	Remote Access Server NBFCP interface
RASPAP.DLL	Remote Access PPP password authentication protocol
RASPHONE.EXE	Remote Access Server Phone application
RASPPP.DLL	Remote Access PPP API library
RASPPPEN.DLL	Remote Access PPP engine

Table 4.4   Dynamic Link Library (.DLL) Files *(continued)*

Filename	Description
RASRES.DLL	Remote Access Server resource library
RASSAUTH.DLL	Remote Access Server authentication library
RASSER.DLL	Remote Access Server serial library
RASSPAP.DLL	Remote Access PPP Shiva password authentication protocol
RASTAPI.DLL	Remote Access TAPI compliance layer
RNAL.DLL	Network monitoring Remote Network Abstraction Layer
RPCDCE4.DLL	RPC transport drivers that allow RPC to communicate with TCP/IP and NetBIOS
RPCDGC3.DLL	Remote Procedure Call UDP client DG DLL
RPCDGC6.DLL	Remote Procedure Call IPX client DG DLL
RPCDGS3.DLL	Remote Procedure Call UDP server DG DLL
RPCDGS6.DLL	Remote Procedure Call IPX server DG DLL
RPCLTC1.DLL	Remote Procedure Call client support for Named Pipes (if using LPC for local communication, these won't be needed for minimal startup)
RPCLTC3.DLL	RPC transport drivers that allow RPC to talk to TCP/IP and NetBIOS
RPCLTC5.DLL	RPC transport driver
RPCLTC6.DLL	RPC transport driver
RPCLTS1.DLL	Remote Procedure Call server support for Named Pipes (if using LPC for local communication, these won't be needed for minimal startup)
RPCLTS3.DLL	RPC transport driver
RPCLTS5.DLL	RPC transport driver
RPCLTS6.DLL	RPC transport driver
RPCNS4.DLL	RPC Name Service support (should not be needed for starting the system)
RPCRT4.DLL	RPC run time (if go to LPC for local communication these won't be needed for minimal startup)
S3.DLL	Video driver library for S3 video chipsets
SAMLIB.DLL	Security Authority Manager API library
SAMSRV.DLL	Security Authority Manager server library
SCHMSG32.DLL	Microsoft Schedule+ message library
SECURITY.DLL	Security support provider client DLL

Table 4.4   Dynamic Link Library (.DLL) Files *(continued)*

Filename	Description
SEIKO.DLL	Printer driver for Seiko Professional ColorPoint 8BPP
SEIKO24E.DLL	Printer driver for Seikosha LT-20, SL-80 IP, SL-92, and SL 92 Plus
SEIKOSH9.DLL	Printer driver for Seikosha SP models 1900, 1900+, 2000, 2400, and 2415
SENDFL32.DLL	Microsoft Mail Send File utility to send attached files
SETUPDLL.DLL	Setup library
SFMAPI.DLL	Services for Macintosh API library
SFMATCFG.DLL	Services for Macintosh AppleTalk protocol configuration library
SFMATMSG.DLL	Services for Macintosh AppleTalk protocol message library
SFMCTRS.DLL	Macintosh file service performance counter
SFMMON.DLL	Services for Macintosh Print Monitor library
SFMMSG.DLL	Services for Macintosh Message library
SFMPSDIB.DLL	Services for Macintosh PostScript Raster Image Processor library
SFMPSFNT.DLL	Services for Macintosh PostScript font library
SFMPSPRT.DLL	Services for Macintosh PostScript print processor library
SFMRES.DLL	Services for Macintosh Setup dialog resources library
SFMUTIL.DLL	Services for Macintosh Setup Utilities library
SFMWSHAT.DLL	Services for Macintosh Windows Sockets Helper AppleTalk protocol library
SHELL.DLL	Win16 Shell library for Win16 application compatibility
SHELL32.DLL	Windows NT 32-bit Shell API library
SIMPTCP.DLL	Simple TCP/IP Services
SNDBLST.DLL	Audio driver library for Creative Labs SoundBlaster, also the Media Vision Thunder Board
SNDSYS32.DLL	Configuration and MIDI patch code
SOCKUTIL.DLL	Berkeley-style UNIX sockets interface support
SOUND.DLL	Control Panel Sound library
SPOOLSS.DLL	Spooling subsystem library support
SRVSVC.DLL	Server service library
STAR24E.DLL	Printer driver for Star LC24-*xxx*, NB24-*xx*, NX-24*xx*, XB-24*xx*, and XB24-*xxx* models of printers
STAR9E.DLL	Printer driver for Star models of printers: LC-*xxx*, NL-10, NX-1*xxx*, XR-1*xxx*, ZA-200, ZA-250

Table 4.4   Dynamic Link Library (.DLL) Files *(continued)*

Filename	Description
STARJET.DLL	Printer driver for Star SJ-48 printer
STORAGE.DLL	OLE version 2.1 16/32 interoperability library
STORE32.DLL	Microsoft Mail store support functions
SYNTH.DLL	Synthesizer library
T1INSTAL.DLL	Type 1 to TrueType converter
TAPISRV.DLL	Remote Access Server WAN connection wrapper library
TCPCFG.DLL	TCP/IP configuration DLL
TCPIPSVC.DLL	TCP/IP service library
TELNET.DLL	Telnet driver library
THINKJET.DLL	Printer driver for HP ThinkJet® (2225 C-D)
TI850.DLL	Printer driver for TI 850 and 855
TOOLHELP.DLL	Windows-16 Tool Helper library
TOSHIBA.DLL	Printer driver for Toshiba® P351 and P1351
TRNSCH32.DLL	Microsoft Schedule+ shared file system transport library
TYPELIB.DLL	OLE version 2.1 16/32 interoperability library
UFAT.DLL	Unicode FAT file system library
UHPFS.DLL	Unicode HPFS library
ULIB.DLL	Windows NT Utilities library
UNTFS.DLL	Unicode NTFS library
UREG.DLL	Registry utility
USER32.DLL	Windows NT User library to provide support for user interface routines
USEREXTS.DLL	User symbolic debugger extensions
USPIFS.DLL	Setup utility that contains Chkdsk and file system code for FAT, HPFS, and NTFS
VCDEX.DLL	Virtual MSCDEX driver; supports MS-DOS-based and Windows-based applications using the Microsoft CD ROM extensions (MSCDEX)
VDMDBG.DLL	Virtual DOS Machine (VDM) debugging library
VDMREDIR.DLL	Multiple VDM network support (named pipes, mailslots, network APIs, NetBIOS, DLC)
VER.DLL	Win16 Windows version library
VERSION.DLL	Windows NT version library
VFORM32.DLL	Microsoft Mail Viewer Forms library

Table 4.4   Dynamic Link Library (.DLL) Files *(continued)*

Filename	Description
VGA.DLL	VGA video driver library
VGA256.DLL	VGA 256-color library
VGA64K.DLL	32K/64K color VGA display driver
VWIPXSPX.DLL	NWCS file
WEITEKP9.DLL	Weitek® P9000 display driver
WGPOMG32.DLL	Windows NT workgroup postoffice manager functions
WIN32SPL.DLL	Windows NT Spooler library
WIN87EM.DLL	Win16 x87 math coprocessor emulation
WINMM.DLL	Windows NT Multimedia DLL
WINMSD.DLL	Windows NT Microsoft Diagnostics
WINPRINT.DLL	Windows NT Print API library
WINSCTRS.DLL	WINS Service performance counters
WINSEVNT.DLL	WINS event log messages
WINSMIB.DLL	WINS SNMP agent
WINSOCK.DLL	16-bit Windows Sockets interface support (thunks through to WSOCK32.DLL) for TCP/IP
WINSRPC.DLL	WINS RPC library
WINSRV.DLL	Contains the server side of the 32-bit User and GDI routines (graphics engine)
WINSTRM.DLL	Windows NT TCP/IP interface for the Route utility
WKSSVC.DLL	Network Workstation service library
WOW32.DLL	32-bit code for Win16 support
WSHISN.DLL	NWLINK2 socket helper
WSHNETBS.DLL	NetBIOS Windows sockets helper
WSHNWLNK.DLL	Windows NT Windows Sockets helper for NWLink
WSHTCPIP.DLL	Windows NT Windows Sockets helper for TCP/IP
WSOCK32.DLL	32-bit Windows Sockets API library
XACTSRV.DLL	Transaction Server, supports remote API calls from downlevel systems
XGA.DLL	XGA video driver library

Executable Files

To free hard disk space, you can delete executable files for accessories and games that you don't intend to use, for example the CD Player accessory or Freecell game. To remove accessory or game files and their corresponding online Help files, delete the files using the Windows NT Setup program.

For more information about removing executable files for accessories and games, see "Adding and Removing Windows NT Components" in Chapter 12, "System Maintenance with Windows NT Setup," in the *Windows NT System Guide*.

Windows NT includes the following executable files.

Table 4.5   Executable (.EXE and .COM) Files

Filename	Description
ACCESS.EXE	Access utility for individuals with motion or hearing impairments
ACLCONV.EXE	Access Control List Conversion utility that converts OS/2 LAN Manager Server ACLs
APPEND.EXE	MS-DOS 5.0 utility
ARP.EXE	TCP/IP network utility to manipulate the ARP cache
AT.EXE	Windows NT scheduling utility that schedules commands and programs to run on a computer
ATSVC.EXE	Windows NT Scheduling service
ATTRIB.EXE	File Attribute utility; displays or changes file attributes
AUTOCHK.EXE	Autocheck utility run during boot sequence
AUTOCONV.EXE	Auto File System Conversion utility
AUTOSETP.EXE	Windows NT Setup extension
BACKUP.EXE	MS-DOS 5.0 backup utility
BOOTOK.EXE	Boot Acceptance application for Registry; part of the Service Controller used for LastKnownGood control set functionality
BOOTVRFY.EXE	Boot Verify application for Registry used for LastKnownGood startup support component
CACLS.EXE	Control ACLs Program
CALC.EXE	Calculator tool
CARDFILE.EXE	Cardfile tool
CCMD.EXE	Windows NT Command Processor
CDPLAYER.EXE	CD-ROM Audio player support
CHARMAP.EXE	Character Map tool
CHCP.COM	MS-DOS utility (Change Code Page); displays or sets the active code page number

Table 4.5 Executable (.EXE and .COM) Files *(continued)*

Filename	Description
CHKDSK.EXE	Check Disk utility that checks a disk and displays a status report
CLIPBRD.EXE	Clipbook Viewer tool
CLIPSRV.EXE	Network DDE Clipbook service
CLOCK.EXE	Clock tool
CMD.EXE	Windows NT single-command shell interpreter
COMMAND.COM	Command interpreter for MS-DOS and Windows 16-bit VDMs
COMP.EXE	MS-DOS Compare utility that compares the contents of two files or sets of files
COMPACT.EXE	File Compression utility
CONTROL.EXE	Control Panel
CONVERT.EXE	FAT to NTFS and HPFS to NTFS file system conversion utility
CSRSS.EXE	Client-server run-time server subsystem; Win32 API support
DDESHARE.EXE	Network dynamic data exchange share support
DEBUG.EXE	MS-DOS 5.0 Debug utility
DHCPADMN.EXE	Dynamic Host Configuration Protocol (DHCP) Manager
DISKCOMP.COM	MS-DOS Disk Compare utility; compares the contents of two floppy disks
DISKCOPY.COM	MS-DOS Disk Copy utility; copies the contents of one floppy disk to another
DISKPERF.EXE	Performance Monitor command-line interface to enable and disable the disk counters
DOSKEY.EXE	MS-DOS 5.0 utility
DOSX.EXE	VDM DOS extender
DRWATSON.EXE	Win16 version of Dr. Watson that records faults in Win16 subsystem
DRWTSN32.EXE	Win32 version of Dr. Watson that records fault in native Windows NT
DUMPBIN.EXE	32-bit linker stub
EDIT.COM	MS-DOS editor
EDLIN.EXE	MS-DOS line editor
EVENTVWR.EXE	Event Viewer
EXE2BIN.EXE	MS-DOS Exe2Bin utility
EXPAND.EXE	Expand utility to decompress files
FASTOPEN.EXE	MS-DOS utility

Table 4.5   Executable (.EXE and .COM) Files *(continued)*

Filename	Description
FC.EXE	File Comparison command utility that compares two files or sets of files, and displays the differences between them
FIND.EXE	Find command utility that searches for a text string in a file or files
FINDSTR.EXE	Find String command utility that searches for strings in files
FINGER.EXE	TCP/IP utility that displays information about a user on a specified system running the Finger service. Output varies based on the remote system
FORCEDOS.EXE	Forces Windows NT to run the specified program as an MS-DOS application when the application executable file contains both the OS/2 and MS-DOS version in a bound executable file
FORMAT.COM	Windows NT command utility that formats a disk for use with Windows NT
FREECELL.EXE	Freecell solitaire game
FTP.EXE	File Transfer Program, a TCP/IP utility
GDI.EXE	Win16 Graphics Device Interface API library, a core Windows component
GRAFTABL.COM	Utility to enable Windows NT to display an extended character set in graphics mode
GRAPHICS.COM	Utility to allow MS-DOS to print screen contents when using CGA, EGA, or VGA display mode
HELP.EXE	Provides Help information for Windows NT
HOSTNAME.EXE	TCP/IP network utility to determine the system's local hostname
INTRO.EXE	Introduction to Windows NT executable
IPCONFIG.EXE	Windows NT IP Configuration
IPXROUTE.EXE	Network IPX
JETPACK.EXE	Off-line Jet database compact application
KB16.COM	Command-line keyboard program for specific language keyboard layouts
KEYB.COM	MS-DOS keyboard program for specific language keyboard layouts
KRNL286.EXE	Win16 Standard-mode kernel routines
KRNL386.EXE	Win16 Enhanced-mode kernel routines
LABEL.EXE	Command-line utility to create, change, or delete the volume label of a disk
LMREPL.EXE	LAN Manager Replicator service

Table 4.5   Executable (.EXE and .COM) Files *(continued)*

Filename	Description
LOADFIX.COM	Windows command-line utility to load MS-DOS programs above the first 64K of memory
LOCATOR.EXE	Supports Remote Procedure Calls (RPC)
LODCTR.EXE	Load Performance Monitor counters
LOGVIEW.EXE	Migration Tool for NetWare Log File Viewer
LPQ.EXE	TCP/IP diagnostic utility used to obtain status of a print queue on a host running the LPD server
LPR.EXE	TCP/IP connectivity utility used to print a file to a host running an LPD server
LSASS.EXE	Local Security Authority server process
MACFILE.EXE	Windows NT Macintosh MacFile command-line user interface
MAILSP32.EXE	Microsoft Mail Spooler (32-bit)
MAPISRV.EXE	Microsoft Message API (MAPI) Server for Microsoft Mail and Microsoft Schedule+; processes internal service requests from other applications using MAPI
MEM.EXE	Command-line utility that displays the amount of used and free memory on the system
MODE.COM	Device Mode command-line command utility
MORE.COM	Command-line command utility that displays output one screen at a time; similar to the MS-DOS MORE utility, but with added functionality
MPLAY32.EXE	Media Player multimedia application
MPNOTIFY.EXE	Run by Winlogon to notify multiple providers (such as Banyan®, Novell, and so on) of security events (such as change password and logon)
MSCDEXNT.EXE	Microsoft CD-ROM extensions
MSMAIL32.EXE	Microsoft Mail (32-bit)
MSRMND32.EXE	Microsoft Schedule+ Reminder utility
MUSRMGR.EXE	User Manager (Windows NT base product)
NBTSTAT.EXE	NetBIOS over TCP/IP networking statistics application
NCADMIN.EXE	Network Client Administrator
NDDEAGNT.EXE	Network DDE
NDDEAPIR.EXE	Network DDE
NET.EXE	Network command-line utility supporting commands such as **net use** and **net print**
NET1.EXE	Net command utility

Table 4.5   Executable (.EXE and .COM) Files *(continued)*

Filename	Description
NETDDE.EXE	Network DDE background application
NETSTAT.EXE	TCP/IP utility for gathering network statistics information
NLSFUNC.EXE	Command-line utility to load country-specific information
NMAGENT.EXE	Network Monitor service that provides remote access to RNAL.DLL
NOTEPAD.EXE	Notepad tool
NTBACKUP.EXE	Windows NT Tape Backup application
NTDETECT.COM	Windows NT hardware detection code
NTGPCEDT.EXE	Windows NT GPC Editor
NTKRNLMP.EXE	Windows NT Multiprocessor kernel
NTOSKRNL.EXE	Windows NT operating system kernel
NTSD.EXE	Symbolic debugger for Windows NT
NTVDM.EXE	MS-DOS and Win16 application support
NW16.EXE	NWCS file
NWCONV.EXE	Migration Tool for NetWare
NWSVC.EXE	NetWare Services
OS2.EXE	OS/2 command shell
OS2SRV.EXE	OS/2 subsystem server
OS2SS.EXE	OS/2 system server
PACKGR32.EXE	Win32 Object Packager
PAX.EXE	POSIX tape archive program
PBRUSH.EXE	Paintbrush tool
PERFMON.EXE	Performance Monitor application
PID.EXE	Used to change the Product Identification Number entered during the Windows NT Setup process
PIFEDIT.EXE	Program Information File Editor that configures MS-DOS program execution attributes
PING.EXE	TCP/IP diagnostic command that verifies connections to one or more remote hosts
PORTUAS.EXE	Utility to Port the OS/2 LAN Manager User Account service to Windows NT
POSIX.EXE	POSIX Console Session Manager
PRINT.EXE	Command-line utility to print a text file
PRINTMAN.EXE	Print Manager facility
PROGMAN.EXE	Program Manager

Table 4.5 Executable (.EXE and .COM) Files *(continued)*

Filename	Description
PSXSS.EXE	POSIX subsystem server
QBASIC.EXE	Command-line Quick Basic application
RASADMIN.EXE	Remote Access Server Administrator
RASDIAL.EXE	Remote Access Server Dial tool
RASMAN.EXE	Remote Access Server Manager
RASMON.EXE	Remote Access Monitor
RASPHONE.EXE	Remote Access user tool
RASSPRXY.EXE	Remote Access Server supervisor proxy
RASSRV.EXE	Remote Access Server supervisor
RCP.EXE	TCP/IP connectivity command that copies files between a Windows NT computer and a system running **rshd**, the remote shell server
RDISK.EXE	Repair Disk utility used to create emergency repair disks
RECOVER.EXE	Command-line utility to recover readable information from a bad or defective disk
REDIR.EXE	Network redirector for Win16 support; not required for startup
REGEDIT.EXE	Win16 Registry Editor
REGEDT32.EXE	Windows NT Registry Editor
REPLACE.EXE	Command-line utility to replace files
RESTORE.EXE	Command-line utility for restoring files backed up using the MS-DOS Backup command
REXEC.EXE	TCP/IP connectivity command that runs commands on remote hosts running the **rexecd** service; authenticates the user name on the remote host by using a password
RLADMIN.EXE	Resource Localization Administrator
RLEDIT.EXE	Resource Localization Editor
RLQUIKED.EXE	Win32 Resource Localization Quick Editor
ROUTE.EXE	TCP/IP diagnostic command used to manipulate network routing tables
RPCSS.EXE	Remote Procedure Call subsystem
RPLCMD.EXE	Remoteboot command-line utility
RPLCNV.EXE	Remoteboot conversion utility
RPLMGR.EXE	Remoteboot Service Manager
RPLSVC.EXE	Remoteboot Service DLL
RSH.EXE	TCP/IP connectivity command that runs commands on remote hosts running the **rsh** service

Table 4.5   Executable (.EXE and .COM) Files *(continued)*

Filename	Description
SAVEDUMP.EXE	Windows NT save dump utility
SCHDPL32.EXE	Microsoft Schedule+
SCM.EXE	OLE 2.1 for Windows NT
SERVICES.EXE	Service controller and services
SETACL.EXE	Assigns ACLs during Setup
SETUP.EXE	Windows NT Setup program
SETVER.EXE	Command-line utility that sets the version number that Command-line reports to a program
SFMPRINT.EXE	Services for Macintosh Print Service
SFMPSEXE.EXE	Services for Macintosh PostScript Raster Image Processor program
SFMSVC.EXE	Services for Macintosh file service
SHARE.EXE	Command-line utility to enable file sharing facilities
SIMPCNTR.EXE	Simple OLE 2.0 In-Place Container
SIMPDND.EXE	Simple OLE 2.0 Drag/Drop Container
SIMPSVR.EXE	Simple OLE 2.0 Server
SMSS.EXE	Session Manager subsystem
SNDREC32.EXE	Sound Recorder application
SNDVOL32.EXE	Sound volume setting tool
SNMP.EXE	SNMP Service; proxy agent that listens for requests and hands them off to the appropriate network provider
SNMPTRAP.EXE	SNMP Trap Service that works with SNMP.EXE to receive Trap Packets
SOL.EXE	Solitaire game
SORT.EXE	Command-line utility that sorts input and writes results to the screen, a file, or another device
SPDND16.EXE	Simple OLE 2.0 Drag/Drop Container
SPOOLSS.EXE	Spooling subsystem for printing support
SRVMGR.EXE	Server Manager application
SUBST.EXE	Command-line utility that associates a path with a drive letter
SYSEDIT.EXE	Win16 System Editor for reading and editing CONFIG.SYS, AUTOEXEC.BAT, WIN.INI, and SYSTEM.INI files
TASKMAN.EXE	Task Manager program
TCPSVCS.EXE	TCP/IP Services application
TELNET.EXE	Starts the Telnet service (if not started already) and Windows Terminal

Table 4.5   Executable (.EXE and .COM) Files *(continued)*

Filename	Description
TERMINAL.EXE	Terminal application
TFTP.EXE	Trivial File Transfer Protocol (TFTP) client over UDP (TCP/IP utility)
TRACERT.EXE	TCP/IP Traceroute command
TREE.COM	Command-line command utility that graphically displays the directory structure of a drive or path
UNLODCTR.EXE	Unloads Performance Monitor counters
UPEDIT.EXE	User Profile Editor application
UPS.EXE	Uninterruptible Power Supply Service
USER.EXE	Win16 User for Win16 application compatibility
USERINIT.EXE	Windows NT logon user interface
USETUP.EXE	Windows NT Setup (user mode portion of character-based phase)
USRMGR.EXE	Windows NT User Manager for Domains
VWIPXSPX.EXE	NWCS file
WIN.COM	Win16 loader (for compatibility)
WINBUG.EXE	Windows NT Bug Reporting tool
WINCHAT.EXE	Windows NT Chat tool
WINDISK.EXE	Disk Administrator tool
WINFILE.EXE	File Manager tool
WINHELP.EXE	Win16 Help engine application file
WINHLP32.EXE	Windows NT Help engine application file
WINLOGON.EXE	Windows NT Logon utility
WINMINE.EXE	Minesweeper game
WINMSD.EXE	Windows NT Microsoft Diagnostics
WINNT.EXE	Network-based Windows NT Installation utility
WINS.EXE	WINS Server
WINSADMN.EXE	Windows Internet Naming Service Manager
WINSPOOL.EXE	WOW spooler driver
WINVER.EXE	Version Reporting utility
WOWDEB.EXE	WOW debug/tool helper application
WOWEXEC.EXE	Win16 shell; used to run 16-bit applications on behalf of Win32 applications
WRITE.EXE	Windows Write application (16-bit)
XCOPY.EXE	Extended Copy utility, a command-line utility that copies files and directory trees

Font and Printer Files

Windows NT includes several fonts for use with various types of applications, display monitors, and code pages. To add screen, plotter, TrueType or Type 1 fonts to Windows NT applications, double-click the Fonts icon in the Control Panel window.

Fonts occupy memory. If you don't intend to use all the fonts you have installed, you can remove the fonts from the system and free memory for use by applications. For more information about removing fonts, see "Removing a Font" in Chapter 5, "Control Panel," in the *Windows NT System Guide*.

Windows NT includes the following raster and vector fonts. For more information about Windows NT fonts, see Chapter 7, "Fonts." For more information about code pages, see Appendix C, "International Considerations."

Table 4.6   Raster and Vector Font (.FON and .FNT) Files

Filename	Description
APP850.FON	MS-DOS application font; uses code page 850
CGA40850.FON	CGA font; uses code page 850
CGA40WOA.FON	CGA font; uses code page 437 (WOA is an acronym for Windows Old Application)
CGA80850.FON	CGA font; uses code page 850 (80 column display)
CGA80WOA.FON	CGA font; uses code page 437 (80 column display)
COURE.FON	Windows 3.0 Courier system font, VGA display compatible; aspect ratio 1:1, 96 ppi x 96 ppi (pixels per inch)
COURF.FON	Windows 3.0 Courier system font, 8514 display compatible; aspect ratio 1:1, 120 ppi x 120 ppi
DOSAPP.FON	MS-DOS application font; uses code page 437
EGA.CPI	EGA ROM international fonts; used for displaying full-screen MS-DOS applications
EGA40850.FON	EGA font; uses code page 850
EGA40WOA.FON	CGA font; uses code page 437
EGA80850.FON	EGA font; uses code page 850 (80 columns)
EGA80WOA.FON	CGA font; uses code page 437 (80 columns)
MODERN.FON	Windows 3.1 vector font
NT.FNT, NT2.FNT	Introduction to Windows NT font files
ROMAN.FON	Vector font
SCRIPT.FON	Vector font

Table 4.6   Raster and Vector Font (.FON and .FNT) Files *(continued)*

Filename	Description
SERIFE.FON	Windows 3.0 serif system font, VGA display compatible; aspect ratio 1:1, 96 ppi x 96 ppi
SERIFF.FON	Windows 3.0 serif system font, 8514 display compatible; aspect ratio 1:1, 120 ppi x 120 ppi
SMALLE.FON	Windows 3.0 small system font, VGA display compatible; aspect ratio 1:1, 96 ppi x 96 ppi
SMALLF.FON	Windows 3.0 small system font, 8514 display compatible ; aspect ratio 1:1, 120 ppi x 120 ppi
SSERIFE.FON	Windows 3.0 sans serif system font, VGA display compatible; aspect ratio 1:1, 96 ppi x 96 ppi
SSERIFF.FON	Windows 3.0 sans serif system font, 8514 display compatible; aspect ratio 1:1, 120 ppi x 120 ppi
SYMBOLE.FON	Windows 3.0 Symbol system font, VGA display compatible; aspect ratio 1:1, 96 ppi x 96 ppi
SYMBOLF.FON	Windows 3.0 Symbol system font, 8514 display compatible; aspect ratio 1:1, 120 ppi x 120 ppi
VGA850.FON	VGA font support for code page 850 (International)
VGA860.FON	VGA font support for code page 860 (Portuguese)
VGA861.FON	VGA font support for code page 861 (Icelandic)
VGA863.FON	VGA font support for code page 863 (French Canadian)
VGA865.FON	VGA font support for code page 865 (Norwegian/Danish)
VGAFIX.FON	VGA fixed font (typically used as a monospace system font)
VGAOEM.FON	VGA OEM font; used to display Clipboard objects in the Clipboard Viewer
VGASYS.FON	VGA System font (proportional)

The TrueType downloadable fonts shipped with Windows NT support the Arial, Courier New, Times New Roman®, Symbol, and Wingdings® font families. Each family requires two files, a font header (.FOT) file, and a TrueType font (.TTF) file.

Caution   The Setup program installs TrueType font and font header files in *%systemroot%*\SYSTEM. Be careful not to delete the TrueType files from this directory because these files are used by Windows NT 32-bit applications as well as 16-bit applications.

Windows NT includes the following TrueType font and font header files.

Table 4.7   TrueType Font and Font Header (.TTF and .FOT) Files

Filename	Description
ARIAL.FOT	Arial TrueType font header
ARIAL.TTF	Arial
ARIALBD.FOT	Arial Bold TrueType font header
ARIALBD.TTF	Arial Bold
ARIALBI.FOT	Arial Bold Italic TrueType font header
ARIALBI.TTF	Arial Bold Italic
ARIALI.FOT	Arial Italic TrueType font header
ARIALI.TTF	Arial Italic
COUR.FOT	Courier TrueType font header
COUR.TTF	Courier
COURBD.FOT	Courier Bold TrueType font header
COURBD.TTF	Courier Bold
COURBI.FOT	Courier Bold Italic font header
COURBI.TTF	Courier Bold Italic
COURI.FOT	Courier Italic TrueType font header
COURI.TTF	Courier Italic
SYMBOL.FOT	Symbol TrueType font header
SYMBOL.TTF	Symbol
TIMES.FOT	Times New Roman TrueType font header
TIMES.TTF	Times New Roman
TIMESBD.FOT	Times New Roman Bold TrueType font header
TIMESBD.TTF	Times New Roman Bold
TIMESBI.FOT	Times New Roman Bold Italic font header
TIMESBI.TTF	Times New Roman Bold Italic
TIMESI.FOT	Times New Roman Italic font header
TIMESI.TTF	Times New Roman Italic
UCLUCIDA.TTF	Unicode Lucida® TrueType
WINGDING.FOT	WingDings TrueType font header
WINGDING.TTF	WingDings

Introducing Windows NT Sequence Files

Windows NT includes an online introduction, Introducing Windows NT. The introduction demonstrates how to use the built-in networking, security, and workgroup features of Windows NT to make your job easier. To view the online introduction, double-click the Introducing Windows NT icon in the Main program group.

Windows NT includes the following Introducing Windows NT sequence files.

Table 4.8   Introducing Windows NT Sequence (.SEQ) Files

CLIP01.SEQ	CONN02.SEQ	NTMENU.SEQ	SETT02.SEQ
CLIP02.SEQ	CREAT01.SEQ	PANEL.SEQ	SETT03.SEQ
CLIP03.SEQ	CREAT02.SEQ	PAUSE.SEQ	SETT04.SEQ
COMM01.SEQ	INTRO1.SEQ	PRINT01.SEQ	SHARE01.SEQ
COMM02.SEQ	INTRO2.SEQ	REVIEW.SEQ	SHARE02.SEQ
CONN01.SEQ	LOG01.SEQ	SETT01.SEQ	

Miscellaneous Files

Windows NT includes the following miscellaneous files.

Table 4.9   Miscellaneous Files

Filename	Description
_DEFAULT.PIF[2]	Default PIF for MS-DOS applications
A221064.PAL	PALcode for DECpc AXP/150 (Jensen - EV4, pass 2) systems
A221066.PAL	PALcode for DECpc AXP/150 (Jensen - EV4, pass 2) systems
A321064.PAL	PALcode for DECpc AXP/150 (Jensen - EV4, pass 3) systems
AUTOEXEC.NT	Default AUTOEXEC.BAT file for Windows NT
BIOS1.ROM, BIOS2.ROM	Required for VDM emulation
CANYON.MID	Multimedia sample file
CLOCK.AVI	Sample AVI file
CMOS.RAM	Required for VDM emulation
CONFIG.NT	Default CONFIG.SYS for Windows NT
DEFAULT	Registry hive
EGA.CPI	ROM fonts, international
FATBOOT.BIN	FAT boot sector

Table 4.9   Miscellaneous Files *(continued)*

Filename	Description
GRAPHICS.PRO	Graphics Profile file; used by the Graphics utility to load printer profile information
HOSTS	Windows Sockets database file; provides hostname and IP address name resolution for Windows Sockets
HOSTS.SHP	Sockets database file
HPFSBOOT.BIN	HPFS boot sector
IDP_XFS.BIN	Network NDIS driver: Digiboard ISDN
IMAADP32.ACM	IMA ADPCM Codec for MSACM
INTRO.ICO	Introduction to Windows NT icon
LMHOSTS	Windows Sockets database file; provides computername and IP address name resolution for Windows Networking
LMHOSTS.SAM	Sockets database file
MIB.BIN	SNMP component; SNMP service
MIDIMAP.CFG	MIDI configuration file; controls the mapping of MIDI sound channels onto instruments
MMTASK.TSK	Multimedia background task support module
MSADP32.ACM	ADPCM Codec for MSACM
MSGSM32.ACM	GSM version 6.10 audio Codec for MSACM
MUSRMGR.IND	User Manager help index
MVOPL3.PAT	Media Vision OPL3 FM Synthesizer patches for OPL3 Synthesizer driver
NETAPI.OS2	OS/2 network API
NETFLX.BIN	Network NDIS driver for COMPAQ NetFlex™/DualSpeed Token Ring adapter card
NETWORKS	Sockets database file; provides network name and net ID resolution for TCP/IP management utilities
NT.DOC	Introduction to Windows NT documentation
NTLDR	Windows NT loader
OSO001.007	OS/2 message file in German
OSO001.009[2]	OS/2 message file in English
OSO001.010	OS/2 message file in Spanish
OSO001.012	OS/2 message file in French
OSO001.016	OS/2 message file in Italian
OSO001.029	OS/2 message file in Swedish
PASSPORT.MID	MIDI sound file

Table 4.9   Miscellaneous Files *(continued)*

Filename	Description
PROFILE.SPC	Needed for MS-DOS and Win16 VDMs
PROTOCOL	Sockets database file; provides protocol name and protocol ID resolution for Windows Sockets applications
QUOTES	Quotes files for Simple TCP/IP; sends arguments, verbatim, to the remote FTP server
SERVICES	Sockets database file; provides service name and port ID resolution for Windows Sockets applications
SETUPLDR	Setup loader
SETUPREG.HIV	System hive for text setup
SFMUAM.IFO	Services for Macintosh user authentication manager volume information file
SFMUAM.RSC	Services for Macintosh user authentication module volume resource file
SOFTWARE	Software hive; default Registry configuration
STDOLE.TLB	16-bit OLE version 2.1
STDOLE32.TLB	32-bit OLE version 2.1
SYNTH.PAT	Synthesizer patch codes
SYSTEM.INI	Win16 system initialization file, for Win16 compatibility
SYSTEM.MDB	??? DHCP MDB
SYSTEM	Windows NT System hive
TAGFILE.TAG	Windows NT Setup uses this file
TELNET.TRM	Windows NT Terminal configuration file for the Telnet driver (used by TELNET.EXE)
TSSOFT32.ACM	DSP Group Truespeech™ Audio Codec for MSACM version 3.5
V7VGA.ROM	Emulation of Video 7 BIOS code required for VDM emulation
WDL.TRM	Terminal file for Microsoft Download Service
WIN.INI	Win16 Windows initialization file (for compatibility)
WINFILE.INI	File Manager initialization file
WINOLDAP.MOD	Launch non-Windows-based Win16 applications from Win16

National Language Support Files

National Language Support files are used to convert code page information to Unicode.

Windows NT includes the following national language support files. For more information about national language support, code pages, and Unicode, see Appendix C, "International Considerations."

Table 4.10   National Language Support (.NLS) Files

Filename	Description
BIG5.NLS	Sorting table for Chinese
C_037.NLS	EBCDIC Latin1
C_10000.NLS	Macintosh Roman
C_10001.NLS	Japanese MAC code page
C_10006.NLS	Macintosh Greek 1
C_10007.NLS	Macintosh Cyrillic
C_10029.NLS	Macintosh Slavic
C_10079.NLS	Icelandic MAC code page
C_10081.NLS	Turkish MAC code page
C_1026.NLS	EBCDIC Latin 1/Turkish
C_1250.NLS	Win 3.1 Eastern European
C_1251.NLS	Win 3.1 Cyrillic
C_1252.NLS	Win 3.1 US (ANSI)
C_1253.NLS	Win 3.1 Greek
C_1254.NLS	Win 3.1 Turkish
C_437.NLS	MS-DOS U.S.
C_500.NLS	EBCDIC Latin 1
C_737.NLS	Greek Primary code page
C_850.NLS	MS-DOS Latin I
C_852.NLS	MS-DOS Latin II
C_855.NLS	IBM Russian
C_857.NLS	IBM Turkish
C_860.NLS	MS-DOS Portuguese
C_861.NLS	MS-DOS Icelandic

Table 4.10   National Language Support (.NLS) Files *(continued)*

Filename	Description
C_863.NLS	MS-DOS French Canadian
C_865.NLS	MS-DOS Nordic
C_866.NLS	MS-DOS "Russian" (former USSR)
C_869.NLS	IBM Modern Greek
C_875.NLS	EBCDIC Greek
CTYPE.NLS	Character type 1 unicode translation data file (always installed)
CTYPE1.NLS	Character type 1 Unicode translation data file (always installed)
CTYPE2.NLS	Character type 2 Unicode translation file (always installed)
CTYPE3.NLS	Character type 3 Unicode translation data file (always installed)
KSC.NLS	Sorting table for Korean
L_ELL.NLS	Greek casing table (upper and lowercase character tables)
L_INTL.NLS	International casing table (upper and lowercase character tables)
L_TRK.NLS	Turkish cashing table
L_TRK.NLS	Turkish casing table (upper and lowercase character tables)
LOCALE.NLS	Locale information for all locales (required for booting)
LOCALE.NLS	Locale information for all locales (required for startup)
SORTKEY.NLS	National Language Support sort keys
SORTTBLS.NLS	National Language Support sort tables
UNICODE.NLS	Unicode translation data file; required for startup
XJIS.NLS	Sorting table for Japanese

Online Help Files

Windows NT provides Help so that you can get useful information quickly while you are working. Help contains a description of each command and dialog box, and explains procedures for most tasks. To see online Help, select an item from the Help menu of the application or tool you are using, or press F1. For a description of how to use online Help, select How To Use Help from the Help menu in Program Manager.

Windows NT includes the following online Help files.

Table 4.11   Online Help (.HLP) Files

Filename	Description
AUDIOCDC.HLP	IMA ADPCM Audio CODEC configuration help
BACKUP.HLP	Windows NT Backup utility help
CALC.HLP	Calculator tool help
CARDFILE.HLP	Cardfile tool help
CDPLAYER.HLP	CD Player help
CHARMAP.HLP	Character Map tool help
CLIPBRD.HLP	Clipbook Viewer help
CONTROL.HLP	Control Panel help
DDESHARE.HLP	DDE Share Conversation Manager help
DECPSMON.HLP	DECPSMON help
DGCONFIG.HLP	Digiboard serial driver help
DHCPADMN.HLP	Dynamic Host Configuration Protocol Administrator help
DOSHELP.HLP	MS-DOS command-line help
DRWTSN32.HLP	Dr. Watson error log help
EDIT.HLP	MS-DOS Editor help
EVENTVWR.HLP	Event Viewer help
FREECELL.HLP	Freecell game help
FTPSMX.HLP	File Transfer Program Manager Extensions help
GLOSSARY.HLP	Windows NT Glossary help
GLOSSON.HLP	Glossary for the Windows NT messages database
HALFTONE.HLP	Halftone printing option help
HELP.HLP	Help file for Help utility
HPMON.HLP	HP Monitor help
ISDNHELP.HLP	Digiboard ISDN help
LOGVIEW.HLP	Migration Tool for NetWare LogView help

Table 4.11   Online Help (.HLP) Files *(continued)*

Filename	Description
MPLAYER.HLP	Media Player help
MSMAIL32.HLP	Microsoft Mail help
MUSRMGR.HLP	Windows NT workstation User Manager help
NCADMIN.HLP	Network Client Administrator help
NET.HLP	Network command-line help
NETWORK.HLP	Network help (Windows help format)
NOTEPAD.HLP	Notepad help
NTCMDS.HLP	Windows NT command-line help
NWCONV.HLP	Migration Tool for NetWare help
NWDOC.HLP	Client Service for NetWare help
NWDOCGW.HLP	Gateway Service for NetWare help
PACKAGER.HLP	Win16 Object Packager help
PBRUSH.HLP	Paintbrush™ help
PERFMON.HLP	Performance Monitor help
PID.HLP	Product Identification Number help
PIFEDIT.HLP	PIF Editor help
PLOTUI.HLP	Plotter Driver help
PRINTMAN.HLP	Print Manager help
PROGMAN.HLP	Program Manager help
PSCRIPT.HLP	PostScript driver help
QBASIC.HLP	Command-line Quick Basic help
RASADMIN.HLP	Remote Access Server Administrator help
RASDDUI.HLP	Raster Printer Device Driver User Interface help
RASGLOSS.HLP	Remote Access Service glossary help
RASPHONE.HLP	Remote Access Server Phone help
RASSETUP.HLP	Remote Access Server Setup help
RDISK.HLP	Repair Disk Utility Help
REGEDIT.HLP	Win16 Registry Editor help
REGEDT32.HLP	Windows NT Registry Editor help
RPLMGR.HLP	Remoteboot Manager help
SCHDPL32.HLP	Microsoft Schedule+ help
SETUPNT.HLP	Windows NT setup help
SFMMGR.HLP	Services for Macintosh Manager help
SNDVOL32.HLP	Sound Volume tool help

Table 4.11   Online Help (.HLP) Files *(continued)*

Filename	Description
SOL.HLP	Solitaire game help
SOUNDREC.HLP	Sound Recorder help
SRVMGR.HLP	Server Manager help
TCPIP.HLP	Transmission Control Protocol/Internet Protocol help
TELNET.HLP	Telnet application help
TERMINAL.HLP	Terminal application help
UPEDIT.HLP	User Profile Editor help
USERCONV.HLP	User Conversion help
USRMGR.HLP	Windows NT server User Manager for Domains help
WINCHAT.HLP	Windows NT Chat help
WINDISK.HLP	Windows NT workstation Disk Administrator help
WINDISKA.HLP	Windows NT Server Disk Administrator help
WINFILE.HLP	File Manager application help
WINHELP.HLP	Win16 Help application help
WINMINE.HLP	Minesweeper help
WINNT.HLP	Windows NT introduction help
WINNT32.HLP	Network-based Windows NT installation utility help
WINNTMSG.HLP	Windows NT system and error message help
WINSADMN.HLP	WINS Manager help
WNTUPMGR.HLP	Windows NT Server Upgrade Manager help
WRITE.HLP	Windows Write help

Deleting Online Help Files

To free hard disk space, you can delete online Help files for components or files that you don't intend to use (for example, accessories and games). To remove an online Help file, delete the file using the Windows NT Setup program.

When you remove online Help files, the files are deleted from your computer. If you want to add them later, you must supply the files from the Windows NT installation disks or from a source directory on your network. For more information about removing files, see "Adding and Removing Windows NT Components" in Chapter 12, "System Maintenance with Windows NT Setup," in the *Windows NT System Guide*.

Because most of the Help files for Windows NT have full-text search functionality, deleting one or more Help files has other than the typical "Cannot open Help file" message seen in Windows 3.1. With Windows NT, if you remove a Help file that is part of a full-text search index, you will still see the full-text search dialog box and its list of all the Help files to search (whether or not the file is available). From there, you can type a search request and get a list of all topics containing the search string. However, if the Help file is not available, you will see the message, "Cannot open Help file."

The following table shows which files are part of each full-text search index (.IND) file. If you remove the index file and then try to use full-text search from a corresponding online Help file, Windows NT displays the message "Old or Missing Index File."

Table 4.12   Full-Text Search Index (.IND) Files for Online Help

Filename	Corresponding Help file	
CALC.IND	Calculator	CALC.HLP
	Cardfile	CARDFILE.HLP
	CD Player	CDPLAYER.HLP
	Character Map	CHARMAP.HLP
	Freecell	FREECELL.HLP
	Media Player	MPLAYER.HLP
	Notepad	NOTEPAD.HLP
	Paintbrush	PBRUSH.HLP
	Solitaire	SOL.HLP
	Sound Recorder	SOUNDREC.HLP
	Sound Volume Control	SNDVOL32.HLP
	Terminal	TERMINAL.HLP
	Chat	WINCHAT.HLP
	Minesweeper	WINMINE.HLP

Table 4.12   Full-Text Search Index (.IND) Files for Online Help *(continued)*

Filename	Corresponding Help file	
MUSRMGR.IND	Disk Administrator for Windows NT workstation	WINDISK.HLP
	User Manager for Windows NT workstation	MUSRMGR.HLP
NTCMDS.IND	Command Reference	NTCMDS.HLP
USRMGR.IND	Disk Administrator for Windows NT Server	WINDISKA.HLP
	User Manager for Windows NT Server	USRMGR.HLP
	User Profile Editor	UPEDIT.HLP
	Server Manager	SRVRMGR.HLP
WINNT.IND	Backup	BACKUP.HLP
	Control Panel	CONTROL.HLP
	Clipbook Viewer	CLIPBRD.HLP
	Event Viewer	EVENTVWR.HLP
	File Manager	WINFILE.HLP
	Microsoft Mail	MSMAIL32.HLP
	Performance Monitor	PERFMON.HLP
	PIF Editor	PIFEDIT.HLP
	Program Manager	PROGMAN.HLP
	Print Manager	PRINTMAN.HLP
	Registry Editor	REGEDT32.HLP
	Schedule+	SCHDPL32.HLP
	Setup	SETUPNT.HLP
	Windows NT Help	WINNT.HLP

Other relationships of the various Help and Index files follow:

- If WINHELP.HLP is removed, errors occur when you choose the Help menu item How To Use Help.

- If NTCMDS.HLP is removed, an error occurs when you choose the Command Reference button from the Windows NT Help file located in the Main program group.

- If GLOSSARY.HLP is removed, the definition popups in nearly every Help file will display an error message.

Plotter Driver Files

A plotter is any device used to draw charts, diagrams and other line-based graphics. To install a new or additional plotter driver, double-click the Printers icon in the Control Panel window.

Windows NT includes the following plotter drivers. For more information about printing, see Chapter 6, "Printing."

Table 4.13   Plotter (.PCD) Driver Files

Filename	Description
HPGL2PEN.PCD	Hewlett-Packard HP-GL/2 Plotter
HP7550PL.PCD	HP 7550 Plus
HPDESIGN.PCD	HP DesignJet (C3180A)
HP20022.PCD	HP DesignJet 200 (C3180A)
HP20036.PCD	HP DesignJet 200 (C3181A)
HP60022.PCD	HP DesignJet 600 (C2847A)
HP60036.PCD	HP DesignJet 600 (C2848A)
HP650C22.PCD	HP DesignJet 650C (C2858A)
HP650C22.PCD	HP DesignJet 650C (C2858B)
HP650C36.PCD	HP DesignJet 650C (C2859A)
HP650C36.PCD	HP DesignJet 650C (C2859B)
HPDMRXMX.PCD	HP Draftmaster® RX/MX
HPDMSX.PCD	HP Draftmaster SX
HPDPP22.PCD	HP Draftpro® Plus (C3170A)
HPDPP36.PCD	HP Draftpro Plus (C3171A)

PostScript Printer Description Files

The Windows NT PostScript driver supports Adobe version 4.0-compatible PostScript printer description files. The files described in this section provide additional PostScript description information for specific printers. To install a new or additional printer driver for your printer, double-click the Printers icon in the Control Panel window.

Windows NT includes the following Adobe PostScript printer description files. For more information about printing, see Chapter 6, "Printing."

Table 4.14   Adobe PostScript Printer Description (.PPD) Files

Filename	Description
ALJII523.PPD	Adobe LaserJet II Cartridge version 52.3
AMCHR518.PPD	Agfa Matrix ChromaScript version 51.8
AC500503.PPD	Agfa TabScript C500 PostScript Printer version 50.3
CG94_493.PPD	Agfa-Compugraphic 9400P version 49.3
LWNTX470.PPD	Apple LaserWriter® II NTX version 47.0
LWNTX518.PPD	Apple LaserWriter II NTX version 51.8
AP_NTXJ1.PPD	Apple LaserWriter II NTX-J version 50.5
APLWIIF1.PPD	Apple LaserWriter IIf version 2010.113
APLWIIG1.PPD	Apple LaserWriter IIg version 2010.113
A_PNT518.PPD	Apple LaserWriter Personal NT version 51.8
APPLE380.PPD	Apple LaserWriter Plus version 38.0
APPLE422.PPD	Apple LaserWriter Plus version 42.2
APTOLLD1.PPD	Apple LaserWriter Pro 600
APTOLLW1.PPD	Apple LaserWriter Pro 630
APLW8101.PPD	Apple LaserWriter Pro 810
APPLE230.PPD	Apple LaserWriter version 23.0
LWNT_470.PPD	Apple LaserWriter II NT version 47.0
APLWNTR1.PPD	Apple Personal LaserWriter NTR version 2010.129
APS08522.PPD	APS-PS PIP with APS-6-108 version 49.3 or 52.2
APS12522.PPD	APS-PS PIP with LZR1200 version 49.3 or 52.2
APS80522.PPD	APS-PSP IP with APS-6-80 version 49.3 or 52.2
APS26522.PPD	APS-PSP IP with LZR2600 version 49.3 or 52.2
AST__470.PPD	AST TurboLaser-PS version 47.0
CNLBP4_1.PPD	Canon LBP-4PS-2 version 51.4
CNLBP8_1.PPD	Canon LBP-8IIIPS-1 version 51.4

Table 4.14   Adobe PostScript Printer Description (.PPD) Files *(continued)*

Filename	Description
CNLBP8R1.PPD	Canon LBP-8IIIRPS-1 version 51.4
CNLBP8T1.PPD	Canon LBP-8IIITPS-1 version 51.4
CN_500_1.PPD	Canon PS-IPU Color Laser Copier version 52.3
CN_500J1.PPD	Canon PS-IPU Kanji Color Laser Copier version 52.3
COLORQ.PPD	ColorAge ColorQ
NCOL_519.PPD	Colormate PS version 51.9
CPPMQ151.PPD	COMPAQ PAGEMARQ 15 version 2012.015
CPPMQ201.PPD	COMPAQ PAGEMARQ 20 version 2012.015
DATAP462.PPD	Dataproducts LZR-2665 version 46.2
DP_US470.PPD	DataproductsLZR1260version 47.0
DPL15601.PPD	DataproductsLZR1560version 2010.127
DPLZ9601.PPD	DataproductsLZR960version 2010.106
DECCOLOR.PPD	Digital Colormate PS version 51.9
DCLF02_1.PPD	Digital DECcolorwriter 1000 with 17 fonts
DCLF02F1.PPD	Digital DECcolorwriter 1000 with 39 fonts
DCD11501.PPD	Digital DEClaser 1150 version 51.4
DC1152_1.PPD	Digital DEClaser 1152 (17fonts) version 2011.113
DC1152F1.PPD	Digital DEClaser 1152 (43fonts) version 2011.113
DC2150P1.PPD	Digital DEClaser 2150 plus version 51.4
DCD21501.PPD	Digital DEClaser 2150 version 51.4
DC2250P1.PPD	Digital DEClaser 2250 plus version 51.4
DCD22501.PPD	Digital DEClaser 2250 version 51.4
DEC3250.PPD	Digital DEClaser 3250 version 47.0
DCLN03R1.PPD	Digital LN03R ScriptPrinter version 47.2
DCLPS171.PPD	Digital PrintServer 17 version 48.3
DCLPS201.PPD	Digital PrintServer 20 version 48.3
DCKPS321.PPD	Digital PrintServer 32 Kanji version 48.3
DCLPS321.PPD	Digital PrintServer 32 version 48.3
DCKPS401.PPD	Digital PrintServer 40 Plus Kanji version 48.3
DCLPS401.PPD	Digital PrintServer 40 Plus version 48.3
DCKPS201.PPD	Digital turbo PrintServer 20 Kanji version 48.3
DCTPS201.PPD	Digital turbo PrintServer 20 version 48.3
EPL75523.PPD	Epson EPL-7500 version 52.3

Table 4.14   Adobe PostScript Printer Description (.PPD) Files *(continued)*

Filename	Description
EPL3KF51.PPD	Epson LP-3000 PS F5 version 52.3
EPL3KF21.PPD	Epson LP-3000PS F2 version 52.3
EP826051.PPD	Epson PostScript CARD version 52.5
F71RX503.PPD	Fujitsu RX7100PS version 50.3
GCBLPEL1.PPD	GCC BLP Elite version 52.3
GCBLP2_1.PPD	GCC BLP II version 52.3
GCBLP2S1.PPD	GCC BLP IIS version 52.3
GCBL4921.PPD	GCC Business LaserPrinter version 49.2
GCBL5141.PPD	GCC Business LaserPrinter version 51.4
GDGL8001.PPD	Gestetner GLP800-Scout version 52.3
HERMES_1.PPD	Hermes H 606 PS with13 fonts
HERMES_2.PPD	Hermes H 606 PS with 35 fonts
HP_650C1.PPD	HP DesignJet 650C version 2013.109
HPLJ_4M.PPD	HP LaserJet 4 PostScript version 2011.110
HP4M3_V1.PPD	HP LaserJet 4/4M PS 300 dpi
HP4M6_V1.PPD	HP LaserJet 4/4M PS 600 dpi
HP4ML_V1.PPD	HP LaserJet 4L/4ML PostScript
HP4MP3_1.PPD	HP LaserJet 4P/4MP PS 300 dpi
HP4MP6_1.PPD	HP LaserJet 4P/4MP PS 600 dpi
HP4SI6_1.PPD	HP LaserJet 4Si or 4SiMXAPS 600dpi
HP4SI3_1.PPD	HP LaserJet 4Si/4SiMX PS 300dpi
HPELI522.PPD	HP LaserJet ELI PostScript version 52.3
HPIID522.PPD	HP LaserJet IID PostScript Cartridge version 52.2
HPIII522.PPD	HP LaserJet III PostScript Cartridge version 52.2
HPLJ_31.PPD	HP LaserJet III PostScript Plus version 2010.118
HP_3D522.PPD	HP LaserJet IIID PostScript Cartridge version 52.2
HPLJ_3D1.PPD	HP LaserJet IIID PostScript Plus version 2010.118
HP_3P522.PPD	HP LaserJet IIIP PostScript Cartridge version 52.2
HPLJ_3P1.PPD	HP LaserJet IIIP PostScript Plus version 2010.118
HP3SI523.PPD	HP LaserJet IIISi PostScript version 52.3
HPIIP522.PPD	HP LaserJet IIP PostScript Cartridge version 52.2
HPPJXL31.PPD	HP PaintJet XL300 version 2011.112
HP3SI523.PPD	HPLaserJetIIISiPostScript version 52.3

Table 4.14   Adobe PostScript Printer Description (.PPD) Files *(continued)*

Filename	Description
IBM17523.PPD	IBM 4019 17fonts version 52.3 or 52.1
IBM39523.PPD	IBM 4019 39 fonts version 52.3 or 52.1
IBM4039P.PPD	IBM 4039 LaserPrinter plus PS
IBM4039.PPD	IBM 4039 LaserPrinter PS
IBM20470.PPD	IBM 4216-020 version 47.0
IBM30505.PPD	IBM 4216-030 version 50.5
IBM4079.PPD	IBM Color Jetprinter PS 4079
40291730.PPD	IBM LaserPrinter 4029 PostScript version 52.3; also known as the IBM LaserPrinter 4029 PS17
40293930.PPD	IBM LaserPrinter 4029 PostScript version 52.3; also known as the IBM LaserPrinter 4029 PS39
KDCOLOR1.PPD	Kodak® ColorEase PS Printer
L200230.PPD	Linotronic® 200 and 230
L200_471.PPD	Linotronic 200 version 47.1
L200_493.PPD	Linotronic 200 version 49.3
L300_471.PPD	Linotronic 300 version 47.1
L300_493.PPD	Linotronic 300 version 49.3
L330_523.PPD	Linotronic 330 version 52.3
L3330523.PPD	Linotronic 330-RIP30 version 52.3
L500_493.PPD	Linotronic 500 version 49.3
L530_523.PPD	Linotronic 530 version 52.3
L5330523.PPD	Linotronic 530-RIP30 version 52.3
LH_630_1.PPD	Linotronic 630 version 52.3
LH930__1.PPD	Linotronic 930 version 52.3
LHPR60_1.PPD	Linotronic Pr60 version 52.3
L100_425.PPD	Linotronic 100 version 42.5
MT_TI101.PPD	Microtek TrueLaser
MOIM1201.PPD	Monotype® ImageMaster 1200 version 52.3
MONO_522.PPD	Monotype Imagesetter version 52.2
NCCPS401.PPD	NEC Colormate PS/40 version 51.9
NCCPS801.PPD	NEC Colormate PS/80 version 51.9
NCSW_951.PPD	NEC SilentWriter 95 version 2010.119
NC95FAX1.PPD	NEC Silentwriter 95 version 2011.111

Table 4.14   Adobe PostScript Printer Description (.PPD) Files *(continued)*

Filename	Description
NC97FAX1.PPD	NEC Silentwriter 97 version 2011.111
N890_470.PPD	NEC Silentwriter LC890 version 47.0
N890X505.PPD	NEC Silentwriter LC890XL version 50.5
N2290520.PPD	NEC Silentwriter2 290 version 52.0
N2090522.PPD	NEC Silentwriter2 90 version 52.2
NCS29901.PPD	NEC Silentwriter2 990 version 52.3
NX_NLP_1.PPD	NeXT™ 400 dpi LaserPrinter version 2000.6
O5241503.PPD	OceColor G5241 PS
O5242503.PPD	OceColor G5242 PostScript Printer version 50.3
OK801PF1.PPD	Oki Microline 801PS+F version 52.3
OL830525.PPD	Oki OL830-PS version 52.5
OL840518.PPD	Oki OL840-PS version 51.8
OKOL8501.PPD	Oki OL850-PS version 52.5
OKOL8701.PPD	Oki OL870-PS version 2013.108
OLIVETI1.PPD	Olivetti PG 306 PS (13 fonts)
OLIVETI2.PPD	Olivetti PG 306 PS (35 fonts)
OLIV5000.PPD	Olivetti PG 308 HS PostScript printer
P4455514.PPD	Panasonic KX-P4455 version 51.4
PAP54001.PPD	Panasonic KX-P5400 version 2013.112
AGFAP400.PPD	PostScript Printer Description file for Agfa Compugraphic 400PS
IBM31514.PPD	Printer driver for IBM Personal Page Printer II-31
QMS2025.PPD	QMS® 2025 Print System
QMS3225.PPD	QMS 3225 Print System
QMS420.PPD	QMS 420 Print System version 2011.22 r15
QMS45252.PPD	QMS 4525 Level 2
QMS4525.PPD	QMS 4525 Print System
QMS860.PPD	QMS 860 Print System version 2011.22 r15
Q860PLS2.PPD	QMS 860+ Level 2
Q30SI503.PPD	QMS ColorScript 100 Mod 30si
QCS10503.PPD	QMS ColorScript 100 Model 10 version 50.3
QCS20503.PPD	QMS ColorScript 100 Model 20 version 50.3
QCS30503.PPD	QMS ColorScript 100 Model 30 version 50.3
QMSCS494.PPD	QMS ColorScript 100 version 49.4

Table 4.14   Adobe PostScript Printer Description (.PPD) Files *(continued)*

Filename	Description
QCS10001.PPD	QMS ColorScript 1000 Level 1
QCS10002.PPD	QMS ColorScript 1000 Level 2
QMSCS210.PPD	QMS ColorScript 210 version 2011.22
QMSCS230.PPD	QMS ColorScript 230 version 2011.22
QMSJP461.PPD	QMS-PS® Jet Plus version 46.1
QMSJ_461.PPD	QMS-PS Jet version 46.1
QM1700_1.PPD	QMS-PS 1700 version 52.4
QM2000_1.PPD	QMS-PS 2000 version 52.4
Q2200523.PPD	QMS-PS 2200 version 51.0 or 52.3
Q2210523.PPD	QMS-PS 2210 version 51.0 or 52.3
Q2220523.PPD	QMS-PS 2220 version 51.0 or 52.3
QMPS4101.PPD	QMS-PS 410 version 52.4
QMS8P461.PPD	QMS-PS 800 Plus version 46.1
QMS8_461.PPD	QMS-PS 800 version 46.1
Q810T517.PPD	QMS-PS 810 Turbo version 51.7
QMS81470.PPD	QMS-PS 810 version 47.0
QM815MR1.PPD	QMS-PS 815 MR version 52.4
QMPS8151.PPD	QMS-PS 815 version 52.4
Q820T517.PPD	QMS-PS 820 Turbo version 51.7
Q820_517.PPD	QMS-PS 820 version 51.7
QM825MR1.PPD	QMS-PS 825 MR version 52.4
QMPS8251.PPD	QMS-PS 825 version 52.4
QMS1725.PPD	QMS 1725 Print System
QUME_470.PPD	Qume ScripTEN version 47.0
R6000505.PPD	Ricoh PC Laser 6000-PS version 50.5
SCG20522.PPD	Scantext 2030-51 version 49.3 or 52.2
S5232503.PPD	Schlumberger 5232 Color PostScript Printer version 50.3
SEIKO_04.PPD	Seiko ColorPoint PS Model 04
SEIKO_14.PPD	Seiko ColorPoint PS Model 14
JX9460PS.PPD	Sharp JX-9460 PS
JX9500PS.PPD	Sharp JX-9500 PS
JX9600PS.PPD	Sharp JX-9600 PS
JX9660PS.PPD	Sharp JX-9660 PS

Table 4.14   Adobe PostScript Printer Description (.PPD) Files *(continued)*

Filename	Description
JX9700PS.PPD	Sharp JX-9700E PS
S746J522.PPD	Shinko Color CHC-746PSJ PostScript Printer version 52.2
TK200172.PPD	Tektronix Phaser 200e with 17 fonts version 2011.108(3)
TK200392.PPD	Tektronix Phaser 200e with 39 fonts version 2011.108(3)
TKP200I2.PPD	Tektronix Phaser 200i version 2011.108(3)
TKP200J1.PPD	Tektronix Phaser 200J
TK220171.PPD	Tektronix Phaser 220e with 17 fonts
TK220391.PPD	Tektronix Phaser 220e with 39 fonts
TKP220I1.PPD	Tektronix Phaser 220i
TKP220J1.PPD	Tektronix Phaser 220J
TKP300I1.PPD	Tektronix Phaser 300i
TKP300J1.PPD	Tektronix Phaser 300J
TKPH4801.PPD	Tektronix Phaser 480
PHIIPX.PPD	Tektronix Phaser II PX
TKPXE171.PPD	Tektronix Phaser II PXe version 2010.128 with 17 fonts
TKPXE391.PPD	Tektronix Phaser II PXe version 2010.128 with 39 fonts
TKPHZR22.PPD	Tektronix Phaser II PXi version 2011.108
TKPHZ2J1.PPD	Tektronix Phaser II PXiJ version 2011.108
TKPHZR31.PPD	Tektronix Phaser III PXi version 2010.116
TKPHZR32.PPD	Tektronix Phaser III PXi version 2011.108
TKPHZ3J1.PPD	Tektronix Phaser III PXiJ version 2011.108
TKPHZR21.PPD	Tektronix Phaser IIPXi version 2010.116
TKPH2SD1.PPD	Tektronix Phaser IISD version 2011.108
TKP2SDJ1.PPD	Tektronix Phaser IISDJ
TKP2SDX1.PPD	Tektronix Phaser IISDX
PX.PPD	Tektronix Phaser PX
TKPHPXI1.PPD	Tektronix Phaser PXi
T1513470.PPD	TI® 2115 13 fonts version 47.0
T1535470.PPD	TI 2115 35 fonts version 47.0
TIM17521.PPD	TI microLaser PS17 version .52.1
TIM35521.PPD	TI microLaser PS35 version .52.1
TIX17521.PPD	TI microLaser XL PS17 version .52.1
TIX35521.PPD	TI microLaser XL PS35 version .52.1

Table 4.14   Adobe PostScript Printer Description (.PPD) Files *(continued)*

Filename	Description
TITRB161.PPD	TI microLaser16 Turbo version 2010.119
TITRBO61.PPD	TI microLaser6 Turbo version 2010.119
TITRBO91.PPD	TI microLaser9 Turbo version 2010.119
TI08_450.PPD	TI OmniLaser 2108 version 45.0
TI15_470.PPD	TI OmniLaser 2115 version 47.0
TRIUMPH1.PPD	Triumph Adler® SDR 7706 PS13
TRIUMPH2.PPD	Triumph Adler SDR 7706 PS35
UNI39521.PPD	Unisys® AP9210 39 Fonts version 52.1
U9415470.PPD	Unisys AP9415 version 47.0
UNI17521.PPD	Unisys AP9210 17 Fonts version 52.1
VT4L3001.PPD	Verityper™ 4000-L300 version 52.3
VT4L3301.PPD	Verityper 4000-L330 version 52.3
VT4L5001.PPD	Verityper 4000-L500 version 52.3
VT4L5301.PPD	Verityper 4000-L530 version 52.3
VT42P522.PPD	Verityper 4200B-P version 49.3 or 52.2
VT43P522.PPD	Verityper 4300P version 49.3 or 52.2
VT530522.PPD	Verityper Series 4000-5300 version 49.3 or 52.2
V5334522.PPD	Verityper Series 4000-5330 version 49.3 or 52.2
VT550522.PPD	Verityper Series 4000-5500 version 52.2
VT600P1.PPD	Verityper VT-600P
VT60P480.PPD	Verityper VT-600P version 48.0
WANG15FP.PPD	Verityper VT-600P version 48.0
VT600W1.PPD	Verityper VT-600W version 48.0
VT60W480.PPD	Verityper VT-600W version 48.0
VT4510A1.PPD	Verityper VT4_510A version 52.3
VT49901.PPD	Verityper VT4990 version 52.3
VT4530A1.PPD	VT4_530A version 52.3
VT4530B1.PPD	VT4_530B version 52.3
VT4530C1.PPD	VT4_530C version 52.3
VT4533B1.PPD	VT4_533B version 52.3
VT4533C1.PPD	VT4_533C version 52.3
VT453EA1.PPD	VT4_53EA version 52.3

Table 4.14   Adobe PostScript Printer Description (.PPD) Files *(continued)*

Filename	Description
VT453EB1.PPD	VT4_53EB version 52.3
VT4550A1.PPD	VT4_550A version 52.3
VT4550B1.PPD	VT4_550B version 52.3
VT4550C1.PPD	VT4_550C version 52.3
VT4551A1.PPD	VT4_551A version 52.3
VT4563A1.PPD	VT4_563A version 52.3
VT4563B1.PPD	VT4_563B version 52.3
WANG15.PPD	Wang® LCS15
XRDT1351.PPD	Xerox® DocuTech 135 version 2010.130
XRDT0901.PPD	Xerox DocuTech 90 version 2010.130
XRDT0851.PPD	Xerox DocuTech 85 version 2010.130

Printer Separator Files

You can use separator files for a variety of purposes. Windows NT includes separator files that print a page at the beginning of each document to make it easy to find a document among others at the printer and separator files that can switch a printer between PostScript and PCL printing.

The Windows NT default separator page is SYSPRINT.SEP. To specify a different separator page, type the name of the separator file, including its path, in the Separator File box of the Printer Details dialog box.

Windows NT includes the following separator files. For more information about printing, see Chapter 6, "Printing."

Table 4.15   Printer Separator (.SEP) Files

Filename	Description
PCL.SEP	Switches printer to PCL printing (compatible with PCL)
PSCRIPT.SEP	Switches printer to PostScript printing (compatible with PostScript)
PSLANMAN.SEP	Prints a page before each document (compatible with PostScript)
SYSPRINT.SEP	Prints a page before each document (compatible with PostScript)

Quick Basic Sample Files

Windows NT includes the following sample files for Quick Basic.

Table 4.16   Quick Basic (.BAS) Sample Files

Filename	Description
GORILLA.BAS	Game
MONEY.BAS	Personal finance manager
NIBBLES.BAS	Game
REMLINE.BAS	Line number removal utility

Screen Saver Files

Screen savers reduce wear on your display and provide security for your system. When Windows NT is installed, a default screen saver is selected. However, several other screen savers are included with Windows NT. To select a screen saver, double-click the Desktop icon in the Control Panel window.

To free hard disk space, you can delete screen savers that you don't intend to use, for example the bezier screen saver. To remove screen savers, delete the files using the Windows NT Setup program. For more information about removing files, see "Adding and Removing Windows NT Components" in Chapter 12, "System Maintenance with Windows NT Setup," in the *Windows NT System Guide*.

Windows NT includes the following screen saver files. For more information about screen savers, see "Working with Screen Savers" in Chapter 5, "Control Panel," in the *Windows NT System Guide*.

Table 4.17   Screen Saver (.SCR) Files

Filename	Description
BLACK16.SCR	Black screen (16-bit)
LOGON.SCR	Randomly-positioned Windows NT Logon dialog box
SCRNSAVE.SCR	Black screen (32-bit)
SS3DFO.SCR	Three-dimensional flying objects
SSBEZIER.SCR	Bezier curves
SSMARQUE.SCR	Marquee display
SSMYST.SCR	Mystify
SSPIPES.SCR	Three-dimensional pipes
SSSTARS.SCR	Star field simulation

Setup Script Files

The TXTSETUP.SIF file and information (.INF) files are what you must modify when you want to customize the Windows NT Setup program to meet the specific needs of your organization. You can customize the Setup program, for example, by adding files and applications to Windows NT or by removing certain unused features, such as OS/2 support, to reduce the amount of disk space needed to install Windows NT.

For more information about .INF files and customizing Windows NT Setup, see Chapter 3, "Customizing Windows NT Setup."

Table 4.18   Setup Script (.INF) Files

Filename	Description
TXTSETUP.SIF	Text-mode installation of core Windows NT components. Used by Setup from CD or floppy disks, or via the **winnt** or **winnt32** utility.
APP.INF	Used when searching the hard drive for existing applications and for automatically configuring MS-DOS application Program Information Files (PIFs)
DOSNET.INF	Contains the list of files copied to your local hard disk during **winnt** or **winnt32** Setup. Used by the MS-DOS portion of **winnt**, and by **winnt32** Setup.
FILELIST.INF	Used to create a network sharepoint for WINNT.EXE Setup
HARDWARE.INF	Hardware configuration file used by Windows NT Setup
INITIAL.INF	Graphical-mode installation of additional Windows NT components. Used by Setup via CD, floppy disks, or the **winnt** or **winnt32** utility.
IPINFOR.INF	TCP/IP default IP address
KEYBOARD.INF	Setup information for keyboards
LANGUAGE.INF	Setup information for installing language-specific support files
LAYOUT.INF	Setup information to install specific keyboard layout support
MMDRIVER.INF	Multimedia drivers setup information
MODEM.INF	Remote Access Server modem setup information file
MONITOR.INF	Monitors setup information file
NBINFO.INF	NetBIOS setup information file
NCPARAM.INF	Network card parameters setup information file
NCPASHEL.INF	Network Control Panel tool shell setup information file
NETDTECT.INF	Network card autodetection setup information file
NTLANMAN.INF	Windows NT LAN Manager setup information file

Table 4.18   Setup Script (.INF) Files *(continued)*

Filename	Description
NTLMINST.INF	Network installation setup information file
OEMNADAM.INF	Network adapter setup script for Advanced Micro Devices AM2100, AM1500T, and PCnet adapters; also Novell/Anthem NE1500T, and NE2100 adapters
OEMNADAR.INF	Network adapter setup script for Advanced Micro Devices AM2100, AM1500T, and PCnet adapters; also Novell/Anthem NE1500T and Novell/Anthem NE2100 adapters
OEMNADD1.INF	Network driver setup script for DEC EtherWORKS LC adapter and Turbo/LC adapter cards
OEMNADD2.INF	Network driver setup script for DEC EtherWORKS Turbo adapter
OEMNADD4.INF	Network driver setup script for DEC EtherWORKS Turbo EISA adapter
OEMNADDE.INF	Network driver setup script for DEC Turbo Channel Ethernet adapter
OEMNADDI.INF	Network driver setup script for Digiboard PCIMAC (ISA, PCIMAC) MC, and PCIMAC/4 adapters (Digiboard ISDN adapters)
OEMNADDP.INF	Network driver setup script for DEC Etherworks DEPCA adapter
OEMNADDS.INF	Digiboard C/X, PC/Xem, PC/8i, PC/2e, PC/4e, PC/8e adapter setup script
OEMNADE1.INF	Network driver setup script for 3Com Etherlink 16 TP adapter
OEMNADE2.INF	Network driver setup script for 3Com Etherlink II® adapter
OEMNADE3.INF	Network driver setup script for 3Com Etherlink III adapter
OEMNADEE.INF	Network driver setup script for 3Com Etherlink III EISA adapter
OEMNADEM.INF	Network driver setup script for 3Com 3C523 Etherlink/MC adapter
OEMNADEN.INF	Network driver setup script for 3Com Etherlink III MCA adapter
OEMNADFD.INF	Network Peripherals FDDI, MCA network adapter setup script
OEMNADIN.INF	Network driver setup script for Intel EtherExpress 16 LAN adapter
OEMNADLB.INF	Network driver setup script for MS Loopback adapter
OEMNADLM.INF	Network driver setup script for DayStar Digital LocalTalk adapter (MCA)
OEMNADLT.INF	Network driver setup script for DayStar Digital LocalTalk adapter
OEMNADN1.INF	Network driver setup script for Novell NE1000 adapter

Table 4.18   Setup Script (.INF) Files *(continued)*

Filename	Description
OEMNADN2.INF	Network driver setup script for Novell NE2000 adapter
OEMNADNE.INF	Network driver setup script for Novell NE3200 EISA adapter
OEMNADNF.INF	Network driver setup script for COMPAQ NetFlex/DualSpeed Token Ring adapter
OEMNADNM.INF	Network driver setup script for Novell NE2000 adapter and compatible MC adapter
OEMNADNP.INF	Network driver setup script for Network Peripherals FDDI EISA adapter
OEMNADP3.INF	Network driver setup script for Proteon P1390 adapter
OEMNADP9.INF	Network driver setup script for Proteon P1990 adapter
OEMNADPM.INF	Network driver setup script for Proteon MCA adapter
OEMNADS1.INF	Network driver setup script for Sonic EISA adapter
OEMNADT2.INF	Network driver setup script for IBM Token Ring Network 16/4 ISA Adapter II
OEMNADTE.INF	Network driver setup script for IBM Token Ring EISA adapter
OEMNADTK.INF	Network driver setup script for IBM Token Ring adapter
OEMNADTM.INF	Network driver setup script for IBM Token Ring adapter/A
OEMNADUB.INF	Network driver setup script for Ungermann-Bass Ethernet NIUpc, NIUpc/EOTP, NIUps adapters
OEMNADUM.INF	Network driver setup script for Ungermann-Bass Ethernet NIUps adapter
OEMNADWD.INF	Network driver setup script for SMC (Western Digital) ISA adapter
OEMNADWM.INF	Network driver setup script for SMC (Western Digital) adapters: 8003E /A, 8003W /A, 8013WP /A, 8013EP /A
OEMNADXM.INF	Network adapter setup script for Ungermann-Bass Ethernet NIUps adapter (XNS®)
OEMNADXN.INF	Network adapter setup script for Ungermann-Bass Ethernet NIUpc and Ethernet NIUpc/EOTP adapters (XNS)
OEMNSVBH.INF	Network service setup script for Network Monitor Agent
OEMNSVCU.INF	Network service setup script for TCP/IP utilities
OEMNSVDH.INF	Network service setup script for Microsoft DHCP Server
OEMNSVFT.INF	Network service setup script for FTP Server
OEMNSVNB.INF	Network service setup script for NetBIOS Transport Interface
OEMNSVNW.INF	Network service setup script for Client Service for NetWare
OEMNSVRA.INF	Network service setup script for Remote Access Server, NetBIOS Gateway, API Layer, RAS Hub, and AsyMAC driver

Table 4.18   Setup Script (.INF) Files *(continued)*

Filename	Description
OEMNSVRC.INF	Network service setup script for Remote Command Server
OEMNSVRI.INF	Network service setup script for Remoteboot Service
OEMNSVRP.INF	Network service setup script for Remote Procedure Call Locator service
OEMNSVSA.INF	Network service setup script for SAP Agent
OEMNSVSM.INF	Network service setup script for AppleTalk protocol
OEMNSVSP.INF	Network service setup script for Simple TCP/IP Services
OEMNSVSV.INF	Network service setup script for Windows NT LAN Manager Server
OEMNSVTP.INF	Network service setup script for TCP/IP Print Server
OEMNSVWI.INF	Network service setup script for Windows Internet Name Service
OEMNSVWK.INF	Network service setup script for Windows NT LAN Manager Workstation
OEMNXPDL.INF	Network transport setup script for DLC protocol
OEMNXPIP.INF	Network transport setup script for NWLink Transport driver and NWLink NetBIOS driver
OEMNXPNB.INF	Network transport setup script for NetBEUI 3.0 Transport
OEMNXPS1.INF	Network transport setup script for SNMP Service
OEMNXPSM.INF	Network transport setup script for Service for Macintosh, including the AppleTalk protocol, File Server for Macintosh, Kernel driver, and Print Server for Macintosh
OEMNXPSN.INF	Network transport setup script for SNMP Network Management Service
OEMNXPST.INF	Network transport setup script for Streams environment
OEMNXPTC.INF	Network transport setup script for TCP/IP protocol, including TCP/IP NetBIOS, Telnet, Loop Support Environment, and TCP/IP NetBIOS helper
OEMNXPTP.INF	Network transport setup script for ISO TP4/CLNP Stack
OEMNXPXN.INF	Network transport setup script for MCS XNS
OEMNXPXS.INF	Network transport setup for Ungermann-Bass XNS 1.0
OTHER.INF	Setup script for "Other Driver" selections
PAD.INF	PAD script information for Remote Access Server configuration (X.25)
PARTIAL.INF	Graphical-mode installation of optional Windows NT components and creation of Program Manager groups. Used by Setup via CD, floppy disks, or the **winnt** or **winnt32** utility.

Table 4.18   Setup Script (.INF) Files *(continued)*

Filename	Description
POINTER.INF	Pointing devices setup script (including mouse)
PRINTER.INF	Printer setup script file; specific printer driver information
PRNSETUP.INF	Printer setup script file
REGISTRY.INF	Registry setup script file
REPAIR.INF	Repair disk setup script file
SCSI.INF	SCSI installation setup script
SETUP.INF	Windows NT Setup script file
SETUP16.INF	Win16 SETUP.INF file
SFMICONS.INF	Services for Macintosh icon information
SFMMAP.INF	Services for Macintosh Type Creator mappings information file
SUBROUTN.INF	Windows NT Setup common subroutines script file
SWITCH.INF	Remote Access Server switch configuration information file
TAPE.INF	Setup script for tape devices
UPDATE.INF	Used to update files when a selection is made from a set of files and the chosen one is copied under a generic name. This can be used to update the following files: HAL.DLL, NTOSKRNL.EXE, NTBOOTDD.SYS, and NTDETECT.COM.
UTILITY.INF	Utility script used for network setup
VIDEO.INF	Video driver setup script
VIRTUAL.INF	Setup information for configuring the Windows NT paging file
XPORTS.INF	Transport customization

Your system might also include other information files. Many of these files are for specific hardware devices provided by original equipment manufacturers (OEMs). Filenames for these files are in the form OEM*xxxyy*.INF, where *xxx* refers to the type of information file in the list below and *yy* represents the specific device(s).

Table 4.19   OEM Setup Script (.INF) Files

Filename	Description	Filename	Description
OEMCPT*yy*.INF	Computer	OEMSND*yy*.INF	Sound
OEMVIO*yy*.INF	Video	OEMDRV*yy*.INF	Driver
OEMPTR*yy*.INF	Pointer	OEMNAD*yy*.INF	NetAdapter
OEMKBD*yy*.INF	Keyboard	OEMNDR*yy*.INF	NetDriver
OEMLA*yy*Y.INF	Layout	OEMNXP*yy*.INF	NetTransport
OEMLNG*yy*.INF	Language	OEMNSV*yy*.INF	NetService
OEMPRN*yy*.INF	Printer	OEMNWK*yy*.INF	Network
OEMSCS*yy*.INF	SCSI	OEMNPR*yy*.INF	NetProvider
OEMTAP*yy*.INF	Tape		

Sound Wave Files

Using the sound wave files included with Windows NT, you can associate sounds to events. To associate sound waves with certain system and application events, double-click the Sound icon in the Control Panel window.

You must have a sound card and a sound driver installed to use the sound wave (.WAV) files. The Sound icon only appears in the Control Panel window if you have the necessary hardware and driver installed.

To free hard disk space, you can delete the sound wave files that you don't intend to use or all of the sound wave files if you do not have a sound card installed on your computer. To remove the sound wave files, use the Windows NT Setup program. For more information about removing files, see "Adding and Removing Windows NT Components" in Chapter 12, "System Maintenance with Windows NT Setup," in the *Windows NT System Guide*.

Windows NT includes the following sound wave files. For more information about sound wave files, see "Using Audio and MIDI Sounds in Windows NT" in Chapter 5, "Control Panel," in the *Windows NT System Guide*.

Table 4.20   Sound Wave (.WAV) Files

Filename	Description
CHIMES.WAV	Chimes
CHORD.WAV	Chord
DING.WAV	Ding
RINGIN.WAV	Chat tool sound file for incoming call
RINGOUT.WAV	Chat tool sound file for outgoing call
TADA.WAV	Windows NT Startup sound

Spelling Lexicon Files

Windows NT includes the following lexicon files. For related information, see Appendix C, "International Considerations."

Table 4.21   Spelling Lexicon (.LEX) Files

Filename	Description
MSP32_AM.LEX	U.S. English spelling
MSP32_BR.LEX	International English spelling
MSP32_DA.LEX	Danish spelling
MSP32_ES.LEX	Spanish spelling
MSP32_FI.LEX	Finnish spelling
MSP32_FR.LEX	French spelling
MSP32_GE.LEX	German spelling
MSP32_IT.LEX	Italian spelling
MSP32_NB.LEX	Norwegian spelling
MSP32_NL.LEX	Dutch spelling
MSP32_PB.LEX	Portuguese spelling
MSP32_SW.LEX	Swedish spelling

Text Files

Windows NT also includes online information in the form of text files. The text files are in ASCII format and can be viewed by using Notepad, Write, or any text editor or word processing package.

The following text files are included with Windows NT.

Table 4.22   Text (.TXT and .WRI) Files

Filename	Description
NETWORK.WRI	Network readme containing information related to networks, such as information on network adapter cards and network interoperability
PRINTER.WRI	Printer readme containing information related to printing, such as information on specific printers
PROBREP.TXT	Bug reporting template
RASREAD.TXT	Remote Access Server readme
README.WRI	Windows NT readme containing hardware- and software-specific information not available in the Microsoft Windows NT *Installation Guide* or in online Help, as well as information on changes that occurred after publication
SETUP.TXT	Setup readme containing additional information you may need prior to installing Windows NT on some hardware configurations
SFMUAM.TXT	Services for Macintosh readme containing information about installing the Macintosh workstation software, quick reference for Macintosh users, and Services for Macintosh User Authentication Module
WINPERMS.TXT	Windows NT permission list

Wallpaper Files

You can display wallpaper on your desktop instead of a solid color or pattern. To select a bitmap to display as wallpaper, double-click the Desktop icon in the Control Panel window.

Windows NT uses more memory when displaying wallpaper than when displaying a solid color or a pattern on the desktop. If you run low on memory when running an application, you can change to a solid color or pattern to free some memory.

To free hard disk space, you can delete the wallpaper files that you don't intend to use. To remove a wallpaper file, delete the bitmap file (.BMP) from the \systemroot directory or use the Windows NT Setup program. For more information about removing files, see "Adding and Removing Windows NT Components" in Chapter 12, "System Maintenance with Windows NT Setup," in the *Windows NT System Guide*.

Windows NT includes the following wallpaper files. For more information about wallpaper, see "Displaying Custom Wallpaper" in Chapter 5, "Control Panel," in the *Windows NT System Guide*.

Table 4.23   Wallpaper (.BMP) Files

Filename	Description
256COLOR.BMP	256-color design
ARCADE.BMP	Gray-textured diamond against light green background
ARCHES.BMP	Roman coliseum effect or aqueduct effect
ARGYLE.BMP	Argyle pattern
BALL.BMP	Three-dimensional ball against checked background
CARS.BMP	Car on street pointing to upper-right corner
CASTLE.BMP	Castle wall
CHITZ.BMP	Random squares-and-squiggles pattern
EGYPT.BMP	Egyptian-style pattern
HONEY.BMP	Honeycomb pattern
LANMANNT.BMP	Windows NT Advanced Server bitmap (for Windows NT Advanced Server only)
LEAVES.BMP	Leave pattern
MARBLE.BMP	Marble pattern
REDBRICK.BMP	Red brick pattern
RIVETS.BMP	Rivets
SQUARES.BMP	Square
TARTAN.BMP	Tartan pattern
THATCH.BMP	Thatch pattern
WINLOGO.BMP	Windows logo
WINNT.BMP	Windows NT logo (for the base Windows NT product only)
ZIGZAG.BMP	Zigzag pattern

Using Windows NT

Part Three describes some of the most basic features of the Windows NT product, including its file systems and printing. This part also examines technical issues related to using fonts, Microsoft Mail, and Microsoft Schedule+ under Windows NT.

C H A P T E R   5

Windows NT File Systems and Advanced Disk Management

Windows NT supports multiple active file systems including the existing FAT and HPFS file systems. It also includes a new file system called NTFS, designed to take advantage of the very large disks and fast processors on current and future computers.

As noted in Chapter 1, "Windows NT Architecture," Windows NT also implements redirectors and servers as file systems. In addition, Windows NT supports the CD file system for use on CD-ROM drives. It also supports the Named Piles File System (NPFS) and the Mailslot File System (MSFS), both used for communication between processes.

These nontraditional file systems are not included in the discussion of this chapter. Instead, this chapter focuses on FAT, HPFS, and NTFS, the three file systems that can be used on read/write hard drives.

This chapter describes FAT and HPFS both as progenitors to NTFS and as file systems that can be used with Windows NT. It also details the features of NTFS and compares features of NTFS, FAT, and HPFS.

This chapter also describes the disk management techniques offered by Windows NT that you can use to organize and safeguard data on your disks.

File System History

In 1981, IBM introduced its first personal computer, which ran a new operating system designed by Microsoft, MS-DOS. The computer contained a 16-bit 8088 processor chip and two drives for low-density floppy disks. The MS-DOS file system, FAT (named for its file allocation table), provided more than enough power to format these small disk volumes and to manage hierarchical directory structures and files. The FAT file system continued to meet the needs of personal computer users even as hardware and software power increased year after year. However, file searches and data retrieval took significantly longer on large hard disks than on the original low-density floppy disks of the first IBM personal computer.

By the end of the 1980s, the prediction of "a computer on every desk and in every home" was less a dream and more a reality. Personal computers now had 16-bit processors and hard disks of 40 MB and more—so big that users had to partition their disks into two or more volumes because the file allocation table's limit was 32 MB per volume. (Later versions of MS-DOS allowed for larger disk volumes.)

In 1990, a high-performance file system (HPFS) was introduced as a part of the OS/2 operating system version 1.x. This file system was designed specifically for large hard disks on 16-bit processor computers. On the heels of HPFS came HPFS386. It was introduced as part of Microsoft LAN Manager and was designed to take advantage of the 32-bit 80386 processor chip.

Today's personal computers include a variety of very fast processor chips and can accommodate multiple, huge hard disks. The new Windows NT file system, NTFS, is designed for optimal performance on these computers.

Because of features such as speed and universality, FAT or HPFS are now popular and widely used file systems. NTFS offers consistency with these two file systems, plus advanced functionality needed by corporations interested in greater flexibility and in data security.

Before discussing how each file system organizes data on the disk, the next section briefly reviews how a disk is organized.

About Disks and Disk Organization

Each disk is divided into top and bottom sides, rings on each side called *tracks*, and sections within each track called *sectors*. A sector is the smallest physical storage unit on a disk, typically 512 bytes in size. The **format** command organizes the disk into tracks and sectors for use by a particular file system. Unless you specify a particular sector size, **format** evaluates your disk and determines an appropriate sector size for you.

As a file is written to the disk, the file system allocates the appropriate number of sectors to store the file's data. For example, if each sector is 512 bytes and the file is 800 bytes, two sectors are allocated for the file. Later, if the file is appended, for example, to twice its size (1600 bytes), another two sectors are allocated. If *contiguous* sectors (sectors that are next to each other on the disk) are not available, the data is written elsewhere on the disk, and the file is considered to be *fragmented*. Fragmentation only becomes an issue when the file system must search several different locations to find all the pieces of the file you want to read. The search causes a delay before the file is retrieved. Allocating larger sectors reduces the potential for fragmentation but increases the likelihood that sectors would have unused space.

The way data is retrieved depends on the indexing methods used by the file system. The following sections provide details about FAT, HPFS, and NTFS, including how each stores, indexes, and retrieves data on the disk.

FAT File System

As mentioned earlier, the FAT file system is named for its method of organization—the file allocation table. This table of values provides links from one allocation unit (one or more sectors) to another, as shown in Figure 5.1.

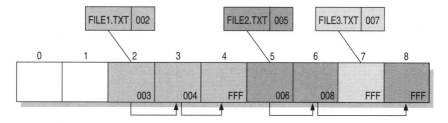

Figure 5.1   File Allocation Table

This illustration includes three files. The file named FILE1.TXT is a file that is large enough to take the space of three allocation units. A small file, FILE3.TXT, takes space in only one allocation unit. The third file, FILE2.TXT, is a large, fragmented file. In each case, the directory entry points to the first allocation unit containing the file. If the file contents go beyond one allocation unit, the first allocation unit points to the next in the chain. FFF indicates the end of the chain.

The FAT file system is a simple file system originally designed for small disks and simple directory structures. Its design has been improved over the years to work more effectively with larger disks and more powerful personal computers. With MS-DOS version 4.0, the FAT entries grew from 12 bits to 16 bits in size, thus allowing for partitions larger than 32 MB.

Figure 5.2 illustrates how the FAT file system organizes the disk.

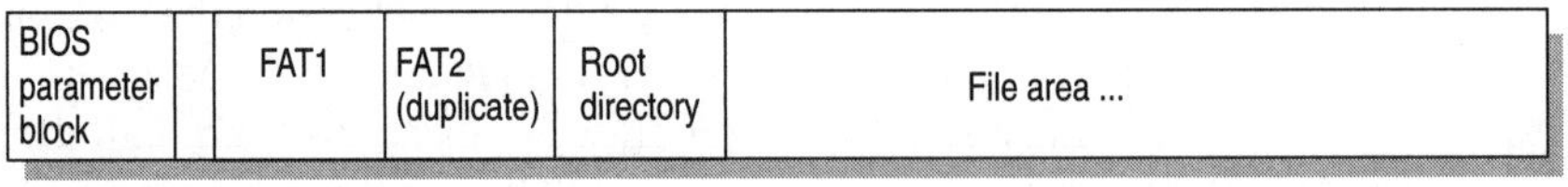

| BIOS parameter block | | FAT1 | FAT2 (duplicate) | Root directory | File area ... |

Figure 5.2   FAT Disk Partition (Volume)

The root directory has a fixed size and location on the disk. Directories are special files with 32-byte entries for each file contained in that directory. The entry for each file includes the following information:

- Filename (eight-plus-three characters)
- Attribute byte (8 bits worth of information, described below)
- Modification time (16 bits)
- Modification date (16 bits)
- Starting allocation unit (16 bits)
- File size (32 bits)

This information is used by all operating systems that support the FAT file system. In addition, Windows NT can store additional time stamps in a FAT directory entry. These time stamps show when the file was created or last accessed and are used principally by POSIX applications.

Bits in the attribute byte of the directory entry of a file indicate whether the file has certain attributes. One bit indicates that the file is a subdirectory, while another bit marks the file as a volume label. Normally, only the operating system controls the settings of these bits. In addition, a FAT files has four special attributes that can be turned on or off by the user—archive file, system file, hidden file, and read-only file.

Windows NT versions 3.5 and later use these attribute bits to support long filenames up to 256 characters on FAT partitions in a way that does not interfere with how MS-DOS or OS/2 access the partition. Whenever a user creates a file with a long filename (that is, a filename that exceeds the eight-plus-three limits of the FAT file system on MS-DOS and OS/2 or that contains extended or mixed-case characters), Windows NT creates a conventional directory entry for the file, supplying an eight-plus-three name in the same manner as for a file on an NTFS volume. (For information about how Windows NT creates the short filename, see "Generating Short Filenames" later in this chapter.) In addition to this conventional entry, Windows NT creates one or more secondary directory entries for the file, one for each 13 characters in the long filename. Each of these secondary directory entries stores a corresponding part of the long filename in Unicode. Windows NT sets the volume, read-only, system, and hidden file attribute bits of the secondary directory entry to mark it as part of a long filename. MS-DOS and OS/2 generally ignore directory entries with all four of these attribute bits set, so these entries are effectively invisible to these operating systems. Instead, MS-DOS and OS/2 access the file using the eight-plus-three filename contained in the conventional directory entry for the file.

Some third-party disk utilities that directly manipulate the FAT might regard the long-filename directory entries created by Windows NT as errors in the logical structure of the disk volume and so may damage the directory entries or even the file itself trying to correct the error. Do not use a third-party disk utility to repair or defragment a FAT partition used by Windows NT unless the disk utility has been certified as being compatible with Windows NT version 3.5 or later. You can, safely use the Scandisk and Chkdsk utilities supplied with MS-DOS version 6.0 and later to repair a damaged FAT partition, but do not use the Defrag utility to defragment a FAT partition containing long filenames because it tends to discard long filename information.

By default, Windows NT 3.5 supports long filenames on FAT partitions. If you want to be able to use third-party disk utilities to repair or defragment FAT partitions used by Windows NT, set the Win31FileSystem parameter of the following Registry entry to 1:

```
HKEY_LOCAL_MACHINE\System\CurrentControlSet\Control\FileSystem
```

Setting this value will prevent Windows NT from creating new long filenames on all FAT partitions; it does not affect existing long filenames. See Chapter 10, "Overview of the Windows NT Registry," and Chapter 11, "Registry Editor and Registry Administration," for information about adding and changing entries in the Registry.

Using the FAT File System with Windows NT

The Windows NT FAT file system works the same as it does with MS-DOS and Windows. In fact, you can install Windows NT on your existing FAT partition.

Note Remember that you cannot use Windows NT with any compression or partitioning software that requires drivers to be loaded by MS-DOS. Rather, you must have Windows NT-specific versions of the drivers to enable Windows NT to read the disk.

You can move or copy files between FAT and NTFS volumes. When you move or copy a file from NTFS to FAT, permissions and alternate streams are lost.

HPFS

HPFS includes features that make it an efficient manager of large hard-disk volumes. HPFS also supports long filenames (up to 255 characters), which allows users to give files descriptive names.

When HPFS formats a volume, it reserves the first 18 sectors for the *boot block*, the *super block*, and the *spare block*. These three structures are used to boot the operating system, maintain the file system, and recover from possible errors.

HPFS also reserves space for a pair of 2K bitmaps at 16 MB intervals throughout the volume. Each bitmap contains one bit for each allocation unit (equal to one sector) in the 8 MB band, showing which allocation units are in use.

Figure 5.3 illustrates how HPFS organizes a volume.

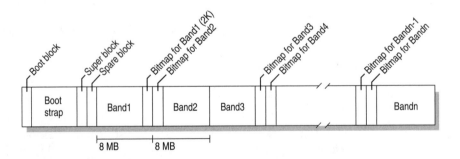

Figure 5.3   An HPFS Volume

The bitmaps are alternately located at the end and beginning of each band to allow a maximum amount of contiguous space for data (almost 16 MB instead of almost 8 MB). In addition, HPFS plans where it writes new files, leaving room between new and existing files so that each has room to expand into contiguous space on the disk. This feature helps HPFS to allow fast data retrieval and to minimize file fragmentation.

Another feature that accounts for fast directory searches is HPFS's use of B-trees. A *B-tree* is a tree structure with a root and several nodes. It contains data organized in some logical way so that the whole structure can be quickly traversed. The root contains a small amount of administrative information, a map to the rest of the structure, and possibly a small amount of data. The nodes contain most of the data. On large directories, B-trees perform much better than the linear lists used by the FAT file system.

HPFS uses B-trees to structure each of its directories and each of its files. Each directory points to Fnodes for files contained in that directory. An *Fnode* is 512 bytes in length and contains a header, the filename (truncated to 15 characters), the file length, extended attributes (EA) and access control list (ACL) information, and the location of the file's data.

Note HPFS ACLs are supported by the OS/2 operating system but not by Windows NT. If you want access control list support, use NTFS.

Figure 5.4 shows the Fnode for a file whose data is contained in Extent1, Extent2, and Extent3 (where an *extent* is a range of contiguous sectors).

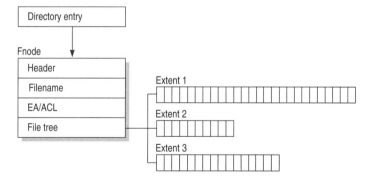

Figure 5.4   An HPFS File

Because of the arrangement of bitmaps on the volume shown in Figure 5.3, a file extent can be almost 16 MB. Depending on the size of the file, the Fnode can point to as many as eight extents. If the file is so large that it cannot be contained within eight extents, the Fnode includes up to 12 pointers to allocation nodes that have space for more file extents.

If the extended attribute and ACL information cannot be contained in the Fnode, the Fnode includes a pointer to that information.

In short, HPFS includes powerful features and works efficiently on disks of up to 2 GB. The HPFS design does have some weaknesses. For example, if something damages the first portion of the volume, which contains boot information and a pointer to the root directory, use of the volume is lost. HPFS's use of **chkdsk** at each system boot and to repair disk errors can be time-consuming. In addition, its design requiring 512-byte sectors is not well-suited for larger volumes.

Using HPFS with Windows NT

Some HPFS features are implemented differently for Windows NT than for OS/2. For example, Windows NT does not support HPFS access control list information or HPFS hot-fixing. (However, these features are available with NTFS.) Also, disk caching and lazy writing are managed by the Windows NT Cache Manager and not the file system.

When you move or copy a file from NTFS to HPFS, any permissions, and alternate streams are lost, and filenames are converted from the Unicode to OEM character set. In addition, the filename becomes case-insensitive.

Windows NT supports HPFS primarily for backwards compatibility for systems that dual-boot OS/2 and Windows NT. NTFS provides all the benefits of HPFS as well as such additional features as security and reliability. Unless a volume must be available to OS/2, the volume should be formatted for NTFS rather than HPFS.

NTFS

NTFS provides a combination of performance, reliability, and compatibility not found in either FAT or HPFS. It is designed to quickly perform standard file operations such as read, write, and search—and even advanced operations such as file-system recovery—on very large hard disks.

It also includes security features required for file servers and high-end personal computers in a corporate environment. NTFS supports data access control and ownership privileges that are important for the integrity of corporate data. While directories shared by a Windows NT Server are assigned particular permissions, NTFS files and directories can have assigned permissions whether they are shared or not. NTFS is the only file system on Windows NT that allows you to assign permissions to individual files.

NTFS has a simple, yet very powerful design. From the file system's perspective, everything on the NTFS volume is a file or part of a file. Every sector on an NTFS volume that is allocated belongs to some file. Even the file system metadata (information that describes the file system itself) is part of a file.

This attribute-based file system supports object-oriented applications by treating all files as objects that have user-defined and system-defined attributes.

Master File Table

Each file on an NTFS volume is represented by a record in a special file called the master file table (MFT). NTFS reserves the first 16 records of the table for special information. The first record of this table describes the master file table itself, followed by a MFT *mirror record*. If the first MFT record is corrupted, NTFS reads the second record to find the MFT mirror file, whose first record is identical to the first record of the MFT. The locations of the data segments for both the MFT and MFT mirror file are recorded in the boot sector. A duplicate of the boot sector is located at the logical center of the disk.

The third record of the MFT is the log file, used for file recovery. The log file is discussed in detail later in this chapter. The seventeenth and following records of the master file table are for each file and directory (also viewed as a file by NTFS) on the volume. Figure 5.5 provides a simplified illustration of the MFT structure.

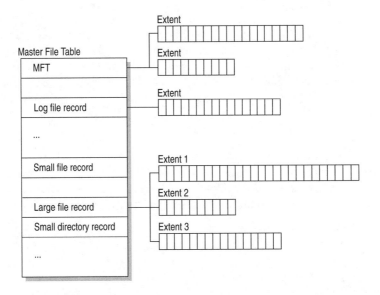

Figure 5.5   Master File Table

The master file table allocates a certain amount of space for each file record. The attributes of a file are written to the allocated space in the MFT. Small files and directories (typically 1500 bytes or smaller), such as the file illustrated in Figure 5.6, can entirely be contained within the master file table record.

Standard information	File or directory name	Security descriptor	Data or index	

Figure 5.6   MFT Record for a Small File or Directory

This design makes file access very fast. Consider, for example, the FAT file system, which uses a file allocation table to list the names and addresses of each file. FAT directory entries contain an index into the file allocation table. When you want to view a file, FAT first reads the file allocation table and assures that it exists. Then FAT retrieves the file by searching the chain of allocation units assigned to the file. With NTFS, as soon as you look up the file, it's there for you to use.

Directory records are housed within the master file table just like file records. Instead of data, directories contain index information. Small directory records reside entirely within the MFT structure. Large directories are organized into B-trees, having records with pointers to external clusters containing directory entries that could not be contained within the MFT structure.

NTFS File Attributes

NTFS views each file (or directory) as a set of file *attributes*. Elements such as the file's name, its security information, and even its data are all file attributes. Each attribute is identified by an attribute type code and, optionally, an attribute name.

When a file's attributes can be written within the MFT file record, they are called *resident* attributes. For example, information such as filename and time stamp are always included in the MFT file record. When a file is too large to fit all of its attributes in the MFT file record, some of its attributes are *nonresident*. The nonresident attributes are allocated one or more runs of disk space elsewhere in the volume. (A *run* of disk space is a contiguous linear area on the disk.)

In general, all attributes can be referenced as a stream of bytes whether they are resident or nonresident.

Table 5.1 lists all of the file attributes currently defined by NTFS. This list is extensible, meaning that other file attributes can be defined in the future.

Table 5.1 NTFS File Attribute Types

Attribute type	Description
Standard Information	Includes time stamps, link count, and so on.
Attribute List	Lists all other attributes in large files only.
Filename	A repeatable attribute for both long and short filenames. The long name of the file can be up to 255 Unicode characters. The short name is the MS-DOS–readable, eight-plus-three, case-insensitive name for this file. Additional names, or *hard links*, required by POSIX may also be included as additional Filename attributes.
Security Descriptor	Shows information about who can access the file, who owns the file, and so on.
Data	Contains file data. NTFS allows for multiple data attributes per file. Each file typically has one unnamed data attribute. In addition, a file can have one or more named data attributes, using a particular syntax.
Index Root	Used to implement directories.
Index Allocation	Used to implement directories.

Table 5.1 NTFS File Attribute Types *(continued)*

Attribute type	Description
Volume Information	Used only in the volume system file and includes, among other things, the version and name of the volume.
Bitmap	Provides a map representing records in use on the MFT or directory.
Extended Attribute Information	Used by file servers that are linked with OS/2 systems. This attribute type isn't useful to Windows NT.
Extended Attributes	Used by file servers that are linked with OS/2 systems. This attribute type isn't useful to Windows NT.

Long and Short Filenames

One of the improvements HPFS implemented on the MS-DOS design was the ability to use long filenames of up to 255 characters. Unfortunately, files with long names on an HPFS volume couldn't be accessed from an MS-DOS operating system, which has an eight-plus-three filename limitation.

Like HPFS, NTFS allows filenames of up to 255 characters. NTFS filenames use the 16-bit Unicode character set but solve the problem of access from MS-DOS. NTFS automatically generates an MS-DOS–readable (eight-plus-three) name for each file. This way, NTFS files are accessible over a network by the MS-DOS and OS/2 operating systems. This is a particularly important feature for file servers, especially in an office using personal computers with two or all three of these operating systems.

By creating eight-plus-three filenames for files, NTFS also allows MS-DOS–based and Windows-based 3.*x* applications to recognize and load files that have NTFS long filenames. In addition, when an MS-DOS-based or Windows-based 3.*x* application saves a file on an NTFS volume, both the eight-plus-three filename and NTFS long filename are retained.

Note When saving a file from an MS-DOS–based or Windows-based 3.*x* application on an NTFS volume, if that application saves to a temporary file, deletes the original file, and renames the temporary file to the original filename, the long filename is lost. Any unique permissions set on that file are also lost. Permissions are propagated again from the parent directory.

If the long name of a file or directory on an NTFS volume contains spaces, be sure to surround the path name with quotation marks. This is true when specifying a path in Program Manager for the application's icon. For example, suppose Word for Windows is installed in D:\WORD FOR WINDOWS. The Program Item Properties Command Line should be set to D:\WORD FOR WINDOWS\WINWORD.EXE. If the quotation marks were omitted, an error message would display, saying "The path D:\Word is invalid."

This is also true when a path typed at the command line includes spaces, as in the following example:

```
move "c:\This month's reports\*.*" "c:\Last month's reports"„
```

Note Remember to use wildcards such as * and ? carefully in conjunction with the **del** and **copy** commands. NTFS searches both long and short filenames for matches to the wildcard combination you specify, which may cause extra files to be deleted or copied.

To copy or move files with case-sensitive long filenames, it is safest to select the files using a mouse in File Manager. That way, you can clearly identify which files you want to copy or move.

Beginning with Windows NT 3.5, files created or renamed on FAT partitions can also have associated long filenames. The rules governing long filenames on NTFS volumes also apply to long filenames on FAT partitions except that filenames on FAT can contain extended characters. For more information about long-filename support on FAT partitions, see "FAT File System" earlier in this chapter.

Generating Short Filenames

Because NTFS uses the Unicode character set for its names, there are potentially several "illegal" characters that MS-DOS cannot read in any filename. To generate a short MS-DOS–readable filename for a file, NTFS deletes all of these characters from the long filename and removes any spaces. Since an MS-DOS–readable filename can have only one period, NTFS also removes all extra periods from the filename. Next, NTFS truncates the filename, if necessary, to six characters and appends a tilde (~) and a number. For example, each nonduplicate filename is appended with **~1**. Duplicate filenames end with **~2**, **~3**, and so on. Filename extensions are truncated to three or fewer characters. Finally, when displaying filenames at the command line, NTFS translates all characters in the filename and extension to uppercase. (File Manager displays these filenames as lowercase.)

Windows NT 3.5 uses a slightly different method for creating short filenames when there are five or more files that would result in duplicate short filenames. For the fifth and subsequent files, Windows NT uses only the first two letters of the long filename and then generates the next four letters of the short filename by mathematically manipulating the remaining letters of the long filename, appending ~5 (or another number if necessary to avoid a duplicate filename) to the result. This method provides substantially improved performance when Windows NT must create short filenames for a large number of files with similar long filenames. Windows NT uses this method to create short filenames for both FAT and NTFS volumes.

By default, Windows NT 3.5 supports MS-DOS–readable filenames on all NTFS volumes. To improve performance on volumes with many long, similar names, you can disable this feature on all volumes. To disable short filename support on all NTFS volumes, set the NtfsDisable8dot3NameCreation parameter of the following Registry entry to 1:

```
HKEY_LOCAL_MACHINE\System\CurrentControlSet\Control\FileSystem
```

Windows NT does not generate short (eight-plus-three) filenames for files created by POSIX applications on an NTFS partition. This means that MS-DOS–based and Windows-based applications cannot view these filenames if they are not valid eight-plus-three filenames. If you want to use files that are created by a POSIX application with MS-DOS–based or Windows-based applications, be sure to use standard MS-DOS eight-plus-three naming conventions.

Viewing Short Filenames

Both File Manager and the **dir** command are able to display either the long NTFS filenames or the short MS-DOS–readable filenames, so you can look up and manipulate files using either long or short filenames.

To see short filenames from File Manager, choose Full File Details.

From the command line, to see both the long and short filenames for each file in the directory, type the following command:

```
dir /x
```

Tip To display both long and short filenames automatically, use the System application in Control Panel to set the **dircmd** variable to the value **/x**.

Multiple Data Streams

NTFS supports multiple data streams. The stream name identifies a new data attribute on the file. Streams have separate opportunistic locks, file locks, allocation sizes, and file sizes, but sharing is per file.

The following is an example of an alternate stream:

```
myfile.dat:stream2
```

This feature permits related data to be managed as a single unit. For example, Macintosh computers use this type of structure to manage resource and data forks. Or, a company might create a program to keep a list of changes to the file in an alternate stream, thus keeping archive information with the current version of the file.

As another example, a library of files might exist where the files are defined as alternate streams, as in the following example:

```
library:file1
       :file2
       :file3
```

Suppose a "smart" compiler creates a file structure like the following example:

```
program:source_file
       :doc_file
       :object_file
       :executable_file
```

Note Because NTFS is not supported on floppy disks, when you copy an NTFS file to a floppy disk, data streams and other attributes not supported by FAT are lost.

POSIX Compliance

POSIX compliance permits UNIX applications to be ported to Windows NT. Windows NT is fully compliant with the Institute of Electrical and Electronic Engineers (IEEE) standard 1003.1, which is a standard for file naming and identification.

The following POSIX-compliant features are included in NTFS:

- *Case-sensitive naming.* Under POSIX, README.TXT, Readme.txt, and readme.txt are all different files.

- *Hard links.* A file can be given more than one name. This allows two different filenames, which can be located in different directories, to point to the same data.

- *Additional time stamps.* These show when the file was last accessed or modified.

Caution   POSIX applications create case-sensitive filenames where two or more filenames can differ only in case (for example, annm.doc and AnnM.Doc).

While NTFS supports both case-preservation and case-sensitivity, you cannot use standard commands with NTFS to manage filenames that differ only in case. (*Standard* commands include those used at the command-line—such as **copy**, **del**, and **move**—and their File Manager equivalents.) For example, both annm.doc and AnnM.Doc are deleted if you type the following at the command prompt:

```
del AnnM.Doc
```

You must use POSIX applications to manage filenames that differ only in case.

For related information, see the section on the POSIX subsystem in Chapter 1, "Windows NT Architecture" and Chapter 17, "POSIX Compatibility."

NTFS Features Used by Macintosh Services Clients

Services for Macintosh is included with Windows NT Server. These services give Macintosh users access to files residing on a Windows NT Server, and since these files are available to Windows NT network users, the file server can be easily used for sharing files across platforms.

You must make an NTFS partition available when you enable Services for Macintosh if you want to automatically create the User Authentication Module volumes for Macintosh clients. (The Network Control Panel uses the first NTFS partition to create these default volumes.)

Macintosh clients can use only files on NTFS volumes. Macintosh resource forks and the Finder information for each Macintosh file are stored as NTFS streams. Because NTFS also supports long names, most Macintosh filenames are preserved.

Services for Macintosh stores File Sharing folder privileges as Windows NT permissions, meaning that there is only one set of permissions on a folder or file, which is enforced both for Windows NT users and Macintosh users. However, Macintosh users cannot see file permissions, since AppleShare® supports only folder permissions.

For more information about Services for Macintosh, see *Windows NT Server Services for Macintosh.*

NTFS System Files

NTFS includes several system files, all of which are hidden from view on the NTFS volume. A *system file* is one used by the file system to store its metadata and to implement the file system. System files are placed on the volume by the Format utility.

The NTFS system files are listed in Table 5.2.

Table 5.2   NTFS System Files

System file	Filename	Description
Master File Table	$Mft	A list of all contents of the NTFS volume.
Master File Table2	$MftMirr	A mirror of the important parts of the MFT, used to guarantee access to the MFT in the case of a single-sector failure.
Log File	$LogFile	A list of transaction steps, used by the Log File System for recoverability.
Volume	$Volume	The name, version, and other information about the volume.
Attribute Definitions	$AttrDef	A table of attribute names, numbers, and descriptions.
Root Filename Index	$.	Root directory.
Cluster Bitmap	$Bitmap	A representation of the volume showing which allocation units are in use.
Boot File	$Boot	Includes the bootstrap for the volume, if this is a bootable volume.
Bad Cluster File	$BadClus	A location where all the bad clusters in the volume are located.

Comparing NTFS with HPFS and FAT

NTFS takes the best parts of both FAT and HPFS and improves upon those designs. From FAT, NTFS borrowed the "simplicity yields performance" philosophy. Performance increases when the number of disk transfers is minimized for common operations. From HPFS, NTFS borrowed techniques for speed and flexibility. For example, NTFS uses B-trees similar to those used by HPFS to maximize performance.

NTFS supports both long and short (eight-plus-three) filenames for compatibility with MS-DOS, HPFS, and other networked clients including OS/2, UNIX, AppleShare, and NFS. NTFS also provides for multiple extended attributes and allows future applications to define other extended attributes.

NTFS offers data security on fixed and removable hard disks, a feature important to corporate users and other power users.

For example, suppose Joe has a removable hard disk on his computer. That hard disk is formatted as an NTFS volume and has security permissions that allow access only to Joe and to one other coworker in his domain, Ann. Ann works at the company's branch office. Joe removes the disk from his computer and sends it to Ann, who installs it in her computer. When she accesses the files on the disk, since Ann's computer is in the same domain as Joe's, she sees that the security mechanisms within the domain for the NTFS volume are intact.

Note Be sure to shut down the system before removing a disk containing an NTFS volume.

In addition to these features, NTFS provides a recovery system that is more reliable than either FAT or HPFS, and NTFS meets POSIX requirements.

The following table summarizes key features of FAT, HPFS, and NTFS as implemented on Windows NT:

Table 5.3   Comparison of FAT, HPFS, and NTFS

	FAT file system	HPFS	NTFS
Filename	Eight-plus-three ASCII characters [one period (delimiter) allowed]; on Windows NT 3.5, 255 Unicode characters [multiple periods (delimiters) allowed]	254 bytes of double-byte characters [multiple periods (delimiters) allowed]	255 Unicode characters [multiple periods (delimiters) allowed]
File size	2^{32} bytes	2^{32} bytes	2^{64} bytes
Partition	2^{32} bytes	2^{41} bytes	2^{64} bytes
Maximum path length	64; on Windows NT 3.5, no limit	No limit	No limit
Attributes	Only a few bit flags, plus a few bytes of extended attribute information on Windows NT 3.5	Bit flags plus up to 64K of extended-attribute information	Everything, including data, is treated as file attributes
Directories	Unsorted	B-tree	B-tree
Philosophy	Simple	Efficient on larger disks	Fast, recoverable, and secure
Built-in security features	No	No	Yes

The next section describes one other difference that distinguishes the FAT, HPFS, and NTFS file systems—that is, the way each file system ensures data integrity on the disk.

Data Integrity and Recoverability with File Systems

Until now, there were two types of file systems—careful-write file systems and lazy-write file systems. NTFS introduces a third type—a recoverable file system.

Careful-write File Systems

A *careful-write file system* is designed around the idea that it is important to keep the volume structure consistent. An example of a careful-write file system is FAT on MS-DOS.

A careful-write file system works in the following manner. When it's modifying the volume structure, it orders the disk writes. Most volume updates are made one at a time. Disk writes for each update are ordered so that if the system failed between two disk writes, the volume would be left in an understandable state with the possibility of an "expected" inconsistency. The disk remains usable. Running utilities such as **chkdsk** is rarely needed for a careful-write file system. (On FAT, for example, **chkdsk** is needed only to recover from system failure and provides a way to restore file system consistency quickly.)

The disadvantage of careful-write file systems is that serialized writes can be slow. This is because the first disk write must be completed and committed before the second disk write can begin, and so on. On a powerful computer, this is not the most efficient use of processing power.

Lazy-write File Systems

A second kind of file system, such as FAT on Windows NT and most UNIX file systems, is called a *lazy-write file system*. This type was designed to speed up disk access. Assuming that disk crashes were not a regular occurrence, a lazy-write file system was designed to use an intelligent cache-management strategy and provide a way to recover data (such as the **chkdsk** utility) should something happen to the disk.

All data is accessed via the disk cache. While the user searches directories or reads files, data to be written to disk is allowed to accumulate in the cache. Thus, the user never has to wait while disk-writes are performed. Plus, the user is able to access all the file-system resources that might otherwise be allocated for disk writing. Data gets written to disk when the computer's resources are in low demand, rather than in serial fashion.

If the same data is modified several times, all those modifications are captured in the disk cache. The result is that the file system needs to write to disk only once to update the data. That is, the file system opens the file once and then performs all of the updates together before closing the file.

The disadvantage of a lazy-write file system is that, in the event of a disk crash, recovery could take much longer than with a careful-write file system. This is because a utility such as **chkdsk** must then scan the entire volume to recover, checking what should have been written to disk against what actually was written.

Recoverable File Systems

NTFS is a third kind of file system—a *recoverable file system*. It combines the speed of a lazy-write file system with virtually instant recovery.

NTFS guarantees the consistency of the volume by using standard transaction logging and recovery techniques. It includes a lazy writing technique plus a system of volume recovery that takes typically only a second or two after the computer is rebooted. The transaction logging, which allows NTFS to recover quickly, requires a very small amount of overhead compared with careful-write file systems.

When used on a partition on a single device, NTFS can recover from a system crash, yet it may lose data as the result of an I/O error. In conjunction with the mirroring or parity striping support implemented by the fault tolerance driver (described later in this chapter), NTFS can survive any single point of failure. The NTFS partition still remains accessible, though potentially not bootable. That is, even if the boot sector is lost and the bootstrap cannot transfer control to the NTFS copy of the boot sector, you can still boot the computer from another partition or another physical drive and can still access the NTFS partition.

NTFS also supports hot-fixing, so that if an error occurs because of a bad sector, the file system moves the information to a different sector and marks the original sector as bad. This is transparent to any applications performing disk I/O. Hot-fixing eliminates error messages such as the "Abort, Retry, or Fail?" error message that occurs when a file system such as FAT encounters a bad sector.

However, when NTFS is used on a fault-tolerant device and an error is detected on one copy of a cluster, data can be recovered. The bad cluster is migrated to the Bad Cluster File, and it is replaced by another cluster. Then a copy of the original data is written to the new cluster.

Note NTFS supports cluster sizes of 512, 1024, 2048, and 4096.

Although the **format** command automatically selects an appropriate cluster size based on its examination of your disk, you can use the **/a** option to specify a particular cluster size. Type **format /?** at the command line for more syntax information.

For more information about using fault tolerance with Windows NT, see "Windows NT Fault-Tolerance Mechanisms," later in this chapter.

Data Integrity and Recoverability with NTFS

Each I/O operation that modifies a file on the NTFS volume is viewed by the file system as a transaction and can be managed as an atomic unit.

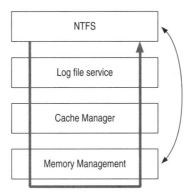

Figure 5.7   Interaction Between NTFS and Other Windows NT Components

When a user updates a file, the Log File Service logs all redo and undo information for the transaction. For recoverability, *redo* is the information that tells NTFS how to repeat the transaction, and *undo* tells how to roll back the transaction that was incomplete or that had an error.

If a transaction completes successfully, the file update is committed. If the transaction is incomplete, NTFS ends or rolls back the transaction by following instructions in the undo information. If NTFS detects an error in the transaction, the transaction is also rolled back.

File system recovery is straightforward with NTFS. If the system crashes, NTFS performs three passes—an *analysis pass*, a *redo pass*, and an *undo pass*. During the analysis pass, NTFS appraises the damage and determines exactly which clusters must now be updated, per the information in the log file. The redo pass performs all transaction steps logged from the last checkpoint. The undo pass backs out any incomplete (uncommitted) transactions.

Lazy Commit

Lazy commit is an important feature of NTFS. It allows NTFS to minimize the cost of logging to maintain high performance.

Lazy commit is similar to lazy write. Instead of using resources to mark a transaction as successfully completed as soon as it is performed, the commitment information is cached and written to the log as a background process. If the power source and/or computer system should fail before the commit is logged, NTFS will recheck the transaction to see whether it was successfully completed. If NTFS cannot guarantee that the transaction was completed successfully, it backs out the transaction. No incomplete modifications to the volume are allowed.

Periodic Log File Checkpoints

Every few seconds, NTFS checks the cache to determine the status of the lazy writer and marks the status as a checkpoint in the log. If the system crashes subsequent to that checkpoint, the system knows to back up to that checkpoint for recovery. This method provides for more expedient recovery times by saving the amount of queries that are required during recovery.

Note This level of recoverability protects metadata. User data can still be corrupted in the case of power and/or system failure.

Disk Organization and Disk Management

Windows NT offers a number of disk management techniques that you can use to organize and safeguard data on your disks:

- You can choose how many physical disks and logical disk partitions your system will have. You can also choose whether you want to use volume sets or stripe sets to organize data across partitions.

- You can choose from among several fault-tolerance options to ensure data reliability on your system.

- You can employ other data backup and recovery techniques, such as tape backups and use of uninterruptible power supplies, to further safeguard against data loss.

The remainder of this chapter discusses using these techniques to improve disk performance and to ensure data reliability and security.

Logical Organization: Partitions, Volume Sets, and Stripe Sets

A physical disk can be arranged into one or more logical partitions. Each partition or set of partitions is formatted for a particular file system as a volume and assigned a drive letter. The *primary partition* is the portion of a physical disk that can be used by an operating system. Each disk can have as many as four partitions, one of which may be an extended partition.

Extended partitions can be subdivided into logical drives; primary partitions can't be subdivided. The free space in an extended partition can also be used to create volume sets or other kinds of volumes for fault-tolerance purposes. (Fault-tolerance options are described later in this chapter.) So long as the disk does not contain the boot partition, it can be used entirely as an extended partition.

Note On RISC–based computers, the primary partition created by the manufacturer's configuration program must be FAT.

Creating a *volume set* is simply a way of combining multiple areas of free space and formatting it into a single logical disk with a single drive letter. You can use the Disk Administrator utility to create and extend volume sets. Each volume set can include up to 32 areas of free space from one or more physical disks or partitions. Volume sets are organized so that the free space on one disk is filled before free space on the next disk in the set is used. Using volume sets does not increase disk performance. Only volume sets formatted with NTFS can be extended. A volume set cannot contain mirrored or striped components in its composition.

Disk striping (that is, the use of *stripe sets*) is a way to increase disk performance, as shown in Figure 5.8. You can create stripe sets using the Disk Administrator utility. This method increases both read and write performance since multiple I/O commands can be active on the drives at the same time. A striped set can have from 2 to 32 disks. If the disks are different sizes, the smallest is used as the common partition size. The remaining free space may be used individually or in a volume set.

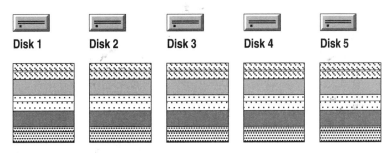

Figure 5.8   Disk Striping Across Physical Disks

Note that disk striping is different from the Windows NT Server method called *disk striping with parity* (described later in this chapter). Disk striping in Windows NT provides no parity stripe. Because the parity stripe is not present, the set is not fault tolerant. Once a stripe has been lost, there is no way to recover it. Some disk drivers do provide i-drive hot-fix capabilities that can be used to help ensure the safety of the data.

Running chkdsk on an NTFS Volume

Each time you boot Windows NT, it performs an autocheck routine. If this routine detects a dirty volume, it automatically runs the **chkdsk /f** command to fix the inconsistency or error. (Note that it is normal for **chkdsk** to report consistency errors on an NTFS drive containing the pagefile.) As long as no specific files are listed as being damaged and no other errors are detected, the volume will be marked clean, and there is rarely a need to force a **chkdsk /f**.

If the **chkdsk** command locates files or directories that have lost pointers to their parent directory, they are named FILE###.CHK and DIR###.CHK, respectively, and housed in the FOUND### directory of the NTFS volume.

If you run **chkdsk /f** from the command line and see the message "Cannot lock the current drive," you should simply make another drive current. For example, if you are trying to run **chkdsk /f** for drive D, type **C:** to make drive C the current drive, and then type the following command:

```
chkdsk d: /f
```

Note If Windows NT is unable to run the **chkdsk /f** command (for example, because you want to run it on the boot partition or because someone is accessing the partition from the network), Windows NT prompts you whether you would like the autocheck routine to run with **chkdsk /f** upon reboot.

Changing the File System on a Partition

There are three ways to establish a new file system on a disk partition:

- Specify the file system for the boot partition during the installation process.
- Use the **format** utility and specify the file system for the partition.
- Use the **convert** utility to convert a partition from FAT or HPFS to NTFS. This leaves the existing files intact.

With the **format** utility, you can format a partition as an NTFS volume by specifying the **/fs:ntfs** option. Using the **format** utility destroys all existing files on the partition.

With the **convert** utility, you can convert an existing partition from FAT or HPFS to NTFS without destroying files. You cannot convert from NTFS to another file system. To convert a volume to the NTFS file system, type the **convert** command using this form, where E: is the partition you want to convert:

```
convert e: /fs:ntfs
```

The **convert** utility can be used on the boot partition of non-RISC–based computers, as well as on secondary partitions. However, the **convert** utility cannot convert the boot partition while it is in use. Instead, if you specify the active partition, an entry is added to the Registry so that the **convert** utility is run the next time the system is booted.

Caution You must not convert the boot partition to NTFS on a RISC–based computer. This is because the firmware on RISC-based computers loads the first system files in the Windows NT boot process, and the firmware understands only the FAT file system. Converting the boot partition would therefore make the computer unable to boot. If you want to use NTFS on a RISC-based computer, create a small boot partition (1 MB or larger) to hold the HAL.DLL and OSLOADER.EXE files. The rest of the disk can be used as an NTFS partition. The installer correctly puts the HAL.DLL and OSLOADER files on the boot partition.

If someone mistakenly converts the RISC–based boot partition to NTFS, run the ARCINST.EXE utility from the install CD-ROM and reformat the boot partition as FAT.

The **convert** utility works in only one direction, so you cannot use it to change your file system from NTFS back to FAT or HPFS format. Instead, you must reformat the NTFS drive using the **format** command. (Be sure to back up any files you want to preserve before using the **format** command.)

Remember, though, that you cannot use the Windows NT **format** command on the system partition. If Windows NT is installed on the NTFS partition, you can reformat the drive by following these steps:

1. Start Windows NT Setup.
2. Choose Custom Installation.
3. When Setup prompts you to select the partition where you would like to install Windows NT, highlight the NTFS drive, and type **P** to delete the partition.
4. Continue using the Setup program to recreate and format the partition.

Windows NT Fault-Tolerance Mechanisms

Windows NT Server offers several fault tolerance mechanisms:

- Tape backup support (available for both Windows NT and Windows NT server)
- Uninterruptible Power Supply support
- Disk mirroring
- Disk duplexing
- Disk striping with parity

Some of these can be used within any file system and some with only specific file systems. Restrictions are specified in the following sections, which provide more details about fault-tolerance mechanisms offered by Windows NT. For more information about how to use Windows NT with uninterruptible power supply (UPS) units and tape backup, see the *Windows NT Server Concepts and Planning Guide.*

Disk Mirroring

Disk mirroring is a method that protects against hard disk failure. Any file system—including FAT, HPFS, and NTFS—can make use of disk mirroring. Disk mirroring uses two partitions on different drives connected to the same disk controller. All data on the first (primary) partition is mirrored automatically onto the secondary partition. Thus, if the primary disk fails, no data is lost. Instead, the partition on the secondary disk is used.

Mirroring is not restricted to a partition identical to the primary partition in size, number of tracks and cylinders, and so on. This eliminates the problem of acquiring an identical model drive to replace a failed drive when an entire drive is being mirrored. For practical purposes, though, the mirrored partitions will usually be created to be the same size as the primary partition. The mirrored partition cannot be smaller. However, if the mirrored partition is larger than the primary, the extra space is wasted.

Disk Duplexing

Disk duplexing is simply a mirrored pair with an additional adapter on the secondary drive. This provides fault tolerance for both disk and controller failure. (The use of multiple adapters connecting to one drive is not supported.) In addition to providing fault tolerance, this can also improve performance.

Like mirroring, duplexing is performed at the partition level. To the Windows NT operating system, there is no difference between mirroring and duplexing. It is simply a matter of where the other partition can be found.

Disk Striping with Parity

Disk striping with parity is a method where multiple partitions are combined as a single logical drive (like disk striping, described earlier). As illustrated in Figure 5.9, the partitions are arranged in a way that ensures multiple single points of failure in the array.

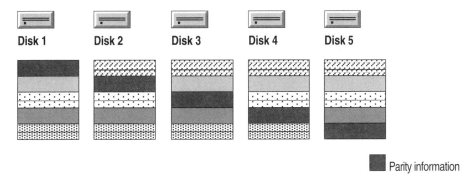

Parity information

Figure 5.9   Disk Striping with Parity

There must be at least three disks and no more than 32 disks in a striped set with parity. A partition of approximately the same size must be selected from each disk. The disks can be on the same or different controllers. SCSI disks (that is, CD-ROMs) are best since advanced recovery features such as bad block remapping can be used during the recovery process. Data is written in stripes across all partitions in the set. In addition to the data, a parity stripe is written interleaved with the data stripes. The parity stripe is simply a byte parity of the data stripes at a given stripe level or row.

For example, suppose you have five disks in the striped set. At level 0, you have stripe block 0 on disk 0, 1 on 1, 2 on 2, and 3 on 3, and the parity (eXclusive OR, XOR) of the stripe blocks on disk 4. The size of the stripes (also called *striping factor*) is currently 64K. The size of the parity stripe is the size of the data stripes. On the next row, the parity stripe is on disk 0. Data is on the rest of the disks. Because the parity stripes are not all on the same disk, there is no single point of failure for the set, and the load is evenly distributed.

When using any of the fault-tolerant disk schemes, Windows NT uses a device driver called FTDISK.SYS to receive commands and respond appropriately based on the type of fault tolerance that is being used. Thus, when the file system generates a request to read a section of a file, the normal disk system receives the request from the file system and passes it to the FTDISK.SYS driver. This driver then determines the stripe the data is in. From this and the information on the number of disks in the set, the disk and location on the disk are located. The data is read into memory. Striping can actually increase read performance since each disk in the set can have an outstanding read at the same time.

Writing to a parity striped set is a little more difficult. First the original data from the stripe that is to be written must be read along with the parity information for that stripe level. The differences in the parity information are calculated. The differences are added to the parity stripe. Finally, both the parity and the new information are written to disks. The reads and the writes can be issued concurrently since they must be on different disks, by design.

Fault Tolerance with Parity Striping

There are two general cases of fault tolerance with parity striping.

The first case is when a data stripe is no longer readable. Though the data stripe is not readable, the system may still function. When the bad data stripe is to be read, all of the remaining good data stripes are read along with the parity stripe. Each data stripe is subtracted (with XOR) from the parity stripe; the order isn't important. The result is the missing data stripe. Writing is a little more complicated but works very much the same way. All the data stripes are read and backed out of the parity stripe, leaving the missing data stripe. The modifications needed to the parity stripe can now be calculated and made. Since the system knows the data stripe is bad, it is not written; only the parity stripe is written.

The other general case is when a parity stripe is lost. During data reads this does not present a problem. The parity stripe is not used during normal reads. Writes become much less complicated as well. Since there is no way to maintain the parity stripe, the writes behave as a data stripe write without parity. The parity stripe can be recalculated during regeneration.

Identifying When a Set Is Broken

The process of error detection and recovery is very similar for both mirrored sets and parity striped sets. The exact system response to the problem depends on when the problem occurred.

A *broken set* is defined as any time one or the other partition in a mirrored or duplexed set cannot be written, or any time a stripe can no longer be written.

When an I/O error is first detected, the system performs some routines in an attempt to keep the set from breaking. The system's first priority is to try reassigning the sector that failed. This is done by issuing a command to remap the sector to the disk.

Windows NT attempts remapping only if the disk is supported by a small computer standard interface (SCSI) controller. SCSI devices are designed to support the concept of remapping. This is why SCSI devices work well as fault-tolerant devices. (Note that some fixed hard disk devices also support the concept of remapping, but there is no standard for this support.)

If the disk does not support sector mapping, or if the other attempts to maintain the set fail, a high severity error is logged to the event log.

The partition that has failed is called an *orphan*. It is important to note that the process of orphaning a partition does not occur during a read, only during writes. This is because the read cannot possibly affect the data on the disks, so performing orphan processing would be superfluous.

During system initialization, if the system cannot locate each partition in a mirrored set, a severe error is recorded in the event log, and the remaining partition of the mirror is used. If the partition is part of a parity striped set, a severe error is recorded in the event log, and the partition is marked as an orphan. The system then continues to function using the fault-tolerant capabilities inherent in such sets.

If all of the partitions within a set cannot be located, the drive is not activated, but the partitions are not marked as orphans. This saves recovery time for simple problems like disconnecting the SCSI chain from the computer.

Recovering Orphans

When a partition is marked as an orphan, the system continues processing until a replacement disk or partition is available to recover from the problem and ensure fault tolerance again. A set with an orphan is not fault tolerant. Another failure in the set can, and most likely will, cause the loss of data.

Recovery procedures should be performed as soon as the problem is discovered.

▶ **To recover**

1. Break the mirror-set relationship using the Break Mirror option in the Disk Administrator utility.

2. This converts the remaining active partition of the set into an "normal" partition. This partition receives the drive letter of the set. The orphan partition receives the next available drive letter.

3. You can then create a new set relationship with existing free space on another disk in the local computer, or replace the orphan drive and reestablish the relationship with space from this disk.

4. Once the relationship is established, restart the computer.

5. During the system initialization, the data from the original good partition is copied over to the new mirrored partition.

When a member of a parity striped set is orphaned, it can be regenerated from the remaining data. This uses the same logic discussed earlier for the dynamic regeneration of data from the parity and remaining stripes. Select a new free space area that is as large as the other members in the set. Then choose the Regenerate command from the Fault Tolerance menu. When the system is restarted, the missing stripes are recalculated and written to the new space provided.

For more information about using Windows NT fault-tolerance features, see the *Windows NT Server Concepts and Planning Guide.*

CHAPTER 6

Printing

Windows NT is the first operating system that truly supports remote printing. There is no need to manually install a printer driver on the local workstation before printing with Windows NT. For Windows NT users, printer resources seem to be provided automatically from each application, and the Windows NT printing model allows users to simply "point and print."

How Windows NT prints a document is somewhat more complicated than the user's "point and print" perspective. The real power of the Windows NT printing model is in the components transparent to the user.

This chapter starts by clarifying the terminology used in Windows NT printing. Next are sections on subjects you should understand before exploring the Windows NT printing model, such as tips on using Print Manager to successfully perform certain tasks, and discussions of Windows NT printer drivers and print job data types. Next is an explanation of what each component of the printing model does, followed by descriptions of the flow of control through this model in several common situations. Finally, the chapter includes information about managing security and manipulating forms on a print server, and a question-and-answer section.

Printing Terms

In Window NT, a *print device* refers to the actual hardware device that produces printed output. A *printer* refers to the software interface between the application and print device.

In Windows NT terminology, a *queue* is just a group of documents waiting to be printed. In the NetWare and OS/2 environments, queues are the primary software interface between the application and print device: users submit print jobs to a queue. However, with Windows NT the printer is that interface—the job is sent to a printer, not a queue.

Network-interface printers are printers with their own network cards; they need not be adjacent to a print server since they are directly connected to the network.

Print device resolution is measured in *dots per inch* (DPI). The greater the DPI, the better the resolution.

Print jobs are classified into *data types* based on what modifications the spooler should make to the job (if any). For instance, one data type implies that the spooler should not modify the job at all; another data type implies that the spooler should add a form feed to the end of the job, and so on.

Rendering means converting a print job from whatever commands the application uses to describe output into commands that a print device understands.

The terms *workstation* and *server* refer to two different roles in over-the-network printing. The workstation is the computer that sends print jobs over the network; the server is the computer that receives print jobs. Do not confuse these terms with Windows NT Workstation and Windows NT Server. Both Windows NT Workstation and Windows NT Server can operate in either workstation or server roles. However, because Windows NT Workstation is limited to 10 connections from other computers, it does not make a practical print server except in small-network situations. Unless otherwise specified, all topics in this chapter apply equally to both Windows NT Workstation and Windows NT Server.

Spooling means writing the contents of a print job to a file on disk. This file is called a *spool file*. *Despooling* means reading the contents from a spool file, and then sending those contents to a print device.

Print Manager Tips

You use Print Manager to create local printers, connect to other servers' printers, install and configure printer drivers, share printers on the network, pause printers and documents, and configure spooler options.

Most of these tasks are straightforward, and you can find the information you need by using the online help or the Windows NT documentation. But a couple of Print Manager issues are a little trickier, and are discussed in the following sections. These issues are deciding which method to use to establish a printer, and determining which printer driver configuration dialog box to use for certain configuration options.

Establishing Printers

There are two ways to establish a printer in Print Manager. Which you should use depends on the location of the print device relative to the computer on which you are establishing the printer.

- To establish a printer for a print device directly attached to your Windows NT-based computer, use the Create Printer command from the Printer menu.

   With this method, you choose the printer driver you want, and then set the initial driver configuration. Thereafter, jobs from locally-run Windows-based applications are assigned the journal data type. In practical terms, this means that applications will regain control quickly after printing; a marked improvement over the way Windows 3.1 manages print jobs. For more information on the data types such as journal, see "Data Types" later in this chapter.

- To establish a printer for a network print server that your Windows NT-based computer sends print jobs to, use the Connect To Printer command from the Printer menu.

   When you use this method, print jobs spool on the print server, not on the local Windows NT-based computer. Jobs sent from locally-run Windows-based applications are assigned the RAW data type, which means that the application does not regain control until the print job is fully rendered. (This situation is essentially the same situation as when using Windows 3.1 or Windows for Workgroups 3.11).

   If the network print server you establish a connection to runs Windows NT, the server automatically downloads the proper printer driver to your computer. This saves you the trouble of installing the driver manually and keeps you from accidentally choosing the wrong driver. If the print server does not run Windows NT, then Print Manager prompts you to manually install the printer driver.

The following table summarizes the differences between using the Create and Connect To commands.

Table 6.1   Using the Create Printer and Connect To Printer Commands

	Create	Connect To
Intended for	Printers under this computer's direct control	Printers controlled by a remote print server
Driver installation	User must manually install driver on the Windows NT-based computer	Windows NT print servers automatically download driver; other print servers cannot download the driver, requiring the user to manually install the driver.
Spool file location	On this Windows NT-based computer	On the print server
Print jobs from locally-run Windows-based applications use which data type	Journal	RAW
Locally-run Windows-based applications regain control	Before job is fully rendered	After job is fully rendered

Configuring the Printer Driver

There are two dialog boxes in Print Manager that you can use to configure Windows NT printer drivers. You access both dialog boxes by selecting the printer you want to configure, and then choosing Properties from the Printer menu.

The resulting Printer Properties dialog box has a Setup button and a Details button, among others. By choosing Details you can then choose several other options, including Job Defaults.

- Choosing the Setup button displays a Printer Setup dialog box that you can use to tell the spooler how the print device's hardware is configured. For instance, you can specify what forms are loaded in the device's trays, or how much memory is installed in the device, or how a plotter's pens are arranged.

- Choosing the Job Defaults button displays a Document Properties dialog box that you can use to define default settings. For instance, it enables you to define which form Windows-based applications should use by default, whether to print portrait or landscape, and at what resolution to print. Many Windows-based applications have a Print Setup option; that option usually displays the Job Defaults dialog box.

As a general rule, use the Setup button to set options that affect every job sent to the print device. Use the Job Defaults option to provide default values that network users are free to change from one job to the next.

For more information on the what Windows NT printer drivers do and how they are composed, see the following section.

Windows NT Printer Drivers

In Windows NT, the printer driver retrieves configuration information from the server and provides WYSIWYG (What You See Is What You Get) support for workstation applications. Some WYSIWYG applications, such as Microsoft Word for Windows, request the printer driver at application startup.

This section details how Windows NT printer drivers work and what components they are made of; for more information on how printer drivers work in the Windows NT print model, see "Clients," later in this chapter.

Printer drivers are composed of three separate files:

- A printer graphics driver (for example, PSCRIPT.DLL, RASDD.DLL, or PLOTTER.DLL). Graphics drivers are responsible for print rendering (converting DDI commands from the graphics engine into printer commands that a printer can understand). Each graphics driver handles different printer languages. For instance, PSCRIPT.DLL deals with the PostScript printer language, PLOTTER.DLL deals with the HPGL/2 language used by many plotters, and RASDD.DLL deals with printer languages based on raster (bitmap) images, including PCL and most dot matrix printer languages.

- A printer interface driver (for example, PSCRPTUI.DLL, RASDDUI.DLL, or PLOTUI.DLL). This DLL includes the user interface you see when you configure a printer in Print Manager. It is called by the client side of the router (WINSPOOL.DRV). For more information on the router, see "Router" later in this chapter.

- A characterization data file (for example, a .PPD file for a PostScript driver, a minidriver for the Universal driver, or a .PCD file for the plotter driver). This component is used by the other two pieces of the print driver as needed. It provides information about the configuration capabilities of a specific make and model of print device. For instance, it knows what resolutions the print device is capable of, whether it can print on both sides of the page (called *duplex printing*), what paper sizes it can accept and what those sizes are named, and so on. Raster minidrivers and .PCD files are source-code compatible across processors and platforms, and .PPD files are binary-compatible across processors and platforms.

These three files work as a unit. For example, when you create a new printer in Print Manager, the interface driver enables you to pick the default resolution. It displays the proper choices because it queries the characterization data file for this information. When you print, the graphics driver queries the interface driver to find what resolution you chose, so that it can create the right printer commands to generate the resolution you specified.

Note The graphics driver, the interface driver, and most characterization data files are not binary compatible across processors. If Windows NT clients are to download the correct driver from a Windows NT print server, you must install drivers on the print server for each processor type that your clients have. For instance, if you have x86-based clients running Windows NT, and you have an Alpha AXP-based print server, you must install x86 printer drivers on the print server.

Printer Drivers Included with Windows NT

Windows NT includes three printer drivers: the Universal printer driver, a PostScript printer driver, and an HPGL/2 plotter driver.

The Universal printer driver is an improved version of the Windows 3.1 driver and supports raster-graphics printing. It includes support for scalable TrueType fonts, device fonts, compression/run length encoding (RLE), and Tag Image File Format (TIFF) version 4.0. It also includes mechanisms that provide for smaller, more efficient bitmaps. These mechanisms include ignoring whitespace and supporting *rules*, which are printable rectangles extracted from the bitmap and sent to the printer as a separate command as supported by Hewlett-Packard LaserJet and compatible printers.

The Windows NT PostScript driver supports Adobe version 4.0-compatible PostScript Printer Description (.PPD) files. (Windows NT does not use the .WPD or .MPD files used by Windows 3.1.) This driver supports key features, including binary transfer compression, from Level II.

The Windows NT plotter driver supports a variety of plotters that use the HPGL/2 language. Note that there is a significant difference between HPGL and HPGL/2, and that the output from the Windows NT plotter driver assumes that plotting device understands all of the enhancements built into the HPGL/2 language.

Characterization Data Files

Characterization data files provide model-specific information about print devices. When hardware vendors release new print devices, a characterization data file for the new device is all you need to use that device with Windows NT. If Windows NT does not supply such a file for your print device, check the device's users' guide for a list of emulations. If your device emulates a device for which Windows NT supplies a driver, then you may be able to use this driver to get output.

Note If you use an emulation and your device does not function *exactly* like the device it emulates, then you may get incorrect output. If this happens, try sending the same output to the device for which the driver was designed. If the problem still occurs, contact the third-party driver vendor. If the problem is solved, contact your hardware vendor for information on correcting their emulation problems.

Raster minidrivers are actually DLLs. The Windows NT Raster printer driver can read most Windows 3.1 minidriver DLLs (those created for UNIDRV.DLL) directly with no porting required. Raster minidrivers contain printer-specific information but do not contain executable code, except for a few rare instances (such as Toshiba and C. Itoh drivers).

The PostScript driver uses standard Adobe PostScript .PPD files as characterization data files. These files include printer-specific information for a particular printer model and are available from the printer's manufacturer. Unlike Windows 3.1, the Windows NT PostScript printer driver can directly interpret .PPD files. Because PostScript printers are included with .PPD files, when new PostScript printers become available, they will be ready for use with Windows NT.

Plotter .PCD files are similar in function to raster minidrivers. They are dynamic link libraries (DLLs), which provide device-specific information to the graphics driver. Unlike raster minidrivers, .PCD files are specific to Windows NT: Windows NT cannot use plotter drivers built for Windows 3.1.

As a general rule, the third-party PostScript hardware vendors are responsible for creating new .PPD files. Included with this resource kit is a PRINTER.INF file you can modify to install newly released .PPD files.

Data Types

Every print job is assigned a data type, which indicates how a Windows NT print server should modify the job (if at all). The data types that Windows NT supports are summarized in the following table:

Table 6.2   The data types for print jobs

Data type	Assumptions	Print Processor's Action
RAW	The job is already fully rendered.	Don't alter the job at all.
RAW [FF Auto]	The job is simple text sent by an application that does not add a form feed to the end of its jobs.	Add a PCL command to produce a form feed at the end of the job.
RAW [FF Appended]	The job is simple text sent by an application that does not add a form feed to the end of its jobs.	Add a PCL command to produce a form feed at the end of the job, unless a simple check indicates a form feed is already there.
TEXT	The job is simple text. This data type is most useful with print devices that don't accept simple text as a valid print job, such as PostScript print devices, or plotters.	Use GDI and the Windows NT printer driver to create a print job that prints the original job's text on the target print device.
Journal (NT JNL 1.000)	A Windows NT-based application running locally on the print server sent this job, and the job is already halfway rendered into printer commands.	Use the graphics engine and the printer driver to finish rendering the job into printer commands.
PSCRIPT1	The job is PostScript code from a Macintosh client, targeted for a non-PostScript print device.	Interpret the PostScript code, creating a bitmap which GDI and the printer driver can convert into the target device's language.

Print clients set their jobs' data type to RAW, journal, or PSCRIPT1. If the job is RAW, then you can use the Default Data type option in Print Manager to use RAW [FF Auto], RAW [FF Appended], or TEXT. However, if the job is already marked journal or PSCRIPT1, the Default Data type setting is ignored.

Windows NT Printing Model

Windows NT has a modular printing architecture. The modularity makes Windows NT an ideal printing platform because third-party software developers can meet specialized needs by adding one or two modules, leaving the others in place. The modular structure is generally transparent to people using the system.

This section describes the Windows NT printing model. The main focus is on how jobs are handled when Windows NT acts as a print server, with additional information about how Windows NT acts as a print client.

Overview of Print Components

Figure 6.1 shows the main components used to process jobs on a Windows NT print server. The components are arranged from top to bottom; the components on top use the services of the components below them. For example, print clients use the services of the router, which in turn uses the services of a print provider, and so on.

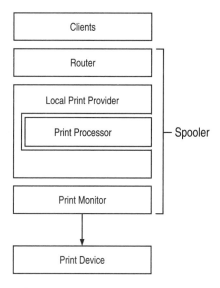

Figure 6.1   Components Used to Process Jobs on a Windows NT Print Server

The components below the clients are collectively called the *spooler*.

Note In Windows NT 3.5, the spooler components are implemented as a service, which you can stop and restart from the Services icon in Control Panel or from the command line by using the **net stop spooler** and **net start spooler** commands.

The following list briefly explains each of the components in Figure 6.1. Following sections discuss each component in more detail.

- *Clients* are any applications that send jobs to the spooler. Clients include locally-run applications (both Windows-based applications and non-Windows-based applications), as well as applications running on other computers, which send print jobs over the network to a Windows NT print server.

- The *router* accepts requests from clients, determines which spooler component should handle the request, and then sends the request to that component.

- There are actually two types of print providers; local and remote. The *local print provider* manages spool files and processes separator pages. It also determines the data type of each job and sends the job to the print processor responsible for that data type. The print provider then determines which print monitor is responsible for the output port. In addition to the local print provider, there are also *remote print providers*, which transfer jobs from the Windows NT print server to MS-Network print servers or NetWare print servers.

- One or more *print processors* are available to modify print jobs of different data types. When they're finished modifying the job, they give control back to the print provider; this is why this component is embedded within the print provider in Figure 6.1.

- *Print monitors* are responsible for transmitting print jobs to different types of print devices. For instance, one print monitor sends jobs to local devices like parallel and serial ports, and other print monitors send jobs to different kinds of network interface printers.

Clients

Clients are those applications which request the spooler's services. These include applications running on the local computer; workstations on the network that send jobs to a Windows NT print server; and the Print Manager application.

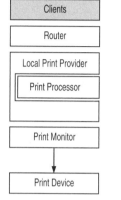

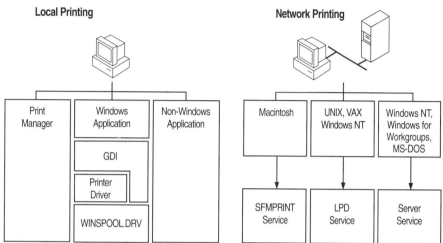

Figure 6.2   The Client Component

Local Applications

Local print clients are any applications running on the local computer that send a print job while running on a Windows NT-based computer. These include both 16-bit and 32-bit Windows-based applications, and non-Windows-based applications.

Windows-based Applications

Windows-based applications are different from nearly all other printing clients, because they depend on the Graphics Device Interface (GDI) and the Windows NT printer driver. These applications rely on Windows NT to create their print jobs, whereas other printing clients rely on Windows NT only to transfer their jobs to the appropriate print device.

The graphics engine (GDI32.DLL) is the printing component that provides WYSIWYG support across devices. The graphics engine communicates with Windows-based applications through the Graphics Device Interface (GDI) and with printer drivers through the Device Driver Interface (DDI).

When a Windows-based application prints, it describes the output it wants in a series of GDI commands. The graphics engine is responsible for translating these GDI commands into the DDI commands understood by components like printer drivers and print processors.

The graphics engine also communicates with the printer driver to find out what the printer's capabilities are. Then the graphics engine instructs the printer driver about which characters, fonts, locations, and point sizes to print and when.

The graphics engine can also query the printer driver about the fonts supported. Then, using that information, the graphics engine uses other DDI commands to specify the positioning of each character in the document by the print device. The graphics engine also uses DDI commands to define how the printer should draw and fill graphics, and how to manipulate and print bitmaps.

The graphics engine provides services to the printer driver, including compatibility with the environment subsystem (MS-DOS, OS/2, and so on), performance optimization, caching, client-server communications, and ANSI-to-Unicode conversion.

The graphics engine communicates with the spooler to determine which data type the graphics engine should spool. If the specified data type is *RAW*, the graphics engine calls the printer driver to render the DDI calls. If the data type is *journal*, the graphics engine writes a journal file and does not call the printer driver to render the DDI calls.

When the graphics engine passes the journal file to the spooler, spooling happens quickly because journal files are small and there is no wait for printer-specific rendering. (Rendering is done later as a background process.) Although journal files contain DDI calls rather than printer commands, they are device-dependent.

The graphics engine calls the printer driver and provides information about the type of printer needed and the data type used. In response, the printer driver provides the graphics engine with the printer's fully qualified path name for the printer and printer-setting information. This information is passed to the spooler.

Journal files differ from metafiles. Windows NT does not spool metafiles because they are device-independent and thus do not translate reliably to an individual printer's page layout. Metafiles are pictures, not pages. In addition, metafiles often contain a list of "acceptable" font and color substitutions for a document. For WYSIWYG accuracy, such color and font substitutions are unacceptable. In contrast, use of journal files guarantees that Windows NT provides true reproduction of spooled document.

Journal files are concise and precise. They only contain calls that make a difference. For example, some applications add hundreds of unnecessary and/or redundant instructions for creating a graphic. The journal file includes only those necessary to draw that picture.

Journal files are tuned for a particular device; they are not device-independent. For example, a journal file created for a 150-DPI LaserJet® printer cannot print on a 300-DPI LaserJet printer. A journal file is created to play back on a specific device and therefore is tuned for the device's specific coordinate space, color space, bits-per-pixel, fonts, and so on.

Non-Windows-based Applications

Non-Windows-based applications running on Windows NT-based computers are not aware of the Windows NT printing model; in particular, they are not aware of Windows NT printer drivers, they cannot make use of them, and the Windows NT driver does not get involved during the job's processing.

If you print from a non-Windows-based application, and the port it prints to is spooled, then the spooler components will take control of the job, much like other client's jobs. However, if the job is sent to a port that isn't spooled, the job goes directly to the device driver responsible for the port, for example, PARALLEL.SYS. A port is spooled if any printer defined in Print Manager prints to that port, or if you have issued a NET USE <portname> command in a Windows NT command prompt.

Remote Print Clients

The second type of print client is remote workstations that send print jobs over the network to a Windows NT print server. The most interesting of these are clients running operating systems other than Windows NT. This section concentrates on those clients: downlevel Microsoft Network clients, Macintosh clients, and UNIX clients. For information on what happens when a Windows NT client sends a print job to a printer controlled by another Windows NT-based computer, see "Remote Print Providers," later in this chapter.

The spooler on the Windows NT print server does not care what kind of application the remote client is running. In most cases, the Windows NT printer driver does not get involved in processing print jobs from remote non-Windows-NT clients. The two exceptions are when jobs sent from Macintosh clients to non-PostScript print devices and when jobs from UNIX or downlevel clients are sent to printers whose default data type has been set to TEXT.

Downlevel Clients

Computers on the network running Windows for Workgroups, Windows 3.1, or MS-DOS are referred to as *downlevel* clients. Any downlevel client that can send a job to a Windows for Workgroups print server or LAN Manager print server can also send jobs to a Windows NT print server.

The Windows NT Server service receives jobs from these clients and passes them to the spooler without alteration. Regardless of what kind of application created the print job on the downlevel client, the job is assigned the RAW data type when it reaches the spooler. In general, the printer driver installed on the Windows NT print server does not get involved with processing jobs from downlevel clients.

Macintosh clients

Because Windows NT Services for Macintosh is required for Macintosh clients to send print jobs to printers controlled by Windows NT-based computers, Macintosh clients cannot print to printers controlled by Windows NT Workstation computers. Windows NT Server, running Services for Macintosh, is required to make printers available to Macintosh clients.

Macintosh clients usually print using a PostScript driver, so their print jobs consist of PostScript commands. Jobs sent to PostScript print devices are assigned the RAW data type, and the Windows NT printer driver does not help process the print job. Macintosh print jobs sent to non-PostScript print devices are assigned the Pscript1 data type, which causes Windows NT Server to convert the job from PostScript to the print device's native language. In this case, the Windows NT printer driver is involved in processing the job.

UNIX

Windows NT can also receive print jobs sent by UNIX systems. To enable this feature, you must first install the TCP/IP network protocol via the Network icon in the Control Panel window, and then install the TCP/IP Network Printing Support option. This procedure installs the LPD service ("daemon" in UNIX terminology), which enables Windows NT to receive print jobs sent by UNIX computers. Once installed, you must start this service by using the Services icon in the Control Panel window or by typing the **net start lpdsvc** command at the command line. Jobs that reach the LPD service are assigned the RAW data type if they contain the "l" control command, or are assigned the TEXT data type if they contain the "f" control command. For more information on these control commands, see "LPR Print Monitor," later in this chapter.

For more information about UNIX print connectivity, see "Print Monitors" later in this chapter.

Print Manager

Because Print manager relies on the spooler components, it is also considered a client. Print Manager is a window into the spooler components; a user interface that lets you configure various options and manipulate print jobs as they are processed.

Router

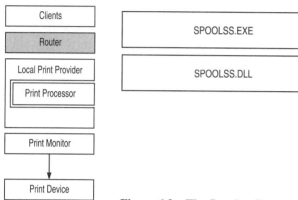

Figure 6.3   **The Spooler Component**

The router provides a single point of contact for clients, receiving service requests and passing those requests to whichever spooler component is best suited to handle the request.

When jobs arrive at the spooler, the client specifies the name of the target printer, and specifies the job's data type. For example, when a locally-run Windows-based application sends a job to local printer port, the graphics engine marks the job journal. The same jobs targeted for remote print servers are always marked with the raw data type. The LPD service marks UNIX print jobs that contain the "l" control command with the RAW data type, and marks UNIX jobs containing the "f" control command with the TEXT data type. Services for Macintosh marks Macintosh print jobs either the raw or Pscript1 data types, depending on the output device. Knowing the data type becomes important when the job reaches the next component, the local print provider.

The router uses the target printer name to determine whether the job should be printed on a local port or should be passed to another print server. If the job should be printed to a local port, then the router gives control to the local print provider. If the job is going to another print server, then the router passes control of the job to the appropriate remote print provider.

Print Providers

The Windows NT local print provider is used to send print jobs to a print device attached locally to the Windows NT-based computer. Remote print providers are used to send print jobs to other computers on the network.

Local Print Provider

A local print provider is used when a Windows NT print server is in charge of printing a job and the output goes to a local device, such as a parallel port or a network-attached printer.

The local print provider, LOCALSPL.DLL, provides the following functions:

- Writes the job to disk as a spool file, and then writes job information to disk as a shadow file. For more information on these files, see the following section, "Spool Files and Shadow Files."

- Passes control of the job to whichever print processor is responsible for that job's data type, so that the print processor can modify the print job, if necessary. When the print processor finishes it returns control to the local print provider.

- Adds separator pages to the job, if the user has requested them in Print Manager. For more information, see "Separator Pages," later in this chapter.

- Uses the destination printer name to look up the port that the job must be sent to, and pass control to whichever print monitor is responsible for that port.

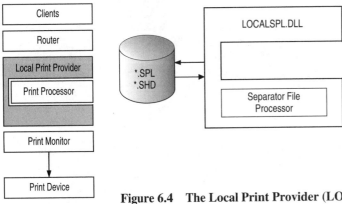

Figure 6.4 The Local Print Provider (LOCALSPL.DLL)

Most of the local print provider's options are configurable in Print Manager, by using the Details button from the Printer Properties dialog box. These options are documented thoroughly in online help, but you should be sure to note some options new to Windows NT in version 3.5:

- You can select whether you want the spooler to hold mismatched jobs. If you do, the spooler makes sure that incoming jobs from locally-run Windows-based applications are requesting features that are currently available. For instance, suppose that you have configured the printer driver assuming Letter-sized paper in the print device. Without the Hold Mismatched Jos option, if an application requests Legal-sized paper, the printer pauses indefinitely, waiting for a human operator to load a Legal paper cassette. With this option enabled, the local print provider holds this job, allowing correctly-configured jobs to print, until a Legal cassette is loaded.

- You can specify whether to keep spool files after the print device accepts the whole print job. This situation is often undesirable, because spool files will accumulate on disk. However, it is possible that between the time that the print device accepts the end of the job and the time it completes printing the job, the print device could be turned off. If you have a very important print job, or one that would be very difficult to recreate, deselecting this option lets you keep the spool file on disk until you're sure the print device has finished printing.

- You can tell the print provider whether it should send data to the print device while the spool file is being written to disk, or wait for the whole spool file to be written before starting to send the job to the print device. Sending data to the device while the spool files is being written can improve printing speed on large jobs.

- You can decide which job to send to the print device first, if two or more are spooling at the same time. You can select whether the job that starts spooling first will print first regardless of how long each job takes to finish spooling, or whether the job that *finishes* spooling will print first.

Spool Files and Shadow Files

For each spooled job, the local print provider creates two files:

- A spool file, which contains the print job itself, without any administrative information about the job. Spool files have an .SPL extension.

- A shadow file, which contains information such as the name of the destination printer, the job's priority, the name of the user who sent the job, and so on. Shadow files have an .SHD extension

If the print server is shut down while print jobs are spooled and waiting to print, the spool and shadow files remain on the disk and are used to restart the print job when the print server is restarted. The local print provider uses the information in the shadow file to determine how to print the print job, and the content of the job is contained in the spool file.

The spool file and shadow file for a job are kept in the same directory on disk. By default, these files are written to *systemroot*\SYSTEM32\SPOOL\PRINTERS. However, you can set a new default location or override the default location on a per-printer basis, by manually editing the Registry.

▶ **To set a new default location by manually editing the Registry**

1. Start the Registry Editor (REGEDT32.EXE) and find the following key: HKEY_LOCAL_MACHINE\SYSTEM\CurrentControlSet\ Control\Print\Printers.

2. Add a DefaultSpoolDirectory setting and as its value provide the full path to the spool directory that all printers should use by default.

   The change in the Registry takes effect after you stop and restart the spooler service.

▶ **To override the default location for one specific printer**

1. Start the Registry Editor (REGEDT32.EXE), and find the following key: HKEY_LOCAL_MACHINE\SYSTEM\CurrentControlSet\Control\Print \Printers.

2. Find the key for the printer.

3. Add a new SpoolDirectory setting, and as its value provide the path to the spool directory that this printer should use.

   The change in the Registry takes effect after you stop and restart the Spooler service.

Remote Print Providers

Remote print providers are used when a Windows NT-based computer sends a print job to another print server. This usually happens when your Windows NT-based computer acts as a workstation on the network, but it can also occur if your Windows NT-based computer acts as a print server which forwards incoming jobs to another print server.

Windows NT supplies two remote print providers.

- WIN32SPL.DLL transfers jobs to Windows Network print servers (such as print servers running Windows NT or Windows for Workgroups).

- NWPROVAU.DLL transfers jobs to Novell NetWare print servers.

Generally, if you are sending a print job to another print server, you have established the printer in Print Manager using the Connect To option. When a client sends a job to such a printer, the router polls each of the remote print providers in turn, in effect asking each one whether it recognizes the printer name. The router passes control to the first network provider that recognizes the printer name. You can set the polling order by using the Network icon in the Control Panel window. After choosing this icon, choose the Networks button. In the Network Providers Search Order dialog box, choose the Print Provider option in the Show Providers For box. Then select the name of a network and use the Up and Down buttons to change the polling order.

Note   Neither of these remote print providers performs spooling. When you send a print job using these remote print providers, the job does not spool locally.

Windows Network Print Provider

If the Windows network print provider, WIN32SPL.DLL, recognizes the printer name, then this print provider makes further decisions based on the type of print server to which the job is going. If the print server is running Windows NT, then WIN32SPL.DLL makes remote procedure calls (RPC) to the router component of the remote server. The remote server's router receives the print job over the network, and then begins processing the job as if one of its own local clients had submitted the job.

If the remote print server is not running Windows NT, then WIN32SPL.DLL contacts the local Windows Network redirector, which forwards the job over the network to the downlevel server. The downlevel server is then responsible for printing the job.

The functions provided by the Windows network print provider are illustrated in the following figure.

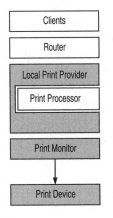

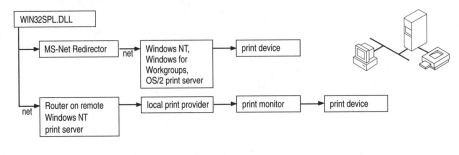

Figure 6.5   The Windows Network Print Provider (WIN32SPL.DLL)

NetWare Print Provider

If the NetWare print provider (NWPROVAU.DLL) recognizes the server name when polled by the router, it takes control of the print job. The NetWare print provider then communicates with the NetWare workstation service, NWWKS.DLL, which in turn passes control to the NetWare redirector. The NetWare redirector then transmits the print job over the network to the NetWare print server. This process is illustrated in the following figure.

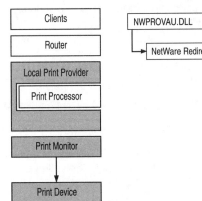

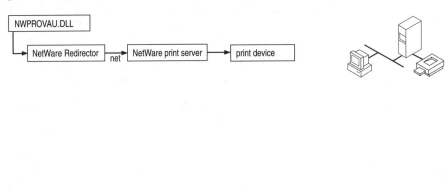

Figure 6.6   How the NetWare Print Provider Interacts with Other Components

Print Processors

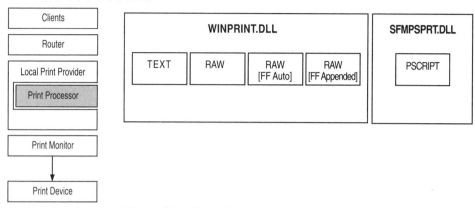

Figure 6.7   The Print Processor Component

Print processors are the components that make necessary alterations to print jobs, based on the data type of the print job. A print processor might recognize only one data type, or it might recognize several data types. Windows NT supplies two print processors, the Windows print processor (WINPRINT.DLL) and the Macintosh print processor (SFMPSPRT.DLL). Third party software vendors may create their own print processors to support custom data types.

Windows Print Processor

The RAW data type indicates that the print job has already been fully rendered, and it does not need any more processing. Most Windows NT printing clients send RAW jobs.

The RAW [FF Auto] and RAW [FF Appended] data types are similar to the RAW data type, but work around one additional problem, as follows.

Many character-mode applications don't send printer-specific commands in their print jobs. Instead, they simply send a stream of ASCII text. This is what happens, for instance, when you copy a text file directly to your computer's parallel port.

Printer languages expect print jobs to contain control commands, but many languages (such as PCL and most dot-matrix printer languages) make an exception when they receive ASCII text without control commands: they feed paper from the default paper source and print the incoming text in the default font with default margins, orientation, and duplexing.

This can cause problems with PCL laser print devices, which only eject a page when one of the following conditions occurs:

- The print device has received enough text to fill the current page
- The print job contains a form-feed command
- Another print job arrives at the print device
- A human operator manually forces a form-feed from the print device's front panel

The character-mode applications described above rarely send a form feed at the end of their jobs, so the last page of these jobs does not eject from the printer until a human operator forces it, or the next job forces the last page out. The RAW [FF Auto] and RAW [FF Appended] data types work around this problem.

If you configure the default data type in Print Manager to be RAW [FF Auto], the print processor assumes the print job is simple text, and adds a form feed to the end of the job. The print processor leaves the rest of the job alone, and then gives control back to the print provider. The RAW [FF Appended] option is similar, but it first looks for a form feed at the end of the job. If it finds one, it does not append another form feed.

The RAW [FF Auto] and RAW [FF Appended] data types work well with printers whose languages accept ASCII text, but if your printer's language requires control commands, then the RAW data types will not produce good output. The PostScript language is a good example. If you send a PostScript device an ASCII text print job, it ignores the job, or prints error messages. The TEXT data type is the solution. If you configure the default data type to be TEXT, the Windows NT print processor sends the incoming job to the graphics engine. The graphics engine returns a print job which, when sent to the print device, prints the original text using the print device's default paper source, with the default font, orientation, margins, and duplexing. This achieves the same result as saving the incoming job to a file, opening that file with Notepad, and then printing the job.

Note If you send a print job that already contains printer commands to a printer whose default data type is TEXT, the best you can hope for is a printout of the control commands. In most cases, the device prints meaningless garbage.

The journal data type (NT JNL 1.000) implies that the job was created by a Windows-based application running on this computer, and that the data in the job is not yet fully rendered. When the application originally sent the print job, the graphics engine partially rendered the job into DDI commands, and then gave control back to the application. From the user's perspective, the print job had completed, and the user could continue using the application. In the background, the router and print provider passed control to the Windows NT print processor. At this point, the Windows NT print processor calls the graphics engine again, requesting that it continue rendering the job from DDI commands into printer commands. Jobs that are first rendered to journal files and later fully rendered by the print processor rarely take longer to begin printing on the print device, and the time savings to the user can be substantial, especially on long, complex jobs.

Macintosh Print Processor

If you have installed Services for Macintosh on a Windows NT Server computer, then you have an additional print processor (SFMPSPRT.DLL), which can interpret the PSCRIPT1 data type. This data type lets Windows NT Server convert a Macintosh client's PostScript print job into other printers' languages.

When a Macintosh client sends a print job to a Windows NT Server print server, the Macintosh print server component, SFMPRINT.DLL, receives the job and checks the targeted printer. If the printer controls a PostScript print device, then SFMPRINT assigns the job the RAW data type, so that the print provider and print processor will pass the print job through to the print device without alteration. However, if the printer controls a non-PostScript print device, SFMPRINT receives the job and assigns the PSCRIPT1 data type. SFMPSPRT has a built-in TrueImage raster image processor (RIP) which reads and interprets the PostScript code and creates bitmaps of each page that the job would have produced on a PostScript print device. SFMPSPRT then sends these bitmaps to the graphics engine to create a print job that produces those bitmaps on the non-PostScript print device.

Note that the RIP produces monochrome bitmaps at 300 DPI, using the fonts available on the Windows NT-based computer. Because of these limitations in the RIP, the bitmaps print at 300 DPI even if the non-PostScript print device and its printer driver support higher resolutions; the bitmaps print in monochrome even if the print device and the printer driver support color.

Print Monitors

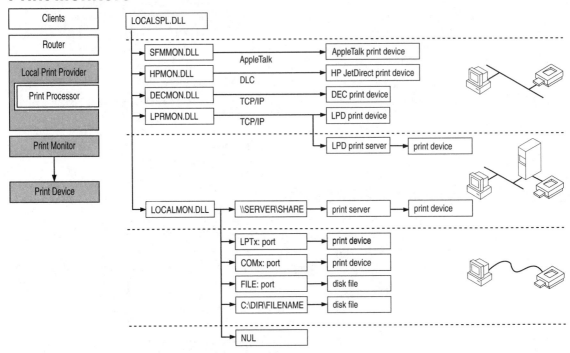

Figure 6.8   The Print Monitor Component

Print monitors are components that the local print provider uses to transmit completed print jobs to various ports and the print devices attached to those ports. The five print monitors supplied with Windows NT—Local, Macintosh, Digital, HP, and LPR—are described in this section.

The next section is an overview of how to use Print Manager to create a port to use one of the Windows NT print monitors. Following sections discuss many of the major configuration issues associated with these monitors, but you can get additional detailed information by choosing the Help button in the dialog box for each monitor.

Using Print Manager to Specify Print Monitors

In the Printer Properties dialog box, the Print To listbox lists the default
Windows NT ports.

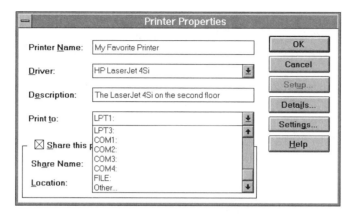

By default, the list in the Print To box includes only standard ports controlled
by the local print monitor, LOCALMON.DLL. When you want to print over other
communications channels (to a network-attached printer, for example), you must
create a new port. To create a port, select Other from the Print To box. The Print
Destinations dialog box then lists the available print monitors.

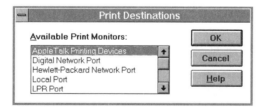

Note Monitors often depend on other software components and do not appear in
this list unless you have loaded the components they require. For example, the
Hewlett-Packard Network Port monitor transmits print jobs using the DLC network
protocol, and you will see this monitor in the list only if you have installed DLC.

Select the monitor that controls the type of communications channel you want to use, and then choose OK. The monitor then displays its own user interface, which you use to create a new port. After you have created the new port and configured a printer to use that port, the Settings option in the Printer Properties dialog launches the monitor user interface again, if the monitor allows reconfiguration of a port.

When you read details about each monitor in the following sections, remember that each print monitor is concerned with a data communications channel, not with the print device at the other end of that channel. In most cases, the print monitor does not know the make or model of print device it is communicating with, nor does it need to know. Also, different print monitors may use the same network protocol, but this does not make them interchangeable. For example, both the Digital Network Port monitor and the LPR Port monitor use the TCP/IP protocol, but they send data over that protocol in very different ways.

Local Print Monitor

The local print monitor, LOCALMON.DLL, is responsible for sending print jobs to local devices. These include familiar ports like LPT1: and COM1:, as well as several others described below.

The FILE: port appears in the default port list in the Printer Properties dialog. When you send jobs to a printer that uses this port, the local print monitor prompts you for the name of a file in which it will store the print job.

If you select Other from the list of ports in the Print To box of the Printer Properties dialog, and then select the Local Port option, the local print monitor prompts you to enter a port name. Some possibilities include:

- An explicit filename, such as C:\DIR\FILENAME. All jobs sent to this port are written to the named file. Each new job overwrites the last one.

- The UNC name of a print share, such as \\SERVER\PRINTER. Jobs sent to this port are transferred over the network to the named share, via the network redirector. This can be useful if you need to send jobs to a network print server, but you want the job to spool locally as well as on the print server.

- The NUL port. You can use this port to test whether network clients are able to send jobs. Simply pause the printer set to use this port, send a job from a network client, look at the printer in Print Manager to confirm that it arrived, and then resume the printer. Jobs sent to NUL are simply deleted from the system, without wasting paper or delaying real print jobs.

Macintosh Print Monitor

The Macintosh print monitor, SFMMON.DLL, is responsible for transmitting jobs over a network, using the AppleTalk protocol, to network-attached print devices such as the Apple LaserWriter family. It also lets you send jobs to AppleTalk spoolers, regardless of the print device that the spooler is attached to.

The configuration dialog for this monitor is shown below. It displays the available network zones, lets you choose a zone, and then shows the available printers in that zone.

This monitor is available on both Windows NT Workstation and Windows NT Server computers, letting any Windows NT-based computer send local print jobs to AppleTalk printers. However, only Windows NT Server has a Macintosh print server component, so only a Windows NT Server computer can receive print jobs from Macintosh clients.

Digital Print Monitor

The Digital Print Monitor, DECMON.DLL, sends print jobs to Digital Equipment Corporation's Digital PrintServer print devices, and other Digital Equipment Corporation print devices such as the DEClaser 5100 and the DECcolorwriter 1000. This monitor's user interface lets you select the print devices you want to print to, and the network protocol to use.

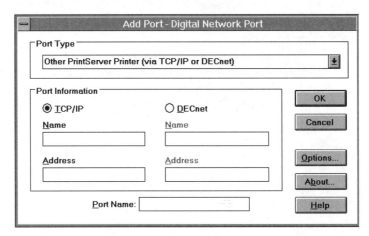

Windows NT supplies the TCP/IP network protocol, but does not supply the DECnet™ protocol. If you want to use DECnet, you must contact Digital Equipment Corporation to obtain it.

HP Print Monitor

The Hewlett-Packard Network Port monitor, HPMON.DLL, is responsible for sending print jobs to HP JetDirect adapters. This includes both the network adapters commonly installed in printers such as the LaserJet 4 Si and the JetDirect EX device, which lets you connect any parallel print device to the network.

Many JetDirect devices can communicate over several different network protocols, including DLC, IPX, TCP/IP, and AppleTalk. HPMON.DLL is specific to DLC: you must load the DLC protocol in order to use this print monitor, and it is not able to transmit jobs over other protocols.

This monitor has several operating parameters to be aware of.

- The DLC protocol is bridgeable, but not routable. This means that if a Windows NT print server is on one physical subnet, and a JetDirect device is on another physical subnet, then the server can send jobs to the JetDirect if the two subnets are joined by a bridge, but cannot send jobs if the two subnets are joined by a router.

- DLC can be bound to multiple network adapters, but the HP Print Monitor software can only manage printers over one network adapter. If your NT computer has multiple network adapters, make sure all the HP JetDirect-equipped printers are on the same physical subnet.

- Each port managed by this print monitor is configurable for either Job Based or Continuous connection. Job Based means that the print server connects to the JetDirect adapter, sends a job, and disconnects, letting other print servers connect to the JetDirect adapter. Continuous connection means that the print server never disconnects from the JetDirect adapter, preventing other servers from connecting and sending jobs, until either the server or the JetDirect's print device is rebooted. The advantage of continuous connection is that all users are validated by the Windows NT security model, and every access can be audited.

Note If you configure two Windows NT print servers to send jobs to the same JetDirect device, configure both servers for Job Based connections. If you configure one of the print servers for Continuous connections, then when it sends its first print job, it will "claim" the JetDirect for itself, preventing the Job Based server from connecting.

LPR Print Monitor

LPR is one of the network protocols in the TCP/IP protocol suite. It was originally developed as a standard for transmitting print jobs between computers running Berkeley UNIX. The LPR standard is published as Request For Comment (RFC) 1179. Windows NT complies with this standard, as do most Berkeley UNIX operating systems. However, most System V UNIX operating systems do not comply with this standard, so in most cases Windows NT will not be able to send print jobs to System V computers, or receive print jobs from them. Exceptions are System V computers that are configured to accept BSD jobs; these computers can accept Windows NT print jobs.

The LPR protocol lets a client application on one computer send a print job to a print spooler service on another computer. The client application is usually named "LPR" and the service (or "daemon") is usually named "LPD." Windows NT 3.5 supplies a command line application, the LPR.EXE utility, and it supplies the LPR Port print monitor. Both act as clients sending print jobs to an LPD service running on another computer. As mentioned previously, Windows NT also supplies an LPD service, so it can receive print jobs sent by LPR clients, including UNIX computers and other Windows NT computers.

The LPR protocol was not designed to pass detailed error status information back to the LPR client. If anything goes wrong, from severe problems (such as the server being too busy to process requests) to print device problems (such as running out of paper), the LPR protocol reports the same error condition. As a result of this protocol limitation, Print Manager cannot provide detailed information when an error occurs printing on an LPR port.

In order to send print jobs, the LPR client needs to know the network address of the LPD server computer, and it needs to know the name that the LPD service associates with its print device. Given this information, LPR sends print jobs to the LPD service, along with instructions on how to process the print job, and the name of the print device that should receive the job. The user interface shown below lets you tell the Windows NT LPR Port monitor which computer should receive the job, and which of the computer's print devices ("queues" in UNIX terminology) the job should go to.

```
┌─────────────────────────────────────────────────────────────────────────┐
│ ─                      Add LPR compatible printer                         │
│                                                                           │
│  Name or address of host providing lpd: [                    ]   [  OK  ] │
│                                                                           │
│  Name of printer on that machine:       [                    ]   [Cancel]│
│                                                                           │
│                                                                  [ Help ] │
│                                                                           │
└─────────────────────────────────────────────────────────────────────────┘
```

Use the Name Or Address of Host Providing LPD box to tell the LPR Port monitor which UNIX computer it should send print jobs to. You can supply either the IP address or the host name of the UNIX computer.

For example, suppose you want to send jobs to a printer named "lablaser" on a UNIX machine whose IP address is 111.222.333.444, and whose name (defined in the hosts file on your Windows NT computer) is "unixbox". In the dialog above, you could enter either "unixbox" or "111.222.333.444" (without the quotation marks) in the Name Or Address Of Host Providing LPD box, and you would enter "lablaser" in the Name Of Printer On That Machine box.

If you don't know a valid name for the printer, you can often find it by looking at the /etc/printcap file on the UNIX computer. The printcap file is a flat-file text database of print queue information. Each entry corresponds to a print queue on the UNIX computer. Fields in these entries are separated by ":" characters, and for readability an entry may be broken over several lines by ending a line with a "\" character and beginning the next line with a space or tab character. The first field of each entry lists valid names for the queue, separated by "|" characters. The remaining lines in each printcap entry describe the queue's characteristics, such as communications parameters, spool file location, error log file location, and so on.

Continuing the lablaser example, we might find entries like the following in the printcap file on the computer named unixbox:

```
lp|lablaser|The_Lab_Printer:\
    :lp=/dev/ttya:br#9600:\
    :lf=/usr/spool/lpd/lablaser-err:\
    :sd=/usr/spool/lpd/lablaser:
```

Note This example is provided for illustrative purposes only. Your UNIX system documentation is your best source of detailed information on your system's printcap file.

The first line in this example defines a print queue with three valid names: "lp", "lablaser", and "The_Lab_Printer". You can use any of these names in the second field of the LPR Port dialog shown above.

Once you tell the LPR Port monitor the LPD server's network address and the proper queue name, it can send print jobs (data files) and processing instructions (control commands contained in a control file). RFC1179 defines 29 control commands, but the three described below are particularly important. Note that all the control commands defined in RFC1179 are case sensitive.

- The **f** command causes the data file to be printed as a plain text file, providing page breaks as necessary. Any ASCII control characters which are not in the following list are discarded: HT, CR, FF, LF, and BS. LPD should filter out most of the non-printing control characters.

- The **l** command causes the specified data file to print without filtering the control characters (as is done with the **f** command).

- The **o** command prints the data file to be printed, treating the data as standard Postscript input.

Note Many printer languages, including PCL, rely heavily on the ESC control character, which the **f** control command causes to be filtered from the print job. Do not use the **f** control command when sending print jobs that contain printer commands.

The LPR Port monitor sends the **l** command by default, while the command line LPR.EXE utility sends the **f** command by default. With the LPR.EXE utility, you can use the **-o** switch if you want to override the default on a job-by-job basis. If you want to change the default command for a particular printer controlled by the LPR Port monitor, you need to modify a registry parameter. Use the Registry Editor (REGEDT32.EXE) to find the key named HKEY_LOCAL_MACHINE\SYSTEM \CurrentControlSet\Control\Print\Monitors\LPR Port\Ports. Next, select the port whose default control command you wish to change, and then select its Timeouts key. In this key, add a value named PrintSwitch with type REG_SZ, and enter the control command you want to use. For instance, enter the letter "f" (without the quotation marks) if you want to use the "f" command by default.

Some UNIX computers do not follow the control commands alone when deciding how to process a print job. For instance, if you send an ASCII text file directly to a PostScript printer, it will not print correctly. As a result, many UNIX systems have additional software that converts ASCII text jobs into PostScript jobs which will print correctly. System administrators are wary of jobs that arrive with a **l** command, because they could be non-PostScript jobs accidentally sent with an **l** command, which would let them bypass the PostScript software and print incorrectly. To avoid this possibility, some LPD services scan jobs that arrive with the **l** control command, looking for known PostScript commands: if the scanner finds these commands, then it passes the job directly to the printer as requested; otherwise, it assumes the user sent the wrong control command, and it sends the job through the PostScript software. If you send PostScript jobs from Windows NT using LPR, and the printer controlled by the UNIX server prints the PostScript code instead of interpreting it, then the UNIX server may have a scanner that does not recognize the output from the Windows NT PostScript driver as valid PostScript code. If this happens, you may need to reconfigure Windows NT to use the "o" control command by default.

Examples of Printing Flow

The following sections trace the flow of printing control when print jobs are sent by different types of network clients.

Tables 6.2 and 6.3 summarize the characteristics of jobs coming from the various types of clients. Table 6.2 is for local clients and the Table 6.3 is for remote clients.

Table 6.3   Characteristics of Print Jobs Sent by Local Clients

	Windows-based Applications	Windows-based Applications	Non-Windows-based Applications	Non-Windows-based Applications
	Connect To	Create	Spooled port	Non spooled port
Is the Windows NT printer driver involved in initial rendering?	Yes	Yes	No	No
Job's data type:	RAW	Journal	RAW	RAW
Does job spool locally?	No	Yes	Yes	No
Does Windows NT alter client's job?	No*	Yes	No*	No*
Does Windows NT printer driver affect job alterations?	Not applicable	Yes	Not applicable	Not applicable

Table 6.4   Characteristics of Print Jobs Sent by Remote Clients

	Macintosh client		LPR client		Downlevel client
	PostScript print device	Non-PostScript print device	"l" control command	"f" control command	
Is the Windows NT printer driver involved in initial rendering?	No	No	No	Yes	No
Job's data type:	RAW	PSCRIPT1	RAW	TEXT	RAW
Does job spool locally?	Yes	Yes	Yes	Yes	Yes
Does Windows NT alter client's job?	No1	Yes	No1	Yes	No1
Does Windows NT printer driver affect job alterations?	Not applicable	Yes	Not applicable	No	Not applicable

1 If the job has RAW data type, and Default Data type in Print Manager is TEXT, FF [Auto], or FF[Appended], then the print processor will alter the print job. Otherwise, the job is not altered.

MS-DOS Client

When an MS-DOS client (including Windows 3.1 and Windows for Workgroups clients) sends a print job, the Server service running on the Windows NT print server receives the job and assigns it the RAW data type. Windows NT does not alter the job unless the Default Data type for the printer has been changed to RAW [FF Auto], or RAW [FF Appended], or TEXT. The Windows NT printer driver is never involved initially creating the print job, and is only involved in altering the job if the printer's default data type is TEXT.

Windows NT Workstation Computer

When a Windows-based application running on a Windows NT Workstation computer sends a job to a printer established by the Connect To command, it uses the graphics engine to create a fully rendered job, with data type RAW. The router sends this job to the router on the Windows NT print server (or sends via the redirector to a Windows for Workgroups, OS/2, or NetWare server).

When you first establish the printer using the Connect To command, if the printer is on a Windows NT print server the server downloads the proper driver to you. If the printer is on a non-Windows NT print server, you must install the printer driver manually.

When a Windows-based application running on a Windows NT Workstation computer sends a job to a printer established by the Connect To command, the application still uses the graphics engine, but the graphics engine only renders the job part-way, into a journal file. The user quickly regains control of the application. In the background, the router always passes journal jobs to the local print provider, which gives control to WINPRINT to complete the rendering into printer commands. The local print provider then gives control to the appropriate print monitor, which transmits jobs to the print device.

Macintosh Client

The Macintosh client sends a job composed of PostScript code. If the target printer is a PostScript device, then SFMPRINT assigns the job the RAW data type, so that when WINPRINT takes control, it will not alter the job. If the target printer is not a PostScript device, then SFMPRINT assigns the job the PSCRIPT1 data type. The local print monitor gives control to the SFMPSPRT print processor, which interprets it into bitmaps of pages, and sends the bitmap to the graphics engine. The graphics engine creates a new job that will print on the non-PostScript print device.

UNIX Client

The UNIX computer sends a job using its LPR utility. If the LPR client specifies the "l" control command, LPD leaves the job alone and assigns it the RAW data type. If the LPR client specifies the "f" command, LPD assigns it the TEXT data type and modifies the file for proper formatting. From this point on, the job is handled the same way that an MS-DOS client's job is handled.

Note that LPD depends entirely on the control command sent with the print job to tell it how to handle the job; it does not parse the rest of the job. For example, if a UNIX client sends a PostScript job and the job contains the "f" command, LPD will not recognize it as PostScript and will treat it as any other job with an "f" command.

Security

Security touches nearly every aspect of Windows NT, and printing is no exception. Security usually comes into play when an administrator uses the Security menu in Print Manager to assign permissions to users and groups. However, security issues can also be important if an administrator assigns permissions to the spool file directory, or to sections of the Registry that affect printing. Finally, security can be an issue when a print server accepts jobs from Macintosh clients, or when a Windows NT print server attempts to forward print jobs to other print servers. Each of these topics is discussed in the following sections.

Printer Security

Windows NT security is integrated into Print Manager so that you can specify which printers have which security attributes. For example, you can specify that everyone in your department can print to this printer, and only one or two specified people can administer it.

There are four categories of permissions you can assign to a person or group for a specific Windows NT printer:

- Full control, which allows a user complete access and administrative control
- Manage documents, which allows a person to change the status of anyone's jobs but not of printers
- Print, which enables the user to print on the printer and have control to pause, resume, or delete his or her own jobs
- No access, which denies access to the printer

By default on Windows NT Server, the Administrators, Server Operators, and Print Operators groups are granted Full Control. On Windows NT Workstation, the Administrators and Power users groups have Full Control. On both types of computer, the Creator Owner group is granted Manage Documents and the Everyone group has the Print permission.

To explicitly deny access to a printer, you must specify No Access for a particular group or user.

Print Manager also provides an auditing option for tracking successful or unsuccessful printing and administrative events for particular groups or individuals. To use this option, you must first enable auditing in User Manager. From the Policies menu, select Audit. Next select the Audit These Events option button and choose OK. (You do not need to specify any events in this dialog box to enable print auditing.)

Spool File Security

If you print to a local printer, the local print provider will spool the job to disk during processing. If the spool directory is on an NTFS partition and you have been denied write access to the spool directory, then you will not be able to print. The Everyone group has Change permission in the default spool directory. If you change the spool directory location, make sure that everyone who should print has Change permission in the new spool directory.

Registry Security

Most printing-related registry settings reside in the subkeys of HKEY_LOCAL_MACHINE\SYSTEM\CurrentControlSet\Control\Print. If an administrator uses the Registry Editor to give you read-only access to this subkey, you will not be able to install or configure printers, because when you run Print Manager you will not be allowed to change these subkeys.

Also, Windows-based applications expect to find information about available printers in the registry at HKEY_CURRENT_USER\Software\Microsoft \Windows NT\CurrentVersion\PrinterPorts. If you do not have permission to write to this subkey, then Windows-based applications will not recognize newly added printers, and may still try to access printers that have been deleted.

Forwarding Jobs

If a workstation sends a print job to a Windows NT print server, which then forwards the job to another Windows NT print server, the print server that forwards the job uses a "null session" to forward the job. Windows NT 3.1 allowed null-session connections by default, so print job forwarding worked. Under Windows NT 3.5, the null-session is disabled by default, preventing job forwarding. You can enable null-session support by manually editing the registry: HKEY_LOCAL_MACHINE\SYSTEM\CurrentControlSet\Services\LanmanServer\Parameters. Here you will find a value named NullSessionShares. Edit this value, and add a new line containing the sharename for the printer. This change does not take effect until you stop and restart the Spooler service.

Macintosh Clients

Although native Macintosh networking imposes security on files, it does not impose security on print devices: if a Macintosh client is physically able to send a job to a print device or print server, then that client implicitly has permission to do so. Because of this, the AppleTalk protocol has no mechanism to let clients supply a user name or password. Because the clients cannot identify themselves to the server, Windows NT cannot impose user-level security on Macintosh clients.

You can, however, enforce one set of printer permissions on all Macintosh users as a group. The MacPrint service must always log on, using a user account, to do its work. By default, it logs on as the System account. This account has Print permission on all local print devices, so by default any Macintosh client can send a job to any of the Windows NT computer's local printers. If you want Macintosh clients to have a different set of permissions, create a new user account and give this user account the printer permissions you want Macintosh users to have. Then set the MacPrint service to log on using this account. To do this, use the Services icon in Control Panel. Select Print Services for Macintosh from the list and choose the Startup button. Then choose the This Account button and type the name of the user account you created in the box.

Note that the System account on one computer does not have permission to access other computers' resources. This means that if MacPrint logs on as System, Macintosh users cannot send jobs to printers which forward jobs to other print servers. The solution is to configure MacPrint to log on as another user, one who has permission to print on all the print servers that jobs are forwarded to.

Managing Forms

A major difference in printing between Windows 3.1 and Windows NT is the move from tray-based printing to forms-based printing. Before the growth of personal computer networks, applications could assume that their target print device was connected directly to the computer. This implied that human users could see what media was loaded in each tray of the print device, and could easily change that media configuration. In a networked environment, these assumptions no longer hold. Print devices are increasingly located beyond the users' line-of-sight, and one user cannot change the print device's media without disrupting other users' work.

Forms-based printing offers a solution. Under this model, the print server administrator configures the Windows NT print server, defining what form is currently loaded in each paper source. A *form* in Windows NT consists of a paper size, margin settings, and a name. Windows-based applications running on a Windows NT-based computer let the user choose the form they want, rather than choosing a tray. When the application prints, the print job requests a specific form rather than a specific tray. The Windows NT print server checks the form-to-tray assignments, and causes the print device to feed paper from the correct tray.

This simplifies printing from the user's perspective. For instance, if a particular print device has multiple trays, and one holds Letter paper and another holds A4 paper, a user on the network can send print jobs requesting either of these forms, and they get the right output. Note that the user does not need to know which tray their form is loaded in, so print server administrators can put the forms in whichever trays they want. Also, the user does not need to know how many trays the print device has, or what those trays are named. All the user needs to know is the name of the form they want to use, and Windows NT takes care of the details.

Through Print Manager, you can define new forms and add them to the print server's database. For example, you could create a form called Customer Receipt Form that uses Letter-size paper and nonstandard margins. You can create multiple forms that use the same paper size, or the same margins, or both.

To create a new form or alter an existing form, choose Forms from the Printer menu in Print Manager. The Forms dialog box appears.

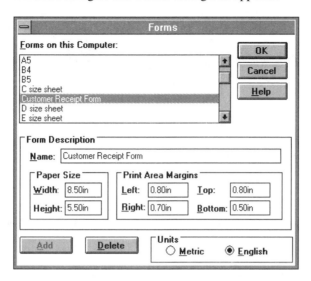

Using the Forms dialog box, anyone with Full Control privilege can add a form and specify the paper size and image area. Forms information is stored per server, not per printer. To create a new form, first select an existing form, and then select any of the Form Description fields. Change its value, and then select Add.

On a per-printer basis, you can use the Printer Properties dialog box to specify the paper tray in which your form is located. The Form drop-down list in this dialog box includes only those forms that can be used by your printer; form sizes your printer cannot accommodate are not listed.

Note that the following dialog boxes do not specify the default form; instead, they define the current mapping of forms to paper sources. If you want to set the default form, choose the Details button in Printer Properties, and then choose Job Defaults. Then, define the default form in the Form field.

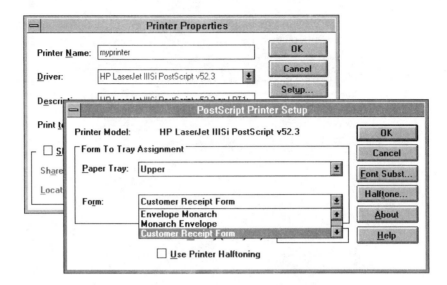

Hint If you want to use an odd-sized form with your printer, specify Manual Feed in the Paper Tray box.

Users who want to print a document can select the new form from the list shown in the application's Print Setup dialog box. The spooler remembers which paper tray contains that form and includes that information in the instructions passed to the print device.

Windows-based applications can use different forms within a document. For example, you might use an envelope for the first page, Letterhead for the second page, and Letter for the third and following pages.

Separator Files

The local print provider contains an interpreter, which reads commands from a separator file and produces one or more pages of text and/or graphics. These pages are then added to the front of the print job. These pages typically show who submitted the job, when the job printed, what server it printed on, and so on. Separator pages are sometimes called *header pages* or *burst pages.*

By default, separator page files are stored in the *systemroot*\\SYSTEM32 directory. To use a separator page file, type its name in the Separator File text box of the Printer Details dialog box in Print Manager. To use no separator file, leave this text box blank.

The following table lists the separator files included with Windows NT. This table supersedes similar tables in the *Windows NT Server System Guide* and the *Windows NT Server Concepts and Planning Guide*.

Table 6.5   Separator Files Included with Windows NT

Filename	Purpose	Compatible with
SYSPRINT.SEP	Prints a page before each document	PostScript
PCL.SEP	Switches dual-language HP printer to PCL printing	PCL
PSCRIPT.SEP	Switches dual-language HP printer to PostScript printing	PostScript

To create your own separator file, you can copy and rename one of the supplied separator files. The following table shows the escape codes you can include in a separator file. The first character of the separator page file must always be the escape character. This character is used throughout the separator page file in escape codes. The separator file interpreter replaces these escape codes with appropriate data, to be sent directly to the printer.

Table 6.6   Escape Codes

Escape code	Function
\N	Prints the user name of the person that submitted the job.
\I	Prints the job number.
\D	Prints the date the job was printed. The representation of the date is the same as the Date Format in the International section in Control Panel.
\T	Prints the time the job was printed. The representation of the time is the same as the Time Format in the International section in Control Panel.
\L*xxxx*	Prints all the characters (*xxxx*) following it until another escape code is encountered.
\Fpathname	Prints the contents of the file specified by path name, starting on an empty line. The contents of this file are copied directly to the printer without any processing.
\H*nn*	Sets a printer-specific control sequence, where *nn* is a hexadecimal ASCII code sent directly to the printer. To determine the specific numbers, see your printer manual.
\W*nn*	Sets the width of the separator page. The default width is 80; the maximum width is 256. Any printable characters beyond this width will be truncated.

Table 6.6   Escape Codes *(continued)*

Escape code	Function
\B\S	Prints text in single-width block characters until \U is encountered.
\E	Ejects a page from the printer. Use this code to start a new separator page or to end the separator page file. If you get an extra blank separator page when you print, remove this code from your separator page file.
\n	Skips *n* number of lines (from 0 through 9). Skipping 0 lines simply moves printing to the next line.
\B\M	Prints text in double-width block characters until \U is encountered.
\U	Turns off block character printing.

Questions and Answers About Printing

- When is the Windows NT printer driver significant?

  There are four cases in which the Windows NT printer driver affects a client's print job:

  - When you are printing from a Windows-based application, which is running on the Windows NT-based computer in question

  - When you're printing from a remote Windows NT client computer that used Connect To to establish a connection to your shared printer (and therefore may have received your printer driver)

  - When you are printing from a remote Macintosh client, and the target printer is not a PostScript device

  - When a print job arrives marked RAW, and the default data type for the printer is TEXT

  In any other case, the Windows NT driver does not get involved.

- When will a Windows NT print server alter an incoming job?

  There are two cases in which Windows NT alters a print job, in addition to the situations listed in the previous question:

  - When a UNIX client uses LPR to send a print job using the "f" control command;

  - When a print job with the RAW data type arrives at a printer that you've configured to use the RAW [FF Auto] or RAW [FF Appended] or TEXT data type by default.

In any other case Windows NT does not alter the job.

- What problems might cause incorrect output?

  Incorrect output is often a symptom of a misconfigured printer driver, a printer driver that does not perfectly match your print device, or a misconfigured default data type. Other possibilities include corrupted documents, corrupted graphics or fonts embedded within a document, or bugs in the application that is generating the print job.

- What problems might prevent output entirely?

  Complete lack of output is often a symptom of problems with a print monitor. Try using a port controlled by another print monitor (FILE: is a good test). If the problem goes away when you access the print device through another port or print monitor, then the port or print monitor may be misconfigured. If the problem does not go away when you test with another port or print monitor, check the print device, and consider printing to another, similar device as a test.

- How can I obtain updated printer drivers?

  Microsoft places all new or updated printer drivers onto its electronic services for public download. These services are listed at the end of your Hardware Compatibility List.

- How do I turn off network popups that occur when print jobs succeed, and how do I keep the print server from beeping when a job arrives that the monitor cannot transmit (for instance, because the target print server is not responding)?

  Use the Registry Editor to find the key: HKEY_LOCAL_MACHINE\SYSTEM \CurrentControlSet\Control\Print\Providers and add a value "NetPopup" with type REG_DWORD and value of zero.

CHAPTER 7

Fonts

This chapter examines technical issues related to fonts, focusing on TrueType, the font technology available in Windows NT. This chapter also presents details about using printer fonts with specific types of printers, and using Adobe Type 1 fonts.

About Typography in Windows NT

A *typeface* is a set of characters that share common characteristics such as stroke width and the presence or absence of serifs. For example, Arial and Courier are both typefaces. Frequently, both the typeface and its name are copyrighted and/or trademarked by the typeface designer or manufacturer.

In Windows NT, a *font* is the name of a typeface, excluding attributes such as bold or italic. This general definition is more widely used than the traditional definition associated with traditional typography. For example, MS Serif is a font in Windows NT.

In Windows NT, a *font family* refers to a group of typefaces with similar characteristics. The families that Windows NT recognizes for font installation and mapping are Roman, Swiss, Modern, Script, and Decorative. For example, the sans serif typefaces Arial, Arial Bold, Arial Bold Italic, Arial Italic, Small Fonts, and MS Sans Serif are all part of the Swiss font family.

For printing and display in a computer system, each font has its own character set according to the ASCII, ANSI, or original equipment manufacturer (OEM) standard or other industry standard that defines what character is represented by a specific keystroke. Windows NT uses the ANSI character set. Many non-Windows NT-based applications use the ASCII character set or the OEM character set.

The following basic terms are used in Windows NT to define the appearance of a font in an application:

- *Font style* refers to specific characteristics of the font. The four characteristics you can define for fonts in Windows NT are italic, bold, bold italic, and roman. (Roman is often referred to as Normal or Regular in font dialog boxes).

- *Font size* refers to the vertical point size of a font, where a point is about 1/72 of an inch. Typical sizes for text are 10-point and 12-point.

- *Font effects* refers to attributes such as underlining, strikeout, and color that can be applied to text in many applications.

The following terms are also used to describe fonts and typefaces:

- *Spacing* can be either fixed or proportional. In a *fixed font*, such as Courier, every character occupies the same amount of space. In *a proportional font*, such as Arial or Times New Roman®, character width varies.

- *Pitch* refers to the amount of horizontal space used for each character of fixed-width fonts. This is often specified in characters-per-inch (CPI), typically where 10-pitch equals 12-point, 12-pitch equals 10-point, and 15-pitch equals 8-point type. (Some fonts use other equivalencies.)

- *Serif* and *sans serif* describe specific characteristics of a typeface. Serif fonts, such as Times New Roman or Courier, have projections that extend from the upper and lower strokes of the letters. Sans serif fonts, such as Arial and MS Sans Serif, do not have serifs.

- *Slant* refers to the angle of a font's characters, which can be italic or roman (no slant).

- *Weight* refers to the heaviness of the stroke for a specific font, such as Light, Regular, Book, Demi, Heavy, Black, and Extra Bold.

- *Width* refers to whether the standard typeface has been extended or compressed horizontally. The common variations are Condensed, Normal, or Expanded.

- *X-height* refers to the vertical size of lowercase characters.

About Windows NT Fonts

Windows NT provides three basic kinds of fonts, which are categorized according to how the fonts are rendered for screen or print output:

- *Raster fonts* are stored in files as bitmaps and are rendered as an array of dots for displaying on the screen and printing on paper. Raster fonts cannot be cleanly scaled or rotated.

- *Vector fonts* are rendered from a mathematical model, where each character is defined as a set of lines drawn between points. Vector fonts can be scaled to any size or aspect ratio.

- *TrueType fonts* are outline fonts. TrueType fonts can be scaled and rotated.

Note Windows NT also supports Adobe Type 1 fonts, although no Adobe Type 1 fonts are included with Windows NT.

In addition, Windows NT fonts are described according to the output device:

- *Screen fonts* are font descriptions that Windows NT uses to represent characters on display devices. (TrueType fonts act as both screen and printer fonts.)

- *Printer fonts* are the font descriptions used by the printer to create a font. Windows NT-based applications can use three kinds of printer fonts—device fonts, downloadable soft fonts, and printable screen fonts, as described in "Printer Fonts and Windows NT," later in this chapter.

As shown in the following illustration, you can identify the different fonts in Windows NT-based applications by the icons associated with the font name.

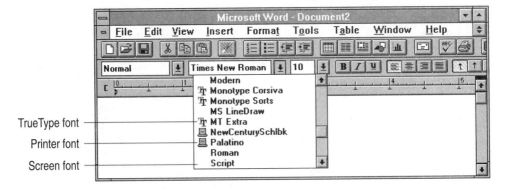

The next sections describe raster, vector, TrueType, and Adobe Type 1 fonts. Later sections in this chapter discuss screen fonts and printer fonts used by Windows NT.

Windows NT Raster Fonts

Raster fonts are bitmaps supplied in different sizes for specific video display resolutions. The Windows NT fonts MS Serif, MS Sans Serif, Courier, System, and Terminal are raster fonts.

A raster font file contains data that describes the style and all the characters of a typeface for a specific display device. Windows NT provides several raster font sizes for various display devices. For example, MS Serif comes in point sizes 8, 10, 12, and 14 for video graphics array (VGA) and 8514 display devices.

Windows NT can scale raster fonts, but if you try to scale them too far from their original size or style, they become jagged. Bold, italic, underline, and strikeout styles can also be generated from a standard raster font.

The following table lists the raster fonts included with Windows NT. Additional raster font sets can be installed by choosing the Fonts icon in Control Panel.

Table 7.1   Windows NT Raster Fonts

Font	Filename	Character set
Courier	COUR*x*.FON	ANSI
MS Sans Serif	SSERIF*x*.FON	ANSI
MS Serif	SERIF*x*.FON	ANSI
Small	SMALL*x*.FON	ANSI
Symbol	SYMBOL*x*.FON	Symbol

Raster Font Sizes

The raster font sets for different display resolutions are distinguished by a letter suffix on the font name (represented as *x* in the previous table). To see the files that Windows NT installs for a given display or printer, add the appropriate letter (displayed in the following table) that identifies the resolution to the raster font filename. For example, the resource file for MS Serif fonts for VGA is named SERIFE.FON.

Table 7.2   Raster Font Sizes

Font set and output device	Horizontal resolution	Vertical resolution	Aspect ratio H:V
E = VGA display	96 dpi	96 dpi	1:1
F = 8514 display	120 dpi	120 dpi	1:1

Printing Raster Fonts on Your Printer

Raster fonts can be printed if their resolution and aspect ratio are close to what your printer requires. If you do not see raster fonts for your printer in a Fonts dialog box, check your printer's horizontal and vertical resolution, and compare it with the preceding table. If there is a close match, choose the Fonts icon in Control Panel, and make sure the appropriate font set is installed. If there is no close match, you cannot print the Windows NT raster fonts on your printer.

Some applications, such as Microsoft Excel for Windows and Microsoft Paintbrush, work around this problem by sending documents to the printer in the form of bitmaps. By using bitmaps, the application can ensure that what prints closely matches what you see on the screen. Other applications, such as desktop publishing packages, allow you to choose only printable fonts.

In general, applications are written so that you can choose either displayable fonts or printable fonts. It is up to the developer of the application to decide which type of font you can choose.

You might be able to print raster fonts in a different resolution, if the other resolution has an aspect ratio that matches your printer. Some printer drivers cannot print raster fonts, regardless of the aspect ratio.

Substituting Fonts Installed by Windows 3.x

In Windows NT, MS Serif and MS Sans Serif replace the identical raster fonts Tms Rmn and Helv that were installed by Windows 3.0 or earlier versions. Windows NT matches MS Serif to Tms Rmn and MS Sans Serif to Helv using the information stored in the FontSubstitutes key in the Registry:

```
HKEY_LOCAL_MACHINE\SOFTWARE\Microsoft\Windows NT
    \CurrentVersion\FontSubstitutes
```

You will still see the Tms Rmn and Helv typeface names in a Fonts dialog box if, for example, your Hewlett-Packard Printer Control Language (HPPCL) printer uses the Microsoft 1Z font cartridge.

Selecting a Readable Screen Font

The raster font named Small Font was designed for readable screen display of small fonts. For sizes under 6 points, Small Font is a better choice than any TrueType font for screen display, because it's easier to read.

Windows NT Vector Fonts

Vector fonts are a set of lines drawn between points, like a pen plotter drawing a set of characters. Vector fonts can be scaled to virtually any size, but generally they do not look as good as raster fonts in the sizes that raster fonts are specifically designed for.

Vector fonts are stored in Windows NT as collections of Graphical Device Interface (GDI) calls and are time-consuming to generate. But these fonts are useful for plotters and other devices where bitmapped characters can't be used. Before TrueType, vector fonts were also used in some applications to create large characters or characters that were rotated or distorted from the baseline.

Some Windows NT-based applications automatically use vector fonts at larger sizes. Some applications allow you to specify at what point size you want to use vector fonts. For example, the Vector Above setting in Aldus® PageMaker® specifies the point size at which PageMaker will switch to vector fonts.

The Windows NT fonts Roman, Modern, and Script are vector fonts. Although the vector fonts use the ANSI character set, they are marked internally as an OEM character set. These fonts are sometimes referred to as *plotter fonts* because, unlike most other fonts, they can be used on plotters.

Note   Third-party, non-TrueType scalable font products that were supported by Windows 3.1 are not supported by Windows NT. These products include Adobe Type Manager® (ATM®), Bitstream® Facelift®, and Atech Publisher's PowerPak.

TrueType and Windows NT

Windows NT includes support for TrueType, an outline font technology. Instead of being composed of bitmaps (such as raster fonts) or lines (such as vector fonts), TrueType fonts are *glyph shapes* that are described by their outlines. A glyph outline consists of a series of contours. A simple glyph may have only one contour. More complex glyphs can have two or more contours. Figure 7.1 shows three glyphs with one, two, and three contours respectively.

Figure 7.1   TrueType Glyphs

Note Windows NT supports all TrueType fonts that are supported by Windows 3.1.

TrueType fonts have many benefits over other kinds of Windows NT fonts:

- What you see is really what you get, because Windows NT can use the same font for both screen and printer. You don't have to think about whether you have a specific point size for a particular printer or for your display.

- You can scale and rotate TrueType fonts. TrueType fonts look good in all sizes and on all output devices that Windows NT supports.

- Your document will look the same when printed on different printers. And, any printer that uses a Windows NT Universal driver can print TrueType fonts.

- Your document will look the same as you move it across platforms. For example, the text you format in Microsoft Word for Windows will look the same as if you opened the same document in Microsoft Word for the Macintosh.

- Each TrueType typeface requires only an .FOT and a .TTF file to create fonts in all point sizes at all resolutions for all output devices. (Many raster font products include one font size per file. The raster fonts included with Windows NT are included within a single file.)

- TrueType fonts are integrated with the operating environment. For this reason, all Windows NT-based applications can use TrueType fonts like they do other Windows NT raster fonts.

The TrueType fonts installed with Windows NT are Arial, Courier New, Times New Roman, Symbol, and Wingdings in regular, bold, bold italic, and italic.

How TrueType Works

TrueType fonts are stored as a collection of points and *hints* that define the character outlines. Hints are algorithms that distort the scaled font outlines to improve how the bitmaps look at specific resolutions and sizes. When a Windows NT application requests a font, TrueType uses the outline and the hints to render a bitmap in the size requested.

Each time you start Windows NT, the first time you select a TrueType font size a bitmap is rendered for display or printing. Windows NT stores the rendered bitmaps in a font cache. Each subsequent time the font is used during that Windows NT session, display or printing have improved performance.

The Windows NT Universal printer driver, PostScript printer driver, and plotter driver all support TrueType fonts. Any printer that works with these printer drivers will support TrueType fonts automatically. For more information about these printer drivers, see Chapter 6, "Printing."

Using TrueType Fonts in Windows NT-based Applications

TrueType fonts give you a broad range of fonts you can use with your application. In many applications, TrueType fonts appear in the Fonts dialog box with a TT logo beside the typeface name. Typefaces that are device fonts have a printer icon beside their names in the list.

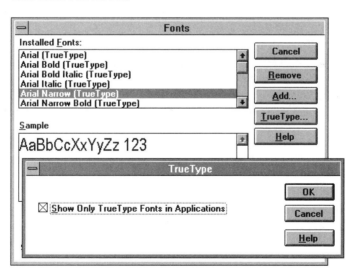

You can specify any size that you want for TrueType fonts, rather than choosing from a limited list of raster or vector font sizes.

Use the TrueType dialog box to specify that you want to use TrueType fonts or restrict all choices to only TrueType.

▶ **To specify that you want to use TrueType fonts**

1. Double-click the Fonts icon in the Control Panel window to display the Fonts dialog box.

2. Select the TrueType fonts that you want to use from the Installed Fonts box.

To ensure that type styles in your documents will print on any dot-matrix, HPPCL, or PostScript printer and that your documents can easily be moved to other platforms, specify that you only want to use TrueType fonts.

▶ **To specify that you want to only use TrueType fonts**

1. Double-click the Fonts icon in the Control Panel window to display the Fonts dialog box.

2. Choose the TrueType button to display the TrueType dialog box.

3. Select the Show Only TrueType Fonts In Application check box.

Windows NT does not automatically change fonts in documents that were produced with earlier font technologies. If you want to update old documents to use TrueType fonts, you must update them manually. You might also contact your application vendor to see if there are new utilities available that will assist automatic upgrading of documents to use TrueType fonts.

Note TrueType fonts use a different character spacing (called ABC widths) than was used for raster fonts. Applications that use this spacing will be able to space characters more accurately, especially for bold and italic text. However, because of this change in spacing, text can sometimes appear inaccurately in applications written for Windows 3.0 or earlier versions. For example, the end of a highlighted text line might look odd on screen.

Using Adobe Type 1 Fonts

Adobe Type 1 fonts are the font technology native to PostScript printers. Like TrueType fonts, Type 1 fonts contain instructions to generate outlines of characters; the outlines are scalable and rotatable. Type 1 fonts are a popular font technology in the desktop publishing industry. These fonts are designed to be downloaded to a PostScript printer, which can interpret their instructions, and thereby produce hardcopy output. Although you can print Type 1 fonts, you cannot directly view them on screen. For this reason, Adobe created an application called *Adobe Type Manager* (ATM), which reads Type 1 font files and creates equivalent raster screen fonts for several platforms.

Windows NT supports Type 1 fonts in two ways. It lets you install Type 1 fonts for use on your PostScript printer. It also provides a font converter that achieves the same goal as ATM by reading Type 1 fonts and creating equivalent TrueType fonts for viewing on screen.

The Windows NT 3.5 Type 1 font converter achieves a very high level of compatibility with ATM 2.5. If you format a document using Type 1 fonts on a computer running Windows for Workgroups 3.11 and ATM 2.5, and then load the same document under Windows NT 3.5 with the same set of Type 1 fonts converted to TrueType fonts, you will see the same character spacing and line breaks and the same output on your printer.

With the Type 1 installation process, you have the following options:

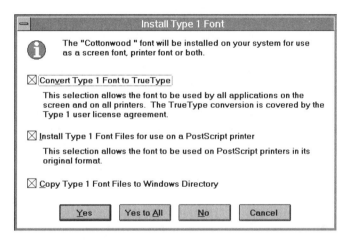

- Convert Type 1 font files to TrueType font files. If you select this option, Windows NT will read the font outline instructions that make up the Type 1 font, convert them into TrueType, and write this equivalent TrueType font to your hard disk.

- Install Type 1 font files for use on a PostScript printer. If you select this option, then when you print to a PostScript printer, Windows NT can send the Type 1 font to the printer. If you choose this option as well as the option described in the preceding paragraph, Windows NT will use the converted TrueType font for screen display, and download the Type 1 font when you print.

- Copy Type 1 Font Files to the Windows directory. If you choose to install the Type 1 font for use on a PostScript printer, then this option lets you copy it to the local computer's \systemroot\SYSTEM directory.

Legal Issues Regarding TrueType Fonts

There are several legal issues to be aware of when converting TrueType fonts.

- With Windows NT 3.5, you can legally convert Type 1 fonts to TrueType fonts only if the third-party font vendor grants permission..

  Windows NT contains a database of the copyright strings that third-party vendors embed within their fonts. If you try to convert a Type 1 font and the font converter does not find a recognized third-party vendor's copyright string in the font, it warns you that you may not have permission to convert this font. You are then advised to contact the third-party vendor to obtain permission to convert the Type 1 font.

  Although none of the third-party vendors that Microsoft contacted refused to allow conversion of their fonts, some vendors did not respond to the request. Those third-party vendors are not listed in the copyright string database, and their fonts will always produce a warning message.

Note The copyright strings that third-party vendors embed within their fonts were never meant to be machine-readable. For this reason, the copyright strings in different fonts from the same vendor sometimes contain different punctuation marks, or extra space characters, and so on. Most of these variations are represented in the copyright string database, but they can sometimes cause the font converter to reject a font, even though the third-party vendor has given their permission to convert it.

- The converted font is bound by the copyright restrictions that apply to the original Type 1 font. For example, if your Type 1 license does not permit you to use the Type 1 font on more than one computer at a time, then you are not permitted to use the converted TrueType font on more than one computer at a time.

- Converted TrueType fonts are only licensed for Windows NT 3.5. It is a copyright violation to copy converted fonts to other platforms, including Windows NT 3.1 or Windows For Workgroups 3.11.

In addition to the legal restrictions, there is a practical reason for not copying converted TrueType fonts to other platforms. Converted fonts are tuned to use features of the Windows NT 3.5 TrueType rasterizer that don't exist on other platforms' TrueType rasterizers. So, using converted fonts on other platforms will produce poor results. This is not a bug, it is an incentive to avoid illegal font copying.

Note All TrueType fonts behave the same way under Windows NT 3.5, whether they were originally created as TrueType or were converted from Type 1 fonts.

Disk Space, Memory Use, and Speed

You may notice a performance decrease if your document uses many fonts in different sizes. Rendering several fonts requires a large font cache, which might cause more swapping to the hard disk.

Hard disk space can be a problem when using multiple raster fonts, but it is not a problem for TrueType fonts. Any soft fonts you already have on your hard disk will not be affected by the installation of TrueType fonts with Windows NT.

The number of TrueType fonts that can exist simultaneously on your system is limited only by hard disk space. However, some printers limit the number of fonts you can use on a single page or in a single document.

Installing Fonts

In Windows NT, fonts can be installed on your system in several ways.

- Windows NT installs TrueType fonts and its screen fonts automatically during system installation. When you specify a printer and other options in the Printer Properties dialog box, Windows NT includes information about font cartridges and built-in fonts for your printer.

- To install additional TrueType fonts or Adobe Type 1 fonts for Postscript printers, choose the Fonts icon in the Control Panel window.

- To install third-party soft fonts on your hard disk, use the utility supplied by the third-party font vendor. To install the third-party soft fonts in Windows NT complete the following steps:

  1. Double-click the Print Manager icon in the Main window.

  2. Choose the Properties command from the Printer menu to display the Printer Properties dialog box.

  3. Choose the Setup button to display the Printer Setup dialog box

  4. Choose the Fonts button to display the Raster Printer Font Installer dialog box.

  5. Indicate the third-party soft fonts you want to install.

- To install a new font cartridge in your printer, complete the following steps:

  1. Double-click the Print Manager icon in the Main window.

  2. Choose the Properties command from the Printer menu to display the Printer Properties dialog box.

  3. Choose the Setup button to display the Printer Setup dialog box.

  4. Select the new font cartridge you want from the Font Cartridges box.

Adding Fonts

To install additional fonts, choose the Fonts icon in the Control Panel window. The following dialog box displays:

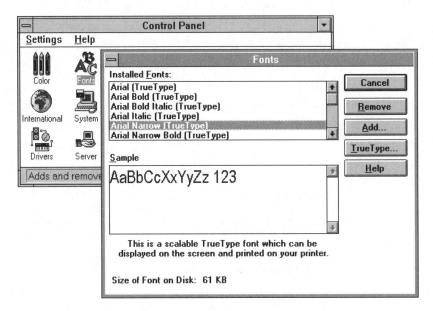

Note Some of the fonts shown here, such as Arial Narrow, are not included with Windows NT but can be purchased separately as part of the Microsoft TrueType Font Pack product.

For more information about installing fonts, choose the Help button in the dialog box.

Information About Installed Fonts

Information about the fonts installed on your system are kept in the Windows NT Registry. As shown in the following illustration, most of the information about installed fonts is kept in the HKEY_LOCAL_MACHINE\SOFTWARE key.

For more information, see "Registry Entries for Fonts" in Chapter 14, "Registry Value Entries."

If you installed Windows NT on a computer that previously had Windows 3.*x* installed, the Registry will include entries showing you where to find that information previously found in the **[Fonts]** and **[FontSubstitutes]** sections of the WIN.INI file. For example, to find information that used to be in the **[Fonts]** section of the WIN.INI file, look in the following location in the Registry:

```
HKEY_LOCAL_MACHINE\SOFTWARE\Microsoft\Windows NT\CurrentVersion\Fonts
```

How Windows NT Matches Fonts

When an application requests characters to print or display, Windows NT must find the appropriate font to use from among the fonts installed on your system. Finding the font can be complex because, for example, your document may contain fonts that aren't available on the current printer, or there may be more than one font with the same name installed on your system.

The basic rules that Windows NT uses for locating a font are as follows:

- If the font is a TrueType font, TrueType renders the character, and the result is sent to the display or to the printer.

- If the font is not a TrueType font, Windows NT uses the font mapping table to determine the most appropriate device font to use.

When Windows NT uses the font mapping table to match screen fonts to printer fonts, the characteristics used to find the closest match are—in descending order of importance—typeface name, character set, variable versus fixed pitch, family, height, width, weight, slant, underline, and strikeout.

The following table shows which types of Windows NT fonts can be printed on different kinds of printers.

Table 7.3   Windows NT Printable Fonts

Printer type	Device fonts	Raster fonts	Vector fonts	TrueType fonts
Dot Matrix	Yes	Yes	Yes	Yes
HPPCL	Yes	No	Yes	Yes
PostScript	Yes	No	Yes	Yes
Plotter	Yes	No	Yes	Yes

The following table lists the character sets installed with Windows NT.

Table 7.4   Windows NT Character Sets

Font	Font type, spacing, and default sizes
Arial Bold Italic	TrueType, proportional, scalable
Arial Bold	TrueType, proportional, scalable
Arial Italic	TrueType, proportional, scalable
Arial	TrueType, proportional, scalable
Courier New Bold Italic	TrueType, fixed, scalable
Courier New Bold	TrueType, fixed, scalable
Courier New Italic	TrueType, fixed, scalable
Courier New	TrueType, fixed, scalable
Courier	Raster, fixed, 10,12,15
Modern	Vector, proportional, scalable
MS Sans Serif	Raster, proportional, 8, 10, 12, 14, 18, 24
MS Serif	Raster, proportional, 6, 7, 8, 10, 12, 14, 18, 24
Roman	Vector, proportional, scalable
Script	Vector, proportional, scalable
Small	Raster, proportional, 2, 3, 4,5, 6, 7
Symbol**	Raster, proportional, 8, 10, 12, 14, 18, 24
Symbol**	TrueType, proportional, scalable
System	Raster, proportional, display-dependent size
Terminal*	Raster, fixed, display-dependent size
Times New Roman Bold Italic	TrueType, proportional, scalable
Times New Roman Bold	TrueType, proportional, scalable
Times New Roman Italic	TrueType, proportional, scalable
Times New Roman	TrueType, proportional, scalable
Wingdings	TrueType, proportional, scalable

* OEM character set, rather than ANSI character set

** Symbol character set, rather than ANSI character set

Screen Fonts and Windows NT

Windows NT uses special raster fonts as the system screen font for menus, window captions, messages, and other text. A set of system, fixed, and OEM terminal fonts is included with Windows NT to match your system's display capabilities (that is, for VGA or 8514 video displays). The default system screen font in Windows NT is System, a proportionally-spaced raster font.

The installed system screen fonts are listed in the following Registry keys:

```
HKEY_LOCAL_MACHINE\SOFTWARE\Microsoft\Windows NT
    \CurrentVersion\Fonts
HKEY_LOCAL_MACHINE\SOFTWARE\Microsoft\Windows NT
    \CurrentVersion\GRE_Initialize
```

By default, code page 437 (U.S.) fonts are installed using the EGA40WOA.FON, EGA80WOA.FON, and DOSAPP.FON files. Other screen font files are included for international language support, identified by the code page number appended to the filename.

Windows NT 3.5 supplies small and large font variations for several display drivers. The major difference between the small and large font variations is the system font set that the Setup program installs. The VGA-resolution system (small) fonts are VGAOEM, VGAFIX, and VGASYS. The 8514-resolution system (large) fonts are 8514OEM, 8514FIX, and 8514SYS.

Printer Fonts and Windows NT

A printer font is any font that can be produced on your printer. There are basically three kinds of printer fonts:

- *Device fonts* are fonts that actually reside in the hardware of your printer. They can be built into the printer itself or can be provided by a font cartridge or font card.

- *Printable screen fonts* are Windows NT screen fonts that can be translated for output to the printer (including TrueType).

- *Downloadable soft fonts* are fonts that reside on your hard disk and are sent to the printer when needed. (Only the characters needed for the particular document are downloaded, not the whole font set.)

Not all printers can use all three types of printer fonts. For example, HPPCL printers cannot print Windows NT screen fonts.

The Windows NT Universal printer driver takes advantage of TrueType fonts and offers other improvements over older dot-matrix and HPPCL printer drivers. The Windows NT Universal printer driver is used instead of specific dot-matrix or HPPCL printer drivers.

For more information about setting up printers, see Chapter 6, "Printing."

Mapping Characters

Windows NT uses the Windows ANSI portion of the Unicode character set. Some printers, such as the IBM Proprinter, use the IBM (OEM) standard for codes above 128. Other printers might use their own proprietary set of extended character codes.

To be sure you get the characters you want, see your printer documentation for the character set supported by the printer. Then see the online Help for Character Map for instructions on entering codes from the keyboard for special characters.

You can also use the Windows NT Character Map to select and insert special characters in your document.

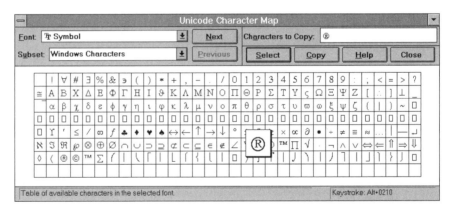

Figure 7.2   Mapping Special Characters

When you insert special characters in a document to print, the character you see on the screen might not be correct because it is displayed using the Windows ANSI portion of the Unicode character set and the best matching screen font for the current printer font. However, the printed document will contain the correct character. Conversely, if you type an ANSI character that appears on screen but is not supported in your printer fonts, some other character will be printed, instead.

Dot-Matrix Printer Fonts

Dot-matrix printers support device fonts and printable screen fonts. Usually, a dot-matrix printer includes only a limited range of internal device fonts. Typically, fixed-spacing fonts are supplied in a variety of characters-per-inch (CPI) sizes and are conventionally named "typeface *xx*CPI," where typeface is the typeface name, and *xx* is the number of characters per inch. Distinguishing a device font on a dot matrix printer is usually as easy as checking for the CPI designation at the end of the font name, such as Courier 10 CPI.

Through the Universal printer driver, dot-matrix printers can also support TrueType. When you use TrueType fonts on a dot-matrix printer, Windows NT sends a rasterized graphics image to the printer.

Dot-matrix printers do not provide any landscape device fonts, but vector and TrueType screen fonts can be printed in any resolution or orientation. Dot-matrix device fonts are faster but less flexible than screen fonts.

Dot-matrix printers are typically distinguished as either 9-pin or 24-pin printers (but not limited to these):

- 9-pin dot-matrix printers such as the Epson 9-pin and IBM Proprinter series usually print in a 1.67:1 aspect ratio. The Windows NT Epson 9-pin driver supports resolutions of 120x72 (1.67:1 aspect ratio), 120x144 (1:1.2), and 240x144 (1.67:1).

- 24-pin dot-matrix printers such as the Epson 24-pin and IBM Proprinter 24 series can print in 120x180 resolution (1:1.5 aspect ratio), 180x180 (1:1), and 360x180 (2:1). Some others, such as the NEC 24-pin, provide a 360x360 resolution. The 180x180 resolution is usually best for printing raster screen fonts. In 180x180 resolution, these printers can print 1:1 aspect ratio screen fonts, such as the E set (96x96 dpi) and the F set (120x120 dpi). E set fonts will be available at about 50 percent, and F set fonts at 75 percent of normal point sizes. A true 180x180 dpi screen font set is available by special order from Epson of America.

Some 24-pin dot-matrix printers such as the Epson and NEC printers also support font cards or cartridges. You can use these fonts if the Windows NT driver for that printer supports them. Use the printer setup dialog box to specify a font cartridge for your printer. (Choose Printer Properties from Print Manager, and then choose Setup.)

HPPCL Printer Fonts

Printers that use the Hewlett-Packard Printer Control Language (HPPCL) can print several different types of fonts. HPPCL printers can use font cartridges, downloadable soft fonts, vector screen fonts, and TrueType fonts.

HPPCL printers cannot print Windows NT raster screen fonts.

When you use TrueType fonts on an HPPCL printer, TrueType performs all the font rendering in the computer and downloads bitmaps of the fonts to the printer. (Windows NT downloads these bitmaps only if the printer has enough memory.) TrueType downloads only the specific characters needed in a document, not the entire font.

Note If you use an HP LaserJet-compatible printer, be sure to specify accurately in the printer driver the amount of memory installed in your printer. This is important because the Windows NT HPPCL minidriver tracks the available memory in your printer. You may get an out-of-printer-memory error or other errors if the memory is specified incorrectly.

Font Cartridges

Hewlett-Packard LaserJet-compatible font cartridges are supplied by numerous manufacturers, including Hewlett-Packard, Pacific Data Products, and IQ Engineering. Some cartridge vendors also produce custom font cartridges to your specifications.

Windows NT treats font cartridges as device fonts because they are always with the printer. Font cartridges can be selected in the Printer Properties dialog box. The HPPCL minidriver available with Windows NT can support all HP font cartridges.

If you want to add a font cartridge that came out after the printer driver was written, you may need a printer cartridge metrics (.PCM) file. A .PCM file tells Windows NT the characteristics of the new font and is installed with the Font Installer in the same way as soft fonts. After a .PCM file is installed, a new entry appears in the Cartridges dialog box of the Printer Properties dialog box.

For new HP cartridges, contact Hewlett-Packard or other cartridge vendor for the appropriate .PCM file.

Downloadable Fonts

You can get HP LaserJet-compatible downloadable soft fonts from a number of sources, including Hewlett-Packard, Bitstream, SoftCraft, and CompuGraphics. Some downloadable font utilities also generate raster screen fonts for Windows NT. If an exact screen font match is not available, Windows NT uses one of its own screen fonts.

Hewlett-Packard downloadable fonts are installed with the Font Installer. (To use the Font Installer, start Print Manager, select the printer, choose Print Properties, choose Setup, and then choose the Fonts button.)

Font Limitations for Older HPPCL Printers

Some older model HPPCL printers have a limit of 16 fonts per page. If you send a page that contains more than 16 fonts to an HPPCL printer, a warning message is displayed.

An Error 20 message might appear on the front panel of the HPPCL printer when printing a document that contains soft fonts. This also indicates that you tried to download more fonts than the printer's memory can hold. You can recover from this error by pressing the Continue button on the printer control panel. The soft font that caused the error is not downloaded and will not print.

To avoid this error, reduce the number of fonts that you try to download, or add more memory to your printer. Also make sure you haven't downloaded any permanent soft fonts that are taking up memory in the printer.

Printer Fonts for HP Printers

Windows NT includes fonts for Hewlett-Packard PCL, DeskJet, and PaintJet printers.

HP LaserJet Printer Fonts

In Windows NT, all HPPCL (LaserJet) printers are supported by the HPPCL.DLL or HPPCL5MS.DLL minidrivers. Additional LaserJet III scalable outline fonts are available from Hewlett-Packard as cartridges or downloadable soft fonts. With the HPPCL drivers in Windows NT, downloadable outline fonts can be installed with the Font Installer.

HP DeskJet Printer Fonts

The HP DeskJet Printers are ink-jet printers. The Windows NT driver for the Hewlett-Packard DeskJet printer family supports Windows NT vector screen fonts, DeskJet internal fonts, soft fonts, and TrueType. DeskJet printers can print at resolutions of 75, 150, and 300 dpi. Without font cartridges, the DeskJet includes only the built-in Courier and LinePrinter fonts. Cartridges can be selected in the Printer Properties dialog box. At this time, font cartridges for DeskJet printers are available only from Hewlett-Packard.

DeskJet soft fonts are installed with the Font Installer. To use downloadable fonts on the DeskJet printers, you must install either HP22707A or HP22707B RAM cartridges. When you set printer memory in the Printer Properties dialog box, make sure to specify the total amount of RAM cartridge memory if more than one cartridge is installed.

DeskJet internal, downloadable, and cartridge fonts will not work in landscape orientation. This is a hardware, not a driver, limitation. For landscape mode, print with Windows NT vector screen fonts such as Modern or Roman.

HP PaintJet Printer Fonts

The HP PaintJet is a color ink-jet printer. The Hewlett-Packard PaintJet driver in Windows NT composes a full page at a time in 180x180 dpi resolution and outputs the page to the PaintJet as a large bitmap. This produces the highest possible quality of output, but results in very large spool files. For improved printing speed, it is recommended that you choose the Print Directly To Ports option in the Details dialog box in Printer Properties. This option prevents the creation of spool files.

The PaintJet driver supports the printing of PaintJet internal fonts, Windows NT raster and vector screen fonts, PaintJet soft fonts, and TrueType. The same considerations apply for printing raster screen fonts on the PaintJet as for using the 24-pin dot matrix printers in 180x180 dpi resolution (see "Dot Matrix Printer Fonts," earlier in this chapter). PaintJet soft fonts are not downloadable fonts. They are used internally by the driver, which places them as necessary into the full-page bitmap during page composition. The font itself is never sent to the printer, except as part of the full-page bitmap.

PaintJet soft fonts, which have a .PJF filename extension, are installed with the Font Installer. Windows NT supports PaintJet soft fonts for Courier 10-CPI and Letter Gothic 12-CPI and 18-CPI. Additional soft fonts can be obtained from Hewlett-Packard. Scalable PaintJet soft fonts are also available from Hewlett-Packard in the HP Color PrintKit (HP part number 17390A).

PostScript Printer Fonts

Adobe Type 1 PostScript fonts are scalable outlines that can be printed at any size. PostScript outline fonts can also be rotated to any angle and can be printed in both portrait and landscape modes. However, font size limits are often imposed by applications. A common PostScript font size limit in an application is 127 points.

Most PostScript printers include either the standard Apple LaserWriter Plus set of 35 scalable fonts or the earlier Apple LaserWriter set of 17 fonts.

Type 1 fonts are installed in the Fonts icon in Control Panel. When you install the font, Windows NT gives you the option of creating an equivalent TrueType font for use as a screen font.

PostScript printers can print Windows NT raster screen fonts, vector screen fonts, TrueType fonts, or Type 1 fonts.

LaserWriter Plus Typefaces

The LaserWriter Plus standard font set includes eleven typefaces, including the following eight, which are available in roman, bold, italic, and bold italic:

- AvantGarde Gothic
- Helvetica
- ITC Bookman®
- Palatino®
- Courier
- Helvetica Narrow
- New Century Schoolbook
- Times

The other three typefaces are Symbol, Zapf Chancery, and Zapf Dingbats. The Symbol typeface contains mathematical and scientific symbols; Zapf Chancery is a calligraphic font; and Zapf Dingbats contains decorative bullet characters and embellishments. These typefaces are available only in roman style.

PostScript Printers and TrueType

TrueType fonts are treated as downloaded fonts by the PostScript driver. When you use TrueType fonts on a PostScript printer, scaling and hints are always performed in the computer. Scan conversion can be done in the computer or in the printer, depending on the point size. At smaller point sizes, TrueType performs scan conversion in the computer; at larger point sizes, scan conversion is done in the printer.

You can map a TrueType font to a PostScript font by using the FontSubst option in Print Manager. (Choose Properties from the Printer menu, and then choose Setup to see this option.) This is helpful to view TrueType as a screen font and to get PostScript for the printout font. This will increase printing speed, but the results on the display may not be exactly the same as the printed output.

Alternately, you can choose to download TrueType fonts as soft fonts to the printer, so that the printed output matches the screen display. (In Print Manager, specify your printer and choose Properties from the Printer menu. Then, in order, choose these three command buttons: Details, Job Defaults, Options. Select the Download TrueType Fonts as Softfont option button.)

Substituting PostScript Fonts

You can edit the Substitution Table to specify which PostScript printer fonts you want to print in place of the TrueType fonts in your documents. The changes you make in the Substitution Table only affect the fonts that are printed. The fonts that appear on the screen will not change; the original TrueType fonts are still used to display TrueType text in your document.

To specify which printer fonts to use, choose FontSubst from the Printer Setup dialog box. Then select the TrueType font you want to replace from the For TrueType Font list in the Substitution dialog box. From the Substitute Printer Font list, select the PostScript printer font you want to use instead of the selected TrueType font.

If your printer supports downloaded fonts, you can choose the Download As Soft Font option, as described in the preceding section. In this case, the selected TrueType fonts will be sent to the printer as soft fonts. Repeat these steps until you have selected printer fonts to use in place of all the TrueType fonts in your document.

PostScript Downloadable Outline Fonts

In addition to installed fonts, PostScript printers also accept downloadable outline fonts, which can be scaled to any size and printed in both portrait and landscape orientations. Downloadable PostScript fonts are available from several suppliers, including Adobe, Agfa, Bitstream, and Monotype.

Although PostScript downloadable outlines can be scaled to any size, Windows NT raster screen fonts cannot. If you specify a PostScript font size that does not have a corresponding screen font, Windows NT substitutes another screen font. This results in a little loss in display quality but no loss in print quality.

Specifying Virtual Printer Memory

You can change the amount of virtual memory that your PostScript printer has available for storing fonts. The PostScript driver uses a default setting recommended by the printer manufacturer for virtual memory.

To adjust the amount of virtual memory for your printer, in the PostScript Printer Setup dialog box, type the amount of virtual memory you want to use in the Printer Memory (kilobytes) box. (Choose the Setup option from the Printer Properties dialog box.) To determine the right value, copy the TESTPS.TXT file (supplied with the Windows NT Resource Kit) to the printer, and enter in this dialog the recommended virtual memory value printed on the resulting page.

Questions and Answers About Fonts

This section answers some common questions about using fonts with Windows NT.

- I printed the same document with TrueType fonts from two different computers to the same PostScript printer. The two printouts are different. Why?

   TrueType font substitution is different on the two computers. Use Print Manager to reconfigure font substitution on one of the computers.

- My document looks fine on the screen but prints with a different font. Why?

   This may be happening for one of two reasons. Either you specified the wrong printer model during setup, or the downloadable font did not download to the print device. Check the Printer Properties dialog box to see that the printer driver you are using matches the print device. Then choose Setup, and check the amount of memory for your printer. Make sure the amount shown in the Setup dialog box accurately reflects the amount of memory for your print device. If there is too little memory, the print device may not be able to download fonts.

- My document prints OK, but it looks funny on the screen. Why?

   There is no direct displayable equivalent of a device font that you are using.

- I can't select a font that I know is provided by a cartridge installed in the printer. Why?

   In Print Manager, make sure that the printer properties lists the correct cartridge.

C H A P T E R   8

Microsoft Mail

Windows NT includes an electronic mail application, Microsoft Mail, that can be used to exchange information with other Windows NT computers. Mail also can work interactively with many other Windows-based applications.

This chapter describes the components that make up Mail and explains how to use Mail functionality from within other Windows-based applications, such as Microsoft Word for Windows and Microsoft Excel for Windows. This chapter also describes customization features you can use to tailor Mail for your office, including custom commands, custom message types, custom menus, and the Messaging Application Program Interface (MAPI).

About Mail

The Mail application provided with Windows NT has a client side, a mail-server side, and an interface between them. The client side includes a visual user interface, made up of viewers for messages, folders, and address lists. The server simply contains a directory structure known as the *postoffice* and has no programmatic components. The interface between the client and server manages message storage and retrieval, name validation, and directory access.

A user sends mail to and receives mail from a *message store* on their own computer. When a user sends a message, it is forwarded from the local computer's message store to the postoffice located on the mail server. The postoffice has a mailbox for each user, giving users access to the messages they've received when they sign in to Mail.

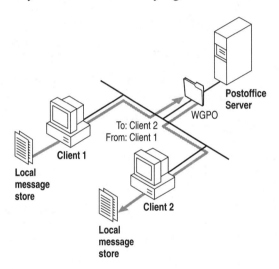

Figure 8.1   Local Message Stores and the WGPO

Mail uses a *shared file system*, which means that the postoffice must reside on a share on a computer running Windows NT to which each user in the workgroup has access. The postoffice is a directory structure in which the main directory is called a *workgroup postoffice* (WGPO). All postoffice file manipulation is handled by the Mail client.

The postoffice is a temporary message store, holding a message until the recipient's workstation retrieves it. Mail is efficient because it stores only one copy of each mail message, even when a message is addressed to multiple recipients. When it is retrieved, the message is removed from the postoffice. A message sent to multiple recipients has a reference count in it. The count decrements each time a recipient retrieves the message, and the message itself is removed when the reference count drops to zero.

For information about how to use Mail, see Chapter 7, "Mail," in the *Windows NT System Guide*.

Mail Postoffice

Figure 8.2 shows the postoffice directory structure.

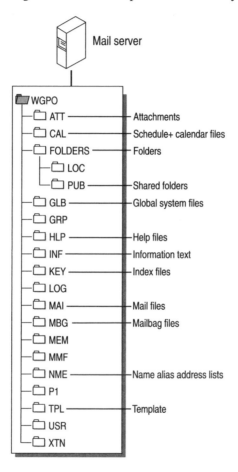

Figure 8.2   Postoffice Directory Structure

All subdirectories must be present for the Mail application to function correctly. The following list describes what is contained in each subdirectory of the Mail postoffice:

- The ATT subdirectory contains encrypted file attachments.
- The CAL subdirectory contains Schedule+ calendar files.

- The FOLDERS\PUB subdirectory contains shared folders.

- The GLB subdirectory contains global system files for Mail. These files contain local user logon information and control files to generate mail files.

- The HLP subdirectory contains Mail help files.

- The INF and TPL subdirectories contain information and template files, respectively. The ADMIN.INF and ADMIN.TPL files contain template information for local postoffice users.

- The KEY subdirectory includes index files that contain pointers to header records in the mailbag (.MBG) files.

- The MAI subdirectory stores mail messages in encrypted form until the recipients retrieve them.

- The MBG subdirectory contains Mail headers that point to the Mail (.MAI) files. For each file in this directory, there is a matching index (.KEY) file.

- The NME subdirectory contains pointer files for the name alias address lists. The ADMIN.NME and ADMINSHD.NME files list members of the postoffice address list.

- The FOLDERS\LOC, GRP, LOG, MEM, MMF, P1, USR, and XTN subdirectories are reserved.

Workgroup Postoffice Administration

The workgroup postoffice administrator is responsible for creating and managing the postoffice. The only difference between the administrator and other Mail users is that the administrator can perform the following tasks:

- Back up the postoffice, which should be done on a regular basis
- Add users to the postoffice
- Change user information, including forgotten passwords
- Check the status of shared folders

The *workgroup postoffice manager library* (WGPOMG32.DLL) is the software component that supports administrative functions such as adding or deleting users and changing passwords.

For more information about performing administrative tasks, see Chapter 7, "Mail," in the *Windows NT System Guide*.

Interface Between the Mail Client and Postoffice

Mail has a modular architecture. While some of the modules comprise the user interface and postoffice, most modules make up the interface between the Mail client and the Mail postoffice. Figure 8.3 shows the key components that make up this interface.

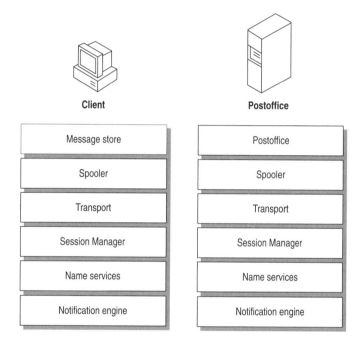

Client   Postoffice

| Message store |
| Spooler |
| Transport |
| Session Manager |
| Name services |
| Notification engine |

| Postoffice |
| Spooler |
| Transport |
| Session Manager |
| Name services |
| Notification engine |

Figure 8.3   Components of the Interface Between Mail Clients and Server

Mail Spooler and Mail Transport

When you have a message to send, the *spooler* (MAILSP32.EXE) notifies the *transport* (MSSFS32.DLL) to move the message from your Outbox to the postoffice. When a message arrives for you at the postoffice, the spooler notifies the transport to deliver the message to your Inbox.

The primary job of the spooler is to parcel out system idle time to the transport. This enables the transport to transfer messages in a timely manner but without interfering with the work you really want to do in the foreground. The spooler provides a safety net for the transport by retrying any operations that fail.

The spooler also resolves address book entries, adds message recipients to the personal address book, generates nondelivery reports, checks for new mail, and deletes mail from the server.

Mail Session Manager

The *Mail Session Manager* (MAILM32.DLL) validates users' identities and manages connections with the Message Store, directory, and transport. It is the component that enables you to work even when the Mail server is unavailable (for example, when you work offline). Mail continues to work with the resources that are available at your computer and automatically connects to the server's resources when the server is available again. Maintaining the security of messages across transitions from offline to online and back is another feature of the Mail Session Manager.

Name Service

The *Name Service* (MAILM32.DLL) manages functions related to browsing and filtering lists of names. At the user interface, the Name Service is apparent whenever you browse file folders, specify search criteria, or ask for a recipient's name to be checked.

With the exception of the personal address book, the Name Service treats the directories it uses as read-only lists. Addresses, as used in Mail, consist of the following parts:

- Display name, which is usually the full descriptive name of a person, group, or resource. This is the name you most often see in the user interface.

- Mail address type, which helps the transport route mail and provides the syntax of the mail address to the Mail client.

- Mail address, which is the part actually used to identify the routing destination for a message.

Notification Engine

When you receive new mail, the *Notification Engine* (STORE32.DLL) lets you know that the mail has arrived.

The Notification Engine also works with the Session Manager when you browse or filter messages. Folder management and message searches use the services of the Notification Engine.

For example, you can have multiple windows viewing the same folder. If you delete a message from the folder in one of the windows, it automatically disappears from the others because each window waits for notification of events like messages being deleted.

When a new message arrives and is written to the *Message Store* by the spooler, the Inbox viewer is updated by the Notification Engine. When you place a message in your Outbox, the Notification Engine alerts the spooler that there is a message to deliver to the postoffice.

Customizing the Mail Client

You can use several Mail features to customize the way Mail works for a user on a Windows NT computer:

- *Custom commands* are commands you add to Mail menus.

- *Custom message types* enable you to define and install mail forms customized for your own requirements.

- *Custom menus* enable you to add a menu name to the Mail menu bar. You may use these menus to group custom commands and/or messages under a single, distinctive menu item.

- The *Messaging Application Program Interface* (MAPI) is a set of calls you can use to easily add Mail-enabled features to other Windows-based applications.

You can install custom commands, message types, and menus for use by a single user on an individual computer or on a network file server to be shared by many users.

Custom Commands

You can add custom functions to your Mail menus with custom commands. A custom command is one that you add to a menu to perform a unique function tailored to your needs.

There is a second type of custom command not associated with any menu, but which can be set to run whenever the user starts Mail, exits Mail, or receives a new message.

A custom command is implemented as a dynamic-link library (DLL). Any executable code—including batch files or applications—can be run from a custom command. Here are some examples of how custom commands can be used to tailor Mail for specific needs:

- Display a window that contains information specific to where the user works, such as a parts list or a list of stock quotes.

- Query a database without leaving Mail.

- Launch another application and open a specific file. For example, users can create a command to open a MEMOS.TXT file in the Windows Notepad application.

Installing Custom Commands

You can install custom commands on the local computer for use by a single user or centrally on the postoffice to be shared by all users. Installing the command on the postoffice eases installation and administrative tasks, and saves space on other users' hard disks.

Once installed, these custom commands can appear to users as built-in features. You can install up to 1000 custom commands in Mail. If you install several custom commands, you can add separator bars between groups of commands to help organize the menu's appearance.

To install custom commands for a user on an individual computer, you need to modify the Registry on that computer for each custom command and supply the appropriate DLLs. To install custom commands for everyone who uses a postoffice, you need to modify the Registry for each user, modify the SHARED32.INI file on the postoffice computer, and add the DLLs to the postoffice computer.

Note Typically, the Setup program that installs the custom commands automatically modifies entries in your computer's Registry and in the postoffice computer's SHARED32.INI file. The information in the following sections is for your reference if you need to make the modifications yourself.

Starting Separate Applications

Mail expects that a custom command will be implemented as a DLL. A custom command can launch an application. The DLL can pass information about the command to the application when it starts.

Although Mail always calls a DLL, the DLL can pass information to an application by using Windows dynamic data exchange (DDE), command-line parameters, or a disk file. If the called application is already running, the DLL transfers information most efficiently using DDE. If the DLL uses a disk file, care should be taken so that multiple temporary files are not added to the user's disk. The application that implements the custom command runs independently of Mail.

Installing a Custom Command for a Single User

To install a custom command for a single user on an individual computer, follow these steps:

1. Copy the DLL for the custom command to the *SystemRoot*\SYSTEM32 directory of your hard drive.

2. Add a custom command entry to the Registry on your computer in HKEY_CURRENT_USER\Software\Microsoft\Mail\Custom Commands. For information on how to do this, see "Custom Command Entries for Mail" in Chapter 14, "Registry Value Entries."

3. Quit Mail if it is running, and then restart it. Mail reads your Registry and adds the custom command.

Installing a Custom Command on the Postoffice

If you have a custom command that you want to make available to multiple users, you can install the command on the postoffice instead of in each user's Registry. When you create a new custom command, you must include a **SharedExtensionsDir** entry in this key in each user's Registry:

```
HKEY_CURRENT_USER\Software\Microsoft\Mail\Microsoft Mail
```

This entry instructs Mail to check the server's SHARED32.INI file for custom command entries.

Mail finds the **SharedExtensionsDir** entry in the user's Registry, then reads entries for custom commands in SHARED32.INI before returning to the user's Registry to read any custom command entries there.

For example in Figure 8.4, Mail reads the **SharedExtensionsDir** entry in the user's Registry first. Then it reads the entries in the **[Custom Commands]** section of SHARED32.INI (in this case, the lines labeled **tagA=** and **tagB=**). After reading all of the custom command entries in SHARED32.INI, Mail reads entries in the key of the user's Registry (in this case, the entries labeled **tag1** and **tag2**):

```
HKEY_CURRENT_USER\Software\Microsoft\Mail\Custom Commands
```

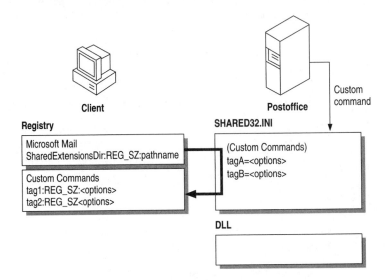

Figure 8.4   File Interaction with Shared Custom Commands

The directory on the postoffice share specified by **SharedExtensionsDir** in the Registry contains the SHARED32.INI file as well as the DLLs that implement shared custom commands.

Mail can check a server for custom commands and custom messages in the following ways:

- When you use a dynamic connection to the postoffice
- When you manually connect to the postoffice before starting Mail

The syntax you use with the **SharedExtensionsDir** entry in the Registry reflects the way you choose to connect. The **SharedExtensionsDir** entry uses the following syntax:

SharedExtensionsDir:REG_SZ:*server******share******pathname* [*password*]

–Or–

SharedExtensionsDir:REG_SZ:*pathname*

When you want to dynamically connect to the server's shared disk, use the *server**share**pathname* option with **SharedExtensionsDir**. Use the *pathname* option with **SharedExtensionsDir** to point to a manual connection to the server's shared disk.

To install a shared custom command, follow these steps:

1. Create a shared Mail extensions directory on the postoffice.
2. Copy the custom command DLL to the shared extensions directory.
3. A sample SHARED32.INI file is included on the *Windows NT Resource Guide* disks. Copy this file to the shared extensions directory.
4. Add custom command entries to the **[Custom Commands]** section of the SHARED32.INI file on the postoffice, using the following syntax:

   tag=*Mail version; menu; name; position; DLL name; command; event map; status text; Help file; Help context*

Note   The custom command entries should be a single command line in the SHARED32.INI file. Don't add any carriage returns even if line-wrapping occurs.

Values are defined in the following table.

Value	Definition
tag	The descriptive identifier for the command.
version	The version of Mail in which the custom command is compatible.
menu	Indicates the menu where the custom command is to be added, such as File or Help.
name	The command name that is to appear on the menu. You may include an ampersand (&) just before the letter that is to serve as an ALT+ key accelerator.

Value	Definition
position	The zero-relative position within its menu where the command is to appear. A value of **-1** places the command at the end of the menu.
DLL name	Name or path of the DLL where the custom command resides. This entry can optionally be followed by a comma and the ordinal of the entry point to call (default is ,**1**).
command	The command string passed as one of the parameters to the DLL entry point for the command.
event map	A sequence of up to 16 digits identifying the Mail events that the custom command supports. Each can be **0** or **1** to indicate if the DLL is to be called for a specific event. Currently, three events are defined; the rest are reserved and must be zero (or this whole section can be empty): The first digit means Mail startup. The second digit means Mail exit. The third digit means the arrival of a new message.
status text	Text to be displayed in the Mail status bar when the user moves the cursor to the command in the menu.
Help file	The Windows NT Help file to be invoked when the user presses F1 while the command is selected. The specified filename is passed to the Windows NT Help program. (This is an optional value.)
Help context	Passed to the Windows NT Help program along with the Help file name. Use **-1** (Help file index) if there is no specific entry in the Help file for this command. (This is an optional value.)
	There is one special token that may appear within certain fields:
<ExtsDir>	Expands to the value of **SharedExtensionsDir** in the user's Registry. Used to refer to DLLs that are installed in a shared extensions directory on the network. Valid for the DLL name, command, and Help file subfields.

5. In the Registry on your computer, add a **SharedExtensionsDir** entry to reference the shared extensions directory in the following key:

```
HKEY_CURRENT_USER\Software\Microsoft\Mail\Microsoft Mail
```

For information about **SharedExtensionsDir**, see "Microsoft Mail Entries" in Chapter 14, "Registry Value Entries."

6. If you have chosen the manual connection method, make the necessary network connection using File Manager.

7. Quit Mail if it is running, and then restart it.

   Mail rereads your Registry and adds the shared custom command to the specified menu.

8. Test the shared custom command.

9. When the custom command works successfully on your computer, modify each user's Registry to have access to the shared extensions directory. (See step 5.)

Custom Message Types

You can install up to 1000 custom message types in Mail. A custom message type is a special type (or class) of message for delivery between two or more Mail recipients or Mail-enabled applications. A custom message type can define a particular way to perform standard Mail operations such as composing, replying to, and forwarding messages. Custom message types can define a message's appearance and content, or the behavior of the forms displayed to the user when sending, reading, and replying to messages of that type.

Most custom message types are received in your Inbox just like standard mail messages. A second kind of custom message type doesn't appear in the Inbox when it arrives and yet is available to other Mail-enabled applications. This allows Mail-enabled applications to define their own message classes.

Custom message types have many similarities to custom commands. Like custom commands, a command for composing a custom message type can be added to a Mail menu. When the Mail user chooses this command, the custom message type DLL displays a dialog box or form that enables the user to compose a message of the corresponding type. These dialog boxes or forms can include features specific to the message type.

When a custom-type message arrives in a Mail folder, it can appear in the message list the same as other standard mail messages. But when read or replied to, the custom dialog boxes or forms associated with the message type can be displayed in place of the standard read or reply form. You can also design a custom message type that doesn't appear in Mail's Inbox when it arrives and yet is available to other Mail-enabled applications.

Note If a custom message type is delivered to a user who does not have that custom message type installed, the message is treated as a standard message type.

Custom message types can provide special messaging functionality such as the following:

- Messages that are composed or read using a special form.
- Messages accessed by the user through an application other than Mail.
- Messages that are preaddressed to a particular recipient.
- Messages that are used to order parts or services or to describe an event. The dialog boxes displayed when the user composes these types of messages can include special structured fields specific to the purpose of the message.
- Messages that help route workflow events.
- Messages that are specific to group scheduling.
- Messages that enable some type of game, such as chess, to be played between two Mail users.

Microsoft Schedule+ is an example of an application that defines its own custom message types. Schedule+ uses the following custom message types:

- IPM.Microsoft Schedule.MtgReq is used to generate the Meeting Request form.
- IPM.Microsoft Schedule.MtgRespP is used to generate the Positive Meeting Response form.
- IPM.Microsoft Schedule.MtgRespN is used to generate the Negative Meeting Response form.
- IPM.Microsoft Schedule.MtgRespA is used to generate the Tentative Meeting Response form.
- IPM.Microsoft Schedule.MtgCncl is used to generate a Meeting Cancellation message.

For more information, see "Custom Message Types for Schedule+" in Chapter 9, "Microsoft Schedule+."

Installing Custom Message Types

Installing a custom message type is similar to installing a custom command. Just like custom commands, you can install custom message types on an individual computer or on the postoffice as shared custom message types. Typically, though, you will install them as shared custom message types because you will want both sending and receiving parties to take advantage of the custom message type.

When you install custom message types on an individual computer, you must modify the Registry on that computer by adding a custom message type entry in this key:

```
HKEY_CURRENT_USER\Software\Microsoft\Mail\Custom Messages
```

For information about how to do this, see "Custom Messages Entries for Mail" in Chapter 14, "Registry Value Entries."

For shared custom message types, you must add a custom message type entry to the postoffice's SHARED32.INI file. Then, on each workstation using the shared custom message type, you must add a **SharedExtensionsDir** entry in the Microsoft Mail subkey Registry. As with custom commands, when Mail sees this entry in the Registry, it reads SHARED32.INI for custom message type entries before reading custom message type entries in the Registry.

Installing Custom Message Types on the Postoffice

To install a shared custom message type on the postoffice, follow these steps:

1. Create a shared Mail extensions directory on the postoffice.

2. Copy the SHARED32.INI file and custom message type DLL (and/or .EXE) to the shared extensions directory.

3. Add custom message type declarations to the **[Custom Messages]** section of the SHARED32.INI file on the postoffice, using this syntax:

   MessageClassName=*Mail version***;** *menu name***;** *command name***;* *command position***;** *ExtsDir DLL name***;** *ExtsDir command string***;* *operation map***;** *status text***;** *ExtsDir Help file name***;** *Help context***;**

Note   The message type declarations should be a single command line in the SHARED32.INI file. Do not add any carriage returns even if line-wrapping occurs.

Values are defined in the following table.

Value	Definition
class	A string uniquely identifying the message type. Mail places this string in messages and calls custom message DLLs based on its value.
Mail version	Identifies the version of Mail in which the custom message is compatible.
menu name	Indicates the menu where the custom command for the message type is to be added, such as File or Mail.

Value	Definition
command name	The command name that is to appear on the menu. As usual, you may include an ampersand (&) just before the letter that is to serve as an ALT+ key accelerator.
command position	The zero-relative position within its menu at which the command is to appear. A value of **-1** places the command at the end of the menu.
ExtsDir DLL name	The name or path of the DLL in which the custom message resides.
command string	The Command string passed as one of the parameters to the DLL entry point for the command.
operation map	A sequence of up to 16 digits. Each can be **0**, **1**, or **2**. **0** indicates that Mail is to perform its standard operation on the custom message. **1** indicates that the DLL is to be called to handle the operation. **2** indicates that the operation is to be completely disabled. Currently, eight operations are defined; the rest are reserved and must be zero. In the following list, **0** is the leftmost digit:
	0 Compose (menu command defined in this entry)
	1 File.Open
	2 Mail.Reply
	3 Mail.Reply to All
	4 Mail.Forward
	5 File.Print
	6 File.Save as
	7 Arrival of new mail
status text	Text to be displayed in the Mail status bar when the user moves the cursor to the command in the menu.
ExtsDir Help file name	The Windows NT Help file to be invoked when the user presses F1 while the command is selected. The specified filename is passed to the Windows NT help program. (This value is optional.)
Help context	Passed to the Windows NT help program along with the Help file name. Use **-1** (Help file index) if there is no specific entry in the Help file for this command. (This value is optional.)
	There is one special token that may appear within certain fields:
<ExtsDir>	Expands to the value of **SharedExtensionsDir** in the user's Registry. Used to refer to DLLs that are installed in a shared extensions directory on the network. Valid for the DLL name, command, and Help file subfields.

4. In the Registry on your computer, add a **SharedExtensionsDir** entry to reference the shared extensions directory in the following key:

```
HKEY_CURRENT_USER\Software\Microsoft\Mail\Microsoft Mail
```

For information about how to do this, see "Microsoft Mail Entries" in Chapter 14, "Registry Value Entries."

5. If you have chosen the manual connection method, make the necessary network connection using File Manager.

6. Quit Mail if it is running, and then restart it.

Mail rereads your Registry and adds the shared custom message to the specified menu.

7. Restart Mail and test the shared custom message type.

8. When the custom message type works successfully on your computer, modify each user's Registry to have access to the shared extensions directory. (See step 4.)

Custom Menus

You can add menu items to the Mail menu bar by putting custom menu entries in the Custom Menus section of your Registry or in the **[Custom Menus]** section of the SHARED32.INI file (in the directory specified by the **SharedExtensionsDir** entry in your Registry). The SHARED32.INI file is examined first.

Each entry specifies a menu name to be added to the Mail menu bar. You may use these menus to group custom commands and/or messages under a single menu item. A description follows of the custom menu entry format for the SHARED32.INI file. Each entry must occupy a single line. Many subfields are optional. For information on how to add equivalent entries to your Registry, see Chapter 14, "Registry Value Entries."

tag=*version*;*name*;*name to follow*;*status text*

For example,

```
tools=3.0;&Tools;Window;Useful development toys
```

Values are defined in the following table.

Value	Definition
tag	Identifies the menu to someone reading the .INI file but serves no other purpose.
version	Identifies the version of Mail in which the command is compatible.
name	The menu name to be added to the menu bar. As usual, you may include an ampersand (&) just before the letter that is to serve as an ALT+ key accelerator.
name to follow	Name of an existing menu. The new menu will be added directly before it.
status text	Text to be displayed in the Mail status bar when the user moves the cursor to the menu.

Messaging Application Program Interface (MAPI)

The Messaging Application Program Interface (MAPI) is a set of functions that developers can use to create Mail-enabled applications. Mail includes a subset of 12 functions called *Simple MAPI*, which enable developers to send, address, and receive messages from within Windows-based applications.

With Simple MAPI functions, developers can easily add the power of messaging to any Windows-based application. Simple MAPI supports the standard interface for simple integration of a Windows-based application with Mail.

All of the Simple MAPI functions are designed to be called from C or C++ programs, but they can also be called from high-level languages, such as Visual Basic®, Actor®, Smalltalk®, and ObjectVision®. Simple MAPI functions can also be called from applications with macro languages that can call a DLL. Two examples of these are Microsoft Excel for Windows or Microsoft Word for Windows.

Some Simple MAPI functions include a user interface (a dialog box) but can also be called without generating an interface. The seamless integration with Mail is convenient for applications such as word processors and spreadsheets, which manipulate files that users may want to exchange through Mail. The style of the user interface is not defined by Simple MAPI, so you can design your own.

An application developer can incorporate Mail functionality into their application by calling the MAPI functions. For example, if an application creates data files that need to be distributed to other users in a workgroup, the application developer can use the **MapiSendDocuments()** function to create a mail message and to send the data files as an attachment to the message. Sending mail messages is fully controlled from the application and the MAPI support library (MAPI32.DLL). The user doesn't need to have the Mail program running to do this.

In this case, one function call is all that is required. The **MapiSendDocuments()** function creates and initializes a message and supplies all the standard Mail dialog boxes for the user to send messages. The function can be compiled into the native code of the application, or if the application includes a macro facility that can link to a DLL, the developer can integrate the DLL as an added macro command.

Simple MAPI consists of the following functions:

Table 8.1   Simple MAPI Functions

Function	Description
MapiAddress()	Addresses a Mail message.
MapiDeleteMail()	Deletes a Mail message.
MapiDetails()	Displays a recipient details dialog box.
MapiFindNext()	Returns the ID of the next (or first) Mail message of a specified type.
MapiFreeBuffer()	Frees memory allocated by the messaging system.
MapiLogoff()	Ends a session with the messaging system.
MapiLogon()	Begins a session with the messaging system.
MapiReadMail()	Reads a Mail message.
MapiResolveName()	Displays a dialog box to resolve an ambiguous recipient name.
MapiSaveMail()	Saves a Mail message.
MapiSendDocuments()	Sends a standard Mail message.
MapiSendMail()	Sends a Mail message.

Integrating Mail and Other Applications

Some applications provide macros and support functions so that users can use the capabilities of Mail directly from within the application. For example, the latest releases of both Microsoft Excel for Windows and Microsoft Word for Windows provide macros to send worksheets and documents, respectively, directly from within these applications.

As an example of how Mail can be integrated with applications, Windows NT provides a File Manager extension to add a Send Mail option to the File Manager menu and toolbar. The Send Mail command displays all the user interface necessary for the user to send the currently selected files or executable files as file attachments to a message. The user can add message text around the file attachment, change the attached files, and address the message as usual.

Tips for Using Mail

This section offers tips for running Mail.

Recreating the Mail Initialization Procedure

When you first run the Mail application, it asks whether you want to use an existing postoffice on the workgroup or to create the postoffice on your computer. If you accidentally select the incorrect option, you will need to reinitialize Mail so that these options are available again. You can also use this procedure to recreate a postoffice.

To reinitialize Mail, follow these steps:

1. Edit your Registry to delete **ServerPath** and **Login** (or edit their values to blank) in the following key:

   ```
   HKEY_CURRENT_USER\Software\Microsoft\Mail\Microsoft Mail
   ```

2. Add or edit the **CustomInitHandler** entry to read as follows:

   ```
   CustomInitHandler:REG_SZ:WGPOMG32.DLL, 10
   ```

3. Run Mail. The initialization process begins and once again prompts you for the location of the workgroup postoffice.

Moving or Changing the Workgroup Postoffice

When the Mail application initializes, the initialization procedure associates the computer running Mail with a particular workgroup postoffice. When a workgroup postoffice must be moved to a different location, it is necessary to change this association. Similarly, a computer that moves to a different workgroup must be associated with the postoffice for that workgroup.

To move a workgroup postoffice, follow these steps:

1. Make sure that the new directory is shared with full access by all users.

2. Use File Manager to move the WGPO directory to its new location, being sure to move all subdirectories.

To change the location of the workgroup postoffice for a computer, perform the following step:

- If the computer is running Windows NT, in the Registry, edit the **ServerPath** entry in HKEY_CURRENT_USER\Software\Microsoft\Mail\Microsoft Mail to indicate the location of the postoffice.

  –Or–

- If the computer is running Windows for Workgroups, edit the MSMAIL.INI file to change the **Serverpath=** line to indicate the location of the postoffice.

Changing the Postoffice Administrator

The postoffice administrator is tied to a specific account that is created when the postoffice is created. To change the postoffice administrator, the person who is using that account must abandon it, and the new administrator must take it over. The two persons involved in the exchange must take their Mail folders and Schedule+ data with them.

To change the postoffice administrator, follow these steps:

1. The future administrator needs to complete the following tasks:

   - Sign in to Schedule+, export your appointments, archive your data, and then exit Schedule+.

   - Sign in to Mail, export your folders, and then exit and sign out of Mail.

- Edit your Registry to include the following entries in HKEY_CURRENT_USER\Software\Microsoft\Mail\Custom Commands.

```
WGPOMgr1:REG_SZ:3.0;Mail;;13
WGPOMgr2:REG_SZ:3.0;Mail;&Postoffice
Manager...;14;WGPOMG32.DLL;0;;
   Administer Workgroup
```

2. The current administrator needs to complete the following tasks:

   - Sign in to Schedule+, export your appointments, archive your data, and then exit Schedule+.

   - Sign in to Mail and export your folders.

   - Remove the present account of the future administrator.

   - Change the details of the postoffice administrator account (Name, Mailbox, Password, etc.) to those of the future administrator.

   - Create a new account for yourself, using the details from the old administrator account.

   - Exit and sign out of Mail.

   - Edit your Registry to remove the **WGPOMgr1** and **WGPOMgr2** entries from HKEY_CURRENT_USER\Software\Microsoft\Mail\Custom Commands.

   - Sign in to your new Mail account and import the folders that you exported.

   - Sign in to Schedule+ and import your appointments.

3. The new administrator needs to complete the following tasks:

   - Sign in to your Mail account, which is now the postoffice administrator account, and import the folders that you exported.

   - Sign in to Schedule+ and import your appointments.

Using the Same Mail File from Different Computers

A user can access the same Mail message (.MMF) file from more than one computer by storing the message file on the postoffice server instead of the user's workstation. Mail message files can become very large, however, and so storing users' message files on the postoffice server may require a great deal of additional disk space beyond the basic requirements of the postoffice itself. Be sure the server has enough available disk space before storing users' message files on it.

To allow a user to access the same message file from more than one computer, the user should perform the following steps on the user's computer:

1. Open Mail on the first computer and select the Options... command from the Mail menu. In the Options dialog box choose the Server... button. Then, in the Server dialog choose the Postoffice option button. Choose OK to close both dialog boxes.

   Windows NT moves the message file to the WGPO\MMF subdirectory and assigns it a name like 00000001.MMF.

2. Select the Address Book... command from the Mail menu. In the Address Book dialog, select the user and choose the Details... button. Make note of the user's mailbox. Close both dialog boxes by choosing the Close button.

3. Select Exit And Sign Out from the File menu.

4. If Mail has already been installed on the other computer from which the user wants to access this message file, follow the procedure outlined in "Recreating the Mail Initialization Procedure" earlier in this chapter on that computer.

5. Start Mail on the other computer. In the Welcome to Mail dialog, choose the Connect To An Existing Postoffice option button and then choose OK.

6. Enter the location of the postoffice and choose OK.

   A message box appears that asks if you have an account on the postoffice.

7. Choose Yes. When the Mail Sign In dialog appears, enter the user's mailbox name and password. Choose OK to close the dialog.

Repeat steps 4 through 6 on any other computer the user will use to access the message file.

Note that the message file can be accessed only by one computer at a time. The user cannot run mail simultaneously on more than one computer.

Packaging Objects with UNC Pointers

Windows NT supports the use of the *uniform naming convention* (UNC) inside packaged objects. This means that you can create an object with the Object Packager utility that includes a pointer to a file located on a network file share.

For example, instead of embedding a 1 MB Word for Windows document into a mail message, you can insert a packaged object that contains a UNC pointer to the document on the network share. When the message is received, the recipient can double-click on the icon created by Object Packager to connect to the share and load the Word for Windows document.

To create a packaged object containing a UNC pointer to a Word for Windows document on a network share, following these steps:

1. In Mail, select Insert Object from the Edit menu.

2. Select Package from the Insert Object list to start the Object Packager utility.

3. In Object Packager, select Command Line from the Edit menu.

4. Type the UNC path and filename of the Word for Windows document file in the command box. For example, you can include something like the following:

   ```
   \\COMPUTER2\WORDDOCS\BUDGET.DOC
   ```

   Note If the network share requires a password, the recipient will have to know the password to retrieve the package.

5. Select the Insert Icon button, and select one of the available icons for this object. Choose OK.

6. From the Edit menu, select Label, and then type a descriptive label for the icon.

7. From the File menu, select Exit. When asked if you want to update the Mail message, choose Yes.

8. Send the Mail message.

Questions and Answers About Mail

This section answers some common questions about Mail.

- How much disk space does the Mail postoffice require?

  You should allow approximately 2 MB of storage on the Mail server to start. As the Mail system is used, the amount of space it requires grows based on the number of users and the size of the messages and attachments being stored.

- Is there a limit on the size or number of attachments you can have in a Mail message?

  There is a limit to the number of attachments you can have in a mail message, not the size. The constraint is the size of a single mail message (not including the size of any attachments). The size of the message text plus the number of attachments must always be less than 32K—allowing for many more attachments than most users need to get their message across.

- Will the Message Finder search attachments to my mail messages?

  No, not currently.

- Can I retrieve deleted messages?

  Mail doesn't actually purge deleted files; it moves them to a Deleted Mail folder. Deleted messages are not deleted until you empty the Deleted Mail folder or quit the program. You can also configure Mail so that messages are not deleted when you quit the program. To keep mail messages from being deleted when you quit Mail, select Options from the Mail menu and then clear the Empty Wastebasket When Exiting check box.

C H A P T E R   9

Microsoft Schedule+

Microsoft Schedule+ is an application that lets you plan and schedule meetings and appointments with others in your workgroup. It works together with Microsoft Mail to perform key functions, such as sending meeting-request messages to other workgroup members.

This chapter describes the components that make up Schedule+ and shows how the application works with Microsoft Mail. It also describes the custom message types used for Schedule+ and includes a section that answers common questions about Schedule+.

For a description of the features of Schedule+ and information about how to use the application, see Chapter 8, "Schedule+" in the *Windows NT System Guide*.

Overview of Schedule+ Architecture

Schedule+ is an example of a Mail-enabled application. It relies on Mail for certain functions, including support for logging on, accessing Mail's address book, and sending and receiving messages.

Because Schedule+ relies on Mail for key functionality, there is no special Schedule+ server. User account information for Mail is automatically translated to Schedule+ accounts.

Figure 9.1 illustrates the key components that make up Schedule+.

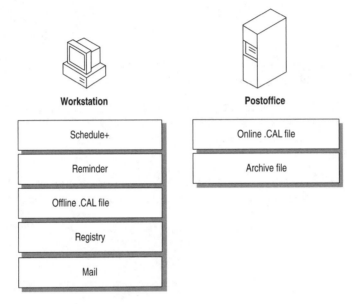

Figure 9.1   Schedule+ Architecture

As shown in Figure 9.1, Schedule+ maintains both an online calendar and an offline calendar, so you can use Schedule+ as a stand-alone application or as a networked application. The *offline calendar* (.CAL) file on your hard disk is read by the program when you start Schedule+ locally. As you make changes to your calendar, those changes are written to disk immediately.

When you use Schedule+ online, it uses the *online calendar* (.CAL) file in the WGPO\CAL directory of the workgroup postoffice. When run online, Schedule+ uses Mail to send meeting messages and to provide name service and logon support.

A separate program, *Reminder* (MSRMND32.EXE), is used to notify you of Schedule+ appointments. This application is typically installed in the Windows NT Startup group and runs in the background (it can alternately be launched by Schedule+). When it is included in the Startup group, as soon as you log on to Windows NT you are prompted to supply your Mail logon name and password. The same logon is shared by Reminder, Schedule+, and Mail.

The next few sections discuss the components shown in Figure 9.1 that make up Schedule+.

Registry Entries

The Registry entries for Schedule+ and Mail are found in the following Registry paths:

```
HKEY_CURRENT_USER\Software\Microsoft\Schedule+
```

```
HKEY_CURRENT_USER\Software\Microsoft\Mail
```

In the Schedule+ entries you will find your preferences, such as colors and general options, and the location of your calendar files and archives. When Schedule+ uses Mail functionality, such as for logging on and using custom message types, Mail reads the necessary information from the Registry. The SCHMSG32.DLL file refers to the Mail entries in the Registry to find out how to launch Schedule+ when you choose the View Schedule button from within the Microsoft Mail client (this button is displayed when you read received meeting requests). For more information, see "Registry Entries for Microsoft Mail" and "Registry Entries for Microsoft Schedule+" in Chapter 14, "Registry Value Entries."

The access privileges you set for Schedule+ are not stored in the Registry. They are stored in your calendar (.CAL) file on the postoffice so that Schedule+ can check for the following types of information:

- When a person wants to look at or modify your calendar—what privileges have you assigned for that person to access your calendar?

- When someone is inviting you to a meeting—do you have an assistant, and what is the assistant's name?

Calendar Files

Schedule+ uses a calendar file, which contains scheduling information. Each user has an offline calendar file (named with the person's logon ID and a .CAL filename extension) and an online calendar file (also having a .CAL filename extension, but with a numeric filename). The offline file resides anywhere you want, by default in your SYSTEM32 directory. The online file location is determined by the Mail transport and resides in the CAL directory on the postoffice.

Whenever you want to access the schedules of another user on the postoffice, Schedule+ reads the data directly from the other user's online .CAL file. (You can prevent others from viewing, reading, or modifying your schedule by setting access privileges for the schedule.) When you schedule a meeting with another user, Schedule+ reads the data in the other user's .CAL file to display his or her busy times.

When you schedule an event with others, Schedule+ automatically creates a Request form that you can send to the others asking them to attend the meeting. For more information about the automatic Request and Response forms, see "Custom Message Types for Schedule+," later in this chapter

Merging Online and Offline Calendars

You can use your online calendar while your computer is connected to the Mail server. If you have an assistant, that person can also make changes to your online calendar. You can also use the offline calendar when the Mail server is unavailable or when you are away from the office.

When you work online, Schedule+ keeps your offline file synchronized with your online file. After you have worked offline and then start up online, Schedule+ merges the calendar files as follows:

- Schedule+ adds all of the appointments that you have added offline to the postoffice file.

- Schedule+ deletes all of the appointments that you have deleted offline from the postoffice file.

- When you change an existing appointment, the changes made to the local file always take precedence over the changes made to the postoffice file. If you change the text of an appointment offline and another person changes the start time, both changes will be applied because these changes are not in conflict. If you change the start time, end time, start date, end date, reminder notification time, or reminder notification date for an appointment, all of these attributes will be set to the values stored in the local file.

- When an overlap occurs as a result of merging the online and offline files, Schedule+ doesn't notify you specifically; instead, both appointments are entered in the calendar. For example, suppose you schedule an appointment on January 1 at noon while working offline and your Schedule+ assistant creates an appointment at the same time on the postoffice file. Because your assistant has authority to add to and modify your scheduled activities, it appears to Schedule+ that you made two changes to the schedule at the same time. Schedule+ enters both appointments in the merged calendar files.

Offsite Calendar Files

As with Microsoft Mail, you can work with Schedule+ offline at home or on a portable computer. You can take a copy of your Schedule+ files from your local computer to work with while you're away from the office.

To take your calendar home or on the road, select the Move Local File command from the File menu to copy the calendar to a floppy disk. Then load Schedule+ on the destination computer and select the Move Local File command again. The command moves the calendar file to the location you specify and changes a Registry entry in the Schedule+ key so that it points to your calendar in the new location.

Archiving Old Calendar Information

A calendar file full of scheduling information soon gets cumbersome. Archiving enables you to remove past data from your calendar and store the data for later reference. This minimizes disk space used on the postoffice without having to completely discard past Schedule+ data. You can open and view your archive file as if it were another appointment book.

Custom Message Types for Schedule+

When you invite people to attend a meeting or when you reserve a resource, Schedule+ automatically prepares a *Request form*. When you respond to someone else's meeting request, Schedule+ generates a *Response form*. This section describes the forms Schedule+ automatically generates and the custom message types associated with each.

Mail enables you to create and use custom message types to send specific kinds of messages, as described in Chapter 8, "Mail." Schedule+ uses this feature to define meeting requests, meeting responses, and meeting cancellations. In the Registry, Schedule+ defines five message types in the Mail\Custom Messages subkey in the Registry:

- Meeting Request (defined as message type IPM.Microsoft Schedule.MtgReq)
- Positive Meeting Response (defined as message type IPM.Microsoft Schedule.MtgRespP)
- Negative Meeting Response (defined as message type IPM.Microsoft Schedule.MtgRespN)
- Tentative Meeting Response (defined as message type IPM.Microsoft Schedule.MtgRespA)
- Meeting Cancellation (defined as message type IPM.Microsoft Schedule.MtgCncl)

These message types create special Request and Response forms that you can use to schedule meetings with others in your workgroup. For example, when you add a new appointment, choose a time, and specify attendees, the Send Request form shown in the following dialog box is displayed automatically.

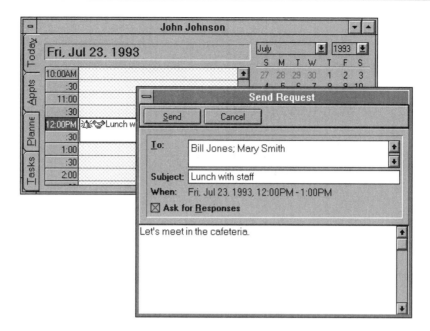

This message is deposited in the Outbox and sent to users just as any Mail message would be sent.

When a meeting attendee accepts the meeting, another automatic form, called the Response form, is generated and sent as a Mail message. Three variations of the Response form (Positive, Negative, and Tentative) are defined by custom message types defined by Schedule+. These three message types define the Response forms and a portion of the response message (such as "I might attend," shown in the Response form). They also add Yes:, No:, or Tentative: to the front of the original request title to create a response-message title. When the messages are displayed in the recipient's Messages window, these custom message types also display symbols (√, **X**, or **?**) to the left of each message to make it easy to see responses at a glance.

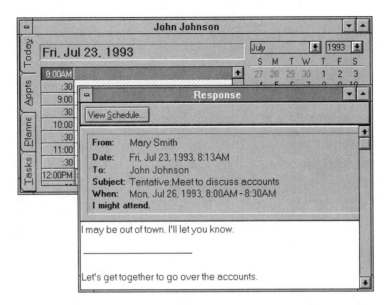

Because meeting messages are sent using Mail facilities, they can be viewed from within Schedule+ or from within Mail. Only one copy of each message is maintained; however, because what appear to be duplicates are really only pointers to the original. So when you delete the message in one view, it is also deleted in the other.

Schedule+ Interoperability

Schedule+ has a flexible architecture that makes communication with other schedule and calendar systems possible. Developers can modify their schedule and calendar software to share information with Schedule+ by using the Schedule+ Interchange format, described below.

The *Schedule+ Interchange* format is a text file with an .SCH extension. An interchange file can be imported to Schedule+ with the File/Import Appointments command; a Schedule+ calendar can be exported with the File/Export Appointments command. The file format supports importing and exporting projects, tasks, appointments, meetings, and notes.

Interchange Format Syntax

The Interchange format file begins with a header describing the owner of the file (the person to whom the schedule belongs) and when it was exported or created. The header is followed by descriptors for projects, tasks, notes, standard appointments, and recurring appointments. Although meetings are supported in the interchange format, they are not documented here. Meetings can be imported as standard appointments by the scheduling or calendar software that is exchanging data with Schedule+. The order of descriptors is not significant, except that projects must precede tasks.

The following section describes the syntax for individual descriptors.

If you export a Schedule+ calendar to the interchange format, you will find that each descriptor begins with a line defining a field called **aid**. This is an appointment ID defined and maintained by Schedule+; it should not be included in the import file.

Table 9.1   Key to Interchange Format Syntax

Item	Description
→	Tab
italic	Required input
nonitalic	Fixed-field definitions
m	Month or minute
d	Day
h	Hour (24-hour format)
y	Year

Header
SCHEDULE+ EXPORT BY *mailbox name* ON *m/dd/yy* AT *hh:mm AM/PM*

Nonprivate Project
FixedAppt:
→szText
project description
→fTask → → → → →T
→aidProject → → → → → →*project id # (integer, number in sequence)*
End

Private Project

FixedAppt:
→szText
project description
→aaplWorld → → → → →Read
→fTask → → → → →T
→aidProject → → → → →→*project id # (integer, number in sequence)*
End

Note The **fTask** line is present for all projects; other lines, like the **aaplWorld** line above, are present only for private projects.

Standard Task

FixedAppt:
→szText
task description
→fTask → → → → →T
→bpri → → → → → →*priority # (1–35, where 1–9 = priority 1–9 and 10–35 = priority A–Z)*
→aidParent → → → → → →*project id # of associated project (integer)*
End

Standard Private Task

FixedAppt:
→szText
task description
→aaplWorld → → → → →Read
→fTask → → → → →T
→bpri → → → → → →*priority # (1–35, where 1–9 = priority 1–9 and 10–35 = priority A–Z)*
→aidParent → → → → →→*project id # of associated project (integer)*
End

Task with Due Date and Start Work Date

FixedAppt:
→dateStart → → → → →→*due date in format m-d-yyyy hh:mm*
→dateEnd → → → → →→*due date in format m-d-yyyy hh:mm*
→szText
task description
→fTask → → → → →T
→nAmtBeforeDeadline → → → → →→*nteger # (with unit below, indicates start work before due date)*
→tunitBeforeDeadline → → → → →*unit: Day, Week, or Month (indicates start work before due date)*

→bpri → → → → →*priority # (1–35, where 1–9 = priority 1–9 and 10–35 = priority A–Z)*
→aidParent → → → → →*project id # of associated project*
End

Note The **dateStart** and **dateEnd** lines ask for *hh:mm*. This must be supplied but won't be used for these date-oriented (rather than time-oriented) tasks. *hh:mm* should be 00:00.

Standard Appointment, Marked Private

FixedAppt:
→dateStart → → → → → →*start date and time in format m-d-yyyy hh:mm (time is 24 hour)*
→dateEnd → → → → → →*end date and time in format m-d-yyyy hh:mm (time is 24 hour)*
→szText
appointment description
→aaplWorld → → → → →Read
End

Standard Appointment with Alarm

FixedAppt:
→dateStart → → → → → →*start date and time in format m-d-yyyy hh:mm (time is 24 hour)*
→dateEnd → → → → → →*end date and time in format m-d-yyyy hh:mm (time is 24 hour)*
→szText
appointment description
→dateNotify → → → → → →*specification of alarm in format m-d-yyyy hh:mm (time is 24 hour)*
→nAmt → → → → → →*integer defining how long before an appointment the alarm should go off*
→tunit → → → → →*the unit (Minute, Hour, Day, Week, Month) defining the alarm*
End

Note The **dateNotify** line asks for *hh:mm*. Place any time here; a value is required. The actual time used for the alarm is set in the **nAmt** and **tunit** lines. If the alarm is in minutes, the **tunit** line is not required.

Recurring Appointment

RecurAppt:
→ymdStart → → → → →*start date of recurrence pattern in format m-d-yyyy*
→ymdEnd → → → → →*end date of recurrence pattern in format m-d-yyyy*
→wgrfValidMonths → → → → →*used to define recurrence pattern (see next section for detail)*
→bgrfValidDows → → → → → →*used to define recurrence pattern (see next section for detail)*
→trecur → → → → → →*used to define recurrence pattern (see next section for detail)*
→timeStart → → → → →*start time in format hh:mm*
→timeEnd → → → → →*end time in format hh:mm*
→σzText
Recurring appointment description
End

Note   The **ymdEnd** line is required only if the recurring appointment has an end date. If it does not, omit the **ymdEnd** line. See the following section for more information about this type of entry.

Notes for One Month

MonthNotes:
→*date of Note in format m-d-yyyy*
note #1 text
→*date of Note in format m-d-yyyy*
note #2 text
End

Note   All notes for the month are listed together in sequence.

Recurrence Patterns

The recurrence pattern is defined by three fields that, in combination, define the following recurrence patterns: daily, weekly, biweekly, monthly defined by a pattern, monthly defined by a date, yearly defined by a pattern, and yearly defined by a date.

The three fields used to define the recurrence types and patterns are describe in the following table.

Table 9.2   Recurrence Pattern Fields

Field	Description
wgrfValidMonths *bbbbbbbbbbbb*	Enumerates valid months of the year, where *bbbbbbbbbbbb* is 12 bits, each being either T or F and representing January through December.
	All bits are T in every recurrence type except yearly. In the yearly case, all but one bit will be F. The T bit indicates which month the yearly appointment falls into in either of the yearly recurrence patterns.
bgrfValidDows *bbbbbbb*	Enumerates valid days of the week where *bbbbbbb* is 7 bits, T or F, representing Sunday through Saturday. (Note that in this syntax the week always starts on Sunday regardless of the user's start of week designation in Schedule+ Options.)
	All bits are T in the case of a monthly or yearly recurrence defined by the specific date. In the daily-every weekday recurrence or the monthly or yearly recurrences defined as the *x* weekday, the first and seventh bits are F, and all others are T. In the monthly or yearly recurrence where field 2 is weekend day (see the description of fields below), the first and seventh bits are T and all others are F. In all other recurrence types, one or more bits are T to indicate the days of the week on which the appointment falls.

Table 9.2   Recurrence Pattern Fields *(continued)*

Field	Description
trecur [**Week** *bb* 0 | **IWeek** *bbbbb* 0 | **Date** *x*]	**trecur** is followed by one of these terms to describe the recurrence type: **Week** *bb* **0**—daily or weekly (*bb* is FF); **trecur** and **bgrfValidDows** are used in conjunction to define the daily or weekly recurrence. The days of the week are indicated as described above. **Week** *bb* **0**—biweekly (if *bb* is TF, this means even weeks; if *bb* is TT, this means odd weeks; based on the start day of the week); **trecur** and **bgrfValidDows** are used in conjunction to define the biweekly recurrence. **IWeek** *bbbbb* **0**—monthly or yearly, defined by a pattern instead of the date. If you look at the choices for the monthly recurrence in Schedule+, you'll see that the pattern is defined by two fields. For example, a monthly appointment can be on the first (field 1) weekday (field 2) of the month. The yearly pattern is defined by three fields. The first two are the same as the monthly fields, and field 3 is the month of the year. **IWeek** is followed by five bits with T or F; only one of these bits can be T. Field 2 of the monthly or yearly recurrence pattern is defined by **bgrfValidDows**. For example, if field 2 is a weekday, **bgrfValidDows** would be FTTTTTF. Field 3 in the yearly pattern is defined by **wgrfValidMonths**. **Date** *x*—monthly or yearly, defined by the date *x* (the day of the month, 1–31). If it is a monthly occurrence, all months are T in **wgrfValidMonths**. If it is a yearly occurrence, one month of the year is indicated by T in **wgrfValidMonths**, and the rest are F.

Sample Schedule+ Interchange Format File

SCHEDULE+ EXPORT BY user1 ON 9/16/1992 AT 10:44 amFixedAppt:

→ szText

Personal Projects

→ aaplWorld→ → → → → Read

→ fTask→ → → → → T

→ aidProject→ → → → → → 1

End

FixedAppt:

→ szText

pay bills (belongs to Personal Project)

→ aaplWorld→ → → → → Read

→ fTask→ → → → → T

→ bpri→ → → → → 4

→ aidParent→ → → → → 1

End

FixedAppt:

→ dateStart→ → → → → → → 9-27-1992 12:00

→ dateEnd→ → → → → → → 9-27-1992 12:00

→ szText

confirm presenters

→ fTask→ → → → → T

→ nAmtBeforeDeadline→ → → → → → 2

→ tunitBeforeDeadline→ → → → → Day

→ bpri→ → → → → → 1

→ aidParent→ → → → → → 2

End

FixedAppt:

→ dateStart→ → → → → → → 10-17-1992 08:00

→ dateEnd→ → → → → → → 10-17-1992 09:00

szText

meeting with John

→ dateNotify→ → → → → → → 10-17-1992 08:00

→ nAmt→ → → → → → 1

→ tUnit→ → → → → Month

End

FixedAppt:
→ dateStart→ → → → → → 9-17-1992 14:00
→ dateEnd→ → → → → → 9-17-1992 15:30
→ szText
phone call with ABC Corp
→ aaplWorld→ → → → → Read
End
RecurAppt:
→ ymdStart→ → → → → 9-16-1992
→ wgrfValidMonths→ → → → → TTTTTTTTTTTT
→ bgrfValidDows→ → → → → → FFFTFFF
→ trecur→ → → → → → Week FF 0
→ timeStart→ → → → → 16:30
→ timeEnd→ → → → → 17:30
szText
Weekly appointment without end date
End
RecurAppt:
→ ymdStart→ → → → → 9-01-1992
→ ymdEnd→ → → → → 6-01-1993
→ wgrfValidMonths→ → → → → TTTTTTTTTTTT
→ bgrfValidDows→ → → → → →TTTTTTT
→ trecur→ → → → → → Date 1
→ timeStart→ → → → → 16:30
→ timeEnd→ → → → → 17:30
szText
Monthly Appointment (the first of each month) with end date
End
MonthNotes:
→ 9-17-1992
call dentist
→ 10-31-1992
Halloween
End

Questions and Answers About Schedule+

This section answers some common questions about Schedule+.

- Does Schedule+ support OLE or attachments (such as a meeting schedule)?

  No, but Mail does. You can create a message to invite attendees to a meeting and refer them to a separate Mail message that includes OLE objects and/or attachments.

- Does Schedule+ include all hours of each day as valid meeting times when the auto-pick feature is used to search for a meeting time?

  To determine a meeting time, auto-pick only looks at weekdays (Monday–Friday) within the time defined by your start-work and end-work settings in the General Options command. Schedule+ looks only at the meeting initiator's settings to determine valid times. Schedule+ doesn't recognize the nonworking hours of other users, and you aren't able to define days other than Saturday or Sunday as nonworking days.

- Does Schedule+ support recurring meetings? For example, I'd like to schedule a weekly meeting with my group.

  Schedule+ supports recurring *appointments*, but not recurring *meetings*. Schedule+ also doesn't support recurring meeting requests. Instead, you must request the meeting for a single occurrence and then remind the attendees to use the Recurring Appointment command to enter it for each week. Alternately, you can ask everyone attending your weekly meeting to set up their own recurring appointment for that time each week.

- Are there options for altering the time and date displays (for example, using a 24-hour clock or a European date format)?

  Yes. From the Windows NT Control Panel, double-click the International icon. In the International dialog box, you can specify the format used for the date and the time, which will affect the displays in Schedule+ also.

- Does Schedule+ support customized reminder sounds?

  Yes. From the Windows NT Control Panel, double-click the Sound icon. In the Sound dialog box, select the sound you want to assign to the Schedule+ Reminders. (You must have a suitable wave output device and driver installed on your computer.)

- Because each resource requires a user account, does this mean that each resource requires a user license?

  No. Microsoft's licensing is per computer running the software, not per user account used.

- What are the dimensions of the print sizes in Schedule+?

  The formats are designed to match the most popular appointment book sizes. They are the following:

  - Standard (8.5 inches by 11.5 inches)
  - Junior (5.5 inches by 8.5 inches)
  - Pocket (3.75 inches by 6.75 inches)

- Are meetings scheduled by somebody else distinguished in any way?

  Yes. If you double-click an appointment created by someone else, the name of the person who created it will be indicated at the bottom of the appointment details. However, the appointment is not identified differently by an icon or special color in the appointment book.

- How can I view or modify someone else's calendar?

  Schedule+ enables you to grant access privileges to other users with the Set Access Privileges command from the Options menu. Once you have assigned privileges to another user, that user can view your calendar while signed in under his or her own account by choosing Open Other's Appt. Book from the File menu.

- What is the difference between the "Modify" and the "Assistant" privileges?

  The modify privilege is part of the set of privileges granted to your assistant. In addition to modifying privileges, the assistant can send meeting messages on your behalf by requesting a meeting while viewing your calendar. The assistant also receives meeting messages designated for you and can respond to them on your behalf.

- When I specify someone as my Schedule+ assistant, do we both receive meeting messages for my meetings, or does only my assistant receive them?

  You have the ability to specify either of the above. If you select General Options from the Options menu, you will see a check box that specifies Send Meeting Messages Only To My Assistant.

- Because I can view the meeting request messages from Mail or Schedule+, does this mean that there are actually two messages?

  No. The Schedule+ Messages box and the Mail Inbox just provide two views of the same message. The message is only stored in one place. When you delete it from one view, it is deleted in the other view.

Windows NT Registry

Part Four explains the organization of the Windows NT Registry and how to use Registry Editor for configuration management in special cases. Chapter 14 contains an encyclopedia of Registry entry values, with definitions and explanations for setting these values.

C H A P T E R   1 0

Overview of the Windows NT Registry

System administrators must meet an enormous challenge in managing hardware, operating systems, and applications on personal computers. In Windows NT, the Registry helps simplify the support burden by providing a secure, unified database that stores configuration data in a hierarchical form, so that system administrators can easily provide local or remote support, using the administrative tools in Windows NT.

This part of the *Windows NT Resource Guide* describes the Registry and shows how to use the information in the Registry for troubleshooting and configuration maintenance.

- This chapter presents background information about the structure and contents of the Registry.

- Chapter 11, "The Registry Editor and Registry Administration," provides details about using Registry Editor for viewing and editing Registry entries.

- Chapter 12, "Configuration Management and the Registry," provides specific problem-solving techniques using the Registry.

- Chapter 13, "Initialization Files and the Registry," describes how Windows NT uses files such as WIN.INI and CONFIG.SYS and how this information is mapped to the Registry.

- Chapter 14, "Registry Value Entries," lists the Registry values that can be used for tuning and troubleshooting the network, system components, and the user environment.

Caution   Wherever possible, use the administrative tools such as Control Panel and User Manager to make configuration changes, rather than using Registry Editor. Using the administrative tools is safer because these applications know how to properly store values in the Registry. If you make errors while changing values with Registry Editor, you will not be warned, because Registry Editor does not understand or recognize errors in syntax or other semantics.

Getting Started with Registry Editor

To get the most out of the material in this chapter, you will want to run Registry Editor so that you can see the contents of the Registry for your computer. The Registry Editor application, REGEDT32.EXE, does not appear in any default program groups in Program Manager, but it is installed automatically when you install Windows NT on any computer.

▶ **To run Registry Editor**

1. Run the REGEDT32.EXE file from File Manager or Program Manager.

   –Or–

   Type the **start regedt32** command at the command prompt, and press ENTER.

2. From the Options menu, choose the Read Only Mode command.

   This command will protect the Registry contents while you explore its structure and become familiar with the entries.

3. Double-click any folder icon to display the contents of that key.

For details about security and backup measures to take with the Registry and other issues, see Chapter 11, "Registry Editor and Registry Administration."

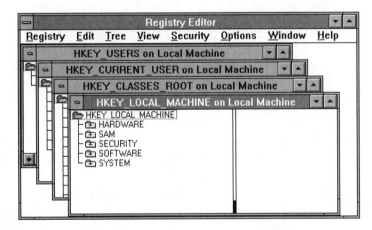

Most simply, the Registry is a database, and Registry Editor displays the four subtrees used to access the contents of the database. The hierarchical structure that appears in Registry Editor is similar to how File Manager displays hierarchical directory structures. The information in this chapter will help you understand where specific kinds of information can be found in the Registry (and where you should or should not make changes).

In this chapter, the Registry keys are described in the order they appear in the Registry Editor windows, with a focus on the parts of the Registry where a system administrator might want to view or change entries. Some information is provided merely to explain what is stored in certain keys.

The content or location of a specific Registry key may differ from what is described in this *Resource Guide*, depending on which services and software are installed, whether a computer is running Windows NT Workstation or Windows NT Server, and other factors. However, the general organization described in this chapter will help you understand how to navigate the Registry.

Note   Most Registry entries that you might need to examine or edit are found under HKEY_LOCAL_MACHINE\SYSTEM\CurrentControlSet, described later in this chapter. Specific entries are defined in Chapter 14, "Registry Value Entries."

How Windows NT Components Use the Registry

Under versions of Windows for MS-DOS, starting the system, connecting to the network, and running applications involves multiple configuration files with some form of synchronization between them. With Windows NT, the operating system stores and checks the configuration information at only one location—the Registry.

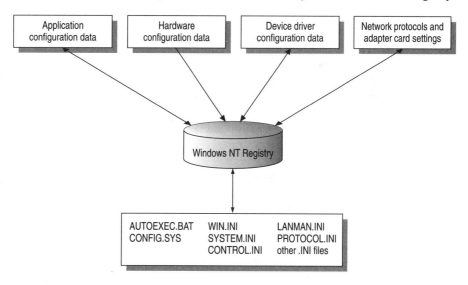

Figure 10.1   Data in the Windows NT Registry

The following figure shows how various Windows NT components and applications use the Registry. The numbered explanations below this illustration provide details.

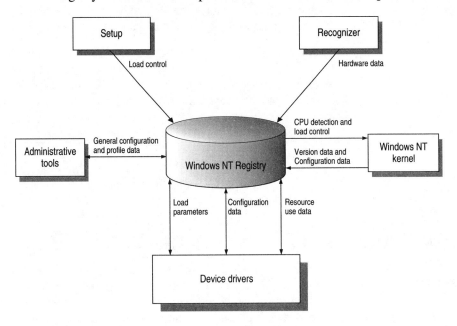

Figure 10.2   How Registry information Is Used by Windows NT

- *Setup*. Whenever you run the Windows NT Setup program or other setup programs for applications or hardware, the Setup program adds new configuration data to the Registry. For example, new information is added when you install a new SCSI adapter or change the settings for your video display.

- *Recognizer*. Each time you start a computer running Windows NT, the Hardware Recognizer places hardware configuration data in the Registry. This information includes a list of hardware detected in your system. On x86-based computers, this is done by a program called NTDETECT.COM and the Windows NT Kernel (NTOSKRNL.EXE). On RISC-based computers, this information is extracted from the ARC firmware.

- *Windows NT kernel*. During system startup, the Windows NT Kernel extracts information from the Registry, such as the device drivers to load and their load order. The NTOSKRNL.EXE program also passes information about itself to the Registry, such as its version number.

- *Device drivers.* Device drivers send and receive load parameters and configuration data from the Registry. This data is similar to what you might find on the DEVICE= lines in the CONFIG.SYS file under MS-DOS. A device driver must report system resources that it uses, such as hardware interrupts and DMA channels, so that the system can add this information to the Registry. Applications and device drivers can read this Registry information to provide users with smart installation and configuration programs.

- *Administrative tools.* The administrative tools in Windows NT, such as those provided in Control Panel and in the Administrative Tools program group, can be used to modify configuration data. The Registry Editor is helpful for viewing and occasionally making detailed changes to the system configuration. You can also use the Windows NT Diagnostics program (WINMSD.EXE) to view configuration information stored in the Registry. For details, see Chapter 11, "Registry Editor and Registry Administration."

The Registry is analogous to the .INI files used under Windows for MS-DOS, with each key in the Registry similar to a bracketed heading in an .INI file, and entries under the heading similar to values in the Registry. However, Registry keys can contain subkeys, while .INI files do not support nested headings. Registry values can also consist of executable code, rather than the simple strings representing values in .INI files. And individual preferences for multiple users of the same computer can be stored in the Registry, which is not possible with .INI files.

Although Microsoft discourages using .INI files in favor of using Registry entries, some applications (particularly 16-bit Windows-based applications) will continue using .INI files for the time being. Windows NT supports .INI files solely for compatibility with those applications and related tools (such as setup programs). Some form of the files AUTOEXEC.BAT and CONFIG.SYS also still exist to provide compatibility with applications created for MS-DOS and Windows 3.1. For details about how Windows NT uses such files in conjunction with the Registry, see Chapter 14, "Initialization Files and the Registry."

Registry Structure

This section describes the hierarchical organization of the Registry and defines the overall structure of keys, value entries, and hives. Following this section, details are provided about specific Registry keys.

The Registry Hierarchy

The Registry is structured as a set of four subtrees of keys that contain per-computer and per-user databases. The per-computer information includes information about hardware and software installed on the specific computer. The per-user information includes the information in user profiles, such as desktop settings, individual preferences for certain software, and personal printer and network settings. In versions of Windows for MS-DOS, per-computer information was saved in the WIN.INI and SYSTEM.INI files, but it was not possible to save separate information for individual users.

In the Windows NT Registry, each individual key can contain data items called *value entries* and can also contain additional *subkeys*. In the Registry structure, keys are analogous to directories, and the value entries are analogous to files.

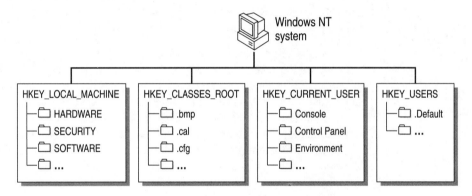

Figure 10.3   The Four Subtrees in the Windows NT Registry

The following table identifies and defines these four subtrees.

Table 10.1   Registry Subtrees

Root key name	Description
HKEY_LOCAL_MACHINE	Contains information about the local computer system, including hardware and operating system data such as bus type, system memory, device drivers, and startup control data.
HKEY_CLASSES_ROOT	Contains object linking and embedding (OLE) and file-class association data (equivalent to the Registry in Windows for MS-DOS).
HKEY_CURRENT_USER	Contains the user profile for the user who is currently logged on, including environment variables, personal program groups, desktop settings, network connections, printers, and application preferences.
HKEY_USERS	Contains all actively loaded user profiles, including HKEY_CURRENT_USER, which always refers to a child of HKEY_USERS, and the default profile. Users who are accessing a server remotely do not have profiles under this key on the server; their profiles are loaded into the Registry on their own computers.

Each of these subtrees is described in detail later in this chapter. Each of the root key names begins with "HKEY_" to indicate to software developers that this is a *handle* that can be used by a program. A handle is a value used to uniquely identify a resource so that a program can access it.

Value Entries in the Registry Keys

Registry data is maintained as value entries under the Registry keys. As shown in the following figure, Registry Editor displays data in two panes. The value entries in the right pane are associated with the selected key in the left pane.

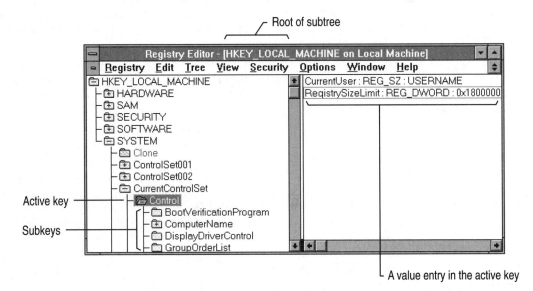

A value entry has three parts: the name of the value, the data type of the value, and the value itself, which can be data of any length. The three parts of value entries always appear in the following order:

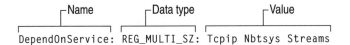

A value entry cannot be larger than about 1 MB. Values from 0 to 0x7fffffff are reserved for definition by the system, and applications are encouraged to use these types. Values from 0x80000000 to 0xffffffff are reserved for use by applications.

The following table lists the data types currently defined and used by the system.

Table 10.2   Data Types for Registry Entries

Data type	Description
REG_BINARY	Raw binary data. Most hardware component information is stored as binary data, and can be displayed in Registry Editor in hexadecimal format, or displayed via the Windows NT Diagnostics program (WINMSD.EXE) in an easy-to-read format. For example: `Component Information : REG_BINARY : 00 00 00...`
REG_DWORD	Data represented by a number that is 4 bytes long. Many parameters for device driver and services are this type and can be displayed in Registry Editor in binary, hex, or decimal format. For example, entries for service error controls are this type: `ErrorControl : REG_DWORD : 0x1`
REG_EXPAND_SZ	An expandable data string, which is text that contains a variable to be replaced when called by an application. For example, for the following value, the string *%SystemRoot%* will be replaced by the actual location of the directory containing the Windows NT system files: `File : REG_EXPAND_SZ : %SystemRoot%\file.exe`
REG_MULTI_SZ	A multiple string. Values that contain lists or multiple values in human readable text are usually this type. Entries are separated by NULL characters. For example, the following value entry specifies the binding rules for a network transport: `bindable : REG_MULTI_SZ : dlcDriver dlcDriver non non 50`
REG_SZ	A sequence of characters representing human readable text. For example, a component's description is usually this type: `DisplayName : REG_SZ : Messenger`

Hives and Files

The Registry is divided into parts called *hives,* named by a Windows NT developer as an analogy for the cellular structure of a beehive. A hive is a discrete body of keys, subkeys, and values that is rooted at the top of the Registry hierarchy. A hive is backed by a single file and a .LOG file. These files are in the *%SystemRoot%*\system32\config directory.

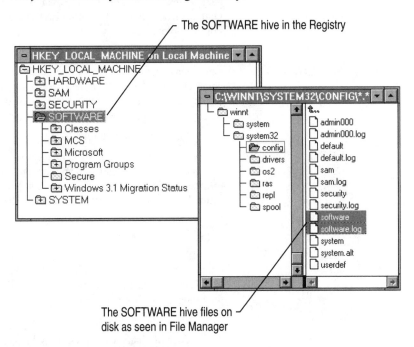

The SOFTWARE hive in the Registry

The SOFTWARE hive files on disk as seen in File Manager

The following table shows the standard hives for a computer running Windows NT.

Table 10.3   Standard Hive Files

Registry hive	Filenames
HKEY_LOCAL_MACHINE\SAM	SAM and SAM.LOG
HKEY_LOCAL_MACHINE\SECURITY	SECURITY and SECURITY.LOG
HKEY_LOCAL_MACHINE\SOFTWARE	SOFTWARE and SOFTWARE.LOG
HKEY_LOCAL_MACHINE\SYSTEM	SYSTEM and SYSTEM.ALT
HKEY_CURRENT_USER	*USER###* and *USER###.LOG* or ADMIN### and ADMIN###.LOG
HKEY_USERS\.DEFAULT	DEFAULT and DEFAULT.LOG

By default, all hives are stored in the *SystemRoot*\SYSTEM32\CONFIG subdirectory, which also includes SYSTEM.ALT and the .LOG files that are backup hive files. The hive files for user profiles can be stored in other locations.

Atomicity and Hive Recovery in the Registry

The Registry ensures *atomicity* of individual actions. This means that any single change made to a value to set, delete, or save either works or does not work—even if the system goes down because of power failure, hardware failure, or software problems. For example, if an application sets values for two entries (A and B), and the system crashes while this change is being made, one of the following situations results:

- You might get a new value for entry A or entry B.
- You might get new values for entries A and B.
- You might not get a new value for either entry.

Because of the atomicity of individual actions, you avoid the situation of getting a corrupted mix of old and new values for an entry. For example, you won't get a corrupted mix of old A and new A. In addition, the key containing entry A and entry B will have a size, time stamp, and other data that are consistent with what is actually there.

Flushing Data

In this version of Windows NT, data is only written to the Registry when a *flush* occurs, which happens after changed data ages past a few seconds, or when an application intentionally flushes the data to the hard disk.

The system performs the following flush process for all hives (except for the System hive):

1. All changed data is written to the hive's .LOG file along with a map of where it is in the hive, and then a flush is performed on the .LOG file. It is now certain that all changed data is written in the .LOG file.
2. The first sector of the hive file is marked to indicate that the file is in transition.
3. The changed data is written to the hive file.
4. The hive file is marked as completed.

Note If a system crash occurs between steps 2 and 4, when the hive is next loaded at startup (unless it's a Profile hive that is loaded at logon), the system sees the mark left in step 2, and proceeds to recover the hive using the changes contained in .LOG file. So, the .LOG files are not used if the hive is not in transition. If the hive is in transition, it cannot be loaded without the .LOG file.

A different flush process is used for the System hive because it is an important element during system startup and is used too early during startup to be recovered as described in the previous flush process.

The SYSTEM.ALT file contains a copy of the data contained in the SYSTEM file. During the flush process, changes are marked, written, and then marked as done, and then the same flush process is followed for the SYSTEM.ALT file. If there is a power failure, hardware failure, or software problems during any point in the process, either the SYSTEM or SYSTEM.ALT files will contain the correct information.

The SYSTEM.ALT file isn't that different from a .LOG file, except that at load time, rather than having to reapply the logged changes, the system just switches to SYSTEM.ALT. You don't need the SYSTEM.ALT file unless the System hive is in transition.

User Profile Hives

Each time a new user logs onto a computer, a new hive is created for that user. Because each user profile is a separate hive, each profile is also a separate file. Profile hives can be stored in other directories. The system administrator can copy a user profile as a file and view, repair, or copy entries using Registry Editor on another computer. For specific information about how to take advantage of this feature, see "Managing User Profiles Through the Registry" in Chapter 13, "Configuration Management and the Registry." For information about the hive for the default profile, see "HKEY_USERS" later in this chapter.

Registry Size Limits

The total amount of space that can be consumed by Registry data (the hives) is restricted by the Registry size limit, which is a kind of "global quota" for Registry space that prevents an application from filling the paged pool with Registry data. Registry size limits affect both the amount of paged pool the Registry can use and the amount of disk space.

You can view or set the value for **RegistrySizeLimit** under the following subkey:

```
HKEY_LOCAL_MACHINE\SYSTEM\CurrentControlSet\Control
```

RegistrySizeLimit must have a type of REG_DWORD and a data length of 4 bytes, or it will be ignored. By default, the Registry size limit is 25 percent of the size of the paged pool, which is 32 MB; so the default **RegistrySizeLimit** is 8 MB (which is enough to support about 5000 user accounts). Setting the **PagedPoolSize** value under the CurrentControlSet\Control\Session Manager\Memory Management subkey also affects the Registry size limit. The system ensures that the value for **RegistrySizeLimit** will be at least 4 MB and no greater than about 80 percent of the size of **PagedPoolSize**.

The **RegistrySizeLimit** limitations are approximate. The **PagedPoolSize** can be set to a maximum of 128 MB, so **RegistrySizeLimit** can be no larger than about 102 MB, supporting about 80,000 users (although other limits prevent a Registry this large from being very useful). Also, **RegistrySizeLimit** sets a maximum, not an allocation (unlike some similar limits in the system). Setting a large value for **RegistrySizeLimit** will not cause the system to use that much space unless it is actually needed by the Registry. A large value also does not guarantee that the maximum space will actually be available for use by the Registry.

The space controlled by **RegistrySizeLimit** includes the hive space, as well as some of the Registry's run-time structures. Other Registry run-time structures are protected by their own size limits or other means.

To ensure that a user can always at least start the system and edit the Registry if the **RegistrySizeLimit** is set wrong, quota checking is not turned on until after the first successful loading of a hive (that is, the loading of a user profile). For more details about **RegistrySizeLimit**, see its entry in Chapter 14, "Registry Value Entries."

HKEY_LOCAL_MACHINE

HKEY_LOCAL_MACHINE contains the configuration data for the local computer. The information in this database is used by applications, device drivers, and the Windows NT system to determine configuration data for the local computer, regardless of which user is logged on and what software is in use.

HKEY_LOCAL_MACHINE contains five subtrees, as listed briefly in the following table. The rest of this section describes these keys.

Note You can read information in any of these keys, but you can only add or change information in the SOFTWARE and SYSTEM keys.

Table 10.4   Subtrees in HKEY_LOCAL_MACHINE

Subtree key name	Contents
HARDWARE	The database that describes the physical hardware in the computer, the way device drivers use that hardware, and mappings and related data that link kernel-mode drivers with various user-mode code. All data in this subtree is recreated each time the system is started. ■ The Description key describes the actual computer hardware. ■ The DeviceMap key contains miscellaneous data in formats specific to particular classes of drivers. ■ The ResourceMap key describes which device drivers claim which hardware resources. The Windows NT Diagnostics program (WINMSD.EXE) can report on its contents in an easy-to-read form.
SAM	The security information for user and group accounts, and for the domains in Windows NT Server. (SAM is the Security Account Manager.)
SECURITY	The database that contains the local security policy, such as specific user rights. This key is used only by the Windows NT security subsystem.
SOFTWARE	The per-computer software database. This key contains data about software installed on the local computer, along with various items of miscellaneous configuration data.
SYSTEM	The database that controls system startup, device driver loading, Windows NT services, and operating system behavior.

By convention, if similar data exists under HKEY_CURRENT_USER and under HKEY_LOCAL_MACHINE, the data in HKEY_CURRENT_USER is considered to take precedence. However, values in this key may also extend (rather than replace) data in HKEY_LOCAL_MACHINE. Also, some items (such as device driver loading entries) are meaningless if they occur outside of HKEY_LOCAL_MACHINE.

HKEY_LOCAL_MACHINE\HARDWARE Subtree

The HKEY_LOCAL_MACHINE\HARDWARE subtree contains the hardware data in the Registry that is computed at system startup. This includes information about hardware components on the system board and about the interrupts hooked by specific hardware devices.

The Hardware subtree contains distinct and important sets of data in three subkeys —Description, DeviceMap, and ResourceMap. These keys are described in the following sections.

All information in HKEY_LOCAL_MACHINE\HARDWARE is *volatile*, which means that the settings are computed each time the system is started and then discarded when the system is shut down. Applications and device drivers use this subtree to read information about the system components, store data directly into the DeviceMap subkey, and store data indirectly into the ResourceMap subkey.

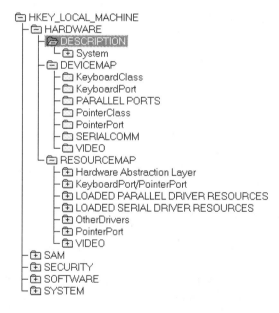

Tip Do not try to edit the data in HKEY_LOCAL_MACHINE\HARDWARE; much of the information appears in binary format, making it difficult to decipher.

To view data about a computer's hardware in an easy-to-read format for troubleshooting, run Windows NT Diagnostics, and choose the Devices button. Windows NT Diagnostics extracts the information from the Registry and renders it in a more readable format.

Description Subkey

The Description subkey under HKEY_LOCAL_MACHINE\HARDWARE displays information from the hardware database built by the firmware, the Hardware Recognizer (NTDETECT.COM), and the Executive itself, which manages the interface between the Kernel and the environment subsystems:

- If the computer is a RISC-based computer, this database is a copy of the ARC configuration database taken from the firmware.

- If the computer is an *x*86-based computer, this database contains the data found by the Hardware Recognizer, which is a program that runs as part of the Windows NT startup sequence. The Hardware Recognizer on *x*86-based computers is NTDETECT.COM.

- If the target computer is not PC-compatible, the OEM provides its own version of NTDETECT.COM as the Hardware Recognizer.

The Hardware Recognizer for *x*86-based computers detects the following items:

Bus/adapter type	Video adapter
Keyboard	Floating point coprocessor
SCSI adapters	Mouse
Communication ports	Floppy drives
Machine ID	Parallel ports

Note Network adapter cards are not detected as part of startup but are instead detected during Windows NT Setup or if you double-click the Network icon in Control Panel to install a new network adapter. For details, see "Network Settings in the Registry," later in this chapter.

HKEY_LOCAL_MACHINE\HARDWARE\Description\System \MultifunctionAdapter contains several other subkeys, each corresponding to specific bus controllers on the local computer. Each of these subkeys describes a class (or type) of controller, including controllers for disk drives, display, keyboard, parallel ports, pointing devices, serial ports, and SCSI devices. The subkey's path describes the type of component. The numbering for hardware components is 0-based, which means that, for example, the first (or only) disk controller appears under the 0 subkey.

The name of the *MultiFunctionAdapter* subkey depends on the bus type. For example, the subkey name for ISA and MCA buses appears as *MultiFunctionAdapter*. For EISA buses, the subkey name is EisaAdapter, and for TurboChannel buses, the subkey name can be TcAdapter.

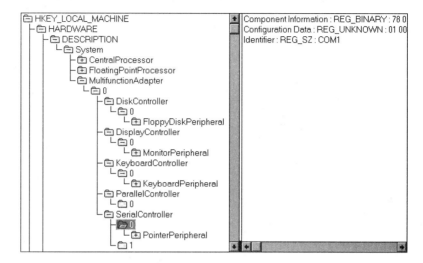

For each detected hardware component, the optional **Component Information** and **Configuration Data** value entries store version and configuration data in binary format. The **Identifier** entry contains the name of a component, if specified. For details about these entries, see "Registry Entries for Device Drivers" in Chapter 14, "Registry Value Entries."

DeviceMap Subkey

Under HKEY_LOCAL_MACHINE\HARDWARE\DeviceMap, each *Device* subkey contains one or more values to specify the location in the Registry for specific driver information for that kind of component.

The following illustration shows an example of the DeviceMap subkey and the value entry for a selected device name.

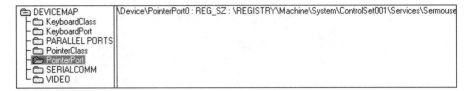

The value for each *Device* subkey describes an actual port name or the path for a *Service* subkey in HKEY_LOCAL_MACHINE\SYSTEM\ControlSet*nnn*\Services, which contains information about a device driver. That *Service* subkey contains the information a system administrator might need for troubleshooting and is also the information presented about the device by Windows NT Diagnostics.

The following shows DeviceMap entries for a computer that has multiple SCSI adapters.

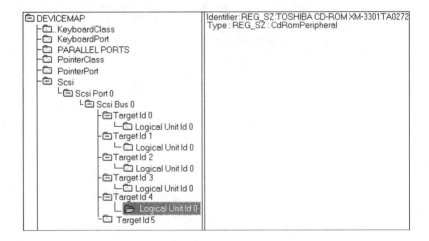

ResourceMap Subkey

The ResourceMap subkey under HKEY_LOCAL_MACHINE\HARDWARE maps device drivers to resources that the drivers use. Each ResourceMap subkey contains data reported by the device driver about its use of I/O ports, I/O memory addresses, interrupts, DMA channels and so on. The data in the ResourceMap subkey is volatile, so this subkey is recreated each time you start Windows NT.

Under the ResourceMap subkey, there are *DeviceClass* subkeys for the general class (or type) of devices. Each of these subkeys contains one or more *DriverName* subkeys with information about a specific driver. For example, in the following illustration, Sermouse is the *DriverName* subkey under the PointerPort *DeviceClass* subkey. (The driver names in these subkeys match the services listed in HKEY_LOCAL_MACHINE\SYSTEM\CurrentControlSet\Services.)

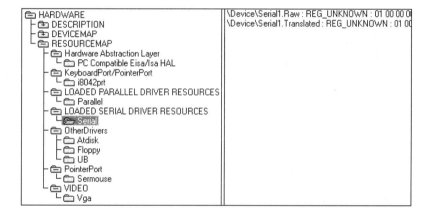

Tip   If you need to resolve resource conflicts, use Windows NT Diagnostics to view the data from these subkeys in an easily readable format.

HKEY_LOCAL_MACHINE\SAM Subtree

The HKEY_LOCAL_MACHINE\SAM subtree contains the user and group account information in the Security Account Manager (SAM) database for the local computer. For a computer that is running Windows NT Server, this subtree also contains security information for the domain. This information is what you see in User Manager, and it also appears in the lists of users and groups when you use the Security menu commands in File Manager.

This subtree is mapped to HKEY_LOCAL_MACHINE\SECURITY\SAM, so changes made in one automatically appear in the other.

If you want to change user account or global group account information, use User Manager or User Manager For Domains to add or remove users or to change information about any account.

Caution The information in this database is in binary format and should not be changed using Registry Editor. Errors in this database may prevent users from being able to log on to the computer—which is another reason why system administrators should not allow typical users to log on as members of the Administrator group.

System Administrators can use User Manager or User Manager For Domains to change security information for the local computer or for the domain.

HKEY_LOCAL_MACHINE\SECURITY Subtree

The HKEY_LOCAL_MACHINE\SECURITY subtree contains security information for the local computer, including user rights, password policy, and the membership of local groups, as set in User Manager.

The subkey HKEY_LOCAL_MACHINE\SECURITY\SAM is mapped to HKEY_LOCAL_MACHINE\SAM, so changes made in one automatically appear in the other.

If you want to change global group membership or other security-related items, use User Manager or User Manager For Domains.

Caution The information in this database is in binary format and should not be changed using Registry Editor. Errors in this database may prevent users from being able to log on to the computer.

HKEY_LOCAL_MACHINE\SOFTWARE Subtree

The HKEY_LOCAL_MACHINE\SOFTWARE subtree contains specific configuration information about software on the local computer. The entries under this handle, which apply for anyone using this particular computer, show what software is installed on the computer and also define file associations and OLE information. The HKEY_CLASSES_ROOT handle is an alias for the subtree rooted at HKEY_LOCAL_MACHINE\SOFTWARE\Classes.

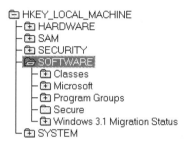

```
🗀 HKEY_LOCAL_MACHINE
  ├─ ⊞ HARDWARE
  ├─ ⊞ SAM
  ├─ ⊞ SECURITY
  ├─ 🗁 SOFTWARE
  │    ├─ ⊞ Classes
  │    ├─ ⊞ Microsoft
  │    ├─ ⊞ Program Groups
  │    ├─ 🗀 Secure
  │    └─ ⊞ Windows 3.1 Migration Status
  └─ ⊞ SYSTEM
```

This subtree contains, for example, the information you add by using the Associate command in File Manager, information added during installation for specific Windows-based applications, and information about applications installed with Windows NT.

The HKEY_LOCAL_MACHINE\SOFTWARE subtree contains several subkeys. The Classes, Program Groups, and Secure subkeys are described here, plus general information about the various *Description* subkeys that might appear in a Registry.

HKEY_LOCAL_MACHINE\SOFTWARE\Microsoft and its subkey Windows NT\CurrentVersion are of particular interest. These subkeys contain information about software that supports services built into Windows NT, as well as data about the version and type of the current release (multiprocessor versus uniprocessor). For example, it is possible to run a Windows NT uniprocessor kernel on a multiprocessor computer, but you don't get any multiprocessor benefits by doing so. To quickly check which kernel type is running on a computer, see the data in the Registry under the Windows NT\CurrentVersion subkey.

Classes Subkey

The Classes subkey defines types of documents, providing information on filename-extension associations and OLE information that can be used by Windows shell applications and OLE applications. HKEY_CLASSES_ROOT displays the same information as stored under this subkey.

Important The OLE information must be created by the specific application, so you should not change this information using Registry Editor. If you want to change filename-extension associations, use the Associate command in File Manager.

The Classes subkey contains two kinds of subkeys:

- Filename-extension subkeys, which specify the application associated with files that have the selected extension, as shown in the following illustration.

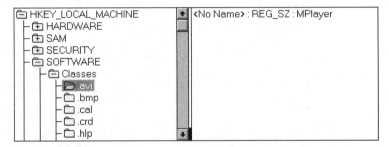

- Class-definition subkeys, which specify the shell and OLE properties of a class (or type) of document. These subkeys can describe shell and protocol properties for each class of document. If an application supports DDE, the Shell subkey can contain Open and Print subkeys that define DDE commands for opening and printing files, similar to the OLE and DDE information stored in the registry database under versions of Windows for MS-DOS. In the following example, **cardfile.exe /p %1** is the print command, and the **%1** parameter stands for the selected filename in File Manager when the command is carried out.

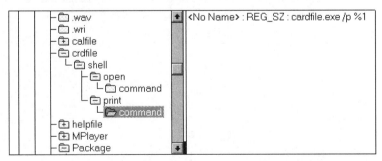

Description Subkeys

The various HKEY_LOCAL_MACHINE\SOFTWARE*Description* subkeys contain the names and version numbers of the software installed on the local computer. (Information about the configuration of these applications is stored on a per-user basis under HKEY_CURRENT_USER.)

During installation, applications record this information in the following form:

```
HKEY_LOCAL_MACHINE\SOFTWARE\<CompanyName>\<ProductName>\<Version>
```

The following example shows some entries under the subkey for Microsoft (a *CompanyName*), which contains entries for the service software installed on the computer:

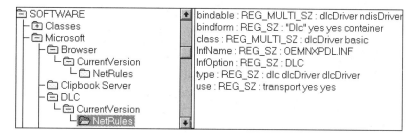

Note The information in each subkey is added by the related application. Do not edit entries in these subkeys unless directed to do so by your application vendor.

Program Groups Subkey

The Program Groups subkey under HKEY_LOCAL_MACHINE\SOFTWARE contains the common program groups—that is, those used in common by all users of the local computer. (The program groups for an individual user can be viewed under HKEY_CURRENT_USER, and the default personal program groups can be viewed in HKEY_USERS\.DEFAULT.) Each subkey under the Program Groups subkey is the name of a common program group, and its value is binary data describing that program group.

If you want to change the content of common program groups, use the menu commands or mouse techniques provided in Program Manager or the User Profile Editor.

Secure Subkey

The Secure subkey provides a convenient place for applications to store configuration information that should not be changed by anyone except an administrator.

If you have a previous version of Windows (Windows 3.x, Windows for Workgroups) installed on your computer, you are permitted to migrate REG.DAT, Program Manager group (.GRP) files, and .INI files to the Windows NT Registry when you first log on to Windows NT. For more information about Windows 3.x migration, refer to Chapter 15, "Windows 3.x Compatibility".

HKEY_LOCAL_MACHINE\SYSTEM Subtree

All startup-related data that must be stored (rather than computed during startup) is saved in the System hive. A complete copy of the data is also stored in the SYSTEM.ALT file. The data in HKEY_LOCAL_MACHINE\SYSTEM—which is the System hive—is organized into control sets that contain a complete set of parameters for devices and services as described in this section. You may occasionally need to change entries in the CurrentControlSet subkey, as described in Chapter 12, "Configuration Management and the Registry."

The following example shows the structure of this subtree:

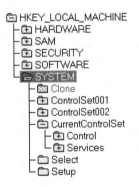

The following sections describe the HKEY_LOCAL_MACHINE\SYSTEM subkeys.

Select, ControlSetnnn, and CurrentControlSet Subkeys

The Registry, particularly data in the System hive, is essential to starting the system. To help ensure that the system can always be started, a kind of backup version is kept, which allows you to undo any configuration changes that did not have the intended effect. This section describes how it works.

All of the data required to control startup is gathered into subtrees called control sets in the Registry. Each control set has two parts, a Control subkey and a Services subkey. The Control subkey contains various data items used to control the system, including such things as the computer's network name and the subsystems to start. The Services subkey contains a list of drivers, file systems, user-mode service programs, and virtual hardware keys. Its data controls the services (drivers, file systems, and so on) to be loaded and their load order. The data in the Services subkey also controls how the services call each other.

Multiple control sets are saved as subtrees of HKEY_LOCAL_MACHINE \SYSTEM under names such as ControlSet001 and ControlSet003. Although as many as four control sets can appear, there are usually two sets. This is similar to having multiple sets of CONFIG.SYS files under MS-DOS — a current one and a backup copy known to start the system correctly. However, the work for creating and maintaining backups is all done automatically by the system.

The Select subkey describes how the control sets are used in four value entries:

- **Default** specifies the number of the control set (for example, 001 = ControlSet001) that the system will use at next startup, barring an error or manual invocation by the user of the LastKnownGood control set.

- **Current** specifies the number of the control set actually used to start the system this time.

- **LastKnownGood** specifies the number of the control set that is a clean copy of the last control set that actually worked.

- **Failed** specifies the control set that was replaced if the LastKnownGood control set was used to start the system this time. You can examine this control set to learn why the replacement was required.

The CurrentControlSet subkey is not the root of an actual control set; rather, it is a symbolic link to the control set indicated by the value of **Current**. It's there so that constant paths can be used to refer to keys in the currently used control set, even though the name of that control set may change.

These multiple control sets are used to allow escape from various problems. Each time the system starts, the control set used to actually start up is saved away (under Clone). If the startup is declared "good," the old LastKnownGood control set is discarded, and the Clone subtree is copied to replace it. Administrators can change how system startup is declared "good," but usually it means no Severe or Critical errors in starting services and at least one successful logon.

If system startup fails in certain ways or if the user chooses LastKnownGood from the Configuration Recovery menu, the LastKnownGood control set will be used to start the system instead of the Default control set. The Default set will be reserved as Failed, and the LastKnownGood set cloned to make a new LastKnownGood set. The LastKnownGood set becomes the new Default set. The effect of all of this is to undo all changes to configuration data stored in a control set since the last time a startup was declared "good." (User profile data is stored elsewhere and is therefore unaffected by this.)

Tip You can choose from among control sets on a computer by pressing the SPACEBAR immediately after selecting Windows NT at the Boot Loader prompt. A message asks if you want to choose to start the system using the current control set or the last known good configuration.

To find out whether Default or Last Known Good was used, see the values in the Select subkey.

You can modify the information stored in these subkeys by choosing the Devices, Network, Server, and Services icons in Control Panel, or by using Server Manager.

If you need to modify the configuration in Registry Editor, make changes under the CurrentControlSet subkey.

The Control and Services keys found in each control set are described in the following sections.

Control Subkey for All Control Sets

The Control subkey contains startup parameters for the system, including information about the subsystems to load, computer-dependent environment variables, the size and location of the paging files, and so on. The following illustration shows the typical Control subkeys, and Table 10.5 describes the contents of some typical subkeys.

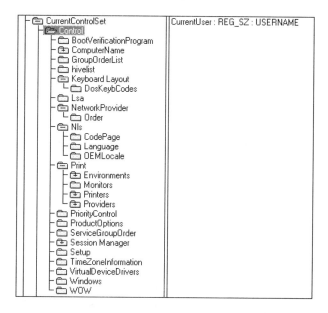

Table 10.5   Typical Subkeys of \CurrentControlSet\Control for All Control Sets

Subkey	Contents
BootVerificationProgram	A value that can be set to define a nonstandard mechanism to declare system startup as "good," as described in Chapter 12, "Configuration Management and the Registry."
ComputerName	The names of the default and active computers, stored in two subkeys, ComputerName and ActiveComputerName. The computer name should be set using the Network icon in Control Panel.
GroupOrderList	Specifies the order to load services for all groups that have one, used in combination with Tags. ServiceGroupOrder specifies the order for loading groups.
ServiceGroupOrder	Specifies the order to load various groups of services. Order within groups is specified using Tags and GroupOrderList.

Table 10.5   Typical Subkeys of \CurrentControlSet\Control for All Control Sets
(continued)

Subkey	Contents
HiveList	The location of the files that contain Registry information. This value should be maintained only by the system.
Keyboard Layout	The DLLs for the keyboard language used as the default layout, plus a subkey named DosKeybCodes that lists the other available keyboard layouts. Settings for keyboard layout should be set by using the International icon in Control Panel.
Lsa	The authentication package for the local security authority. This value should be maintained only by the system—errors may prevent anyone from being able to log on to the computer.
NetworkProvider	Two subkeys, Active and Order, that specify the network provider and the order in which to load providers. Settings for network providers should be set by choosing the Network icon in Control Panel.
Nls	Information on national language support in three subkeys: CodePage, Language, and OEMLocale. Preferences about language and locale in Windows NT should be set using the International icon in Control Panel.
Print	Information about the current printers and printing environment, contained in several subkeys: ■ Environments, which contains subkeys defining drivers and print processors for system environments such as Windows NT Alpha_AXP, Windows NT R4000, and Windows NT *x*86. ■ Monitors, which can contain subkeys with data for specific network printing monitors. ■ Printers, which can contain subkeys describing printer parameters for each installed printer. ■ Providers, which can contain subkeys describing DLLs for network print services. Printing parameters should be changed by using Print Manager.
PriorityControl	The Win32 priority separation. This value should be set only by using the System icon in Control Panel.
ProductOptions	The product type, such as Winnt. These values should be maintained only by the system.

Table 10.5   Typical Subkeys of \CurrentControlSet\Control for All Control Sets (*continued*)

Subkey	Contents
Session Manager	Global variables used by Session Manager and these keys:
	• DOS Devices, which defines the MS-DOS devices AUX, MAILSLOT, NUL, PIPE, PRN, and UNC.
	• Environment, which defines the **ComSpec**, **Path**, **Os2LibPath**, and **WinDir** variables. User environment variables can be set using the System icon in Control Panel. If you want to change or add to the computer's default path, or add default system environment variables, you must change values in this subkey. For an example, see Chapter 14, "Registry Value Entries."
	• FileRenameOperations, which are used during startup to rename certain files so that they can be replaced. These values should be maintained only by the system.
	• KnownDLLs, which defines the directories and filenames for the Session Manager DLLs. These values should be maintained only by the system.
	• MemoryManagement, which defines paging options. The paging file should be defined by using the System icon in Control Panel.
	• SubSystems, which defines information for the Windows NT subsystems. These values should be maintained only by the system.
Setup	Hardware setup options. These values should be maintained only by the system. Users can make choices by running Windows NT Setup.
TimeZoneInformation	Values for time zone information. These settings should be set by using the Date/Time icon in Control Panel.
VirtualDeviceDrivers	Virtual device drivers. These values should be maintained only by the system.
Windows	Paths for the Windows NT directory and system directory. These values should be maintained only by the system.
WOW	Options for 16-bit Windows-based applications running under Windows NT. These settings should be maintained only by the system.

Services Subkey for All Control Sets

The Services subkey in each control set lists all of the Kernel device drivers, file system drivers, and Win32 service drivers that can be loaded by the Boot Loader, the I/O Manager, and the Service Control Manager. The Services subkey also contains subkeys that are static descriptions of hardware to which drivers can be attached. Table 10.6 describes some typical Services subkeys for a Windows NT computer.

Entries that appear under the DeviceMap subkeys include values that refer to entries in the Services subkey in the control set. For example, for a serial mouse, the following entry might appear under the DeviceMap\PointerPort subkey in HKEY_LOCAL_MACHINE\HARDWARE:

```
\Device\PointerPort0 : \REGISTRY\Machine\System\ControlSet001
    \Services\Sermouse
```

A related Services subkey named Sermouse will define values for the serial mouse driver. For example:

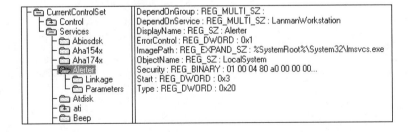

To view this information in an easily readable format, run Windows NT Diagnostics, and then choose the Drivers button and review details about a selected driver. You can choose the Devices icon in Control Panel to change startup and other information for a driver. For suggestions about how a system administrator can use this information for troubleshooting, see Chapter 12, "Configuration Management and the Registry."

Each subkey includes several standard (but optional) entries as shown in the following example, where Alerter is the name of a service that appears in the Services Control database.

The value entries that govern the behavior of a service include **ErrorControl**, **Group**, **DependOnGroup**, **DependOnService**, **ImagePath**, **ObjectName**, **Start**, **Tag**, and **Type**. For definitions of these value entries, see "CurrentControlSet\Services Subkeys" in Chapter 14, "Registry Value Entries."

The optional Linkage subkey specifies the binding options for the driver using the **Bind** and **Export** values. The **OtherDependencies** value that appears in the Linkage subkey for some services allows nodes to be loaded in an order related to other specific nodes with which they are closely associated. For example, the NBF transport depends on an NDIS driver. Therefore, to load the NBF protocol stack successfully, an NDIS network card driver must be loaded first. For details about loading order dependencies for network components, see "Dependency Handling for Network Components," later in this chapter.

The Parameters subkey (optional for some Services subkeys such as an adapter entry) contains a set of values to be passed to the driver. These values vary for each device driver. The following shows parameters for the serial mouse driver.

Because the entries in the Services list are Registry keys, no assumptions can be made about their order in an enumeration, so services can explicitly specify load ordering by grouping services and drivers in order by type. For example, the SCSI port driver can be loaded before any of the miniport drivers. The ordering is specified under the \Control\ServiceGroupOrder subkey in a control set.

Settings for the drivers that appear under the Services subkeys can be changed using the Devices, Network, or Services icons in Control Panel or, for network services, User Manager For Domains in Windows NT. Specific parameters for drivers and services are described in Chapter 14, "Registry Values Entries."

Table 10.6   Descriptions of Typical Services Subkeys for a Windows NT Computer

Service name	Description
Abiosdsk	Primary disk[1]
Ahaxxx	Adaptec SCSI adapters[1]
Alerter	Alerter service for the workstation[3]
AtDisk	Primary disk driver for non-SCSI hard disks[1]
Ati	ATI video display[1]
Beep	Base sound driver[1]
Bowser	Network[1]
Browser	Computer browser used by Workstation and Server services[3]
BusLogic	BusLogic SCSI adapter[1]
Busmouse	Bus mouse pointer[1]
Cdaudio	Filter[1]
Cdfs	SCSI CD-ROM class file system driver[1]
Cdfs_Rec	Recognizer for SCSI CD-ROM class file system[1]
Cirrus	Cirrus Logic video display[1]
ClipSrv	ClipBook (NetDDE service)[3]
Cpqarray	Compaq array driver (no additional Registry values)
Dell_DGX	Dell DGX video display[1]
Diskperf	Filter[1]
DLC	DLC transport[2]
DptScsi	DPT SCSI adapter[1]
Et4000	Tseng ET4000 video display[1]
EventLog	Event log service[3]
Fastfat	FAT boot file system driver[1]
Fat_Rec	Recognizer for FAT boot file system[1]

[1] Change settings for this driver using the Devices icon in Control Panel.

[2] Change settings for this driver using the Network icon in Control Panel.

[3] Change settings for this driver using the Services icon in Control Panel or using Server Manager in Windows NT Services.

Table 10.6   Descriptions of Typical Services Subkeys *(continued)*

Service name	Description
Fd16_700	Future Domain MCS 600/700, TMC-7000ex, 800-series SCSI adapters[1]
Floppy	Primary disk[1]
Ftdisk	Filter[1]
Hpfs_Rec	Recognizer for HPFS boot file system[1]
i8042pt	Keyboard driver[1]
Inport	Microsoft InPort Mouse pointer[1]
Jazzg*xxx*	Video display[1]
Jzvxl484	Video display[1]
Kbdclss	Keyboard class driver[1]
LanmanServer	Server service[3]
Lanman Workstation	Workstation service[3]
Messenger	Messenger service for workstation[3]
Mouclass	Mouse class driver[1]
Mup	Network[1]
Nbf	NetBEUI transport protocol[1, 2]
Ncr*xxx*	NCR SCSI controllers and adapters[1]
NetBIOS	NetBIOS transport interface[1, 2]
NetDDE et al.	Network DDE and Network DDE DSDM[3]
NetDetect	Network detection[1]
NetLogon	Network logon for workstation[3]
Ntfs	NTFS file system driver[1]
Nfts_Rec	Recognizer for NTFS file system[1]
Null	Base driver for null port[1]
Oliscsi	Olivetti SCSI adapter[1]
Parallel	Parallel port[1]
Pinball	HPFS file system driver[1]
Qvision	Qvision video display driver[1]
RAS	Remote Access Service[3]
Rdr	Network redirector[1]

[1] Change settings for this driver using the Devices icon in Control Panel.

[2] Change settings for this driver using the Network icon in Control Panel.

[3] Change settings for this driver using the Services icon in Control Panel or using Server Manager in Windows NT Services.

Table 10.6   Descriptions of Typical Services Subkeys *(continued)*

Service name	Description
Replicator	Directory replicator for workstation and server[3]
RPCLocator	Remote Procedure Call (RPC) locator (name service provider)[3]
RPCSS	Remote Procedure Call (RPC) service[3]
S3	S3 video display[1]
Schedule	Network schedule service[3]
Scsi*xxx*	SCSI class devices, which do not add parameters to the Registry, including Scsicdrm, Scsidisk, Scsiflip, Scsiprnt, and Scsiscan
Serial	Serial port[1]
Sermouse	Serial mouse[1]
Sgikbmou	Silicon Graphics keyboard and mouse driver[1]
Sgirex	Silicon Graphics video display driver[1]
Simbad	Filter[1]
Sparrow	SCSI adapter[1]
Spock	SCSI adapter[1]
Srv	Network server[3]
T128, T13B	Trantor SCSI adapters[1]
Trident	Trident video display[1]
UB*xxx*	Ungermann-Bass NDIS drivers[1, 3]
Ultra*xxx*	UltraStore SCSI adapters[1]
UPS	Uninterruptible power supply (UPS)[3, 4]
V7vram	Video Seven VRAM video display[1]
Vga	VGA video display[1]
Videoprt	Video display[1]
Wd33c93	Maynard SCSI adapter[1]
Wdvga	Western Digital/Paradise video display[1]
Xga	IBM XGA video display[1]

[1] Change settings for this driver using the Devices icon in Control Panel.

[2] Change settings for this driver using the Network icon in Control Panel.

[3] Change settings for this driver using the Services icon in Control Panel or using Server Manager in Windows NT Services.

[4] Change settings for this driver using the UPS icon in Control Panel.

Setup Subkey

The Setup subkey under HKEY_LOCAL_MACHINE\SYSTEM is used internally by Windows NT for the Setup program. Do not change these value entries. These settings should be maintained only by the system.

HKEY_CLASSES_ROOT

HKEY_CLASSES_ROOT contains information about file associations and OLE. As shown in the following illustration, this is the same data as in the Classes subkey under HKEY_LOCAL_MACHINE\SOFTWARE.

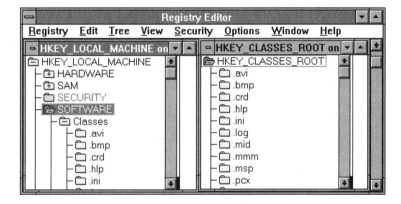

The sole purpose for HKEY_CLASSES_ROOT is to provide compatibility with the Windows 3.1 registration database.

As with Windows for MS-DOS, the Windows NT File Manager includes an Associate dialog box for associating a filename extension with a specific application. Windows NT stores these associations in the Windows NT Registry. The Associate dialog box should be used whenever possible to define filename associations.

HKEY_CURRENT_USER

HKEY_CURRENT_USER contains the database that describes the user profile for the user who is currently logged on the local computer. A user profile contains information that defines the appearance and behavior of the individual user's desktop, network connections, and other environment settings. A user profile ensures that Windows NT will look and act the same at any computer where that user logs on, if that person's profile is available at that computer or on the same domain in Windows NT Server.

HKEY_CURRENT_USER contains all the information necessary to set up a particular user environment on the computer. Information such as program groups, application preferences, screen colors, and other personal preferences and security rights are included. Many of these settings are the same kind of information that was stored in the WIN.INI file under Windows for MS-DOS.

HKEY_CURRENT_USER includes the default subkeys described in the following table. For details about managing the hives for user profiles, see "Managing User Profiles through the Registry" in Chapter 12, "Configuration Management and the Registry." For details about the contents of subkeys in HKEY_CURRENT_USER, see "Registry Entries for User Preferences" in Chapter 14, "Registry Value Entries."

Table 10.7   Default Subkeys in HKEY_CURRENT_USER

Subkey	Contents
Console	Subkeys that define the options and window size for a console (the interface between the user and character-mode applications). This includes settings for the Windows NT command prompt. These settings should be changed by using the commands in the Control menu for each of the specific non-Windows–based applications. (The subkey for the command prompt does not appear unless the font or screen colors have been changed by the current user.)
Control Panel	Subkeys that have parameters adjusted by applications in Control Panel, for example, the Windows NT Desktop. This includes information that was stored in the WIN.INI and CONTROL.INI files under Windows for MS-DOS.
Environment	Value entries that correspond to the current user's settings for environment variables. This includes information that was stored in the AUTOEXEC.BAT file under MS-DOS. Values should be set by using the System icon in Control Panel.
Keyboard Layout	The value entry that gives the current active keyboard layout. This value should be set by using the International icon in Control Panel.

Table 10.7   Default Subkeys in HKEY_CURRENT_USER *(continued)*

Subkey	Contents
Printers	Subkeys that describe the printers installed for the current user. These values should be set by using Print Manager.
Program Groups	Subkeys that describe the names and settings for the current user's program groups. Values defining common program groups are stored in HKEY_LOCAL_MACHINE\SOFTWARE\ProgramGroups. Personal program groups should be set by using the menu commands or mouse techniques in Program Manager.
Software	Subkeys that describe the current user's configurable settings for installed software that the user can use. This information has the same structure as HKEY_LOCAL_MACHINE\SOFTWARE. This information contains application-specific information that was stored in the WIN.INI file or private initialization files under Windows for MS-DOS.

Whenever similar data exists in HKEY_LOCAL_MACHINE and HKEY_CURRENT_USER, the data in HKEY_CURRENT_USER takes precedence, as described earlier, in "HKEY_LOCAL_MACHINE." The most significant example is environment variables, where variables defined for the user who is currently logged on take precedence over system variables, as defined by using the System icon in Control Panel.

HKEY_CURRENT_USER is mapped to HKEY_USER*SID_#*, where *SID_#* is the Security ID string of the current user, as shown in the following example from Registry Editor. The Windows NT logon process builds a user's personal profile environment based upon what it finds in HKEY_USER*SID_#*. If no such data is available, HKEY_CURRENT_USER is built from the data in HKEY_USER\.DEFAULT.

Note   To find the name of the file that goes with a hive, see the HiveList subkey in HKEY_LOCAL_MACHINE\SYSTEM\CurrentControlSet\Control. To find which hive file goes with a user profile (whether or not the user is logged on), see the ProfileList subkey under HKEY_LOCAL_MACHINE\SOFTWARE\Microsoft \Windows NT\CurrentVersion. You can use the Find Key command from the View menu in Registry Editor to locate a specific key quickly.

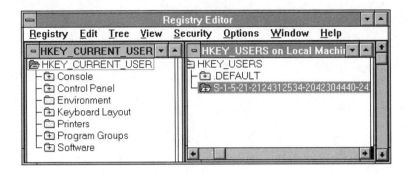

HKEY_USERS

HKEY_USERS contains all actively loaded user profiles. HKEY_USERS has at least two subkeys: .DEFAULT and the Security ID string for the user who is currently logged on. The information in the .DEFAULT subkey is used to create the user profile for a user who logs on without a personal user profile.

The .DEFAULT subtree contains the Console, Control Panel, Environment, Keyboard Layout, Program Groups, and Software subkeys as described in Table 10.7. For details about the contents of subkeys in HKEY_USERS, see "Registry Entries for User Preferences" in Chapter 14, "Registry Value Entries."

To delete profiles from a computer, choose the Delete User Profiles command from the Options menu in Windows NT Setup.

Network Settings in the Registry

When a network component is installed, various information is added to the Registry. Each network component is represented in two distinct areas of the Registry:

- Software registration keys for the component's driver and adapter card under HKEY_LOCAL_MACHINE\SOFTWARE
- Service registration keys for the component's driver and adapter under HKEY_LOCAL_MACHINE\SYSTEM

The following sections describe the general organization and content of the software and service registration information for network components and then conclude with information about bindings for network components and dependency handling.

Note   The information in this section is provided for informational purposes, so that you can easily find entries in the Registry. All changes to settings for network adapters and supporting software should be made by choosing the Network icon in Control Panel, not by directly editing values in the Registry.

Network Component Types in the Registry

The following table describes the network component types.

Table 10.8   Network Component Types

Component type	Meaning
Adapter	A piece of hardware
Driver	A software component associated directly with a piece of hardware
Transport	A software component used by services
Service	A software component providing capability directly to user applications
Basic	A token used to represent a fundamental class name (that is, a class with no parent)

Each type of network component requires a subkey for both software and services. Therefore, the installation of a single network card will usually result in the creation of four distinct subkeys in the Registry:

- The software registration subkey for the driver, found in HKEY_LOCAL_MACHINE\SOFTWARE*Company**ProductName**Version*.

  For example, the path for the driver for an Etherlink adapter will be HKEY_LOCAL_MACHINE\Software\Microsoft\Elinkii\CurrentVersion.

- The software registration subkey for the network adapter card, found in HKEY_LOCAL_MACHINE\SOFTWARE\Microsoft\Windows NT\CurrentVersion\NetworkCards*netcard#*.

- The service registration subkey for the driver, found in HKEY_LOCAL_MACHINE\SYSTEM\CurrentControlSet\Services.

- The service registration subkey for the network adapter card, found in HKEY_LOCAL_MACHINE\SYSTEM\CurrentControlSet\Services.

Software Registration Information for Network Components

Because installation of a network adapter card results in separate Registry entries for the driver and for the adapter, the Software subtree will contain several subkeys to describe the network component. For each network component, a special subkey named NetRules is created in the appropriate driver or adapter registration subkeys. The NetRules subkey identifies the network component as part of the network ensemble.

For example, the standard software registration entry for the Etherlink II driver will appear under this path:

```
HKEY_LOCAL_MACHINE\SOFTWARE\Microsoft   \Elinkii\CurrentVersion
```

The standard entries for the driver might include the following values:

```
Description = 3Com Etherlink II Adapter Driver
InstallDate = 0x2a4e01c5
...
RefCount = 0x1
ServiceName = Elnkii
SoftwareType = driver
Title = 3Com Etherlink II Adapter Driver
```

And under the Etherlink II driver's related NetRules subkey, these value entries might appear:

```
bindable = elnkiiDriver elnkiiAdapter non exclusive
bindform = "ElnkIISys" yes no container
class = REG_MULTI_SZ "elnkiiDriver basic"
Infname = OEMNADE2.INF
InfOption = ELNKII
type = elnkiiSys ndisDriver elnkiiDriver
use = driver
```

The Etherlink adapter is described in a NetworkCards subkey under this path:

```
HKEY_LOCAL_MACHINE\SOFTWARE\Microsoft
    \Windows NT\CurrentVersion\NetworkCards\netcard#
```

The standard entries for the adapter might include these values:

```
Description = 3Com Etherlink II Adapter
InstallDate = 0x2a4e01c5
Manufacturer = Microsoft
ProductName = Elnkii
ServiceName = Elnkii02
Title = [01] 3Com Etherlink II Adapter
```

And these value entries might appear under the adapter's related NetRules subkey:

```
bindform = "Elnkii02" yes yes container
class = "elnkiiAdapter basic"
Infname = OEMNADE2.INF
InfOption = ELNKII
type = elnkii elnkiiAdapter
```

The value entries for the NetRules subkeys are defined in Chapter 14, "Registry Entry Values." The information in the main entries for network adapters and drivers is maintained by the system and should not be changed by users.

Service Registration Information for Network Components

The HKEY_LOCAL_MACHINE\SYSTEM\CurrentControlSet\Services subkey is the service registration area that contains the information used to load a network component into memory. These subkeys contain certain required information, such as the location of the executable file, the service type, and its start criterion.

Each network component's software registration information (as described in the previous section) contains an entry named **ServiceName**, whose value is the name of the service corresponding to the network component. This name acts as a symbolic link to the CurrentControlSet\Services parameters.

Some network components are actually sets of services, each of which has its own subkey in the Services subkey. There is usually a "main" service, with the other services listed as its dependencies.

For example, as shown in the previous section, the Etherlink driver's **ServiceName** is Elnkii, and this name would appear as a Services subkey that defines the location of the driver file, dependencies, and other startup information. The Elnkii subkey in turn contains other subkeys that define the parameters and linkage rules for the driver.

The Etherlink adapter's **ServiceName** is Elnkii02, which also appears as a Services subkey that defines linkage rules for bindings plus physical parameters of the network card, such as its I/O address and interrupt request (IRQ) number, as specified in the Network dialog in Control Panel.

The value entries for the subkeys describing adapters and drivers are defined in "Registry Entries for Network Adapter Cards" in Chapter 14, "Registry Value Entries."

Bindings for Network Components

For the networking software in a computer to operate properly, several different pieces of software must be loaded, and their relationships with other components must be established. These relationships are often called *bindings*. To determine the complete set of optimal bindings among an ensemble of configured network components, the system checks the following information in the Registry:

- The set of network components to be configured
- The types of network components in this set
- The constraining parameters for the network components and their bindings
- The possible bindings that could occur
- The proper way to inform each network component about its bindings

During system startup, the CurrentControlSet\Services subkey is checked for binding information for each service. If any is found, a Linkage subkey is created, and values are stored. For example, these two strings might appear in a value entry under the CurrentControlSet\Services\LanmanWorkstation\Linkage subkey:

```
Bind = \Device\Nbf_Elnkii01  \Device\Nbf_Elnkii02
```

This entry describes the binding information used by the Windows NT Redirector when two separate network cards are present. Each network card's symbolic name is suffixed with a network card index number. This name is joined to the name of the transport through which the network card is accessed. The names are generated by the system according to the constraints defined by the network component's rules.

Bindings have a *usability* requirement that means the binding must terminate at either an adapter (that is, a physical device) or at a *logical end-point*, which is simply a software component that manages all further interconnection information internally. This requirement avoids loading software components that can never be of actual use. For example, a user might have a running network and then choose to remove the adapter card. Without the usability restriction, the bindings would still connect components and prepare them for loading even though the network was entirely unusable.

The following example uses NBF.SYS and SRV.SYS in an ensemble with two Etherlink II network cards and an IBM Token Ring card. First, in the values in the CurrentControlSet\Services\Nbf\Linkage subkey are the following:

```
Bind=   "\Device\ElnkII1"
        "\Device\ElnkII2"
        "\Device\IbmTok1"
Export= "\Device\Nbf\ElnkII1"
        "\Device\Nbf\ElnkII2"
        "\Device\Nbf\IbmTok1"
Route=  "ElnkIISys ElnkII1"
        "ElnkIISys ElnkII2"
        "IbmtokSys IbmTok1"
```

Under the CurrentControlSet\Services\Srv\Linkage subkey, the following might appear:

```
Bind   = "\Device\Nbf\ElnkII1"
         "\Device\Nbf\ElnkII2"
         "\Device\Nbf\IbmTok1"
Export = "\Device\Srv\Nbf\ElnkII1"
         "\Device\Srv\Nbf\ElnkII2"
         "\Device\Srv\Nbf\IbmTok1"
Route  = "Nbf ElnkIISys ElnkII1"
         "Nbf ElnkIISys ElnkII2"
         "Nbf IbmtokSys IbmTok1"
```

The names in the **Bind** and **Export** entries are based upon the object names defined in the component's NetRules subkey; these entry values can therefore be different from the actual names of the services, although in the previous example, for the sake of clarity, they are not. The names in the **Route** entry are the names of the Services subkeys comprising the full downward route through the bindings protocol.

When the system finishes computing the bindings for network components and the results are stored in the Registry, some network components might need to be informed of changes that occurred. For example, TCP/IP needs to ask the user for an IP address for any network adapter that has been newly configured. If the NetRules subkey for a network component has a value entry named **Review** set to a nonzero value, the .INF file for the network component will be checked every time the bindings are changed.

Dependency Handling for Network Components

Services can be dependent upon other services or drivers, which can be dependent upon others, and so on. The system can establish these types of dependencies:

- Specific dependencies, which are represented by the names of the services upon which a service is dependent
- Group dependencies
- Static dependencies, which are required in all circumstances

Specific Dependencies

A specific dependency is simply the name of a necessary service. By default, the system generates explicit names for all dependent services discovered during bindings generation. Specific dependencies are marked in the Registry as a value of the **Use** entry under the component's NetRules subkey.

For example, assume the Workstation service is dependent upon NBF. NBF is connected to two adapter cards and so is dependent upon their drivers. The system will mark NBF as dependent upon the two network card drivers and will mark the Workstation service as dependent upon the network card drivers and NBF.

Group Dependencies

It often happens that a service should be loaded if any member of a set of dependencies successfully loads. In the previous example, the Workstation service would fail to load if either of the network card drivers failed to initialize.

Groups are used to support this approach. Any service (driver, transport, or whatever) can identify itself as being a member of a service group. All Windows NT network card drivers, for example, are treated as members of the group NDIS.

Group dependencies are marked in the Registry as a value of the **Use** entry under the component's NetRules subkey. Groups are symbolic names listed in the CurrentControlSet\Control\GroupOrderList subkey.

Static Dependencies

A *static dependency* is a required service in all circumstances and is unrelated to how the system otherwise determines bindings.

When the system computes dependencies, it discards any previously listed dependencies. To guarantee that a service is always configured to be dependent upon another service, the value entry **OtherDependencies** can be created under the component's Linkage subkey. **OtherDependencies** is a REG_MULTI_SZ value, so it can contain the names of as many services as needed.

C H A P T E R   1 1

Registry Editor and Registry Administration

You can use the Registry Editor to view Registry entries for the various components in Windows NT. You can also use Registry Editor to modify or add Registry entries. This chapter describes what Registry Editor is and how to use it, with an emphasis on protecting the Registry contents and using Registry Editor to monitor and maintain the system configuration on remote computers. The following topics are included in this chapter:

- Using Registry Editor and Windows NT Diagnostics (WINMSD.EXE)
- Viewing the Registry for a remote computer
- Editing Registry value entries
- Maintaining the Registry

For more information about the commands and dialog box options that appear in Registry Editor, press F1 to view the online Help.

It is recommended that, wherever possible, you make changes to the system configuration by using Control Panel or the applications in the Administrative Tools group in Program Manager.

Caution   You can impair or disable Windows NT with incorrect changes or accidental deletions if you (or other users) use Registry Editor to change the system configuration. Wherever possible, you should use the graphical tools in Windows NT to make changes, and use Registry Editor only as a last resort.

To protect the system configuration, administrators can restrict users' access to the Registry, as described in "Maintaining Registry Security," later in this chapter.

Using Registry Editor and Windows NT Diagnostics

Registry Editor

The Registry Editor application, REGEDT32.EXE, does not appear in any default program groups in Program Manager, although it is installed automatically when you set up Windows NT.

▶ **To run Registry Editor**

- Run REGEDT32.EXE from File Manager or Program Manager.

   –Or–

   At the command prompt, type **start regedt32**, and press ENTER.

You can also run Registry Editor from your desktop by dragging the REGEDT32.EXE file from File Manager into any program group.

Your ability to make changes to the Registry using Registry Editor depends on your access privileges. In general, you can make the same kinds of changes in Registry Editor as your privileges allow for Control Panel or other administrative tools.

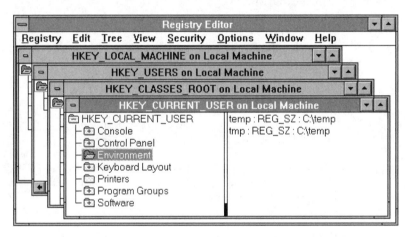

Working in the Registry Editor Windows

You can use the mouse or commands to manipulate the windows and panes in the Registry Editor in the same way as in File Manager. For example:

- Double-click a key name to expand or collapse that entry. Or, choose commands from the View and Tree menus to control the display of a selected key and its data.

- Use the mouse or arrow keys to move the vertical split bar in each window to control the size of the left and right panes.

- Choose the Tile or Cascade command from the View menu to arrange the Registry Editor windows. Click the Minimize button, or double-click the particular window icon for the Registry to reduce or restore a window.

- Choose Auto Refresh from the Options menu to update the display continuously. You can also choose one of the Refresh commands from the View menu to update the display of Registry information when Auto Refresh is turned off.

Tip Turning off Auto Refresh improves the performance of Registry Editor.

The following table shows some keyboard methods for managing the display of data in each of the Registry Editor windows.

Table 11.1   Keyboard Actions for Viewing Registry Data

Procedure	Keyboard action
Expand one level of a selected Registry key	Press ENTER.
Expand all of the levels of the predefined handle in the active Registry window	Press CTRL + *.
Expand a branch of a selected Registry key	Press the asterisk (*) key on the numeric keypad.
Collapse a branch of a selected Registry key	Press ENTER or the minus (-) sign on the numeric keypad.

Using Windows NT Diagnostics to View System Configuration Data

Windows NT
Diagnostics

You can also use the Windows NT Diagnostics tool (WINMSD.EXE) to view configuration information stored in the Registry. Windows NT Diagnostics is placed in your *SystemRoot*\SYSTEM32 directory when you set up Windows NT. You can run this tool like any executable file in Windows NT. It's a good idea to place a program-item icon for Windows NT Diagnostics in either the Main group or Administrative Tools group in Program Manager.

When you want to browse for system information, Windows NT Diagnostics is the best tool to choose.

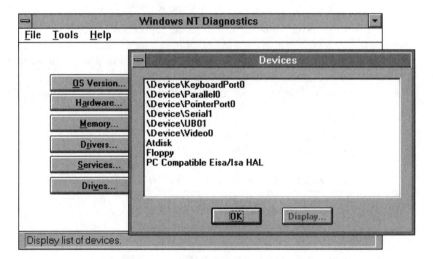

With Windows NT Diagnostics, you choose a button to display specific data from the Registry in an easily readable format.

Tip You cannot edit value entries using Windows NT Diagnostics, so the Registry contents are protected while you browse for information. However, you can select and copy any value if you want to paste information in a Registry Editor edit box or in a text editor.

Viewing the Registry for a Remote Computer

In the same way that you can use Event Viewer or User Manager to view details on another computer, you can use Registry Editor to view and change the contents of another computer's Registry if the Server services on the remote computer are running.

This ability to remotely view a computer's configuration allows you, as a system administrator, to examine a user's startup parameters, desktop configuration, and other parameters. So you can provide troubleshooting or other support assistance over the telephone while you view settings on the other computer from your own workstation.

Note Auto Refresh is not available when you are viewing the Registry from a remote computer. If Auto Refresh is on, manual refresh is disabled. Therefore, when you open a remote registry, Registry Editor checks to see if Auto Refresh mode is on. If it is, Registry Editor displays the message "Auto Refresh is not available for remote registries; Registry Editor will disable Auto Refresh mode".

▶ **To view the Registry for a remote computer**

- From the Registry menu, choose the Select Computer command, and then select or type the name of the computer whose Registry you want to access.

  –Or–

  Double-click the name of a computer in the Select Computer list. Under a Windows NT Server, the first name in this list represents the name of a domain. If no computer name appears after this domain name, double-click the domain name to view a list of the computers in that domain.

Two Registry windows appear for the remote computer, one for HKEY_USERS and one for HKEY_LOCAL_MACHINE. You can view or modify the information on keys for the remote computer if the access controls defined for the keys allow you to perform such operations. If you are logged on as a member of the Administrators group, you can perform actions on all keys.

Loading Hives from Another Computer

You can use the Load Hive and Unload Hive commands in Registry Editor to display and maintain another computer's Registry without viewing it remotely. You might want to do this to view specific values or to repair certain entries for a computer that is not configured properly or cannot connect to the network.

The hives that make up your computer's Registry are loaded automatically when you start the computer, and you can view the content of these hives in Registry Editor. If you want to view or change the contents of other hive files, you must use the Load Hive command to display its contents in Registry Editor.

The following examples use the Load Hive command:

- Repairing a hive on a computer that temporarily cannot run Windows NT. For details, see "Backing Up and Restoring Registry Hives," later in this chapter.

- Looking at or repairing hives for profiles of people who aren't currently logged on, either on the same computer or a remote PC. For details and examples, see "Managing User Profiles Through the Registry" in Chapter 12, "Configuration Management and the Registry."

- Creating a custom LastKnownGood and other startup controls. For details and examples, see "Making Sure the System Always Starts" in Chapter 12, "Configuration Management and the Registry."

The Load Hive and Unload Hive commands affect only the Registry windows that display HKEY_USERS and HKEY_LOCAL_MACHINE. To use these commands, you must have Restore and Backup privileges, which you have if you are logged on as a member of the Administrators group. The Load Hive command is available only when HKEY_USERS or HKEY_LOCAL_MACHINE is selected. The Unload Hive command is available only when a subkey of one of these handles is selected.

▶ **To load a hive into the Registry Editor**

1. Select the HKEY_LOCAL_MACHINE or HKEY_USERS root.

2. From the Registry menu, choose the Load Hive command.

3. Use the File Name, Drives, and Directories boxes and the Network button of the Load Hive dialog box to select the file that contains the hive you want to load, and then choose the OK button.

   If you are loading a hive on a remote computer, the drive and path in the filename is relative to the remote computer.

   Tip You can find the directory location and names of hives on a computer in HKEY_LOCAL_MACHINE\SYSTEM\CurrentControlSet\Control\Hivelist.

   This file must have been created with the Save Key command (as described later in this chapter), or it must be one of the default hives. Under the FAT file system, the filename cannot have an extension.

   If you are unable to connect to another computer over the network, you can load a hive file that you copied to a floppy disk.

4. In the second Load Hive dialog box, type the name you want to use for the key where the hive will be loaded, and then choose the OK button.

   This name creates a new subkey in the Registry. You can specify any name using any characters and including blank spaces. You cannot load to an existing key.

Data from the loaded hive appears as a new subkey under HKEY_USERS or HKEY_LOCAL_MACHINE (whichever handle you selected before loading the hive). A loaded hive remains in the system until it is unloaded.

The Load Hive command creates a new hive in the memory space of the Registry and uses the specified file as the backing hive file (*filename*.LOG) for it. The specified file is held open, but nothing is copied to the file unless the information in a key or value entry is changed. Likewise, the Unload Hive command does not copy or create anything; it merely unloads a loaded hive.

▶ **To unload a hive from the Registry Editor**

- Select the key that represents a hive that you previously loaded, and then from the Registry menu, choose the Unload Hive command.

  The selected key is removed from the window and is no longer actively available to the system or for editing in Registry Editor.

You cannot unload a hive that was loaded by the system. Also, you won't be able to unload a hive that contains an open key.

Saving and Restoring Keys

The Save Key command lets you save the information in a key and all its subkeys in a hive file. This hive file can then be used by the Restore and Load Key commands.

Changes in the Registry are saved automatically, whether you make changes by using Registry Editor or by changing settings in applications. The Save Key command is used specifically to save portions of the Registry as a file on disk.

To use the Save Key command, you need Backup privileges, which you have if you are logged on as a member of the Administrators group.

You can use the Save Key command on any key. However, this command will not save volatile keys, which are destroyed when you shut down the system. For example, the HKEY_LOCAL_MACHINE\HARDWARE key is volatile, so it is not saved as a hive file. If you want to view the Hardware hive for debugging, you can save it in a text file by choosing the Save Subtree As command from the Registry menu, as described at the end of this chapter.

▶ **To save a Registry key**

1. Select the key that you want to save as a hive file on a disk.

2. From the Registry menu, choose the Save Key command, and then complete the filename information in the Save Key dialog box.

   Under the FAT file system, this filename cannot have an extension.

   If the key that you are saving is in the Registry of a remote computer, the drive and path that you specify for the filename is relative to the remote computer.

The selected key is now saved as a file. When you use the Load Hive command, you can select the filename for any files saved using the Save Key command.

For example, as part of system maintenance, you might use the Save Key command to save a key as a file. When the key that you saved is ready to be returned to the system, you use the Restore command.

You can use the Restore or Restore Volatile command to make a hive file a part of the system configuration. The Restore and Restore Volatile commands let you copy information in a hive file over a specified key. This information copied from the file will overwrite the contents of the specified key, except for the key name.

To use the Restore or Restore Volatile commands, you need Restore privilege—which you have if you are logged on as a member of the Administrators group.

▶ **To restore a key**

1. Select the key where you want to restore the hive.

2. From the Registry menu, choose the Restore command, and then complete the filename information in the Restore Key dialog box to specify the hive you want to restore.

   Under the FAT file system, this filename cannot have an extension.

   If you are restoring a key on a remote computer, the drive and path of the filename is relative to the remote computer.

Note If you want to add a key temporarily to a system, however, you use the Restore Volatile command. If you use this command, the Registry will make a volatile copy, which will disappear when the system is restarted.

You cannot restore a key that has opened handles or that has subkeys with opened handles. This is why you cannot restore the SAM or SECURITY subtrees, because Windows NT always has handles open in these keys. So the Restore command is used only for special conditions, such as restoration of user profiles on a damaged system. Usually, to switch in a backup version of a hive, you can use the ReplaceKey function in REGREST.EXE (included on the Resource Guide disk).

Editing Registry Value Entries

Within the Registry, you can alter the value entries for a selected key or assign new value entries to keys. This section describes how to find keys and add, edit, or delete keys and value entries.

Finding a Key in the Registry

The location of a Registry key may be different in the tree structure from what is described in this *Resource Guide*, depending on whether a computer is running Windows NT as a workstation or a server, and other factors.

You can search for a specific key name in the Registry tree. Key names appear in the left pane of the Registry Editor windows. The search begins from the currently selected key. Searching from a predefined key will search all its descendant keys.

Each search is local to the tree where the search begins. That is, if you are searching in the windows for HKEY_LOCAL_MACHINE, the search will not include keys found under HKEY_CURRENT_USER.

▶ **To search for a key in Registry Editor**

1. From the View menu, choose the Find Key command.

2. In the Find What box of the Find Key dialog box, type the name of the key that you want to find.

   ▪ If you want to restrict the scope of the search or define the search direction, select the Match Whole Word Only box, the Match Case option, or select Up or Down in the Direction box.

   ▪ To see the next occurrence of the key name you specified, choose the Find Next button.

3. Choose the Find button.

   Because key names are not unique, it's a good idea to search for additional occurrences of a specific key name, to be sure you find the key you want.

Tip Some key names include spaces (such as Session Manager), while others use underscores (such as Ntfs_rec) or a continuous string (such as EventLog). To ensure that you find the key you want, search for a portion of the name, and make sure that the Match Whole Word Only check box is cleared in the Find dialog box.

You can also use the Registry database provided in the Resource Guide disk to find specific keys or value entries related to specific topics.

▶ **To use the Windows NT Registry Entries database**

• In File Manager, double-click the REGENTRY.HLP file.

Editing Values in the Registry

Each value entry in Registry Editor appears as a string that consists of three components, as shown in the following figure.

Figure 11.1   The Three Components of a Value Entry

The following rules govern the content of these three value entry components:

- The name of the value is a string of up to 16,000 Unicode characters (32K). This name can contain backslash (\) characters. The name itself can be null (that is, " ").

- The data type of the value is REG_BINARY, REG_DWORD, REG_EXPAND_SZ, REG_MULTI_SZ, or REG_SZ, as described in Table 10.2 in Chapter 10, "Overview of the Windows NT Registry." Other data types can be defined by programs, but editing of only these five specific data types is supported in Registry Editor.

- The value itself can be data of a size up to 1 MB in any format except DWord, including arbitrary strings and raw binary data. However, for the sake of efficiency, values larger than 2048 bytes should be stored as files, with the filenames stored in the Registry.

The Registry preserves case as you type it for any entry but ignores case in evaluating the data. The names are case-insensitive. However, the data is defined by specific applications (or users), so it might be case-sensitive, depending on how the program that uses it treats the data.

▶ **To edit any value**

1. In the right pane of the Registry Editor window, double-click the value entry.

   –Or–

   From the Edit menu, choose the String, Binary, DWord, or Multi String command as appropriate for the selected value.

2. Edit the value that appears in the related Editor dialog box, and then choose the OK button.

The Binary and DWord editors give you the flexibility to select the base of a number system in which you want to edit your data. In the Binary editor, you can edit your data as binary (base 2) or hex (base 16). In the DWord editor, you can edit your data in binary, hex, or decimal (base 10). Hex is the default base for both editors. These types of data will always be displayed in hex in the right pane of the Registry Editor.

Tip To view numbers in decimal format, double-click the value entry and select the Decimal format option. Cancel the dialog box when you finish checking the value.

Information stored in a nonvolatile key remains in the Registry until you delete it. Information stored in a volatile key is discarded when you shut down the system. Everything under a volatile key is also volatile. Everything stored under the HKEY_LOCAL_MACHINE\HARDWARE key is volatile.

Note If your Registry becomes quite large, you will want to set a larger value for the value entry named RegistrySizeLimit, as described in "The CurrentControlSet\Control Subkeys" in Chapter 14, "Registry Value Entries."

Adding a Key

You can add a key to store data in the Registry. For example, you might add a subkey under CurrentControlSet\Services to start a service process you have written or to install a device driver that doesn't have an installation program.

To do this, you must have Create Subkey access permission for the key under which you are adding a subkey, as described in "Assigning Access Rights to Registry Keys," later in this chapter.

▶ **To add a key to the Registry**

1. Select the key or subkey under which you want the new key to appear, and then choose the Add Key command from the Edit menu, or press the INS key.

2. In the Key Name box of the Add Key dialog box, type the name that you want to assign your key.

   The key name cannot contain a backslash (\), and it must be unique in relation to other subkeys at the same level in the hierarchy. That is, Key1 and Key2 can each have a subkey named Key3, but Key1 cannot have two subkeys named Key3.

3. Leave the Class box blank, as this entry is reserved for future uses.

4. Choose the OK button to display the new key in the Registry Editor window.

Adding a Value Entry to a Registry Key

In Registry Editor, you can assign a new value entry to a key or edit the value entry of an existing key. When you do this, the value that you add appears in the data pane of the selected Registry window.

You may want to add value entries based on tuning and troubleshooting information you find in Chapter 14, "Registry Value Entries".

▶ **To add a value entry to a Registry key**

1. Select the subkey to which you want to add a value entry.

2. From the Edit menu, choose the Add Value command.

   The Value Name box is displayed.

   Tip To quickly open the Value Name box, move the focus to the right pane using the TAB key or the mouse, and then press the INS key.

   ---

3. In the Value Name box, type the name you want to assign to the new value entry.

4. In the Data Type box, select the type that you want to assign to the value entry, as described in Table 10.2 in Chapter 10, "Overview of the Windows NT Registry."

5. Choose the OK button, and then type the value in the Editor dialog box that appears. Choose the OK button again to display the new entry in the Registry Editor window.

Deleting a Key or a Value Entry

You can use either the Delete command from the Edit menu or press the DELETE key to remove selected keys or value entries from the Registry. However, you cannot delete any of the predefined subtrees or change the name of a key.

Caution There is no Undo command for deletions. Registry Editor asks you to confirm the deletions if the Confirm On Delete option is checked under the Options menu. However, the message does not include the name of the key you are deleting. Check your selection carefully before proceeding when you delete a key.

The only way to retrieve a key that you mistakenly delete is to restart the computer. Press the spacebar immediately after selecting Windows NT at the Boot Loader prompt, and then choose the Last Known Good option to roll back to an earlier configuration.

You can protect the Registry from accidental deletions in these ways:

- Protect data through read-only mode

  To do this, choose the Read Only command from the Options menu. When this command is checked, Registry Editor will not save any changes made, protecting the data from accidental changes.

- Protect data through confirmation

  To do this, choose the Confirm On Delete command from the Options menu. When this command is checked, the Registry Editor asks you to confirm deletion of any key or value.

Maintaining the Registry

Windows NT enforces access control on Registry files, so it is difficult for users to accidentally or intentionally damage or delete hives on a running system. While the system is running, hive files are kept open by the system for exclusive access on all file systems. If the Windows NT *SystemRoot* is not on an NTFS volume, the Registry files can be tampered with—specifically, users can remove hives for user profiles that aren't currently loaded. With NTFS, such tampering can be prevented.

You should plan how you will protect the Registry for each Windows NT computer at your site. This section describes how to ensure that you will have working Registry files under most conditions.

For more details about how to ensure recoverability under all conditions, see "Making Sure the System Always Starts" in Chapter 12, "Configuration Management and the Registry."

Maintaining Registry Security

Don't allow users to log on as members of the Administrators group unless a specific individual has administrative duties.

You might also choose not to put REGEDT32.EXE on workstations, since you can easily administer any workstation from a remote computer. You can also place access controls in File Manager on REGEDT32.EXE, limiting the rights of users to start this program.

This section describes the following additional steps you can take to protect the Registry:

- Protecting Registry files
- Assigning access rights to Registry keys
- Auditing Registry activities

Protecting Registry Files for User Profiles

You can protect the Registry hive files for user profiles in the same way that you protect other files in Windows NT—by restricting access through File Manager. If the files are stored on an NTFS volume, you can use the commands on the Security menu in File Manager to assign permissions. For details about using these commands, see the online Help in File Manager.

Caution   You should only change permissions for user profile hives. The permissions for other hives are maintained automatically by the system and should not be changed.

For information about safeguarding files with backups, see "Backing Up and Restoring Registry Hives," later in this chapter.

Assigning Access Rights to Registry Keys

To determine who has access to specific Registry data, set permissions on the Registry keys to specify the users and groups that can access that key. This is sometimes called *changing ACLs*, in reference to the Access Control Lists that govern who has access to data. You can also add or remove names from the list of users or groups authorized to access the Registry keys.

You can assign access rights to Registry keys regardless of the type of file system on the partition where the Windows NT files are stored.

Caution   Changing the permissions to limit access to a Registry key can have severe consequences. If, for example, you set No Access permissions on a key that the Network Control Panel application needs for configuration, it will cause the application to fail.

At a minimum, ensure that Administrators and the System have full access to the key, to ensure that the system starts and that the Registry key can be repaired by an administrator.

If you change permissions on a Registry key, you should audit the key for failed access attempts. For details, see "Auditing Registry Activities," later in this chapter.

Because assigning permissions on specific keys can have drastic consequences, you should reserve this action for keys that you add to accommodate custom applications or other custom settings. After you change permissions on a Registry key, be sure to turn on auditing in User Manager, and then test the system extensively through a variety of activities while logged on under different user and administrative accounts.

In the Registry Editor, the commands on the Security menu for assigning permission and ownership of keys work the same as similar commands in File Manager for assigning access rights for files and directories. For details about these commands, see the online Help in Registry Editor. For a detailed discussion of permissions and ownership, see "Securing Directories and Files" in Chapter 4, "File Manager," in the *Windows NT System Guide*.

▶ **To assign permission on a key**

1. Make a backup copy of the Registry key before making changes.

2. Select the key for which you want to assign access permission, and then from the Security menu, choose the Permissions command.

3. In the Registry Key Permissions dialog box, assign an access level to the selected key by selecting an option in the Type of Access box as described in the following table, and then choose the OK button.

Type of access	Meaning
Read	Allows users on the Permissions list to read the key's contents, but prevents changes from being saved.
Full Control	Allows users on the Permissions list to access, edit, or take ownership of the selected key.
Special Access	Allows users on the Permissions list some custom combination of access and edit rights for the selected key. For a description of the Special Access types, see "Auditing Registry Activities," later in this chapter.

4. Turn on auditing in User Manager, and then test the system extensively to ensure that the new access control does not interfere with system or application operations.

As a system administrator, you may need to take ownership of a key to protect access to that key. You take ownership of a Registry key by choosing the Owner command from the Security menu in Registry Editor, and then completing the Ownership dialog box. You can also add users or groups to the Permissions list by following the same procedure for managing lists of users and groups as appears throughout Windows NT.

You (or any user) can take ownership of any Registry key if you log onto the computer as a member of the Administrator group. However, if an Administrator takes ownership of a key without being assigned full control by its owner, the key cannot be given back to its original owner, and the event is audited.

Auditing Registry Activities

Auditing Registry activities requires several separate activities:

- Turning on auditing and setting the audit policies in User Manager or User Manager for Domains for the activities you want to audit

- Specifying the groups and users whose activities you want to audit for selected keys, by choosing the Auditing command in Registry Editor

- Viewing the Security log in Event Viewer for a selected computer to see the results of auditing

For each of these activities, you must be logged on as a member of the Administrators group for the specific computer you are auditing. Auditing policies are set on a per-computer basis. Before you can audit activities in Registry keys, you must turn on security auditing for the computer.

▶ **To turn on auditing**

1. In User Manager or User Manager for Domains, choose the Audit command from the Policies menu, and select the Audit These Events option to turn on auditing.

2. Check Success and Failure options for each type of event to be audited, and then choose the OK button.

Note At a minimum, you should check the Failure option for File And Object Access. Choosing the Success option for many items may produce an abundance of meaningless entries in the event log.

You may want to audit actions for a specific Registry key. For example, you might want to audit the following:

- Keys where you want to know about changes being made by users or applications

- Keys you added that you want to test

▶　**To audit user actions for a selected Registry key**

1. From the Security menu in Registry Editor, choose the Auditing command, and then complete the dialog box.

   This command in Registry Editor is similar to the Auditing command in File Manager. For details about the Auditing dialog box, choose online Help in Registry Editor. For a discussion of general issues related to the Auditing command, see "Auditing Files and Directories" in Chapter 4, "File Manager," in the *Windows NT System Guide.*

2. Check the Success or Failure check box for the following activities:

Audit option	Audit events that attempt to
Query Value	Open a key with Query Value access
Set Value	Open a key with Set Value access
Create Subkey	Open a key with Create Value access
Enumerate Subkeys	Open a key with Enumerate Subkeys access (that is, events that try to find the subkeys of a key)
Notify	Open a key with Notify access
Create Link	Open a key with Create Link access
Delete	Delete the key
Write DAC	Determine who has access to the key
Read Control	Find the owner of a key

▶　**To view the results of auditing**

- Run Event Viewer, select the computer that you are interested in, and then choose the Security command from the Log menu.

Note　If you change permission for any Registry key, you should turn on Auditing in User Manager and specify the Failure attempts for File And Object Access to be audited. Then you can check the Security event log for details if any application isn't working because of changes in permissions.

Backing Up and Restoring Registry Hives

You might at some time find it necessary to restore backed up versions of Registry hives. This might occur, for example, when a new computer is to replace an old one, when a disk controller or hard disk has gone bad, or when an electrical failure erased large parts of a disk. This section describes how to back up and restore Registry hives.

How this restoration is done depends on what hardware is available and what file system is in use. You can, of course, only restore what you have backed up.

Important Make frequent and consistent backup sets of all important files, including system files.

Your regular backup routine should include using the Configuration Save command in Disk Administrator to maintain an up-to-date Emergency Repair disk for restoring the Windows NT system. For details, see Chapter 18, "Disk Administrator" in the *Windows NT System Guide*.

Backing Up Registry Hives

You might make a Registry hive backup in one of four ways:

- Using a tape drive and the Windows NT Backup program, and select the Backup Local Registry option in the Backup Information dialog box to automatically include a copy of the local Registry files in the backup set. This is the preferred method for creating backups if you have a tape drive. For details, see Chapter 16, "Backup", in the *Windows NT System Guide*.

- If you don't have a tape drive, run the REGBACK.EXE or REPAIR.EXE program from the Resource Guide disk, or use another tool that uses the same techniques to back up Registry files.

- Start the computer using a different operating system. Then copy all files in the *SystemRoot*\SYSTEM32\CONFIG directory to a safe backup location. For example, use another instance of Windows NT if the Registry is stored on an NTFS partition, or use MS-DOS if the Registry is stored on a FAT partition.

- Use the Save Key command in Registry Editor, which essentially performs t he RegBack procedure manually.

  To do this, for each direct subkey of HKEY_LOCAL_MACHINE and HKEY_USERS, you must choose the Save Key command from the Registry menu, specifying filenames that match the key names. For example, save the SYSTEM key to \BACKDIR\SYSTEM. On the FAT file system, the filename should not have an extension.

  Don't use Save Key with the Hardware hive, which is volatile. You won't get any data, because Save Key cannot save volatile keys to disk.

Restoring Hives from Backup Files

If you have a good set of backup files, which you update regularly, you can restore Registry hives that are damaged or missing.

But you cannot use Registry Editor to fully restore hives, because active parts of the Registry require use of the ReplaceKey operation for restoration, which Registry Editor cannot perform.

To restore a damaged system, you must first restore the basic operating system installation. You might do this by using the Emergency Repair disk to restore your system to what it looked like just after installation, or simply run Windows NT Setup again. Such a restoration results in a system that starts the computer (which is good) but that lacks changes made since you first set it up (which isn't good). Most of those changes are recovered by copying files from backups by using the Windows NT Backup program for tape backups or by copying from disk backups.

However, you cannot merely copy the backups of Registry hive files, because those files are protected while Windows NT is running. So, after the system and all of the additional files such as device drivers are restored, you must restore the Registry. You might do this in one of the following ways, depending on which backup mechanism you used:

- For tape backups, you can use the Windows NT Restore program to restore the Registry. Then restart the computer. For details, see Chapter 14, "Backup," in the *Windows NT System Guide.*

- Start the computer using an alternate instance of the operating system (or using MS-DOS if the system files are on a FAT partition). Copy back the files to the *SystemRoot*\SYSTEM32\CONFIG directory. Then restart the computer using the regular operating system.

- Use the REPAIR.EXE program from the Resource Guide disk.

- Use the REGREST.EXE program from the Resource Guide disk. The RegRest program performs a ReplaceKey operation, which swaps backup files for the default files that the Emergency Repair or Windows NT Setup programs installed, and saves the default files under other filenames. Restart the computer after running the RegRest program to see the restored Registry.

Compacting Registry Data

The memory used for the Registry is approximately equal to the size of a hive when it is loaded into memory. Hives vary in size on disk from 20K to over 500K. The amount of space used depends chiefly on how many local user profiles are retained and how much information is stored in each profile.

You should remove unused or out-of-date user profiles from a computer by choosing the Delete User Profiles command in Windows NT Setup. (The Setup program protects you from deleting the profile for the currently logged on user.)

You can use the Save Key command to save a user hive, and then use the Restore command so you can use this smaller hive. How much space you gain depends on how much was stored in various user profiles.

This procedure is useful only for user profiles, not for the SAM, Security, Software, or System hives.

Viewing and Printing Registry Data as Text

You might want to examine the contents of a Registry key as text for troubleshooting. You can save a key as a text file, and you can print data from Registry Editor, including a key, its subkeys, and all of the value entries of all of its subkeys.

The Save Subtree As command also works for the HKEY_LOCAL_MACHINE \HARDWARE subtree, which you cannot otherwise save as a hive file.

▶ **To save a Registry key as a text file**

- In a Registry window, select the key you want to save as a text file. Then choose the Save Subtree As command from the Registry menu, and specify a filename.

▶ **To print a Registry key**

- In a Registry window, select the key you want, and then choose the Print Subtree command from the Registry menu.

Summary of Administrative Tools for the Registry

The following table summarizes the tools provided with Windows NT (in addition to Registry Editor and Windows NT Diagnostics) that you can use to administer the Registry.

Table 11.2   Tools in Windows NT for Registry Management

Tool	Description
Backup	Back up Registry hives as part of a tape backup routine
Emergency Repair disk	Restore default hives to the system
File Manager	Apply access controls to Registry Editor and hive files

The following table summarizes the tools on the Resource Guide disk that you can use to administer the Registry. For details about these and other utilities provided with the *Windows NT Resource Kit*, see the RKTOOLS.HLP file on your *Resource Kit* disk.

Table 11.3   Tools on the Resource Kit Disk

Tool	Description
REGBACK.EXE	Creates backups of Registry files
REGENTRY.HLP	Documents Windows NT Registry entries
REGINI.EXE	Makes Registry changes by script
REGREST.EXE	Restores Registry hives using the ReplaceKey function

C H A P T E R   1 2

Configuration Management and the Registry

This chapter provides some examples of problem-solving tasks that involve changes made to the Registry using Registry Editor. The topics in this chapter include the following:

- Solving users' environment problems with the Registry
- Making sure the system always starts
- Changing driver and service configuration data
- Managing user profiles through the Registry

Caution Editing entries in the Registry is equivalent to editing raw sectors on a hard disk. This is a dangerous undertaking—you can easily make mistakes so that the computer can no longer be started.

Wherever possible, you should use Control Panel, the programs in the Administrative Tools group, and Windows NT Setup to change the system configuration.

Use extreme care if you follow any procedures described here for changing the Registry directly using Registry Editor.

Solving Users' Environment Problems with the Registry

Using Registry Editor to view the contents of the Registry for a remote computer makes it easier for a system administrator to solve users' configuration problems. Select the troublesome computer using the Select Computer command in Registry Editor, and then you can browse through Registry entries to find where problems may exist.

You can also load a copy of a hive from another computer to view and change entries, as described in "Loading Hives from Another Computer" in Chapter 11, "Registry Editor and Registry Administration."

This is probably how you will use Registry Editor most often—to find the source of problems, not to edit value entries. After you find the source of a problem, Control Panel or other tools can be used to solve the problem.

For example, you can check the user's desktop settings easily by examining the values under the Console and Control Panel subkeys for the user. The Console subkeys define settings for the command prompt and other character-based applications. The Control Panel subkeys in the Registry define the appearance and behavior of items in the Windows NT desktop.

▶ **To view a user's desktop settings**

1. Focus on the user's computer by choosing the Select Computer command from the Registry menu.

2. Under HKEY_USERS for the selected computer, select the key that represents the profile for the user who is having problems.

Tip To determine which *SID_#* key represents which user, see the values for ProfileImagePath under the ProfileList key in the following Registry path:

`HKEY_LOCAL_MACHINE\SOFTWARE\MICROSOFT\WINDOWS NT\CurrentVersion`

The hive filename that is the value for ProfileImagePath includes a portion of the username associated with that *SID_#* key, so that you can identify the user to which it belongs.

---

3. Double-click either the Console or Control Panel subkey, depending on whether the problem is with a character-based screen or a Windows NT window.

4. Check values as described in the Help topic, "Registry Entries for User Components," in the REGENTRY.HLP file, which is included on the *Resource Kit* disk.

For example, suppose a user asks for help, complaining that their screen goes black whenever the icon for the command prompt is clicked in Program Manager. You can select this computer in Registry Editor, and then select the following subkey:

```
HKEY_USERS\SID_#\Console\Command Prompt
```

In this example, if the value of ScreenColors is 0, both the text and the screen background have been set to black, and this is the source of the user's problem. The user can fix this by running Command Prompt and pressing ALT+SPACEBAR to display the Control menu and choosing the Screen Colors command to select new colors.

Tip To change the colors or the bitmap that appears on the CTRL+ALT+DEL logon screen, change the entries under HKEY_USERS\.DEFAULT\Control Panel\Desktop. For example, if you want a bitmap of your company's logo on the logon screen, change the value of Wallpaper to specify the path and filename for that bitmap.

As another example, any user with sufficient access permission can use the System icon in Control Panel to change user environment variables, but the system environment variables can only be set by changing values in the Registry. Such changes to the system environment variables affect all users and can only be made in the Registry if you are logged on as a member of the Administrators group.

▶ **To change system environment variables**

1. In Registry Editor, select the Environment subkey under this Registry path:

   ```
   HKEY_LOCAL_MACHINE\SYSTEM\CurrentControlSet
       \Control\Session Manager\Environment
   ```

2. Double-click an environment variable and change its value, as described in "The CurrentControlSet\Control Subkeys" in REGENTRY.HLP, which is included on the *Resource Kit* disk.

3. Restart the system for these changes to take effect.

For example, if you want to change the path for the Microsoft OS/2 version 1.*x* libraries, change the value of OS2Lib under the Environment subkey to specify a new path name, such as D:\OS2\DLL.

Making Sure the System Always Starts

This section discusses the following three topics:

- Starting a system with configuration problems
- Reconstructing a system with damaged files
- Creating a custom startup verification program

The goal in all of these topics is to make sure a Windows NT system starts correctly each time you turn on the switch. The obvious preliminary steps, of course, involve planning ahead for system safety, with the following activities:

- Protect the Registry hive files on disk and maintain a regular backup program, including backups of Registry hive files, as described in "Maintaining the Registry" in Chapter 11, "Registry Editor and Registry Administration."
- Maintain a handy copy of the Emergency Repair disk created when you installed Windows NT. Each Emergency Repair disk works only for the computer where it was made during Setup.
- Install a redundant copy of the operating system to make the system more robust, as described in Chapter 3, "Customizing Windows NT Setup."

You can also rely on Windows NT to automatically recover from damages to startup data. Specifically, to protect from bad sectors occurring in the System hive file, Windows NT automatically creates a backup of the system hive named the SYSTEM.ALT file, which is stored in the *SystemRoot*\SYSTEM32\CONFIG directory. If any problems are encountered while reading the System hive during startup such as damage to the file, the Boot Loader automatically switches to the SYSTEM.ALT file to continue starting the system. For more information about the SYSTEM.ALT file, see "Hives and Files" in Chapter 10, "Overview of the Windows NT Registry."

Starting a System with Configuration Problems

This section describes how to start a computer when hardware or software problems prevent normal system startup.

For a Windows NT computer, the Registry includes several control sets. Each control set is a complete set of system parameters that define startup, system recovery, and driver load controls plus service parameters and other system configuration data. The control set represented as the CurrentControlSet in the Registry is a link to the control set used to start the system for the current session. For details about control sets, see "HKEY_LOCAL_MACHINE\SYSTEM Subtree" in Chapter 10, "Overview of the Windows NT Registry."

Whenever you start Windows NT, the Boot Loader automatically tries to boot using the CurrentControlSet described in the HKEY_LOCAL_MACHINE \SYSTEM\Select subkey. If the system cannot start using this control set (because of erroneous user changes or bad-sector errors on a file), the Boot Loader automatically tries the LastKnownGood control set, as defined in the Select subkey.

You can also switch to a previous system configuration manually, bypassing the automatic process.

▶ **To manually switch to a previous system configuration**

1. Press ENTER to select Windows NT at the startup prompt, and then immediately press the spacebar.
2. From the Configuration Recovery menu, choose the command named Use Last Known Good Configuration, and then press ENTER.

Note Choosing the Last Known Good option at startup causes the system to discard all configuration changes made since the computer's last successful startup.

During system startup, you can only choose between the current and the LastKnownGood control set. For information about how the LastKnownGood control set is selected and stored, see "HKEY_LOCAL_MACHINE\SYSTEM Subtree" in Chapter 10, "Overview of the Windows NT Registry."

Reconstructing a System with Damaged Files

You might need to restore a user's system configuration and working environment, either because of hardware failure or replacement, or because files have been damaged on the hard disk. You can use the Emergency Repair disk created during Windows NT installation to restore the system files. If you use the Emergency Repair disk to repair files such as the Registry hives, you will lose any changes that were made to the system after installation (unless you update your Emergency Repair disk using the REPAIR.EXE program from the *Resource Kit* disk).

You can use one of the following methods to reconstruct the system from backups, as described in "Backing Up and Restoring Registry Hives" in Chapter 11, "Registry Editor and Registry Administration":

- Use the Windows NT Restore program to restore the Registry from tape backups.
- Start the computer using another instance of the operating system (or with MS-DOS for a FAT partition), and then copy the backup files to the *SystemRoot*\SYSTEM32\CONFIG directory.

If you are attempting to restore damaged SAM or Security hives, you must use this method. You cannot replace these hives while Windows NT is running. This means that if your system files are on an NTFS volume, you must have another instance of Windows NT available on that system to be able to restore the SAM and security hives. Or, you can use the Emergency Repair disk to restore the default SAM and Security hives (and subsequently lose any security changes made since Windows NT was installed).

Creating a Custom Startup Verification Program

System startup is usually declared good if the following two procedures are complete:

- All startup drivers are loaded.

  When a service fails to load during startup, its ErrorControl value is checked, as defined in the CurrentControlSet\Services*serviceName* subkeys. Whether the system startup process continues or halts depends on this value.

- At least one user successfully logs on the computer by pressing CTRL+ALT+DEL and supplying a valid username, domain, and password.

This basic standard for verifying system startup will suit the needs for most situations; however, your site might require additional steps before considering a computer to be successfully started and ready to participate in the network.

For example, you might want to redefine startup validation for a server where, normally, no one logs on or where you want system startup to be validated as successful only after a particular process has started.

Or, for a server running Microsoft SQL Server, you might want a system startup to be marked as good only after the SQL server responds to a request. To do this, you might write a program that queries the SQL server and checks the response. If the response is not as expected, the program can call the NotifyBootConfigStatus() function with FALSE, causing the system to restart using the LastKnownGood control set. Or, the program might cause the system to run without saving the current configuration as the LastKnownGood control. Conversely, if the SQL server responds as expected, the program can call the NotifyBootConfigStatus() function with TRUE, causing the current configuration to be saved as the LastKnownGood control.

You can run such a verification program from the command prompt. Or, you can have the program run automatically during startup by specifying value entries under BootVerificationProgram in the Registry.

▶ **To create a custom startup verification program**

1. Change the value of ReportBootOK to 0 under the following Registry path:

   ```
   HKEY_LOCAL_MACHINE\SOFTWARE\Microsoft\Windows NT\CurrentVersion
       \WinLogon
   ```

   The data type for ReportBootOK is REG_SZ. When this value is 0, it disables the automatic startup acceptance that happens after the first successful logon.

2. Create the executable program that you want to run as part of startup verification. Then specify its filename as a value for ImagePath in the BootVerificationProgram subkey under this Registry path:

   ```
   HKEY_LOCAL_MACHINE\SYSTEM\CurrentControlSet
       \Control\BootVerificationProgram
   ```

   The data type for ImagePath must be REG_SZ or REG_EXPAND_SZ.

As another example, a computer setup for a turnkey application is a candidate for a custom startup verification routine, where the computer doesn't usually interact directly with users and you therefore don't want a successful user logon to be part of the system startup.

If you want a good system startup to be accepted from a remote computer (either manually or automatically), you can use the service program, BOOTVRFY.EXE, that is supplied with Windows NT. In this case, the remote computer accepts the system startup by starting the BOOTVRFY.EXE service. You can also write your own verification service that can reject the system startup and revert to the LastKnownGood control set to restart the computer.

▶ **To verify system startup from a remote computer**

1. For the local computer, add a BootVerification key under the following Registry path:

   ```
   HKEY_LOCAL_MACHINE\SYSTEM\CurrentControlSet\Services
   ```

2. Add the following value entries under this new **BootVerification** key:

   ```
   Start : REG_DWORD : 0x00000003
   Type : REG_DWORD : 0x00000020
   ErrorControl : REG_DWORD : 0x00000001
   ImagePath : REG_EXPAND_SZ : bootvrfy.exe
   ObjectName : REG_SZ : LocalSystem
   ```

   For more information about these entries, see "BootVerification Service Entries" in Chapter 14, "Registry Value Entries."

3. Change the value of ReportBootOK to 0 under the following Registry path:

```
HKEY_LOCAL_MACHINE\SOFTWARE\Microsoft\Windows NT\CurrentVersion
    \WinLogon
```

4. Start the BootVerification service from a remote computer.

   This service tells the service controller on the local computer to save the current startup configuration as the LastKnownGood configuration, and then the service terminates itself.

Important   You cannot use the BootVerification service in conjunction with settings in the BootVerificationProgram key. These are mutually exclusive methods.

You might also want a good system startup to depend on whether a specific service or driver loads. For example, for a server you might want to cause the Boot Loader to choose the LastKnownGood control set if the Server service doesn't start on the computer.

▶   **To change system startup to depend on a service or driver**

1. Select the subkey for the service under the following Registry path:

```
HKEY_LOCAL_MACHINE\SYSTEM\CurrentControlSet\Services\ServiceName
```

   ServiceName can be any service upon which you want successful system startup to depend.

2. Double-click the service's ErrorControl entry, and then specify a new value of 2 (to switch to LastKnownGood if the service doesn't start).

   On a few rare occasions, you might want to specify a value of 3 (to fail the attempted startup if the service doesn't start); however, this ErrorControl value is usually reserved for critical services such as file system drivers.

3. For the new values to take effect, close Registry Editor, shut down the system, and restart the computer.

4. If you do not get the intended effect, restart the computer, and manually choose the LastKnownGood control set as described in "Starting a System with Configuration Problems," earlier in this chapter. All changes in the last session will be discarded.

Customizing Windows NT Logon

You can change the Windows NT logon process in the following two ways:

- Create a custom logon message, especially for secure sites
- Allow automatic logon for a computer

During Windows NT logon, the first message that appears instructs the user to press CTRL+ALT+DEL to log on, and then the Welcome dialog box appears so the user can type a username, domain, and password.

You can define a custom message to display after the user presses CTRL+ALT+DEL. For example, you might want to warn users that a particular computer is restricted to only certain users. Or, for all computers on the network, you might want to warn against unauthorized attempts to log on.

▶ **To create a custom logon message**

1. In Registry Editor, select the following subkey:

   ```
   HKEY_LOCAL_MACHINE\SOFTWARE\Microsoft\Windows NT\CurrentVersion
       \Winlogon
   ```

2. Add a value entry named LegalNoticeCaption of type REG_SZ, and type text that will be the caption for the message.

3. Add a value entry named LegalNoticeText of type REG_SZ, and type text for the message.

If either LegalNoticeCaption or LegalNoticeText is defined in the Registry, a user cannot log on to the computer without acknowledging the message by clicking the OK button.

For some computers such as a print server or other special-use systems, you may want to be able to start the system without a user having to supply a username or password. You can define automatic logon for a computer by adding some value entries in the Registry.

▶ **To allow automatic logon for a computer**

1. In Registry Editor, select the following subkey:

   ```
   HKEY_LOCAL_MACHINE\SOFTWARE\Microsoft\Windows NT\CurrentVersion
       \Winlogon
   ```

2. Add a value entry named AutoAdminLogon of type REG_SZ, and specify a value of 1.

3. Add a value entry named DefaultPassword of type REG_SZ, and enter the password of the user listed under the value DefaultUserName.

Changing Driver and Service Configuration Data

The hardware detected on a computer is stored in the volatile HKEY_LOCAL_MACHINE\HARDWARE key. Because this key is destroyed and recreated each time the system starts, you cannot usefully edit hardware settings.

You can use Windows NT Diagnostics to view hardware data in an easy-to-read format. Based on this information, you can discover conflicts and their causes or determine how to set up new hardware before installing it. You can also get information about conflicts by looking at the System event log in the Event Viewer.

This section presents some suggestions for solving hardware and related driver problems using Registry Editor.

To carry out some procedures described in this section, you need to follow the instructions for saving keys in "Saving and Restoring Keys" in Chapter 11, "Registry Editor and Registry Administration."

Recovering from an Unsuitable Video Display Choice

You can choose the Windows NT Setup icon in Program Manager to change the type of video driver, the color depth, or the resolution for a display adapter. If you make an unsuitable choice, one of the following two events occurs:

- The driver will not recognize the card and will, therefore, fail to load at system startup. By default, the system tries to load VGA in base mode as a kind of reserve. So, if your video choice fails, the computer will start in VGA. Screen resolution will not be what you'd like, but you can run Windows NT Setup from Program Manager to try another option. (This only happens on an x86-based computer.)

- Or, the driver will recognize the card and proceed as though the parameters selected are acceptable. But because they're not (for example, you tried to use 1280x1024 resolution on a monitor that is only capable of 1024x768), you can't see anything on your screen, although the system starts just fine. (This is what always happens on a RISC-based computer when an inappropriate option is chosen but can also occur on an x86-based computer.)

If you can't see anything on screen after changing the display settings, do not attempt to log on. Instead, wait for the disk activity to stop, and then use the power switch to restart the computer; then follow the instructions in "Starting a System with Configuration Problems," earlier in this chapter. Then you can run Windows NT Setup from Program Manager to try another choice.

Changing Driver Loading Controls in the Registry

Under most circumstances, you should define the startup behavior of a device or a service by choosing the Devices icon or the Services icon in Control Panel, or by using Server Manager in Windows NT Server. Use these procedures in specific cases where you cannot define behavior using the other administrative tools.

You can change the basic value entries in the Registry for a specific driver to control driver loading. For example, you can change these things:

- When the driver is loaded or the service is started, including turning off driver loading during startup
- The load order for a driver, a service, or a group during system startup
- Error control for a driver or service, so that startup continues or halts, depending on whether the item is initialized
- Parameters that can be set for a driver or service

▶ **To change the behavior of a driver or service**

1. Select the subkey for the driver or service in the following Registry path:

   ```
   HKEY_LOCAL_MACHINE\SYSTEM\CurrentControlSet
       \Services\DriverName
   ```

2. If you want to change how system startup proceeds if the driver is not loaded or the service is not started, change the value of **ErrorControl** as follows:

Error control	Value	Meaning
Critical	0x3	Fail the attempted system startup
Severe	0x2	Switch to LastKnownGood or, if already using LastKnownGood, continue on in case of error
Normal	0x1	Continue startup if the driver fails to load, but display a message noting the failure
Ignore	0x0	—

3. If you want to change the dependencies for loading the service, specify new values under DependOnGroup, DependOnService, or Tag.

4. If you want to change when the service is started or the driver is loaded, change the Start value as follows:

Start type	Value	Meaning
Boot	0x0	Loaded by the Boot Loader
System	0x1	Loaded at Kernel initialization
Auto load	0x2	Loaded or started automatically at startup
Load on demand	0x3	Available, but started only by the user
Disabled	0x4	Not to be started under any conditions

5. Close Registry Editor, shut down, and restart the computer for these values to take effect.

For details about Start and ErrorControl values, see their definitions in "CurrentControlSet\Services Subkeys" in Chapter 14, "Registry Value Entries."

You can also set parameters for many drivers and services, as described in Chapter 14. For example, a modem that includes a National Semiconductor 16550 AUART chip can take advantage of FIFO buffer support. This capability is not turned on by default in Windows NT, however. If you are using such a modem, you can change the value of ForceFifoEnable to 1 to turn on FIFO support, under this subkey:

```
HKEY_LOCAL_MACHINE\SYSTEM\CurrentControlSet
    \Services\Serial\Parameters
```

Controlling Multiport Serial I/O Cards

The Microsoft serial driver can be used to control many *dumb* multiport serial cards. *Dumb* indicates that the control includes no onboard processor. Each port of a multiport board has a separate subkey under the CurrentControlSet\Services \Serial subkey in the Registry. In each of these subkeys, you must add values for DosDevices, Interrupt, InterruptStatus, PortAddress, and PortIndex, because these are not detected by the Hardware Detector. (For descriptions and ranges for these values, see "Disk, Serial, and Parallel Port Entries" in Chapter 14, "Registry Value Entries.")

For example, if you have a four-port COMTROL Hostess 550 board configured to use address 0x500 with an interrupt of 0x2, the values in the Registry would be as follows:

Serial2 subkey:

```
PortAddress = REG_DWORD 0x500
Interrupt = REG_DWORD 2
DosDevices = REG_SZ COM3
InterruptStatus = REG_DWORD 0x507
PortIndex = REG_DWORD 1
```

Serial4 subkey:

```
PortAddress = REG_DWORD 0x510
Interrupt = REG_DWORD 2
DosDevices = REG_SZ COM5
InterruptStatus = REG_DWORD 0x507
PortIndex = REG_DWORD 3
```

Serial3 subkey:

```
PortAddress = REG_DWORD 0x508
Interrupt = REG_DWORD 2
DosDevices = REG_SZ COM4
InterruptStatus = REG_DWORD 0x507
PortIndex = REG_DWORD 2
```

Serial5 subkey:

```
PortAddress = REG_DWORD 0x518
Interrupt = REG_DWORD 2
DosDevices = REG_SZ COM6
InterruptStatus = REG_DWORD 0x507
PortIndex = REG_DWORD 4
```

Certain multiport boards, such as Digiboard non-MCA bus cards, use a different scheme to determine which port is interrupting. These boards should include the Indexed value entry in the configuration data for each port under its subkey in CurrentControlSet\Services\Serial. This entry indicates that the board uses an indexed interrupt notification scheme as opposed to a bitmapped method.

For example, if you have an eight-port Digiboard communications board configured to be at address 0x100 with an interrupt of 0x3, the values in the Registry would be as follows:

Serial2 subkey:

```
PortAddress = REG_DWORD 0x100
Interrupt = REG_DWORD 3
DosDevices = REG_SZ COM3
InterruptStatus = REG_DWORD 0x140
Indexed = REG_DWORD 1
PortIndex = REG_DWORD 1
```

Serial3 subkey:

```
PortAddress = REG_DWORD 0x108
Interrupt = REG_DWORD 3
DosDevices = REG_SZ COM4
InterruptStatus = REG_DWORD 0x140
Indexed = REG_DWORD 1
PortIndex = REG_DWORD 2
```

Serial4 subkey:

```
PortAddress = REG_DWORD 0x110
Interrupt = REG_DWORD 3
DosDevices = REG_SZ COM5
InterruptStatus = REG_DWORD 0x140
Indexed = REG_DWORD 1
PortIndex = REG_DWORD 3
```

Serial5 subkey:

```
PortAddress = REG_DWORD 0x118
Interrupt = REG_DWORD 3
DosDevices = REG_SZ COM6
InterruptStatus = REG_DWORD 0x140
Indexed = REG_DWORD 1
PortIndex = REG_DWORD 4
```

Serial6 subkey:

```
PortAddress = REG_DWORD 0x120
Interrupt = REG_DWORD 3
DosDevices = REG_SZ COM7
InterruptStatus = REG_DWORD 0x140
Indexed = REG_DWORD 1
PortIndex = REG_DWORD 5
```

Serial7 subkey:

```
PortAddress = REG_DWORD 0x128
Interrupt = REG_DWORD 3
DosDevices = REG_SZ COM8
InterruptStatus = REG_DWORD 0x140
Indexed = REG_DWORD 1
PortIndex = REG_DWORD 6
```

Serial8 subkey:

```
PortAddress = REG_DWORD 0x130
Interrupt = REG_DWORD 3
DosDevices = REG_SZ COM9
InterruptStatus = REG_DWORD 0x140
Indexed = REG_DWORD 1
PortIndex = REG_DWORD 7
```

Serial9 subkey:

```
PortAddress = REG_DWORD 0x138
Interrupt = REG_DWORD 3
DosDevices = REG_SZ COM10
InterruptStatus = REG_DWORD 0x140
Indexed = REG_DWORD 1
PortIndex = REG_DWORD 8
```

Deleting Serial Ports

You can configure communication ports as described in the previous section or as described in "Serial Subkey Entries in the Services Subkey" in Chapter 14, "Registry Value Entries." You might also need to delete one or more COM ports, which you can only do by deleting the related Registry information in the DeviceMap and Services areas of the Registry. To delete entries in the DeviceMap subkey, you must be logged on as a member of the Administrators group.

▶ **To delete a COM port**

1. In Registry Editor, delete the appropriate value entry for the COM port under the following Registry path:

   ```
   HKEY_LOCAL_MACHINE\Hardware\DeviceMap\SerialComm
   ```

   The value entries in this subkey are used to determine all the communication ports available on the system. The values are of the form **Serial**yyy=COMx, where COMx can be COM1 to COM256, and **Serial**yyy can be from Serial0 through any large positive number such as Serial15000.

   You can identify the value entry you want to delete based on the list that appears when you choose the Ports icon in Control Panel.

2. Delete the COM port's related Serialyyy key in the following Registry path:

   ```
   HKEY_LOCAL_MACHINE\System\CurrentControlSet\Services
       \Serial\Parameters\Serialyyy
   ```

If you do not delete the related Services subkey for **Serial**yyy, the COMx port continues to appear in the Ports list in Control Panel each time the system starts, even though there is no related DeviceMap subkey.

Managing User Profiles Through the Registry

Each user on a Windows NT system is assigned a user profile, which can be set up on a local or remote computer. This user profile contains all the individual preferences and settings for items such as personal program groups, desktop settings, printer connections, user environment variables, and other items.

With Windows NT Server, you can use the User Profile Editor to move user profiles to other computers, and you can use User Manager for Domains to assign mandatory or individual profiles to users. For information about creating and assigning profiles on local and remote computers, see the *Windows NT Server System Guide*.

However, you need to use Registry Editor to edit a profile offline or to manage user profiles when you want to examine a profile on a remote computer (as described earlier in this chapter).

When you edit a profile offline, you need to copy both the related hive and .LOG files, and load them on the computer where you will be working, as described in "Loading Hives from Another Computer" in Chapter 11, "Registry Editor and Registry Administration."

This section describes how hive files are created and how you can move a user profile to another computer when User Profile Editor is not available.

Creating User Profile Hives

With the appropriate access permission, a user can save a locally cached copy of a user profile. The directory and filename of the hive are added as a value under the following Registry key, where *SID_#* represents a key with the same name as the security ID assigned to the user:

```
HKEY_LOCAL_MACHINE\SOFTWARE\Microsoft\Windows NT\CurrentVersion
   \ProfileList\SID_#
```

When the user logs on, the hive defined in the particular ProfileList*SID_#* subkey is loaded, with a root key whose name matches the *SID_#* as a child key of HKEY_USERS. HKEY_CURRENT_USER points to this key.

The available user profile hives on a computer will consist of any hives created using User Profile Editor or saved locally by a user who logged on with appropriate permissions, as defined in User Manager for Domains. The ProfileList subkeys define all the known user hives on the local computer.

The hive that is loaded when a user logs on depends on whether the user has an assigned profile, as described in the following tables.

Table 12.1   Creating a Hive for a User Without an Assigned Profile

Scenario	How hive is created
If the user has permission to keep a local copy of a profile	A copy of the User Default profile (USERDEF) is loaded under the key HKEY_USERS*SID_#*, and a local copy of this profile is saved as the user's profile. This hive is created when you install Windows NT and is saved as *SystemRoot*\\SYSTEM32\\CONFIG\\USERDEF.
	The user's local copy resides in the same directory. When the user logs off, all changes made to the profile are saved to the local profile just created.
If the user doesn't have permission to keep a local copy of a profile (that is, Guest accounts)	USERDEF is copied to a temporary file (*SystemRoot*\\SYSTEM32\\CONFIG\\TMPDEF00) and this copy will be used by the user. When the user logs off, all changes made to the profile are lost.

For a user with an assigned profile, that profile is used whenever possible. Otherwise, the rules shown in the following tables are used to create a hive.

Table 12.2   Creating a Hive with an Assigned Profile on a Local Computer

Scenario	How hive is created
If the user has a mandatory profile (with a .MAN file-name extension) on a local and on a remote computer	The profile is copied to a temporary file in the *SystemRoot*\\SYSTEM32\\CONFIG directory, and the user will use this temporary profile. All changes made to this profile are lost when the user logs off.
	If the mandatory profile is not accessible (for example, if the server is down or if there is no access permission for the file), the user is not able to log on.
If the user has a personal profile on a local computer but the profile is not accessible	The user will get a copy of USERDEF.

Table 12.2   Creating a Hive with an Assigned Profile on a Local Computer
(continued)

Scenario	How hive is created
If the user has a personal profile on a remote computer but doesn't have permission to save a local copy	▪ If the remote profile is accessible, it is saved as a temporary file in *SystemRoot*\SYSTEM32\CONFIG directory. The user's changes are saved back to the remote profile when the user logs off. ▪ If the remote profile is not accessible (for example, if the server is down or if there is no access permission for the file) and there is no local copy of the user's profile, a copy of USERDEF is saved as a temporary file in the \CONFIG directory. This temporary profile is used for the user's entire logon session. Changes made to the profile are lost when the user logs off.

This last table shows how a hive is created if the user has a personal profile on a remote computer and has permission to save a local copy.

Table 12.3   Creating a Hive for a User with a Profile on a Remote Computer

Scenario	How hive is created
If the remote profile is accessible and there are no local copies of the profile on the local computer	The remote profile is copied as *SystemRoot*\SYSTEM32\CONFIG\USER002. Then this local copy is loaded into the Registry as the user's profile. At logoff, the changes are saved to the local copy, and the local copy is copied back to the remote profile file.
If the remote profile is accessible and a local copy exists	The newest file overwrites the older version, and the file is treated as described above.
If the remote profile is not accessible but a local copy exists	The local copy is loaded into the Registry and used as the user's profile. At logoff, the changes are saved to the local copy, which is copied to the remote profile file at the next log on (if the remote profile is accessible and if the date on the local copy is newer than that for the remote profile).
If the remote profile is not accessible and the local copy does not exist	A copy of USERDEF is saved to the local profile copy path and is loaded in the Registry to be used as the user's profile. At logoff time, the changes made to the profile are saved in the local profile.

Moving User Profile Hives

The hives for user profiles can be located anywhere on a local or remote computer. In some circumstances, you might want to move a user profile hive to another computer when User Profile Editor is not available. You can move a user profile by copying the hive to the new location, and then changing the Registry to specify the new location.

▶ **To change a user profile location in the Registry**

1. Log on under a username other than the one for the profile you want to move.

2. Use File Manager to copy the hive and .LOG files for the profile you want to move. This file can be on a floppy disk or on a shared network drive.

3. In Registry Editor, display the Registry for the computer where this hive will be used, and change the value of ProfileImagePath under the appropriate ProfileList*SID_#* subkey to specify the new path and filename for the new hive. The full Registry path for this subkey is the following:

```
HKEY_LOCAL_MACHINE\SOFTWARE\Microsoft\Windows NT\CurrentVersion
    \ProfileList\SID_#
```

The data type for ProfileImagePath is REG_EXPAND_SZ, so you can specify a value in the form of %SystemRoot%\system32\config*hiveFilename*. Do not include the double backslash (\\\\) to specify the UNC path name.

The next time that user logs on, the new user profile will be used.

Important For secure installations, user profile hives should be stored on an NTFS volume where they can be secured by specifying access permission in File Manager.

For more information about the ProfileList subkey, see the REGENTRY.HLP file, which is included on the *Resource Kit* disk.

C H A P T E R   1 3

Initialization Files and the Registry

Although the Registry replaces the initialization (.INI) files used in versions of Microsoft Windows created for MS-DOS, some .INI files still appear in the Windows NT system directory. Also, applications created for 16-bit Microsoft Windows must still be able to read and write .INI values that previously were stored in the WIN.INI or SYSTEM.INI file.

This chapter describes how .INI files and other configuration files are used under Windows NT and how these values are stored in the Registry. The following topics are discussed in this chapter:

- How Windows NT uses MS-DOS configuration files
- How .INI files are mapped to the Registry
- Microsoft OS/2 version 1.*x* entries in the Registry
- POSIX entries in the Registry

Related topics are discussed in the following chapters of the *Windows NT Resource Guide*:

- For details about the SHARED32.INI file, see Chapter 8, "Mail."
- For details about Registry entries for Microsoft Mail and Microsoft Schedule+ initialization values, see Chapter 14, "Registry Value Entries."

How Windows NT Uses MS-DOS Configuration Files

During system startup, Windows NT adds any Path, Prompt, and Set commands from the C:\AUTOEXEC.BAT file to the Windows NT environment variables and then ignores the rest of the contents of C:\AUTOEXEC.BAT and C:\CONFIG.SYS. If these files are not present when you install Windows NT, the Setup program creates them.

For a RISC-based computer, default AUTOEXEC.NT and CONFIG.NT files are created.

The path and other Windows NT environment information are stored under the following Registry key:

```
HKEY_LOCAL_MACHINE\SYSTEM\CurrentControlSet
    \Control\Session Manager\Environment
```

When an MS-DOS–based application is started, Windows NT executes files specified in the application's PIF or the AUTOEXEC.NT and CONFIG.NT files in the *SystemRoot*\SYSTEM32 directory. Any changes made in one of these files take effect as soon as the file is saved and a new MS-DOS–based application is started that uses that file. You do not need to restart your system after changing the *.NT files.

File	Use in Windows NT
C:\AUTOEXEC.BAT	Path and environment variables are added to the Windows NT environment at system startup.
C:\CONFIG.SYS	Not used by Windows NT.
AUTOEXEC.NT and CONFIG.NT in *SystemRoot*\SYSTEM32	Used every time an MS-DOS–based application is run with the _DEFAULT.PIF. (Custom *.NT files can be created and used when starting an application from another PIF.)

You can use Windows NT Diagnostics to view the contents of the AUTOEXEC.NT files and the CONFIG.NT files by choosing commands from the File menu. You can edit the contents of these files using any text editor.

Commands in the AUTOEXEC.BAT and CONFIG.SYS files for starting applications and initializing drivers are ignored in Windows NT. If you want an application to run automatically when you start Windows NT, place an icon for the application in the Startup group in Program Manager, as described in Chapter 3, "Program Manager," in the *Windows NT System Guide*. For a service or driver, use the Services icon in Control Panel to define the startup type. This setting is saved as the **Start** value in the service's subkey under HKEY_LOCAL_MACHINE \SYSTEM\CurrentControlSet\Services in the Registry.

VDM Sessions

Each MS-DOS-based and 16-bit Windows-based application runs in a Windows NT virtual MS-DOS machine (VDM). Windows NT includes the necessary virtual device drivers (VDDs) for the mouse, keyboard, printer, COM ports, and network support. The VDDs are loaded into every VDM based on values stored in the Registry. Information about VDDs is found in the following registry path:

```
HKEY_LOCAL_MACHINE\SYSTEM\CurrentControlSet\Control\VirtualDeviceDrivers
```

Any changes to the VDD entries are managed automatically by the system when you add a device driver using Windows NT Setup.

Windows for MS-DOS on Windows NT

Windows NT is a 32-bit environment, and Windows 3.*x* for MS-DOS is a 16-bit environment. For a 16-bit Windows-based application, Windows NT runs the application using a VDM and VDDs. This process is called WOW, for *Win16 on Win32*. Using a Win16 VDM, Windows NT translates Windows 3.1-based application calls in standard mode for RISC-based computers and in 386 enhanced mode for *x*86 based-computers.

Control parameters for WOW startup and for the WOW application environment are found under the following Registry path:

```
HKEY_LOCAL_MACHINE\SYSTEM\CurrentControlSet\Control\WOW
```

The settings in this key are maintained automatically by the system and should not require manual changes.

The environment settings equivalent to the SYSTEM.INI file for Windows 3.*x* are found in this Registry path:

```
HKEY_LOCAL_MACHINE\SOFTWARE\Microsoft\Windows NT\CurrentVersion\WOW
```

The WOW subkeys have the same names as headings in the SYSTEM.INI file, and the values are the same items as contained in the old SYSTEM.INI file. For details about these entries, see the REGENTRY.HLP file on the Resource Guide disk.

How .INI Files Are Mapped to the Registry

If you install Windows NT as an upgrade over Windows 3.1, all the settings from various initialization files are copied into the Registry, including CONTROL.INI, PROGMAN.INI, SYSTEM.INI, WIN.INI, WINFILE.INI, and others. You can see where the Windows initialization files are mapped in the Registry by viewing the subkeys and value entries under this path:

```
HKEY_Local_Machine\SOFTWARE\Microsoft
    \Windows NT\CurrentVersion\IniFileMapping
```

When you install an application created for 16-bit Microsoft Windows, the application's setup program creates its own .INI file or creates entries for the WIN.INI or SYSTEM.INI file in the same way that it does for any versions of Windows for MS-DOS. These entries are not updated in the Registry, because these applications do not know how to access the Windows NT Registry. For this reason, basic SYSTEM.INI, WIN.INI, and WINFILE.INI files appear in the *SystemRoot* directory in Windows NT.

If a Windows-based application tries to write to WIN.INI, SYSTEM.INI, or any other section listed in the IniFileMapping key, and if the application uses the Windows NT Registry APIs, the information is stored in the Registry. If the application writes to other sections of the .INI file or tries to open the .INI file directly without using the Windows NT Registry APIs, the information is saved in an .INI file.

To find mapping information in the HKEY_LOCAL_MACHINE\Software key, the system looks up the *filename.ext* of the initialization file. If a match is found, it looks under the mapped key for the specific application name and a variable name, and if necessary it continues to look for keys whose value entries are the variable names. If no mapping for either the application name or filename is found, the system looks for an .INI file to read and write its contents.

Tables 13.1 through 13.3 show where system settings are saved in the Registry in comparison to initialization files used with Windows 3.1 for MS-DOS.

In the entries in the IniFileMapping key and in Tables 13.1 through 13.3, the following symbols are used:

Symbol	Description
!	Forces all writes to go to both the Registry and to the .INI file on disk.
#	Causes the Registry value to be set to the value in the Windows 3.1 .INI file whenever a new user logs in for the first time after Setup, if Windows NT was installed on a computer that had Windows 3.1 already installed.
@	Prevents any reads from going to the .INI file on disk if the requested data is not found in the Registry.
USR	Stands for HKEY_CURRENT_USER, and the text after the prefix is relative to that key.
SYS	Stands for HKEY_LOCAL_MACHINE\Software, and the text after the prefix is relative to that key.

WIN.INI Settings in the Registry

The information stored in the keys described in Table 13.1 is used by applications that expect to find this information in a WIN.INI file.

Table 13.1   Registry Paths for WIN.INI Sections

WIN.INI section	Registry path	Description
[colors]	#USR\Control Panel\Colors[1]	Defines colors for the Windows display as set using the Colors icon in Control Panel.
[compatibility]	#SYS...\Compatibility[3]	—
[desktop]	#USR\Control Panel\Desktop[1]	Specifies appearance of the desktop as set using the Desktop icon in Control Panel.
[embedding]	#SYS...\Embedding[3]	Lists the server objects used in Object Linking and Embedding (OLE); created during software setup.
[extensions]	#USR...\Extensions[2]	Associates types of files with applications as set by choosing Associate in File Manager.
[fonts] and [fontSubstitutes]	#SYS...\Fonts and \FontSubstitutes[3]	Describes the screen font files loaded by Windows as set using the Fonts icon in Control Panel.
[intl]	#USR\Control Panel\International[1]	Describes items for languages and locales as set using the International icon in Control Panel.
[mci extensions]	SYS...\MCI Extensions[3]	Associates file types with Media Control Interface devices as set using the Control Panel Drivers icon.
[network]	USR...\Network\Persistent Connections[2]; network printers in HKEY_LOCAL_MACHINE \SYSTEM\Control\Print	Describes network printer port settings as set using Print Manager and the persistent network connections as set using File Manager.
[ports]	SYS...\Ports[3]	Lists all available printer and communications ports as set using the Ports icon in Control Panel.
[printerPorts] and [devices]	SYS...\PrinterPorts and \Devices[3]	Lists active and inactive output devices to be accessed by Windows as set using Printer Manager.
[sounds]	#USR \Control Panel\Sounds[1]	Lists the sound files assigned to each system event as set using the Sound icon in Control Panel.
[TrueType]	#USR...\TrueType[2]	Describes options for using TrueType fonts as set using the Fonts icon in Control Panel.
[Windows Help]	USR\Software \Microsoft\Windows Help[1]	Lists settings for the Help window as set using the mouse or menus in any Help window.
[Windows]	#SYS...\Winlogon[3]	Specifies the Windows environment and user startup options as set using the Desktop, Keyboard, and Mouse icons in Control Panel.

[1] Full path = HKEY_CURRENT_USER

[2] Full path = HKEY_CURRENT_USER\SOFTWARE\Microsoft\Windows NT\CurrentVersion

[3] Full path = HKEY_LOCAL_MACHINE\SOFTWARE\Microsoft\Windows NT\CurrentVersion

SYSTEM.INI Settings in the Registry

Entries from a SYSTEM.INI file in Windows for MS-DOS on the computer when you install Windows NT will be preserved as entries under this key:

`HKEY_LOCAL_MACHINE\Software\Microsoft\Windows NT\CurrentVersion\WOW`

The following table describes where you can view or edit entries for similar purposes in Windows NT. These entries are used by applications that look for values in the SYSTEM.INI file.

Table 13.2   Registry Paths for SYSTEM.INI Sections

SYSTEM.INI section	Registry path	Description
[boot] and **[boot.description]**	#SYS...\WOW\Boot and \Boot.description[3]; replaced by ...CurrentControlSet\Control	Lists drivers and Windows modules as set using the System icon in Control Panel.
[drivers]	Replaced by #SYS...\Drivers32[3]	Contains a list of aliases (or names) assigned to installable driver files as set using the Drivers and Devices icons in Control Panel.
[keyboard]	#SYS...\WOW\Keyboard[3]; #USR\Keyboard Layout[1]	Contains information about the keyboard as set using the International icon in Control Panel or identified by the Hardware Detector.
[mci] and **[mci32]**	Replaced by #SYS...\MCI and \MCI32[3] and #SYS...\Drivers.desc[3]	Lists Media Control Interface (MCI) drivers as set using the Drivers icon in Control Panel.
[NonWindows App]	#SYS...\WOW\NonWindowsApp[3]	Contains information used by non-Windows–based applications as defined in PIFs for specific applications or in CONFIG.NT.
[standard]	Standard in #SYS...\WOW[3]	Contains information used by Windows for MS-DOS in standard and 386 enhanced mode. All memory management is handled automatically by Windows NT.

[1] Full path = HKEY_CURRENT_USER

[2] Full path = HKEY_CURRENT_USER\SOFTWARE\Microsoft\Windows NT\CurrentVersion

[3] Full path = HKEY_LOCAL_MACHINE\SOFTWARE \Microsoft\Windows NT\CurrentVersion

Other Initialization File Settings in the Registry

The following table describes where you can view or edit Registry entries equivalent to CONTROL.INI, PROGMAN.INI, and WINFILE.INI entries.

Table 13.3 Registry Paths for Other Initialization Files

.INI file section	Registry path	Description
CONTROL.INI **[Current]**, **[Color Schemes]**, **[Custom Colors]**	Color Schemes, Current, and Custom Colors subkeys in #USR \Control Panel[1]	Describes color schemes and custom colors as set using the Colors icon in Control Panel.
CONTROL.INI **[Patterns]** and **[Screen Saver*]**	Patterns and Screen Saver.x subkeys in #USR\Control Panel[1]	Describes elements of desktop appearance and behavior as set using the Desktop icon in Control Panel.
CONTROL.INI **[MMCPL]**, **[Drivers.Desc]**, **[Userinstallable.drivers]**	#USR\Control Panel\MMCPL[1]; #SYS...\Drivers.Desc and \Userinstallable.drivers[3]	Contains values for installable drivers and devices used for multimedia as set using the Drivers icon in Control Panel.
PROGMAN.INI **[groups]**, **[restrictions]**, **[settings]**	Groups, Restrictions, and Settings subkeys in #USR...\Program Manager[2]	Describes window appearance, groups and the icons in the groups, and restrictions on Program Manager operations as set using Program Manager; restrictions are set in User Manager for Domains.
MSMAIL32.INI	USR...\Mail[2]	Contains parameters that can be set for Mail.
SCHDPL32.INI	#USR...\Schedule+[2]	Contains parameters that can be set for Schedule+.
WINFILE.INI **[settings]**	#USR...\File Manager[2]	Describes the appearance and behavior of items in File Manager as set using File Manager.

[1] Full path = HKEY_CURRENT_USER

[2] Full path = HKEY_CURRENT_USER\SOFTWARE\Microsoft\Windows NT\CurrentVersion

[3] Full path = HKEY_LOCAL_MACHINE\SOFTWARE \Microsoft\Windows NT\CurrentVersion

3.5-INCH FLOPPY DISK ORDER CARD

The core set of utilities for the Intel® platform found on the *Microsoft® Windows NT* ™ *Resource Kit* CD are also available on a set of 3.5-inch floppy disks—for only **$15.95** (including shipping and handling).

To order, please fill out this card and enclose it in an envelope along with your check for $15.95 (U.S. funds only) and send to: **Microsoft Press**
Attn: Windows NT Resource Kit Disks
P.O. Box 3011
Bothell, WA 98041-3011

Name

Address

City   State   ZIP

Offer valid in the U.S. only.
Please allow 2-3 weeks for delivery.

1-55615-657-XA   **Microsoft® Windows NT™ Resource Kit**   Owner Registration Card

Register Today!

Return this **Microsoft Windows NT Resource Kit** registration card for:

☑ a Microsoft Press catalog
☑ exclusive offers on specially
priced books

Name

Company (if applicable)

Address

City   State   ZIP

U.S. and Canada addresses only. Fill in information above and mail postage-free.

3.5-INCH FLOPPY DISK ORDER CARD

Complete Technical
Information and
Tools for the
Support Professional

Windows NT
Resource Kit SECOND EDITION

For Windows NT Workstation and Windows NT Server Version 3.5

Microsoft OS/2 Version 1.x Entries in the Registry

The Microsoft OS/2 version 1.x subsystem starts whenever a user starts an OS/2 character-based application on an x86-based computer. The Registry entries for the OS/2 subsystem are found under this key:

```
HKEY_LOCAL_MACHINE\SYSTEM\CurrentControlSet
    \Control\Session Manager\SubSystems
```

The Os2 entry in this subkey describes the path to the executable file used to start the OS/2 subsystem. The directory path for the OS/2 library is the Os2LibPath value defined under the Session Manager\Environment subkey.

When Windows NT is installed on a computer, if Setup finds a copy of CONFIG.SYS for OS/2, a copy is placed in the *SystemRoot*\SYSTEM32 directory. This information is used to configure the OS/2 subsystem whenever an OS/2 application is started. If a CONFIG.SYS file is not found, a substitute is created in the Registry, with the following values:

```
PROTSHELL=C:\os2\pmshell.exe c:\os2\os2.ini c:\os2\os2sys.ini
    %SystemRoot%\system32\cmd.exe
SET COMSPEC=%SystemRoot%\system32\cmd.exe
```

The OS/2 CONFIG.SYS information is stored in the following Registry entry, which appears only after an OS/2 application has been run on the system:

```
HKEY_LOCAL_MACHINE\SOFTWARE\Microsoft\OS/2 Subsystem for NT\config.sys
```

The other subkeys under the OS/2 Subsystem key do not contain entries.

If you subsequently edit the C:\CONFIG.SYS file using a text editor, LIBPTH=, SET PATH=, and Set WINDIR= entries are appended to the end of the file from the Windows NT environment. Any changes made to the path or environment variables take effect after the system is shut down and restarted.

For details about managing this environment under Windows NT, see Chapter 11, "Other Application Environments," in the *Windows NT System Guide*.

You can disable an OS/2 subsystem in Windows NT and still run a bound application under a VDM. Many bound applications run better under a VDM than under the OS/2 subsystem.

▶ **To disable the OS/2 subsystem in Windows NT**

- In Registry Editor, change the value of GlobalFlag to 20100000 in the following Registry path:

```
HKEY_LOCAL_MACHINE\SYSTEM\CurrentControlSet\SessionManager
```

You can also use FORCEDOS.EXE, a utility supplied with Windows NT in the *SystemRoot*\SYSTEM32 subdirectory. This allows you to run a bound application under a VDM. To see how to use the ForceDOS utility, type **forcedos /?** at the command prompt.

POSIX Entries in the Registry

The POSIX subsystem starts whenever a user starts a POSIX application. The Registry entries for the POSIX subsystem are found under this key:

```
HKEY_LOCAL_MACHINE\SYSTEM\CurrentControlSet
    \Control\Session Manager\SubSystems
```

The **Posix** entry in this subkey describes the path to the executable file used to start the POSIX subsystem. The POSIX subsystem does not have any parameters or environmental variables that the user can set.

C H A P T E R   1 4

Registry Value Entries

Wherever possible, you should use the Control Panel and the applications in the Administrative Tools program group to make changes to the system configuration. For those occasions when you need to view or adjust a setting, this chapter identifies the Registry entries that you can add or change using the Registry Editor.

In this chapter, entries for Registry values are listed alphabetically within the following groups of topics:

- Summaries of entries in the Select, Control, and Services subkeys in HKEY_LOCAL_MACHINE\SYSTEM\CurrentControlSet

- Network adapter cards, drivers, and bindings

- Device drivers, with entries for disk, serial, and parallel port devices; keyboard and mouse devices; SCSI miniport devices; and video display devices

- Services, with entries for the Alerter, AppleTalk and Macfile, DLC, Eventlog, NetBEUI (NBF) transport, Netlogon, Replicator, Server, NWLink, TCP/IP, UPS, and Workstation services

- Mail and Schedule+

- User preferences

- Fonts and printing

- Windows NT subsystems

Caution Using Registry Editor incorrectly can cause serious problems, including corruption that may make it necessary to reinstall Windows NT.

Not all entries that appear here may be found in the Registry for a particular computer. For many entries, the system uses the default value unless you add the entry to the Registry and specify another value.

The information in this chapter appears in the following format:

Entry Name   REG_type   Range for value entry
A description of the entry, usually including the conditions under which you might change the value.

Default: *value*
(For value ranges that are Boolean, the value can be **1** for true or "enabled," or **0** for false or "disabled.")

In general, if you change values for any entries in the CurrentControlSet, you must restart the computer for the changes to take effect.

If you change values for entries under HKEY_CURRENT_USER using Registry Editor, you may have to log off and log back on for the changes to take effect.

Note You'll find a navigational hint at the bottom corner of each page, indicating which service or portion of the Registry is described on that page.

CurrentControlSet\Select Subkey

The Select subkey under HKEY_LOCAL_MACHINE\SYSTEM maintains information about the control sets for the currently selected computer. The Select subkey contains the following named values:

Current   REG_DWORD   *0xN, where N identifies a control set*
Identifies the control set from which the CurrentControlSet subkey is derived. If this value is 0x1, for example, the subkey producing the CurrentControlSet is ControlSet001.

Default   REG_DWORD   *0xN, where N identifies a control set*
Identifies the default control set. If this value is 0x1, for example, the default control set is ControlSet001.

Failed   REG_DWORD   *0xN, where N identifies a control set*
Identifies the control set number of the control set that was last rejected and replaced with a LastKnownGood control set.

LastKnownGood   REG_DWORD   *0xN, where N identifies a control set*
Identifies the last control set that successfully started the system. If this value is 0x1, for example, the last control set known to be good is ControlSet001.

CurrentControlSet\Control Subkeys

This subkey contains parameters that control system startup, such as subsystems to load, the size and location of paging files, and so on.

Note The system must be restarted for any changes in the Control subkey to take effect.

The Control subkey itself can contain the following value entries:

Current User   REG_SZ   *Username*

Specifies the username for the currently logged-on user.

Default: *Username*

RegistrySizeLimit   REG_DWORD   *4 bytes to unlimited*

Limits both the amount of paged pool the Registry may use, and the amount of disk space.

If the value of **RegistrySizeLimit** is less than 4 MB, it will be forced up to 4 MB. If it is greater than about 80% of the size of **PagedPoolSize**, it will be set down to 80% of the size of **PagedPoolSize**. (It is assumed that **PagedPoolSize** will always be bigger than 5 MB.)

RegistrySizeLimit sets a maximum, not an allocation, meaning a large **RegistrySizeLimit** value will be used only if it is actually needed by the Registry. It does not guarantee that much space will be available for use in the Registry.

Setting **RegistrySizeLimit** to 0xffffffff will effectively set it to be as large as **PagedPoolSize** allows (80% of **PagedPoolSize**). **PagedPoolSize** can be set to a maximum of 128 MB, thus limiting **RegistrySizeLimit** to 102 MB.

Default: 8 MB (That is, 25 percent of the default **PagedPoolSize**.)

SystemStartOptions   REG_SZ   *String*

Contains the text of system arguments passed to the system by the firmware. These values can be used to determine whether the debugger is enabled, the options set for ports and speed, and so on. For example, the following value could be defined for **SystemStartOptions**:

```
c:\winnt="Windows NT" /DebugPort=com1 /DebugBaudRate=56000
```

In this example, "Windows NT" in the first part of the string indicates the *SystemRoot* specified under the Windows NT\CurrentVersion subkey in the Software area of the Registry. The remaining portion of this string is interpreted by the system to define the COM port and baud rate for debugging.

The following standard Control subkeys are found under this Registry path:

```
HKEY_LOCAL_MACHINE\SYSTEM\CurrentControlSet\Control
```

BootVerificationProgram	Lsa[1]	Session Manager
ComputerName[1]	NetworkProvider	Setup[1]
DisplayDriverControl[1]	Nls	TimeZoneInformation[1]
GroupOrderList	Print[2]	VirtualDeviceDrivers
ServiceGroupOrder	PriorityControl[1]	Windows
HiveList	ProductOptions[1]	WOW
Keyboard Layout		

[1] These keys contain information used only by the system and should not be edited by users. Because these entries should be maintained only by the system, they are not described here.

[2] See "Registry Entries for Printing," later in this chapter.

BootVerificationProgram Control Entries

The BootVerificationProgram subkey is used to update the last known good configuration during system startup. This entry describes a program that will be called by the service controller to establish the last known good configuration. Such a program can be written by the system administrator.

The Registry path of this subkey is the following:

```
HKEY_LOCAL_MACHINE\SYSTEM\CurrentControlSet
    \Control\BootVerificationProgram
```

Any entry added under this subkey must have the following format:

ImagePath   Reg_SZ or REG_EXPAND_SZ   *Filename*
Specifies the filename for a startup verification program.

Default: (no entry)

You must also specify a value of 1 for the **ReportBootOK** entry under the following Registry path:

```
HKEY_LOCAL_MACHINE\Software\Windows NT\CurrentVersion\WinLogon
```

When the value of **ReportBootOK** is set to 0, it disables the automatic (default) startup acceptance, which happens after the first successful logon.

As an alternative, if you want to verify system startup from a remote location, the BootVerification service supplied with Windows NT can be used instead of the BootVerificationProgram, as described later in this chapter. The BootVerification service cannot be used in conjunction with entries in the BootVerificationProgram subkey.

Note Do not change values in the BootVerificationProgram subkey unless you need a custom verification program to satisfy specific startup criteria at your site. Otherwise, accept the default procedures for verifying system startup.

FileSystem Control Entries

The entries in the FileSystem subkey specify the behavior of NTFS and FAT, respectively, under the following Registry path:

```
HKEY_LOCAL_MACHINE\SYSTEM\CurrentControlSet\Control\FileSystem
```

NtfsDisable8dot3NameCreation   REG_DWORD *0 or 1*

Controls whether NTFS will create a short name for a filename that is not in the format *xxxxxxxx.yyy*, contains extended characters, or both. Creating short names impacts performance, so some sites may want to set this value to 1 (true) if they do not intend to either use DOS applications on long names, or share disks with different code page machines (i.e., machines in the U.S.). For example, in the Far East, where all native file names generate short names, set this value to 1.

You must reboot the system for a change to this value to take effect.

Default: 0 (false)

Win31FileSystem   REG_DWORD *0 or 1*

Controls whether the FAT will allow creation, enumeration, opening, or querying of long file names, and whether extended time stamp information (CreationTime and LastAccessTime) is stored and reported. Set this value to 1 (true) to revert to basic Win3*x* (and Windows NT 3.5) semantics.

Note Changing this value does not change any disk structures. It simply changes how the system behaves from now on.

You must reboot the system for a change to this value to take effect.

Default: 0 (false)

GroupOrderList Control Entries

The entries in the GroupOrderList subkey specify the ordering of services within groups, under the following Registry path:

```
HKEY_LOCAL_MACHINE\SYSTEM\CurrentControlSet\Control\GroupOrderList
```

For a service listed under CurrentControlSet\Services, the value of the **Group** entry plus any **Tag** entry determines the order in which the service is loaded. But not all services have a **Tag** entry, and not all groups have an entry in the GroupOrderList subkey. The ServiceGroupOrder subkey described later in this section specifies the order for loading groups.

The entries in the subkey are all of type REG_BINARY. The default entries that define the order within groups are listed below:

Base	Pointer Class	Video
Ndis	SCSI Miniport	Keyboard Port
Primary Disk	Keyboard Class	
Filter	Pointer Port	

HiveList Control Entries

The location of the files that contain Registry information is reported under the following Registry path:

```
HKEY_CURRENT_MACHINE\SYSTEM\CurrentControlSet\Control\hivelist
```

All data types are REG_SZ. The following are the default entries:

\REGISTRY\MACHINE\HARDWARE

\REGISTRY\MACHINE\SAM=
\Device\Harddisk0\Partition1*SystemRoot*\SYSTEM32\CONFIG\SAM

\REGISTRY\MACHINE\SECURITY=
\Device\Harddisk0\Partition1*SystemRoot*\SYSTEM32\CONFIG\SECURITY

\REGISTRY\MACHINE\SOFTWARE=
\Device\Harddisk0\Partition1*SystemRoot*\SYSTEM32\CONFIG\SOFTWARE

\REGISTRY\MACHINE\SYSTEM=
\Device\Harddisk0\Partition1*SystemRoot*\SYSTEM32\CONFIG\SYSTEM

\REGISTRY\USER\.DEFAULT=
\Device\Harddisk0\Partition1*SystemRoot*\SYSTEM32\CONFIG\DEFAULT

\REGISTRY\USER*SID_#*=
\Device\Harddisk0\Partition1*SystemRoot*\SYSTEM32\CONFIG\ADMIN000

Keyboard Layout Control Entries

The Keyboard Layout subkey maintains the mapping of keyboard layout names to keyboard layout DLL names, under the following Registry path:

```
HKEY_LOCAL_MACHINE\SYSTEM\CurrentControlSet\Control\Keyboard Layout
```

The Keyboard Layout subkey is used by the system to determine which DLL to load. The mapping may contain duplicated keyboard layout DLL names if that DLL implements the layout for more than one language (in other words, a keyboard layout may have more than one name). Individual preferences are stored under HKEY_CURRENT_USER\Keyboard Layout.

The Keyboard Layout subkey contains an entry in this format:

KeyboardLayout   **REG_SZ**   *DLL filename*

By convention, a keyboard layout name is a null-terminated string of 8 hexadecimal digits representing a language ID (in the last four digits) and a variation number (in the first four digits).

For example, the language ID of Swiss German is 0x807, so, by convention, keyboard layout names could be 00000807, 00010807, and so on.

The DosKeybCodes subkey is used by the system to convert Windows NT keyboard layout names into MS-DOS–style two-character keyboard layout names as used by the **kb16** command (equivalent to **keyb** in MS-DOS). The system must automatically switch the VDM keyboard layout whenever the Windows NT keyboard layout is changed. Entries are found under this Registry path:

```
HKEY_LOCAL_MACHINE\SYSTEM\CurrentControlSet\Control
  \Keyboard Layout\DosKeybCodes
```

KeyboardLayout   **REG_SZ**   *Two-character code*

These entries define the two-character equivalent for each keyboard layout. This list summarizes the entries under DosKeybCodes:

00000405=cz	**00000414**=no	**0000080C**=be
00000406=dk	**00000415**=pl	**00000813**=be
00000407=gr	**00000416**=br	**00000816**=po
00000409=us	**00000419**=ru	**00000C0C**=cf
0000040A=sp	**0000041A**=yu	**00001009**=us
0000040B=su	**0000041B**=sl	**0000100C**=sf
0000040C=fr	**0000041D**=sv	**00010409**=dv
0000040E=hu	**00000807**=sg	**0001040A**=sp
0000040F=us	**00000809**=uk	**00010C0C**=cf
00000410=it	**0000080A**=la	**00020409**=us
00000413=nl		

NetworkProvider Control Entries

Windows NT supports a common interface that allows networks from several different vendors (that is, network providers) to operate on a single computer at the same time. The NetworkProvider subkey provides a list of the available network providers that use the Microsoft network-independent APIs. The following value for the Order subkey appears under this Registry path:

```
HKEY_LOCAL_MACHINE\SYSTEM\CurrentControlSet\Control
    \NetworkProvider\Order
```

ProviderOrder   **REG_SZ**   *Comma-separated list of key names*

Specifies the order for accessing available network providers, as defined by choosing the Networks button in the Network dialog box in Control Panel. Each entry in this list is in the form of a Registry Services subkey name for a service or driver that is associated with a particular network provider. The Services subkey associated with a network provider should contain a **Group** entry with the value of NetworkProvider, and must also contain a NetworkProvider subkey with information for the Multiple Provider Router. For more information, see "NetworkProvider" in the "Registry Entries for Network Services" section later in this chapter.

Default: LanmanWorkstation (when a single network is installed)

Nls Control Entries

This subkey contains other subkeys that define information for languages and code pages.

In the Code Page and Language subkeys, all code pages and languages supported under Windows NT are listed, so applications can check these keys to find all "supported" languages. However, only the entries with filenames in the data fields are actually installed in the system. So applications must check the data fields to find out if a specific code page is actually installed in the system.

CodePage Entries

The entries under the following Registry path identify the files for available code pages. If there is no value following the entry name, that code page is not installed in the system.

```
HKEY_LOCAL_MACHINE\SYSTEM\CurrentControlSet\Control\Nls\CodePage
```

Each entry has the following format:

CodePageID   **REG_SZ**   *Filename*

As shown in the following list, **437**=C_437.NLS indicates the file for code page 437, and **1252**=C_1252.NLS indicates the file for code page 1252, and so on. **ACP** is the default ANSI code page; **OEMCP** is the default OEM code page; and **MACCP** is the default Macintosh code page.

10000=c_10000.nls	**1253**=	**861**=
10006=	**1254**=	**863**=
10007=	**437**=c_437.nls	**865**=
10029=	**500**=	**866**=
1026=	**850**=c_850.nls	**869**=
1250=	**852**=	**875**=
1251=	**855**=	**ACP**=1252
1252=c_1252.nls	**857**=	**MACCP**=10000
	860=	**OEMCP**=437

Language Entries

The entries under the following Registry path identify the files for available languages. If there is no value following the entry name, that language is not installed in the system.

```
HKEY_LOCAL_MACHINE\SYSTEM\CurrentControlSet\Control\Nls\Language
```

Each entry has the following format:

LanguageID*   REG_SZ   *Filename

As shown in the following table, l_INTL.NLS is the file for language 0409, l_INTL.NLS is the file for language 0809, and so on.

Default: 0409 (the default language ID)

0405=l_intl.nls	**0414**= l_intl.nls	**0813**=l_intl.nls
0406= l_intl.nls	**0415**=l_intl.nls	**0814**=l_intl.nls
0407=l_intl.nls	**0416**=l_intl.nls	**0816**=l_intl.nls
0408=	**0419**=l_intl.nls	**0c07**= l_intl.nls
0409=l_intl.nls	**041b**=l_intl.nls	**28**=l_intl.nls
040a=l_intl.nls	**041d**=l_intl.nls	**0c0a**=l_intl.nls
040b= l_intl.nls	**041f**=	**0c0c**=l_intl.nls
040c=l_intl.nls	**0807**=l_intl.nls	**1009**=l_intl.nls
040e=l_intl.nls	**0809**=l_intl.nls	**100c**=l_intl.nls
040f=l_intl.nls	**080a**=l_intl.nls	**1409**=l_intl.nls
0410=l_intl.nls	**080c**=l_intl.nls	**1809**=l_intl.nls
0413=l_intl.nls	**0810**=l_intl.nls	

OEMLocale Entries

The following subkey, if present, can contain entries that an OEM adds to customize its locale:

```
HKEY_LOCAL_MACHINE\SYSTEM\CurrentControlSet\Control\Nls\OEMLocale
```

This section of the Registry is only checked if a specific locale ID is not found in the default locale file (LOCALE.NLS). If this subkey is present, each entry has the following format:

OEMlocale*   REG_SZ   *filename

Specifies the locale ID and a filename for the OEM locale.

Default: This subkey is not present, so there is no default.

LPR Print Monitor Control Entries

One value can be set for the LPR Print Monitor, in the following registry path:

```
HKEY_LOCAL_MACHINE\SYSTEM\CurrentControlSet\Control\Print\
    Monitors\LPR Port\Ports\<portname>\Timeouts
```

PrintSwitch   REG_SZ   *Control character string*

Specifies the format control character that the LPR Print Monitor should send to the print server via the control file. By default, this parameter doesn't exist in the registry, and "l" (lowercase L) is sent as the control character. You can set it to any string. If set, the first character of the string is taken as the format control character and sent to the print server. The rest of the string is ignored. In situations, you may need to use "f" instead of "l".

Default: (none)

ServiceGroupOrder Control Entries

The ServiceGroupOrder subkey specifies the order to load various groups of services.

Order within groups is specified using the value of **Tag** under the specific Services subkeys and the values in the GroupOrderList subkey. For example, when you start Windows NT, the Boot Loader scans the Registry for drivers with a **Start** value of 0 (which indicates that these drivers should be loaded but not initialized before the Kernel) and a **Type** value of 0x1 (which indicates a Kernel device driver such as a hard disk or other low-level hardware device driver). The drivers are then loaded into memory in the order specified as the **List** value in the ServiceGroupOrder subkey.

```
HKEY_LOCAL_MACHINE\SYSTEM\CurrentControlSet\Control\ServiceGroupOrder
```

List   REG_MULTI_SZ   *Group names*

Specifies the order for loading drivers into memory.

Default:

SCSI miniport
port
Primary disk
SCSI class
SCSI CDROM
class filter
boot file system
Base
Keyboard Port
Pointer Port
Keyboard Class
Pointer Class
Video
file system
Event log
Streams Drivers
NDIS
TDI
NetBIOSGroup
NetDDEGroup
extended base network

Session Manager Control Entries

The Session Manager subkey contains the global variables used by the Session Manager. These values are stored under the following Registry path:

```
HKEY_LOCAL_MACHINE\SYSTEM\CurrentControlSet\Control\Session Manager
```

BootExecute   REG_MULTI_SZ

Specifies programs to run during startup. For example, if CONVERT.EXE has been used to convert the file system on a hard disk drive, this value is added to **BootExecute** so that conversion occurs when the system is restarted:

```
BootExecute = autocheck autoconv \DosDevices\x: /FS:NTFS
```

Default: autocheck autochk *

CriticalSectionTimeout   REG_DWORD

Specifies the deadlock time-out for critical sections. Usually, retail installations of Windows NT will not time-out and detect deadlocks.

Default: 0x278d00

GlobalFlag   REG_DWORD

Controls various Windows NT internal operations. You can change this value to disable the OS/2 subsystem if you want to run bound applications in a VDM, rather than under the OS/2 subsystem. Set this value to 20100000 to disable the OS/2 subsystem.

Default: 0x21100000

ObjectDirectories   REG_MULTI_SZ

Lists the object directories to create during startup. Do not edit these entries.

Default: \DosDevices
\Windows
\RPC Control

DOS Devices Control Entries

The DosDevices subkey lists the built-in symbolic links to create at startup. The values are stored under this subkey:

```
HKEY_LOCAL_MACHINE\SYSTEM\CurrentControlSet
    \Control\Session Manager\DOS Devices
```

Entries in this subkey have the data type of REG_SZ. The following list shows the default entries under this subkey.

AUX=\DosDevices\COM1
MAILSLOT=\Device\MailSlot
NUL=\Device\Null
PIPE=\Device\NamedPipe
PRN=\DosDevices\LPT1
TELNET=\Device\Telnet
UNC=\Device\Mup

Environment Control Entries

The Environment subkey defines environment variables that the system creates and that are used by Windows NT Logon and Program Manager.

Caution Use extreme care in changing these entry values. If the operating system cannot find the files specified for a subsystem, you will not be able to run non-Windows NT-based applications.

The Registry path for these values is the following:

```
HKEY_LOCAL_MACHINE\SYSTEM\CurrentControlSet
    \Control\Session Manager\Environment
```

ComSpec   REG_EXPAND_SZ   *Filename*

Defines the path and filename for the Windows NT command interpreter (the equivalent of MS-DOSCOMMAND.COM in MS-DOS).

Default: %systemRoot%\SYSTEM32\CMD.EXE

Os2LibPath   REG_EXPAND_SZ   *Filename*

Defines the path for the Microsoft OS/2 version 1.*x* library.

Default: %systemRoot%\SYSTEM32\os2\dll

Path   REG_EXPAND_SZ   *Filename*

Defines the path variable for Windows NT logon and Program Manager.

Default: %systemRoot%\SYSTEM32; %SystemRoot%

Windir   REG_EXPAND_SZ   *Filename*

Defines the path for the executable for WOW, as used by Windows NT logon and Program Manager.

Default: %systemRoot%\SYSTEM32\CMD.EXE

KnownDLLs Control Entries

The KnownDlls subkey defines the set of DLLs that are first searched during system startup. In general, these are system DLLs that are loaded from disk into a section of memory and are checked for integrity. These DLLs consume some resources, even if no application loads them. These appear as separate entries under this Registry path:

```
HKEY_LOCAL_MACHINE\SYSTEM\CurrentControlSet\Control\Session
Manager\KnownDLLs
```

driverName   **REG_SZ**   *DLL Filename*

This series of entries defines a driver name and the corresponding DLL filename. The following shows the default entries:

advapi32=advapi32.dll   **olecli32**=olecli32.dll
comdlg32=comdlg32.dll   **olesvr32**=olesvr32.dll
crtdll=crtdll.dll   **rpcrt4**=rpcrt4.dll
DllDirectory=%SystemRoot%\system32   **shell32**=shell32.dll
gdi32=gdi32.dll   **user32**=user32.dll
kernel32=kernel32.dll   **version**=version.dll
lz32=lz32.dll

Memory Management Control Entries

The Memory Management subkey defines paging options under the following Registry path:

```
HKEY_LOCAL_MACHINE\SYSTEM\CurrentControlSet\Control
    \Session Manager\Memory Management
```

The paging file parameters should be defined by using the System icon in Control Panel and choosing the Virtual Memory button.

IoPageLockLimit   **REG_DWORD**   *Number of bytes*

Specifies the limit of the number of bytes that can be locked for I/O operations. When this value is 0, the system uses the default (512K). The maximum value is about the equivalent of physical memory minus pad, which is 7 MB for a small system and grows as the amount of memory grows. For a 64 MB system, pad is about 16 MB; for a 512 MB system, pad is about 64 MB.

Default: 512K

LargeSystemCache   **REG_DWORD**   *Number*

Specifies, for a nonzero value, that the system favor the system-cache working set rather than the processes working set. Set this value by choosing the Windows NT ServerWindows NT Server installation base.

Default: 0

NonPagedPoolSize   **REG_DWORD**   *Number of bytes*

Specifies the size of nonpaged pool in bytes. When this value is 0, the system uses the default size (based on physical memory). The maximum amount is about 80 percent of physical memory.

Default: 0

PagedPoolSize   REG_DWORD   *0 to 128 MB*

Specifies the size of paged pool in bytes. When this value is 0, the system uses the default size (32 MB). See also the entry for **RegistrySizeLimit** at the beginning of this section.

Default: 0x3000000 (32 MB)

PagingFiles   REG_MULTI_SZ   *System_Paging_Files*

Specifies page file information set by choosing the System icon in Control Panel.

Default: C:\pagefile.sys 27

Subsystem Startup Control Entries

The following is the Registry path for the subsystem settings established at startup:

```
HKEY_LOCAL_MACHINE\SYSTEM\CurrentControlSet
    \Control\Session Manager\SubSystems
```

These values should only be maintained by the system. You should not need to manually define these settings.

Debug   REG_EXPAND_SZ   *Names*

Default: (no value)

Optional   REG_MULTI_SZ   *Subsystem names*

Defines subsystems that are only loaded when the user starts an application that requires this subsystem.

Default: Os2 Posix

Os2   REG_EXPAND_SZ   *Path and filename*

Defines the path to the executable file used to start the Microsoft OS/2 version 1.*x* subsystem.

Default: %SystemRoot%\system32\os2ss.exe

Posix   REG_EXPAND_SZ   *Path and filename*

Defines the path to the executable file used to start the POSIX subsystem. (There are no additional POSIX entries in the Registry.)

Default: %SystemRoot%\system32\psxss.exe

Required   REG_MULTI_SZ   *Name*

Default: Debug Windows

SystemPages   REG_DWORD   *Number of entries*

Defines the number of system page table entries reserved for mapping I/O buffers and other information into the system address space. Each entry maps a single page. The value 0 indicates that the default number of entries is to be used.

Default: TBD

Windows   REG_EXPAND_SZ   *Path and filename*

Defines the path to the executable file used to start the Win32 subsystem.

Default: %SystemRoot%\system32\csrss.exe ObjectDirectory=\Windows SharedSection=1024,3072 Windows=On SubSystemType=Windows ServerDll=basesrv,1 ServerDll=winsrv:GdiServerDllInitialization,4 ServerDll=winsrv:UserServerDllInitialization,3 ServerDll=winsrv:ConServerDllInitialization,2 ServerDll=mmsndsrv,5 ProfileControl=Off MaxRequestThreads=16

VirtualDeviceDrivers Control Entries

The VirtualDeviceDriver subkey contains a list of Win32 DLLs that serve as virtual device drivers (VDD). Each **VDD** entry results in loading that VDD when a virtual MS-DOS machine (VDM) is being created for running an application created for MS-DOS or 16-bit versions of Microsoft Windows. This is the Registry path:

```
HKEY_LOCAL_MACHINE\SYSTEM\CurrentControlSet\Control\VirtualDeviceDrivers
```

VDD   REG_MULTI_SZ   *Filenames*

Specifies valid Win32 DLLs that are virtual device drivers.

Default: None—the Windows NT VDDs are built into the system.

Windows Startup Control Entries

This subkey contains entries that define the system directories for the Win32 subsystem (32-bit Windows) under this path:

```
HKEY_LOCAL_MACHINE\SYSTEM\CurrentControlSet\Control\Windows
```

Directory   REG_EXPAND_SZ   *Directory name*

Defines the directory for Windows NT.

Default: %SystemRoot%

SystemDirectory   REG_EXPAND_SZ   *Directory name*

Defines the directory for the Windows NT system files.

Default: %SystemRoot%\system32

The Registry entries for starting the Win32 subsystem are defined under the **Required** and **Windows** value entries in the Session Manager\Subsystem subkey, as described earlier in this section.

WOW Startup Control Entries

The following values control startup parameters that affect MS-DOS–based applications and applications created for 16-bit Windows 3.1. The Registry path for these values is the following:

```
HKEY_LOCAL_MACHINE\SYSTEM\CurrentControlSet
    \Control\WOW
```

Cmdline   REG_EXPAND_SZ   *Path and switches*

Defines the command line that runs when an MS-DOS–based application runs under Windows NT. This command line continues to run until the related application is closed. The following switches can be included:

Switch	Meaning
-a	Specifies a command to pass to the VDM
-f	Specifies the directory to find NTVDM.EXE
-m	Hides the VDM console window
-w	Specifies the WOW VDM

Default: %SystemRoot%\system32\ntvdm -f%SystemRoot%\system32 -a

KnownDLLs   REG_SZ   *DLL filenames*

Defines a list of known DLLs for use by the WOW VDM that provide compatibility for non-Win32 applications. When the system searches for DLLs to load, it compares the requested DLL with those in the **KnownDLLs** list and then loads the matching DLL from the *SystemRoot*\SYSTEM32 directory.

If you want to replace a DLL, you must delete the name from this list, so that the system will search elsewhere for the DLL. The files USER.DLL, GDI.DLL, and SYSTEM.DRV are not included in this list, because these are required Windows NT system files and their location cannot be changed.

Default: shell.dll commdlg.dll mmsystem.dll olecli.dll olesvr.dll ddeml.dll win87em.dll toolhelp.dll lanman.drv netapi.dll pmspl.dll wowdeb.exe

LPT_timeout **REG_SZ** *Number of seconds*

Defines how many seconds after the LPT port has been used that Windows NT waits before grabbing the port, closing it, and flushing the output. This value should only be needed for MS-DOS-based applications that use BIOS and do not close the port.

Default: 15

Size **REG_SZ** *Number in megabytes*

Defines the amount of memory to be given to each individual MS-DOS VDM. The default of 0 gives the VDM as much memory as Windows NT determines is necessary, depending upon the memory configuration.

To change this value, change the related value in the PIF file for the application.

Default: 0

Wowcmdline **REG_EXPAND_SZ** *Path and switches*

Defines the command line that runs when a 16-bit Windows-based application is started. The switches instruct Windows NT to start either an MS-DOS VDM or a WOW VDM. See the definitions for allowable switches under **Cmdline**.

Default: %SystemRoot%\system32\ntvdm -m -w -f%SystemRoot%\system32
   -a %SystemRoot%\system32\krnl386

Wowsize **REG_SZ** *Up to 16 megabytes*

For RISC-based computers, defines the amount of memory provided in a VDM when a WOW session is started. This value is not used on *x*86-based computers, where Windows NT allocates the memory needed when it is asked for.

The default size chosen for a RISC-based computer depends on the amount of system memory on the computer. For each megabyte specified, the system uses 1.25 MB, so setting **Wowsize** to 4 MB causes the VDM to allocate 5 MB, although applications can only use 4 MB. You can override the following defaults:

System memory size	Default VDM size
Less than 12 MB (small)	3 MB
12–16 MB (medium)	6 MB
More than 16 MB (large)	8 MB

Caution Setting **Wowsize** to a value lower than 3 MB will cause most applications to fail.

Default: Depends on RISC-based computer's system memory

CurrentControlSet\Services Subkeys

The Services subkeys under the following Registry path contain parameters for the device drivers, file system drivers, and Win32 service drivers:

```
HKEY_LOCAL_MACHINE\SYSTEM\CurrentControlSet\Services
```

The name of each Services subkey is the name of the service, which is also the root of the name of the file from which the service is loaded. For example, for the serial mouse, the service name and Services subkey name is Sermouse. The file from which this is loaded is *SystemRoot*\SYSTEM32\DRIVERS\SERMOUSE.SYS.

All service names are defined under HKEY_LOCAL_MACHINE\SOFTWARE. The names of the Windows NT built-in network services such as the Alerter and Browser services are defined under the Microsoft\Windows NT\CurrentVersion subkey in the Software area of the Registry.

Each Services subkey can have additional subkeys. Many services have a Linkage subkey, which provides data for binding network components, as described in "Linkage Subkey Entries for Network Components," later in this chapter. Many services also have a Parameters subkey that contains entries defined by the service with values for configuring the specific service.

Values for Parameters subkeys and other service-specific entries are described in these sections in this chapter:

- Registry Entries for LPDSVC
- Registry Entries for Network Adapter Cards
- Registry Entries for Device Drivers
- Registry Entries for Network Services

The following standard value entries appear for each Services subkey:

ErrorControl   **REG_DWORD**   *Error constant*

Specifies the level of error control for the service as follows:

Error control level	Meaning
0x3 (Critical)	Fail the attempted system startup. If the startup is not using the LastKnownGood control set, switch to LastKnownGood. If the startup attempt is using LastKnownGood, run a bug-check routine.
0x2 (Severe)	If the startup is not using the LastKnownGood control set, switch to LastKnownGood. If the startup attempt is using LastKnownGood, continue on in case of error.
0x1 (Normal)	If the driver fails to load or initialize, startup should proceed, but display a warning.
0x0 (Ignore)	If the driver fails to load or initialize, start up proceeds. No warning is displayed.

Group   **REG_DWORD**   *Group name*

Specifies the name of the group of which the particular service is a member.

Default: (null)

DependOnGroup   **REG_DWORD**   *Group name*

Specifies zero or more group names. If one or more groups is listed, at least one service from the named group must be loaded before this service is loaded.

Default: (empty)

DependOnService   **REG_DWORD**   *Service name*

Specifies zero or more Services subkey names. If a service is listed here, that named service must be loaded before this service is loaded.

Default: (empty)

ImagePath   **REG_DWORD**   *Path and filename*

Specifies a path name. For adapters, this value is ignored.

Default: For a driver, *systemroot*\SYSTEM32\DRIVERS*driverName*.SYS. For a service, *systemroot*\SYSTEM32*serviceName*.EXE (where *driverName* or *serviceName* is the same as the related Services subkey name)

ObjectName   REG_DWORD   *Object name*

Specifies an object name. If **Type** specifies a WIN32 Service, this name is the account name that the service will use to log on when the service runs. If **Type** specifies a Kernel driver or file system driver, this name is the Windows NT driver object name that the I/O Manager uses to load the device driver.

Default: *subkeyName*

Start   REG_DWORD   *Start constant*

Specifies the starting values for the service as follows:

Start type	Loader	Meaning
0x0 (Boot)	Kernel	Represents a part of the driver stack for the boot (startup) volume and must therefore be loaded by the Boot Loader.
0x1 (System)	I/O subsystem	Represents a driver to be loaded at Kernel initialization.
0x2 (Auto load)	Service Control Manager	To be loaded or started automatically for all startups, regardless of service type.
0x3 (Load on demand)	Service Control Manager	Available, regardless of type, but will not be started until the user starts it (for example, by using the Devices icon in Control Panel).
0x4 (Disabled)	Service Control Manager	Not to be started under any conditions.

The **Start** value is ignored for adapters. If **Type** is a Win32 Service value (as described below), the **Start** value must specify an Auto, Demand, or Disabled value.

Tag   REG_DWORD

Specifies a load order within a given group. The value of **Tag** specifies a number that is unique within the group of which the service is a member. The related *GroupName* entry under the Control\GroupOrderList subkey specifies a list of tags, in load order.

For example, the following services that are members of the Primary Disk group could have these values: **Tag**=4 for the Abiosdsk subkey, **Tag**=2 for Atdisk, **Tag**=1 for Cpqarray, and **Tag**=3 for Floppy. The value for **Primary Disk** under the GroupOrderList subkey will use these **Tag** values to specify the defined order for loading these services. As another example, each SCSI miniport service has a unique **Tag** value that is used as an identifier in the **SCSI miniport** value under the GroupOrderList subkey to define which SCSI adapter to load first.

Type   **REG_DWORD**   *Type constant*

Specifies the type of service as follows:

Service type	Description
0x1	A Kernel device driver.
0x2	File system driver, which is also a Kernel device driver.
0x4	A set of arguments for an adapter.
0x10	A Win32 program that can be started by the Service Controller and that obeys the service control protocol. This type of Win32 service runs in a process by itself.
0x20	A Win32 service that can share a process with other Win32 services.

For example, when you start Windows NT, the Boot Loader scans the Registry for drivers with a **Start** value of 0 (which indicates that these drivers should be loaded but not initialized before the Kernel) and a **Type** value of 0x1 (which indicates a Kernel device driver such as a hard disk or other low-level hardware device driver). The drivers are then loaded into memory in the order specified as the **List** value in CurrentControlSet\Control\ServiceGroupOrder.

Registry Entries for LPDSVC

The binding information is stored in three value entries in the Linkage subkey for a component under the Services subkey. The Registry path for each Linkage subkey is the following:

```
HKEY_LOCAL_MACHINE\SYSTEM\CurrentControlSet\Services
    \LPDSVC\Parameters
```

AllowJobRemoval   **REG_DWORD**   *0 or 1*

Setting this parameter to 0 disables job removal. If it is required that LPDSVC not delete a job from the queue once it is submitted, set this to 0. The default (1) allows a job to be removed if the removal request comes from the machine that originally submitted it.

Default: 1

AllowPrinterResume   **REG_DWORD**   *0 or 1*

If set to 1 (default), anyone can cause a paused printer to resume by sending the appropriate LPR command. If set to 0, all resume commands are ignored.

Default: 1

MaxconcurrentUsers   REG_DWORD   *0 to 0x64 users*

Specifies how many users can concurrently send a job to LPDSVC.

Default: 0x64 (100)

Registry Entries for Network Adapter Cards

This section describes specific Registry entries related to network adapter cards and the drivers for network adapters. Windows NT supports network adapter drivers under the NDIS 3.0 specification (Network Device Interface Specification).

The CurrentControlSet\Services subkey for a network driver or adapter card includes the standard entries found in the Services subkeys, with the following default values:

Value entry	Value
ErrorControl	0x1 (normal)
Start	0x3 (load on demand)
Type	0x1 or 0x4 (driver or adapter)

The following sections describe entries in the other areas of the Registry that contain configuration information for network adapter cards and their drivers, including:

- NetRules subkeys under HKEY_LOCAL_MACHINE\SOFTWARE for drivers and adapters.
- Linkage subkey entries under HKEY_LOCAL_MACHINE\SYSTEM for drivers and adapters, defining information about bindings for the component.
- Parameter subkey entries under HKEY_LOCAL_MACHINE\SYSTEM for network card adapters, defining specific information such as the IRQ number, I/O base address, and other details.

The information provided here is chiefly to be used for informational and troubleshooting purposes. The settings for either the NDIS driver or the network adapter card should be changed using the Network icon in Control Panel.

For information about Registry values other network services, see "Registry Entries for Network Services," later in this chapter. Entries for TCP/IP that are specific to network adapter cards can be found under "TCP/IP Transport Entries," later in this chapter.

NetRules Subkey Entries

During network reconfiguration (that is, when you use the Network icon in Control Panel to make changes), the system reads the values stored in the NetRules subkeys for information used to bind the network components. The Registry path for these value entries is the following:

- For adapter card drivers and network services, where the *driverName* subkey is the name of the network card's driver, as defined by the system:

```
HKEY_LOCAL_MACHINE\SOFTWARE\Microsoft
    \driverName\CurrentVersion\NetRules
```

- For network adapter cards, where the *netcard#* subkey is a number, beginning with 01 for the first network adapter:

```
HKEY_LOCAL_MACHINE\SOFTWARE\Microsoft\Windows NT\CurrentVersion
    \NetworkCards\netcard#\NetRules
```

Bindable   REG_MULTI_SZ   *fromClass toClass Yes|No Yes|No value*

Defines a possible binding and its constraints. For example:

```
bindable = ndisDriver ndisAdapter non exclusive 100
```

This example specifies that components of class "ndisDriver" can be bound to those of class "ndisAdapter." For the other fields in this example:

- Non indicates that the component of class ndisDriver can accept other bindings

- Exclusive indicates that the component of class ndisAdapter cannot accept other bindings

- 100 indicates the relative importance (weight) of this binding; that is, in cases of competition, it will be discarded in favor of other bindings whose weight is greater.

Because this value entry is a REG_MULTI_SZ, as many criteria for binding as necessary can be defined by a single component.

This value entry is optional, because there are a few predefined binding rules, and binding rules defined anywhere in the system apply to all network component classes.

Bindform   REG_SZ   *ObjectName Yes|No Yes|No [container|simple|streams]*

The *ObjectName* field contains the name (or name prefix) by which the component is identified by the system. This value must be the same as the name in the related CurrentControlSet\Services subkey. Names for adapters are created by the system and override the **Bindform** setting.

The first Yes|No pair indicates whether the component is to receive binding information directly in its Linkage subkey. The second Yes|No pair indicates whether the device name is supposed to appear in generated binding strings.

The final optional value in this entry indicates how binding device names are constructed. This value is required for software components.

Class   REG_MULTI_SZ   *NewClassName OldClassName|basic [Yes|No]*

Allows a component to define a new class. As many new classes as necessary can be defined by any component.

Note These classes are not related to the OLE and DDE classes defined under HKEY_LOCAL_MACHINE\SOFTWARE\Classes.

Class names do not need to be defined within any particular component. The system adds the new definition to its database without regard to origin. The order of **Class** entries is irrelevant. However, results are indeterminate if classes are referred to that are not defined anywhere in the system.

This entry is optional, because there are a few predefined classes, and class definitions made anywhere in the system apply to all network components. Because any network component can define new classes, be careful that the names used are unique within all possible installable network components. The following shows the predefined class names in the first release of Windows NT. This list, of course, cannot be exhaustive.

Predefined class	Adapter card type
ee16Driver; ee16Adapter	Intel EtherExpress 16 LAN adapter
elnkiiAdapter; elinkiiDriver	3Com Etherlink II® adapter
ibmtokDriver; ibmtokAdapter	IBM Token Ring adapter
lanceDriver; dec101Adapter	DEC Lance adapter
lt200Driver; lt200Adapter	Daystar Digital LocalTalk adapter
ne2000Driver; ne2000Adapter	Novell NE2000 adapter
proteonDriver; p1390Adapter	Proteon adapter
ubDriver; ubAdapter	Ungermann-Bass Ethernet NIUpc adapter
wdlanDriver; smcisaAdapter	SMC® (WD) adapter

The final optional value indicates whether this class is a "logical end-point" for the bindings protocol; the default value is No.

NetRules Subkey Entries

Hidden   REG_DWORD   *0 or 1*

Suppresses the display of the component (adapter or network software) in the Network dialog box in Control Panel.

Usually, all networking components discovered in the Registry are displayed in the two list boxes in the Network dialog box in Control Panel. Setting this value to 1 prevents the item from being displayed, which means it cannot be configured or removed by the user.

Interface   REG_MULTI_SZ

Allows a single component to make available more than one type of capability to other components in the system. The format for this value is:

```
Interface = interfaceName upperClass "objectName" namingMethod
```

Value	Meaning
interfaceName	The tokenized name of the secondary interface.
upperClass	The class to which the interface belongs. (*LowerClass* is the same as the primary interface.)
objectName	The Windows NT device name to be created.
namingMethod	Determines how the bindings appear.

Review   REG_DWORD   *0 or 1*

Indicates whether a component requests bindings review. If set to 1 (or nonzero), the system reinvokes this component's .INF file after bindings have been changed. This allows network components to modify the binding information or request additional information from administrators about the new or altered connections.

Type   REG_SZ   *component className [lowerClass]*

Defines the type of the component in terms of abstract network component classes. If the optional lower class name is absent, the first (or upper level) class type name is used for both its upper and lower classes.

This value is required for network software and network adapter cards.

Component type	Meaning
Adapter	A piece of hardware
Driver	A software component associated directly with a piece of hardware
Transport	A software component used by services
Service	A software component providing capability directly to user applications
Basic	A token used to represent a fundamental class name (that is, a class with no parent)

Use   REG_SZ   *service\driver\transport\adapter   [Yes\No]   [Yes\No]*

Defines the role played by the component. If this entry is absent, the value of Service is assumed. This value entry only appears for software items.

A hardware device is automatically assumed to be an adapter. Each network component may identify itself as a driver, transport, or service to clarify its role. This distinction is as follows (note the lowercase for the values):

Value	Meaning
driver	Exists only to support one or more adapters. If no bindings are generated (or permitted by the user) that include a particular driver, that driver is not loaded. However, no error is generated, since no "denial of service" has occurred.
service	Provides end-user functionality, and every attempt is made to support its operation. An EventLog entry is generated if a service is present in the system for which there is no available transport (the number of possible bindings is zero).
transport	Exists only to support services. Like a driver, it is not loaded unless necessary.

The final two Yes\No values in this entry are optional; if present; each must be either Yes or No. The first value indicates whether driver group names are used instead of specific driver dependencies. The second value indicates whether transport group names are used instead of specific transport dependencies. These values cause the system to generate references to dependencies based upon their group names, not by their specific service names.

For example, the LanmanServer is marked as Yes Yes; this means that its transport and driver dependencies are at the group level; so LanmanServer will be loaded if any one of its transport dependencies and any one of its driver dependencies successfully load.

Linkage Subkey Entries for Network Components

Each network component that the system determines to be required can be given bindings, which establish the relationships between network software components, as described in "Bindings for Network Components" in Chapter 11, "Overview of the Windows NT Registry." All bindings are created by the system and should not be changed by the user, except by choosing the Bindings button in the Network dialog box in Control Panel.

Whether the bindings actually appear in the Registry depends upon the **Bindform** value for the component in its NetRules subkey.

The binding information is stored in three value entries in the Linkage subkey for a component under the Services subkey. The Registry path for each Linkage subkey is the following:

```
HKEY_LOCAL_MACHINE\SYSTEM\CurrentControlSet\Services
    \ServiceName\Linkage
```

If a binding is disabled, the settings are stored under a Disabled subkey under the Linkage subkey. These values are in exactly the same format as for active bindings.

For a network component, there might be more than one subkey under its Services subkey: one for the driver and one for the network adapter card, plus additional subkeys for services that might be installed with the network adapter. Also, entries for adapter cards for AppleTalk, DLC (Data Link Control), NWLink, and TCP/IP are described in their respective sections in "Registry Entries for Network Services," later in this chapter.

Bind   REG_MULTI_SZ   *ObjectName ObjectName ...*

Each string in this value entry is the name of a Windows NT object created by the underlying software. The names are based on the object names declared in the **Bindform** entry under the NetRules subkey.

Export   REG_MULTI_SZ   *ObjectName ObjectName ...*

Each string in this value entry indicates the name that should be added in the system to allow access to the corresponding bound object. The names are based on the object names declared in the **Bindform** entry under the NetRules subkey.

Route   REG_MULTI_SZ   *"Name of service" "Name of service"...*

Each string in this value entry indicates the exact path through the binding protocol represented by the binding. The names of services are used, surrounded by quotation marks.

Each element of these multistring values has a one-to-one correspondence with the others; that is, **Bind[1]** is to **Export[1]** and **Route[1]** as **Bind[2]** is to **Export[2]** and **Route[2]**.

In addition to generating binding information, the system determines each network component's complete set of dependencies, and stores them in the related subkey in the CurrentControlSet\Services subkey. For examples using these value entries, see "Bindings for Network Components" in Chapter 11, "Overview of the Windows NT Registry."

Parameters Subkey Entries for Network Adapter Cards

Each network adapter card has a Parameters subkey with value entries that contain the settings for interrupt number, I/O port, and other parameters. These entries are found under subkeys for specific adapter cards in this Registry path:

```
HKEY_LOCAL_MACHINE\SYSTEM\CurrentControlSet
    \Services\adapter name#\Parameters
```

These values should all be set by choosing the Network icon in Control Panel. These value entries are provided here for informational purposes only. For a list of default values for network adapter card settings, see the table at the end of this section.

BusNumber   REG_DWORD   *Number*

Defines the bus number, beginning with 0 in the common case where the computer has one bus type, whether it is ISA, EISA, MCA, or TurboChannel. For the rare computer that has more than one bus, bus number 2 has the value of 1, and so on.

Note   If you install an ISA network adapter card on a PCI bus computer and the network is not recognized, set **BusNumber** to 0 and your network adapter card will be recognized.

Default: Usually 0 (depends on the installation)

BusType   REG_DWORD   *Number*

Specifies the bus type for the computer, as in the following list:

Value	Bus type
0	MIPS (Jazz-Internal bus)
1	ISA bus
2	EISA bus
3	MCA bus
4	TcChannel bus

This value should be maintained by the system. You cannot change it using the Network dialog box in Control Panel.

CableType   REG_DWORD   *1 or 2*

Specifies the cable type as unshielded twisted pair (UTP=1) or shielded twisted pair (STP=2), for Proteon 1390 adapter cards.

CardSpeed   REG_DWORD *4 or 16 megabits per second*

Specifies card speed as 4 or 16 megabits per second in hex (0x4 or 0x10), for Proteon 1390 adapter cards.

CardType   REG_DWORD *Number*

Specifies the card installed in the system. For some manufacturers, all their network cards use the same driver, which checks the value of **CardType** to determine the network card model number of the installed card. For example:

CardType value	Network card model number
DEC:	
1	DEC100
2	DEC20x
3	DEC PC
4	DEC Station
5	DEC422
7	DEC101
Proteon:	
1	Proteon 1390
2	Proteon 1990
Ungermann-Bass:	
2	UB PC
3	UB EOTP
4	UBPS

This value should be maintained by the system. You cannot change it using the Network dialog box in Control Panel.

DMAChannel   REG_DWORD *5, 6, or 7*

Specifies the DMA channel used by the adapter card.

InterruptNumber   REG_DWORD *IRQ number*

Specifies the interrupt level (IRQ) for the adapter card. IRQ5 is a common choice (0x5).

IoBaseAddress   REG_DWORD   *Number in hex*

For some adapters, this entry specifies the I/O port base address as a hexadecimal string. For other adapters, this entry specifies whether this is the primary adapter card (1) or a secondary card (2).

MediaType   REG_DWORD   *Number*

Specifies the network type, as follows:

Value	Network type
1	Ethernet
2	IBM Token Ring
3	ARCnet
4	FDDI network
5	Apple LocalTalk

This value should be maintained by the system. You cannot change it using the Network dialog box in Control Panel.

MaximumPacketSize   REG_DWORD   *Number*

Specifies the maximum packet size that the IBM Token Ring adapter is allowed to transmit. Use this parameter when sending data across bridges that may have smaller packet sizes available on the destination network than on the native network. You cannot change this parameter using the Network dialog box in Control Panel.

MemoryMapped   REG_DWORD   *0 or 1*

Specifies whether the adapter card is memory mapped.

MemoryMappedBaseAddress   REG_DWORD   *Memory address in hex*

Specifies the base memory (I/O) address used by the adapter card. This number must match the card's memory address settings as specified by its manufacturer.

NetworkAddress   REG_SZ   *Number*

Specifies the address the network adapter should use instead of the burned-in address. For example, for the IBM Token Ring card, this value is 40000000203. You can change this value for Token Ring adapters using the Network dialog box in Control Panel, but not for Ethernet adapters.

Transceiver   REG_DWORD   *1 or 2*

Specifies the transceiver as External (1) or OnBoard (2). This value should be 1 for a DEC/Intel/Xerox (DIX) connection.

Parameters Subkey Entries for Network Adapter Cards

The following table summarizes default settings for various card types.

Card name	Default setting
3Com [1]**:**	
EtherLink® II, EtherLink II / TP, EtherLink II/ 16, or EtherLink II/ 16 TP	**InterruptNumber** = 3 **IoBaseAddress** = 0x300 **Transceiver** = Internal **MemoryMapped** = Off
EtherLink 16/16 TP	**InterruptNumber** = 5 **IoBaseAddress** = 0x300 **MemoryMappedAddress** = 0xD0000 **MemorySize** = 16 **Transceiver** = Internal
DEC [1]**:**	
EtherWORKS Turbo EISA	**SlotNumber** = 1
EtherWORKS LC, EtherWORKS Turbo, or EtherWORKS Turbo / TP	**InterruptNumber** = 5 **MemoryAddress** = 0xD0000 **IoBaseAddress** = Primary
IBM [1]**:**	
Token Ring 16/4	**IoBaseAddress** = Primary
Novell [1]**:**	
NE2000	**InterruptNumber** = 3 **IoBaseAddress** = 0x300
Proteon [1]**:**	
P1390	**InterruptNumber** = 5 **IoBaseAddress** = 0xa20 **DMAChannel** = 5 **CableType** = STP **CardSpeed** = 16
SMC®/Western Digital™**:**	
8003EP, 8013EWC, or 8013WB	**InterruptNumber** = 3 **MemoryBaseAddress** = 0xD000 **IoBaseAddress** = 0x300
Ungermann-Bass®[1]**:**	
Ethernet NIUpc (long) or Ethernet NIUpc/EOTP (short)	**InterruptNumber** = 5 **IoBaseAddress** = 0x368 **MemoryMappedAddress** = 0xD8000

1 Settings are not required for EtherLink / MC, DEC PC, IBM Token Ring 16/4A, Proteon P1990, Novell NE3200, SMC/Western Digital 8013EA, and the Ungermann-Bass Ethernet NIUps (MC) or Ethernet NIUps/EOTP (short MC).

Parameters Subkey Entries for Network Adapter Cards

Registry Entries for Device Drivers

The following device drivers have additional value entries that can be specified in the Registry, in addition to changes that you can make using the Devices or Drivers icon in Control Panel. These types of services and drivers appear in the Registry and are described in this section:

- File system drivers and recognizers
- Disk, serial, and parallel port devices
- Keyboard and mouse devices
- SCSI miniport devices
- Sound cards
- Video display devices

Tip You can view current settings for these device drivers by choosing the Devices button in WinMSD.

File System Drivers and Recognizers

Each file system supported by Windows NT is made up of three components: the file system driver, the file system utility DLL, and the file system recognizer used during startup to determine the file systems present on the system. All necessary elements and settings are recognized automatically by Windows NT. You can configure file system drivers by choosing the Devices icon in Control Panel.

File system driver and recognizer	File System
Cdfs and Cdfs_Rec	Compact disc file system (CDFS)
Fastfat and Fat_Rec	File Allocation Table (FAT)
Ntfs and Ntfs_Rec	Windows NT file system (NTFS)
Pinball and HPFS_Rec	High-performance file system (HPFS)

The Registry path for settings that control file system drivers is the following, where *DriverName* is the file system driver minus the filename extension:

```
HKEY_LOCAL_MACHINE\SYSTEM\CurrentControlSet\Services\DriverName
```

The standard entries for the file system drivers are the following:

Value entry	Default value
ErrorControl	0x1 (Normal)
Group	Boot file system
Start	0x4 (disabled)
Type	0x2 (file system driver)

The file system recognizer determines whether the file system should be loaded. The Registry path for file system recognizers is the following, where *RecognizerName* is the file system driver minus the filename extension:

```
HKEY_LOCAL_MACHINE\SYSTEM\CurrentControlSet\Services\RecognizerName
```

The standard entries for the file system recognizers are the following:

Value entry	Default value
ErrorControl	0 (startup halts)
Group	Boot file system
Start	0x1 (system)
Type	0x8 (file system recognizer)

The file system drivers and recognizers do not add any additional Registry entries besides the standard entries described in "CurrentControlSet\Services Subkeys," earlier in this chapter.

Note If CONVERT.EXE has been used to convert the file system on a hard disk drive, this value is added to CurrentControlSet\Control\SessionManager so that conversion occurs when the system is restarted:

```
BootExecute = autocheck autoconv \DosDevices\x: /FS:NTFS
```

File System Drivers and Recognizers

Disk, Serial, and Parallel Port Entries

This section provides general information about the Description entries for adapters in the Hardware subtree. Then specific information is presented about the DeviceMap subkey entries for AtDisk and for serial and parallel ports. Finally, Services subkey entries for parallel and serial ports are described, including specific entries for multiport serial I/O cards.

Description Entries for Adapters

The following shows the path for all *MultifunctionAdapter* entries:

```
HKEY_LOCAL_MACHINE\HARDWARE\Description\System
    \MultifunctionAdapter\0\ControllerName\0.
```

The entries in this portion of the Registry contain data discovered by the Hardware Recognizer (NTDETECT.COM) or provided from the ARC database that describes controllers for hard disks, display devices, the keyboard, pointing devices, and serial and parallel ports. Administrators cannot usefully modify entries in the Hardware subtree. This data is volatile (destroyed and recreated each time the system starts) and is useful only for informational purposes. You can use WinMSD to view this information in a more usable format.

Each subkey contains information in the following format:

Component Information   REG_BINARY   *System-defined*
Identifies version information plus other data for the associated subkey entry.

Configuration Data   REG_UNKNOWN   *System-defined*
Contains binary information related to the hardware component, such as I/O port addresses and IRQ number. This entry is not present if no such data is available for a particular subkey.

Identifier   REG_SZ   *Device type name*
Contains the name of a component, if specified.

The following samples from the *MultifunctionAdapter* subkeys describe a system that has a keyboard, a Microsoft InPort® bus mouse or Microsoft Mouse Port mouse, and a Microsoft serial mouse (on COM1), all connected to the ISA bus. This sample is for informational purposes only, since these subkeys are volatile and are therefore recreated each time you start Windows NT.

In the following example, the **Identifier** value specifies the keyboard type name, which is typically PCAT_ENHANCED to indicate a 101/102-key enhanced keyboard. The keyboard type name is mainly informational, since the actual keyboard type and subtype are retrieved from the keyboard-specific data in **Configuration Data**.

```
HKEY_LOCAL_MACHINE\HARDWARE\Description\System\MultifunctionAdapter
    \0\KeyboardController\0\KeyboardPeripheral\0

Configuration Data : REG_UNKNOWN : Device data (keyboard type, subtype)
Identifier : REG_SZ : PCAT_ENHANCED
```

The following two examples show typical **Identifier** values for two basic types of pointer devices. For the first example, the **Identifier** value for the pointer type name can also be MICROSOFT PS2 MOUSE (also known as the Mouse Port mouse) or MICROSOFT BUS MOUSE under this subkey:

```
HKEY_LOCAL_MACHINE\HARDWARE\Description\System\MultifunctionAdapter
    \0\PointerController\0\PointerPeripheral\0

Identifier : REG_SZ : MICROSOFT INPORT MOUSE
```

This example shows a typical entry for a serial mouse, under this subkey:

```
HKEY_LOCAL_MACHINE\HARDWARE\Description\System\MultifunctionAdapter
    \0\SerialController\0\PointerPeripheral\0

Identifier : REG_SZ : MICROSOFT SERIAL MOUSE
```

DeviceMap Subkey Entries for AtDisk

AtDisk is the driver for non-SCSI hard disk controllers on x86-based computers.

Note The Abiosdsk driver has no Hardware key and no parameters that users can set under CurrentControlSet\Services.

The following Registry path can contain subkeys named Controller$x$, where x starts at 0 and increases:

```
HKEY_LOCAL_MACHINE\HARDWARE\DeviceMap\AtDisk
```

These Controller$x$ subkeys are created for each non-SCSI hard disk controller on the system. As with all hardware data, these subkeys are volatile and so are recreated each time you start the system.

Under the Controller*x* subkeys are subkeys named Disk*y*, where *y* starts at 0 (zero) and increases. These subkeys are created for each actual disk controlled by the particular controller.

Under the Disk*y* subkeys are the following value entries, which can be extremely helpful in reporting disk problems:

Firmware revision   REG_SZ   *Free format*
Defined by the disk manufacturer to identify the version of the on-board code used to control the disk.

Identifier   REG_SZ   *Free format*
Defined by the disk manufacturer to identify the make and model of the disk.

Number of cylinders   REG_DWORD   *A hex value*
The number of cylinders on the drive.

Number of heads   REG_DWORD   *A hex value*
The number of heads on the drive.

Sectors per track   REG_DWORD   *A hex value*
The number of sectors that exist on a track. These are typically 512-byte sectors.

The standard entries for AtDisk under the CurrentControlSet\Services subkey are the following:

Value entry	Default value
ErrorControl	0 (startup halts)
Group	Primary disk
Start	0x0 (boot)
Tag	0x2
Type	0x1 (Kernel driver)

DeviceMap Subkey Entries for Serial and Parallel Ports

Remember that the entries in HKEY_LOCAL_MACHINE\HARDWARE are recreated each time the system is started. The entries in these subkeys are described here for informational purposes only.

Parallel*X*   REG_SZ   *A string, typically LPTy*
HKEY_LOCAL_MACHINE\HARDWARE\DEVICEMAP\PARALLEL PORTS

Specifies that the Windows NT Parallel device *X* is the actual device for the
MS-DOS name LPT*y*. These value entries are used to determine all the parallel
ports available on the system.

Serial*X*   REG_SZ   *A string, typically COMy*
HKEY_LOCAL_MACHINE\HARDWARE\DeviceMap\Serialcomm

Specifies that the Windows NT Serial device *X* is the actual device for the
MS-DOSMS-DOS name COM*y*. These value entries are used to determine all
the communication ports available on the system.

Parallel Subkey Entries in the Services Subkey

The following subkeys and values can be found under the following subkey:

HKEY_LOCAL_MACHINE\System\CurrentControlSet\Services\Parallel

Subkeys and values under the Parallel subkey can be used to configure parallel
(printer) ports in addition to information that the Hardware Recognizer finds at
system startup.

This can also be used to override values determined by the Hardware Recognizer. If
the **PortAddress** value entry is the same as a system-detected port, this data in the
current control set will be used instead of the data found by the system. Entries
appear in the System log in Event Viewer if this is occurring.

The Parallel subkey contains a subkey named Parameters, under which is a set
of subkeys typically named Parallel*x* where *x* is some whole number. A system
administrator must place these subkeys and values into the Registry. There exists
no tool other than Registry Editor to define and manipulate these values.

For example, under the Parallel2 subkey, the following value entries can appear.

The first two of these value entries are required. If the section does not include both,
the port is not configured and an error appears in the System log in Event Viewer. If
an entry is placed into the Registry with just these values, the port will be driven
using polling algorithms.

DosDevices   REG_SZ   *Free-form string*
Specifies the name used to access the parallel port from the command prompt or
from within an application. A typical value would be LPT3.

PortAddress   REG_DWORD   *A hex value*
Denotes the address of the first register of the parallel port. A typical
PortAddress in this case would be 0x278.

The following values are optional:

DisablePort   REG_DWORD   *0 or 1*

If the value is a 1, the device will be deleted after the port is reset during initialization. No access to the port will be allowed.

Default: 0

Interrupt   REG_DWORD   *A hex value*

Denotes the IRQ that the particular device would interrupt on. A typical **Interrupt** value in this case would be 0x5.

The standard entries for the Parallel subkey are the following:

Value entry	Default value
ErrorControl	0 (startup halts)
Group	Extended base
Start	0x2 (autoload)
Type	0x1 (Kernel device driver)

Serial Subkey Entries in the Services Subkey

The values for serial ports are under the following Registry path:

`HKEY_LOCAL_MACHINE\System\CurrentControlSet\Services\Serial`

Subkeys and values under the CurrentControlSet\Services subkey can be used to configure serial ports in addition to information that the Hardware Recognizer finds at system startup. This can also be used to override values determined by the Hardware Recognizer. If the **PortAddress** value entry is the same as a system-detected port, this data in the current control set will be used instead of the data found by the system. Entries appear in the System log in Event Viewer if this is occurring.

The Serial subkey contains a subkey named Parameters, under which is a set of subkeys typically named Serial*X* where *X* is a whole number. A system administrator must place these subkeys and values into the Registry. You can only define and manipulate these values by using Registry Editor.

For example, under the Serial2 subkey, the following value entries can appear.

The first three of these value entries are required. If the subkey does not include all three, the port is not configured, and an error appears in the System log in Event Viewer.

DosDevices   REG_SZ   *Free-form string*

Specifies the name used to access the communication port from the command prompt or from within an application. A typical value would be COM3.

Interrupt   REG_DWORD   *A hex value*

Denotes the IRQ that the particular device would interrupt on. A typical **Interrupt** value in this case would be 0x4.

PortAddress   REG_DWORD   *A hex value*

Denotes the address of the first register of the serial device. A typical **PortAddress** in this case would be 0x3e8.

The following entry values are optional:

DisablePort   REG_DWORD   *0 or 1*

If the value is 1, the device will be deleted after the port is reset during initialization. No access to the port will be allowed.

Default: 0

ForceFifoEnable   REG_DWORD   *0 or 1*

If the value is 1 and the hardware supports a FIFO buffer (for example, the NS 16550AFN), the driver enables the FIFO. Not all FIFOs are reliable. If the application or the user notices lost data or no data transmission, it is recommended that this value be set to 0.

Default: 1

The standard entries for the Serial subkey are the following:

Value entry	Default value
ErrorControl	0 (startup halts)
Group	Extended base
Start	0x2 (autoload)
Type	0x1 (Kernel device driver)

Multiport Serial I/O Card Entries in the Services Subkey

In addition to controlling the standard serial ports included with most personal computers, the Microsoft serial driver can be used to control many *dumb* multiport serial cards. Dumb denotes that the control includes no onboard processor.

At least the following two additional value entries are used for each port on the multiport card. Each of these two entries must be included for each port of the multiport board under subkey entries in CurrentControlSet\Services:

InterruptStatus   REG_DWORD   *A hex value*

Denotes the address of the interrupt status register that indicates which port on the multiport card is actually requesting an interrupt. To determine the appropriate value, consult the manufacturer's installation guide.

PortIndex   REG_DWORD   *A hex value*

Denotes which port on the card this information is for. These values start at 1 and increase. Typically these would be the same as the values inscribed on the connector for the multiport.

Certain multiport boards, such as Digiboard non-MCA bus cards, use a different scheme to determine which port is interrupting. These boards should include the following value entry in the configuration data:

Indexed   REG_DWORD   *Should be 1*

Denotes that this board uses an indexed interrupt notification scheme as opposed to a bitmapped method. To determine whether this entry should be included, consult the board's manufacturer.

For detailed examples describing entries for four-port and eight-port communications boards, see "Controlling Multiport Serial I/O Cards" in Chapter 12, "Configuration Management and the Registry."

Mouse and Keyboard Driver Entries

Parameters in this section are for the mouse and keyboard class and port drivers, including these drivers:

Busmouse	Mouclass	Kbdclass
Inport	i8042prt	Sermouse

Microsoft Bus Mouse Port Driver Entries

The following value entries for the Microsoft bus mouse are found in this subkey:

```
HKEY_LOCAL_MACHINE\SYSTEM\CurrentControlSet\Services\Busmouse\Parameters
```

MouseDataQueueSize   REG_DWORD   *>= 0x1*

Specifies the number of mouse events to be buffered internally by the driver, in nonpaged pool. The allocated size, in bytes, of the internal buffer is this value times the size of the MOUSE_INPUT_DATA structure (defined in NTDDMOU.H). Consider increasing the size if the System log in Event Viewer frequently contains this message from the Busmouse source: "The ring buffer that stores incoming mouse data has overflowed (buffer size is configurable via the Registry)."

Default: 0x64 (100)

NumberOfButtons   REG_DWORD   *>= 0x1*

Specifies the number of buttons on the bus mouse. If the number of buttons detected at startup time and placed in the Registry is incorrect, this value can be used to override it.

Default: 0x2 (two buttons)

PointerDeviceBaseName   REG_SZ   *Base port device name*

Specifies the base name for the device object(s) created by the bus mouse port device driver. The device driver also writes information about the device objects into HKEY_LOCAL_MACHINE\HARDWARE\DeviceMap so that the pointer class driver can locate the pointer port device objects.

Default: PointerPort

SampleRate   REG_DWORD   *Mouse sample rate in Hz*

Specifies the sample rate for the bus mouse. Intended for future use. This value might have no effect in the first release of Windows NT.

Default: 0x32 (50 Hz)

Intel 8042 Port Driver Entries

The i8042prt driver handles the keyboard and mouse port mouse (also known as a PS/2-compatible mouse) for the Intel 8042 controller. These value entries are found in the following subkey:

```
HKEY_LOCAL_MACHINE\SYSTEM\CurrentControlSet\Services\i8042prt\Parameters
```

KeyboardDataQueueSize   REG_DWORD   *>= 0x1*

Specifies the number of keyboard events to be buffered internally by the driver, in nonpaged pool. The allocated size, in bytes, of the internal buffer is this value times the size of the KEYBOARD_INPUT_DATA structure (defined in NTDDKBD.H). Consider increasing the size if the System log in Event Viewer contains the following message from the i8042prt source: "The ring buffer that stores incoming keyboard data has overflowed (buffer size is configurable via the Registry)."

Default: 0x64 (100)

KeyboardDeviceBaseName   REG_SZ   *Base keyboard port device name*

Specifies the base name for the keyboard device object(s) created by the i8042prt device driver. The device driver also writes information about the device objects into HKEY_LOCAL_MACHINE\HARDWARE\DeviceMap so that the keyboard class driver can locate the keyboard port device objects.

Default: KeyboardPort

MouseDataQueueSize   REG_DWORD   *>= 0x1*

Specifies the number of mouse events to be buffered internally by the driver, in nonpaged pool. Consider increasing the size if the System log in Event Viewer contains the following message from the i8042prt source: "The ring buffer that stores incoming mouse data has overflowed (buffer size is configurable via the Registry)."

Default: 0x64 (100)

MouseResolution   REG_DWORD   *Mouse resolution specifier*

Used in specifying the mouse port mouse resolution, where 2 to the power of **MouseResolution** specifies counts-per-millimeter.

Default: 0x3

MouseSynchIn100ns   REG_DWORD   *Time, in 100 nanosecond units*

Specifies the length of time after which the next mouse interrupt is assumed to indicate the start of a new mouse packet (partial packets are discarded). This allows the driver to synchronize its internal notion of the mouse packet state with the hardware state, in the event that a mouse interrupt has been lost. Consider modifying this value if the system behaves as if there are random mouse events occurring (for example, button clicks when no mouse button has been pressed).

Default: 10000000 (1 second)

NumberOfButtons   REG_DWORD   *>= 0x1*

Specifies the number of buttons on the mouse port mouse. If an incorrect number of buttons is detected at startup time and placed in the Registry, this value can be used to override it.

Default: 0x2

PointerDeviceBaseName   REG_SZ   *Base mouse port device name*

Specifies the base name for the pointer device object(s) created by the mouse port mouse driver. The device driver also writes information about the device object into HKEY_LOCAL_MACHINE\HARDWARE\DeviceMap so that the pointer class driver can locate the pointer port device objects.

Default: PointerPort

PollStatusIterations   REG_DWORD   *Number*

Specifies the maximum number of times to check the i8042 controller status register for interrupt verification before dismissing the interrupt as spurious. This value can be used to work around a problem experienced on some hardware (including the Olivetti MIPS computers) where the keyboard interrupt is raised before the Output Buffer Full bit is set in the i8042 status register.

Increase this value if the system seems to suddenly stop taking keyboard interrupts. This can happen if a keyboard interrupt is mistakenly dismissed as spurious, when instead it just took too long to set Output Buffer Full after raising the interrupt. Increasing the value of **PollStatusIterations** results in a longer execution time for the Interrupt Service Routine if the keyboard interrupt truly is spurious (there is a 1 microsecond delay following each check for Output Buffer Full).

To determine whether the driver is taking keyboard interrupts, press the NUMLOCK key. If the NumLock light on the keyboard turns on or off, this indicates that the i8042prt driver handled the keyboard interrupt correctly.

Default: 1

Mouse and Keyboard Driver Entries

OverrideKeyboardType   REG_DWORD   >= *0x0*

This entry is not usually present. When present, it specifies the keyboard type (overriding the keyboard type detected during system initialization). Add this value entry if the detected keyboard type is incorrect in the Registry. Type values 0x2 and 0x4 indicate an enhanced 101-key or 102-key keyboard, or compatible; other values typically indicate an old-style AT keyboard (83, 84, or 86 keys), or compatible.

Default: 0x4 (Enhanced 101-key or 102-key keyboard)

OverrideKeyboardSubtype   REG_DWORD   >= *0x0*

This entry is not usually present. When present, it specifies the OEM-dependent keyboard subtype (overriding the keyboard subtype detected during system initialization).

Default: 0x0

PollingIterations   REG_DWORD   >= *0x400*

Specifies the standard number of times to poll the hardware (in polling mode) before giving up and timing out the operation. Consider increasing this value if the driver fails to initialize or work correctly and the System log in Event Viewer contains the following message from the i8042prt source: "The operation on ... timed out (time out is configurable via the Registry)."

Default: 0x400

PollingIterationsMaximum   REG_DWORD   >= *0x400*

Specifies the maximum number of times to poll the hardware (in polling mode) before giving up and timing out the operation. This value is used instead of **PollingIterations** when an old-style AT keyboard is detected (see **OverrideKeyboardType**).

Consider increasing this value if the driver fails to initialize or work correctly and the System log in Event Viewer contains the following message from the i8042prt source: "The operation on ... timed out (time out is configurable via the Registry)."

Default: 0x2EE0

ResendIterations   REG_DWORD   >= *0x1*

Specifies the maximum number of times a hardware operation will be retried before timing out. Consider increasing this value if the driver fails to initialize or work correctly and the System log in Event Viewer contains the following message from the i8042prt source: "Exceeded the allowable number of retries (configurable via the Registry) on device ..."

Default: 0x3

SampleRate   REG_DWORD   *Mouse sample rate in Hz*

Specifies the sample rate for the mouse. Intended for future use. This value might have no effect in the first release of Windows NT.

Default: 0x3C (60 Hz)

Microsoft InPort Bus Mouse Port Driver Entries

The value entries for the Microsoft InPort bus mouse are found in the following subkey:

HKEY_LOCAL_MACHINE\SYSTEM\CurrentControlSet\Services\Inport\Parameters

HzMode   REG_DWORD   *Mouse sample rate mode specifier*

Specifies the value written to the Microsoft InPort mode register to set the mouse sample rate. Might be used in the first release of Windows NT, but should become obsolete.

Default: 0x2 (selects 50 Hz)

MouseDataQueueSize   REG_DWORD   *>= 0x1*

Specifies the number of mouse events to be buffered internally by the driver, in nonpaged pool. The allocated size, in bytes, of the internal buffer is this value times the size of the MOUSE_INPUT_DATA structure (defined in NTDDMOU.H). Consider increasing the size if the System log in Event Viewer contains the following message from the InPort source: "The ring buffer that stores incoming mouse data has overflowed (buffer size is configurable via the Registry)."

Default: 0x64 (100)

NumberOfButtons   REG_DWORD   *>= 0x1*

Specifies the number of buttons on the Microsoft InPort bus mouse. If the number of buttons detected at startup time and placed in the Registry is incorrect, this value can be used to override it.

Default: 0x2

PointerDeviceBaseName   REG_SZ   *Base port device name*

Specifies the base name for the device object(s) created by the Microsoft InPort bus mouse device driver. The device driver also writes information about the device objects into HKEY_LOCAL_MACHINE\HARDWARE\DeviceMap so that the pointer class driver can locate the pointer port device objects.

Default: PointerPort

Mouse and Keyboard Driver Entries

SampleRate   REG_DWORD   *Mouse sample rate in Hz*

Specifies the sample rate for the Microsoft InPort bus mouse. Intended for future use. This value might have no effect in the first release of Windows NT.

Default: 0x32 (50 Hz)

Microsoft Serial Mouse Port Driver Entries

The value entries for the Microsoft serial mouse are found in the following subkey:

```
HKEY_LOCAL_MACHINE\SYSTEM\CurrentControlSet\Services\Sermouse\Parameters
```

MouseDataQueueSize   REG_DWORD   *>= 0x1*

Specifies the number of mouse events to be buffered internally by the driver, in nonpaged pool. The allocated size, in bytes, of the internal buffer is this value times the size of the MOUSE_INPUT_DATA structure (defined in NTDDMOU.H). Consider increasing the size if the System log in Event Viewer contains the following message from the Sermouse source: "The ring buffer that stores incoming mouse data has overflowed (buffer size is configurable via the Registry)."

Default: 0x64 (100)

NumberOfButtons   REG_DWORD   *>= 0x1*

Specifies the number of buttons on the serial mouse. If the number of buttons detected at startup time and placed in the Registry is incorrect, this value can be used to override it.

Default: 0x2

OverrideHardwareBitstring   REG_DWORD   *0x1 or 0x2*

This entry is not usually present. When present, it specifies that regardless of whether it was actually detected, a serial mouse is present on the system. Add this value to tell the driver to assume the serial mouse is on COM1 (specified by the value 0x1) or COM2 (specified by the value 0x2). This entry is useful if the serial mouse has not been automatically detected.

PointerDeviceBaseName   REG_SZ   *Base port device name*

Specifies the base name for the device object(s) created by the serial mouse device driver. The device driver also writes information about the device objects into HKEY_LOCAL_MACHINE\HARDWARE\DeviceMap so that the pointer class driver can locate the pointer port device objects.

Default: PointerPort

SampleRate   REG_DWORD   *Mouse sample rate in Hz*

Specifies the sample rate for the serial mouse. Intended for future use. This value might have no effect in the first release of Windows NT.

Default: 0x28 (1200 baud)

Mouse Class Driver Entries

The value entries for the mouse class driver are found in the following subkey:

HKEY_LOCAL_MACHINE\SYSTEM\CurrentControlSet\Services\Mouclass\Parameters

ConnectMultiplePorts   REG_DWORD   *0x0 or 0x1*

Specifies the type of connection between class and port device objects. This parameter is mainly of interest to device driver writers.

The value 0x0 specifies a 1:1 relationship between class device objects and port device objects. (That is, one class device object is created by the driver and connected to one port device object; the maximum number of objects created and connected to an associated port object is determined by the value of **MaximumPortsServiced**.) The value 0x1 specifies a 1:many relationship between a single class device object and multiple port device objects. (That is, one class device object is created by the driver and then connected to multiple port device objects, up to a maximum specified by **MaximumPortsServiced**.)

Default: 0x1 (The events generated by up to the **MaximumPortsServiced** number of pointing devices on the system will all be fed to the Windows subsystem in a single input stream.)

MaximumPortsServiced   REG_DWORD   *>= 0x1*

Specifies the number of port devices the mouse class device driver will connect to and service. The class device driver handles hardware-independent operations on a specific class of devices (in this case, the mouse and other pointing devices). The port drivers manage the hardware-specific operations.

Default: 0x3 (The class driver will service up to three pointing devices.)

MouseDataQueueSize   REG_DWORD   *>= 0x1*

Specifies the number of mouse events to be buffered internally by the driver, in nonpaged pool. The allocated size, in bytes, of the internal buffer is this value times the size of the MOUSE_INPUT_DATA structure (defined in NTDDMOU.H). Consider increasing the size if the System log in Event Viewer frequently contains the following message from the Mouclass source: "The ring buffer that stores incoming mouse data has overflowed (buffer size is configurable via the Registry)."

Default: 0x64 (100)

PointerDeviceBaseName   REG_SZ   *Base class device name*

Specifies the base name for the device object(s) created by the mouse class device driver. The device driver also writes information about the device object into HKEY_LOCAL_MACHINE\HARDWARE\DeviceMap so that the pointer class device object(s) can be easily located.

Default: PointerClass

Keyboard Class Driver Entries

The value entries for the keyboard class driver are found in the following subkey:

```
HKEY_LOCAL_MACHINE\SYSTEM\CurrentControlSet\Services\Kbdclass\Parameters
```

ConnectMultiplePorts   REG_DWORD   *0x0 or 0x1*

Specifies the type of connection between class and port device objects. This parameter is mainly of interest to device driver writers.

The value 0x0 specifies a 1:1 relationship between class device objects and port device objects. (That is, one class device object is created by the driver and connected to one port device object; the maximum number of objects created and connected to an associated port object is determined by the value of **MaximumPortsServiced**.) The value 0x1 specifies a 1:many relationship between a single class device object and multiple port device objects (That is, one class device object is created by the driver and then connected to multiple port device objects, up to a maximum specified by **MaximumPortsServiced**.)

Default: 0x0 (The events generated by up to the **MaximumPortsServiced** number of keyboard devices on the system will feed separate input streams. In the first release of Windows NT, the Windows subsystem only reads from a single keyboard input stream.)

KeyboardDataQueueSize   REG_DWORD   *>= 0x1*

Specifies the number of keyboard events to be buffered internally by the driver, in nonpaged pool. The allocated size, in bytes, of the internal buffer is this value times the size of the KEYBOARD_INPUT_DATA structure (defined in NTDDKBD.H). Consider increasing the size if the System log in Event Viewer contains the following message from the Kbdclass source: "The ring buffer that stores incoming keyboard data has overflowed (buffer size is configurable via the Registry)."

Default: 0x64 (100)

KeyboardDeviceBaseName   REG_SZ   *Base class device name*

Specifies the base name for the keyboard device object(s) created by the keyboard class device driver. The device driver also writes information about the device objects into HKEY_LOCAL_MACHINE\HARDWARE\DeviceMap so that the keyboard class device objects are easily located.

Default: KeyboardClass

MaximumPortsServiced   REG_DWORD   *>= 0x1*

Specifies the number of port devices the keyboard class device driver will connect to and service. The class device driver handles hardware-independent operations on a specific class of devices (in this case, keyboard devices). The port drivers manage the hardware-specific operations.

Default: 0x3 (The class driver will service up to three keyboard devices.)

DeviceMap Entries for the Keyboard and Mouse

The following DeviceMap descriptions are for informational purposes only, since the DeviceMap subkeys are volatile and are recreated each time you start Windows NT. Administrators cannot modify DeviceMap entries.

These DeviceMap entries are used by the Windows subsystem to locate the pointer and keyboard class devices, and by the pointer and keyboard class drivers to locate the associated pointer and keyboard port devices. Information is placed in the DeviceMap subkey by the keyboard and pointer class and port drivers.

The format for each of these entries is the following:

Name of class device object **: REG_SZ :** *Registry path to driver's Services*

The keyboard class information appears in the following Registry path:

```
HKEY_LOCAL_MACHINE\HARDWARE\DeviceMap\KeyboardClass
```

There can be one or more of these entries. Each entry specifies the name of a device object created by the keyboard class driver to represent the class device, followed by the Registry path to the driver's Services subkey.

Default:

```
\Device\KeyboardClass0 : REG_SZ :
\Registry\Machine\System\ControlSet001\Services\Kbdclass
```

The keyboard port information appears in the following Registry path:

```
HKEY_LOCAL_MACHINE\HARDWARE\DeviceMap\KeyboardPort
```

There can be one or more of these entries. Each entry specifies the name of a device object created by the keyboard port driver(s) to represent the physical keyboard (port) device, followed by the Registry path to the driver's Services subkey.

Default:

```
\Device\KeyboardPort0 : REG_SZ :
\Registry\Machine\System\ControlSet001\Services\i8042prt
```

The mouse class information appears in the following Registry path:

```
HKEY_LOCAL_MACHINE\HARDWARE\DeviceMap\PointerClass
```

There can be one or more of these entries. Each entry specifies the name of a device object created by the pointer (mouse) class driver to represent the class device, followed by the Registry path to the driver's Services subkey.

Default:

```
\Device\PointerClass0 : REG_SZ :
\Registry\Machine\System\ControlSet001\Services\Mouclass
```

The mouse port information appears in the following Registry path:

```
HKEY_LOCAL_MACHINE\HARDWARE\DeviceMap\PointerPort
```

There can be one or more of these entries. Each entry specifies the name of a device object created by the pointer port driver(s) to represent the physical pointing (port) device, followed by the Registry path to the driver's Services subkey.

Default (assumes mouse port, Microsoft InPort, and serial pointing devices are connected):

```
\Device\PointerPort0 : REG_SZ :
    \Registry\Machine\System\ControlSet001\Services\i8042prt
\Device\PointerPort1 : REG_SZ :
    \Registry\Machine\System\ControlSet001\Services\Inport
\Device\PointerPort2 : REG_SZ :
    \Registry\Machine\System\ControlSet001\Services\Sermouse
```

Mouse and Keyboard Driver Entries

SCSI Miniport Driver Entries

The basic SCSI miniport driver entries in the Registry are found under subkeys in the following path:

```
HKEY_LOCAL_MACHINE\System\CurrentControlSet\Services
```

Each subkey's name is the same as the driver's filename minus the .SYS filename extension; for example, FD8XX, which is the entry for all Future Domain 800-series SCSI adapter. The Registry includes entries for at least the following SCSI miniport device drivers:

Driver name	Description
Aha*xx*	Adaptec 154x and 174x SCSI adapters
DptScsi	DPT SCSI adapter
Fd16_700, Fd7000ex, Fd8xx	Future Domain MCS 600/MCS 700, TMC-7000ex, and 800-series SCSI adapters
Ncr53c9x, Ncrc700, Ncrc710	NCR SCSI controller and adapters
Oliscsi	Olivetti SCSI adapter
Sparrow	SCSI adapter
Spock	SCSI adapter
T128 and T13B	Trantor SCSI adapters
Ultra*xx*	UltraStor 124, 14f, and 24f SCSI adapters
Wd33c93	Maynard SCSI adapter

The contents of a SCSI miniport subkey are standard for all SCSI miniport drivers, with these basic value entries:

Value entry	Value
ErrorControl	0x01—which is the preferred value for **ErrorControl**. With a value of 0x01, the startup process continues if the SCSI miniport driver fails to initialize.
Group	SCSI Miniport.
Start	0x00 (Auto Start).
Tag	Optional (determines the load order of SCSI miniport drivers).
Type	0x01 (device driver).

For each SCSI miniport subkey, there can be one or more other subkeys named Parameters\Device or Parameters\Device$N$, where $N = 0, 1, 2$, and so on. The value of N corresponds to the SCSI host adapter number. If the subkey name is Device, the value is globally defined. If the subkey name is Device$N$, the value only pertains to the particular SCSI host adapter.

The SCSI miniport driver recognizes several optional value entries that can be defined under these subkeys, as described in this section.

InitiatorTargetId   REG_DWORD   *Number*

Sets the SCSI bus host adapter ID. It is used by host adapters that can set the initiator ID from software.

Default: Uninitialized

MaximumLogicalUnit   REG_DWORD   *Number*

Controls the number of logical units per target controller that are scanned for by the SCSI miniport driver. Most devices only support one logical unit, and some devices may fail if more than one logical unit is scanned for.

Default: 8

ScsiDebug   REG_DWORD   *Number*

This value is used to set the value of the ScsiDebug variable, which controls the verbosity of DebugPrint, with 0 being the least verbose. This is used for debugging.

Default: 0

The following value entries are used to fix problems such as device time-outs or controller detection errors but will reduce I/O performance. These value entries can be abbreviated. For example, a value entry of **Disable** will cause **DisableSynchronousTransfers**, **DisableTaggedQueuing**, **DisableDisconnects**, and **DisableMultipleRequests** to be set.

Note The system must be restarted before these options take effect.

BreakPointOnEntry   REG_DWORD   *0 or 1*

A DbgBreakPoint() call is immediately made inside of SpParseDevice. This is used for debugging.

Default: 0 (disabled)

DisableDisconnects   REG_DWORD   *0 or 1*

Disables disconnects on the SCSI bus. It causes all requests to be executed sequentially.

Default: 1 (enabled)

DisableMultipleRequests   REG_DWORD   *0 or 1*

Prevents the SCSI miniport driver from sending more than one request at a time per SCSI device.

Default: 1 (enabled)

DisableSynchronousTransfers   REG_DWORD   *0 or 1*

Disables synchronous data transfers on the SCSI bus.

Default: 1 (enabled)

DisableTaggedQueuing   REG_DWORD   *0 or 1*

Disables SCSI-II tagged command queuing on the host adapter.

Default: 1 (enabled)

DriverParameter   *Data type is specific to driver   A string*

A pointer to this data is passed to the SCSI miniport driver in a miniportFindAdapter routine. It is the fourth parameter, ArgumentString. A miniport driver uses this data to define the IRQ number for the SCSI host adapter, but other applications for the data are possible.

The data type for this value is defined by the specific SCSI miniport driver developer. If the data type is REG_SZ, the Unicode string is converted to an ANSI string before transferring it to the SCSI miniport driver.

The following drivers currently use the **DriverParameter** value entry:

Driver	Values	Meaning
Wd33c93	**IRQ**=*xx*; **DMA**=*yy*	*xx* is the IRQ the card should use. Valid values are: 3, 4, 5, 10, 11, 12, and 15. The default is 10. *yy* is the DMA channel the card should use. Valid values are: 5, 6, and 7. The default is 6.
Aha154*x*	**BusOnTime**=*xx*	*xx* is the bus on time in microseconds for the card. Valid values are 2–15. The default is 7. The value is usually adjusted downward when DMA transfers from the Adaptec card are interfering with other DMA transfers.
FD8*XX*	**IRQ**=*xx*	*xx* is the IRQ the card should use. Valid values are 0, 3, 4, 5, 10, 11, 12, 14, 15. This value should match the jumper settings on the card. Numbers 0, 3, and 5 are for the short cards (850, 845); the rest are for the 885 card only. A value of 0 indicates the card should not use any interrupts and will poll. The default is 5.

Driver *(continued)*	Values *(continued)*	Meaning *(continued)*
T128	**IRQ**=*xx*	*xx* is the IRQ the card should use. Valid values are: 0, 3, 5, 7 , 10, 12, 14, and 15. This value should match the jumper settings on the card. Numbers greater than 7 are for the T128F card only. A value of 0 indicates the card should not use any interrupts and will poll. The default is 5.
T13B	**IRQ**=*xx*	*xx* is the IRQ the card should use. Valid values are 0, 3, 5, and 7. This value should match the jumper settings on the card. A value of 0 indicates the card should not use any interrupts and will poll. The default is 5.
TMV1	**IRQ**=*xx*	*xx* is the IRQ the card should use. Valid values are: 2, 3, 4, 5, 6, 7, 10, 11, 12, and 15. The default is 10.

Sound Card Driver Entries

Usually, sound drivers consist of two parts: a front-end for installation and request processing, consisting of files such as SNDBLST.DLL or SYNTH.DLL; and a kernel driver for communicating with the hardware, consisting of files such as SNDBLST.SYS or SYNTH.SYS.

There is also a helper driver named MMDRV.DLL that transforms most low-level calls to Wave, MIDI, and AUX devices into calls to kernel mode drivers.

The installable sound kernel drivers for Windows NT are listed in the following table:

Sound driver	Comment
MIPSSND.SYS	MIPS ARCSystem 100/150 built-in sound
MVAUDIO.SYS	Media Vision Pro Audio Spectrum 16 and Pro Studio 16
MVOPL3.SYS	Synthesizer driver for Media Vision Pro Audio Spectrum 16 and Pro Studio 16
SNDBLST.SYS	Sound Blaster™ 1.5 and compatibles
SNDSYS.SYS	Windows sound system and COMPAQ® Business Audio
SYNTH.SYS	Ad Lib and OPL3 MIDI synthesizer driver

For each installed sound driver, several parameters are stored in the Registry, based on choices made by using the Drivers icon in Control Panel. The following shows the Registry path for sound system driver entries:

```
HKEY_LOCAL_MACHINE\SYSTEM\CurrentControlSet\  Services
    \SoundDriverName\Parameters\Device0
```

The actual subkey name in the Registry is the same as the filename of the related kernel driver. For example, for SNDBLST.SYS, the subkey name is Sndblst.

Some drivers can write over the values they receive on the basis of information read from the hardware. The following shows some typical values found in the Parameters subkey for sound cards:

Configuration Error   REG_DWORD   *0, 1, 2, 3, or 4*

Specifies an error that occurred during install. This value is only relevant if the driver fails to load. (Not all drivers write this information into the Registry.)

Value	Meaning
0	Nonspecific error
1	Hardware not found (usually the wrong I/O port was assumed)
2	Specified interrupt was incorrect or did not work
3	Specified DMA channel was incorrect or did not work
4	Hardware is present but not working

DmaChannel   REG_DWORD

Defines the DMA channel settings for transferring digitized sound.

Default: Depends on the sound card—not user-configurable.

Interrupt   REG_DWORD   *Interrupt number*

Defines the interrupt number used by the hardware.

Default: 0xa (configured for Interrupt 10)

LeftLineInAtten   REG_DWORD   *Number*

Specifies the current volume level of the left channel of the line-in input.

Port   REG_DWORD   *Address*

Defines the I/O port start address used to communicate with the hardware.

Default: 0x220 for SNDBLST.SYS

RightLineInAtten   REG_DWORD   *Number*

Specifies the current volume level of the right channel of the line-in input.

Video Device Driver Entries

This section describes the entries for video device drivers under the DeviceMap subkey and under the CurrentControlSet\Services subkeys for specific video drivers.

Video Information in the DeviceMap Subkey

The hardware device mapping for video is under the following subkey:

```
HKEY_LOCAL_MACHINE\Hardware\DeviceMap\Video
```

This information is volatile and is reconstructed at startup by the video port driver. It can change from startup to startup based on external factors, such as failure to initialize a video adapter or the addition of other video cards to the system.

This subkey contains the mappings from Windows NT logical video devices to the physical device they represent in the CurrentControlSet\Services subkey. This mapping allows the system to find the right display driver for the currently installed video device.

%device_object_name%   **REG_SZ**   *Registry path for device*
Indicates the first logical video device is the first physical adapter. For example, the following entry indicates that the first logical video device is the second physical XGA adapter:

```
Video\Device0 =
\Registry\Machine\CurrentControlSet\Services\XGA\Device1
```

In this example, the value indicates that the second logical video device is the first physical VGA adapter:

```
Video\Device1 =
\Registry\Machine\CurrentControlSet\Serivces\Vga\Device0
```

These values point to entries in the Services subkey, as described in the next section.

Video Driver Entries in the Services Subkey

The port driver portion of the video driver is hardware-independent and contains operating system-specific code. Therefore, the port driver, VIDEOPRT.SYS, can support one or more video devices. The Services\Videoprt subkey has no added parameters, and its standard entries are the following:

Value entry	Default value
ErrorControl	0x1 (Normal)
Group	Video
Start	0x1 (system)
Type	0x1 (Kernel driver)

The specific subkey for each video driver contains all the information required to initialize and program the device properly. If several adapters can be handled by a single driver, the subkeys Device1, Device2, and so on will contain information for the other devices. The Registry path looks like this, where *VideoDriverName* is the name of a specific video device driver:

```
HKEY_LOCAL_MACHINE\SYSTEM\CurrentControlSet\Services
    \VideoDriverName\Device0
```

The *VideoDriverName* subkeys for drivers in Windows NT include the following. This is not an exhaustive list:

Ati	ET4000	Jazzg*xxx*
S3	Trident	Vga
Wdvga	Xga	

For example, the following subkey contains information for the first logical device of type VGA:

```
HKEY_LOCAL_MACHINE\SYSTEM\CurrentControlSet\Services\Vga\Device0
```

The following values can be set in a video driver subkey.

DefaultSettings.BitsPerPel   REG_DWORD   *Number of bits per pixel*

Contains the number of colors for the mode requested by the user. For example, for the v7vram miniport, the following value yields a 256-color mode:

```
DefaultSettings.BitsPerPel = 8
```

DefaultSettings.Interlaced   REG_DWORD   *0 or 1*

Determines whether the mode requested by the user is interlaced. For example, for the v7vram miniport:

```
DefaultSettings.Interlaced = 0x0 (FALSE)
```

DefaultSettings.VRefresh   REG_DWORD   *Number Hz*

Contains the refresh rate of the mode requested by the user. For example, for the et4000 miniport:

```
DefaultSettings.VRefresh = 72
```

DefaultSettings.XResolution   REG_DWORD   *Number of pixels*

Contains the width of the mode requested by the user. For example, for the et4000 miniport:

```
DefaultSettings.Xresolution = 1024
```

DefaultSettings.YResolution   REG_DWORD   *Number of pixels*

Contains the height of the mode requested by the user. For example, for the et4000 miniport:

```
DefaultSettings.Yresolution = 768
```

DeviceData   REG_BINARY   *Binary code*

Contains binary data specific to the Windows display driver. For example, for the VGA miniport:

```
DeviceData = 05a0 5075 8ef0 8456 c8dd
```

InstalledDisplayDrivers   REG_MULTI_SZ   *Driver names*

Contains a list of names of display drivers that can function with this miniport, depending on which mode is selected by the user.

Note Display driver names do not contain the .DLL filename extension.

The system attempts to initialize the adapter by calling each display driver, using the user-selected parameter. If the combination of display driver and monitor do not support the mode requested by the user, the display driver fails to initialize and the system tries the next display driver. If all display drivers fail to initialize, the system calls the first display driver again to set the adapter to any mode it can.

For example, for the et4000 miniport:

```
InstalledDisplayDrivers = "vga" "vga256" "vga64k"
```

For the S3 miniport:

```
InstalledDisplayDrivers = "s3"
```

Monitor   REG_SZ   *Monitor name*

This entry is reserved to contain the name of the VESA VDIF monitor information file for the monitor connected to the adapter. No such files are provided with Windows NT in the current version.

If a file is supplied and a value is added, the miniport can load this file to determine the exact timings of the monitor connected to the physical device.

For example, for the XGA miniport, if a NEC4FS monitor was attached to the XGA card:

```
Monitor = "NEC4fg.vdb"
```

VgaCompatible   REG_DWORD   *0 or 1*

Determines whether the driver supports all of the VGA functionality required to perform full-screen operations.

If this value is 1, the driver supports full-screen applications in *x*86-based computers. If this value is 0, the VGA miniport (described under the Vga subkey) will also be used to enable and disable full-screen modes for non-Windows-based applications.

As a general rule, all drivers for SVGA adapters should set this value to 1, because they must implement all the VGA functionality to perform extended save/restore of all registers. A video accelerator designed as an accelerator working independently of the VGA miniport (via pass-through) can set this to 0 and let the VGA miniport do all the full-screen work.

For example, for the et4000 miniport:

```
VgaCompatible = 0x1 (TRUE)
```

For the S3 miniport:

```
VgaCompatible = 0x0 (FALSE)
```

This functionality is not required for other computer platforms, such as RISC-based computers, because the VDM sessions are emulated using NTVDM.EXE, and there are no full-screen sessions.

Video Driver Entries in the Software Subkey

The optional entries for open graphics libraries (OpenGL) are under the following subkey:

```
HKEY_LOCAL_MACHINE\Software\Microsoft\WindowsNT
  \CurrentVersion\OpenGLDrivers
```

%display_driver_name%   **REG_SZ**   *%OpenGL_client_driver_name%*

For example, suppose that MYOPENGL.DLL is the OpenGL client driver for the display driver MYDISP.DLL. Then the OpenGLDrivers subkey would have the value-data pair:

```
mydisp: REG_SZ: myopengl
```

The subkey may be empty if no OpenGL client drivers are installed. This value can be changed via the Control Panel Display option. Manual modification should not be necessary except for manual installation or uninstallation of OpenGL client drivers (which is different from the OpenGL built into the GDI). Only one client driver is allowed for each unique display driver name.

Registry Entries for Network Services

The following services have additional value entries that can be specified in the Registry, in addition to changes that you can make using the Services icon in Control Panel or Server Manager in Windows NT ServerWindows NT Server. You can view current settings for these services by choosing the Services button in WinMSD.

Alerter service	NWLink transport
AppleTalk and MacFile services	Redirector (Rdr) service
BootVerification service	Remote Access Service (RAS)
Browser service	Replicator service
DiskPerf service	Schedule service
DLC transport	Server service
EventLog service	TCP/IP (FTP, NetBt, Streams, WinSock)
NetBEUI (NBF) transport	UPS service
NetLogon service	Workstation service
NetworkProvider service	

Services that are not included in this section do not have hidden parameters that you can set.

This section describes parameters for these services under the HKEY_LOCAL_MACHINE\SYSTEM\CurrentControlSet\Services subkey.

Some of these services also have configuration information stored under HKEY_LOCAL_MACHINE\SOFTWARE. These values are described in "NetRules Subkey Entries," earlier in this chapter.

Note Wherever possible, choose the Services icon in Control Panel or use Server Manager in Windows NT ServerWindows NT Server to change values for these services.

Alerter Service Entries

Entries for this service appear under the following subkey:

`HKEY_LOCAL_MACHINE\SYSTEM\CurrentControlSet\Services\Alerter\Parameters`

AlertNames   REG_MULTI_SZ   *List*

Specifies the list of users to whom administrator alerts are sent. This value can be set using the Server Manager.

Default: NULL

AppleTalk and MacFile Service Entries for SFM

Services For Macintosh (SFM) does not appear in the Registry until you install SFM using the Network icon in Control Panel. After installation, the SFM value entries appear under several Services subkeys: AppleTalk, MacFile, MacPrint, and MacSrv. You should let the system maintain entries in the MacPrint or MacSrv services. However, the AppleTalk and MacFile services contain definable parameters described in this section.

You should use the Network icon in Control Panel to configure SFM, and use File Manager to administer file services, Server Manager to administer server services, and Print Manager to administer print services for SFM.

SFM is included with Windows NT ServerWindows NT Server and the AppleTalk transport service is on the *Windows NT Resource Guide* disk.

AppleTalk Entries for SFM

The values for the AppleTalk service are found in the following Registry path:

`HKEY_LOCAL_MACHINE\SYSTEM\CurrentControlSet\Services\AppleTalk`

For changes to take effect, you must restart the File Server for Macintosh using the Devices icon in Control Panel.

Values for the AppleTalk Parameters and Adapters subkeys are described here. The settings in the Linkage subkey and the TCP/IP settings in the Winsock subkey for AppleTalk are maintained by the system and should not be changed by the user.

AppleTalk Parameter Entries

This is the Registry path for the AppleTalk parameters:

```
HKEY_LOCAL_MACHINE\SYSTEM\CurrentControlSet\Services
    \AppleTalk\Parameters
```

These values set port, zone, and router information.

DefaultPort   EG_SZ   *Adapter name*

Specifies the network on which the SFM service names are registered. If the AppleTalk protocol is not routing, only Macintosh workstations connected to this network can see the file and print services. During initial installation, the default port is set automatically to the first Ethernet adapter found, or to the first Token Ring adapter, or to a LocalTalk adapter (in that order).

Default: the first adapter found.

DesiredZone   REG_SZ   *Zone name*

Specifies the zone in which the SFM service is present. If this value is not set, SFM is present in the default zone for that network.

There is no default.

EnableRouter   REG_DWORD   *0 or 1*

Tells the AppleTalk protocol whether routing needs to be started on this computer. If routing is started, Macintosh workstations connected to any of the networks that this computer is on should be able to use the file and print servers for Macintosh.

Important This value is critical. Unless absolutely essential, do not set this value to 1.

Default: 0

Adapter Card Entries for AppleTalk

The entries for AppleTalk that are specific to network adapter cards are found under the following Registry path:

```
HKEY_LOCAL_MACHINE\SYSTEM\CurrentControlSet\Services
    \AppleTalk\Adapters\adapter_name
```

There is one subkey for each adapter that is AppleTalk-compatible on the computer. These entries are found in each *Adapter_Name* subkey.

AarpRetries   REG_DWORD   *Number*

Specifies the maximum number of AppleTalk address-resolution protocol packets to be sent by the AppleTalk protocol.

Default: 0xa

DdpCheckSums   REG_DWORD   *0 or 1*

Tells the AppleTalk protocol whether to compute checksums in the DDP layer. If this entry is 1, the AppleTalk protocol uses sums in the DDP layer.

Default: 0

DefaultZone   REG_SZ   *Zone name*

Contains the default zone for this network if this adapter is seeding the network. If the adapter is seeding the network, the default zone is chosen when you configure SFM using the Network icon in Control Panel.

There is no default.

NetworkRangeLowerEnd   REG_DWORD   *1 to 65279*

Specifies the lower network number of the network range if this adapter is seeding the network. If the adapter is seeding the network, this number is set by using the Network icon in Control Panel to configure SFM.

There is no default.

NetworkRangeUpperEnd   REG_DWORD   *1 to 65279*

Specifies the upper network number of the network range for this network if this adapter is seeding the network. If the adapter is seeding the network, this number is set by using the Network icon in Control Panel to configure SFM.

There is no default.

PortName   REG_SZ   *AdapterName@ComputerName*

Specifies the name used to identify the AppleTalk protocol running on a particular adapter on a computer.

There is no default.

SeedingNetwork   REG_DWORD   *0 or 1*

Used by the AppleTalk protocol during startup. If this value is 0, this adapter is not seeding the network and the AppleTalk protocol ignores any seeding information for the adapter, if specified. If this value is 1, the AppleTalk protocol reads all seeding information and seeds the network, if valid.

Default: 0.

ZoneList   REG_MULTI_SZ   *List of zones*

This value is relevant only when the adapter is seeding the network. The network is seeded with this list of zones by the AppleTalk protocol. Changes can be made by using the Network icon in Control Panel to configure SFM.

There is no default.

MacFile Entries for SFM

The MacFile subkey contains the main entries for the AppleTalk File Protocol (AFP) server. All configuration information for the file server is in the following subkey:

```
HKEY_LOCAL_MACHINE\SYSTEM\CurrentControlSet\Services\MacFile
```

For changes to take effect, you must restart the computer.

The MacFile\Parameters subkey includes Type_Creators, Icons, and Extensions subkeys. You should let the system maintain entries in the Icons or Extensions subkeys. This section describes value entries for the Parameters and Parameters\Type_Creator subkeys.

MacFile Parameters Entries

The Registry path for MacFile parameters is the following:

```
HKEY_LOCAL_MACHINE\SYSTEM\CurrentControlSet\Services\MacFile\Parameters
```

The following value entries specify server options, which can be set from the Server Manager. All other entries are added to the Registry when changes to the default values occur.

For information about the Macintosh codepage, see the entry for MacCP in the NLS\CodePage subkey.

LoginMsg   REG_SZ   *1–198 characters*

Specifies the message you want Macintosh users to see when they log on to the Windows NT ServerWindows NT Server network.

There is no default.

MaxSessions   REG_DWORD   *1 to unlimited (0xffffffff)*

Specifies the maximum number of user sessions that the file server for Macintosh can accommodate.

Default: 0xff (255in decimal)

PagedMemLimit   REG_DWORD   *1000K to 256000K*

Specifies the maximum amount of page memory that the file server for Macintosh uses. Performance of the MacFile service increases with an increase in this value. However, the value should not be set lower than 1000K. It is especially important that you are well acquainted with memory issues before changing this resource parameter. You cannot change this value from Server Manager.

Default: 0x4e20 (20000 in decimal)

NonPagedMemLimit   REG_DWORD   *256K to 16000K*

Specifies the maximum amount of RAM that is available to the file server for Macintosh. Increasing this value helps performance of the file server, but decreases performance of other system resources.

Default: 0xfa0 (4000 in decimal)

ServerName   REG_SZ   *Server name*

Specifies the name of the server running SFM on a Windows NT ServerWindows NT Server network. Use the server's Windows NT ServerWindows NT Server name as the default if you need to add this entry.

There is no default.

ServerOptions   REG_DWORD

Specifies server options that are set in Server Manager. If needed for repair purposes, change Bits 1 through 3; do not change any of the other bits. When on, Bit 1 allows guest logons, Bit 2 allows cleartext passwords, and Bit 3 allows Macintosh users to save passwords on their workstations.

The defaults are bit 1, 2, and 3 set to on.

Volume **REG_MULTI_SZ** *MaxUses Properties Password Path*

Each entry specifies information about a Macintosh-accessible volume on the server on a Windows NT ServerWindows NT Server network. You should add Macintosh-accessible volumes using File Manager.

Value	Meaning
MaxUses	Specifies the maximum number of simultaneous workstations that can be connected to the file server. The upper limit is unlimited. The practical limits are based on the server hardware and network media.
Properties	Specifies security options. When Bit 1 is set to On, the volume is read-only. When Bit 16 is set to On, guests can use this volume. The default is 1000000000000000 (in binary notation) (the volume is read-only; guests can use this volume).
Password	Contains the encrypted password. Do not change this value. If a user forgets a password, you can delete this entry, thus removing a password requirement from the user's account. Then the user can specify a new password at logon.
Path	Specifies the path of the volume's root directory. If a volume has been deleted, the path may still be valid; consequently, you should not delete this value. If volumes are deleted using File Manager, you can delete this value.

Type_Creators Entries for MacFile

The values in the following Registry subkey list all the Macintosh type-creators that are associated with MS-DOS–style filename extensions:

```
HKEY_LOCAL_MACHINE\SYSTEM\CurrentControlSet\Services
    MacFile\Parameters\Type_Creators
```

Change these values using File Manager by choosing the **Associate** command from the MacFile menu. The value entries that appear in the Registry for each type of creator have the following format:

**REG_MULTI_SZ** **Creator=***Value* **Type=***Value* **Comment=***Value*

The three values appear for each entry. The value for Creator= must have from 1 through 4 characters. The value for Type= must have from 1 through 4 characters. The value for Comment= must have from 0 through 29 characters.

BootVerification Service Entries

The Services subkey for the BootVerification service does not appear by default in the Registry. You can add this subkey if you want to verify system startup from a remote location using the BOOTVRFY.EXE program provided with Windows NT. This service can be started from a remote computer. The service tells the Windows NT service controller that it should save the current startup system configuration as the LastKnownGood control set, and then the service terminates itself.

When you add the BootVerification subkey using Registry Editor, add the following value entries:

Value entry	Data type	Value	Comment
ErrorControl	REG_DWORD	0x1	Normal
ImagePath	REG_EXPAND_SZ	bootvrfy.exe	—
ObjectName	REG_SZ	LocalSystem	—
Start	REG_DWORD	0x3	Demand
Type	REG_DWORD	0x2	Win32 shared process

You must also specify a value of 1 for the **ReportBootOK** entry under the following Registry path:

```
HKEY_LOCAL_MACHINE\Software\Windows NT\CurrentVersion\WinLogon
```

When the value of **ReportBootOK** is set to 0, it disables the automatic (default) startup acceptance, which happens after the first successful logon.

This alternative method of verifying system startup cannot be used in conjunction with BootVerificationProgram (as described earlier in this chapter). See Chapter 12, "Configuration Management and the Registry" for the procedure for verifying system startup from a remote computer.

Browser Service Entries

The parameters that control network bindings for the Browser service are described in "NetRules Subkey Entries," earlier in this chapter.

Under the following Registry path, two parameters are found:

```
HKEY_LOCAL_MACHINE\SYSTEM\CurrentControlSet\Services\Browser\Parameters
```

CacheHitLimit   REG_DWORD   *0 to 256*

Describes the number of NetServerEnum requests required to qualify that the response to a NetServerEnum request be cached. If the browser receives more than **CacheHitLimit** NetServerEnum requests with a particular set of parameters, it caches the response and returns that value to the client.

Default: 1

CacheResponseSize   REG_DWORD   *0 to xffffffff*

Specifies the maximum number of responses kept for each transport. To disable this feature, set this value to 0.

Default: 10

IsDomainMasterBrowser   REG_SZ   *Boolean*

For TCP/IP, specifies a workstation within a workgroup which can be included in global LMHOSTS file. When this parameter is set to Yes, it forces the elevation of a workstation's priority for the browser. This helps with WAN browsing.

This value should be set on a few systems for the workgroup, placing mappings for each in the global LMHOSTS file. For example, in a workgroup with 20 members, set this value on three of the computers to earn a better chance to act as master browsers. This facilitates remote browsing ability for workstations in remote domains whose domain master browser has successful mappings for these special workgroup members.

MaintainServerList   REG_SZ   *Boolean or Auto*

If this value is No, this server is not a browse server. If this value is Yes, this server becomes a browse server. It attempts to contact the Master Browse Server to get a current browse list. If it cannot find the Master Browse Server, it forces an election and is, of course, a candidate to become the master.

If **MaintainServerList** is Auto, this server may or may not become a browse server, depending on the results of the Registry exchange with the Master Browse Server.

If **MaintainServerList** is set to Yes, the computer is configured to always be a backup browser.

Default: Auto, if none is present. (This server contacts the Master Browse Server, and the Master Browse Server tells this server whether it should become a browse server.)

QueryDriverFrequency   REG_DWORD   *0 to 900*

Indicates the time after which a browser master will invalidate its NetServerEnum response cache and the frequency that a master browser will query the browser driver to retrieve the list of servers. Increasing this time makes browsing somewhat faster, but browse information will not necessarily be 100 percent accurate to the minute. Lowering this time makes browse response more accurate, but will increase the CPU load on the browse master.

Default: 30

The following Browser driver parameters are found under this Registry path for the Datagram Receiver:

```
HKEY_LOCAL_MACHINE\SYSTEM\CurrentControlSet\Services\DGRcvr\Parameters
```

BrowserServerDeletionThreshold   REG_DWORD
BrowserDomainDeletionThreshold   REG_DWORD *0 to 0xffffffff*

If more than **BrowserServerDeletionThreshold** servers (or **BrowserDomainDeletionThreshold**) servers (or domains) are flushed in a 30-second interval, this will cause an event to be generated.

Default: 0xffffffff

FindMasterTimeout   REG_DWORD   *0 to 0xffffffff*

Specifies the maximum number of seconds that FindMaster requests should be allowed to take. If you have a slow LAN, you may want to increase this value (but only if directed by Microsoft Product Support services).

Default: 0xffffffff

GetBrowserListThreshold   REG_DWORD   *Number*

Represents the threshold that the Browser uses before logging an error indicating that too many of these requests have been "missed." If more requests than the value of **GetBrowserServerList** are missed in an hour, the Browser logs an event indicating that this has happened.

Default: 0xffffffff (That is, never log events.)

MailslotDatagramThreshold   REG_DWORD   *Number*

Represents the threshold that the Browser uses before logging an error indicating that too many of these requests have been "missed." If more mailslots than the value of **MailslotDatagramThreshold** are missed in an hour, the Browser logs an event indicating that this has happened.

Default: 0xffffffff (That is, never log events.)

DiskPerf Service Entries

The DiskPerf subkey entries determines whether disk performance statistics are maintained by the system. If the **Start** value is 0 (boot), then statistics are counted and are reported by Performance Monitor and similar tools. Collecting disk performance statistics can take up to 1.5 percent of the disk throughput on a system with a slow processor (such as an 20 MHz 80386 computer) but should have negligible impact on a system with a faster processor (such as a 33 MHz i486 and above).

Turn DiskPerf on or off only by using the Diskperf utility; for example, type **diskperf -y** at the command prompt.

The Registry path is the following:

```
HKEY_LOCAL_MACHINE\SYSTEM\CurrentControlSet\Services\DiskPerf
```

There are no parameters that users can set. The following are the default values for the standard entries:

Value entry	Value
ErrorControl	0x1 (Normal)
Group	Filter
Start	0x4 (disabled)
Type	0x1 (Kernel driver)

DLC System Driver Entries

The DLC subkey does not appear unless this service is installed. In Windows NT, the Data Link Control (DLC) protocol only needs to be installed on computers that access IBM mainframes (usually with 3270 applications) or on print servers that print directly to Hewlett-Packard printers. Network printers such as the HP III si use the DLC protocol, for example, because the frames received are easy to take apart.

The DLC driver depends on an having an NDIS group service available and is bound to the network adapter card through the NDIS device driver. Each adapter that supports the DLC protocol has a subkey under the DLC\Parameters subkey. With Registry Editor, you can modify the following parameters for the DLC system driver. The path for these parameters is the following:

```
HKEY_LOCAL_MACHINE\SYSTEM\CurrentControlSet\Services
    \DLC\Parameters\adapter name
```

The following **TxTick** parameters are multipliers for the T1, T2, and Ti values, which represent time periods in milliseconds that are used when a station or SAP is opened. If the time period value is between 1 and 5, the time delay is computed as follows:

```
(time period) * TxTickOne * 40 milliseconds
```

If the time period value is between 6 and 10, the time delay is computed as follows:

```
(time period - 5) * TxTickTwo * 40 milliseconds
```

When computing the short-tick values (_One) and the long-tick values (_Two), the resulting values for T1, T2, and Ti should generally follow this rule: T2 < T1 < Ti.

T1Tick{One|Two} REG_DWORD *1 to 255 milliseconds*

Specifies the delay before retransmitting an I frame if not acknowledged.

Default: **T1TickOne** = 5; **T1TickTwo** = 25

T2Tick{One|Two} REG_DWORD *1 to 255 milliseconds*

Specifies the delay before acknowledging frames in the receive window if the receive window has not been filled.

Default: **T2TickOne** = 1; **T2TickTwo** = 10

TiTick{One|Two} REG_DWORD *1 to 255 milliseconds*

Specifies the delay before testing an inactive station to determine if it is still active.

Default: **TiTickOne** = 25; **TiTickTwo** = 125

Swap   REG_DWORD   *0 or 1*

Used when talking over Ethernet to support certain Token Ring-to-Ethernet bridges in swapping of the Destination Address when using DLC over a Token Ring network. If this value is 0, the adapter addresses presented at the API interface are not bit-flipped before being put online.

Default: 1

UseDixOverEthernet   REG_DWORD   *0 or 1*

Specifies the default mode for the connection-oriented and connectionless 802.2 LLC (Logical Link Control) frames sent on Ethernet. If this value is 1, the DLC driver users DIX encoding in the frames to be transmitted instead of the 802.3 Ethernet format.

Default: 0

Note Additional parameters that were included in the Microsoft LAN Manager COMTOKR utility are not defined for DLC, because Windows NT does not have the same memory limitations as MS-DOS.

EventLog Service Entries

The Services subkey for EventLog contains at least three subkeys for the three types of logs—Application, Security, and System. These *Logfile* subkeys contain subkeys that define the location of the related event message file and the supported types of events, as follows:

- The Application subkey contains subkeys for installed applications and services that write to the Application event log.
- The Security subkey contains subkeys for each of the security subsystem components.
- The System subkey contains subkeys for device drivers.

Each of the three *Logfile* subkeys for the EventLog service can contain the value entries described in this section. The Registry path for these entries is the following, where *logfile* is System, Application, or Security.

```
HKEY_CURRENT_MACHINE\SYSTEM\CurrentControlSet\Services
    \Eventlog\logfile
```

These entries are described for informational purposes only. This information is usually maintained by Event Viewer. New keys under the Application subkey can only be added in meaningful ways by using the Win32 Registry APIs.

File   REG_SZ   *Path and filename*

Specifies the fully qualified path name of the file for this log. This value can be set in Event Viewer.

Default: *SystemRoot*\system32\config*filename*

MaxSize   REG_DWORD   *Number in kilobytes*

Specifies the maximum size of the log file. This value can be set using the Event Viewer.

Default: 512

Retention   REG_DWORD   *Number of seconds*

Specifies that records that are newer than this value will not be overwritten. This is what causes a log full event. This value can be set using the Event Viewer.

Default: 604800 (7 days)

Sources   REG_MULTI_SZ   *Names of source applications*

Specifies the applications, services, or groups of applications that write events to this log. Each source is a subkey of the *Logfile* subkey.

Default: None. This value is dynamically maintained by the EventLog service.

The *Source* subkeys under a *Logfile* subkey are created by the applications that write events in the related event log. These subkeys contain information specific to the source of the event under the following types of value entries.

EventMessageFile   REG_EXPAND_SZ   *Filename*

Specifies the path and filename for the event identifier message file.

CategoryMessageFile   REG_EXPAND_SZ   *Filename*

Specifies the path and filename for the category message file. The category and event identifier message strings may be in the same file.

CategoryCount   REG_DWORD   *Number*

Specifies the number of categories supported.

TypesSupported   REG_DWORD   *Number*

Specifies a bitmask of supported types.

NBF (NetBEUI) Transport Entries

The startup parameters for the NetBEUI (NBF) transport are found under the following subkey:

```
HKEY_LOCAL_MACHINE\SYSTEM\Services\NBF\Parameters
```

Note The parameters that control network bindings for this service are described in "NetRules Subkey Entries," earlier in this chapter. You should set the Export and Bind parameters by using the Network application in Control Panel.

The **Init*xxx*** entries for NBF define the initial allocation and the size of free memory for items. The **Max*xxx*** entries define the upper limits. Within these ranges, the system autotunes performance. By default, the NBF service uses all the resources necessary to handle client requests, and when it is not actively working, it doesn't use many resources. Set **Init*xxx*** values to control initial allocation, which can make the system a little faster when you know a server will be busy. Set the **Max*xxx*** values to control limits when you don't want the server to be too busy or to use too much memory for networking.

With Registry Editor, you can modify the following startup parameters for the NBF transport:

AddNameQueryRetries   **REG_DWORD**   *Number*

Specifies the number of times that NBF will retry sending ADD_NAME_QUERY and ADD_GROUP_NAME_QUERY frames. Adjust this parameter only if NBF is registering addresses on a network that drops many packets.

Default: 3

AddNameQueryTimeout   **REG_DWORD**   *100-nanosecond units*

Specifies the time-out between NBF sending successive ADD_NAME_QUERY and ADD_GROUP_NAME_QUERY frames. Adjust this parameter only if NBF is registering addresses on a network with slow computers or over a slow network.

Default: 5000000

GeneralRetries   **REG_DWORD**   *Number*

Specifies the number of times that NBF will retry sending STATUS_QUERY and FIND_NAME frames. Adjust this parameter only if NBF is operating on a network that drops many packets.

Default: 3

DefaultT1Timeout   REG_DWORD   *100-nanosecond units*

Specifies the initial value for the T1 timeout. T1 controls the time that NBF waits for a response after sending a logical link control (LLC) poll packet before resending it. Adjust this parameter only if NBF will be connecting over slow networks or to slow remote computers (although NBF does adapt).

Default: 6000000 (600 milliseconds)

DefaultT2Timeout   REG_DWORD   *100-nanosecond units*

Specifies the initial value for the T2 timeout. T2 controls the time that NBF can wait after receiving an LLC poll packet before responding. It must be much less than T1; one-half or less is a good general rule. Adjust this parameter only if NBF will be connecting over slow networks or to slow remote computers.

Default: 1500000 (150 milliseconds)

DefaultTiTimeout   REG_DWORD   *100-nanosecond units*

Specifies the initial value for the Ti timeout. Ti is the inactivity timer. When it expires, NBF sends an LLC poll packet to ensure that the link is still active. Adjust this parameter only if NBF is connecting over networks with unusual reliability characteristics, or over slow networks or to slow computers.

Default: 300000000 (30 seconds)

GeneralTimeout   REG_DWORD   *100-nanosecond units*

Specifies the time-out between NBF sending successive STATUS_QUERY and FIND_NAME requests. Adjust this parameter only if NBF is operating on a network with slow computers or over a slow network.

Default: 5000000

InitAddresses   REG_DWORD   *1 or higher; 0 = no limit*

Specifies the number of initial addresses to allocate within any memory limits that might imposed on NBF. Addresses correspond to NetBIOS names. An address is for the actual name, and an address file is for a TDI (Transport Driver Interface) client using that name; so usually you have the same number, but if two users open the same address, that is two address files but only one address.

Set this parameter if you know that a large number of addresses are needed. Otherwise, the system automatically allocates space for addresses as needed.

Default: 0 (no limit)

InitAddressFiles   REG_DWORD   *1 or higher; 0 = no limit*

Specifies the number of initial address files to allocate within any memory limits that might imposed on NBF. Set this parameter if you know that a large number of address files are needed. Otherwise, the system automatically allocates space for address files as needed.

Default: 0 (no limit)

NBF (NetBEUI) Transport Entries

InitConnections   **REG_DWORD**   *1 or higher; 0 = no limit*

Specifies the number of initial connections (NetBIOS sessions) to allocate within any memory limits that might imposed on NBF. Set this parameter if you know that a large number of connections are needed. Otherwise, the system automatically allocates space for connections as needed.

Default: 1

InitLinks   **REG_DWORD**   *1 or higher; 0 = no limit*

Specifies the number of initial LLC links to allocate within any memory limits that might imposed on NBF. Typically, you have one connection per LLC link to another network adapter card, because the redirector puts all links to a computer into one connection. However, you may have more if two computers are communicating with each other or if a NetBIOS application is running. Set this parameter if you know that a large number of links are needed. Otherwise, the system automatically allocates space for links as needed.

Default: 2

InitReceiveBuffers   **REG_DWORD**   *1 or higher; 0 = no limit*

Specifies the number of initial receive buffers to allocate. Receive buffers are used by NBF when it calls NDIS TransferData for received datagrams. Usually, this value is allocated as needed, but you can use this parameter to preallocate memory if you know a large number of datagram frames will be received.

Default: 5

InitReceivePackets   **REG_DWORD**   *1 or higher; 0 = no limit*

Specifies the number of initial receive packets to allocate. Receive packets are used by NBF when it calls NDIS TransferData for received data. Usually, this value is allocated as needed, but you can use this parameter to preallocate memory if you know a large number of UI frames will be received.

Default: 10

InitRequests   **REG_DWORD**   *1 or higher; 0 = no limit*

Specifies the number of initial requests to allocate within any memory limits that might imposed on NBF. Requests are used for in-progress connect requests, remote adapter status requests, find name requests, and so on. Set this parameter if you know that a large number of requests are needed. Otherwise, the system automatically allocates space for requests as needed.

Default: 5

InitSendPackets   **REG_DWORD**   *1 or higher; 0 = no limit*

Specifies the number of initial send packets to allocate. Send packets are used by NBF whenever it sends connection-oriented data on behalf of a client. Usually, this value is allocated as needed, but you can use this parameter to preallocate memory if you know a large number of data frames are needed or if you see a lot of "send packets exhausted" messages when using Performance Monitor.

Default: 30

InitUIFrames   **REG_DWORD**   *1 or higher; 0 = no limit*

Specifies the number of initial UI frames to allocate. UI frames are used by NBF to establish connections and for connectionless services such as datagrams. Usually, this value is allocated as needed, but you can use this parameter to preallocate memory if you know a large number of UI frames are needed.

Default: 5

LLCMaxWindowSize   **REG_DWORD**   *Number of frames*

Specifies the number of LLC I-frames that NBF can send before polling and waiting for a response from the remote. Adjust this parameter only if NBF is communicating over a network whose reliability often changes suddenly.

Default: 10

LLCRetries   **REG_DWORD**   *1 or higher; 0 = no limit*

Specifies the number of times that NBF will retry polling a remote workstation after receiving a T1 timeout. After this many retries, NBF closes the link. Adjust this parameter only if NBF is connecting over networks with unusual reliability characteristics.

Default: 8

MaxAddresses   **REG_DWORD**   *1 or higher; 0 = no limit*

Specifies the maximum number of addresses that NBF allocates within any memory limits that might imposed on NBF. Addresses are NetBIOS names that are registered on the network by NBF. An address is for the actual name, and an address file is for a TDI client using that name.

Use this optional parameter to fine-tune use of NBF memory. Typically this parameter is used to control address resources with an unlimited NBF.

Default: 0 (no limit)

MaxAddressFiles   REG_DWORD   *1 or higher; 0 = no limit*

Specifies maximum number of address files that NBF allocates within any memory limits that might imposed on NBF. Each address file corresponds to a client opening an address.

Use this optional parameter to fine-tune use of NBF memory. Typically this parameter is used to control address files with an unlimited NBF.

Default: 0 (no limit)

MaxConnections   REG_DWORD   *1 or higher; 0 = no limit*

Specifies the maximum number of connections that NBF allocates within any memory limits that might imposed on NBF. Connections are established between NBF clients and similar entities on remote computers.

Use this optional parameter to fine-tune use of NBF memory. Typically this parameter is used to control connection resources with an unlimited NBF.

Default: 0 (no limit)

MaximumIncomingFrames   REG_DWORD   *1 or higher; 0 = off*

Used in some cases to control how many incoming frames NBF will receive before it sends an acknowledgment to a remote machine. In general, NBF automatically senses when to sends acknowledgments, however when communicating with some Microsoft LAN Manager or LAN Server remote computers configured with a very low value for **maxout**, this parameter can be set to an equal or lower value to improve network performance. (This parameter corresponds roughly to the Microsoft LAN Manager **maxin** parameter.) A value of 0 turns off this hint, causing NBF to revert to usual behavior. For communication with most all remotes, this parameter isn't used.

Default: 2

MaxLinks   REG_DWORD   *1 or higher; 0 = no limit*

Specifies the maximum number of links that NBF allocates within any memory limits that might imposed on NBF. Links are established for every remote adapter to which NBF communicates.

Use this optional parameter to fine-tune use of NBF memory. Typically this parameter is used to control link resources with an unlimited NBF.

Default: 0 (no limit)

NBF (NetBEUI) Transport Entries

MaxRequests   REG_DWORD   *1 or higher; 0 = no limit*

Specifies the maximum number of requests that NBF allocates within any memory limits that might imposed on NBF. Requests are used by NBF to control send, receive, connect, and listen operations.

Use this optional parameter to fine-tune use of NBF memory. Typically this parameter is used to control request resources with an unlimited NBF.

Default: 0 (no limit)

NameQueryRetries   REG_DWORD   *Number*

Specifies the number of times that NBF will retry sending NAME_QUERY frames. Adjust this parameter only if NBF is connecting to computers over a network that drops many packets.

Default: 3

NameQueryTimeout   REG_DWORD   *100-nanosecond units*

Specifies the time-out between NBF sending successive NAME_QUERY frames. Adjust this parameter only if NBF is connecting to slow computers or over a slow network.

Default: 5000000

QueryWithoutSourceRouting   REG_DWORD   *0 or 1*

When you are using NBF over a Token Ring driver, this parameter instructs NBF to send half the queries without including source routing information when connecting to a remote computer. This supports bridging hardware that cannot forward frames that contain source routing information.

Default: 0 (false)

UseDixOverEthernet   REG_DWORD   *0 or 1*

Specifies whether NBF should use DIX encoding when bound to an Ethernet MAC. When using DIX encoding is enabled, NBF cannot talk to computers that use the standard IEEE 802.3 encoding.

Default: 0 (false)

WanNameQueryRetries   REG_DWORD   *Number*

Specifies the number of times that NBF will retry sending NAME_QUERY frames when connecting with RAS. Adjust this parameter only if NBF is connecting to computers over a network that drops many packets.

Default: 5

NBF (NetBEUI) Transport Entries

NetLogon Service Entries

The Registry path for the parameters for the NetLogon service is the following:

```
HKEY_LOCAL_MACHINE\SYSTEM\CurrentControlSet\Services\Netlogon\Parameters
```

Note The NetLogon share name should also be in the path for logon scripts.

ChangeLogSize   REG_DWORD   *64K to 4 MB*

Defines the size (in bytes) of the change log. The change log exists both in memory and on disk, %SystemRoot%\netlogon.chg. Since this parameter setting does not degrade system performance, it is advisable to leave it at the 0x4000000 (4 MB) setting, rather than returning it to the 64K default setting. The 4 MB setting ensures that the domain's database will not be completely replicated when large changes are made in the future.

ChangeLogSize should be the same on all BDCs to ensure that when a BDC is promoted to a PDC, it will have that same **ChangeLogSize** value.

Default: 64K

The minimum (and typical) size of an entry is 32 bytes. Therefore, a 64K change log holds about 2000 changes.

MaximumMailslotMessages   REG_DWORD   *1 to 0xffffffff messages*

Specifies the maximum number of mailslot messages that will be queued to the Netlogon service. Even though the Netlogon service is designed to process incoming mailslot messages immediately, it can get backed up processing requests on a heavily loaded system. Each mailslot message consumes about 1500 bytes of non-paged pool until it is processed. By setting this parameter low, you can govern the maximum amount of non-paged pool that can be consumed. If this parameter is set too low, Netlogon may miss important incoming mailslot messages.

Default: 500

MaximumMailslotTimeout   REG_DWORD   *5 to 0xffffffff seconds*

Specifies the maximum acceptable age (in seconds) of an incoming mailslot message. If Netlogon receives a mailslot messages that arrived longer ago than this, it ignores the message. This allows Netlogon to process messages that are more recent. If this parameter is set too low, Netlogon will ignore important incoming mailslot messages. Ideally, Netlogon processes each mailslot message in a fraction of a second. This parameter is only significant if the Windows NT server is overloaded.

Default: 10

MailslotDuplicateTimeout   REG_DWORD   *0 to 5 seconds*

Specifies the interval (in seconds) over which duplicate incoming mailslot messages will be ignored. Netlogon compares each mailslot message received with the previous mailslot message received. If the previous message was received within this many seconds and the messages are identical, this message will be ignored. Set this parameter to 0 to disable this feature. You should disable this feature if your network is configured such that this machine can see certain incoming mailslot messages but cannot respond to them. For instance, a DC may be separated from a Windows NT workstation by a bridge/router. The bridge/router might filter outgoing NBF broadcasts, but allow an incoming one. As such, Netlogon might respond to an NBF mailslot message (only to be filtered out by the bridge/router) and not respond to a subsequent NBT mailslot message. Disabling this feature (or preferably reconfiguring the bridge/router) solves this problem. If you set this parameter too high, Netlogon will ignore retry attempts from a client.

Default: 2

Pulse   REG_DWORD   *60 to 3600 seconds*

Defines the typical pulse frequency (in seconds). All SAM/LSA changes made within this time are collected together. After this time, a pulse is sent to each BDC needing the changes. No pulse is sent to a BDC that is up to date.

When this value is not specified in the Registry, NetLogon determines optimal values depending on the domain controller's load.

Default: 300 (5 minutes)

PulseConcurrency   REG_DWORD   *1 to 500 pulses*

Defines the maximum number of simultaneous pulses the Primary Domain Controller (PDC) will send to Backup Domain Controllers (BDCs). Netlogon sends pulses to individual BDCs. The BDCs respond asking for any database changes. To control the maximum load these responses place on the PDC, the PDC will only have **PulseConcurrency** pulses "pending" at once. The PDC should be sufficiently powerful to support this many concurrent replication RPC calls. Increasing **PulseConcurrency** increases the load on the PDC. Decreasing **PulseConcurrency** increases the time it takes for a domain with a large number of BDCs to get a SAM/LSA change to all of the BDCs.

Default: 20

PulseMaximum   REG_DWORD   *60 to 86,400 seconds*

Defines the maximum pulse frequency (in seconds). Every BDC will be sent at least one pulse at this frequency regardless of whether its database is up to date.

Default: 7200 (2 hours)

NetLogon Service Entries

PulseTimeout1   REG_DWORD   *1 to 120 seconds*

Defines how long (in seconds) the PDC waits for a non-responsive BDC. When a BDC is sent a pulse, it must respond within this time period. If not, the BDC is considered to be non-responsive. A non-responsive BDC is not counted against the **PulseConcurrency** limit allowing the PDC to send a pulse to another BDC in the domain. If this number is too large, a domain with a large number of non-responsive BDCs will take a long time to complete a partial replication. If this number is too small, a slow BDC may be falsely accused of being non-responsive. When the BDC finally does respond, it will partial replicate from the PDC unduly increasing the load on the PDC.

Default: 5

PulseTimeout2   REG_DWORD   *60 to 3600 seconds*

Defines how long (in seconds) a PDC waits for a BDC to complete partial replication. Even though a BDC initially responds to a pulse (as described for **PulseTimeout1**), it must continue making replication progress or the BDC will be considered non-responsive. Each time the BDC calls the PDC, the BDC is given another **PulseTimeout2** seconds to be considered responsive. If this number is too large, a slow BDC (or one that has its replication rate artificially governed) will consume one of the **PulseConcurrency** slots. If this number is too small, the load on the PDC will be unduly increased because of the large number of BDCs doing a partial sync.

Note This parameter only affects the cases where a BDC cannot retrieve all the changes to the SAM/LSA database in a single RPC call. This will only happen if a large number of changes are made to the database.

Default: 300 (5 minutes)

Randomize   REG_DWORD   *0 to 120 seconds*

Specifies the BDC back off period (in seconds). When the BDC receives a pulse, it will back off between zero and **Randomize** seconds before calling the PDC. The pulse is sent to individual BDCs, so this parameter should be small. **Randomize** should be smaller than **PulseTimeout1**. Consider that the time to replicate a SAM/LSA change to all the BDCs in a domain will be greater than:

```
[(Randomize/2) * NumberOfBdcsInDomain] / PulseConcurrency
```

When this value is not specified in the Registry, NetLogon determines optimal values depending on the domain controller's load.

Default: 1

ReplicationGovernor   REG_DWORD   *0 to 100 percent*

Defines both the size of the data transferred on each call to the PDC and the frequency of those calls. For instance, setting **ReplicationGovernor** to 50% will use a 64K buffer rather than a 128K buffer and will only have a replication call outstanding on the net a maximum of 50% of the time. Do not set the **ReplicationGovernor** too low, or replication may never complete. A value of 0 will cause Netlogon to *never* replicate. The SAM/LSA database will be allowed to get completely out of sync.

BDCs can be configured for the variances of WAN types. **ReplicationGovernor** allows the administrator to control the partial synchronization parameters. This parameter must be set individually on each BDC.

Note It is also possible to configure different replication rates at different times of the day using a script file with the AT command (for example, net stop netlogon, regini scriptfile, net start netlogon). The script file contains the path to the **RegistrationGovernor** parameter and the new Registry entries. REGINI.EXE is part of the Windows NT Resource Kit.

Default: 100

Scripts   REG_SZ   *Pathname*

Specifies the fully qualified path name to where logon scripts reside. This value can be set using the Services icon in Control Panel or the Server Manager.

Default: NULL

Update   REG_SZ   *Yes or No*

When this value is set to Yes, NetLogon fully synchronizes the database each time it starts.

Default: No

NetworkProvider Service Entries

If more than one network is present under Windows NT, each network has a Services subkey that include a value for **Group** of NetworkProvider plus its own subkey named NetworkProvider, under the following Registry path:

```
HKEY_LOCAL_MACHINE\SYSTEM\CurrentControlSet
    \Services\Service or Driver Key Name\NetworkProvider
```

The following entry values should appear under the NetworkProvider subkey for each network the computer can use:

ProviderName   **REG_SZ**   *Name*

Specifies the name of the Provider, which is displayed as the network name in Browse dialog boxes. This name is defined by the network vendor, and is usually some variation of the product name.

Default: Defined by network vendor

ProviderPath   **REG_SZ**   *DLL pathname*

Specifies the full path of the DLL that implements the network provider.

Default: Defined by network vendor

The NetworkProvider subkey under CurrentControlSet\Control provides a list of the available network providers.

NWLink Transport Entries (IPX/SPX)

NWLink is an implementation of the IPX/SPX protocols popular in NetWare networks. In addition, the module NWNBLink provides support for the Novell implementation of the NetBIOS protocol. With the Registry Editor, you can modify the following:

- The NetBIOS component of NWNBLink, including modification of parameters supporting the Microsoft extensions to Novell NetBIOS
- The IPX/SPX component of NWLink
- Parameters that affect the use of NWLink in a Token Ring network

---

Caution All entries have reasonable defaults that usually should not need to be modified. Be careful when modifying an entry, because any change can easily affect the performance of a conversation between the sender and receiver.

The NWLink keys do not appear in the Registry unless this service is installed using the Network icon in Control Panel. After the service is installed, not all entries appear by default in the Registry. If the entry is not there, the default value for that entry is used.

NWNBLink Entries for Microsoft Extensions to Novell NetBIOS

The Microsoft Extensions to Novell NetBIOS are included to enhance the performance of the traditional Novell NetBIOS protocol. NWNBLink can detect automatically whether it is talking to a Novell NetBIOS implementation that does not understand these extensions; in such a case, NWNBLink will fall back to the standard Novell NetBIOS protocol currently used in NetWare networks. However, significant performance gains can be realized if the extensions are used (for example, if the NetBIOS conversation occurs between two Windows NT computers).

The Registry path for these value entries is the following:

```
HKEY_LOCAL_MACHINE\SYSTEM\CurrentControlSet
    \Services\NWNBLink\Parameters
```

AckDelayTime   REG_DWORD   *50 to 65535 milliseconds*

Determines the value of the delayed acknowledgment timer.

Default: 250 (no entry = default)

AckWindow   REG_DWORD   *0 to 65535 frames*

Specifies the number of frames to receive before sending an acknowledgment. The **AckWindow** entry is used as a clocking mechanism on networks in which the sender is networked on a fast LAN, but the receiver is networked on the other side utilizing a slower link. By automatically forcing acknowledgments, the sender can keep sending frames continually. If both the sender and receiver are located on a fast link, you can set **AckWindow** to 0 to turn off sending an acknowledgment to the sender. Alternatively, NWNBLink can be set to dynamically determine whether to use the **AckWindow** parameter based on the setting of **AckWindowThreshold**. Related parameter: **AckWindowThreshold**.

Default: 2 (no entry = default)

AckWindowThreshold   REG_DWORD   *0 to 65535 milliseconds*

Specifies the threshold value for the round-trip time that defines when **AckWindow** will be ignored. The round trip time is an estimate of how long it takes for a frame to be sent and received from a workstation. NWNBLink determines this estimate and uses it as a basis for determining whether it is necessary to send automatic acknowledgments. If **AckWindowThreshold** is set to 0, NWNBLink relies on the **AckWindow** entry. Related parameters: **AckWindow**.

Default: 500

EnablePiggyBackAck   REG_DWORD   *0 or 1*

Allows the receiver to piggyback acknowledgments. Piggybacking acknowledgments can occur when the receiver has detected the end of a NetBIOS message. When the sender and receiver are not participating in two-way NetBIOS traffic, you should set **EnablePiggyBackAck** to 0. An example of one-way traffic is a stock update application, where a server constantly sends NetBIOS messages to clients but the client does not need to respond.

If **EnablePiggyBackAck** is set to 1 but there is no back traffic, NWNBLink waits the number of milliseconds determined by **AckDelayTime** before sending the acknowledgment, and then it turns off support for piggybacking acknowledgments. If the workstation at some point starts sending as well as receiving data, NWNBLink turns support back on for piggybacking acknowledgments. Related parameter: **AckDelayTime**.

Default: 1 (true—enable piggybacking acknowledgments; no entry = default)

Extensions   REG_DWORD   *0 or 1*

Specifies whether to use NWNBLink extensions discussed in this section.

Default: 1 (true; no entry = default)

RcvWindowMax   REG_DWORD   *1 to 49152 frames*

Specifies the maximum number of frames the receiver can receive at one time. The value specified by **RcvWindowMax** is sent to the sender during session initialization to give the sender an upper bound on the number of frames that can be sent at one time. Related parameters: **AckDelayTime**, **AckWindow**, **AckWindowThreshold**, **EnablePiggyBackAck**, and **RcvWindowMax**.

Default: 4 (no entry = default)

NWNBLink Entries for Novell NetBIOS or Microsoft Extensions

The Registry path for these value entries is the following:

```
HKEY_LOCAL_MACHINE\SYSTEM\CurrentControlSet
   \Services\NWNBLink\Parameters
```

**BroadcastCount   REG_DWORD   *1 to 65535*

Specifies the number of times to send a broadcast. If **Internet** is set to 1, the **BroadcastCount** is doubled. Related parameter: **BroadcastTimeout**.

Default: 3 (no entry = default)

**BroadcastTimeout   REG_DWORD   *1 to 65535 half-seconds*

Specifies the time between sending find-name requests. This value is not affected if **Internet** is set to 1. Related parameter: **BroadcastCount**.

Default: 1 (no entry = default)

**ConnectionCount   REG_DWORD   *1 to 65535*

Specifies the number of times to send a connection probe. A connection probe is sent by the initiator of a session if a connection could not be made to the remote computer. If **Internet** is set to 1, the **ConnectionCount** is doubled. Related parameter: **ConnectionTimeout**.

Default: 5 (no entry = default)

**ConnectionTimeout   REG_DWORD   *1 to 65535 half-seconds*

Specifies the time between sending connection probes when initiating a session.

Default: 2 (no entry = default)

**InitialRetransmissionTime   REG_DWORD   *1 to 65535 milliseconds*

Specifies the initial value for the retransmission time. Related parameter: **RetransmitMax**.

Default: 500 (no entry = default)

**Internet   REG_DWORD   *0 or 1*

Specifies whether to change the packet type from 0x04 to 0x14 (Novell WAN broadcast).

Default: 1 (true; no entry = default)

NWLink Transport Entries (IPX/SPX)

KeepAliveCount   REG_DWORD   *1 to 65535*

Specifies the number of times to send a session-alive frame before timing out if there is no response. Related parameter: **KeepAliveTimeout**.

Default: 8 (no entry = default)

KeepAliveTimeout   REG_DWORD   *1 to 65535 half-seconds*

Specifies the time between sending session-alive frames. Related parameter: **KeepAliveCount**.

Default: 60 (no entry = default)

RetransmitMax   REG_DWORD   *1 to 65535*

Specifies the maximum number of times the sender should retransmit before assuming that something is wrong with the link. Related parameter: **InitialRetransmissionTime**.

Default: 8 (no entry = default)

NWLink Entries for IPX/SPX:
NWLink Parameters for the Network Adapter Card

These parameters are specific for each binding of NWLink to a network adapter card. The Registry path for these value entries is the following:

```
HKEY_LOCAL_MACHINE\SYSTEM\CurrentControlSet\Services
    \NWLinkIPX\NetConfig\<adapter name>
```

AdapterName   REG_DWORD   *Name*

Specifies the name of the adapter that NWLink will use. This parameter is set when you choose a network adapter card to bind NWLink using the Network icon in Control Panel. In this release, only one card is supported.

BindSap   REG_DWORD   *Type field*

Specifies the Ethertype if the frame format is Ethernet II. The Ethertype field is only relevant if Ethernet II frames are to be sent or received. You can choose the frame type using the Network icon in Control Panel. For more information, see the explanation for the **PktType** entry. Related parameter: **PktType**.

Default: 8137 (in hex)

DefaultAutoDetectType   REG_DWORD   *0, 1, 2, 3, or 4*

Specifies the packet type to use if IPX cannot detect any servers when detecting the network on startup. If a new packet type is detected, this value is updated by the transport. The valid values are the following:

Value	Packet form
0	Ethernet_II
1	Ethernet_802.3
2	802.2
3	SNAP
4	ArcNet

Default: 2 (802.2)

EnableFuncaddr   REG_DWORD   *Boolean*

When set to 1, this parameter specifies that the IPX functional address will be enabled if this card is a Token Ring card. If this value is 0, the IPX functional address will not be added. The IPX functional address is C00000800000 (hex). Novell has been phasing out use of this, but it is still in use in some places. It is up to the application to take advantage of the IPX functional address. In most instances, the broadcast address (ffffffffffff hex) is used instead.

Default: 1 (true)

EnableWanRouter   REG_DWORD   *Boolean*

When set to 1 (true), the RIP router should be enabled for this adapter.

Default: 1 (true)

MaxPktSize   REG_DWORD   *0 to 65535*

Specifies the maximum frame size the network adapter card should be allowed to transmit. If this number is 0, NWLink will get this information from the card driver. This parameter allows the administrator to make the maximum transmit size for a card smaller than the card driver allows. A scenario in which you might want to change this entry is in an environment in which the network adapter card on one side of a conversation is on a link that has a larger frame size than the link on the other side of a conversation—for example, if the sending station is linked to a 16 Mbps Token Ring and the receiving station is linked to an Ethernet network.

Default: 0

NetworkNumber   REG_DWORD   *Number*

Specifies the network number (in hex) to be used for this adapter. If this number is 0, the NWLink will get the network number from the network as it is running. This parameter is set using the Network icon in Control Panel. IPX network numbers are 4 bytes (8 hex characters) long. An example of an IPX network number is AABBDDFF. You should not have to enter a specific value because NWLink will determine it for you. Make sure to get the network number for your IPX subnet from the network administrator if you want to enter a specific number.

Default: 0

PktType   REG_DWORD   *0, 1, 2, 3,4, or 0xFF*

NWLink supports Ethernet, Token Ring, FDDI, and ARCnet topologies. The **PktType** parameter specifies the packet form to use. The valid values are the following:

Value	Packet form
0	Ethernet_II
1	Ethernet_802.3
2	802.2
3	SNAP
4	ARCnet
0xFF	Auto-detect

If multiple packet types are used for an adapter, the network number for each can be specified by adding corresponding entries in the **NetworkNumber** multistring.

If the adapter is an Ethernet adapter, choose between values 0 through 3. If the adapter is either a Token Ring or FDDI adapter, choose between s 2 and 3. If you are using an ARCnet adapter, choose value 4. If the adapter is a Token Ring or FDDI adapter, values 0 and 1 will work the same as value 2. Related parameter: **BindSap**.

Default: 1 (802.3)

SourceRouteBcast   REG_DWORD   *0 or 1*

Specifies the source route to be used when transmitting a packet to the broadcast MAC (Media Access Control) address (ffffffffFFF hex). If this value is 0, the packet will be transmitted to the single-route broadcast (0xC2, 0x70). If the value is 1, the packet will be transmitted to the all-routes broadcast (0x82, 0x70). Related parameters: **SourceRouteDef**, **SourceRouting**, and **SourceRouteMCast**.

Default: 0

SourceRouteDef **REG_DWORD** *0 or 1*

Specifies the source route to be used when transmitting a package to a unique MAC address that is not in the source routing table. If the MAC address is in the source routing table, the route in the table will be used. If this value is 0, the packet will be transmitted to the single-route broadcast (0xC2, 0x70). If the value is not 0, the packet will be transmitted to the all-routes broadcast (0x82, 0x70). Related parameters: **SourceRouteBcast**, **SourceRouting**, and **SourceRouteMCast**.

Default: 0

SourceRouteMcast **REG_DWORD** *Boolean*

Specifies the source route to be used when transmitting a packet to a multicast MAC address (C000xxxxxxxx). If this value is 0, the packet will be transmitted to the single-route broadcast (0xC2, 0x70). If the value is not 0, the packet will be transmitted to the all-routes broadcast (0x82, 0x70). Related parameters: **SourceRouteBcast**, **SourceRouteDef**, and **SourceRouting**.

Default: 0

SourceRouting **REG_DWORD** *Boolean*

Specifies whether to use source routing. This parameter is only used if the adapter is a Token Ring adapter. If there are no source routing bridges on the Token Ring, disable this entry to disable all of the source routing logic. Related parameters: **SourceRouteBcast**, **SourceRouteDef**, and **SourceRouteMCast**.

Default: 0 (false—do not use source routing)

NWLink Entries for IPX/SPX: Global IPX Parameters

The following parameters are global for the entire transport. The Registry path for these value entries is the following:

```
HKEY_LOCAL_MACHINE\SYSTEM\CurrentControlSet
    \Services\NWLinkIPX\Parameters
```

ConnectionCount **REG_DWORD** *1 to 65535*

Specifies the number of times the probe will be sent when SPX is trying to connect to a remote node. If no response is received after the probes are sent, an error will occur. Related parameter: **ConnectionTimeout**.

Default: 10

ConnectionTimeout   **REG_DWORD**   *1 to 65535 half-seconds*

Specifies the time between connection probes when SPX is trying to connect to a remote node. Related parameter: **ConnectionCount**.

Default: 2 (1 second)

DedicatedRouter   **REG_DWORD**   *Boolean*

When set to 1 (true), this computer is a dedicated router and will not have services running on it.

Default: 0 (false)

DisableDialinNetbios   **REG_DWORD**   *Boolean*

When set to 1 (true), IPX should prevent NetBIOS type 20 packets from going out over dial-in WAN lines. This setting prevents unneeded traffic on the WAN. The only case where **DisableDialinNetbios** should be false is when a NetBIOS application on the local computer needs to connect to a remote computer over a dial-in WAN line.

Default: 1 (true)

DisableDialoutSap   **REG_DWORD**   *Boolean*

When set to 1 (true), IPX should disable SAP announcements and responses on dial-out WAN lines. This prevents the WAN line from being tied up with router to router SAP traffic and allows the Gateway Service for NetWare or the Client Service for NetWare on the machine to correctly discover servers on the WAN.

Default: 0 (false)

EthernetPadToEven   **REG_DWORD**   *Boolean*

When set to 1 (true), Ethernet sends should be padded to an even length to accommodate ODI card drivers that can receive only even-length frames.

Default: 1 (true)

InitDatagrams   **REG_DWORD**   *1 to 65535*

Specifies the number of datagrams initially allocated by IPX. Related parameter: **MaxDatagrams**.

Default: 10

KeepAliveCount   **REG_DWORD**   *1 to 65535*

Specifies how many times to send a keep-alive probe before timing out if there is no response. Related parameter: **KeepAliveTimeout**.

Default: 8

KeepAliveTimeout   REG_DWORD   *1 to 65535 half-seconds*

Specifies the time that the local side should wait before sending a probe to the remote to verify that the SPX connection is still alive. Related parameter: **KeepAliveCount**.

Default: 12 (6 seconds)

MaxDatagrams   REG_DWORD   *1 to 65535*

Specifies the maximum number of datagrams that IPX will allocate. Related parameter: **InitDatagrams**.

Default: 50

RipAgeTime   REG_DWORD   *1 to 65535 minutes*

IPX maintains an RIP cache in order to locate computers on a remote network. The **RipAgeTime** entry informs IPX how long to wait before requesting an RIP update for an entry. This timer is reset when an RIP announcement is received for an entry in the RIP cache.

Default: 5 minutes

RipCount   REG_DWORD   *1 to 65535*

When the RIP protocol layer is trying to find a route on the network, this parameter specifies how many times to send a request before giving up. Related parameter: **RipTimeout**

Default: 5

RipTableSize   REG_DWORD   *1 to 65535*

Specifies the number of buckets in the RIP hash table.

Default: 7

RipTimeout   REG_DWORD   *1 to 65535 half-seconds*

Specifies the timeout between RIP request packets being sent out when the RIP protocol layer is trying to find a route on the network. Related parameter: **RipCount**.

Default: 1 (1 half-second)

RipUsageTime   REG_DWORD   *1 to 65535 minutes*

IPX maintains a RIP cache in order to locate computers on a remote network. The **RipUsageTime** entry informs IPX how many minutes to wait before an entry in the RIP cache will be deleted from the cache. This timer is reset when a packet is sent to the remote computer.

Default: 15 minutes

NWLink Transport Entries (IPX/SPX)

SingleNetworkActive   REG_DWORD   *Boolean*

When set to 1 (true), either the LAN or the WAN line can be active on the computer, but not both at once. This setting allows the Gateway Service for NetWare or the Client Service for NetWare to correctly locate NetWare servers on the WAN when dialed in.

Default: 0 (false)

SocketStart   REG_DWORD   *0 to 65535*

Specifies the start of the range that IPX uses to auto-assign sockets. Related parameters: **SocketEnd**, **SocketUniqueness**.

Default: 0x4000

SocketEnd   REG_DWORD   *1 to 65535*

Specifies the end of the range that IPX uses to auto-assign sockets. Related parameters: **SocketStart**, **SocketUniqueness**.

Default: 0x8000

SocketUniqueness   REG_DWORD   *1 to 65535*

Specifies the number of sockets that IPX sets aside when auto-assigning a socket. For example, if **SocketUniqueness** is 8 and **SocketStart** is 0x4000, IPX will set aside the range 0x4000-0x4007. Related parameter: **SocketStart**, **SocketEnd**.

Default: 8

SourceRouteUsageTime   REG_DWORD   *1 to 65535 minutes*

Range: Specifies the number of minutes an unused entry can remain in the Token Ring source routing cache before it is flushed.

Default: 10

VirtualNetworkNumber   REG_DWORD   *0 to 4294967295*

Specifies the virtual network number of this computer.

Default: 0

WindowSize   REG_DWORD   *1 to 10 SPX packets*

Specifies the window to use in the SPX packets. SPX uses the Allocation field of the SPX packet to tell the remote how many receives are available for receiving data. The **WindowSize** entry specifies what value to put in the SPX Allocation field.

Default: 4

NWLink Transport Entries (IPX/SPX)

NWLink Entries for IPX/SPX: Global SPX Parameters

The following parameters are global for the entire transport. The Registry path for these value entries is the following:

```
HKEY_LOCAL_MACHINE\SYSTEM\CurrentControlSet
    \Services\NWLnkSPX\Parameters
```

ConnectionCount   REG_DWORD   *1 to 65535*

Specifies the number of times the probe will be sent when SPX is trying to connect to a remote node. If no response is received after the probes are sent, an error will occur. Related parameter: **ConnectionTimeout**.

Default: 10

ConnectionTimeout   REG_DWORD   *1 to 65535 half-seconds*

Specifies the time between connection probes when SPX is trying to connect to a remote node. Related parameter: **ConnectionCount**.

Default: 2 (1 second)

InitPackets   REG_DWORD   *1 to 65535*

Specifies the initial number of packets that SPX allocates.

Default: 5

InitialRetransmissionTime   REG_DWORD   *1 to 65535 milliseconds*

Specifies the amount of time that SPX will wait for an acknowledgment before sending a probe.

Default: 500 milliseconds

KeepAliveCount   REG_DWORD   *1 to 65535*

Specifies how many times to send a keep-alive probe before timing out if there is no response. Related parameter: **KeepAliveTimeout**.

Default: 8

KeepAliveTimeout   REG_DWORD   *1 to 65535 half-seconds*

Specifies the time that the local side should wait before sending a probe to the remote to verify that the SPX connection is still alive. Related parameter: **KeepAliveCount**.

Default: 12 (6 seconds)

MaxPackets   REG_DWORD   *1 to 65535*

Specifies the maximum number of packets that SPX will allocate.

Default: 30

MaxPacketSize   REG_DWORD   *1 to 65535*

Specifies the maximum packet size that SPX-2 will use when negotiating packet size with the remote network node. SPX-2 will use the correct size for the network if it is smaller than **MaxPacketSize**.

Default: 4096

RetransmissionCount   REG_DWORD   *1 to 65535*

Specifies the number of probes that SPX sends while awaiting an acknowledgment for data.

Default: 8

SpxSocketEnd   REG_DWORD   *1 to 65535*

Specifies the end of the range that SPX uses to auto-assign sockets.

Default: 0x7fff

SpxSocketStart   REG_DWORD   *0 to 65535*

Specifies the start of the range that SPX uses to auto-assign sockets

Default: 0x4000

SpxSocketUniqueness   REG_DWORD   *1 to 65535*

Specifies the number of sockets that SPX sets aside when auto-assigning a socket. For example, if **SpxSocketUniqueness** is 8 and **SpxSocketStart** is 0x4000, SPX will set aside the range 0x4000-0x4007.

Default: 8

WindowSize   REG_DWORD   *1 to 10 SPX packets*

Specifies the window to use in the SPX packets. SPX uses the Allocation field of the SPX packet to tell the remote how many receives are available for receiving data. The **WindowSize** entry specifies what value to put in the SPX Allocation field.

Default: 4

NWLink Transport Entries (IPX/SPX)

Redirector (Rdr) Service Entries

The subkey for the Rdr (redirector) service has the following Registry path:

```
HKEY_LOCAL_MACHINE\SYSTEM\CurrentControlSet\Services\Rdr\Parameters
```

For the search buffer sizes defined in the following entries: If the buffer passed for the search is less than the **LowerSearchThreshold** value, the system requests **LowerSearchThreshold** bytes of data from the server. If the buffer size is between the value of **LowerSearchThreshold** and **UpperSearchBufferSize**, the system uses the buffer size. On a slow link (such as a RAS link), if it will take more than five seconds to retrieve data, the Redirector service uses the user's requested buffer size.

ConnectTimeout   REG_DWORD   *Number of seconds*

Specifies the maximum amount of time the redirector will wait for a connect or disconnect to complete.

Default: 300 (5 minutes)

LowerSearchBufferSize   REG_DWORD   *Number of kilobytes*

Specifies the number of bytes the redirector will use for small searches.

Default: 16K

LowerSearchThreshold   REG_DWORD   *Number of kilobytes*

Specifies the number of bytes below which the redirector will request a search of **LowerSearchBufferSize**. If the search size is larger than this (but below the **UpperSearchBufferSize**), the redirector will use the **UpperSearchBufferSize**.

Default: 16K

StackSize   REG_DWORD   *Number of kilobytes*

Sets the default IRP stack size for the redirector.

Default: 4

UpperSearchBufferSize   REG_DWORD   *Number of kilobytes*

Specifies the number of bytes the redirector will use for large searches.

Default: 32K

UseAsyncWriteBehind   REG_DWORD   *0 or 1*

Enables the asynchronous-write-behind variation of the write-behind optimization.

Default: 1 (true)

UseWriteBehind   **REG_DWORD**   *0 or 1*

Enables the write-behind optimization.

Default: 1 (true)

Remote Access Service (RAS) Entries

The RemoteAccess subkey is created in the Registry when you install RAS on a server, using the Network icon in Control Panel. The default values in RemoteAccess and its subkeys work well for all Windows NT operations such as copying files, using network resources, and sending and receiving electronic mail. However, for some systems, you may want to adjust individual parameters to suit your particular performance and security needs.

Initially, there are no value entries in the Registry for the Remote Access subkey or its subkeys until you add them with new settings. (The only exception is **EnableNetbiosGateway**, the NetBIOS parameter.) Unlisted value entries are set to their default values, as described in this section.

For information on Remote Access configuration files and other parameters, see Appendix B, "Configuration Files," in the *Windows NT Remote Access Service Administrator's Guide.*

The subkeys under the Remote Access subkey in HKEY_LOCAL_MACHINE \SYSTEM\CurrentControlSet\Services\ include the following:

- RemoteAccess\Parameters
- RemoteAccess\Parameters\NetbiosGateway
- AsyncMac*n*\Parameters
- RasHub\Parameters
- RasMan\Parameters

See also **WanNameQueryRetries** in "NBF (NetBEUI) Transport Entries," earlier in this chapter.

Remote Access Parameters Subkey Entries

The Parameters subkey for Remote Access has the following Registry path:

```
HKEY_LOCAL_MACHINE\SYSTEM\CurrentControlSet\Services
    \RemoteAccess\Parameters
```

For changes to take effect, you must stop and restart the Remote Access service. The functions and settings of these value entries are as follows:

AuthenticateRetries   REG_DWORD   *0 to 10*

Sets the maximum number of unsuccessful retries allowed if the initial attempt at authentication fails.

Default: 2

AuthenticateTime   REG_DWORD   *20 to 600 seconds*

Sets the maximum time limit within which a user must be successfully authenticated. If the client does not initiate the authentication process within this time, the user is disconnected.

Default: 120 seconds

CallbackTime   REG_DWORD   *2 to 12 seconds*

Sets the time interval that the server waits before calling the client back when the Callback feature has been set. Each client communicates the value of its own callback time when connecting to a Remote Access server. If this value is not communicated (that is, if the client does not communicate a value for the callback time, as with Remote Access 1.0 and 1.1 clients), the value of the **CallbackTime** parameter becomes the default.

Default: 2 seconds

EnableAudit   REG_DWORD   *0 or 1*

Determines whether Remote Access auditing is turned on or off. If this feature is enabled, all audits are recorded in the Security event log, which you can view using Event Viewer.

Default: 1 (enabled)

NetbiosGatewayEnabled   REG_DWORD   *0 or 1*

Caution   Do not change this value in Registry Editor, because various network bindings must also be changed. This parameter should only be changed by using the RAS Setup program.

Makes the server function like a NetBIOS gateway, allowing clients to access the LAN. If disabled, remote clients can access only the resources on the Remote Access server in a point-to-point connection; dial-in users cannot see the network or access network resources.

Default: 1 (enabled)

RAS NetBIOSGateway Subkey Entries

The Registry path for these entries is the following:

```
HKEY_LOCAL_MACHINE\SYSTEM\CurrentControlSet\Services
    \RemoteAccess\Parameters
```

AutoDisconnect   **REG_DWORD**   *0 to 1000 minutes*

Sets the time interval after which inactive connections are terminated. Inactivity is measured by lack of NetBIOS session data transfer, such as copying files, accessing network resources, and sending and receiving electronic mail. You may want to set this value to 0 seconds if clients are running NetBIOS datagram applications. Setting this value to 0 turns off **AutoDisconnect**.

Default: 20 minutes

DisableMcastFwdWhenSessionTraffic   **REG_DWORD**   *0 or 1*

Allows NetBIOS session traffic (for example, Windows NT-based applications) to have priority over multicast datagrams (such as server messages). In other words, multicast datagrams are transferred only when there is no session traffic. Unless you're using an application that depends on multicast datagrams, leave this parameter enabled.

Default: 1 (enabled)

EnableBroadcast   **REG_DWORD**   *0 or 1*

Determines whether broadcast datagrams are forwarded to remote workstations. Broadcast datagrams are not often useful and take up too much bandwidth on a slow link. Unless you're using an application that relies on broadcast datagrams, leave this parameter disabled.

Default: 0 (disabled)

EnableNetbiosSessionsAuditing   **REG_DWORD**   *0 or 1*

Enable this parameter to record in the event log the establishment of NetBIOS sessions between the remote clients and the LAN servers. Enable this parameter to track the NetBIOS resources accessed on the LAN.

Default: 0 (disabled)

MaxBcastDgBuffered   **REG_DWORD**   *16 to 255*

Sets the number of broadcast datagrams that the gateway buffers for a client. If you're using an application that communicates extensively through multicast or broadcast datagrams, increase this parameter so that the Remote Access server can deliver all datagrams reliably.

Default: 32

MaxDgBufferedPerGroupName   REG_DWORD   *1 to 255*

Sets the number of datagrams that can be buffered per group name. Increasing this value buffers more datagrams per group name but also takes up more virtual memory.

Default: 10

MaxDynMem   REG_DWORD   *131072 to 4294967295*

Sets the amount of virtual memory used to buffer NetBIOS session data for each remote client.

Because the Remote Access server is a gateway between the slow line and the LAN, data is stored (buffered) in its memory when coming from the fast line (LAN) before it is forwarded to the slow line (asynchronous line).

The Remote Access server minimizes the usage of the system's physical memory by locking only a minimal set of pages (about 64K per client) and making use of virtual memory (up to **MaxDynMem**) to buffer the rest of the data. So, as long as there is enough space on the hard disk to expand PAGEFILE.SYS, you can increase this value if needed.

If you have an application with a LAN (fast) sender and an asynchronous (slow) receiver, and if the sender is sending more data at a time than the Remote Access server can buffer in **MaxDynMem**, the Remote Access server tries to apply a form of NetBIOS level flow control by not submitting NCB.RECEIVE on the session until it has enough buffer space to get incoming data. For this reason, if you have such an application, you should increase your NetBIOS SEND/RECEIVE time-outs so that the fast sender can keep pace with the slow receiver.

Default: 655350

MaxNames   REG_DWORD   *1 to 255*

Sets the number of unique NetBIOS names each client can have, with a limit of 255 names for all clients together.

Remote clients running Windows NT and Windows for Workgroups may need as many as seven or eight names each. To accommodate these workstations, set the **MaxNames** value to 8 and reduce the number of ports on the Remote Access server. If you have Windows NT or Windows for Workgroups clients dialing in to servers running Remote Access version 1.1 or earlier, set this parameter to 8 or greater.

Default: 255

MaxSessions **REG_DWORD** *1 to 255*

Sets the maximum number of simultaneous NetBIOS sessions each client can have, with a limit of 255 sessions for all clients together. If you have multiple clients connecting simultaneously with each running 4 or 5 sessions, decrease the value of this parameter so that the total number of sessions does not exceed 255.

Default: 255

MultiCastForwardRate **REG_DWORD** *–1 (disabled); 0 to 32,676 seconds*

Governs the multicasting of group name datagrams to all remote workstations. This parameter filters datagrams sent on group names by forwarding them at a specified time interval.

The value –1 disables forwarding. The value 0 guarantees delivery of group name datagrams. The value *n* forwards datagrams every *n* seconds, when $1 \leq n \leq 32,676$.

If the **EnableBroadcast** parameter is set to 0, broadcasts are not forwarded even if the **MultiCastForwardRate** parameter is set to a positive number (in this case, only multicast datagrams are forwarded). The line becomes overloaded. If **MultiCastForwardRate** is set to –1, broadcasts are still not forwarded even if **EnableBroadcast** is set to 1. See also **EnableBroadcast**.

To save bandwidth for session traffic, filter the datagrams. However, if you have an application based on multicast datagrams, set this parameter to 0. This value guarantees delivery of all datagrams sent on group names from the LAN to the remote client.

Default: 5

NumRecvQueryIndications **REG_DWORD** *1 to 32*

Allows a Remote Access client to initiate multiple network connections simultaneously. If a remote client is running a NetBIOS application that does multiple NCB.CALL commands simultaneously, increase this parameter to improve performance.

Default: 3

RcvDgSubmittedPerGroupName **REG_DWORD** *1 to 32*

Determines the number of NetBIOS commands of the type Receive Datagram that can be submitted simultaneously per group name on the LAN stack. Keep this setting as small as possible to minimize the amount of memory consumed by system resources. Each datagram command received locks about 1.5K of physical memory in the system.

Default: 3

Remote Access Service (RAS) Entries

RemoteListen   REG_DWORD   *0 to 2*

Sets the remote NCB_LISTEN capability.

Value	Meaning
0	Disables a client's ability to post NCB_LISTEN for any NetBIOS name. Because every remote listen posted consumes one session, setting this parameter to 0 saves sessions.
1	Messages. Allows clients to post NCB_LISTEN on Windows NT ServerWindows NT Server message aliases only. If a remote client is running the Messenger service, it can then receive messages from LAN users, printers, and the like.
2	All. Enables NCB_LISTEN for all remote client NetBIOS names, allowing clients to run NetBIOS server applications. This setting allows all clients to function as NetBIOS servers on the network.

It is best to leave the **RemoteListen** parameter set to the default, 1 (messages). Allowing NCB_LISTEN capability on remote clients can significantly drain system resources and therefore is not recommended.

If the **RemoteListen** parameter is set to 2, Remote Access posts an NCB_LISTEN on all NetBIOS names of Remote Access clients. Because the average Windows NT ServerWindows NT Server workstation has about seven or eight NetBIOS names assigned to it, the total number of NetBIOS names for which an NCB_LISTEN would be posted is 7 or 8 * 64 (the maximum number of clients per Remote Access server), which exceeds the 255 maximum.

Default: 1 (messages)

SizWorkBufs   REG_DWORD   *1024 to 65536*

Sets the size of work buffers. The default setting is optimized for the server message block (SMB) protocol, the protocol between the workstation and the server running on the Windows NT ServerWindows NT Server system.

Default: 4500

RAS AsyncMAC Subkey Entries

The Registry path for these entries is the following:

```
HKEY_LOCAL_MACHINE\SYSTEM\CurrentControlSet\Services
    \AsyncMacn\Parameters
```

For changes to take effect, you must restart the computer.

MaxFrameSize   REG_DWORD *576 to 1514*

Determines the maximum frame size. Use smaller frames for noisy links. A lower setting sends less data per frame, slowing performance. Do not change this parameter for previous versions of the Remote Access service. The value is negotiated between the server and Windows NT clients.

Default: 1514

RAS PPP Subkey Entries

The Registry path that contains entries for the Point-to-Point Protocol (PPP) service is the following:

```
HKEY_LOCAL_MACHINE\SYSTEM\CurrentControlSet\Services\Rasman\PPP
```

ForceEncryptedPassword   REG_DWORD *Boolean*

This is a server-side parameter only. It is used to force the use of the Crypto-Handshake Authentication Protocol while authenticating clients. This means that the cleartest password will not get sent on the wire during authentication.

Default: 1 (enabled)

MaxConfigure   REG_DWORD *Number*

Indicates the number of Configure-Request packets sent without receiving a valid Configure-Ack, Configure-Nak or Configure-Reject before assuming that the peer is unable to respond.

Default: 10

MaxFailure   REG_DWORD *Number*

Indicates the number of Configure-Nak packets send without sending a Configure-Ack before assuming that the configuration in not converging.

Default: 10

MaxReject   REG_DWORD *Number*

Indicates the number of Config-Rejects sent before assuming that the PPP negotiation will not converge.

Default: 5

MaxTerminate   REG_DWORD   *Number*

Indicates the number of Terminate-Request packets sent without receiving a Terminate-Ack before assuming that the peer is unable to respond.

Default: 2

Additional PPP entries are found in the following subkey:

```
HKEY_LOCAL_MACHINE\SYSTEM\CurrentControlSet\Services\Rasman\PPP
    \IPCP
```

PriorityBasedOnSubNetwork   DWORD   *0 or 1*

Local and remote subnets are part of the same network number range. By default, RAS forwards packets over the RAS link when the two interfaces belong to the same network. RAS forwards packets based on the subnet number and lets you see this machine on the LAN even when called in over RAS if this value is set to 1.

Default: 0

RAS RasHub Subkey Entries

The Registry path for the RasHub subkey is the following:

```
HKEY_LOCAL_MACHINE\SYSTEM\CurrentControlSet\Services\RasHub\Parameters
```

For changes to take effect, you must restart the computer.

The subkeys RasHub01 and RasHub02 show, for example, that this installation of Remote Access is configured for two COM ports. In configuring ports, you can determine whether clients have access to the Remote Access server only (point-to-point connection) or to the network.

NetworkAddress   REG_SZ   *"xxxxxx"*

Reassigns the first four bytes of the 6-byte IEEE address. For example, for the address "03-1F-2C-81-92-34" only the first four bytes are looked at.

Some applications depend on an IEEE adapter address being available. However, because the Remote Access Service uses modems (not real Ethernet adapters), it does not have an IEEE Ethernet address per se. This parameter lets you manually set an IEEE adapter address for Remote Access adapter bindings where applications demand it.

Remote Access Service (RAS) Entries

RAS RasMan Subkey Entries

The Registry path for the RasMan subkey is the following:

```
HKEY_LOCAL_MACHINE\SYSTEM\CurrentControlSet\Services\RasMan\Parameters
```

Logging   REG_DWORD   *0 or 1*

Turns on information tracking for the modem using the DEVICE.LOG file. Set this value to 1 if you have modem problems that you cannot solve following documented procedures in the *Microsoft Windows NT Remote Access Administrator's Guide.* Logging begins the next time you dial in to connect through RAS. You do not need to restart your computer for the DEVICE.LOG file to be created.

Replicator Service Entries

The Registry path that contains entries for the Replicator service is the following:

```
HKEY_LOCAL_MACHINE\SYSTEM\CurrentControlSet\Services
    \Replicator\Parameters
```

CrashDir   REG_SZ   *First-level directory name*

This item is temporarily recorded in the Registry by the Replicator service. If it remains after a system repair, you can delete this entry using Registry Editor.

ExportList   REG_SZ   *List*

Lists an unlimited number of servers or domains that receive notices when the export directory is updated. These servers subsequently replicate from the export server. If no *List* value is specified, the export server sends a notice to its domain. Separate multiple *List* names with a semicolon (;). This value is ignored if the value of **Replicate** is 2 (Import).

Do not use the UNC name when you specify a computername; that is, do not include two backslashes (\\) at the beginning of the name.

Use the Replicator controls in Server Manager or the Server icon in Control Panel to set this value.

Default: (none)

ExportPath   REG_SZ or REG_EXPAND_SZ   *Pathname*

Specifies the export path. All files to be replicated must be in a subdirectory of the export directory. This value is ignored if the value of **Replicate** is set to 2 (Import). Use the Replicator controls in Server Manager or the Server icon in Control Panel to set this value, which cannot be a UNC name.

Default: %SystemRoot%\System32\Repl\Export

GuardTime   REG_DWORD   *0 to one-half of Interval minutes*

Sets the number of minutes an export directory must be stable (no changes to any files) before import servers can replicate its files.

Default: 2 minutes

ImportList   REG_SZ   *List*

Lists an unlimited number of servers or domains that receive notices when the import directory is updated. These servers subsequently replicate from the import server. If no *List* value is specified, updates come from the import server's domain. Separate multiple *List* names with a semicolon (;). This value is ignored if the value of **Replicate** is 1 (Export).

Do not use the UNC name when you specify a computername; that is, do not include two backslashes (\\) at the beginning of the name.

Use the Replicator controls in Server Manager or the Server icon in Control Panel to set this value.

ImportPath   REG_SZ or REG_EXPAND_SZ   *Pathname*

Specifies the path on the import server to receive replicas from the export servers. This value is ignored if the value of **Replicate** is 1 (Export). Use the Replicator controls in Server Manager or the Server icon in Control Panel to set this value, which cannot be a UNC name.

Default: %SystemRoot%\System32\Repl\Import

Interval   REG_DWORD   *1 to 60 minutes*

Sets how often an export server checks the replicated directories for changes. This option is ignored on import servers.

Default: 5 minutes

Pulse   REG_DWORD   *1 to 10 cycles*

Specifies how often the export server repeats sending the last update notice. These repeat notices are sent even when no changes have occurred, so that import servers that missed the original update notice can receive the notice. The server waits the equivalent of (**Pulse** * **Interval**) minutes before sending each repeat notice.

Default: 3

Random   REG_DWORD   *1 to 120 seconds*

Specifies the maximum time that the import servers can wait before requesting an update. An import server uses the export server's value of **Random** to generate a random number of seconds (from 0 to the value of **Random**). The import server waits this long after receiving an update notice before requesting the replica from the export server. This prevents the export server from being overloaded by simultaneous update requests.

Default: 60

Replicate   REG_DWORD   *1, 2, or 3*

Specifies the Replicator action, according to the following:

Value	Meaning
1	Export—the server maintains a master tree to be replicated.
2	Import—the server receives update notices from the export server.
3	Both— the server is to export and import directories or files.

Use the Replicator controls in Server Manager or the Server icon in Control Panel to set this value.

Default: 3

Schedule Service Entries

There are no parameters that can be added for the Schedule service in this path:

```
HKEY_LOCAL_MACHINE\SYSTEM\CurrentControlSet\Services
    \Schedule
```

You use the Schedule service to submit a job such as an executable or batch file to run at a later time. You must define access controls on the Schedule subkey itself if you want to run in an account that is not an Administrator account.

Server Service Entries

With Registry Editor, you can modify the startup parameters for the Server service. Unless otherwise noted, these parameters are found in this path:

```
HKEY_LOCAL_MACHINE\SYSTEM\CurrentControlSet\Services
    \LanmanServer\Parameters
```

The parameters that control network bindings for this service are described in "NetRules Subkey Entries," earlier in this chapter.

AlertSched   REG_DWORD   *1 to 65535 minutes*

Specifies in Microsoft LAN Manager and in Windows NT how often the server checks alert conditions and sends needed alert messages.

Default: 5

BlockingThreads   REG_DWORD   *1 to 9999 for NTAS*

Specifies the number of threads set aside by the server to service requests that can block the thread for a significant amount of time. Larger values can increase performance but use more memory. A value that is too large can impede performance by causing excessive task switching.

Default: (depends on configuration; max. 4 for Windows NT Workstation)

ConnectionlessAutoDisc   REG_DWORD   *15 minutes to infinity*

Disconnect time for clients using direct hosted IPX. If the client does not send a request to the server during this interval, the client is disconnected regardless of whether it has open files or pipes.

Default: 15

CriticalThreads   REG_DWORD   *1 to 9999*

Special-purpose threads used for time-critical tasks.

Default: 1

DiskSpaceThreshold   REG_DWORD   *0 to 99 percent*

Specifies the percentage of free disk space remaining before an alert is sent.

Default: 10 percent

EnableFCBopens   REG_DWORD   *0 or 1*

Specifies whether MS-DOS File Control Blocks (FCBs) are folded together, so multiple remote opens are performed as a single open on the server. This saves resources on the server.

Default: 1 (true)

EnableOplockForceClose   REG_DWORD   *0 or 1*

If a client has an opportunistic lock (oplock) and does not respond to an oplock break, there are two possible behaviors that this parameter selects:

Value	Meaning
0 (false)	Fail the second open, thereby limiting access to the file. (This is typical behavior for a client running LAN Manager version 2.0.)
1 (true)	Force closed the open instance of the client that has the oplock, risking the loss of cached data. (This is typical behavior for a client running LAN Manager version 2.1.)

Default: 0 (false)

Server Service Entries

EnableOplocks   REG_DWORD   *0 or 1*

Specifies whether the server allows clients to use oplocks on files. Oplocks are a significant performance enhancement, but have the potential to cause lost cached data on some networks, particularly wide-area networks.

Default: 1 (true)

EnableRaw   REG_DWORD   *0 or 1*

Specifies whether the server processes raw Server Message Blocks (SMBs). If enabled, this allows more data to be transferred per transaction and improves performance. However, it is possible that processing raw SMBs can impede performance on certain networks. This parameter is automatically tuned by the server.

Default: 1 (true)

EnableSharedNetDrives   REG_DWORD   *0 or 1*

If NWCS is installed, set this value to 1 to reshare the drives connected via NWCS (i.e. Novell drives) as NT shares. It does not allow resharing of NT shares.

Default: 1

EnableSoftCompat   REG_DWORD   *0 or 1*

Specifies whether the server maps a request to a normal open request with shared-read access when the server receives a compatibility open request with read access. Mapping such requests allows several MS-DOS-based computers to open a single file for read access. However, this feature can potentially cause functionality problems with some MS-DOS-based applications.

Default: 1 (true)

EnableWFW311DirectIpx   REG_DWORD   *True or false*

Specifies whether the server should allow old direct-hosted IPX clients to connect. Some old WFW clients provide inadequate named pipe support when running over direct-hosted IPX, causing named pipe applications to hang. If the user does not need named pipe support, this flag can be set to true to allow normal file I/O.

Default: false

ErrorThreshold   REG_DWORD   *1 to 65535*

Sets the number of errors that can occur within an **AlertSched** interval before the server sends an alert message.

Default: 10

Server Service Entries

Hidden   REG_DWORD   *0 or 1*

If this parameter is disabled, the server's name and comment can be viewed by others on the domain. If enabled, the server's name and comment will not be announced.

Default: 0 (false)

InitConnTable   REG_DWORD   *1 to 128*

Specifies the initial number of tree connections to be allocated in the connection table. The server automatically increases the table as necessary, so setting the parameter to a higher value is an optimization.

Default: 8

InitFileTable   REG_DWORD   *1 to 256*

Specifies the initial number of file entries to be allocated in the file table of each server connection.

Default: 16

InitSearchTable   REG_DWORD   *1 to 2048*

Specifies the initial number of entries in the connection's search table.

Default: 8

InitSessTable   REG_DWORD   *1 to 64*

Specifies the initial number of session entries to be allocated in the session table of each server connection.

Default: 4

InitWorkItems   REG_DWORD   *1 to 512*

Specifies the initial number of receive buffers, or work items, used by the server. Allocating work items costs a certain amount of memory initially, but not as much as having to allocate additional buffers later.

Default: (depends on configuration)

IRPstackSize   REG_DWORD   *1 to 12*

Specifies the number of stack locations in I/O Request Packets (IRPs) used by the server. It may be necessary to increase this number for certain transports, MAC drivers, or local file system drivers. Each increment costs 36 bytes of memory per work item (that is, #work items * 36 bytes = total memory cost).

Default: 5

Server Service Entries

LinkInfoValidTime   **REG_DWORD**   *0 to 100,000 seconds*

Specifies the amount of time during which the transport link information is still valid. If more than this amount of time has passed since the last query, the server requires transport link information.

Default: 60

MaxFreeConnections   **REG_DWORD**   *2 to 8 items*

Specifies the maximum number of free connection blocks maintained per endpoint.

Default: Depends upon configuration

MaxGlobalOpenSearch   **REG_DWORD**   *1 to infinity*

The maximum number of core searches that can be active in the server at one time. This is to ensure that resources used by active core searches cannot exceed a certain limit. A high value allows more searches to be active, but can use up more server resources. A low value would save server resources, but can affect clients that needs a lot of searches to be active.

Default: 4096

MaxLinkDelay   **REG_DWORD**   *0 to 100,000 seconds*

Specifies the maximum time allowed for a link delay. If delays exceed this number, the server disables raw I/O for this connection.

Default: 60

MaxKeepSearch   **REG_DWORD**   *10 to 10000 seconds*

Specifies the maximum time during which an incomplete MS-DOS search will be kept by the server. Larger values ensure better interoperability with MS-DOS utilities such as tree-copy and delete-node. However, larger values can cause unusual local behavior (such as a failure of a local directory-delete operation) and higher memory use on the server.

Default: 1800

MaxMpxCt   **REG_DWORD**   *1 to 100 requests*

Provides a suggested maximum to clients for the number of simultaneous requests outstanding to this server. A higher value can increase server performance but requires higher use of server work items.

Default: 50

MaxNonpagedMemoryUsage   **REG_DWORD**   *1 MB to infinite bytes*

Specifies the maximum size of nonpaged memory that the server can have allocated at any time. Adjust this parameter if you want to administer memory quota control.

Default: (depends on system and server configuration)

Server Service Entries

MaxPagedMemoryUsage   REG_DWORD   *1 MB to infinite bytes*

Specifies the maximum size of pageable memory that the server can have allocated at any time. Adjust this parameter if you want to administer memory quota control.

Default: (depends on system and server configuration)

MaxRawWorkItems   REG_DWORD   *1 to 512 items*

Sets the maximum raw work items the server can allocate. If this limit is reached, then the server will reject raw I/O operations from the client.

Default: (depends on configuration)

MaxWorkItems   REG_DWORD   *1 to 512 items*

Specifies the maximum number of receive buffers, or work items, the server can allocate. If this limit is reached, the transport must initiate flow control at a significant performance cost.

Default: (depends on configuration; max. 64 for Windows NT Workstation)

MaxWorkItemIdleTime   REG_DWORD   *10 to 1800 seconds*

Specifies the amount of time that a work item can stay on the idle queue before it is freed.

Default: 30

MinFreeConnections   REG_DWORD   *2 to 5 items*

Specifies the minimum number of free connection blocks maintained per endpoint.

Default: (depends upon configuration)

MinFreeWorkItems   REG_DWORD   *0 to 10 items*

Specifies the minimum number of available receive work items that are needed for the server to begin processing a potentially blocking SMB. A larger value for this parameter ensures that work items are available more frequently for nonblocking requests, but it also increases the likelihood that blocking requests will be rejected.

Default: 2

MinLinkThroughput   REG_DWORD   *0 to infinite bytes per second*

Specifies the minimum link throughput allowed by the server before it disables raw and opportunistic locks for this connection.

Default: 0

MinRcvQueue   **REG_DWORD**   *0 to 10 items*

Specifies the minimum number of free receive work items needed by the server before it begins allocating more. A larger value for this parameter helps ensure that there will always be work items available, but a value that is too large is simply inefficient.

Default: 2

NetworkErrorThreshold   **REG_DWORD**   *1 to 100 percent*

Triggers an alert whenever the percentage of failing network operations relative to total network operations exceeds this value during the **AlertSched** interval.

Default: 5 percent

NonBlockingThreads   **REG_DWORD**   *1 to 9999*

Specifies the number of threads set aside by the server to service requests that cannot block the thread for a significant amount of time. Larger values can increase performance but use more memory. A value that is too large can impede performance by causing excessive task switching.

Default: (depends on configuration; max. 8 for Windows NT Workstation)

NullSessionPipes   **REG_DWORD**   *List of pipes*

List of pipes that the client is allowed to access using the null session. If a pipe is not on this list, the request to access it will be denied. Used with **RestrictNullSessionAccess** and **NullSessionShares**.

Default: (none)

NullSessionShares   **REG_DWORD**   *List of shares*

List of file shares the client is allowed to access using the null session. If a share is not on this list, the request to access it will be denied. Used with **RestrictNullSessionAccess** and **NullSessionPipes**.

Default: (none)

OpenSearch   **REG_DWORD**   *1 to 2048 searches*

Specifies the maximum number of outstanding searches on the server, per connection. A single client can have up to the **OpenSearch** number of active searches. This includes all types of searches, including MS-DOS, OS/2, and Windows NT.

Default: 2048

OplockBreakWait   **REG_DWORD**   *10 to 180 seconds*

Specifies the time that the server waits for a client to respond to an oplock break request. Smaller values can allow detection of crashed clients more quickly but can potentially cause loss of cached data.

Default: 35

Server Service Entries

RawWorkItems **REG_DWORD** *1 to 512 items*

Specifies the number of special work items for raw I/O that the server uses. A larger value for this parameter can increase performance but costs more memory.

Default: (depends on configuration)

RemoveDuplicateSearches **REG_DWORD** *True or false*

Specifies whether the server should close duplicate searches from the same client. This lessens the likelihood of the server hitting the MaxGlobalOpenSearch limit by closing identical searches. This must be set to False if a client needs multiple identical searches to be active.

Default: true

RestrictNullSessionAccess **REG_DWORD** *True or false*

Specifies whether the server should limit access to requests coming in through the null session. If true, NullSessionPipes and NullSessionShares are used. Used with NullSessionPipes and NullSessionShares.

Default: true

ScavTimeout **REG_DWORD** *1 to 300 seconds*

Specifies the time that the scavenger remains idle before waking up to service requests. A smaller value for this parameter improves the response of the server to various events but costs CPU cycles.

Default: 30

ScavQosInfoUpdateTime **REG_DWORD** *0 to 100,000 seconds*

Specifies the time that can pass before the scavenger goes through the list of active connections to update the link information.

Default: 300

SessConns **REG_DWORD** *1 to 2048 connections*

Specifies the maximum number of tree connections that can be made on the server via a single virtual circuit.

Default: 2048

SessOpens **REG_DWORD** *1 to 2048 files*

Specifies the maximum number of files that can be open on a single virtual circuit.

Default: 2048

SessUsers   REG_DWORD   *1 to 2048 users*

Specifies the maximum number of users that can be logged on to a server via a single virtual circuit.

Default: 2048

SharingViolationRetries   REG_DWORD   *0 to 1000*

The number of times the server retries an operation when it gets sharing violation back from the file system. Operations affected include opens, renames, and deletes. This minimizes network traffic in cases where the client keeps retrying these operations whenever it gets a sharing violation.

Default: 5

SharingViolationDelay   REG_DWORD   *0 to 1000 milliseconds*

The number of milliseconds that the server delays for each retry. If this value is too low, then a sharing violation error is more likely at the server's next retry. If set too high, then the response to the client might get delayed much more than what is necessary and will negatively affect performance.

Default: 200

SizReqBuf   REG_DWORD   *512 to 65536 bytes*

Specifies the size of request buffers that the server uses. Small buffers use less memory; large buffers may improve performance.

Default: 4356

ThreadPriority   REG_DWORD   *0, 1, 2, or 15*

Specifies the priority of all server threads in relation to the base priority of the process. Higher priority can give better server performance at the cost of local responsiveness. Lower priority balances server needs with the needs of other processes on the system. Values 0 to 2 are relative to normal or background processes. The default value of 1 is equivalent to the foreground process. A value of 15 runs the server threads at real-time priority—which is not recommended.

Default: 1

Users   REG_DWORD   *1 to infinite*

Specifies the maximum number of users that can be simultaneously logged on to the server.

Default: 0xffffffff (infinite); max. 10 for Windows NT Workstation

Server Service Entries

XactMemSize   REG_DWORD   *64K to 16 MB*

Specifies the maximum amount of virtual memory used by the Xactsrv service. A larger value for this parameter helps ensure that memory is available for downlevel clients but costs virtual address space and potentially costs pageable memory.

Default: 1 MB

TCP/IP Transport Entries

The various TCP/IP keys do not appear in the Registry unless TCP/IP is installed using the Network icon in Control Panel.

With Registry Editor, you can modify the following parameters for the TCP/IP transport. This section does not include all the TCP/IP parameters that can be set using the Networks application in Control Panel. You must restart your machine for a change in any of these parameters to take effect.

The startup parameters defined in this section are found in these subkeys of HKEY_LOCAL_MACHINE\SYSTEM\System\CurrentControlSet\Services:

- TCPIP\Parameters
- *adapter_name#*\Parameters\TCPIP, where *adapter_name#* indicates a Services subkey for a network adapter card
- DHCP\Parameters
- Ftpsvc\Parameters
- NetBt\Parameters
- Streams\Parameters
- Windows Sockets\Parameters
- WINS\Parameters

Parameters for network bindings for this service are described in "NetRules Subkey Entries," earlier in this chapter. See also **IsDomainMasterBrowser** in "Browser Service Entries," earlier in this chapter.

TCP/IP Parameters Subkey Entries

The entries for TCP/IP parameters appear under the following Registry path:

```
HKEY_LOCAL_MACHINE\SYSTEM\CurrentControlSet\Services\Tcpip\Parameters
```

ArpCacheLife   **REG_DWORD**   *Number of Seconds*

Determines the default lifetime for entries in the ARP cache table. Once an entry is placed in the ARP cache, it is allowed to remain there until its lifetime expires or until its table entry is reused because it is the oldest entry.

Default: 600 (10 minutes)

ArpCacheSize   **REG_DWORD**   *Number*

Determines the maximum number of entries that the ARP cache table can hold. The ARP cache is allowed to grow dynamically until this size is reached. After the table reaches this size, new entries can only be added by replacing the oldest entries that exist.

Default: 62

ArpUseEtherSNAP   **REG_DWORD**   *Boolean*

If set to 1 (true), TCP/IP is forced to transmit ethernet packets using 802.3 SNAP encoding. By default, the stack transmits packets in DIX ethernet format. It will always receive both formats.

Default: 0 (false)

DatabasePath   **REG_EXPAND_SZ**   *Valid Windows NT path*

Specifies the path to the standard Internet database files (hosts, lmhosts, networks, protocols). It is used by the Windows Sockets interface.

Default: %SystemRoot%\system32\drivers\etc

DefaultTOS   **REG_DWORD**   *0 to 255*

Specifies the default Type of Service (TOS) value set in the header of outgoing IP packets. See RFC 791 for a definition of values.

Default: 0

DefaultTTL   **REG_DWORD**   *1 to 255 seconds*

Specifies the default Time To Live (TTL) value set in the header of outgoing IP packets. The TTL determines the maximum amount of time an IP packet may live in the network without reaching its destination. It is effectively a bound on the number of routers an IP packet may pass through before being discarded.

Default: 32

EnableDeadGWDetect   REG_DWORD   *0 or 1*

Setting this parameter to 1 causes TCP to perform Dead Gateway Detection. With this feature enabled, TCP will ask IP to change to a backup gateway if it retransmits a segment several times without receiving a response. Backup gateways may be defined in the Advanced section of the TCP/IP configuration dialog in the Network Control Panel option.

Default: 1 (true)

EnablePMTUBHDetect   REG_DWORD   *0 or 1*

Setting this parameter to 1 (True) causes TCP to try to detect "Black Hole" routers while doing Path MTU Discovery. A "Black Hole" router does not return ICMP Destination Unreachable messages when it needs to fragment a TCP packet with the Don't Fragment bit set. TCP depends on receiving these messages to perform Path MTU Discovery. With this feature enabled, TCP will try to send segments without the Don't Fragment bit set if several retransmissions of a segment go unacknowledged. If the segment is acknowledged as a result, the MSS will be decreased and the Don't Fragment bit will be set in future packets on the connection. Enabling black hole detection increases the maximum number of retransmissions performed for a given segment.

Default: 0 (false)

EnablePMTUDiscovery   REG_DWORD   *0 or 1*

Setting this parameter to 1 (True) causes TCP to attempt to discover the Maximum Transmission Unit (MTU or largest packet size) over the path to a remote machine. By discovering the Path MTU and limiting TCP segments to this size, TCP can eliminate fragmentation at routers along the path which connect networks with different MTUs. Fragmentation adversely affects TCP throughput and network congestion.

Default: 1 (true)

ForwardBufferMemory   REG_DWORD   *Number of bytes*

This parameter determines how much memory IP allocates to store packet data in the router packet queue. When this buffer space is filled, the router begins discarding packets at random from its queue. Packet queue data buffers are 256 bytes in length, so the value of this parameter should be a multiple of 256. Multiple buffers are chained together for larger packets. The IP header for a packet is stored separately. This parameter is ignored and no buffers are allocated if the IP router is not enabled.

Default: 74240 (enough for fifty 1480-byte packets, rounded to a multiple of 256).

IGMPLevel   REG_DWORD   *0, 1, or 2*

This parameter determines to what extent the system supports IP multicasting and participates in the Internet Group Management Protocol. At level 0, the system provides no multicast support. At level 1, the system may only send IP multicast packets. At level 2, the system may send IP multicast packets and fully participate in IGMP to receive multicast packets.

Default: 2

IpReassemblyTimeout   REG_DWORD   *Number of seconds*

Determines how long IP accepts fragments when attempting to reassemble a previously fragmented packet. That is, if a packet is fragmented, all of the fragments must make it to the destination within this time limit; otherwise, the fragments will be discarded and the packet will be lost.

Default: 60 seconds

KeepAliveInterval   REG_DWORD   *1 to 0xffffffff milliseconds*

This parameter determines the interval separating keep alive retransmissions until a response is received. Once a response is receive, the delay until the next keep alive transmission is again controlled by the value of KeepAliveTime. The connection will be end after the number of retransmissions specified by TcpMaxDataRetransmissions have gone unanswered.

Default: 1000 (1 second)

KeepAliveTime   REG_DWORD   *1 to 0xffffffff milliseconds*

The parameter controls how often TCP attempts to verify that an idle connection is still intact by sending a keep alive packet. If the remote system is still reachable and functioning, it will acknowledge the keep alive transmission. Keep alive packets are not sent by default. This feature may be enabled on a connection by an application.

Default: 7,200,000 (two hours)

NumForwardPackets   REG_DWORD   *Less than 0xffffffff*

This parameter determines the number of IP packet headers which are allocated for the router packet queue. When all headers are in use, the router will begin to discard packets at random from the queue. This value should be at least as large as the ForwardBufferMemory value divided by the maximum IP data size of the networks connected to the router. It should be no larger than the ForwardBufferMemory value divided by 256, since at least 256 bytes of forward buffer memory are used for each packet. The optimal number of forward packets for a given ForwardBufferMemory size depends on the type of traffic carried on the network and will be somewhere in between these two values. This parameter is ignored and no headers are allocated if the router is not enabled.

Default: 50

TcpDisableReceiveChecksum   REG_DWORD   *0 or 1*

Specifies whether Checksums is disabled on receive.

Default: 0 (false, that is, checksums will be checked on receives)

TcpDisableSendChecksum   REG_DWORD   *0 or 1*

Specifies whether Checksums is disabled on send.

Default: 0 (false, that is, checksums will be generated on sends)

TcpKeepCnt   REG_DWORD   *Number in seconds*

Specifies how often TCP/IP will generate keep-alive traffic. When TCP/IP determines that no activity has occurred on the connection within the specified time, it generates keep-alive traffic to probe the connection. After trying **TcpKeepTries** number of times to deliver the keep-alive traffic without success, it marks the connection as down.

Default: 120

TcpKeepTries   REG_DWORD   *Number*

Specifies the maximum number of times that TCP/IP will attempt to deliver keep-alive traffic before marking a connection as down.

Default: 20

TcpLogLevel   REG_DWORD   *Number*

Specifies how verbose TCP/IP should be about logging events in the event log. The highest level of verbosity is 16, and 1 is the lowest level. The following shows general information about these levels.

Level	Events to be included
1	Only the most critical errors
4	Serious protocol violations
8	Nonserious protocol violations
12	Information about unusual events
16	Information about unusual events that some networks normally allow

Default: 16 (log everything)

TcpMaxConnectAttempts   REG_DWORD   *Number*

Specifies the maximum number of times TCP/IP attempts to establish a connection before reporting failure. The initial delay between connection attempts is 3 seconds. This delay is doubled after each attempt.

Default: 3

TcpMaxConnectRetransmission   **REG_DWORD**   *0 to 0xffffffff*

This parameter determines the number of times TCP will retransmit a connect request (SYN) before stoping the attempt. The retransmission timeout is doubled with each successive retransmission in a given connect attempt. The initial timeout value is three seconds.

Default: 3

TcpMaxDataRetransmissions   **REG_DWORD**   *0 to 0xffffffff*

This parameter controls the number of times TCP will retransmit an individual data segment (non connect segment) before ending the connection. The retransmission timeout is doubled with each successive retransmission on a connection. It is reset when responses resume. The base timeout value is dynamically determined by the measured round-trip time on the connection.

Default: 5

TcpMaxRetransmissionAttempts   **REG_DWORD**   *Number*

Specifies the maximum number of times that TCP/IP attempts to retransmit a piece of data on an established connection before ending the connection. The initial delay before retransmitting is based on the current estimate TCP/IP makes of the round-trip time on the connection. This delay is doubled after each retransmission. Acknowledgment of the data results in a recalculation of the estimate for the round-trip time.

Default: 7

TcpNumConnections   **REG_DWORD**   *0 to 0xfffffFE*

This parameter limits the maximum number of connections that TCP may have open simultaneously.

Default: 0xfffffFE

TcpRecvSegmentSize   **REG_DWORD**   *Bytes*

Specifies the maximum receive segment size.

Default: 1460

TcpSendDownMax   **REG_DWORD**   *Number*

Specifies the maximum number of bytes queued by TCP/IP.

Default: 16384

TcpSendSegmentSize   **REG_DWORD**   *Bytes*

Specifies the maximum send segment size.

Default: 1460

TcpUseRFC1122UrgentPointer   REG_DWORD   *0 or 1*

This parameter determines whether TCP uses the RFC 1122 specification for urgent data or the mode used by BSD-derived systems. The two mechanisms interpret the urgent pointer in the TCP header and the length of the urgent data differently. They are not interoperable. Windows NT defaults to BSD mode.

Default: 0 (false)

TcpWindowSize   REG_DWORD   *Number*

This parameter determines the maximum TCP receive window size offered by the system. The receive window specifies the number of bytes a sender may transmit without receiving an acknowledgment. In general, larger receive windows will improve performance over high delay or high bandwidth networks. For maximum efficiency, the receive window should be an even multiple of the MTU of the underlying network less the size of the standard TCP and IP headers (40 bytes).

Default: The smaller of: 0xffff OR the larger of: four times the maximum TCP data size on the network OR 8192 rounded up to an even multiple of the network TCP data size

UdpDisableReceiveChecksum   REG_DWORD   *0 or 1*

Specifies whether Checksums is disabled on receive.

Default: 0 (false, that is, checksums will be checked on receives)

UdpDisableSendChecksum   REG_DWORD   *0 or 1*

Specifies whether Checksums is disabled on send.

Default: 0 (false, that is, checksums will be generated on sends)

UdpNumConnections   REG_DWORD   *Number*

Specifies the maximum number of UDP endpoints.

Default: 64

Adapter Card Parameters for TCP/IP

These parameters for TCP/IP are specific to individual network adapter cards. These appear under the following Registry path, where *adapter name#* refers to the Services subkey for the specific adapter card:

```
HKEY_LOCAL_MACHINE\SYSTEM\CurrentControlSet\Services
    \adapter name#\Parameters\Tcpip
```

BroadcastType   REG_DWORD   *0 or 1*

Determines whether broadcast packets contain all 0's or all 1's as the broadcast address. The most common broadcast type is all 1's. The all-0's setting is provided for compatibility with BSD 4.2 systems.

Default: 1 (all 1's)

ForwardBroadcasts   REG_DWORD   *0 or 1*

Specifies whether broadcasts should be forwarded between adapters. If enabled, broadcasts seen by this interface are forwarded to other IP interfaces.

Default: 0 (false)

KeepAlive   REG_DWORD   *0 or 1*

Determines whether TCP connections that request keep-alive packets result in keep-alive packets being sent. This feature is used to determine when inactive connections can be disconnected. When a connection becomes inactive, keep-alive packets are periodically exchanged. When 20 consecutive keep-alive packets go unanswered, the connection is broken. This disconnect is initiated by the endpoint that is sending keep-alive packets.

Default: 1 (true)

MTU   REG_DWORD   *Number in octets*

Specifies the maximum transmission unit size of an interface. Each interface used by TCP/IP may have a different MTU value specified. The MTU is usually determined through negotiation with the lower driver, using that lower driver's value. However, that value may be overridden.

Ideally, the MTU should be large enough to hold any datagram in one frame. The limiting factor is usually the technology making the transfer. Some technologies limit the maximum size to as little as 128; Ethernet limits transfers to 1500; and proNet-10 allows as many as 2044 octets per frame.

Datagrams larger than the MTU value are automatically divided into smaller pieces called fragments; size is a multiple of eight octets. Fragmentation usually occurs somewhere through which the traffic must pass whose MTU is smaller than the encapsulated datagram. If fragmentation occurs, the fragments travel separately to the destination computer, where they are automatically reassembled before the datagram is processed.

Default: 0 (That is, use the value supplied by the adapter.)

RouterMTU   REG_DWORD   *Number in octets*

Specifies the maximum transmission unit size that should be used when the destination IP address is on a different subnet. Each interface used by TCP/IP may have a different **RouterMTU** value specified. In many implementations, the value of **RouterMTU** is set to 576 octets. This is the minimum size that must be supported by any IP node. Because modern routers can usually handle MTUs larger than 576 octets, the default value for this parameter is the same value as that used by **MTU**.

Default: 0 (That is, use the value supplied by the lower interface.)

Trailers   REG_DWORD   *0 or 1*

Specifies whether the trailer format is used. This feature provides compatibility with BSD 4.2 systems. When this feature is enabled, TCP/IP header information follows the data area of IP packets.

Default: 0 (false)

UseZeroBroadcast   REG_DWORD   *0 or 1*

If set to 1 (true), TCP/IP uses zeros for the host portion of the broadcast address. The ones-flavored local broadcast address is 255.255.255.255, while the zeros-flavored is 0.0.0.0. Most systems use ones-flavored broadcasts, but some systems derived from BSD implementations use zeros-flavored. Systems which use different flavors will not interoperate well on the same network.

Default: 0 (false)

DHCP Server Service Entries for TCP/IP

You must restart the Microsoft DHCP Server service whenever you change any of these parameters.

The Registry parameters for DHCP servers are specified under the following key:

```
..SYSTEM\current\currentcontrolset\services\DHCPServer\Parameters
```

APIProtocolSupport   REG_DWORD   *1, 2, 4, 5, 7*

Specifies the supported protocols for the DHCP server. You can change this value to ensure that different computers running different protocols can access the DHCP server. The values for this parameter can be the following:

0x1   For RPC over TCPIP protocols
0x2   For RPC over named pipes protocols
0x4   For RPC over local procedure call (LPC) protocols
0x5   For RPC over TCPIP and RPC over LPC
0x7   For RPC over all three protocols (TCP/IP, named pipes, and LPC)

Default = 0x5

BackupDatabasePath   REG_EXPAND_SZ   *filename*

Specifies the location of the backup database file where the database is backed up periodically. The best location for the backup file is on another hard drive, so that the database can be recovered in case of a system drive crash. Do not specify a network drive, because DHCP Manager cannot access a network drive for database backup and recovery.

Default = %SystemRoot%\system32\dhcp\backup

BackupInterval   REG_DWORD   *Interval*

Specifies the interval (unlimited) for backing up the database.

Default = 60 minutes

DatabaseCleanupInterval   REG_DWORD   *Interval in minutes*

Specifies the interval (unlimited) for cleaning up expired client records from the DHCP database, freeing up those IP addresses for reuse.

Default = 1440 minutes (1 day)

DatabaseLoggingFlag   REG_DWORD   *0 or 1*

Specifies whether to record the database changes in the JET.LOG file. This log file is used after a system crash to recover changes that have not been made to the database file defined by **DatabaseName**. Database logging affects system performance, so **DatabaseLogging** can be turned off if you believe the system is highly stable and if logging is adversely affecting system performance.

Default = 1 (true—that is, database logging is enabled)

DatabaseName   REG_SZ   *filename*

Specifies the name of the database file to be used for the DHCP client information database.

Default = dhcp.mdb

DatabasePath   REG_EXPAND_SZ   *pathname*

Specifies the location of the database files that have been created and opened.

Default = %SystemRoot%\System32\dhcp

RestoreFlag   REG_DWORD   *0 or 1*

Specifies whether to restore the database from the backup directory. This flag is reset automatically after the successful restoration of the database.

Default = 0 (false—that is, do not restore)

DHCP Clients Service Entries for TCP/IP

The Registry parameters for DHCP clients are specified under the following key:

`..SYSTEM\current\currentcontrolset\services\DHCP\Parameter\<option#>`

The *Option#* keys are a list of DHCP options that the client can request from the DHCP server. For each of the default options, the following values are defined:

RegLocation   REG_SZ   *location*

Specifies the location in the Registry where the option value is written when it is obtained from the DHCP server. The "?" character expands to the adapter name for which this option value is obtained.

Default = Depends on the Registry location for the specific option

KeyType   REG_DWORD   *type*

Specifies the type of Registry key for the option.

Default = 0x7

FTP Server Service Entries for TCP/IP

The following Registry path contains parameters that affect the behavior of the FTP server service component:

`HKEY_LOCAL_MACHINE\SYSTEM\CurrentControlSet\Services\Ftpsvc\Parameters`

The Ftpsvc subkey does not appear until you install the FTP service using the Network icon in Control Panel. Also, you must restart the FTP server service (Ftpsvc) using the Services icon in Control Panel for any changes to these values to take effect.

There can also be an AccessCheck subkey under Ftpsvc, which allows access to FTP for new users. If the AccessCheck subkey exists, but cannot be opened, the user is refused FTP services. If the subkey exists but can only be opened for read access, the user is granted read-only FTP access. If the subkey does not exist, it is not used to influence FTP access. By default, this subkey does not exist and therefore has no impact on FTP operations. An administrator can create this Registry subkey and attach specific access controls. which will serve to control user access to the FTP service.

AllowAnonymous   REG_DWORD   *0 or 1*

Controls anonymous logons. Anonymous logons are only allowed if this value is nonzero (true).

Default: 1 (true — anonymous logons are allowed)

AnnotateDirectories   REG_DWORD   *0 or 1*

When this value is 1, every time a user changes directories (that is, sends the server a CWD command), an attempt is made to open a file named ~FTPSVC~.CKM in the new directory. If this file is found, its contents are sent to the user as part of the successful reply to the CWD command. This may be used to attach annotations to specific directories.

This value is used as a default for new users. Users can toggle their own personal annotate directories flag with the site-specific CKM command (SITE CKM).

Default: 0 (false —do not send directory annotations)

AnonymousOnly   REG_DWORD   *0 or 1*

When this value is 1, only anonymous logons are allowed. Otherwise, nonanonymous logons are allowed as well.

Default: 0 (false —nonanonymous logons are allowed)

AnonymousUserName   REG_SZ   *UserName*

Contains the anonymous login alias. When a user attempts an anonymous login, the username specified ("anonymous") is mapped to this Registry value for authentication and impersonation.

Default: "Guest"

ConnectionTimeout   REG_DWORD   *Seconds*

Specifies the time to allow clients to remain idle before forcibly disconnecting them. This prevents idle clients from consuming server resources indefinitely.

This value may be set to 0 if time-outs are not to be enforced. If set to 0, idle clients may remain connected indefinitely.

Default: 600 (10 minutes)

ExitMessage   REG_SZ   *Message*

Specifies a signoff message sent to an FTP client upon receipt of a QUIT command.

Default: "Goodbye."

GreetingMessage   REG_MULTI_SZ   *Strings*

Specifies the message (if this value exists in the Registry) to be sent to new clients after their account has been validated. In accordance with de facto Internet behavior, if a client logs on as anonymous and specifies an identity starting with a "-" (minus), then this greeting message is not sent.

Default: None (no special greeting message)

HomeDirectory   REG_EXPAND_SZ   *Path*

Specifies the initial home directory for new clients. After a new client is validated, an attempt is made to change to this directory with the Chdir command. If this directory is inaccessible, the client is refused FTP services. If Chdir is successful, then an attempt is made to change to a directory with the same name as the client's username. If this fails, an attempt is made to change to a directory called DEFAULT. If this fails, the current directory is left at home.

If a new client connects and finds the home directory is inaccessible, an event is written to the event log.

Default: C:\

LogAnonymous   REG_DWORD   *0 or 1*

When this value is 1, all successful anonymous logons are logged to the system event log.

Default: 0 (false —do not log successful anonymous logons)

LogFileAccess   REG_DWORD   *0, 1, or 2*

Specifies log file access method. Syntax is as follows:

Value	Description
0	Do not log file accesses (default).
1	Log file accesses to FTPSVC.LOG
2	Log file accesses to FT*yymmdd*.LOG, where *yy* is the current year, *mm* is the current month, and *dd* is the current day. New log files are opened daily as necessary.

Default: 0

LogFileDirectory   REG_SZ   *directory path*

Specifies the target directory for the log file(s). This allows the log file(s) to be moved off of the system partition.

Default: %SystemRoot%\System32

LogNonAnonymous   REG_DWORD   *0 or 1*

When this value is 1, all successful nonanonymous logons are logged to the system event log.

Default: 0 (false, that is, do not log successful nonanonymous logons)

MaxClientsMessage   REG_SZ   *Message*

Specifies the message (if this value exists in the Registry) to be sent to a client if the maximum number of clients has been reached or exceeded. This indicates that the server is currently servicing the maximum number of simultaneous clients and is refusing additional clients. See **MaxConnections**.

Default: "Maximum clients reached, service unavailable."

MaxConnections   REG_DWORD   *0 or 1*

Specifies the maximum number of simultaneous clients the server will service. This value may be set to 0 if there is to be no limit on simultaneous clients.

Default: 20

MsdosDirOutput   REG_DWORD   *0 or 1*

When this value is 1, the output of the LIST command (usually sent as a result of a DIR command from the client) will look like the output of the MS-DOS **dir** command. If this value is 0, the output of the LIST command looks like the output of the UNIX **ls** command.

This value also controls slash flipping in the path sent by the PWD command. When this value is 1 (true), the path contains backward slashes (\). If this value is 0 (false), the path contains forward slashes (/).

This value is used as a default for new users. Users can toggle their own personal MS-DOS directory output flag with the site-specific DIRSTYLE command (SITE DIRSTYLE).

Default: 1 (true—directory listings will look like MS-DOS)

ReadAccessMask   REG_DWORD   *BitFields*

This value is a bitmask and controls the read ability of the various disk volumes in the system. Drive A corresponds to bit 0, drive B corresponds to bit 1, drive C corresponds to bit 2, and so on. A user may only read from a specific volume if the corresponding bit is set.

Default: 0 (all read access denied)

WriteAccessMask   REG_DWORD   *BitFields*

This value is a bitmask and controls the write ability of the various disk volumes in the system. Drive A corresponds to bit 0, drive B corresponds to bit 1, drive C corresponds to bit 2, and so on. A user may only write to a specific volume if the corresponding bit is set.

Default: 0 (all write access denied)

NetBt Parameters for TCP/IP

NetBt is the NetBIOS over TCP/IP service. Parameters for TCP/IP are also configured under NetBt in the following Registry path:

`HKEY_LOCAL_MACHINE\SYSTEM\CurrentControlSet\Services\NetBt\Parameters`

BcastNameQueryCount   REG_DWORD   *1 to 0xffff repetitions*

This value determines the number of times NBT broadcasts a query for a given name without receiving a response.

Default: 3

BcastQueryTimeout   REG_DWORD   *100 to 0xffffffff milliseconds*

This value determines the time interval between successive broadcast name queries for the same name.

Default: 750 msec

BroadcastAddress   REG_DWORD   *0 to 0xffffffff*

This parameter can be used to force NBT to use a specific address for all broadcast name related packets. By default, NBT uses the ones-flavor subnet broadcast address appropriate for each net (i.e. for a net of 11.101.0.0 with a mask of 255.255.0.0, the subnet broadcast address would be 11.101.255.255). This parameter would be set, for example, if the network uses the zeros-flavor broadcast address (set using the **UseZeroBroadcast** TCP/IP parameter). The appropriate subnet broadcast address would then be 11.101.0.0 in the example above. This parameter would then be set to 0x0b650000. Note that this parameter is global and will be used on all subnets to which NBT is bound.

Default: The ones-flavored subnet broadcast address for each network

CacheTimeout   REG_DWORD   *60000 to 0xffffffff milliseconds*

This value determines the time interval that names are cached in the remote name table.

Default: 0x927C0 (10 minutes)

EnableProxyCheck   REG_DWORD   *0 or 1*

When this is enabled, the proxy will check name registrations from Bnodes against the WINS database by doing a name query to WINS. If it finds the name in WINS with a different IP address, the proxy will send a name registration failure message to the Bnode. Set this value to 1 to verify that Bnodes do not claim names that Pnodes have.

Default: 0 (disabled)

EnableProxyRegCheck   REG_DWORD   *0 or 1*

If this parameter is set to 1 (True), then the proxy name server will send a negative response to a broadcast name registration if the name is already registered with WINS or is in the proxy's local name cache with a different IP address. The hazard of enabling this feature is that it prevents a system from changing its IP address as long as WINS has a mapping for the name. For this reason it is disabled by default.

Default: 0 (false)

InitialRefreshTimeout   REG_DWORD   *960,000 to 0xffffffff milliseconds*

This parameter specifies the initial refresh timeout used by NBT during name registration. NBT tries to contact the WINS servers at 1/8th of this time interval when it is first registering names. When it receives a successful registration response, that response will contain the new refresh interval to use.

Default: 960,000 (16 minutes)

LmhostsTimeout   REG_DWORD   *1000 to 0xffffffff milliseconds*

This parameter specifies the timeout value for Lmhosts and DNS name queries. The timer has a granularity of the timeout value, so the actual timeout could be as much as twice the value.

Default: 6000 (6 seconds)

MaxDgramBuffering   REG_DWORD   *0 to 0xffffffff bytes*

This parameter specifies the maximum amount of memory that NBT will dynamically allocate for all outstanding datagram sends. Once this limit is reached, further sends will fail due to insufficient resources.

Default: 0x20,000 (128K)

MaxPreload   REG_DWORD   *Number*

Specifies the maximum NetBt number of entries for LMHOSTS that are preloaded into the NetBt NetBIOS name cache. LMHOSTS is a file located in the directory specified by **DatabasePath**.

Default: 100

NameServerPort   REG_DWORD   *0 to 0xffff (UPD port number)*

This parameter determines the destination port number to which NBT will send name service related packets such as name queries and name registrations to WINS. The Microsoft WINS listens on port 0x89. Netbios Name Servers from other vendors may listen on different ports.

Default: 0x89

NameSrvQueryCount   REG_DWORD   *0 to 0xffff milliseconds*

This value determines the number of times NBT sends a query to a WINS server for a given name without receiving a response.

Default: 3

NameSrvQueryTimeout   REG_DWORD   *0 to 0xffffffff milliseconds*

This value determines the time interval between successive name queries to WINS for a given name.

Default: 750 msec

NbtKeepAlive   REG_DWORD   *Number in seconds*

Specifies how often NetBT will generate keep-alive traffic. When NetBt determines that no activity has occurred on a connection for the specified time interval, it will generate keep-alive traffic to probe the connection. If TCP/IP is unable to deliver this traffic, it marks the connection as down and notifies NetBT.

Default: 1 (Generate NetBt keep-alive traffic.)

NodeType   REG_DWORD   *1, 2, 4, or 8*

1 = Bnode, 2 = Pnode, 4 = Mnode, 8 = Hnode. A Bnode system uses broadcasts. A Pnode system uses only point-to-point name queries to a name server (WINS). An Mnode system broadcasts first, then queries the name server. An Hnode system queries the name server first, then broadcasts. Resolution via Lmhosts and/or DNS, if enabled, will follow the these methods. If this key is present it will override the DhcpNodeType key. If neither key is present, the system defaults to Bnode if there are no WINS servers configured for the network. The system defaults to Hnode if there is at least one WINS server configured.

Default: 1 or 8 based on the WINS server configuration.

PermanentName   REG_SZ   *Unique name*

Specifies the permanent name of the NetBIOS node for NetBt. In many NetBIOS implementations, this is the MAC address. This name must be unique.

Default: The value of *IPAddress* in dotted decimal

RandomAdapter   REG_DWORD   *0 or 1*

This parameter applies to a multihomed machine only. If it is set to 1 (True), then NBT will randomly choose the IP address to put in a name query response from all of its bound interfaces. Normally, the response contains the address of the interface on which the query arrived. This feature would be used by a server with two interfaces on the same network for load balancing. The SingleResponse parameter must be set to a value of 1 (True) for this parameter to take effect.

Default: 0 (false)

RefreshOpCode   REG_DWORD   *8 or 9*

This parameter forces NBT to use a specific opcode in name refresh packets. The specification for the NBT protocol is somewhat ambiguous in this area. Although the default of 8 used by Microsoft implementations appears to be the intended value, some other implementations, such as those by Ungermann-Bass, use the value 9. Two implementations must use the same opcode to interoperate.

Default: 8

SessionKeepAlive   REG_DWORD   *60,000 to 0xffffffff*

This value determines the time interval between keep alive transmissions on a session. Setting the value to 0xffffffff disables keep alives.

Default: 60,000 (1 hour)

SingleResponse   REG_DWORD   *0 or 1*

This parameter applies to a multihomed machine only. If this parameter is set to 1 (True), then NBT will only supply an IP address from one of its bound interfaces in name query responses. By default, the addresses of all bound interfaces are included. This parameter must be set to 1 (True) to enable the RandomAdapter feature.

Default: 0 (false)

Size/Small/Medium/Large   REG_DWORD   *1, 2, or 3*

This value determines the size of the name tables used to store local and remote names. In general, Small (1) is adequate. If the system is acting as a proxy nameserver, then the value is automatically set to Large to increase the size of the name cache hash table. Large (3) sets the number of hash buckets to 256, Medium (2) to 128, Small to 16.

Default: 1 (Small)

WinsDownTimeout   REG_DWORD   *1000 to 0xffffffff milliseconds*

This parameter determines the amount of time NBT will wait before again trying to use WINS after it fails to contact any WINS server. This feature primarily allows machines which are temporarily disconnected from the network, such as laptops, to proceed through boot processing without waiting to timeout out each WINS name registration or query individually.

Default: 15,000 (15 seconds)

Streams Parameters for TCP/IP

The TCP/IP parameter for Streams are found under the following Registry path:

```
HKEY_LOCAL_MACHINE\SYSTEM\CurrentControlSet\Services\Streams\Parameters
```

MaxMemoryUsage   REG_DWORD   *Number of bytes*

Specifies the maximum amount of memory that can be allocated to the Streams environment. Once this limit is reached, Streams will fail allocation requests made by Streams-based drivers.

Default: No limit

Windows Sockets Entries for TCP/IP

All Windows Sockets parameters can be set by choosing the Network icon in Control Panel. These parameters are found in two locations, as shown here.

```
HKEY_LOCAL_MACHINE\SYSTEM\CurrentControlSet \Services
    \Winsock\Parameters
```

Transports   REG_Multi_SZ   *Strings*

Contains the Registry key names of installed transports that support Windows Sockets. If TCP/IP is the only installed transport that supports Windows Sockets, then this value is Tcpip. The Windows Sockets DLL uses the strings in **Transports** to find information about each transport.

Default: Depends on installation

```
HKEY_LOCAL_MACHINE\SYSTEM\CurrentControlSet \Services
    \TCPIP\Parameters\Winsock
```

HelperDllName   REG_EXPAND_SZ   *Path and filename*

Specifies the name of the Windows Sockets helper DLL for the TCP/IP transport. This value is set by the Windows Sockets DLL and is not a user defined parameter.

Default: Depends on the transport; %SystemRoot%\system32\wshtcpip.dll for TCP/IP.

IRPStackSize   REG_DWORD   *Number*

Specifies the number of IRP stack locations needed by AFD, the driver used for Windows Sockets. The default is sufficient for all existing transports, but new transports may be developed that need more IRP stack locations.

Default: 4

Mapping   REG_BINARY

Identifies the address families, socket types, and protocols supported by the transport. This value is set by the Windows Sockets DLL and is not a user defined parameter.

Default: Depends on transport

MaxSockAddrLen   REG_DWORD   *Octets*

Specifies the maximum length of socket addresses for the INET sockets family. This value is set by the Windows Sockets DLL and is not a user defined parameter.

MinSockAddrLen   REG_DWORD   *Octets*

Specifies the minimum length of socket addresses for the INET sockets family. This value is set by the Windows Sockets DLL and is not a user defined parameter.

AFD is the driver that handles Winsock. These values are in the following Registry path:

`HKEY_LOCAL_MACHINE\SYSTEM\CurrentControlSet \Services\Afd\Parameters`

Some of these values have three defaults, depending on amount of RAM:

Default	Amount of RAM
First	12.5 MB or less
Second	12.5 to 20 MB
Third	More than 20 MB

BufferMultiplier   REG_DWORD   *Multiplier*

DefaultReceiveWindow and DefaultSendWindow get divided by this value to determine how many massages can be sent/received before flow control is imposed.

Default: 512

TCP/IP Transport Entries

DefaultReceiveWindow   REG_DWORD   *Bytes*

The number of receive bytes AFD will buffer on a connection before imposing flow control. for some applications. A larger value here will give slightly better performance at the expense of increased resource utilization. Note that applications can modify this value on a per-socket basis with the SO_RCVBUF socket option.

Default: 8192

DefaultSendWindow   REG_DWORD   *Bytes*

Same as DefaultReceiveWindow, but for the send side of connections.

Default: 8192

InitialLargeBufferCount   REG_DWORD   *Buffer count*

The count of large buffers allocated by AFD at system startup. Allocate more buffers to improve performance at the cost of physical memory.

Default: 0, 2, or 10 depending on RAM amount.

InitialMediumBufferCount   REG_DWORD   *Buffer count*

Initial count of medium buffers.

Default: 2, 10, or 30 depending on RAM amount.

InitialSmallBufferCount   REG_DWORD   *Buffer count*

Initial count of small buffers.

Default: 5, 20, or 50 depending on RAM amount.

LargeBufferSize   REG_DWORD   *Bytes*

The size in bytes of large buffers used by AFD. Smaller values use less memory, larger values can improve performance.

Default: 4096

MediumBufferSize   REG_DWORD   *Bytes*

The size in bytes of medium buffers used by AFD. Smaller values use less memory, larger values can improve performance.

Default: 1504

PriorityBoost   REG_DWORD   *Priority*

The priority boost AFD gives to a thread when it completes I/O for that thread. If a multithreaded application experiences starvation of some threads, reducing this value may remedy the problem.

Default: 2

TCP/IP Transport Entries

SmallBufferSize   **REG_DWORD**   *Bytes*

The size in bytes of small buffers used by AFD. Smaller values use less memory, larger values can improve performance.

Default: 64

StandardAddressLength   **REG_DWORD**   *Length*

The length of TDI addresses typically used for the machine. If the customer has a transport protocol like TP4 which uses very long addresses, then increasing this value will result in a slight performance improvement.

Default: 24

WINS Entries for TCP/IP

The Registry parameters for WINS servers are specified under the following subkey:

```
..\SYSTEM\CurrentControlSet\Services\Wins\Parameters
```

This subkey lists all the nonreplication-related parameters needed to configure a WINS server. It also contains a \Datafiles subkey, which lists all the files that should be read by WINS to initialize or reinitialize its local database.

DbFileNm   **REG_EXPAND_SZ**   *path name*

Specifies the full path name for the WINS database file.

Default = %SystemRoot%\system32\wins\wins.mdb

DoStaticDataInit   **REG_DWORD**   *0 or 1*

If this parameter is set to a non-zero value, the WINS server will initialize its database with records listed in one or more files listed under the \Datafiles subkey. The initialization is done at process invocation and whenever a change is made to one or more values of the \Parameters or \Datafiles keys (unless the change is to change the value of **DoStaticDataInit** to 0).

Default = 0 (false—that is, the WINS server does not initialize its database)

InitTimePause   **REG_DWORD**   *1-40*

Set to 1 to instruct WINS to remain in the paused state until the first replication. If set to 1, it is recommended that WINS\Partners\Pull\InitTimeReplication be either set to 1 or removed. Either method ensures that WINS replicates with its listed partners on starting. Paused state means that WINS will not accept any name registrations/releases until the above replication happens.

Default: 0

LogFilePath   REG_SZ or **REG_EXPAND_SZ**   *Directory*

Specifies the directroy for WINS log files.

Default: %SystemRoot%\System32\WINS

NoOfWrkThds   REG_DWORD   *1-40*

Specifies the number of worker threads (to handle name query packets from clients). This can be changed without restarting the WINS computer.

Default: Number of processors on the system

PriorityClassHigh   REG_DWORD   *0-1*

Specifies the priority class of WINS. Set to 1 for high priority class. This can be changed without restarting the WINS computer.

Default: 0

Also, the HKEY_LOCAL_MACHINE\SYSTEM\CurrentControlSet\Services \Wins\Parameters\Datafiles subkey lists one or more files that the WINS server should read to initialize or reinitialize its local database with static records. If the full path of the file is not listed, the directory of execution for the WINS server is assumed to contain the data file. The parameters can have any names (for example, DF1 or DF2). Their data types must be REG_SZ or REG_EXPAND_SZ.

The HKEY_LOCAL_MACHINE\SYSTEM\CurrentControlSet\Services \Wins\Partners key has two subkeys, \Pull and \Push, under which are subkeys for the IP addresses of all push and pull partners, respectively, of the WINS server.

A push partner, listed under the \Partners\Pull key, is one from which a WINS server pulls replicas and from which it can expect update notification messages. The following parameter appears under the IP address for a specific push partner. This parameter can be set only by changing the value in Registry Editor:

OnlyDynRecs   REG_DWORD   *0 or 1*

If set to 1, specifies that only dynamically registered records be replicated to WINS pulling replicas. The default setting of 0 means that all records (dynamic and static) be replicated.

Default: 0

MemberPrec   REG_DWORD   *0 or 1*

Specifies the relative precedence of addresses in an Internet group (name with 16th byte being 0x1c). Addresses in the 0x1c names pulled from a WINS partner will be given the precedence assigned to the WINS. The value can be 0 (low) or 1 (high). The locally registered addresses always have a high precedence. Set this value to 1 if this WINS partner is serving a geogrphic location that is nearby.

Default: 0

TCP/IP Transport Entries

UPS Service Entries

The Registry does not contain information for the UPS service until the user checks the Uninterruptible Power Supply Is Installed checkbox in the UPS dialog box and then chooses the OK button. Changes to settings should be made by using the UPS icon in Control Panel.

The UPS service will not start unless the UPS subkey is present in the Registry, all parameters are present in the Registry, and all values are within the correct range. If any of these elements are missing or in error, a message announces that the UPS service is not correctly configured. All corrections can be made using the UPS icon in Control Panel.

The UPS parameters remain in the Registry if the user uninstalls UPS.

The path for the UPS subkey is the following:

`HKEY_LOCAL_MACHINE\SYSTEM\CurrentControlSet\Services\UPS`

BatteryLife   REG_DWORD   *2 to 720 minutes*

Specifies the life of the UPS backup battery when fully charged.

Default: 2 (minutes)

CommandFile   REG_EXPAND_SZ   *Filename*

Specifies the name of a command file to execute immediately before shutting down.

Default: (empty)

FirstMessageDelay   REG_DWORD   *0 to 120 seconds*

Specifies the number of seconds between initial power failure and the first message sent to the users. If power is restored within the **FirstMessageDelay** time, no message is sent, although the event is logged.

Default: 5 (seconds)

MessageInterval   REG_DWORD   *5 to 300 seconds*

Specifies the number of seconds between messages sent to users to inform them of power failure.

Default: 120 (seconds)

Options   REG_DWORD   *Value*

Defines the bit mask for messages related to options in the UPS dialog box, as the following:

Installed	0x00000001
PowerFailSignal	0x00000002
LowBatterySignal	0x00000004
CanTurnOff	0x00000008
PosSigOnPowerFail	0x00000010
PosSigOnLowBattery	0x00000020
PosSigShutOff	0x00000040
CommandFile	0x00000080

There are no default values in the registry for **Options**. They are set in the UPS application of Control Panel. For example, if you select only Power Failure Signal, Low Battery Signal At Least 2 Minutes Before Shutdown, and Remote UPS Shutdown, then the registry value will be 0xf. However, if you also change all UPS Interface Voltages from negative (default) to positive, then the registry value will be 0x7f.

Port   REG_SZ   *Port name*

Specifies the name of the serial port the UPS is connected to.

Default: COM1:

RechargeRate   REG_DWORD   *1 to 250 minutes*

Specifies the recharge rate of the UPS backup battery.

Default: 100 (minutes)

Workstation Service Entries

You can modify the startup parameters for the Workstation service using the Registry Editor. Unless otherwise indicated, these value entries are found in the following Registry path:

```
HKEY_LOCAL_MACHINE\SYSTEM\CurrentControlSet\Services
    \LanmanWorkstation\Parameters
```

The parameters that control network bindings for this service are described in "NetRules Subkey Entries," earlier in this chapter.

BufFilesDenyWrite   REG_DWORD   *0 or 1*

Specifies whether the redirector should cache files that are opened with only FILE_SHARE_READ sharing access. Usually, if a file is opened with FILE_SHARE_READ specified, the file cannot be buffered because other processes may also be reading that file. This optimization allows the redirector to buffer such files. This optimization is safe because no process can write to the file.

Disable this parameter if it is necessary to preserve the strict semantics of the sharing modes specified.

Default: 1 (true)

BufNamedPipes   REG_DWORD   *0 or 1*

Indicates whether the redirector should buffer character-mode named pipes.

Disable this parameter to guarantee that all pipe write operations are flushed to the server immediately and to disable read ahead on character-mode named pipes.

Default: 1 (true)

BufReadOnlyFiles   REG_DWORD   *0 or 1*

`...\CurrentControlSet\Services\LanmanWorkstation`

Specifies whether the redirector should cache files that are read-only. Usually, if a read-only file is opened, the file cannot be buffered because other processes may also be reading that file. This optimization allows the redirector to buffer such files. This optimization is safe because no process can write to the file. However, another user can modify the file to enable writing to the file, causing loss of data.

Disable this parameter if it is necessary to preserve the strict semantics of the sharing modes specified.

Default: 1 (true)

CacheFileTimeout   REG_DWORD   *Number of seconds*

Specifies the maximum time that a file will be left in the cache after the application has closed the file.

Increase the value of this parameter if you are performing operations on the server that could cause files to be reopened more than 10 seconds after the application has closed them. For example, if you are performing a build over the network, you should increase this parameter's value.

Default: 10

Workstation Service Entries

CharWait   **REG_DWORD**   *0 to 65535 milliseconds*

Specifies time to wait for an instance of a named pipe to become available when opening the pipe.

Increase this value if your pipe server application is typically very busy.

Default: 3600

CollectionTime   **REG_DWORD**   *0 to 65535000 milliseconds*

Specifies the maximum time that write-behind data will remain in a character-mode pipe buffer.

Changing this value may cause a named pipe application's performance to improve (but it does not affect SQL Server applications).

Default: 250

DormantFileLimit   **REG_DWORD**   *Number of files*

Specifies the maximum number of files that should be left open on a share after the application has closed the file.

This parameter exists because the default configuration of LAN Manager servers only allow a total of 60 open files from remote clients and 50 from each client workstation. Because the Windows NT redirector may keep files open in the cache after an application has closed the file, this means that the redirector may overload a misconfigured LAN Manager server. To correct this problem, either reduce this value, or increase the values for the LAN Manager server's **maxSessopens** and **maxOpens** parameters.

Default: 45

IllegalDatagramResetTime   **REG_DWORD**   *Number of seconds*

Specifies the span of time during which the number of illegal datagram events is counted. Because Windows NT logs all illegal datagrams, it is possible for the event log to be filled with a proliferation of these in a short amount of time. This entry and the **NumIllegalDatagramEvents** entry work together to limit the number of illegal datagrams that are recorded in the log within a certain span of time.

Default: 60

KeepConn   **REG_DWORD**   *1 to 65535 seconds*

Specifies the maximum amount of time that a connection can be left dormant. This parameter is the redirector equivalent of the **Disc** parameter in the Services\LanmanServer\Parameters subkey.

As a general rule, try increasing this value if your application closes and opens UNC files to a server less frequently than 10 minutes apart. This decreases the number of reconnections made to a server.

Default: 600

Workstation Service Entries

LockIncrement   REG_DWORD   *Number of milliseconds*

This parameter is not used for Win32 applications. However, if OS/2-based applications request that a lock operation waits forever, and if the lock cannot be immediately granted on a non-LAN Manager version 2.0 server, this parameter controls the rate at which the redirector ramps back the failed lock operations.

This parameter should not be changed unless you are running an OS/2-based application that requests lock operations that might fail.

Default: 10

LockMaximum   REG_DWORD   *Number of milliseconds*

Used to configure the lock backoff package. This parameter exists to prevent an errant application from "swamping" a server with nonblocking requests where there is no data available for the application.

Default: 500

LockQuota   REG_DWORD   *Bytes of data*

Specifies the maximum amount of data that is read for each file using this optimization if the **UseLockReadUnlock** parameter is enabled.

Increase this value if your application performs a significant number of lock-and-read style operations. (This means performing lock operations and immediately reading the contents of the locked data.) It is conceivable that you could cause the system to run out of paged pool, but only by increasing this value to a few megabytes and by using an application that locks millions-of-byte ranges.

Default: 4096 (bytes)

LogElectionPackets   REG_DWORD   *0 or 1*

Specifies whether the Browser should generate events when election packets are received.

Default: 0 (false)

MailslotBuffers   REG_DWORD   *Number of buffers*

Specifies the maximum number of buffers available to process mailslot messages. If your application uses many mailslot operations, set this higher to avoid losing mailslot messages.

Default: 5

MaxCmds   REG_DWORD   *0 to 255*

Specifies the maximum number of work buffers that the redirector reserves for performance reasons.

Increase this value to increase your network throughput. If your application performs more than 15 simultaneous operations, you might want to increase this value. Because this parameter actually controls the number of execution threads that can be simultaneously outstanding at any time, your network performance will not always be improved by increasing this parameter. Each additional execution threads takes about 1K of nonpaged pool if you actually load up the network. Resources will not be consumed, however, unless the user actually makes use of them.

Default: 15

MaxCollectionCount   REG_DWORD   *0 to 65535 bytes*

Specifies the threshold for character-mode named pipes writes. If the write is smaller than this value, the write will be buffered. Adjusting this value may improve performance for a named-pipe application (but it will not affect SQL server applications).

Default: 16

NumIllegalDatagramEvents   REG_DWORD   *Number of events*

Specifies the maximum number of datagram events to be logged within the span of time specified by the **IllegalDatagramResetTime** parameter. Because Windows NT logs all illegal datagrams, the event log can be filled with a proliferation of these in a short time. This entry and the **IllegalDatagramResetTime** entry work together.

Default: 5

OtherDomains   REG_SZ   *DomainNames*

Specifies the Microsoft LAN Manager domains to be listed for browsing.

Default: (none)

PipeIncrement   REG_DWORD   *Number of milliseconds*

Controls the rate at which the redirector "backs off" on failing nonblocking pipe reads.

This parameter is used to prevent an errant application from swamping a server with nonblocking requests where there is no data available for the application. You can use the backoff statistics to tune this parameter to be more efficient for an application that uses nonblocking named pipes (except for SQL Server applications).

Default: 10

Workstation Service Entries

PipeMaximum   REG_DWORD   *Number of milliseconds*

Controls the maximum time at which the redirector "backs off" on failing nonblocking pipe reads.

This parameter exists to prevent an errant application from swamping a server with nonblocking requests where there is no data available for the application. You can use the backoff statistics to tune this parameter to be more efficient for an application that uses nonblocking named pipes (except for SQL Server applications).

Default: 500

ReadAheadThroughput   REG_DWORD   *Kilobytes per second*

Specifies the throughput required on a connection before the cache manager is told to enable read ahead.

Default: 0xffffffff

ServerAnnounceBuffers   REG_DWORD   *Number*

Specifies the maximum buffers used to process server announcements. If your network has many servers, you can increase this value to avoid losing server announcements.

This parameter is found under the LanmanWorkstation\Parameters\Static subkey.

Default: 20

SessTimeout   REG_DWORD   *10 to 65535 seconds*

Specifies the maximum amount of time that the redirector allows an operation that is not long-term to be outstanding.

Default: 45

SizCharBuf   REG_DWORD   *64 to 4096 bytes*

Specifies the maximum number of bytes that will be written into a character-mode pipe buffer. Adjusting this value may improve performance for a named-pipe application (but it will not affect SQL server applications).

Default: 512

Transports   REG_MULTI_SZ   *List*

Lists the transports that the redirector services and is found under the LanmanWorkstation\Linkage subkey. You should modify it by choosing the Network icon in Control Panel.

Default: None

Workstation Service Entries

Use512ByteMaxTransfer   REG_DWORD   *0 or 1*

Specifies whether the redirector should only send a maximum of 512 bytes in a request to an MS-Net server regardless of the servers-negotiated buffer size. If this parameter is disabled, request transfers from the Windows NT redirector could cause the MS-Net server to crash.

Default: 0 (false)

UseLockReadUnlock   REG_DWORD   *0 or 1*

Indicates whether the redirector uses the lock-and-read and write-and-unlock performance enhancements.

When this value is enabled, it generally provides a significant performance benefit. However, database applications that lock a range and don't allow data within that range to be read will suffer performance degradation unless this parameter is disabled.

Default: 1 (true)

UseOpportunisticLocking   REG_DWORD   *0 or 1*

Indicates whether the redirector should use opportunistic-locking (oplock) performance enhancement. This parameter should be disabled only to isolate problems.

Default: 1 (true)

UseRawRead   REG_DWORD   *0 or 1*

Enables the raw-read optimization. This provides a significant performance enhancement on a local area network

Default: 1 (true)

UseRawWrite   REG_DWORD   *0 or 1*

Enables the raw-write optimization. On a LAN, this provides a significant performance enhancement.

Default: 1 (true)

UseUnlockBehind   REG_DWORD   *0 or 1*

Indicates whether the redirector will complete an unlock operation before it has received confirmation from the server that the unlock operation has completed. Disable this parameter only to isolate problems or to guarantee that all unlock operations complete on the server before completing the application's unlock request.

Default: 1 (true)

Workstation Service Entries

UseWriteRawData   REG_DWORD   *0 or 1*

Enables the raw-write-with-data optimization. This allows the redirector to send 4K of data with each write-raw operation. This provides a significant performance enhancement on a local area network.

Default: 1 (true)

UtilizeNtCaching   REG_DWORD   *0 or 1*

Indicates whether the redirector uses the cache manager to cache the contents of files. Disable this parameter only to guarantee that all data is flushed to the server immediately after it is written by the application.

Default: 1 (true)

Registry Entries for Microsoft Mail

The parameters used by the Microsoft Mail application provided with Windows NT appear under this subkey:

```
HKEY_CURRENT_USER\Software\Microsoft\Mail
```

This key includes the following subkeys:

Subkey	Purpose
Address Book	Specifies entries used by the Address Book support functions for the Mail program.
Custom Commands	Specifies a custom command that can be installed into one of the Mail menus at run-time.
Custom Messages	Specifies a custom message type that is installed into a Mail menu at run-time.
Custom Menus	Specifies a custom menu name to be added to the Mail menu bar.
Microsoft Mail	Defines the configuration of the Mail program, and the Microsoft Mail transport and name service.
MMF	Affects the automatic compression of the Mail message file.
Mac File Types	Defines the mapping from Macintosh file type and creator tags to eight-plus-three character filename extensions.
MS Proofing Tools	Defines settings for the speller.
Providers	Defines settings that service providers use with Microsoft Mail front-end programs.

Many of the entries in these subkeys have default values and won't be present in the Mail subkeys. To change the appearance and behavior of the Mail application, use the Mail menu commands instead of editing the Mail entries directly. Some of the options that you specify in the Mail application are stored in your mail message file (.MMF) instead of the Mail Registry entries.

These keys are created in HKEY_CURRENT_USER when you first run Mail. If your system previously contained a Windows for MS-DOS version of MSMAIL.INI, its contents are migrated to the Registry when you first run Mail under Windows NT.

Address Book Entries for Mail

Entries in this subkey are used by the Address Book support functions in the Mail program. Most of the entries for this subkey use default values specified by the Mail program, and the Address Book subkey might not be present under the Mail key. The entries in this subkey control the default address directory displayed in the Address Book. Do not change any of these entries if they appear.

This is the Registry path for this subkey:

```
HKEY_CURRENT_USER\Software\Microsoft\Mail\Address Book
```

Custom Commands Entries for Mail

Each entry under this key specifies a custom command that can be installed into one of the Mail menus at run-time. These entries can appear both in the Microsoft Mail key and in the SHARED32.INI file in the directory defined under the Microsoft Mail subkey as the value of **SharedExtensionsDir**.

This is the Registry path for this subkey:

```
HKEY_CURRENT_USER\Software\Microsoft\Mail\Custom Commands
```

The Custom Commands subkey can contain one or more of the following entries:

tag   **REG_SZ**

This specifies the descriptive identifier for the command in the following format:

```
tag= version;menu;name;position;DLL name, ordinal;command;
    event map;status text;Help file;help context;
```

For example:

```
IC1= 3.0;help;&Out of Office;10;<ExtsDir>BIN-EXT\OOF32.DLL;3;;
    Out of Office Email Notification
```

Value	Meaning
version	The version of Mail in which the custom command is compatible.
menu	The menu where the custom command is to be added, such as File or Help.
name	The command name to appear on the menu. Include an ampersand just before the letter that is to serve as an ALT+*key* accelerator.
position	The zero-relative position within its menu where the command is to appear. A value of –1 places the command at the end of the menu.
DLL name	Name or path of the DLL where the custom command resides. This entry can optionally be followed by a comma and the ordinal of the entry point to call (default is ,1).
command	The command string passed as one of the parameters to the DLL entry point for the command.
event map	A sequence of up to 16 digits identifying the Mail events that the custom command supports. Each can be 0 or 1 to indicate if the DLL is to be called for a specific event. Currently three events are defined; the rest are reserved and must be zero (or, as in the examples above, this whole section can be empty): • The first digit means Mail startup. • The second digit means Mail exit. • The third digit means the arrival of a new message.
status text	Text to be displayed in the Mail status bar when the user highlights the command in the menu.
Help file	Windows NT Help file to be invoked when the user presses F1 while the command is selected. The specified filename is passed to the Windows NT Help program. (optional)
help context	Passed to the Windows NT help program along with the Help file name. Use –1 (Help file index) if there is no specific entry in the Help file for this command. (optional)
<ExtsDir>	A special token that can appear within certain fields. Expands to the value of **SharedExtensionsDir** in the Microsoft Mail key. Used to refer to DLLs that are installed in a shared extensions directory on the network. Valid for the *DLL name, command,* and *Help file* subfields.

Custom Messages Entries for Mail

This subkey is similar in many ways to the Custom Commands subkey. Each entry specifies a custom message type to be installed into a Mail menu at run-time.

These entries can appear both in the Microsoft Mail key and in the SHARED32.INI file in the directory defined by the **SharedExtensionsDir** entry under the Microsoft Mail key.

This is the Registry path for this subkey:

```
HKEY_CURRENT_USER\Software\Microsoft\Mail\Custom Messages
```

The Custom Messages subkey can contain one or more of the following entries.

class   REG_SZ

Specifies a string uniquely identifying the message type. Mail places this string in messages and calls custom message DLLs based on its value. Each entry is in the following format:

```
class = version;menu;name;position;DLL name;command;operation map;
    status text;Help file;help context;
```

Value	Meaning
version	The version of Mail in which the custom message is compatible.
menu	The menu where the custom command for the message type is to be added, such as File or Mail.
name	The command name to appear on the menu. Include an ampersand just before the letter that is to serve as an ALT+k*ey* accelerator.
position	The zero-relative position within its menu at which the command is to appear. A value of –1 places the command at the end of the menu.
DLL name	Name or path of the DLL in which the custom command resides.
command	Command string passed as one of the parameters to the DLL entry point for the command.

Value *(continued)*	Meaning *(continued)*
operation map	Sequence of up to 16 digits. Each can be 0, 1, or 2, where 0 indicates that Mail is to perform its standard operation on the custom message. 1 indicates that the DLL is to be called to handle the operation. 2 indicates that the operation is to be completely disabled. Currently eight operations are defined; the rest are reserved and must be zero. In the following list, 0 is the leftmost digit:

0	Compose (menu command defined in this entry)
1	File.Open
2	Mail.Reply
3	Mail.Reply to All
4	Mail.Forward
5	File.Print
6	File.Save as
7	Arrival of new mail

Value	Meaning
status text	Text to be displayed in the Mail status bar when the user highlights the command in the menu.
Help file	Windows NT Help file to be invoked when the user presses F1 while the command is selected. The specified filename is passed to the Windows NT Help program. (optional)
help context	Passed to the Windows NT Help program along with the Help filename. Use –1 (Help file index) if there is no specific entry in the Help file for this command. (optional)
<ExtsDir>	A special token that can appear within certain fields. Expands to the value of **SharedExtensionsDir** in the Microsoft Mail key. Used to refer to DLLs that are installed in a shared extensions directory on the network. Valid for the *DLL name, command,* and *Help file* fields.

Custom Menus Entries for Mail

This subkey can contain any number of entries (within reason). You can use these menus to group custom commands and/or messages under a single, distinctive menu item.

This is the Registry path for this subkey:

```
HKEY_CURRENT_USER\Software\Microsoft\Mail\Custom Menus
```

The following information can appear both in the Microsoft Mail key and in SHARED32.INI in the directory defined by **SharedExtensionsDir** under the Microsoft Mail key. The SHARED32.INI file is examined first.

tag   **REG_SZ**

Identifies the menu to someone reading these values but serves no other purpose. Specifies a menu name to be added to the Mail menu bar. This is the format:

```
Tag=version;name;name to follow;status text
```

For example:

```
tools=3.0;&Tools;Window;Useful development toys
```

Value	Meaning
version	The version of Mail with which the menu is compatible; 3.0 is the current version.
name	The menu name to be added to the menu bar. Include an ampersand just before the letter that is to serve as an ALT+*key* accelerator.
name to follow	Name of an existing menu. The new menu is added directly before it.
status text	Text to be displayed in the Mail status bar when the user highlights the menu name.

Microsoft Mail Entries

This subkey is used to define the appearance and behavior of the Mail program. This is the Registry path for this subkey:

```
HKEY_CURRENT_USER\Software\Microsoft\Mail\Microsoft Mail
```

This key also appears under HKEY_USERS\.DEFAULT, but its only contents are **MigrateIni and MigrateIniPrint**.

These are the value entries that can appear in this key:

CheckLatencyInterval   REG_SZ   *seconds*

Affects the mail spooler's latency checking, which is intended to prevent spooler background processing from interfering with foreground work. If the specified length of time passes without the spooler having any work to do, the latency algorithm is reinitialized.

Default: 30 seconds

DemosEnabled   REG_SZ   *0 or 1*

Specifies whether the Demos menu option is to be displayed in the Help menu. If the value of the entry is 1, the Demos menu option is displayed in the Help menu. If this entry is 0, the Demos menu option is not shown.

Default: 0 (The Mail demos are not provided with Windows NT.)

ExportMmfFile   REG_SZ   *filename*

Identifies the path and filename for a .MMF file pointing to the last place a mail folder was exported to. This entry is written by the Mail program and is used as a default value for display in the Export Folder dialog box when you choose Export Folders from the File menu in Mail.

FixedFont   REG_SZ   *facename, size, 0 or 1, 0 or 1*

Identifies the fixed-pitch font used to display the body text of a mail message. This entry has four parts, each separated by a comma: typeface name (not the font file name), point size, flag for bold, and flag for italic. The Change Font command on the View menu toggles between the Normal font and the Fixed font.

Default: Courier New, 9, 0, 0

ForceScanInterval   REG_SZ   *seconds*

Affects the mail spooler's latency checking, which is intended to prevent the spooler background processing from interfering with foreground work. If the designated length of time passes without the spooler getting an opportunity to do outstanding work, idle time is requested more frequently (based on the value of **ScanAgainInterval**), and eventually idle time is used whenever it can.

Default: 300 seconds (5 minutes)

GALOnly   REG_SZ   *0 or 1*

If this entry is set to 1, the Mail address book displays only the Global Address List and the personal address book, thereby providing a flat address list of all the users visible from your postoffice. You must be running against a PC Mail 3.0 or higher postoffice with global address list support for this to work. **GALOnly** is currently supported only by the PC Mail name service provider.

Default: 0

IdleRequiredInterval   REG_SZ   *seconds*

Affects the mail spooler's latency checking, which is intended to prevent the spooler's background processing from interfering with foreground work. The spooler defers its work temporarily if the system has serviced an interactive request such as a keyboard entry or mouse movement within this interval, to avoid starting a transfer when the user is busy.

Default: 2 seconds

Lang   REG_SZ   *String*

This value is specific to Japanese Windows NT in order to give better interoperability with U.S. mail clients. If you specify anything other than "USA" for <String>, Japanese is used in the prefix.

Default: (none)

Microsoft Mail Entries

LocalMMF   REG_SZ   *0 or 1*

Specifies the location where the user's mail message file (.MMF) is created when the user runs Mail for the first time. If this entry is 0, the user's Mail messages are stored in the postoffice on the server. If this entry is 1, the user's .MMF file is created locally in the *SystemRoot* directory rather than on the postoffice the first time Mail is run. Also, this value set to 1, in conjunction with the **NoServerOptions** entry, prevents .MMF files from being stored in the postoffice.

Default: 1

Login   REG_SZ   *mailbox name*

Identifies the default User Name (up to 10 characters) displayed in the Mail Sign In dialog box used to log into Mail. If you set both the **Login** and **Password** entries, the Login dialog is not displayed when you start Mail, and your mailbox is immediately displayed. If you set just **Login**, Mail prompts for your password only.

Default: (blank)

MailBeep   REG_SZ   *filename*

Specifies the path name of a .WAV file to change the sound that Mail uses to notify the user when new mail arrives. This entry is ignored if the Sound Chime option in the Mail Options dialog box is not checked.

Mail looks at this entry only if it can't find a **MailBeep** entry in the HKEY_CURRENT_USER\Control Panel\Sounds subkey.

Default: (blank)—Mail beeps twice when new mail arrives.

MailTmp   REG_SZ   *Pathname*

Set this entry to a directory where Mail can place temporary copies of attached files. When you launch an application by double-clicking a file attached to a mail message, Mail copies the file to this directory and runs the application.

Default: The value of the TEMP environment variable. If there is no TEMP variable, the default is the *SystemRoot* directory.

MAPIHELP   REG_SZ   *filename*

Specifies the MAPI Help file to be used when the user requests help in any of the dialog boxes displayed by the MAPI support functions. This entry is defined when the Mail program is run for the first time.

Default: The MSMAIL32.HLP file in the user's *SystemRoot*\SYSTEM32 directory (for example, C:\WINNT\SYSTEM32\MSMAIL32.HLP).

MigrateIni   REG_SZ   *0 or 1*

Specifies whether to migrate the Mail .INI files created by a Windows for MS-DOSMS-DOS version of Mail for use under Windows NT. This entry is saved in the HKEY_USERS\.DEFAULT\Software\Microsoft\Mail subkey. In HKEY_CURRENT_USER, this entry is deleted after the user first runs Mail.

Default: 1 (yes)

MigrateIniPrint   REG_SZ   *0 or 1*

Specifies whether to migrate the Mail .INI print information created by a Windows for MS-DOS version of Mail for use under Windows NT. This entry is saved in the HKEY_USERS\.DEFAULT\Software\Microsoft\Mail subkey. In HKEY_CURRENT_USER, this entry is deleted after the user first runs Mail.

Default: 1 (yes)

Multi-Message   REG_SZ   *0 or 1*

Defines the last setting chosen for the Print Multiple Notes On A Page check box in the Print dialog box, which appears when you print messages from Mail. Set this entry to 0 for that option to appear unchecked by default.

Default: 1 (That is, the check box is checked by default.)

NetBios   REG_SZ   *0 or 1*

Enables NetBIOS notification of new mail delivery. When NetBIOS notification is used, the Windows NT computer sending a mail message to another Windows NT computer sends a NetBIOS notification message to the destination computer to tell the Mail program running on that machine that a new mail message was sent to the computer. The Mail program on the destination computer can then check the workgroup postoffice for the new mail message. This entry set to 1 to enable NetBIOS notification also provides quicker response to the arrival of new mail from users on your local postoffice. If this entry is 0 to disable NetBIOS notification, the Mail client needs to regularly check for the arrival of new mail messages on the postoffice.

Default: 1

NewMsgsAtStartup   REG_SZ   *0 or 1*

Specifies whether Mail is to check for new mail messages in the foreground as soon as the user logs in. Set this entry to 1 to have Mail download new messages as quickly as possible when it is started. If this entry is 0, Mail checks for new messages in the background (as is usually the case when the Mail application is being used).

Default: 0

NextOnMoveDelete   REG_SZ   *0 or 1 or –1*

If this entry is 1, Mail automatically opens the next message in a folder after you delete or move an open message. If set to –1, mail automatically opens the previous message. This facilitates quick scanning through the Inbox. If set to 0, Mail closes the Read Note window after you move or delete the message, and you must press ENTER or double-click to open the next message. Use 1 for messages sorted in ascending order (in the order received) and –1 for messages sorted in descending order (most recent message first).

Default: 1

NormalFont   REG_SZ   *facename, size, 0 or 1, 0 or 1*

Identifies the default font (normally proportionally spaced) used to display Mail messages. This entry has four parts, each separated by a comma: typeface name (not the font file name), point size, flag for bold, and flag for italic. The Change Font command in the View menu toggles between the Normal font and the Fixed font. The latter is useful for viewing messages that were created using a fixed-pitch font. Both entries affect only message body text, not the message envelope text or folder lists; Mail uses Helv 8 for that purpose.

Default: Helv, 10, 0, 0 (The FontSubstitutes subkey defines the mapping of the Helv font to a font present on the local computer.)

NoServerOptions   REG_SZ   *0 or 1*

If this entry is 1, the Server button in the Mail Options dialog box is unconditionally disabled. On the Mail server, this button calls up another dialog box that enables the user to relocate the .MMF file. Together with the **LocalMMF** entry, this entry prevents .MMF files from being stored on the postoffice.

Default: 0

OfflineMessages   REG_SZ   *Pathname*

Defines the file location when you choose to store your message file somewhere other than the postoffice. When you start up without connecting to the postoffice, this entry locates the file quickly (without presenting a File Browse dialog box). The entry is removed when you store your message file at the postoffice.

Note If you start online and your .MMF file is not on the postoffice, this entry is not used. Use the Mail Server Options dialog box to move your .MMF file.

Default: The path specified in the Mail Options Server dialog for a local message file.

Microsoft Mail Entries

OldStorePath   **REG_SZ**   *Pathname*

Contains the original path to a file that was originally stored in a place other than the postoffice. This entry is written temporarily by the Mail transport while you are moving your message file (using the Mail Options Server dialog box). This entry is removed after the move completes successfully and only appears if the system crashes during a move.

Password   **REG_SZ**   *password*

Use this entry and the **Login** entry to provide Mail with your account information, without being required to type this information into the Mail Sign In dialog box each time. If there is no password, leave the value for this entry blank, but do not omit the entry. Omitting the entry means you want to type your password each time in the Mail Sign In dialog box when you start Mail.

Default: (blank)—you are prompted for a password by the Mail program.

PollingInterval   **REG_SZ**   *minutes*

Gives the default for the Check for New Mail Every *n* Minutes option in the Mail Options dialog box. The value the user enters in the dialog box is written to the user's mail message file (.MMF)—this value is used to define how often the Mail spooler checks for new mail messages.

Default: 10

Printer   **REG_SZ**   *printer name, driver name, port*

This is the printer that appears in the Mail Print dialog box and is used by Mail when printing messages.

Default: the default printer specified in Print Manager

PumpCycleInterval   **REG_SZ**   *seconds*

Permits the spooler to check for new mail more often than once per minute, or to override the polling interval value defined in the user's mail message file.

Default: 60 seconds, or the number of minutes specified in the Mail Options dialog box

ReplyPrefix   REG_SZ *String*

If this entry is present, Mail distinguishes your comments from the original message when you reply to mail. When you reply, the original message text is copied to the body of the reply message, and each line of the original is prefixed with the string specified by this entry. If the string contains a space, enclose it within double quotation marks (for example, "| "—a vertical bar followed by a space).

Default: (blank)

ScanAgainInterval   REG_SZ *seconds*

Affects the mail spooler latency checking to prevent spooler background processing from interfering unduly with foreground work. When the spooler defers work because of higher priority, interactive tasks, it rechecks the availability of the system at this interval.

Default: 2

Security   REG_SZ *0 or 1*

If this entry is 1, Mail prompts for your password whenever its window is restored from its iconic state. That is, if Mail is minimized and you double-click on the icon, you must re-enter your password before you (or anyone else) can see your messages.

Default: 0

ServerPassword   REG_SZ *password*

Identifies the password used to connect to the server specified by the **ServerPath** entry. This entry should be used to specify the password for the file share if the form of the **ServerPath** entry is specified using the universal naming conventions (UNC) and the server, share, or the path name contains spaces. If this entry is present, the value for the **ServerPath** entry is interpreted literally, and any spaces present in the value for the entry is used when dynamically connecting to the workgroup postoffice.

If the **ServerPassword** entry is used, do not specify a password for the **ServerPath** entry (the password will be misinterpreted, and the resulting path to the workgroup postoffice will be invalid). The **ServerPassword** entry is written by the Mail program when connecting for the first time to the workgroup postoffice and is stored in the Microsoft Mail key file in encrypted format. Do not change this entry.

Microsoft Mail Entries

ServerPath	**REG_SZ**	*Pathname*
ServerPath	**REG_SZ**	*\\server\share\path password*
ServerPath	**REG_SZ**	*server/share:path*

If this entry is present, Mail searches for the postoffice in the specified directory. The first form, with a normal path name, works on all networks—the connection to the file share containing the network postoffice must be made before running the Mail program. The second form (UNC) works only on Windows NT and on Microsoft networks and compatibles. If you use the UNC form, Mail connects dynamically (without using a drive) to the file server where the postoffice resides. (If the specified UNC name contains any spaces, the password for the share needs to be specified for the **ServerPassword** entry.) The third form works only on Novell NetWare networks and uses an unused drive letter to connect dynamically to the NetWare file server where the postoffice resides. If no value is specified for the **ServerPath** entry, Mail asks the user for a path to the workgroup postoffice and writes a new value for this entry.

SharedExtensionsDir	**REG_SZ**	*Pathname*
SharedExtensionsDir	**REG_SZ**	*\\server\share\path password*

If this entry is present, Mail searches for shared custom commands and messages in the specified directory. The SHARED32.INI file in that directory identifies the shared extensions to load. Additional extensions can be entered in the Microsoft Mail key. Administrators often provide a common share point for extensions to Mail to simplify updating the extensions, and this entry makes it work. The first form with a normal path name works on all networks. The second form works only on Windows NT and on Microsoft networks and compatibles. If the second form is used, Mail connects dynamically (without using a drive) to the file server where the shared extensions reside.

Default: (blank)

SharedFolders   REG_SZ   *0 or 1*

Enables the use of Mail shared folders. If this entry is 1, the user can access shared folders. If this entry is 0, shared folders are unavailable to the user.

Default: 1

SpoolerBackoffInterval   REG_SZ   *milliseconds*

Specifies the amount of time the mail spooler waits before retrying an operation that has failed because of a transient mail server error condition, such as a locked file.

Default: 2000 (two seconds)

SpoolerReconnectInterval   REG_SZ   *seconds*

Specifies the amount of time the mail spooler waits before retrying an operation that has failed because of a fatal mail server error condition, such as a lost network connection.

Default: 60 (one minute)

StripGatewayHeaders   REG_SZ   *0 or 1*

If this entry is 1, message header text that appears above the dashed line is stripped from PC Mail messages that arrive via a gateway. Set this value to 0 if you want to see the extended information supplied by the gateways, which typically includes items such as message identifiers specific to the foreign mail system.

Message header text supplied by native PC Mail clients is always stripped. Only the PC Mail transport supports this entry.

Default: 1 (That is, you don't see gateway information.)

WG   REG_SZ   *0 or 1*

Specifies whether the version of the Mail program running on the computer is the Mail program provided with Windows NT. This entry is used internally by the Mail application and is written by the Mail program when it is executed.

Default: 1

Window   REG_SZ   *Left Top Right Bottom Zoom Toolbar Statusbar Scrollbars*

Specifies the zero-relative position within its menu where the main Mail window is to appear. This entry consists of eight numbers that govern the display of the main Mail window. This information is written when you exit Mail, and the changes you made while Mail was running are lost.

The format for this entry is as follows:

Value	Definition
Left Top *Right Bottom*	The first four numbers are pixel coordinates for the four sides of the main window in this order: left, top, right, and bottom.
Zoom	The zoom value is:
	1 main window is in a normal (restored) state 2 maximized (zoomed) 3 minimized (by icon)
Toolbar *Statusbar* *Scrollbars*	Determines when the toolbar, status bar, and scroll bars are displayed on the main window:
	0 corresponding bar is not displayed 1 bar is displayed

Default: window size and location determined by Windows NT, zoom state normal (restored), toolbar on, status bar on, scroll bars on.

Microsoft Mail Entries

MMF Entries for Mail

Most entries under this key affect automatic compression of the Mail message file, which by default has the filename extension of .MMF. When enabled, automatic compression uses idle time on your PC to recover disk space freed by the deleted messages and returns the disk space to the file system. You should not need to change the default values for entries in this subkey.

This is the Registry path for this subkey:

```
HKEY_CURRENT_USER\Software\Microsoft\Mail\MMF
```

Kb_Free_Start_Compress   REG_SZ   *kilobytes*

Background compression starts when at least this much recoverable space is detected in your message file. Both **Percent_Free_Start_Compress** and this entry are always active. The first entry to trigger starts the compression.

Default: 300

Kb_Free_Stop_Compress   REG_SZ   *kilobytes*

Background compression stops when there is less than the indicated amount of recoverable space in your message file. This avoids the unnecessary difficulty in trying to recover the last little bit of free space. Both this entry and **Percent_Free_Stop_Compress** are always active. The first entry to trigger stops the compression.

Default: 100.

No_Compress   REG_SZ   *0 or 1*

Specifies whether background compression is to be disabled. A value of 1 disables background compression of the .MMF message store.

Default: 0 (That is, background compression is enabled.)

Percent_Free_Start_Compress   REG_SZ   *percent*

Background compression starts when the amount of recoverable space rises above this percentage of the total file size. Both **Kb_Free_Start_Compress** and this entry are always active. The first one to trigger starts the compression.

Default: 10

Percent_Free_Stop_Compress   REG_SZ   *percent*

Background compression stops when the amount of recoverable space falls below this percentage of the total .MMF file size. Both this entry and **Kb_Free_Stop_Compress** are always active. The last one to trigger stops the compression.

Default: 5

Secs_Till_Fast_Compress   REG_SZ   *seconds*

The background compression algorithm has a fast mode and a slow mode. Background compression begins in the slow mode to avoid slowing system response time. After a number of seconds of system inactivity indicated by this entry, the compression switches to fast mode. Any user activity changes the setting back to slow mode.

Default: 600 seconds (That is, ten minutes of system inactivity.)

See also the entry for **AppInit_DLLs** in "Windows Software Registration Entries."

Mac FileTypes Entries for Mail

Entries in this subkey map the Macintosh file type and creator tags to MS-DOS eight-plus-three filenames. This is the Registry path for this subkey:

```
HKEY_CURRENT_USER\Software\Microsoft\Mail\Mac FileTypes
```

Mail uses these entry values to determine what application to launch on a file attachment that has been sent from a Macintosh mail client. There are two alternate forms for the entries:

```
creator:type=extension      or      :type=extension
```

Both the creator and type are sequences of four characters (possibly including blanks). For example,

```
:TEXT=DOC
```

launches the application associated with the extension .DOC (Word for Windows, for example) on any Macintosh file of type TEXT.

MS Proofing Tools Entries for Mail

The MS Proofing Tools subkey defines spelling values for Mail. This is the Registry path for this subkey:

```
HKEY_CURRENT_USER\Software\Microsoft\Mail\MS Proofing Tools
```

CustomDict   **REG_SZ**   *entry name*

Specifies the name of an entry in the [MS Proofing Tools] section of the WIN.INI file. That entry in turn gives the fully qualified path to a file containing your custom dictionary. The custom dictionary contains spellings not found in the standard dictionary but that were added using the Add button in the Spelling dialog box. This entry lets Mail take advantage of a custom dictionary you may have already created with another Microsoft application, such as Microsoft Word for Windows.

Default: (no default)

Spelling   **REG_SZ**   *keyname*

Specifies the name of an entry in the MS Proofing Tools subkey that defines filenames for the spelling checker DLL and dictionary. The entries for **Spelling** are in this format:

```
Spelling NNNN,M
```

There is no space after the comma. In this format, *NNNN* is the four-digit language identifier of the current Windows NT version as defined in the Control\NLS\Language subkey, and *M* is the spelling dictionary type.

The Registry path for the key that this entry refers to is the following, by default:

```
HKEY_CURRENT_USER\Software\Microsoft\Mail\MS Proofing Tools
```

This subkey contains an entry in the following form:

Spelling *NNNN*,0   **REG_SZ**   *DLLfilename, Dictionary filename*

Specifies the fully qualified path to the spelling checker DLL and dictionary. This entry lets Mail use the same dictionary you may already be using with another Microsoft application, such as Microsoft Word for Windows. Windows NT does supply a dictionary.

Default: MSPELL32.DLL,MSP32_*XX*.LEX (In these values, *XX* is usually the two letters identifying the language version of Windows NT defined in the DosKeybCodes subkey, as described in "Keyboard Layout Entries," earlier in this chapter.)

Providers Entries for Mail

Entries in the Providers subkey for Mail define settings that service providers use with Microsoft Mail front-end programs. For this release, there are service providers for Microsoft Mail for PC LANs. Service providers for other mail systems may be available later.

This is the Registry path for this subkey:

```
HKEY_CURRENT_USER\Software\Microsoft\Mail\Providers
```

Logon   REG_SZ   *DLL name*

Identifies a single DLL that contains the logon and session management code for your mail system. This value is often, but not necessarily, the same as the **Transport** and **Name** entries. This value is the base name of the DLL, without the .DLL filename extension, but include a path if the DLL is not in a directory on the user's path or in the directory containing the Mail executable file.

Default: MSSFS32

Name   REG_SZ   *DLL name*

Identifies one or more DLLs that contain functions required to browse system and personal user lists. One of the values is often, but not necessarily, the same as the **Logon** and **Transport** entries. Enter the base name of the DLL, without the .DLL filename extension, but include a path if the DLL is not in a directory on the user's path or in the directory containing the Mail executable file.

The order of providers in this entry is significant. When Mail is attempting to resolve ambiguous names typed in a message and finds an exact match in the first provider in the list, it will not go on to query the rest. Placing the personal address book provider first can save time in that process.

Default: MSSFS32 PABNSP32

SharedFolders   REG_SZ   *DLL name*

Identifies a single DLL that contains functions required to read and write messages in Microsoft PC Mail shared folders.

Default: MSSFS32 (It is unlikely that any DLL other than MSSFS will have this functionality.)

Transport   REG_SZ   *DLL name*

Identifies a single DLL that contains the functions necessary to send and receive mail on your mail system. It is often, but not necessarily, the same as the **Logon** and **Name** entries. Enter the base name of the DLL, without the .DLL filename extension, but include a path if the DLL is not in a directory on the user's path or in the directory containing the Mail executable file.

Default: MSSFS32

Registry Entries for Microsoft Schedule+

The settings used by Microsoft Schedule+ to track basic information about the user's schedule, such as display and general option settings, current window positions, and printer information are stored under the following key:

HKEY_CURRENT_USER\Software\Microsoft\Schedule+

The Schedule+ key contains the following subkeys:

Subkey	Purpose
Microsoft Schedule	Defines the appearance and behavior of Schedule+.
Microsoft Schedule+ Appt Books	Indicates the number and list of other users' Appointment Books that were open when you exited Schedule+.
Microsoft Schedule+ Archives	Indicates the number and list of Archive files that were open when you exited Schedule+.
Microsoft Schedule+ Exporters	Specifies DLL filenames for exporters.
Microsoft Schedule+ Importers	Specifies DLL filenames for importers.

Most of these entries have built-in defaults. You should not need to change the Schedule+ settings. To change the appearance and behavior of Schedule+, use the appropriate Schedule+ menu commands. Many values are for saving settings between sessions.

These keys are created in HKEY_CURRENT_USER when you first run Schedule+. If your system previously contained a Windows for MS-DOS version of SCHDPLUS.INI, the contents are migrated to the Registry when you first run Schedule+ under Windows NT.

Microsoft Schedule+ Entries

This key defines the appearance and behavior of Microsoft Schedule+. This is the Registry path for this subkey:

```
HKEY_CURRENT_USER\Software\Microsoft\Schedule+\Microsoft Schedule+
```

This key also appears under HKEY_USERS\.DEFAULT, but its only contents are **MigrateIni and MigrateIniPrint**.

These are the value entries that can appear in this key:

AppointmentView   REG_SZ   *state left top right bottom*

Specifies the state (1=normal, 2=maximized, 3=iconic) and the coordinates for the position of the Appointment Book window on the screen. These five numbers are written by the Schedule+ application when you exit and are used to restore the window to the last displayed position. The coordinates are pixel coordinates for the four sides of the Appointment Book window.

AppPath   REG_SZ   *Pathname*

Specifies the location of the Schedule+ program and execution files. Microsoft Mail uses this path to find Schedule+ when you receive a meeting request.

Default: *SystemRoot*\SYSTEM32 directory

ApptBookColor   REG_SZ   *colornumber(1-17)*

Specifies the preference setting for the background color of the Appointment Book. The color number corresponds (in order) to the colors shown in the Display dialog box available from the Options menu, as follows:

1=Black	7=Red	13=Bright green
2=White	8=Violet	14=Bright blue-green
3=Yellow	9=Khaki	15=Bright red
4=Blue	10=Dark gray	16=Bright violet
5=Green	11=Light gray	17= Bright yellow
6=Blue-green	12=Bright blue	

Default: 3 (Yellow)

ApptBookLinesColor   REG_SZ   *colornumber(1-17)*

Specifies the preference setting for the color of the lines in the Appointment Book. The color number corresponds to nondithered colors in the Display dialog box available from the Options menu (as described in the **ApptBookColor** entry).

Default: 1 (Black)

CopyTime   REG_SZ   *minutes*

Specifies the time interval that Schedule+ copies your online .CAL file to your local .CAL file (occurs in idle time).

Default: 15 minutes

CreateFileFirstTime   REG_SZ   *0 or 1*

Specifies whether an online calendar (.CAL) file should be created for a first-time Schedule+ user. If this entry is 1, an online calendar (.CAL) file is created the first time a user signs on to Schedule+. If 0 (as set automatically the first time you run Schedule+), an online calendar file is not created automatically.

Default: 0

DefaultPrinter   REG_SZ   *printer name, driver name, port*

Indicates the current default printer port and its network path as specified in Print Manager. This is the default printer Schedule+ uses for printing schedule information.

DefaultRemindAgain   REG_SZ   *0 or 1*

Defines the default state of the Remind Again check box. If this entry is 1, you are reminded again of your appointments at the requested intervals. If this entry is 0, you are reminded of your appointment only once.

Default: 0

DefaultRemindAgainAmount   REG_SZ   *timeunits*

Specifies the default number of time units to wait (interval) before reminding you of appointments again.

Default: 5

DefaultRemindAgainUnits   REG_SZ   *minutes, hours, days, weeks, or months*

Specifies the type of time units used in the **DefaultRemindAgainAmount** entry.

Default: minutes

DemosEnabled   REG_SZ   *0 or 1*

Specifies whether the Demos menu option is to be displayed in the Help menu. If the entry is 1, the Demos menu option is displayed in Help menu. If this entry is 0, the Demos menu option is not shown.

Default: 0 (The Schedule+ demos are not provided with Windows NT.)

ExportNoNotes   REG_SZ   *0 or 1*

Indicates whether the user chose to export notes. If this entry is 0, notes are exported. If this entry is 1, the notes are not exported.

Default: 0

ExportRange   REG_SZ   *0 or 1*

Indicates the range of schedule information to be exported. If this entry is 0, the entire schedule file is exported. If this entry is 1, a particular range is exported.

ExportType   REG_SZ   *0 or 1*

Indicates the current default file type for exporting your schedule. If this entry is 0, the default file type for exporting your schedule is the Schedule+ format. If the entry is 1, the file type for export is Text.

Default: 0

ImportDoNotAddDuplicates   REG_SZ   *0 or 1*

Indicates whether the user chose to import duplicate appointments. If this entry is 0, duplicate appointments are imported. If this entry is 1, your duplicate appointments are not imported.

Default: 0

ImportDoNotAskAboutConflicts   REG_SZ   *0 or 1*

Indicates whether the user chose to be asked about conflicting appointments during the import process. If this entry is 0, you are prompted for each conflicting appointment during the import process—in this case, you are asked whether to add each conflicting appointment. A value of 1 indicates that you are not asked about conflicts; they are added automatically.

Default: 0

ImportType   REG_SZ   *0 or 1*

Indicates the current default file type for importing a schedule file. If this entry is 0, the file type for importing your schedule is the Schedule+ format. If the entry is 1, the file type is the Windows NT Calendar format.

Default: 0

LargeFont   REG_SZ   *0 or 1*

Specifies the preference setting for the font size of text displayed in the Appointment Book and Planner. If this entry is 1, the font size of text is 10 points. If this entry is 0, the font is 8 points.

Default: 0

LocalPath   REG_SZ   *Pathname*

Specifies the location of the last user's local calendar (.CAL) file.

LocalUser   REG_SZ   *username*

Specifies the name of the last user to use the Schedule+ software on this computer.

MainWindow   REG_SZ   *state left top right bottom*

Specifies the state (1=normal, 2=maximized, 3=iconic) and the coordinates for the position of the Schedule+ application window on the screen. These five numbers are written by the Schedule+ application when you exit, and are used to restore the Schedule+ window to the last displayed position. The coordinates are pixel coordinates for the four sides of the main window.

MigrateIni   REG_SZ   *0 or 1*

Specifies whether to migrate the Schedule+ .INI files created by a Windows for MS-DOS version of Schedule+ for use under Windows NT. This entry is saved in the HKEY_USERS\.DEFAULT\Software\Microsoft\Mail subkey. In HKEY_CURRENT_USER, this entry is deleted after the user first runs Mail.

Default: 1 (yes)

MigrateIniPrint   REG_SZ   *0 or 1*

Specifies whether to migrate the Schedule+ .INI print information created by a Windows for MS-DOS version of Schedule+ for use under Windows NT. This entry is saved in the HKEY_USERS\.DEFAULT\Software\Microsoft\Mail subkey. In HKEY_CURRENT_USER, this entry is deleted after the user first runs Mail.

Default: 1 (yes)

NoStatusBar   REG_SZ   *0 or 1*

Indicates the preference setting for displaying the status bar. If this entry is 1, status bar is not displayed. If set to 0, the status bar is displayed.

Default: 0

OtherColor   REG_SZ   *colornumber(1-17)*

Specifies the preference setting for the color of other users' appointments in the Planner. The color number corresponds to nondithered colors in the Display dialog box available from the Options menu (as described in the **ApptBookColor** entry).

Default: 7 (Red)

PageBackgroundColor   REG_SZ   *colornumber(1-17)*

Specifies the preference setting for the background color of the Schedule+ window. The color number corresponds to nondithered colors in the Display dialog box available from the Options menu (as described in the **ApptBookColor** entry).

Default: 11 (Gray)

PlannerColor   REG_SZ   *colornumber(1-17)*

Specifies the preference setting for the background color of the Planner window. The color number corresponds to colors in the Display dialog box available from the Options menu (as described in the **ApptBookColor** entry).

Default: 2 (White)

PlannerLinesColor   REG_SZ   *colornumber(1-17)*

Specifies the preference setting for the color of the lines in the Planner. The color number corresponds to nondithered colors in the Display dialog box available from the Options menu (as described in the **ApptBookColor** entry).

Default: 1 (Black)

PollTime   REG_SZ   *centiseconds*

Specifies the frequency for checking the server for schedule file changes.

Default: 6000 centiseconds (one minute)

ReminderPollTime   REG_SZ   *minutes*

Specifies the frequency for polling the server for alarm changes.

Default: 15

RequestSummary   REG_SZ   *state left top right bottom*

Specifies the state (1=normal, 2=maximized, 3=iconic) and the coordinates for the position of the Messages window on the screen. These five numbers are written by the Schedule+ application when you exit and are used to restore the Messages window to the last displayed position. The coordinates are pixel coordinates for the four sides of the Messages window.

ShowActiveTasks   REG_SZ   *0 or 1*

Indicates whether the Task list is showing all tasks or only active tasks, as specified from the Tasks menu. If only active tasks are displayed, this value is 1.

Default: 0 (That is, all tasks are displayed.)

StartupOffline   REG_SZ   *0 or 1*

Specifies whether Schedule+ should start up using the offline scheduling information, or whether the online schedule should be used. If this entry is 1, Schedule+ is started offline.

Default: 0 (That is, Schedule+ is started online.)

**TaskSortOrder   REG_SZ   *0, 1, 2, –1, –2, or –3*

Specifies the current sort order for tasks, according to the following:

Value	Meaning
0	Tasks are sorted by priority.
1	Tasks are sorted by due date.
2	Tasks are sorted by description.
–1	Tasks are sorted by reverse description.
–2	Tasks are sorted by reverse due date.
–3	Tasks are sorted by reverse priority.

Default: 0

**TaskSortSecond   REG_SZ   *0, 1, 2, –1, –2, or –3*

Specifies the secondary sort order for tasks. If this entry is 0, the second sort order is by priority; if 1 the second sort order, using the same values as specified for **TaskSortOrder**.

Default: 0

**UpdatePostOfficeTime   REG_SZ   *centiseconds*

Specifies the frequency for updating the postoffice on the server after a change is made.

Default: 6000 centiseconds (one minute)

**UserColor   REG_SZ   *colornumber(1-17)*

Specifies the preference setting for the color of your own appointments in the Planner. The color number corresponds to nondithered colors in the Display dialog box available from the Options menu (as described in the **ApptBookColor** entry).

Default: 4 (Blue)

**ViewNotByProject   REG_SZ   *0 or 1*

Indicates whether the tasks in the Task list are currently displayed by project. If this entry is 1, the tasks are not displayed by project.

Default: 0

**WindowOrder   REG_SZ   *0 1 or 1 0*

Indicates the current display order of Schedule+ windows. The Schedule+ window is represented by 0, and the Messages window is 1. The first value for the **WindowOrder** entry indicates the window on top, and the second entry identifies the window behind the top window.

Default: 0 1

Microsoft Schedule+ Entries

Microsoft Schedule+ Appt Books Entries

Schedule+ uses this subkey to track the Appointment books of other Schedule+ users that you had open when you exited Schedule+. The following is the Registry path for this subkey:

```
HKEY_CURRENT_USER\Software\Microsoft
    \Schedule+\Microsoft Schedule+ Appt Books
```

Count   REG_SZ   *number*

Indicates the number of other users' Appointment Books you had open when you exited Schedule+. More entries appear in this subkey when the number is nonzero.

Microsoft Schedule+ Archives Entries

Schedule+ uses this subkey to track the Archive files that you had open when you exited Schedule+. This is the Registry path for this subkey:

```
HKEY_CURRENT_USER\Software\Microsoft
    \Schedule+\Microsoft Schedule+ Archives
```

Count   REG_SZ   *number*

Indicates the number of Archive files you had open when you exited Schedule+. More entries appear in this subkey when the number is nonzero.

Microsoft Schedule+ Exporter Entries

Schedule+ uses this subkey to specify settings for exporters. This is the Registry path for this subkey:

```
HKEY_CURRENT_USER\Software\Microsoft
    \Schedule+\Microsoft Schedule+ Exporters
```

Key   REG_SZ   *DLL name*

Identifies a single exporter DLL for Schedule+. The available files can be found on CompuServe. The *Key* name of this entry can be any string.

Microsoft Schedule+ Importer Entries

Schedule+ uses this subkey to specify settings for importers. This is the Registry path for this subkey:

```
HKEY_CURRENT_USER\Software\Microsoft
    \Schedule+\Microsoft Schedule+ Importers
```

***Key* REG_SZ**   *DLL name*

Identifies a single importer DLL for Schedule+. The available files can be found on CompuServe. The *Key* name of this entry can be any string.

Registry Entries for User Preferences

Information about Registry entries for user preferences about the following topics can be found in this section:

Hive information for user profiles	International
Console	Keyboard and keyboard layout
Colors, patterns, and screen savers	Mouse
Cursors	Multimedia and sound
Desktop	Network
Environment variables	Program Manager
File Manager	Windows

The information presented here is primarily for troubleshooting, showing the default entry values and explaining the meaning of important entries. There are no hidden values that you can set for user preferences. All of these values can be set using the icons in Control Panel or the tools in the Administrative Tools group, or other programs provided with Windows NT.

All Registry paths shown here are for HKEY_CURRENT_USER, to show how you can view entries for the currently logged on user. However, most of these entries also appear in HKEY_USERS\.DEFAULT, where changing entries will change values for the default user profile.

Hive Information for User Profiles

Information about user profile files appears in the following keys:

- The HiveList subkey lists all hives that are active but not profiles that are not active. (See its entry in "CurrentControlSet\Control Subkeys," earlier in this chapter.)

- The ProfileList subkey lists all the profiles known on the computer, whether or not the profiles are active, under the following Registry path:

```
HKEY_LOCAL_MACHINE\SOFTWARE\Microsoft\Windows NT\CurrentVersion
    \ProfileList\SID_#
```

Each installed user profile has its own subkey under the ProfileList subkey, and that subkey contains the following entry:

ProfileImagePath   REG_EXPAND_SZ   *Profile hive filename*
Specifies the path and filename for the hive for this user. The hive file name that is the value for **ProfileImagePath** includes a portion of the username associated with that *SID_#*, so that you can identify the user to which it belongs.

Default: %SystemRoot%\system32\config*hiveFilename*

Sid   REG_BINARY   *Number assigned by system*

Backup Entries for Users

Windows NT Backup may have a problem restoring files from a Sytos Plus tape if the file is in a backup session that spans two Sytos Plus tapes and the file itself is entirely on the second tape. If this occurs, you can restore the file by rerunning Backup after setting the following Windows NT Registry key to 0:

```
HKEY_CURRENT_USER\Software\Microsoft\Ntbackup
    \Backup Engine\Use fast file restore
```

After restoring the file, reset the key to 1.

When restoring or cataloging a Sytos Plus tape under Windows NT, you might get the error "An error occurred during translation of data to or from the tape in the drive." This is because the backup error correction code (ECC) flag value in the Registry has been incorrectly set by the data on the tape. The value in the Registry is an override. To correct this problem, edit the following Registry key:

```
HKEY_CURRENT_USER\SOFTWARE\Microsoft\Ntbackup\Translators
    \Sytos Plus ECC flag
```

Sytos Plus ECC Flag   REG_DWORD   *0, 1, or 2*

Valid values are as follows:

Value	Description
0 (Off)	NTBACKUP assumes that there is no software ECC on the tape.
1 (On)	NTBACKUP assumes that there is software ECC on the tape.
2 (Auto)	NTBACKUP determines whether a Sytos tape was written with software ECC by checking the data on the tape.

Values should be set accordingly for the following types of tape:

Tape	Value
4mm DAT	0
8mm DAT	0
1/4 in. 525	0
1/4 in. 150	1

Default: 2

Note If you have previously run the version of Windows NT Backup included with Windows NT 3.1, delete the Windows NT Backup entries in the Registry prior to running the upgrade version of Windows NT Backup. Otherwise, the ECC flag will not appear.

Console Entries for Users

The Console key contains font, cursor, and screen control values under the following Registry path:

HKEY_CURRENT_USER\Console

CursorSize   REG_DWORD   *Percentage*

Specifies percentage of character cell filled by the cursor.

Default: 0x19

FullScreen   REG_DWORD   *0 or 1*

1 = full screen mode, 0 = windowed mode. Valid only on x86 machines.

Default: 0x0

FaceName   REG_SZ   *Name*

Specifies name of console font.

Default: Null

FontFamily   REG_DWORD   *Family*

Specifies console font family (TrueType, raster, etc.).

Default: 0

FontSize   REG_DWORD   *Size*

Specifies console font size. Low word is character width, high word is character height.

Default: 0

FontWeight   REG_DWORD   *Number*

Specifies console font weight.

Default: 0

HistoryBufferSize   REG_DWORD   *Number*

Specifies number of commands stored in command history buffer.

Default: 0x32

InsertMode   REG_DWORD   *0 or 1*

Enables insert mode (1) or overtype mode (0).

Default: 0

NumberOfHistoryBuffers   REG_DWORD   *Number*

Specifies number of history buffers associated with console.

Default: 0x4

PopupColors   REG_DWORD   *Colors*

Specifies colors to use for popup windows. The four low-order bits are foreground, and the next four are background.

Default: 0xf5

QuickEdit   REG_DWORD   *0 or 1*

Specifies 1 (enabled) for quick-edit mode, 0 (disabled) for normal edit mode.

Default: 0

ScreenBufferSize   REG_DWORD   *Buffer size*

Specifies console screen buffer size. Low word is width, high word is height.

Default: 0x00190050

Console Entries for Users

ScreenColors   REG_DWORD   *Colors*

Specifies colors to use for console text windows. The four low-order bits are foreground, and the next four are background.

Default: 0x7

WindowSize   REG_DWORD   *Size*

Specifies console window size. Low word is width, high word is height.

Default: 0x00190050

WindowPosition   REG_DWORD   *Position*

Specifies console window position. Low word is X, high word is Y.

Default: Not set

You can also create subkeys under HKEY_CURRENT_USER\CONSOLE which are the names of console windows. These subkeys can contain any of the preceding values. When you open a console window, Windows NT looks in the registry for a subkey with the same name as the window title (for example, "Command Prompt"). If the subkey is found, any values stored there override the values stored in the \CONSOLE key for that console.

The Console key also contains several subkeys that define screen size and buffer size for character-based screens in Windows NT. These subkeys appear under the following Registry path:

`HKEY_CURRENT_USER\Console\subkeyNames`

The Command Prompt subkey does not appear unless the current user has changed the screen colors or font for the command prompt and also checked the Save Configuration options. Use the commands on the Control menu in the command prompt to change these values.

Console subkey	Default value entries
Command Prompt (All data types are REG_DWORD)	**FontFamily**=0x30 **FontSize**=0xc0008 **FullScreen**=0x1 **PopupColors**=0xf5 **QuickEdit**=0 **ScreenBufferSize**=0x190050 **ScreenColors**=0x9f **WindowsPosition**=0x150004 **WindowSize**=0x190050
Introducing Windows NT	**FullScreen**=0x1
Microsoft QBASIC	**FullScreen**=0x1

Color, Pattern, and Screen Saver Entries for Users

This section describes the subkeys that contain settings for user preferences related to the desktop.

Colors Entry Values

The Colors subkey specifies the color as a series of three numbers for each area of the Windows screen, in the following Registry path:

```
HKEY_CURRENT_USER\Control Panel\Colors
```

Each entry has a REG_SZ data type. The following lists the defaults for each entry under the Colors subkey:

ActiveBorder=192 192 192
ActiveTitle=0 0 128
AppWorkSpace=255 255 255
Background=255 255 255
ButtonFace=192 192 192
ButtonHilight=255 255 255
ButtonShadow=128 128 128
ButtonText=0 0 0
GrayText=128 128 128
Hilight=0 0 128
HilightText=255 255 255
InactiveBorder=192 192 192
InactiveTitle=192 192 192
InactiveTitleText=0 0 0
Menu=255 255 255
MenuText=0 0 0
Scrollbar=192 192 192
TitleText=255 255 255
Window=255 255 255
WindowFrame=0 0 0
WindowText=0 0 0

Color Schemes Entry Values

The entries in the Color Schemes subkey define the colors for each element of specific color schemes, as set by choosing the Color icon in Control Panel. These entries appear under the following Registry path:

```
HKEY_CURRENT_USER\Control Panel\Color Schemes
```

The Current subkey specifies the current color scheme, based on those listed in the Color Schemes subkey.

The Custom Colors subkey defines the custom colors in the color palette, as set by choosing the Color icon in Control Panel. The entries are designated ColorA through ColorP, and all have the value ffffFF by default.

Each entry in these subkeys has a REG_SZ data type.

Patterns Entry Values

The Patterns subkey contains entries that define the color values for the bitmap patterns, as set by choosing the Desktop icon. Each value is a set of eight numbers, corresponding to the colors in the eight basic elements of the pattern.

Each entry has a REG_SZ data type.

Screen Saver Subkey Entry Values

The various *Screen Saver* subkeys define user preferences for specific screen savers. All entries have a REG_SZ data type. The following table summarizes the default entries under the *Screen Saver* subkeys.

Screen Save subkey	Default value entries
Screen Saver.Bezier	—
Screen Saver.Marquee	**BackgroundColor**=0 0 128 **CharSet**=0 **Font**=Times New Roman **Mode**=1 **Size**=24 **Speed**=14 **Text**=Your text goes here. **TextColor**=255 0 255
Screen Saver.Mystify	**Active1**=1 **Active2**=1 **Clear Screen**=1 **EndColor1**=255 255 255 **EndColor2**=255 255 255 **Lines1**=7 **Lines2**=12 **StartColor1**=0 0 0 **StartColor2**=0 0 0 **WalkRandom1**=1 **WalkRandom2**=1
Screen Saver.Stars	**Density**=50 **WarpSpeed**=10

Additional screen saver settings are defined in the Desktop subkey, described later in this section.

Cursors Entry Values for Users

The Cursor subkey contains entries that specify the .ANI or .CUR files containing custom cursors defined using the Cursor icon in Control Panel. There are no entries in this key unless the user changes cursor styles in Control Panel. All data types are REG_SZ. The following lists the names for possible default entries: **<NEW TABLE>**

3D-Bronze	**Hands 1 or 2**	**SizeNS**
3D-White	**IBeam**	**SizeNWSE**
AppStarting	**Magnified**	**SizeWE**
Arrow	**No**	**Variations**
Conductor	**Old Fashioned**	**Wait**
CrossHair	**SizeAll**	**Windows Animated**
Dinosaur	**SizeNESW**	**Windows Default**

Desktop Entry Values for Users

The Desktop key contains entries that control the appearance of the screen background and the position of windows and icons on the screen. The following shows the Registry path:

```
HKEY_CURRENT_USER\Control Panel\Desktop
```

To change most of these entries, use the Desktop icon in Control Panel. The Desktop subkey can contain the following entries:

BorderWidth   REG_SZ   *number*

Sets the width of the borders around all the windows that have sizable borders. The possible range is 1 (narrowest) to 49 (widest).

Default: 3

CoolSwitch   REG_SZ   *Boolean*

Turns fast task switching on or off. To change this entry, choose the Desktop icon from Control Panel, and check or clear the Fast ALT+TAB Switching option in the Task List dialog box.

Default: 1

CursorBlinkRate   REG_SZ   *milliseconds*

Indicates how much time elapses between each blink of the selection cursor.

Default: 530

GridGranularity   REG_SZ *number*

Specifies the size of the grid used to position windows on the screen. The possible range is 0 through 49, in units of 8 pixels.

Default: 0

IconSpacing   REG_SZ *pixels*

Specifies the number of pixels that appear horizontally between icons. A larger number increases the space between icons.

Default: 75

IconTitleFaceName   REG_SZ *fontname*

Specifies the font used to display icon titles. Change this value if the icon title is difficult to read.

Default: Helv

IconTitleSize   REG_SZ *number*

Specifies the size of the font used to display icon titles. Change this value if the icon title is difficult to read.

Default: 9

IconTitleStyle   REG_SZ *Boolean*

Default: 0

IconTitleWrap   REG_SZ *Boolean*

Specifies whether to wrap icon titles. A value of 1 allows icon title wrapping and increases icon vertical spacing by three lines; 0 turns off icon title wrapping.

Default: 1

Pattern   REG_SZ *b1 b2 b3 b4 b5 b6 b7 b8*

Specifies a pattern for the screen background. The 8 numeric values define a bitmap 8 pixels wide and 8 pixels high. Each decimal value represents a byte, and each byte represents a row of 8 pixels, where 0 sets the corresponding pixel to the background color, and 1 sets the corresponding pixel to the foreground color (specified by the **Background** and **WindowText** values in the Colors subkey, respectively).

For example, if you set the *b1* value to the decimal value 175, the top row of pixels in the bitmap appears as the binary equivalent (10101111).

Default: (None) (This string appears when no pattern is specified.)

ScreenSaveActive   REG_SZ   *Boolean*

Specifies whether a screen saver should be displayed if the system is not actively being used. Set this value to 1 to use a screen saver; 0 turns off the screen saver.

Default: 0

ScreenSaverIsSecure   REG_SZ   *Boolean*

Specifies whether a password is assigned to the screen saver.

Default: 0

ScreenSaveTimeOut   REG_SZ   *seconds*

Specifies the amount of time that the system must be idle before the screen saver appears.

Default: 900

SCRNSAVE.EXE   REG_SZ   *Filename*

Specifies the screen saver executable filename.

Default: (None)

TileWallpaper   REG_SZ   *Boolean*

Specifies that the desktop wallpaper is tiled across the screen if this value is 1, or centered if this value is 0.

Default: 0

Wallpaper   REG_SZ   *bitmap-filename*

Supplies the filename for the bitmap on the screen background. Include the path if the file is not in the *SystemRoot* or *SystemRoot*\SYSTEM32 directory.

Default: "(None)" (This string appears when no pattern is specified.)

Environment Variable Entries for Users

The Environment subkey contains the user environment variables, as defined by choosing the System icon in Control Panel. Changes to these variables take effect the next time a non-Windows NT–based application is run or the command prompt is used. These value entries are found under the following path:

```
HKEY_CURRENT_USER\Environment
```

The default is the environment variables defined in the user's profile at startup.

File Manager Entries for Users

This section describes settings for user preferences in File Manager.

File Manager Software Settings

The File Manager subkey under this Registry path contains the user preferences for the appearance of items in File Manager:

```
HKEY_CURRENT_USER\Software\Microsoft\File Manager\Settings
```

The following entries can appear. Most items have a default setting and do not appear unless the user makes changes in File Manager.

AddOns   REG_SZ   *Boolean*

Default: (none)

ConfirmDelete   REG_SZ   *Boolean*

Specifies whether the user is to be prompted to confirm file deletion requests.

Default: 1 (enabled)

ConfirmFormat   REG_SZ   *Boolean*

Specifies whether the user is to be prompted to confirm formatting requests.

Default: 1 (enabled)

ConfirmMouse   REG_SZ   *Boolean*

Specifies whether the user is to be prompted to confirm mouse drag-and-drop requests.

Default: 1 (enabled)

ConfirmReplace   REG_SZ   *Boolean*

Specifies whether the user is to be prompted to confirm file replacement requests.

Default: 1 (enabled)

ConfirmSubDel   REG_SZ   *Boolean*

Specifies whether the user is to be prompted to confirm subdirectory deletion requests.

Default: 1 (enabled)

ConfirmSystemHiddenReadOnly **REG_SZ** *Boolean*

Specifies whether the user is to be prompted to confirm for system, hidden, or read-only file changes.

Default: 1 (enabled)

dir1 **REG_SZ** *Comma-separated list*

The current directory settings.

Default: 0,0,522,249,-1,-1,1,0,202,2033,261,C:\WINNT*.*

Face **REG_SZ** *Typeface*

Specifies the name of the typeface used for desktop items.

Default: MS Sans Serif.

FaceWeight **REG_SZ** *Number*

Specifies 700 for bold or bold italic, 400 for regular or italic.

LowerCase **REG_DWORD** *0, 1, 4, 8*

Specifies values for lowercase variables checked in the Fonts dialog box, as follows:

Value	Meaning
0	No options checked
0x1	Lowercase for FAT drives
0x4	Italic
0x8	Lowercase for all drives

NumButtons **REG_SZ** *Number*

Default: 15000000

Size **REG_SZ** *Number*

The point size for the typeface.

Default: 8

ToolbarWindow **REG_SZ**

Contains user-defined settings for the toolbar, as defined in the Options menu in File Manager.

Default:
CD000000CE000000ffffffffFE000000FF000000ffffffff9101000092010000fffff
fff940100009501000096010000970100000ffffffff52040000ffffffff6B0000006A
0000006C000000ffffffff5D020000

Window   REG_SZ   *Numbers*

Specifies the size and position of the window and whether it is maximized when opened. Use the mouse to move and size the window.

Default: 0,0,640,480, , ,2

Extensions Entries for Users

The Extensions subkey identifies personal preferences for document files with corresponding command lines, so that opening a document file in File Manager automatically starts the application. The extensions are found in the following Registry path:

```
HKEY_CURRENT_USER\Software\Microsoft\Windows NT\CurrentVersion
    \Extensions
```

The following default entries are defined. All have a REG_SZ data type.

bmp=pbrush.exe ^.bmp
crd=cardfile.exe ^.crd
ini=notepad.exe ^.ini
pcx=pbrush.exe ^.pcx
rec=recorder.exe ^.rec
trm=terminal.exe ^.trm
txt=notepad.exe ^.txt
wri=write.exe ^.wri

Note   The extension information for all users can be viewed and modified in HKEY_CLASSES_ROOT. This is where you will find the file types and extension information for File Manager.

International Entry Values for Users

The International subkey describes how to display dates, times, currency, and other items for a specific country, under the following Registry path:

```
HKEY_CURRENT_USER\Control Panel\International
```

The International\Sorting Order key is not used in this version of Windows NT.

The following table summarizes entry values under this subkey. All data types are REG_SZ. To change any of these items, choose the International icon in Control Panel.

iCountry   REG_SZ   *country*

Specifies the country code. This number matches the country's international telephone code, except for Canada, which is 2. The U.S. English default is 1.

iCurrDigits   REG_SZ   *number*

Specifies the number of digits to put after the decimal separator in currency. The U.S. English default is 2.

iCurrency   REG_SZ   *number*

Specifies a positive currency format, where 0 = $2, 1 = 2$, 2 = $ 2, and 3 = 2 $. The U.S. English default is 0. The actual currency symbol is specified by the **sCurrency** value.

iDate   REG_SZ   *number*

Specifies a numerical date format for compatibility with Windows 2.x, where 0 = 12/31/90, 1 = 31/12/90, and 2 = 90/12/31. The U.S. English default is 0. The actual date divider is specified by the **sShortDate** value.

iDigits   REG_SZ   *number*

Specifies the number of digits to display after the decimal separator in numbers. The U.S. English default is 2.

iLZero   REG_SZ   *0 or 1*

Specifies whether to put leading zeros in decimal numbers, where 0 = .7 and 1 = 0.7. The U.S. English default is 1. The actual decimal separator is specified by the **sDecimal** value.

iMeasure   REG_SZ   *0 or 1*

Specifies the measurement system as metric or English, where 0 = metric and 1 = English. The U.S. English default is 1.

iNegCurr   REG_SZ   *number*

Specifies a negative number format, where:

0 = ($1)	4 = (1$)	8 = –1 $	12 = $ -1.1
1 = –$1	5 = –1$	9 = –$ 1	13 = 1.1- $
2 = $–1	6 = 1–$	10 = 1 $–	14 ($ 1.1)
3 = $1–	7 = 1$–	11 = $ 1–	15 = (1.1 $)

The U.S. English default is 1. The actual currency symbol is specified by the **sCurrency** value.

iTime   **REG_SZ**   *number*

Specifies whether to format time using a 12-hour or 24-hour clock, where 0 = 1:00 (12-hour clock) and 1 = 13:00 (24-hour clock). The U.S. English default is 0. The actual time separator is specified by the **sTime** value.

iTLZero   **REG_SZ**   *number*

Specifies whether to put leading zeros in time, where 0 = 9:15 and 1 = 09:15. The U.S. English default is 0. The actual time separator is specified by the **sTime** value.

Locale   **REG_SZ**   *number*

Specifies the current user's locale ID for the local language preferences, based on values defined in CurrentControlSet\Control\Nls\Language. The U.S. English default is 00000409.

s1159   **REG_SZ**   *string*

Specifies the time marker to use in time strings before noon in the 12-hour time format. The U.S. English default is AM.

s2359   **REG_SZ**   *string*

Specifies the time marker to use in time strings after noon in the 12-hour format or that follows all times in the 24-hour format. The U.S. English default is PM.

sCountry   **REG_SZ**   *string*

Specifies the name of the country whose standard value you want to use. The U.S. English default is United States.

sCurrency   **REG_SZ**   *string*

Specifies the currency symbol you want to use. The U.S. English default is $.

sDate   **REG_SZ**   *string*

Specifies the symbol separating numbers for the short date. The U.S. English default is /.

sDecimal   **REG_SZ**   *string*

Specifies the punctuation used to separate the fractional part of a decimal number from the whole number part. The U.S. English default is a period (.).

sLanguage   REG_SZ   *string*

Specifies the language you want to work in. Windows-based applications that provide language specific tasks, such as sorting or spell checking, use this entry. The U.S. English default is **enu**. Values for the locales supported for the first version of Windows NT are the following:

csy = Czech	frc = French (Canadian)
dan = Danish	frs = French (Swiss)
deu = German	hun = Hungarian
des = German (Swiss)	isl = Icelandic
dea = German (Austrian)	ita = Italian
ell = Greek	its = Italian (Swiss)
ena = English (Australia)	nlb = Dutch (Belgian)
enc = English (canada)	nld = Dutch
eng = English (U.K.)	non = Norwegian (Nynorsk)
eni = English (Irish)	nor = Norwegian (Bokmal)
enu = English (U.S.)	plk = Polish
enz = English (New Zealand)	ptb = Portuguese (Brazilian)
esm = Spanish (Mexican)	ptg = Portuguese
esn = Modern Spanish	rus = Russian
esp = Castilian Spanish	sky = Slovak
fin = Finnish	svc = Swedish
fra = French	trk = Turkish
frb = French (Belgian)	

sLiisl = Icelandic   st   REG_SZ   *string*

ita = ItalianSpecifies the character used to separate items in a list. In U.S. English, the nld = Dutchmost common separator is a comma. The U.S. English default is , (comma).

sLonor = Norwegian   ngDate   REG_SZ   *format*

ptg = Portuguese   Specifies your choices for the long date formats, including abbreviations for the sve = Swedish words and separators. Control Panel accepts only certain format combinations. Therefore, you should use Control Panel to change these entries. The U.S. English default is dddd, MMMM dd, yyyy (that is, Friday, June 1, 1990). Values are:

d = Day (1–31)
dd = Day (01–31)
ddd = Day (Mon–Sun)
dddd = Day (Monday–Sunday)
M = Month (1–12)
MM = Month (01–12)
MMM = Month (Jan–Dec)
MMMM = Month (January–December)
yy = Year (00–99)
yyyy = Year (1900–2040)

International Entry Values for Users

sShortDate   **REG_SZ**   *format*

Specifies a choice for the short date format, including abbreviations for the words and separators, according to the list described for **sLongDate**. Control Panel accepts only certain format combinations. Therefore, you should use Control Panel to change this setting. The U.S. English default is M/d/yy (that is, 6/1/90).

sThousand   **REG_SZ**   *string*

Specifies the symbol used to separate thousands. For example, if the value is a comma, the number appears as 3,000. The U.S. English default is , (comma).

sTime   **REG_SZ**   string

Specifies the character used to separate the hours, minutes, and seconds in time. For example, if the value is a colon, the time appears as 15:29:31. The U.S. English default is : (a colon).

Keyboard and Keyboard Layout Entries for Users

The Keyboard entry contains user preferences as defined by choosing the Keyboard icon in Control Panel. Entries are found under this Registry path:

```
HKEY_CURRENT_USER\Control Panel\Keyboard
```

InitialKeyboardIndicators   **REG_SZ**   *Number*

Specifies initial values for keys. 0 means that NUMLOCK is turned off after the user logs on; 2 means NUMLOCK is turned on after the user logs on. This value is set during log off or shutdown to preserve the state of the NUMLOCK key at that time.

Default: 0

KeyboardDelay   **REG_SZ**   *0 to 3*

Establishes how much time elapses after you hold down a key before the key starts to repeat. The values 0 through 3 provide a linear scale from the smallest delay supported by the keyboard driver to the largest delay. Typically, 0 represents 250 milliseconds, and 3 represents 1 second, with a 20 percent accuracy.

Default: 1

KeyboardSpeed   **REG_SZ**   *0 to 31*

Sets how much time elapses between repetitions of a character on the display when you hold down a keyboard key. The values 0 through 31 provide a linear scale from the slowed repeat rate supported by the keyboard driver to the fastest repeat rate. Typically, 0 represents 2 per second, and 31 represents 30 per second.

Default: 31

The Keyboard Layout key records the user's preferred layout, which is loaded and activated by the system when the user logs on. Entries are found under this Registry path:

```
HKEY_CURRENT_USER\Control Panel\Keyboard Layout
```

When the user logs off, the user's current keyboard layout is stored here. The value for the entry is based on those defined in CurrentControlSet\Control\NLS\KeyboardLayout. To change the keyboard layout, choose the Windows NT Setup icon from the Main program group.

Active   REG_SZ   *KeyboardLayout*
Default: 00000409 (for standard U.S. English)

The Keyboard Layout\Substitutes key is empty by default. This subkey records a mapping between keyboard layout names. The system checks the user's Substitutes subkey when loading the keyboard driver, and if a substitute is specified, the corresponding layout name is substituted. For example, an entry such as the following under the Keyboard Layout\Substitutes subkey indicates that the user prefers the Dvorak U.S. English keyboard layout (00010409) to the standard U.S. English keyboard layout (00000409).

```
00000409 : REG_SZ : 00010409
```

Mouse Entries for Users

To change these entries, choose the Mouse icon from Control Panel.

DoubleClickSpeed   REG_SZ   *milliseconds*
Sets the maximum time between clicks of the mouse button that the system permits for one double-click. The lower the value for this entry, the less time you have to click twice to double-click.
Default: 686

MouseSpeed   REG_SZ   *0 or 1 or 2*
Sets the relationship between mouse and cursor movement when the value of either **MouseThreshold1** or **MouseThreshold2** is exceeded. When this occurs, cursor movement accelerates according to the value of **MouseSpeed**.

Value	Meaning
0	No acceleration.
1	The cursor is moved twice the normal speed when mouse movement exceeds the value of **MouseThreshold1**.
2	The cursor is moved twice the normal speed when the mouse movement exceeds the value of **MouseThreshold1**, or four times the normal speed if mouse movement exceeds **MouseThreshold2**.

Default: 1

MouseThreshold1   REG_SZ   *pixels*
MouseThreshold2   REG_SZ   *pixels*

These entries set the maximum number of pixels that the mouse can move between mouse interrupts before the system alters the relationship between mouse and cursor movement. If the mouse movement exceeds the threshold defined by **MouseThreshold1** and if **MouseSpeed** is greater than 0, the system moves the cursor at twice the normal speed. If the mouse movement exceeds the threshold defined by **MouseThreshold2** and if **MouseSpeed** is 2, the system moves the cursor at four times the normal speed.

Default: **MouseThreshold1=6**
          MouseThreshold2=10

SwapMouseButtons   REG_SZ   *Boolean*

Specifies whether to swap the right and left mouse buttons. If the value is 1, the buttons are swapped.

Default: 0

Multimedia and Sound Entries for Users

Values related to user preferences for multimedia items in Control Panel are found in the following Registry path:

HKEY_CURRENT_USER\Control Panel

The information here is for troubleshooting reference. All changes should be made using the Devices, Drivers, MIDI Mapper, and Sound icons in Control Panel. The following lists the default entries. All are REG_SZ data types.

Multimedia subkey	Default value entries
MMCPL	**H**=230 **NumApps**=20 **W**=442 **X**=88 **Y**=84
Sound	**Beep**=yes
Sounds	**Enable**=1 **SystemAsterisk**=chord.wav,Asterisk **SystemDefault**=ding.wav,Default Beep **SystemExclamation**=chord.wav,Exclamation **SystemExit**=chimes.wav,Windows Logoff **SystemHand**=chord.wav,Critical Stop **SystemQuestion**=chord.wav,Question **SystemStart**=tada.wav,Windows Logon

Network Entries for Users

This section describes the user preferences and settings for the network.

Network Administration Entries for Users

The following Registry path contains values used by administrators to remember the last server and client share points used by the NCADMIN.EXE application between executions:

```
HKEY_CURRENT_USER\SOFTWARE\Microsoft\WindowsNT\CurrentVersion\Network
    \NCAdmin
```

LastClientServer   **REG_SZ**   *0 to 15 characters*

Remembers the last server used for the creation of network client installation disks or Over the Network Installation startup disks.

Default: (none)

LastClientSharepoint   **REG_SZ**   *0 to 8 characters (MS-DOS); 0 to 80 characters (Windows NT)*

Remembers the last share used for the creation of network client installation disks or Over the Network Installation startup disks.

Default: (none)

LastToolsServer   **REG_SZ**   *0 to 15 characters*

Remembers the last server that referenced the network administration tools directory path.

Default: (none)

LastToolsSharepoint   **REG_SZ**   *0 to 8 characters (MS-DOS); 0 to 80 characters (Windows NT)*

Remembers the last share that referenced the network administration tools directory path.

Default: (none)

Note **LastToolsSharepoint** plus **LastToolsServer** must be less than MAX_PATH - 3. (The 3 accounts for the two backslashes (\)at the beginning of the path and the one between the server and the share.) This same rule applies to **LastClientSharepoint** and **LastClientServer**.

Characters may be any legal UNICODE character that can be used in a server or share name. The NCAdmin subkey and these values do not appear until NCAdmin has been run at least once by the current user.

Network Connection Entries for Users

The following Registry path contains the list of specific shares to reconnect when the user logs on:

```
HKEY_CURRENT_USER\Network
```

The Network subkey does not appear unless you are connected to a shared directory when the Reconnect At Logon option was checked in File Manager. There is a subkey for each shared directory to be reconnected at system startup. The name of the subkey is the drive-letter designated for the connection. Each such subkey can contain the following entries:

ConnectionType   **REG_DWORD**   *0x1 or 1x2*

Specifies connection types as 0x1 for drive redirection or 0x2 for print redirection.

Default: 0x1

ProviderName   **REG_SZ**   *Network name*

Specifies the network provider for the path to the shared directory.

Default: Microsoft Windows Network

RemotePath   REG_SZ   *UNC sharename*

Specifies the UNC name for the shared directory.

UserName   REG_SZ   *username*

Specifies the username under whose authority the connection was established. The password is not remembered. This name can appear in the Connect As box in the Connect Network Drive dialog box in File Manager.

Default: (blank) (That is, the name of currently logged on user is assumed.)

Network Software Entries for Users

The following path contains subkeys with settings for user preferences related to Event Viewer, Server Manager, User Manager, and User Manager for Domains:

```
HKEY_CURRENT_USER\SOFTWARE\Microsoft\Windows NT\CurrentVersion\Network
```

The following table summarizes default settings in the Network subkeys. All entries have REG_SZ data types.

Network subkey	Default value entries
Event Viewer	**Filter=** (as chosen in the Filter dialog box) **Find=**: (string from Find dialog box) **FontFaceName=**(none) **FontHeight=**0 **FontItalic=**0 **FontWeight=**0 **IfNT=**1 (1=focused on Windows NT server) **LogType=**0 (0=system; 1=security; 2=application; 4=read from a file) **Module=**System (or Security or Application) **SaveSettings=**1 **SortOrder=**0 (0=new events first; 1=old events first) **Window=**132 126 504 282 0 (position and minimize)
Remote Boot Manager	**Confirmation=**1 **FontFaceName=**(none) **FontHeight=**0 **FontItalic=**0 **FontWeight=**0 **SaveSettings=**1 **Window=**132 126 504 282 0 (position and minimize)

Network subkey *(continued)*	Default value entries *(continued)*
Server Manager	**AccountsOnly**=0 **FontFaceName**=(none) **FontHeight**=0 **FontItalic**=0 **FontWeight**=0 **SaveSettings**=1 **View** = 4 (1=view workstations; 2=view servers) **ViewExtension** (file being viewed if **View**=0)
User Manager	**FontFaceName**=(none) **FontHeight**=0 **FontItalic**=0 **FontWeight**=0 **ListBoxSplit**=667 **SaveSettings**=1
User Manager for Domains	**Confirmation**=1 **FontFaceName**=(none) **FontHeight**=0 **FontItalic**=0 **FontWeight**=0 **GroupCommentsCutoffMsec**=(none) **ListBoxSplit**=667 **SaveSettings**=1 **SortOrder**=0 (for sort by full name) **Window**=132 90 480 258 0

The following defines most of the common parameters for these applications:

Confirmation   REG_SZ   *Boolean*

Specifies whether the application requests user confirmation for actions such as deletions or other value changes.

FontFaceName   REG_SZ   *Name*

Specifies font to use in the application main window, for example, Times New Roman.

Default: (none)

FontHeight   REG_SZ   *Number*

Specifies point size of font in the application main window.

Default: 0

FontItalic   REG_SZ   *0 or 1*

Specifies normal (0) or italic (1) font style in the application main window.

Default: 0

FontWeight   **REG_SZ**   *0 to 900*

Specifies the font weight (thin to heavy) of the font used in the application main window, where 400 is normal, 700 is bold, and 900 is heavy.

Default: 0

Note **FontFaceName**, **FontHeight**, **FontItalic**, and **FontWeight** apply only to the application main window, not to any dialog boxes.

GroupCommentsCutoffMsec   **REG_SZ**   *Number of milliseconds*

Separate remote API calls must be made for each group comment, which many be excessively slow for some installations. Setting this value to greater than zero suppresses the loading of local group comments (and global group comments against a non-Windows NT target), if loading the user list took more than the defined number of milliseconds. Set this value lower if you experience long User Manager for Domains startup, listbox refresh, or heavy network traffic over slow links.

ListBoxSplit   **REG_SZ**   *0 to 1000*

In User Manager and User Manager for Domains only, specifies the vertical space (in thousandths) devoted to the user listbox as opposed to the group listbox.

Default: 667 (That is, the top two-thirds of the display is given to the user listbox.)

SaveSettings   **REG_SZ**   *Boolean*

Specifies whether options selected in the application are saved when the application is closed.

SortOrder   **REG_SZ**   *Boolean*

Specifies the sort order followed by the application, where 1 specifies sort by username, and 0 specifies sort by full name.

Window   **REG_SZ**   *Pixel location for window*

Specifies window location when application was last closed as four numbers plus 1 or 0 to indicate whether the window was iconized.

The Persistent Connections subkey contains entries that control the restoration of network connections, under this Registry path:

```
HKEY_CURRENT_USER\SOFTWARE\Microsoft\Windows NT\CurrentVersion
    \Network\Persistent Connections
```

DriveMappingLetter   **REG_SZ**   *UNC sharename*

An entry appears for each connection to a shared network directory.

Network Entries for Users

Order   REG_SZ   *drive-letter order*

Specifies the order for the shared directory connections.

For example, set the order to "abcdefghijklmnopqrstuvwxyz" to save up to 26 previously connected server paths.

Default: (none)

SaveConnections   REG_SZ   *Yes or No*

Contains the value set by the Reconnect At Logon check box in the Connect Network Drive dialog box in File Manager.

Default: Yes

The following Network parameter is found in this Registry path:

```
HKEY_LOCAL_MACHINE\SOFTWARE\Microsoft\Windows NT\CurrentVersion
    \Network\SMAddOns
```

.DLL Name   REG_SZ   *String*

Contains a pointer to Server Manager extension .DLLs used to augment RAS.

Default: (none)

The following Network parameter is found in this Registry path:

```
HKEY_LOCAL_MACHINE\SOFTWARE\Microsoft\Windows NT\CurrentVersion
    \Network\UMAddOns
```

.DLL Name   REG_SZ   *String*

Contains a pointer to User Manager extension .DLLs used to augment RAS.

Default: (none)

The following Network parameter is found in this Registry path:

```
HKEY_LOCAL_MACHINE\SOFTWARE\Microsoft\Windows NT\CurrentVersion
    \Network\World Full Access Shared Parameters
```

ExpandLogonDomain   REG_SZ   *Yes or No*

Specifies whether the Shared Directories list is expanded by default in the Connect Network Drive dialog box. This is the value set in the Connect Network Drive dialog box in File Manager by checking the Expand By Default check box.

Default: Yes

The following parameter is used by the Windows NT administrative applications:

```
HKEY_LOCAL_MACHINE\SOFTWARE\Microsoft\Windows NT\CurrentVersion
    \Network\Shared Parameters
```

Slow Mode   REG_SZ   *String*

Stores information about which servers and domains are across a Low Speed Connection. User Manager for Domains, Server Manager, and Event Viewer read this information unless explicitly told whether to start in Low Speed Connection mode. The cache is updated each time one of these applications is started or set to a new, nonlocal focus, or when the user explicitly changes the Low Speed Connection setting. This is an LRU cache of up to 20 focus targets. The first entry is the most recently used.

This is a shared state between users, so if one user changes the cached setting for a target focus, other users get that setting by default. The user must be a member of a group with Power Users or better privileges to have access to this subkey.

Default: "CLOSEDOMAIN;h;FARDOMAIN;l;\\CLOSEMACHINE;h; \\FARMACHINE;1"

SortHyphens   REG_DWORD   *0 or 1*

Specifies whether to ignore hyphens when sorting lists of users. For example, set **SortHyphens** to 1 (true) if you want "a-test" to sort after "Administrator". The default setting of 0 (false) causes the hyphen to be ignored, and "a-test" would sort before "Administrator".

Note Although **SortHyphens** will primarily be of interest for User Manager for Domains, it also changes the base sort order for Event Viewer, Remote Boot Manager, Server Manager, and User Manager. In addition to these executables, the base sort order of the Control Panel tools for customizing network settings (NCPA.CPL), server, services, and devices (SRVMGR.CPL), and the FTP server services (FTPMGR.CPL) can be thus controlled as well.

Default: 0

Performance Monitor Entries for Users

The Perfmon subkey contains values under the following Registry path:

```
HKEY_CURRENT_USER\SOFTWARE\Microsoft\Perfmon
```

Only one value in this subkey should be altered:

DataTimeOut   REG_DWORD   *Value (msec)*

Used by the Performance Monitor data collection thread. If the thread does not return data within the time defined by *Value*, Performance Monitor ignores the data. Use a large value when remote monitoring over a slow link, as RAS.

Default: 20000 msec

The Monitor subkey contains values under the following Registry path:

```
HKEY_LOCAL_MACHINE\SYSTEM\\CurrentControlSet\Services\Monitor
```

Note Use MONITOR.EXE in the Windows NT Resource Kit to set up parameters for this subkey.

DataTimeOut   REG_DWORD   *Value (msec)*

This is the same as the Performance Monitor DataTimeOut value. Monitor Service uses it to determine when to give up on performance data collection from a remote machine.

Default: 20000 msec

Program Manager Entries for Users

UNICODE Program Groups Entries

The UNICODE Program Group key contains subkeys that define the contents of all personal program groups in Program Manager, under this Registry path:

```
HKEY_CURRENT_USER\UNICODE Program Groups
```

Common groups are defined under the following key:

```
HKEY_LOCAL_MACHINE\SOFTWARE\Program Groups
```

The information stored in these subkeys is in binary format, so you cannot easily edit it from Registry Editor. To change the content of program groups, use the mouse and keyboard techniques in Program Manager.

Program Manager Software Groups Entries

The Groups key specifies group numbers for the defined program groups, under this Registry path:

```
Software\Microsoft\Windows NT\CurrentVersion\Program Manager
    \UNICODE Groups
```

These are the default entries. All data types are REG_SZ.

Group1=Main
Group2=Accessories
Group3=Administrative Tools
Group4=Games
Group5=Startup

Restrictions Entries for Program Manager

The Restrictions subkey defines restrictions for activities in Program Manager, under this Registry path:

```
Software\Microsoft\Windows NT\CurrentVersion
    \Program Manager\Restrictions
```

Restrictions can be defined for users in User Profile Editor.

EditLevel   REG_DWORD   *Number*

Sets restrictions for what users can modify in Program Manager. You can specify one of the following values.

Value	Meaning
0	Allows the user to make any change. (This is the default value.)
1	Prevents the user from creating, deleting, or renaming groups. If you specify this value, the New, Move, Copy, and Delete commands on the File menu are not available when a group is selected.
2	Sets all restrictions in **EditLevel=1** and prevents the user from creating or deleting program items. If you specify this value, the New, Move, Copy, and Delete commands on the File menu are not available at all.
3	Sets all restrictions in **EditLevel=2** and prevents the user from changing command lines for program items. If you specify this value, the text in the Command Line box in the Properties dialog box cannot be changed.
4	Sets all restrictions in **EditLevel=3** and prevents the user from changing any program item information. If you specify this value, none of the areas in the Properties dialog box can be modified. The user can view the dialog box, but all of the areas are dimmed.

Default: 0

NoClose   REG_DWORD   *0 or 1*

Disables the Exit Windows command on the File menu if this value is 1. Users cannot quit Program Manager through the File Menu or the Control menu (the Exit Windows and Close commands will be dimmed), or by using ALT+F4.

Default: 0

NoFileMenu   REG_DWORD   *0 or 1*

Removes the File menu from Program Manager if this value is 1. All of the commands on that menu are unavailable. Users can start the applications in groups by selecting them and pressing ENTER, or by double-clicking the icon. Unless you have also disabled the Exit Windows command, users can still quit Windows by using the Control menu or ALT+F4.

Default: 0

NoRun   REG_DWORD   *0 or 1*

Disables the Run command on the File menu if this value is 1. The Run command is dimmed on the File menu, and the user cannot run applications from Program Manager unless the applications are set up as icons in a group.

Default: 0

NoSaveSettings   REG_DWORD   *0 or 1*

Disables the Save Settings on Exit command on the Options menu if this value is 1. The Save Settings command is dimmed on the Options menu, and any changes that the user makes to the arrangement of windows and icons are not saved when Windows NT is restarted. This setting overrides the **SaveSettings** value in the Program Manager subkey.

Default: 0

Restrictions   REG_DWORD   *0 or 1*

Turns restrictions on or off.

Default: 0

ShowCommonGroups   REG_DWORD   *0 or 1*

Controls whether common program groups are displayed.

Default: 0x1

Program Manager Settings Entries

AutoArrange   REG_DWORD   *0 or 1*

If the AutoArrange command is checked on the Options menu in Program Manager, this value is 1, and the icons in each group are automatically arranged when you run Program Manager.

Default: 0x1

CheckBinaryTimeout   REG_DWORD   *0 to 4294967295 milliseconds*

Allows you to configure the auto-check delay. When you bring up either the Run dialog box, the New Item dialog box, or the Edit Item dialog box, the "Run in Separate Memory Space" checkbox automatically turns on and off depending on the executable name being typed in. The delay between the last character typed and before the autochecking starts is this value. For example, if you are in a network environment and are concerned about network traffic caused by autochecking the binary type, increase this value to reduce the number of times the file is checked.

Default: 500

CheckBinaryType   REG_DWORD   *0 or 1*

Allows you to turn off the binary type checking. When you bring up either the Run dialog box, the New Item dialog box, or the Edit Item dialog box, the "Run in Separate Memory Space" checkbox automatically turns on and off depending on the executable name being typed in. If you want this auto-checking feature turned off (and the checkbox always enabled), set this value to 0. For example, you might set this value to 0 if you frequently use a floppy disk drive to run programs, or if you are concerned about network traffic caused by auto-checking files on the server.

Default: 1

display.drv   REG_SZ   *filename*

Defines the video display driver used.

Default: vga.drv

MinOnRun   REG_DWORD   *0 or 1*

If the Minimize On Use command is checked on the Options menu in Program Manager, this value is 1, and Program Manager is iconized when you run another application.

Default: 0x1

SaveSettings   REG_DWORD   *0 or 1*

If the Save Settings On Exit command on the Options menu is checked in Program Manager, this value is 1, and Program Manager saves the current configuration when you close Windows.

Default: 0x1

UNICODE Order   REG_SZ   *Order*

List the order (Z order) in which the UNICODE groups and common groups appear in Program Manager.

Default: (none)

Window   REG_SZ

Four numbers that indicate the pixel position of the window when Program Manager is opened, followed by a 1 if the window is maximized.

Default: 68 63 636 421 1

Recovery Entries for Users

In the System option of Control Panel, there is a Recovery dialog box in which you make settings that control what happens in the event of a system lock-up. This section describes values for the Recovery dialog box, found in the following Registry path:

`HKEY_LOCAL_MACHINE\SYSTEM\CurrentControlSet\Control\CrashControl`

AutoReboot   REG_DWORD   *0 or 1*

Specifies whether the system is to automatically reboot upon failure or lock-up.

Default: 1 (enabled) for NTAS, 0 (disabled) for NT Workstation

CrashDumpEnabled   REG_DWORD   *0 or 1*

Specifies whether debugging information is to be written to a log file.

Default: 1 (enabled) for NTAS, 0 (disabled) for NT Workstation

DumpFile   REG_EXPAND_SZ   *Path and* file

Specifies the file to which degugging information is to be written.

Default: %SystemRoot%\MEMORY.LOG

LogEvent   REG_DWORD   *0 or 1*

Tells the system to write events to a system log.

Default: 1 (enabled) for NTAS, 0 for NT Workstation

Overwrite   REG_DWORD   *0 or 1*

Specifies whether an existing log file is to be overwritten by the new one.

Default: 1 (enabled) for NTAS, 0 (disabled) for NT Workstation

SendAlert   REG_DWORD   *0 or 1*

Controls whether an administrative alert is sent.

Default: 1 (enabled) for NTAS, 0 (disabled) for NT Workstation

If Overwrite is disabled and the LogEvent is enabled, the system displays a message saying that the log is full. All further log attempts are ignored.

If this is unacceptable, create the CrashOnAuditFail value (REG_DWORD) in the following Registry path:

```
HKEY_LOCAL_MACHINE\SYSTEM\CurrentControlSet\Control\Lsa
```

Set CrashOnAuditFail to 1. Now when a log attempt fails, the system will halt and not reboot.

Note A new feature in Windows NT 3.5 is the TXTSETUP.SIF file. This file controls the text mode portion of Setup, including changes to the Registry when you are upgrading from an earlier version of Windows NT. Because the TXTSETUP.SIF file lists all of the files supplied for a specific platform, you can use it to repair your system if it becomes damaged. For more information, see *"About Windows NT Information Files"* in Chapter 3, "Customizing Windows NT Setup."

Windows Entries for Users

This section describes values for personal preferences for items that were formerly stored in WIN.INI for versions of Windows for MS-DOS.

```
HKEY_CURRENT_USER\Software\Microsoft\Windows NT\CurrentVersion\Windows
```

device   REG_SZ   *output-device-name, device-driver, port-connection*
Defines the default printer. An explicit port and driver must be assigned to the device. The *device-driver* is the filename (without the extension) of the device driver file. To change this entry, use Print Manager.

Default: *printerName*,winspool,LPT1:

Documents   REG_SZ   *extensions*
Defines files to be considered "documents" by Windows NT. Use this entry to define only document file extensions not listed in the Extensions subkey, because those extensions are automatically considered documents. The extensions listed in this entry are not associated with any application. Separate the filename extensions with a space, and do not include the preceding periods.

Default: (empty)

DosPrint   REG_SZ   *Boolean*
Specifies whether to use MS-DOS interrupts when printing. When this entry is Yes, MS-DOS interrupts are used; if the value is No, printing output is sent directly to the port that the printer is assigned to. The default is No. To change this entry, clear Print Direct To Ports option in the Printer Details dialog box in Print Manager.

Default: No

ErrorMode   REG_DWORD   *0, 1, or 2*

Controls the behavior of hard error popups.

The format for this entry is as follows:

Value	Definition
Mode 0	Current operating mode. Errors are serialized and wait for a response.
Mode 1	If the error does not come from the system, then normal operating mode. If the error comes from the system, then log the error to the event logger, and return OK to the hard error. No intervention is required and the popup is not seen.
Mode 2	Always log the error to the event logger and return OK to the hard error. Popups are not seen.

In all modes, system-originated hard errors are logged to the system log. To run an unattended server, use mode 2.

Default: 0

fPrintFileLine   REG_SZ   *Boolean*

Default: False

fPrintVerbose   REG_SZ   *Boolean*

Default: False

fPromptOnError   REG_SZ   *Boolean*

Default: True

fPromptOnVerbose   REG_SZ   *Boolean*

Default: False

fPromptOnWarning   REG_SZ   *Boolean*

Default: False

load   REG_SZ   *filename(s)*

Specifies the applications to be run as icons when Windows NT is started. This entry is a list of application filenames, or documents associated with an application, with each filename separated by a space. Make sure to specify the path if the file is not located in the *SystemRoot* directory. To change this entry, add the application to the Startup group in Program Manager, and then check Minimize On Use in the Properties dialog box.

Default: (empty)

NetMessage   REG_SZ *Boolean*

Specifies whether to display a warning message if the system is configured to run a network and the network is not running or the wrong network is running. All Windows network-related options are disabled if the network is disabled or incorrect. Setting this value to 0 turns off the warning message. The default is 1.

Default: no

NullPort   REG_SZ *string*

Specifies the name used for a null port. This name appears in the Printers Connect dialog box in Print Manager when a device is installed (that is, the device driver is present) but is not connected to any port.

Default: None

Programs   REG_SZ *extensions*

Defines which files Windows NT regards as applications. Separate the filename extensions with a space and do not include the preceding periods.

Default: com exe bat pif cmd

run   REG_SZ *filename(s)*

Tells Windows NT to run the specified applications when Windows NT is started. The value is a list of application filenames or documents associated with applications, with each filename separated by a space. Make sure you specify the complete path if the file is not in the *SystemRoot* directory. To change this entry, add the application to the Startup group in Program Manager.

Default: (none)

Registry Entries for Winlogon

The Registry value entries that control the logon sequence for starting Windows NT are found under the following Registry key:

```
HKEY_LOCAL_MACHINE\SOFTWARE\Microsoft\Windows NT\CurrentVersion\Winlogon
```

AutoAdminLogon   REG_SZ *0 or 1*

Specifies automatic logon if this value is 1. You must also add the value entry **DefaultPassword** with a value for the user listed under **DefaultUserName** for automatic logon to work.

When **AutoAdminLogon** is used, Windows NT automatically logs on the specified user when the system is started, bypassing the CTRL+ALT+DEL logon dialog box.

DefaultDomainName **REG_SZ** *Domain name*

Specifies the name of the last successfully logged on domain.

Default: NEWDOMAIN

DefaultPassword **REG_SZ** *Password*

Specifies the password for the user listed under **DefaultUserName**. Used during automatic logon.

DefaultUserName **REG_SZ** *Username*

Specifies the name of the last successfully logged on user. If values are defined for **DefaultPassword** and **AutoAdminLogon**, this is the user who is logged on by default during automatic logon.

DontDisplayLastUserName   **REG_SZ**   *0 or 1*

By default, Windows NT displays the name of the last person to log on in the Username space of the Welcome dialog box. Set this value to 1 (true) if you want the Username space to be blank.

Default: 0 (false)

LegalNoticeCaption   **REG_SZ**   *String*

Specifies a caption for a message to appear when the user presses CTRL+ALT+DEL during logon. Add this value entry if you want to add a warning to be displayed when a user attempts to log on to a Windows NT system. The user cannot proceed with logging on without acknowledging this message.

To specify text for the message, you must also specify a value for **LegalNoticeText**.

Default: (none)

LegalNoticeText   **REG_SZ**   *String*

Specifies for a message to appear when the user presses CTRL+ALT+DEL during logon. Add this value entry if you want to add a warning to be displayed when a user attempts to log on to a Windows NT system. The user cannot proceed with logging on without acknowledging this message.

To include a caption for the logon notice, you must also specify a value for **LegalNoticeCaption**.

Default: (none)

ParseAutoexec   **REG_SZ**   *0 or 1*

If the value is set to 1, AUTOEXEC.BAT is parsed when you log on to Windows NT. If the value is set to 0, AUTOEXEC.BAT is not parsed. This has no effect on the parsing of AUTOEXEC.NT or CONFIG.NT.

Default: 1

PowerdownAfterShutdown   **REG_SZ**   *0 or 1*

If the value is set to 1, you can select Shutdown and Power Off from the Shutdown and Logoff menus. If the value is 0, the Power Off button does not appear.

Default: 0 on NTAS, 1 on NT

ShutdownWithoutLogon   **REG_SZ**   *0 or 1*

If the value is set to 1, you can select Shutdown without Power Off from the Welcome dialog box. If the value is 0, the Shutdown without Power Off button does not appear.

Default: 0 on Windows NT Server, 1 on Windows NT Workstation

ReportBootOk   **REG_SZ**   *0 or 1*

When this value is set to 0, it disables the automatic (default) startup acceptance, which happens after the first successful logon. This value must be 0 if you use alternate settings in the BootVerification or BootVerificationProgram keys.

Default: 1

Shell   **REG_SZ**   *Executable names*

Specifies executables that are run by USERINIT and that are expected to be in the user's shell program. If for some reason WinLogon cannot start the entries listed in **Userinit**, then WinLogon will execute the entries in **Shell** directly.

Default: taskman,progman,wowexec

System   **REG_SZ**   *Executable names*

Specifies executables to be run by WinLogon in the system context. These are activated during system initialization.

Default: lsass.exe,spoolss.exe

Taskman   **REG_SZ**   *Executable name*

Allows you to specify a different task manager.

Default: (none)

Userinit   **REG_SZ**   *Executable names*

Specifies executables to be run by WinLogon when a user logs on. These executables are run in the user context. The first entry (USERINIT) is responsible for executing the shell program. NDDEAGNT.EXE is needed to run NetDDE.

Default: USERINIT,NDDEAGNT.EXE

The Registry values that allow you to specify and retain your shutdown settings are in the following Registry path:

```
HKEY_CURRENT_USER\SOFTWARE\Microsoft\WindowsNT\CurrentVersion\Shutdown
```

LogoffSetting   REG_DWORD   *0, 1, 2, or 3*
Default: 0

ShutdownSetting   REG_DWORD   *1, 2, or 3*
Default: 0

Both these settings represent selections for the Logoff and Shutdown dialog boxes, allowing you to keep your favorite selections. The values are:

0 = Logoff
1 = Shutdown
2 = Shutdown and Restart
3 = Shutdown and Power Off

Selection 3 is available only if the computer hardware supports it.

Registry Entries for Fonts

This section describes entries in subkeys that concern the fonts available to all users on a computer.

FontCache Entries

The FontCache subkey in the following Registry path contains entries that define parameters for font caching:

```
HKEY_LOCAL_MACHINE\SOFTWARE\Microsoft\Windows NT\CurrentVersion
    \FontCache
```

The value entries in the FontCache subkey can greatly influence the amount of memory used by the system. However, these values should not be modified, except in the rare case where you must tune the performance for an international version of Windows NT or for specialized cases such as a print shop, where you may be manipulating large character sets.

MaxSize   REG_DWORD   *Number of kilobytes*
Specifies the maximum amount of address space reserved per font cache.
Default: 0x80

MinIncrSize   REG_DWORD   *Number of kilobytes*

Specifies the minimum amount of memory committed each time a font cache is grown.

Default: 0x4

MinInitSize   REG_DWORD   *Number of kilobytes*

Specifies the minimum amount of memory initially committed per font cache at the time of creation.

Default: 0x4

FontDPI Entries

The FontDPI subkey in the following Registry path indicates the default number of dots per inch (DPI):

```
HKEY_LOCAL_MACHINE\SOFTWARE\Microsoft\Windows NT\CurrentVersion
   \FontDPI
```

LogPixels   REG_DWORD   *0x78 or 0x60*

Determines the resources used by the system, such as bitmap resolution for icons and toolbar buttons, as well as the system font size.

120 DPI (0x78) is what is generally called "Large Fonts" and 96 DPI (0x60) is "Small Fonts."

This value only indicates to the system which fonts and resources to use. Reboot the machine for the changes to apply. You can also change this value by using the Display option in Control Panel.

Default: 0x60

Font Drivers Entries

The Font Drivers subkey in the following Registry path can contain references to external font drivers:

```
HKEY_LOCAL_MACHINE\SOFTWARE\Microsoft\Windows NT\CurrentVersion
   \Font Drivers
```

You should not need to modify this entry directly. Your font vendor should supply an installation program for adding and removing drivers.

Driver description   **REG_SZ**   *Driver filename or pathname*

Lists external font drivers installed on the system. Windows NT does not include any external font drivers. The bitmap, vector, and TrueType drivers are built in and do not appear on this list.

Fonts Entries

The following Registry path is for entries describing the fonts used for displaying information in applications created for Windows NT or versions of Windows for MS-DOS:

```
HKEY_LOCAL_MACHINE\SOFTWARE\Microsoft\Windows NT\CurrentVersion\Fonts
```

Entries in the Fonts key have the following format:

Font Name   **REG_SZ**   *font filename*

These value entries define the installed fonts and their related filenames. The default value entries are listed below:

Arial=ARIAL.FOT
Arial Bold=ARIALBD.FOT
Arial Bold Italic (TrueType)=ARIALBI.FOT
Arial Italic (TrueType)=ARIALI.FOT
Courier 10,12,15 (VGA res)=COURE.FON
Courier New (TrueType)=COUR.FOT
Courier New Bold (TrueType)=COURBD.FOT
Courier New Bold Italic (TrueType)=COURBI.FOT
Courier New Italic (TrueType)=COURI.FOT
Modern (Plotter)=MODERN.FON
MS Sans Serif 8,10,12,14,18,24 (VGA res)=SSERIFE.FON
MS Serif 8,10,12,14,18,24 (VGA res)=SERIFE.FON
Roman (Plotter)=ROMAN.FON
Script (Plotter)=SCRIPT.FON
Small Fonts (VGA res)=SMALLE.FON
Symbol (TrueType)=SYMBOL.FOT
Symbol 8,10,12,14,18,24 (VGA res)=SYMBOLE.FON
Times New Roman (TrueType)=TIMES.FOT
Times New Roman Bold (TrueType)=TIMESBD.FOT
Times New Roman Bold Italic (TrueType)=TIMESBI.FOT
Times New Roman Italic (TrueType)=TIMESI.FOT
WingDings (TrueType)=WINGDING.FOT

GRE_Initialize Entries

The following Registry path is for entries describing the fonts used for character-based programs:

```
HKEY_LOCAL_MACHINE\SOFTWARE\Microsoft\Windows NT\CurrentVersion
    \GRE_Initialize
```

The FONTS.FON and FIXEDFON.FON entries do not affect the console, but they do affect menus and dialog boxes and some applications such as Notepad.

Caution Editing these entries can cause menus and dialog boxes to display improperly.

Unlike versions of Windows from MSD, changing these default fonts will render poor results, because the font set under Windows NT is closely tied to the driver.

FONTS.FON   REG_SZ   *Filename*

Specifies the filename of the default system font.

FIXEDFON.FON   REG_SZ   *Filename*

Specifies the filename of the default system fixed-width font.

OEMFONT.FON   REG_SZ   *Filename*

Specifies the filename of the default OEM (or console) font.

FontSubstitutes Entries

The entries in the FontSubstitutes subkey define substitute typeface names for fonts under the following Registry path:

```
HKEY_LOCAL_MACHINE\SOFTWARE\Microsoft\Windows NT\CurrentVersion
    \FontSubstitutes
```

You should not need to modify these entries. This subkey is usually used by applications with a special need to equate font names.

Alternate name   **REG_SZ**   *Actual name*

Specifies the alternate typeface name. For example, the following entry means that Helv is an alternative typeface name that can be used to refer to the MS Sans Serif font:

```
Helv=MS Sans Serif
```

Default:
Helv=MS Sans Serif
Helvetica=Arial
Times=Times New Roman
Tms Rmn=MS Serif

TrueType Entries for Users

The entries in the TrueType subkey describe options that affect the use and display of TrueType fonts in Windows-based applications. This is the Registry path:

```
HKEY_CURRENT_USER\Software\Microsoft\Windows NT\CurrentVersion\TrueType
```

The TrueType subkey can contain the following entries:

TTEnable   **REG_SZ**   *Boolean*

Controls whether TrueType fonts are available. Setting this value to 1 makes TrueType fonts available in your Windows-based applications. Setting this value to 0 turns off TrueType fonts so they are unavailable in applications.

Default: 1

TTonly   **REG_SZ**   *Boolean*

Specifies whether to make only TrueType fonts available in Windows-based applications. If this value is set to 1, only TrueType fonts are available. If this value is set to 0, all fonts installed on your system are available. To change this entry, choose the Fonts icon from Control Panel.

Default: 0

Registry Entries for Printing

Note Before making any changes to the Registry, stop the print spooler via either the Control Panel or by typing "net stop spooler" at the command prompt. After you have made changes to the Registry, restrart the spooler, via either the Control Panel or by typing "net start spooler" at the command prompt.

The Registry contains printer information in these locations:

- The per-user settings for the current default printer are stored under this key:
  ```
  HKEY_CURRENT_USER\Printers
  ```

- The hardware-specific information about drivers and print processors is stored under this key, where *Hardware* represents the subkey for a specific Windows NT platform, such as Windows NT x86 or Windows NT R4000:
  ```
  HKEY_LOCAL_MACHINE\SYSTEM\CurrentControlSet
      \Control\Print
  ```

- The default spool directory is *SystemRoot*\SYSTEM32\Spool\Printers. However, you can specify an alternate path in which to store print jobs. To specify an alternate path for all printers to spool to, add the value DefaultSpoolDirectory, with the type REG_SZ, and set it to the new spool path under the following Registry key:

```
HKEY_LOCAL_MACHINE\SYSTEM\CurrentControlSet
    \Control\Print\Printers
```

By default, this will apply to all printers. However, if you want to override the spool setting on a per-printer basis, add the value SpoolDirectory, type REG_SZ, and set it to the spool path for the printer under the following key:

```
HKEY_LOCAL_MACHINE\SYSTEM\CurrentControlSet
    \Control\Print\Printers\[printer name]
```

Restart the system for this change to take effect.

The following illustration indicates what can be found in *Print* subkeys.

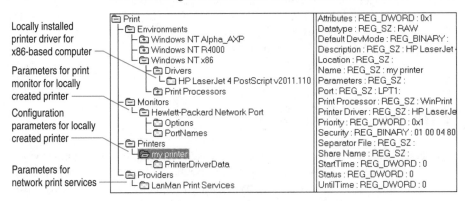

With the exception of spool directories, always use Print Manager to change configuration settings for all printers.

Values that control print spooling and other aspects of printer support are found in the following Registry path:

```
HKEY_LOCAL_MACHINE\SYSTEM\CurrentControlSet
    \Control\Print
```

BeepEnabled   REG_DWORD   *0 or 1*

When remote jobs get an error on a print server, you can enable beeping each time the job is retried (every 10 seconds).

Default: 0 (disabled)

TrueType Entries for Users

DisableServerThread   REG_DWORD   *0 or 1*

Set this to 1 (true) to disable the browse thread on the current machine. This thread is used to call other printer servers to notify them that this printer exists.

Default: 0 (false)

FastPrintSlowDownThreshold   REG_DWORD   *Milliseconds*

Default: **FastPrintWaitTimeout** divided by **FastPrintThrottleTimeout**

FastPrintThrottleTimeout   REG_DWORD   *Milliseconds*

When **JobPrintsWhilstSpooling** is enabled, some printers pause if they don't receive data for a timeout period (usually 15 seconds for a Postscript printer). To counteract this, the spooler throttles back on data sent to the printer when **FastPrintSlowDownThreshold** is reached. At that point, **FastPrintThrottleTimeout** causes 1 byte per defined period to be sent to the printer until the threshold defined by **FastPrintSlowDownTheshold** is exceeded.

Default: 2,000 (2 seconds)

FastPrintWaitTimeout   REG_DWORD   *Milliseconds*

When **JobPrintsWhilstSpooling** is enabled, the port thread must synchronize with the spooling application. This value determines how long the port thread waits before giving up, pausing the current print job, and moving to the next print job.

Default: 24,000 (4 minutes)

NetPrinterDecayPeriod   REG_DWORD   *Milliseconds*

Specifies how long to cache a network printer. The cache is used to present the list of printers when the browse dialog is used.

Default: 3,600,000 (1 hour)

PortThreadPriority   REG_DWORD   *Priority*

Allows you to set the priority of the port threads. These are the threads that do the output to the printers.

Default: THREAD_PRIORITY_NORMAL

PriorityClass   REG_DWORD   *Class*

Sets the priority class for the spooler. 0 or no value indicates the default (7 for workstations, 9 for servers). Any other value becomes the priority class for the server.

Default: 0

SchedulerThreadPriority   REG_DWORD   *Priority*

Allows you to set the priority of the scheduler thread, which is used to assign jobs to ports.

Possible values are THREAD_PRIORITY_NORMAL, THREAD_PRIORITY_ABOVE_NORMAL, and THREAD_PRIORITY_BELOW_NORMAL.

Default: THREAD_PRIORITY_NORMAL

To control network popups for remote print jobs, add the value **NetPopup** to the key found in the following Registry path:

```
HKEY_LOCAL_MACHINE\SYSTEM\CurrentControlSet
    \Control\Print\Providers
```

NetPopup   REG_DWORD   *0 or 1*

Specifies whether to display a popup message for remote print jobs.

Default: 1

EventLog   REG_DWORD   *0 or 1*

Specifies whether event logging occurs from the spooler.

Default: 0

The following values control print and point features of Windows NT so that drivers can only be loaded from a trusted print server, rather than from the server to which the user is connected. These values are in the following Registry path:

```
HKEY_LOCAL_MACHINE\SYSTEM\CurrentControlSet\Control\Print
    \Providers\LanMan Print Services
```

LoadTrustedDrivers   REG_DWORD   *0 or 1*

If set to 1 (enabled), drivers are not installed from the remote print server, but are taken only from the path specified in **TrustedDriverPath**.

Default: 0 (disabled)

TrustedDriverPath   REG_SZ   *String*

Specifies the path from which you can install printer drivers. The path represents the trusted print server shares. Note that even though you connect to a particular server, you will not get the printer drivers from that server. You will only get the driver settings from that server. The drivers are copied only from the **TrustedDriverPath**.

Default: (none)

TrueType Entries for Users

Registry Entries for Software Classes

Various HKEY_LOCAL_MACHINE\SOFTWARE subkeys contain the names and version numbers of the software installed on the local computer. (Information about the configuration of these applications is stored on a per-user basis under HKEY_CURRENT_USER.)

During installation, applications record this information in the following form:

```
HKEY_LOCAL_MACHINE\SOFTWARE\CompanyName\ProductName\Version
```

Registry Entries for Subsystems

This section describes software registration entries related to Windows NT subsystems.

Microsoft OS/2 Version 1.x Software Registration Entries

The basic software information for the Microsoft OS/2 version 1.x subsystem is found in the following Registry path:

```
HKEY_LOCAL_MACHINE\SOFTWARE\Microsoft\OS/2 Subsystem for NT
```

The OS/2 Subsystem key contains several subkeys, but initially only the \config.sys subkey contains an entry. This subkey contains the OS/2 CONFIG.SYS information stored after an OS/2 application has been run on the system.

If there is no OS/2 CONFIG.SYS file, this subkey contains the following entry:

```
PROTSHELL=C:\os2\pmshell.exe c:\os2\os2.ini c:\os2\os2sys.ini
    %SystemRoot%\system32\cmd.exe
SET COMSPEC=%SystemRoot%\system32\cmd.exe
```

The Os2 subkey under CurrentControlSet\Control\Session Manager\SubSystems defines the path to the executable file used to start the OS/2 subsystem. The **Os2LibPath** value under the Session Manager\Environment subkey defines the directory path for the OS/2 library. These entries are described in "CurrentControlSet\Control Subkeys," earlier in this chapter.

To disable the OS/2 subsystem, set the value of **GlobalFlag** to 20100000 in the following subkey:

```
HKEY_LOCAL_MACHINE\SYSTEM\CurrentControlSet\Control\Session Manager
```

Windows Software Registration Entries

The Windows subkey under the following path defines some values used by applications created to run under Windows for MS-DOS:

`HKEY_LOCAL_MACHINE\SOFTWARE\Microsoft\Windows NT\CurrentVersion\Windows`

AppInit_DLLs   REG_SZ

Causes all the specified DLLs (one or many) to be attached to all Windows-based applications. This means that once this is set for a session, upon restarting the system, all the Windows-based applications that run in that session will load the specified DLLs. For example, an applications developer can use it to attach the Microsoft Call/Attributive Profiler to all Windows-based applications by calling CAPSETUP.EXE, which sets the **AppInit_DLLs** so the user doesn't have to do it through Registry Editor.

Default:

DeviceNotSelectedTimeout   REG_SZ   *Seconds*

Specifies how much time the system waits for a device to be switched on. If the device is not switched on during this time, the system won't print to the device. For some devices, the system immediately posts an error message if the device is not already switched on. This entry only defines the system default value. To change the value for a particular printer, use Print Manager.

Default: 15

Spooler   REG_SZ   *Boolean*

Specifies whether output to the printer is to be sent through Print Manager. Changing this value to No turns off Print Manager.

Default: Yes

swapdisk   REG_SZ   *drive:directory*

Provides the name of the disk drive and directory to which Windows for MS-DOSMS-DOS in standard mode swaps non-Windows–based applications.

Default: The directory pointed to by the TEMP environment variable; if there is no TEMP variable, the default is the boot directory of your first hard disk (usually C:).

TransmissionRetryTimeout   REG_SZ   *Seconds*

Specifies the default amount of time for attempted transmission retries. If a successful transmission does not occur during this time, Print Manager displays a message stating that the printer is not receiving characters. This setting serves only as the system default value. To change the value for a particular printer, use Print Manager.

Default: 45

WOW Software Registration Entries

Software registration values for the WOW subsystem appear under the following Registry key:

```
HKEY_LOCAL_MACHINE\SOFTWARE\Microsoft\Windows NT\CurrentVersion\WOW
```

The WOW subkeys have the same names as headings in the SYSTEM.INI file, and the values are the same items as were contained in the Windows for MS-DOS SYSTEM.INI file. All are REG_SZ value types.

The information provided here is for troubleshooting only.

WOW subkey	Description and defaults
Boot	Lists drivers and Windows 3.*x* modules, with these entries and default values to map Windows 3.*x* drivers to Windows NT.
	Provided for applications that seek this information. Mostly ignored, but drivers are loaded from this source, such as MMSYSTEM.DLL.
	comm.drv = comm.drv **display.drv** = vga.drv **drivers** = mmsystem.dll **fixedfon** = vgafix.fon **keyboard.drv** = keyboard.drv **language.dll** = (empty) **mouse.drv** = mouse.drv **network.drv** = lanman.drv **oemfonts.fon** = vgaoem.fon **shell** = progman.exe **sound.drv** = sound.drv **system.drv** = system.drv

WOW subkey	Description and defaults *(continued)*
boot.description	Provided for applications that seek this information. Not actually used by the WOW subsystem. Lists names of devices that can be changed using Windows 3.*x* Setup, with these kinds of entries and default values: **display.drv** = VGA **keyboard.typ** = Enhanced 101/102 key U.S. and Non U.S. keyboards **language.dll** = English (American) **network.drv** = LAN Support **system.drv** = MS-DOS or PC-DOS System
Compatibility	Used to translate 16-bit Windows APIs and messages to 32-bit equivalents. **MAILSPL** = 0x40000000 (for MS Mail) **SHOPPER** = 0x20000000 (for Clip-Art Windows Shopper) **SHADOW** = 0x10000000 (for BeyondMail installation) **WINPROJ** = 0x80000000 (for Microsoft Project) **ESCAPES** = 0x1000000 (for Micrographix Escapes) **HIRES** = 0x00100000 (for HIRES display cards)
Keyboard	Contains information about the keyboard, provided for applications that seek this information, with these kinds of entries and default values: **keyboard.dll** = (empty) **subtype** = (empty) **type** = 4
NonWindowsApp	Contains information used by non-Windows–based applications. This is handled automatically by Windows NT. Unless you manually added values to SYSTEM.INI in Windows 3.*x*, this subkey is empty.
Standard	Contains entries specific to running Windows 3.*x* in standard mode. Unless you manually added values to SYSTEM.INI in Windows 3.*x*, this subkey is empty.

The [386Enh] section is read from the SYSTEM.INI file for 16-bit Windows-based applications that need it. There is no Registry equivalent, because Windows NT ignores this information.

WOW Software Registration Entries

P A R T V

Migration and Compatibility

Part Five discusses migration and compatibility issues for Windows 3.*x* for MS-DOS, Microsoft OS/2 version 1.*x*, and POSIX applications. These chapters describe details about running applications and how the subsystems are implemented.

C H A P T E R   1 5

Windows 3.x Compatibility

This chapter discusses the compatibility of the 16-bit Windows subsystem with the actual Windows 3.1 product. It explains how the subsystem is implemented and describes the restrictions on applications run under it.

Running Applications

The 16-bit Windows subsystem runs 16-bit Windows-based applications, which you can launch from Program Manager, File Manager, or the command prompt. There are no user-visible distinctions between 16-bit and 32-bit Windows-based applications.

Restrictions

This section describes the few restrictions that apply to running applications under the 16-bit Windows subsystem.

- Direct access to floppy disk drives is supported. Direct access to a hard disk is supported, if the user is an administrator and no one else is using the disk at that time.

- All MS-DOS functions except task-switching APIs (application programming interface functions) are supported.

- Block mode device drivers are not supported. (Block devices are not supported, so MS-DOS IOCTL APIs that deal with block devices and SETDPB functions are not supported).

- Interrupt 10 function 1A returns 0; all other functions are passed to read-only memory (ROM).

- Interrupt 13 calls that deal with prohibited disk access are not supported.

- Interrupt 18 (ROM BASIC) generates a message that says ROM BASIC is not supported.

- Interrupt 19 will not reboot the computer, but will cleanly terminate the current virtual DOS machine (VDM).

- Interrupt 2F dealing with the DOSKEY program call outs (AX = 4800) is not supported.

- Microsoft CD-ROM Extensions (MSCDEX) functions 2, 3, 4, 5, 8, E, and F are not supported.

- The 16-bit Windows subsystem on an X86 computer supports Enhanced mode applications; it does not, however, support 16-bit VXDs (virtual device drivers). The subsystem on a non-X86 computer supports only Standard mode 16-bit applications.

Terminating the Subsystem

If an ill-behaved application locks up the 16-bit Windows subsystem, you can terminate the subsystem.

▶ **To terminate the 16-bit Windows subsystem**

1. Press CTRL+ESC to bring up the Task List.

2. From the Task List, select the application.

3. Choose End Task.

4. If problems persist, press CTRL+ALT+DEL to display the Windows NT Security dialog box.

5. In the Windows NT Security dialog box, choose Logoff to display the Logoff Windows NT dialog box.

6. In the Logoff Windows NT dialog box, choose OK to log off Window NT and display the Welcome box.

7. Press CTRL+ALT+DEL to log back in to Windows NT.

Interoperating with a Previous Version of Windows

If you have a previous version of Windows (Windows 3.x, Windows for Workgroups) installed on your computer, and you want to run your installed applications from both the previous version of Windows and from Windows NT, then install Windows NT in the same directory as the previous version of Windows. This allows Windows NT to configure the Windows environment based on the existing environment and allows Windows NT to support the features of currently installed applications.

When the first logon occurs on the newly-installed Windows NT computer, the system migrates REG.DAT and portions of the WIN.INI file from the previous version of Windows to the Registry in Windows NT. The status of each step in the migration is recorded in the Application Log, which can be viewed with Event Viewer.

The first time each new user logs in, Windows NT presents a dialog box that lets him or her select the parts of the previous version of Windows to migrate into the Windows NT environment. The user can select whether to migrate the .INI files and/or the Program Manager .GRP files to the Registry. If the user cancels the dialog box and later would like to migrate the files, he or she must delete the following key from the Registry and then log off and log back into Windows NT:

```
HKEY_CURRENT_USER\Windows 3.1 Migration Status
```

Refer to Part IV, "Windows NT Registry," for information on the Registry and its entries.

Note The per-user dialog box and migration do not happen for the usernames Administrator, Guest, and System.

If a user chooses to migrate the .INI files, then each time he or she logs into Windows NT, the system reads the WIN.INI file and the SYSTEM.INI file and stores the information in the Registry. When the user logs off from Windows NT, the system updates the WIN.INI file and the SYSTEM.INI file with any changes made to the environment. This keeps the configuration of Windows NT and the previous version of Windows synchronized with each other.

If Windows NT is not installed in the same directory as the previous version of Windows, then configuration changes made under one version of Windows are not available to the other version. The same is true if the previous version of Windows is installed after Windows NT. In these situations, a user in Windows NT may not be able to run some applications installed under the previous version of Windows. The applications will have to be reinstalled under Windows NT (into the same directories into which they are installed under the previous version of Windows).

Regardless of where Windows NT is installed, changes made to the Desktop or to the arrangement of the Program Groups are not synchronized with the previous version of Windows.

Caution   Setup installs TrueType font and font header files in *SystemRoot*\SYSTEM. Be careful not to delete the TrueType files from this directory. These files are used by Windows NT 32-bit applications as well as 16-bit applications. For more information on the TrueType font and font header files included with Windows NT, refer to Chapter 4, "Windows NT Files."

What Is Migrated at the First Logon

The following items are migrated to the Registry when the first logon occurs on a newly-installed Windows NT computer.

- All of the OLE (Object Linking and Embedding) information kept in the Windows 3.x registry (REG.DAT)

- The following sections and variables from the WIN.INI file:

  [Compatibility]

  [Embedding] (except SoundRec, Package, and PBrush)

  [Fonts]

  [FontSubstitutes]

  [Windows]
  DeviceNotSelectedTimeout
  Spooler
  TransmissionRetryTimeout

When Each User First Logs On

What Is Not Migrated

The following items are not migrated:

- Persistent shares and users from Windows for Workgroups.

- Default domain and user ID from Windows for Workgroups or the LANMAN.INI file.

- Per-user profiles maintained by the WINLOGIN add-on product for Windows for Workgroups.

- Any changes that the user has made to his or her Accessories, Games, Main, and Startup groups in Windows 3.x. These groups are not migrated because their names match the names of 32-bit Windows NT groups.

- MS-DOS drive letters. If you have FAT partitions and HPFS or NTFS partitions on a computer that dual-boots MS-DOS and Windows NT, use Disk Administrator to assign drive letters to your non-FAT partitions. Begin with the first drive letter after the one that MS-DOS assigns to your last FAT partition. This ensures that the FAT partition drive letters are the same for both systems and that any migrated path names are valid.

- The options Auto Arrange, Minimize on Run, and Save Settings on Exit from the PROGMAN.INI file.

- Font information for character-mode command windows.

- The Language and Keyboard settings in the International applications.

- The default screen saver (SCRNSAVE.EXE) in the **[BOOT]** section of the SYSTEM.INI file. 16-bit screen savers are ill-behaved under Windows NT.

What Is Migrated

The following items are migrated the first time each new user logs in, if he selects to migrate the .INI files and the .GRP files. This per-user migration does not happen for the usernames Administrator, Guest, and System.

- The following sections and variables from the WIN.INI file:

  [Clock]

  [Colors]

  [Cursors]

  [DeskTop]

  [Extensions]

  [Intl]

  [Sounds]

  [Terminal]

  [TrueType]

  [Windows]
      Beep
      BorderWidth
      CursorBlinkRate
      DoubleClickSpeed
      KeyboardDelay
      KeyboardSpeed
      MouseSpeed
      MouseThreshold1
      MouseThreshold2
      ScreenSaveActive
      ScreenSaveTimeOut
      SwapMouseButtons

- The following sections and variables from the CONTROL.INI file:

  [Color Schemes]

  [Current]

  [Custom Colors]

  [Patterns]

  [Screen Saver.Marquee]

  [Screen Saver.Mystify]

  [Screen Saver.Stars]

- The **[Settings]** section from the WINFILE.INI file.

- All 16-bit Windows 3.*x* Program Manager group files listed in the PROGMAN.INI file. If a group name (contained in the group file, not the actual .GRP filename) matches the name of a 32-bit Windows NT Personal or Common group, then that 16-bit group will not be migrated (for example, Accessories, Games, Main, and Startup). Each group is migrated "as is", and the show state is set to Minimized.

- The Country setting in the international applications.

Implementation of the Subsystem

VDM Structure

The 16-bit Windows subsystem is implemented as a virtual MS-DOS machine (VDM) with a layer that emulates Windows 3.1 functionality. All 16-bit Windows-based applications run in the same VDM, a multithreaded Win32 process in which each application runs in its own thread. Below is a diagram of the 16-bit Windows subsystem VDM. A description of each layer follows.

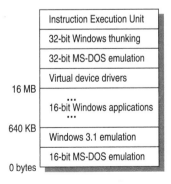

Figure 15.1   16-bit Windows Subsystem VDM

The 16-bit MS-DOS emulation layer contains all the information to emulate BIOS calls and tables. Some 16-bit Windows applications depend upon BIOS calls, since 16-bit Windows is built on top of MS-DOS.

The Windows 3.1 emulation layer provides the functionality of the Windows 3.1 kernel and 16-bit API stubs. A 16-bit application cannot call a 32-bit API routine. When an application calls a 16-bit API routine, that call is made to a stub routine, which in turn calls a 32-bit API routine. The 32-bit API routine performs the required action, and the result is transformed back into the format expected by the 16-bit API stub, which returns the result to the application. The transformation between 16-bit and 32-bit formats is known as *thunking*, and is carried out by a separate layer in the VDM.

16-bit Windows-based applications use the memory from 640K to 16 MB for their own purposes.

Windows NT does not support 16-bit device drivers that have unrestricted access to hardware (character-mode device drivers that do not depend on special hardware are supported). A secure and robust multitasking operating system cannot let user-level applications talk directly with the hardware because they could completely bypass security and crash the system. (There are exceptions to this, however; refer to "Restrictions," at the beginning of this chapter). The VDM contains a layer of virtual device drivers (VDDs) that allow the sharing of hardware and provide the necessary functionality in a way that is consistent with the design of Windows NT.

The 32-bit MS-DOS emulation layer is for the DOS Protect Mode Interface (DPMI) and 32-bit memory access. This layer replaces calls made to the MS-DOS-level functions for extended and expanded memory with Windows NT memory calls. Windows NT then makes the appropriate conversions so that the 16-bit application sees segmented memory as it normally would.

The purpose of the 32-bit Windows thunking layer was described above.

For Windows NT running on a non-X86 computer, the Instruction Execution Unit emulates the Intel 80286 instruction set, which lets the computer run the binary application. The 16-bit Windows subsystem (or any other VDM) on a non-x86 computer supports only Standard mode 16-bit applications.

On an x86 computer the Instruction Execution Unit acts as a trap handler, capturing instructions that cause hardware traps and transferring control to the code that handles them. A VDM (such as the 16-bit Windows subsystem) on an x86 computer supports Enhanced mode applications; it does not, however, support 16-bit VXDs (virtual device drivers).

Input Queue

Under Windows NT, each application has its own input queue. This eliminates lockups due to programs halting the queue. Under Windows 3.*x*, all applications receive input from the same queue. As in Windows 3.*x*, the 16-bit Windows-based subsystem provides just one input queue. A 16-bit Windows application can lock up the subsystem by halting the queue. This does not affect any 32-bit applications running under Windows NT, as they each have their own input queue.

Scheduling

Within the 16-bit Windows subsystem, the applications (threads) are scheduled non-preemptively. Because the applications share memory, a single input queue, and are scheduled non-preemptively, an ill-behaved application can cause the subsystem to lock up. This will not affect the rest of Windows NT, since Windows NT treats the 16-bit Windows subsystem as a whole just like any other 32-bit Windows NT-based application. The subsystem is scheduled preemptively along with all of the other 32-bit applications.

Files Used

The following are the principal files used by the 16-bit Windows subsystem.

File	Purpose
NTVDM.EXE	The main loader for a VDM.
WOWEXEC.EXE	Provides the Windows 3.1 emulation for the VDM. When you log onto Windows NT, the WOWEXEC program is loaded by running the NTVDM program, which makes that VDM the 16-bit Windows subsystem.
WOW32.DLL	Provides the DLL portion of the Windows 3.1 emulation layer. When you use the PViewer utility to look at running NTVDM processes, you can identify the one that is the 16-bit Windows subsystem by WOW32.DLL being listed in its memory detail.
AUTOEXEC.NT CONFIG.NT	Used to boot the files necessary for running 16-bit Windows applications. The AUTOEXEC.NT and CONFIG.NT files are usually in the \SYSTEM32 directory, but you can change this location by using _DEFAULT.PIF. Windows NT creates the AUTOEXEC.NT file from the AUTOEXEC.BAT file and creates the CONFIG.NT file from scratch. It writes comments to the AUTOEXEC.BAT and CONFIG.SYS files that describe the .NT versions. Refer to the *Windows NT System Guide* for more information.

Communication with Other Subsystems

An application running under the 16-bit Windows subsystem can communicate with applications in other subsystems (as well as 32-bit applications running under Windows NT) through the usual mechanisms of Object Linking and Embedding (OLE), Dynamic Data Exchange (DDE), and named pipes.

C H A P T E R   1 6

OS/2 Compatibility

This chapter describes the OS/2 subsystem in Windows NT. It describes the types of applications that the subsystem currently supports, as well as those that it does not support. It describes the supported, unsupported, and partially supported OS/2 application programming interfaces (APIs). This chapter also describes how the OS/2 subsystem is implemented and the Win32 thunking mechanism.

Running Applications

The OS/2 subsystem allows OS/2 16-bit character-based applications to run directly with Windows NT with essentially no modification. You can launch a character-based or video I/O (VIO) application from the Windows NT command prompt, from the File Manager, from the Program Manager, or indirectly from within a Win32 or OS/2 application. You can create a single batch file that can launch any combination of MS-DOS, Windows, or OS/2 programs. Windows NT recognizes an OS/2 application from information stored in the header of the executable file; it then calls the OS/2 subsystem to load the application.

If you never run an OS/2 application, the subsystem does not use any Windows NT resources. When you run an application, the OS2SRV process is loaded and continues to exist even after you've quit the application. To free up the minimal resources that the OS2SRV process uses, run the PViewer utility (which is provided with the *Windows NT Resource Kit*) and quit the OS2SRV process. If you later run another OS/2 application, the OS2SRV process is reloaded.

Supported Applications

You can run the following types of applications with the OS/2 subsystem:

- OS/2 1.*x* 16-bit applications on X86 computers only
- Character-based applications

Unsupported Applications

You cannot run the following types of applications with the OS/2 subsystem:

- OS/2 2.*x* applications.
- Presentation Manager (PM) applications (unless you install the Windows NT Add-On Subsystem for Presentation Manager)
- Advanced video I/O (AVIO) applications (unless you install the Windows NT Add-On Subsystem for Presentation Manager)
- OS/2 applications on RISC-based computers.

- Applications that directly access hardware memory or I/O ports at Ring 2 or below.

  For example, applications that directly access video memory to manipulate text or graphics are not supported. Some OS/2 applications, which rely on the statement IOPL=YES in the CONFIG.SYS file to run Ring 2 code segment, will run nevertheless under the OS/2 subsystem as long as the privileged instructions they issue in those segments are CLI/STI instructions and not IN/OUT instructions. For more details, see "I/O Privilege Mechanism" later in this chapter.

- You cannot run custom device drivers (those not included with OS/2 itself). These must be rewritten to the Windows NT device driver interface.

If you want to run an OS/2 application that is not supported, you have the following choices:

- If this is a bound application (one that can run under both OS/2 and MS-DOS), you can try to run it with the MS-DOS subsystem. To do so, run the **forcedos** command from the command line:

```
FORCEDOS [/D directory] filename [parameters]
```

  where */directory* is the current directory for the application to use, *filename* is the application to start, and *parameters* is the parameters to pass to the application.

- If this is not a bound application and you have the source code, you can recompile the source without the unsupported APIs, which are specified in the error message that is displayed when you try to run the application. If you don't have the source, contact the application's developer.

Partially Supported Applications

Video input/outputx (VIO) applications are partially supported. Some will work and some will not, depending on the API functions that the applications use. The robustness and security of Windows NT restrict access to physical hardware, which restricts the use of VIO physical buffer APIs, certain **DosDevIOCtl** functions, and I/O privilege level (IOPL). For more information, see the following section on APIs.

Note Presentation Manager and AVIO applications are supported by the Windows NT Add-on Subsystem for Presentation Manager, available from Microsoft.

APIs

A complete list of the APIs that are supported, unsupported, or partially supported is provided in the OS2API.TXT file on the *Resource Kit* disk.

Supported APIs

APIs with the following prefixes are supported:

- **Dos** (except **DosDevIOCtl** and **DosDevIOCtl2**, which are partially supported)
- **Kbd** (except those that conflict with the security and robustness of Windows NT)
- **Mou** (except those that require Presentation Manager or AVIO)
- **Vio** (except those that conflict with the security of Windows NT by accessing the physical video hardware and those that require PM or AVIO)
- **WinQueryProfile** and **WinWriteProfile**
- **Net** (selected APIs based on their commercial use)

Unsupported APIs

APIs with the following prefixes are not supported:

- **Dev**
- **Gpi**
- **Kbd** (those that conflict with the security and robustness of Windows NT)
- **Mou** (those that require PM or AVIO)
- **Vio** (those that conflict with the security of Windows NT by accessing the physical video hardware and those that require PM or AVIO)
- **Win** (except **WinQueryProfile** and **WinWriteProfile** APIs)

Partially Supported APIs

The following APIs are partially supported:

- **DosDevIOCtl** and **DosDevIOCtl2**
- **VioGetConfig**

- **VioGetMode** and **VioSetMode**

- **VioGetState** and **VioSetState**

Note APIs with the **Mou** or **Vio** prefixes that require Presentation Manager (PM) or advanced video I/O (AVIO) are supported by the Windows NT Add-on Subsystem for Presentation Manager, available from Microsoft.

Implementation of the OS/2 Subsystem

This section describes how the OS/2 subsystem is implemented.

Memory Map of an OS/2 Application

The following is a map of memory usage while the OS/2 subsystem is running an application.

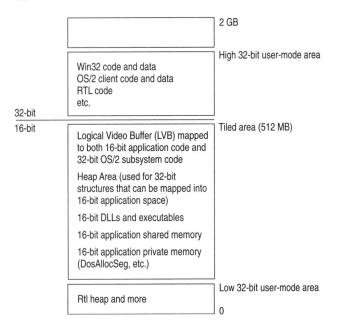

Figure 16.1   OS/2 Subsystem Memory Map

The *tiled area* is 512 MB of virtual address space that is reserved up-front and then committed or decommitted when 16-bit applications need segments. The OS/2 subsystem maintains a local descriptor table (LDT) for each process, with shared memory segments at the same LDT slot for all OS/2 processes.

Architecture Diagram

The OS/2 subsystem is implemented as a protected server; OS/2 applications communicate with the subsystem by using the local procedure call (LPC) message-passing facility. The subsystem and each application run in their own protected address spaces, which protects them from other processes running with Windows NT.

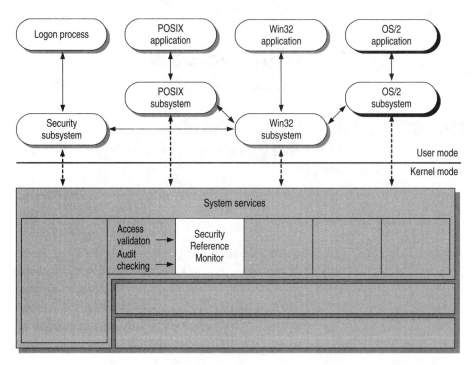

Figure 16.2   OS/2 Subsystem in Windows NT

In native OS/2, applications run in user mode (Ring 3) and communicate with the OS/2 kernel by using calls to the DLLs. Some application programs and DLLs contain I/O privilege segments and are allowed to perform I/O operations in Ring 2. The OS/2 subsystem will attempt to run such programs but those using the I/O privilege to perform IN/OUT instructions (to access some hardware device) violate the robustness features of Windows NT and thus will be terminated with a general protection fault. For more information, see "I/O Privilege Mechanism" later in this chapter.

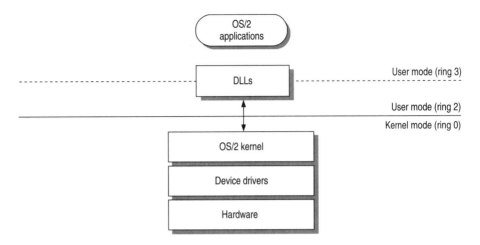

Figure 16.3   Native OS/2

Multitasking

Process

The OS/2 subsystem uses OS/2 semantics to maintain the various OS/2 objects. Examples of this include process IDs, the process tree, handles, local and global **infosegs**, thread-1 semantics, exit-list processing, signals, and semaphores. Windows NT objects are used only when they are relevant; they are then embedded inside OS/2 objects (for example, file handles).

The process tree records the descendant processes of a given process. The subsystem uses the process tree in all related operations, such as ending a program by pressing CTRL+C.

Thread

Every thread created by an OS/2 application is implemented with a Windows NT thread in the same process. The thread receives the priority and ID that are relevant in OS/2. The exact OS/2 semantics (such as contents of the register and the stack) are retained when the thread function starts.

Scheduler

The Windows NT scheduler handles the scheduling of OS/2 threads, with the OS/2 priorities 0–63 mapping to Windows NT variable priorities 0–15. (OS/2 priorities are changed only by the application; they are not changed by the scheduler). OS/2 threads never receive Windows NT real-time priorities 16–31.

VIO User Interface

The VIO user interface is partially supported. Applications cannot get direct control of the video hardware. The use of a logical video buffer, as opposed to a physical video buffer, is allowed. For specific information, see the lists of APIs earlier in this chapter.

Dynamic Linking

The OS/2 subsystem implements a full OS/2 loader, which loads DLLs, executables, and resources in exactly the same way as in OS/2. Static linking, load-time dynamic linking, and run-time dynamic linking all function as they do in OS/2.

Memory Management

Protection Model

The OS/2 subsystem implements the protection between OS/2 applications. It constructs their address spaces (both the flat address space and LDTs) and implements the same protection as exists in OS/2.

Some of the memory management limitations of OS/2 1.x are removed. The most important of these is the limit of 16 MB of physical RAM; the OS/2 subsystem uses the large memory capability of Windows NT. This translates into increased performance for applications that can use the additional memory, such as Microsoft's SQL Server. SQL Server asks for the physical memory available in the system at setup time. It then uses this number to determine the level of caching it will use. In OS/2, you can't use more than 16 MB; however, in the OS/2 subsystem in Windows NT, you can use 32 MB (for example) and double your caching capability.

Segment Swapping

The OS/2 subsystem uses the Windows NT paging mechanism; no segment swapping is performed. Segment swapping is inferior to paging and exists in OS/2 only to support the 80286 processor, which is not supported for Windows NT.

Interprocess Communication

The OS/2 subsystem implements all OS/2 IPC mechanisms (semaphores, pipes, shared memory, queues, and signals).

Named Pipes

The OS/2 subsystem implements named pipes on top of the Windows NT named pipe file system. These are supported transparently between Win32, MS-DOS, Win16, and OS/2 applications, both locally and remotely. Microsoft LAN Manager 2.x named pipe functionality is supported in its entirety.

Anonymous Pipes

Anonymous pipes, including inheritance, are fully supported. They are integrated into the OS/2 file handle space.

Shared Memory

The full functionality of OS/2 1.x shared memory, including Get and Give semantics, is implemented using Windows NT shared memory features. The discardable segments property is ignored. (It is invisible to the OS/2 application).

Semaphores

The OS/2 subsystem supports the full range of OS/2 1.x semaphore APIs, including RAM semaphores in private and shared memory, system semaphores, and fast-safe RAM semaphores. Association of semaphores with timers and named pipes is fully supported. The OS/2 subsystem uses a combination of the Windows NT semaphore object and the Windows NT event object to implement an OS/2 semaphore.

Queues

OS/2 1.x queues are fully supported, using shared memory between OS/2 processes and OS/2 semaphores as required.

Signals

OS/2 signals are fully supported, using Windows NT APIs to manipulate thread context. The OS/2 subsystem controls the address space of OS/2 processes and uses it to manipulate the register content and the stack of thread 1 of the process to be signaled.

I/O Architecture

Device Drivers

Existing private OS/2 device drivers will not be supported in the OS/2 subsystem directly, but must be rewritten for the Windows NT device driver model. In this context, *private device driver* means a driver that a particular application requires but that is not included in the OS/2 operating system itself.

Examples of such drivers include those that provide custom support for security, fax, MIDI, or 3270 communication cards. Once an OS/2 device driver has been rewritten for the Windows NT model, however, an OS/2 application can communicate with that device driver using the same OS/2 API, **DosDevIoctl**; no changes will be required within the application itself. Additionally, support exists for the native device drivers included with Windows NT, such as the display, printer, disk, communications, keyboard, and mouse devices.

For example, suppose that a corporation has written a custom device driver to control a security card. The OS/2 device driver for this card uses an internal name, SECDEV, and an entry for this device driver appears in the CONFIG.SYS file. In OS/2, the operating system reads the CONFIG.SYS file and adds SECDEV to the device driver list. When an application calls the OS/2 API, **DosOpen**, this list is searched first. The OS/2 subsystem will read this file during initialization and add symbolic links that will allow the OS/2 application to call the Windows NT device driver from the subsystem. For information about how to set the CONFIG.SYS file for the OS/2 subsystem to load a Windows NT device driver, see "OS/2 Configuration" later in this chapter.

The OS/2 application code, as opposed to the device driver code, can still load and run in a binary-compatible manner because the device-specific parameters passed by **DosDevIoctl**(2) APIs are just PVOID buffers. Of course, the new Windows NT version of the ported device driver would have to be made compatible with the original by accepting the same set of parameters within the buffers. Other related OS/2 APIs, such as **DosOpen**, are supported compatibly, just as they are for supporting native Windows NT system device drivers such as the communications device, the keyboard, and the screen.

File System Name Space

OS/2 HPFS supports long names. The OS/2 subsystem supports long names and extended attributes. The subsystem treats an NTFS volume as an HPFS volume. (It does not utilize or expose recoverability and C2 security functions).

Network Connectivity

The OS/2 subsystem implements many LAN Manager APIs. It also implements NetBIOS (both version 2.x and version 3.0 functionality), named pipes, and mail slots.

The OS/2 subsystem maintains remote drives compatible with OS/2. With these, any OS/2 application can use redirected drives transparently with the file I/O APIs. Uniform naming convention (UNC) naming is supported as well. Redirected drives of various network operating systems can be used, provided that the related Win32 Windows NT device drivers (redirectors) have been installed.

I/O Privilege Mechanism

Under native OS/2, if the statement IOPL=YES is present in the CONFIG.SYS file, applications may include Ring 2 segments in which it is possible to execute privileged instructions:

- CLI/STI instructions (disable-enable hardware interrupts)
- IN/OUT to hardware ports

The OS/2 subsystem of Windows NT allows OS/2 applications to run Ring 2 code segments (no special statement required in the OS/2 C:\CONFIG.SYS) but with the following important restrictions:

- CLI/STI instructions will work.

  The OS/2 subsystem will suspend all the other OS/2 applications in the system and all the other threads in the OS/2 process issuing the CLI instructions, until an STI instruction follows. This emulation of CLI/STI instruction is much more costly in run-time overhead than on native OS/2 (where the CPU simply disables external interrupts, which would violate the Windows NT robustness design rules) and also much more costly than semaphore calls. Therefore, when it is possible to modify the OS/2 application, semaphore calls are the preferred way to implement critical sections.

- IN/OUT instructions are *not* supported.

  Such instructions will cause a general-protection fault and the application will be terminated.

Filters

Filters are supported and are integrated with Win32 and MS-DOS; that is, you can redirect input and output between OS/2, MS-DOS, and Win32 applications transparently.

Device Monitors

Device monitors are a feature that OS/2 provides in the device driver level, which violates Windows NT security if given across the system. Therefore, the OS/2 subsystem implements device monitors within an OS/2 session (an OS/2 application and all of its descendants). Within the session the implementation of device monitors is complete and compatible with OS/2. The vast majority of OS/2 applications use monitors within a session already.

Printing

Printing from the OS/2 subsystem is identical to base-level printing on OS/2. For example, you can connect to a remote printer by typing the following at the command prompt:

NET USE LPT1: *myprinter\pscript*

You can then use the dialog boxes within an application to set up a printer and print.

Security

The OS/2 subsystem is subject to the security measures imposed by Windows NT. OS/2 processes, among themselves, have only the security restrictions of OS/2 (no ACLs attached, and so on). OS/2 processes run under the logged-on user token, just as Win32 processes do.

Communication with Other Subsystems

Subsystems communicate by passing messages to one another. When an OS/2 application calls an API routine, for example, the OS/2 subsystem receives a message and implements it by calling Windows NT system services or by passing messages to other subsystems. When it's finished, the OS/2 subsystem sends a message containing the return values back to the application. The message passing and other activities of the subsystem are invisible to the user.

Communication between OS/2 and Windows NT processes can be accomplished by means of named pipes, mail slots, NetBIOS, files, and COM devices. The Win32 subsystem directs user input to an OS/2 application; it handles all screen I/O for OS/2 applications.

Calling 32-bit DLLs

The OS/2 subsystem provides a general mechanism to allow 16-bit OS/2 and PM applications to load and call any Win32 DLL. This feature could be extremely useful in the following cases:

- When you need to call from your OS/2 application some functionality available under Windows NT only as Win32 code.

  Without the ability to call Win32 DLLs, the alternative would be to split the application into an OS/2 application and a Win32 application, then communicate between them using, for example, named pipes. This would be much more complicated to implement and may not yield a good performance.

- When you want to port your OS/2 application to Win32 but would like to do so in stages, by porting only part of the application at first.

A small set of new APIs is provided. See "Win32 Thunking Mechanism" later in this chapter.

OS/2 Configuration

The OS/2 subsystem handles OS2.INI compatibly with OS/2. The WIN*xxx* APIs supported in this release of Windows NT are provided for this purpose. STARTUP.CMD is just a batch file; if you want to run the batch file, add it to the Startup group in the Windows NT Program Manager.

When the OS/2 subsystem starts for the first time, it checks the Registry for OS/2 subsystem configuration information. If it doesn't find any, it looks for information in the original CONFIG.SYS file and adds the information to the Registry. If the original CONFIG.SYS file does not exist or is not an OS/2 configuration file, the subsystem adds the following default information to the Registry:

```
PROTSHELL=c:\os2\pmshell.exe c:\os2\os2.ini c:\os2\os2sys.ini
    %SystemRoot%\system32\cmd.exe
SET COMSPEC=%SystemRoot%\system32\cmd.exe
```

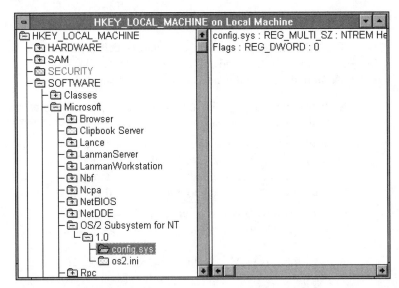

The subsystem updates the environment variable, **Os2LibPath**, with LIBPATH information found in the original CONFIG.SYS file. The updated **Os2LibPath** is *<systemroot>*\SYSTEM32\OS2\DLL concatenated with the list of directories specified in the LIBPATH line of the original CONFIG.SYS file.

The PATH information found in the original CONFIG.SYS file is not entered automatically into the default Windows NT path. To add the location of OS/2 applications, use the System applet in the Control Panel to add a PATH variable to the user environment variables. This information is appended automatically by Windows NT each time a user logs on to the system.

Windows NT supports the OS/2 configuration commands shown in the following table. If you use commands that are not supported, Windows NT ignores them.

Table 16.1 OS/2 Configuration Commands Supported by Windows NT

Command	Function
protshell	Specifies the command interpreter. Only the Windows NT command interpreter is supported.
devicename	Specifies a user-defined Windows NT device driver used by OS/2 applications.
libpath	Specifies the location of OS/2 16-bit dynamic-link libraries.
set	Sets environment variables.
country	Sets a country code that defines country-dependent information such as time, date, and currency conventions.
codepage	Specifies the code pages your system is prepared to use.
devinfo=KBD	Specifies the information the keyboard needs in order to use a particular code page.

The **libpath**, **set**, and **devicename** commands are processed as follows:

- The **libpath** command appends path information to the OS/2 library path in the Windows NT environment. At the command prompt, you can change the library path for OS/2 applications by using the **os2libpath** command.

- The following **set** commands are ignored:

set path	**set comspec**	**set video_devices**
set vio_ibmvga	**set vio_vga**	**set prompt**

- The **devicename** command specifies a device driver compatible with Windows NT for use with an OS/2 application. The syntax for the **devicename** command is as follows:

```
DEVICENAME=OS/2devicename [[path][NTdevicename]]
```

Devicename is the logical name that OS/2 applications use to address the device. *Path* and *NTdevicename* specify the Windows NT device driver to which the OS/2 device name is mapped. If these are not specified, the device is mapped to \DEVICE*os/2devicename*.

Changing OS/2 Configuration Information

Although the OS/2 configuration information is stored in the Registry, you can edit that information just as you would edit an OS/2 CONFIG.SYS file. To edit the information, you must use an OS/2 text editor.

Note   To change configuration information, you must be logged on as a member of the Administrators group.

▶ **To change configuration information**

1. While running Windows NT, start an OS/2 text editor in a window.

2. Open a file called C:\CONFIG.SYS.

   Windows NT retrieves the configuration information from the Registry and stores it in a temporary file that you can edit.

3. Edit the configuration information.

4. Save and close the file.

5. Quit the editor.

   Windows NT stores the new information in the registry.

6. Log off from Windows NT, and restart your computer.

File List

The main files that make up the OS/2 subsystem are listed in the following table. Many additional files, not listed here, are needed when running the Windows NT Add-On Subsystem for Presentation Manager.

Table 16.2   OS/2 Subsystem Files

File	Purpose
OS2SRV.EXE	This file is the subsystem server. It is invoked when you run the first OS/2 application, and it remains to serve new applications as they are run.
OS2.EXE	This file is the client side of every OS/2 application. There is an instance of OS2.EXE for each OS/2 application that is running.
DOSCALLS.DLL[1]	This file contains the DOS*xxx* APIs. The other DLLs that are used in OS/2, such as KBDCALLS and VIOCALLS, are provided in memory by the OS/2 subsystem.
NETAPI.DLL[1]	This file contains the LM APIs.

[1] This file is located in the SYSTEM32\OS2\DLL or C:\OS2\DLL directories when running the Windows NT Add-On Subsystem for Presentation Manager.

Win32 Thunking Mechanism

As mentioned earlier in this document, the OS/2 subsystem provides a general mechanism to allow 16-bit OS/2 and PM applications to load and call any Win32 DLL. To take advantage of this feature, you typically need to complete the following tasks:

- Write a small Win32 DLL thunking layer that will be called by the 16-bit OS/2 application.

  This Win32 thunking layer will in turn call the real Win32 API, using the parameters passed by the 16-bit code. The need for such a thunking layer (rather than calling the real Win32 DLL directly from 16-bit) stems from the fact that the OS/2 subsystem thunking mechanism allows only for one generic pointer parameter. Most Win32 APIs require more parameters or of different type so that a small Win32 thunking layer is required to retrieve parameters via the parameter pointer. This parameter pointer points to application-defined data, which will typically be a structure with the parameters for the actual call to the real Win32 API.

- Change your 16-bit application to include calls to the Win32 thunking APIs described below.

The following 16-bit APIs are to be used by the OS/2 application code. (These APIs are defined in the same manner as OS/2 APIs. See OS/2 1.2 *Programmer's Reference Manual*.)

```
USHORT pascal far Dos32LoadModule (
    PSZ DLLName,
    PULONG pDllHandle);
```

Purpose: Load a Win32 thunk DLL that will intermediate between an OS/2 application and Win32 APIs.

Returns: If NO_ERROR is returned, the value pointed to by **pDllHandle** is used for other Win32 thunk APIs as described below. It is invalid for usage with regular OS/2 APIs. If ERROR_MOD_NOT_FOUND is returned, the value pointed to by **pDLLHandle** is undefined.

```
USHORT pascal far Dos32GetProcAddr (
    ULONG DllHandle,
    PSZ pszProcName,
    PULONG pWin32Thunk);
```

Purpose: Get a cookie (flat pointer) to a routine in a Win32 thunk DLL, previously opened by **Dos32LoadModule**. For example, if the OS/2 application wants to call the **WinSocketFoo** API, it builds a Win32 intermediate DLL, named MYSOCK.DLL, that exports **MyWinSocketFoo**. The application calls **Dos32LoadModule** with MYSOCK.DLL and then **Dos32GetProcAddr** with **pszProcName** of value **MyWinSocketFoo**. If no error is returned, it can use the value pointed to by **pWin32Thunk** in a later call to **Dos32Dispatch**, for calling the **MyWinSocketFoo** routine, which in turn will call a real Win32 API (for example, **WinSocketFoo**).

Returns: NO_ERROR if the **pszProcName** is exported by the Win32 intermediate DLL which relates to **DllHandle**. If ERROR_PROC_NOT_FOUND or ERROR_INVALID_HANDLE is returned, the value pointed to by **pWin32Thunk** is undefined.

```
USHORT pascal far Dos32Dispatch (
    ULONG Win32Thunk,
    PVOID  pArguments,
    PULONG pRetCode);
```

Purpose: **Dos32Dispatch** calls the 32-bit thunk routine **Win32Thunk**, previously obtained by **Dos32GetProcAddr**. It returns the error code returned by **Win32Thunk** in **pRetCode**. It translates the **pArguments** 16:16 pointer to a flat pointer and passes it to the **Win32Thunk** call. The structure pointed to by **pArguments**, and the values of **pRetCode** are application specific and are not interpreted or modified by the OS/2 subsystem.

On the Win32 side, i.e. in the Win32 DLL, the Win32 thunk has to be defined as follows:

```
ULONG MyWinSocketFoo (
    PVOID pFlatArg);
```

The return code from **MyWinSocketFoo** is application-defined and is copied by the OS/2 subsystem to **pRetCode**.

Returns: NO_ERROR if the **pFlatArg** argument is a valid pointer and no exception occurred in the call to it.

```
USHORT pascal far Dos32FreeModule (
    ULONG DllHandle);
```

Purpose: Unload a Win32 thunk DLL that intermediates between an OS/2 application and Win32 APIs.

Returns: NO_ERROR if **DllHandle** indeed corresponds to a Win32 DLL previously loaded by **Dos32LoadModule** (after the call, **DllHandle** is no longer valid). Otherwise, ERROR_INVALID_HANDLE is returned.

```
USHORT pascal far FarPtr2FlatPtr(
    ULONG FarPtr,
    PULONG pFlatPtr);
```

Purpose: Translates the segmented pointer FarPtr to a flat pointer pointed to by **pFlatPtr**.

Returns: NO_ERROR if **FarPtr** is a valid 16:16 pointer: in this case, upon completion of the call **pFlatPtr** contains a valid 32-bit flat pointer to be used by Win32 code. ERROR_INVALID_PARAMETER is returned if the 16:16 pointer is not valid: in this case the value pointed to by **pFlatPtr** is undefined.

```
USHORT pascal far FlatPtr2FarPtr(
    ULONG FlatPtr,
    PULONG pFarPtr);
```

Purpose: Translates the flat pointer **FlatPtr** to a far pointer which it stores into **pFarPtr**.

Returns: NO_ERROR if the 32-bit **FlatPtr** maps to a valid 16:16 pointer in the 16-bit application's context: in this case, upon completion of the call **pFarPtr** contains a valid 16:16 segmented pointer to be used by the 16-bit OS/2 code. Otherwise, i.e. if the 16:16 pointer is not a valid address in the 16-bit application's context, ERROR_INVALID_PARAMETER is returned and **pFarPtr** is undefined.

The following are the .H file and .DEF file that should be compiled and linked with the 16-bit OS/2 application:

The .H File

```
//
// Definition of WIN32 thunk APIs.
//

extern USHORT pascal far
Dos32LoadModule(PSZ DllName, PULONG pDllHandle);

extern USHORT pascal far
Dos32GetProcAddr(ULONG Handle, PSZ pszProcName, PULONG pWin32Thunk);

extern USHORT pascal far
Dos32Dispatch(ULONG Win32Thunk, PVOID pArguments, PULONG pRetCode);

extern USHORT pascal far
Dos32FreeModule(ULONG DllHandle);

extern USHORT pascal far
FarPtr2FlatPtr(ULONG FarPtr, PULONG pFlarPtr);

extern USHORT pascal far
FlatPtr2FarPtr(ULONG FlatPtr, PULONG pFarPtr);
```

The .DEF File

```
IMPORTS
    DOSCALLS.DOS32LOADMODULE
    DOSCALLS.DOS32GETPROCADDR
    DOSCALLS.DOS32DISPATCH
    DOSCALLS.DOS32FREEMODULE
    DOSCALLS.FARPTR2FLATPTR
    DOSCALLS.FLATPTR2FARPTR
```

C H A P T E R   1 7

POSIX Compatibility

This chapter discusses the Windows NT implementation of a POSIX subsystem. It includes information about the following topics:

- Definition of POSIX
- Conformance and compliance to POSIX.1
- Running applications
- Implementation of subsystem
- Windows NT POSIX files

Note This chapter is not intended to be a POSIX tutorial.

Definition of POSIX

POSIX, which stands for *Portable Operating System Interface* for computing environments, began as an effort by the IEEE community to promote the portability of applications across UNIX environments by developing a clear, consistent and unambiguous set of standards. POSIX is not limited to the UNIX environment, however. It can be implemented on non-UNIX operating systems, as was done with the IEEE Std. 1003.1-1990 (POSIX.1) implementation on the VMS, MPE, and CTOS operating systems. POSIX actually consists of a set of standards that range from POSIX.1 to POSIX.12.

As the following table shows, most of these standards are still in the proposed state. This section deals with the Windows NT implementation of a POSIX subsystem to support the international ISO/IEC IS 9945-1:1990 standard (also called *POSIX.1*). POSIX.1 defines a C-language source-code-level application programming interface (API) to an operating system environment.

Table 17.1   Family of POSIX Standards

Standard	ISO Standard	Description
POSIX.0	No	A guide to POSIX Open Systems Environment. This is not a standard in the same sense as POSIX.1 or POSIX.2. It is more of an introduction and overview of the other standards.
POSIX.1	Yes	Systems application programming interface (API) [C language]
POSIX.2	No	Shell and tools (IEEE approved standard)
POSIX.3	No	Testing and verification
POSIX.4	No	Real-time and threads
POSIX.5	Yes	ADA language bindings to POSIX.1
POSIX.6	No	System security
POSIX.7	No	System administration
POSIX.8	No	Networking A. Transparent file access B. Protocol-independent network interface C. Remote Procedure Calls (RPC) D. Open system interconnect protocol-dependent application interfaces
POSIX.9	Yes	FORTRAN language bindings to POSIX.1
POSIX.10	No	Super-computing Application Environment Profile (AEP)
POSIX.11	No	Transaction Processing AEP
POSIX.12	No	Graphical user interface

POSIX Conformance

For a system to be given a certificate of POSIX.1 conformance, it must meet the following requirements:

- The system must support all of the interfaces as defined in the ISO/IEC 9945-1.

- The vendor must supply a *POSIX.1 Conformance Document* (PCD) with the vendor's implementation as specified in ISP/IEC 9945-1.

- The implementation must pass the appropriate *National Institute of Standards and Technology* (NIST) test suite.

Windows NT version 3.1 Workstation and Windows NT Server have been tested using the official NIST PCTS for *Federal Information Processing Standard* (FIPS) 151-2 and NIST has validated the test results. Windows NT version 3.5 is in the process of being verified for POSIX.1 compliance and will also be submitted to NIST for FIPS 151-2 certification. FIPS 151-2 incorporates POSIX.1 as a reference standard and also requires a number of the optional features defined in POSIX.1 to promote application portability among conforming implementations. An implementation that conforms to FIPS 151-2 also conforms to POSIX.1. Note that conformance is specific to the manufacturer, hardware platform, and model number on which the implementation is tested.

POSIX.1 is a source-level standard; it does not provide any binary compatibility.

Application Compliance to POSIX.1

For POSIX.1, there are four categories of compliance, ranging from a very strict compliance to a very loose compliance. The various categories are described in this section.

The current release of Windows NT supports strictly conforming POSIX.1 applications and ISO/IEC conforming POSIX.1 applications. Windows NT supports the latter by virtue of the fact that only 110 of the 149 functions of standard C are part of POSIX.1, and standard C is itself an ISO standard (ISO/IEC 9899).

Strictly Conforming POSIX.1 Applications

A *strictly conforming POSIX.1 application* requires only the facilities described in the POSIX.1 standard and applicable language standards. This type of application accepts the following conditions:

- Any behavior described in ISO/IEC 9945-1 as unspecified or implementation-defined

- Symbolic constants

- Any value in the range permitted in ISO/IEC 9945-1

This is the strictest level of application conformance, and applications at this level should be able to move across implementations with just a recompilation. At this time, the only language interface that has been standardized for POSIX.1 is the C-language interface. (As shown in the figure below, a strictly conforming POSIX application can use 110 calls from the standard C libraries.)

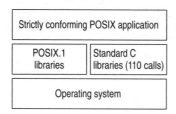

Figure 17.1   A Strictly Conforming POSIX Application

Applications Conforming to ISO/IEC and POSIX.1

An *ISO/IEC-conforming POSIX.1 application* is one that uses only the facilities described in ISO/IEC 9945-1 and approved conforming language bindings for the ISO or IEC standard. This type of application must include a statement of conformance that documents all options and limit dependencies, and all other ISO or IEC standards used.

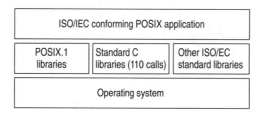

Figure 17.2   An ISO/IEC-conforming POSIX.1 Application

This level of conformance is not as strict as the previous one for two reasons. First, it allows a POSIX.1 application to make use of other ISO or IEC standards, such as GKS. Second, it allows POSIX.1 applications within this level to require options or limit values beyond the minimum. For example, such an application could require that the implementation support filenames of at least 16 characters. The POSIX.1 minimum is 14 characters.

Applications Conforming to POSIX.1 and <National Body>

A *<National Body> conforming POSIX.1 application* differs from an ISO/IEC-conforming POSIX.1 application in that this type of application may also use specific standards of a single ISO/IEC organization, such as ANSI or British Standards Institute (BSI). This type of application must include a statement of conformance that documents all options and limit dependencies, and all other *<National Body>* standards used.

For example, you could have a *<National Body>* conforming POSIX application that uses calls from a BSI-standard set of calls.

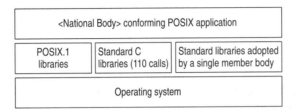

Figure 17.3   A National Body Conforming POSIX.1 Application

POSIX.1-Conformant Applications that Use Extensions

A *conforming POSIX.1 application using extensions* is an application that differs from a conforming POSIX.1 application only because it uses nonstandard facilities that are consistent with ISO/IEC 9945-1. Such an application must fully document its requirements for these extended facilities.

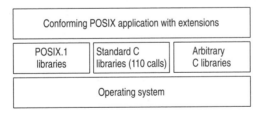

Figure 17.4   A Conforming POSIX.1 Application Using Extensions

This is the lowest level of conformance; almost any C program could satisfy this with the appropriate documentation.

Running Applications

POSIX applications can be started from a Windows NT console window (command prompt), the File Manager, Program Manager, or by invocation from within another POSIX application.

File Systems

POSIX requires a certain amount of functionality from the file system, such as the ability for a file to have more than one name (or *hard links*) and case-sensitive file naming. Neither FAT nor HPFS supports these features, which is another reason why a new file system was required for Windows NT. NTFS supports both hard links and case-sensitive naming. If you want to run in a POSIX-conforming environment, you need at least one NTFS disk partition on your computer.

You can run POSIX applications from any Windows NT file system. If the application does not need to access the file system, the application will run with no problems. However, if the application does require access to the file system, it may not behave correctly on a non-NTFS disk partition.

Bypass Traverse Checking

By default, when you install Windows NT for the first time, the user right *Bypass Traverse Checking* is granted to everyone. This right allows a user to change directories through a directory tree even if the user has no permission for those directories.

If you want to run in a POSIX-conforming environment, you must disable this privilege for your account by using either the User Manager or User Manager for Domains tool.

Note You must be an administrator to do this.

▶   **To disable the Bypass Traverse Checking right for an account**

1. Select the account.

2. From the Policies menu, select User Rights.

   The User Rights Policy dialog box is displayed. Be sure the Show Advanced User Rights check box is marked.

The User Rights Policy dialog box

3. Specify the Bypass Traverse Checking right.

4. Choose Remove.

Printing

The POSIX subsystem itself does not directly support printing, but Windows NT supports redirection and piping between subsystems. If your POSIX application writes to **stdout**, and you have connected or redirected either your serial or parallel ports to a printer, you can redirect the output of a POSIX application to that printer. For example, the following sequence of commands will send to a network printer the output of a POSIX application that writes to **stdout**.

```
NET USE LPT1: \\MYSERVER\PRINTER
POSIXAPP.EXE > LPT1:
```

Network Access

The POSIX.1 specification does not have a requirement for access to remote file systems, but as with any of the other subsystems, the POSIX subsystem and POSIX applications have transparent access to any Win32 remotely connected file system.

Restrictions on POSIX Applications

With this release of Windows NT, POSIX applications have no direct access to any of the facilities and features of the Win32 subsystem, such as memory mapped files, networking, graphics, or dynamic data exchange.

Implementation of Subsystem

The POSIX subsystem is implemented in Windows NT as a protected server. POSIX applications communicate with the POSIX subsystem through a message-passing facility in the Executive known as a *Local Procedure Call* (LPC).

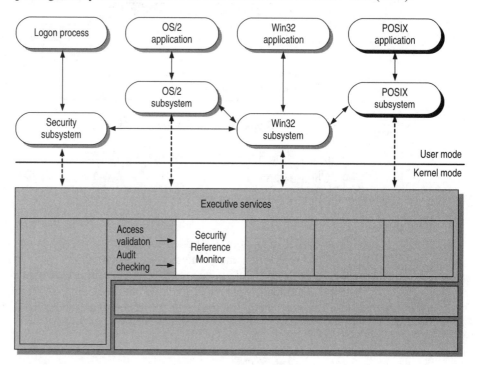

Figure 17.5   POSIX Subsystem in Windows NT

The POSIX subsystem and each POSIX application run in their own protected address space, which protects them from any other application that might be running on Windows NT. POSIX application are preemptively multitasked with respect to each other, and with respect to other applications running in the system.

Files Used

The following table lists the principal files used by the POSIX subsystem, and the figure shows how they interact.

File	Purpose
PSXSS.EXE	The POSIX subsystem server
POSIX.EXE	The POSIX console session manager
PSXDLL.DLL	The POSIX dynamic link library

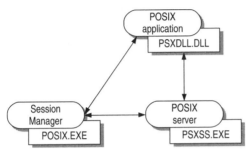

Figure 17.6   How POSIX Subsystem Files Interact

Communicating with Other Subsystems

Windows NT supports a common command processor that can run commands from any of the subsystems. In addition, Windows NT supports piped input and output between commands of different subsystems. For example, you could run the **ls** utility and pipe the results through the **more** command to the console:

```
ls -l | more
```

Further Information

For further information on the POSIX standards, contact either or both of the following resources.

- For information on POSIX.1 (ANSI/IEEE 1003.1-1990, ISO/IEC 9945-1:1990), contact:

  Publication Sales
  IEEE Service Center
  P.O. Box 1331445
  Hoes Lane Piscataway, NJ 08855-1331

- For information on other POSIX standards, contact:

  IEEE Computer Society
  Attention Assistant Director/Standards
  1730 Massachusetts Avenue Northwest
  Washington, DC 20036

P A R T V I

Troubleshooting

Part Six provides specific information for troubleshooting problems with Windows NT, showing the key steps for isolating and solving common problems.

C H A P T E R   1 8

Troubleshooting

Careful record keeping is essential to successful troubleshooting. You should have records of your network layout, cabling, previous problems and their solutions, dates of installation of hardware and software, and so on, all readily accessible. (Remember that you can add your own notes to the Messages database that is included with Windows NT and with this *Resource Kit*.)

Many problems can be avoided with routine virus checks. You should make a special point of checking for viruses before installing or upgrading Windows NT on a computer that is already in use.

Sources of Troubleshooting Information

Your Windows NT documentation set is a valuable source of troubleshooting information. The *Installation Guide* for Windows NT Workstations, the *Installation Guide* for Windows NT Server, and the *Upgrade Guide* each have a chapter titled "Troubleshooting."

The Messages database and book that is shipped with Windows NT and with this resource kit is another source of troubleshooting information. Thousands of messages are documented, with the probable cause and recommended solution to each of them. In particular, the STOP messages that appear when the system fails with a blue screen are documented in *Windows NT Messages*.

The Event Log lets you examine the events that preceded the problem. Use the Event Viewer to examine this log, as described in your *Windows NT System Guide*.

The Knowledge Base is a database of tips, hints, and solutions to known problems. It is created and maintained by Microsoft Product Support, and is included with this resource kit. See the /KB directory in your *Windows NT Resource Kit* distribution files.

Some of the chapters in this *Resource Guide* end with a "Question and Answer" section that is often a good source of troubleshooting information.

Hardware Problems

By far, the most common cause of hardware problems is using hardware that is not listed on the Hardware Compatibility List (HCL), which lists the supported hardware components that have been tested and have passed compatibility testing with Windows NT version 3.5 as of October, 1994. A copy of the most current HCL is included in Appendix D, "Hardware Compatibility List." It is especially important for you to refer to the HCL if you plan to use any of the following hardware components: modems, tape backup units, and SCSI adapters.

Make sure that you are using a make and model that is listed on the HCL. If several models from one manufacture are included in the HCL, only those models are supported; a slightly different model might cause problems. Where special criteria are required for a model to be supported (for example, if a particular version of driver is required) this is noted as a footnote in the HCL. Be sure that your configuration meets these criteria. As additional hardware is tested, the HCL is updated, and additional drivers are created if needed. The updated list and additional drivers are available through the electronic services listed at the end of the HCL.

If you are sure your particular hardware is supported, and you are still having problems, always begin by checking that the physical connections are secure. This simple step is easy to overlook when you are thinking in terms of compatibility issues, resource conflicts, and configuration parameters.

If you are using a SCSI device, double and triple-check the SCSI termination. Even if you are sure the termination is correct, if you are having problems that could be due to incorrect termination, open the computer case and check again.

Next, check your hardware configuration. Windows NT is more exacting than most other operating systems. So I/O conflicts and interrupt conflicts that went unnoticed under another operating system must be resolved when you switch to Windows NT. Likewise, you must pay much closer attention to CMOS and EISA configuration parameters when using Windows NT.

If you encounter video problems, such as an incorrect display or very slow screen updates, you can usually determine whether the problem is with the video component or with some other component by switching from super VGA to plain VGA. For example, restart the computer, and choose plain VGA during the boot sequence. If the problem goes away, look to the video component for the source of the problem.

Software Problems

Obtaining Debugging Information

The Crashdump utility dumps the contents of memory to a Crashfile on the drive. The information in this file can be studied to determine the cause of the crash. The system must be properly installed and configured for Crashdump to work.

You can add switches to your BOOT.INI file to cause debugging output to be sent to a COM port even before the operating system loads. The switches should be added to the end of the line specifying the location of the files for the operating system you want to debug; these lines are listed in the **[operating systems]** section of the BOOT.INI file. The switches are as follows:

/NODEBUG
This is the default; no debugging information will be collected or transmitted during installation.

/DEBUG
The customary switch to enable debugging. The last standard COM port found will be used, unless a port is specified with the /DEBUGPORT=COMx switch.

/DEBUGPORT=COMx
Sends debug output to the specific COM port.

/BAUDRATE=nnnnn

Specifies the baud rate at which data is sent through the COM port, for remote debugging using a modem. Default is 19200.

/CRASHDEBUG

Enables a certain amount of stack pages to be accessible via the debugger. For remote debugging using a modem, the default number of stack pages is 9600. The pages are accessible only after the system encounters a fatal error and begins checking for bugs.

/SOS

Use this switch to show the names of the drivers as they are loaded during system startup. This information can be distracting during routine startups, but if startup is failing while loading drivers this switch allows you to find out which driver is triggering the failure.

/NoSerialMice

Disables the serial mouse detection on certain COM ports. It is mostly used to exclude ports used by Uninterruptible Power Supply (UPS) system. The detection signal causes some UPS units to power down, thereby turning off the computer.

You can use multiple /NoSerialMice switches. The format is
/NoSerialMIce=[COM*x* | COM*x*,COM*y*,COM*z*,...]

- If **/NoSerialMice** is specified without parameters, serial mouse detection will be disabled on all the serial ports.

- If **/NoSerialMice=COM*x*** is specified, serial mouse detection will only be disabled on COM*x*.

- If **/NoSerialMice=COM*x*,COM*y*,COM*z* ...** is specified, serial mouse detection will be disabled on each of the specified ports.

UPS Turns Off When the Computer Starts

Normally, Windows NT sends a detection signal to each port in order to recognize hardware attached to that port. However, some UPS units using serial monitoring implementations respond to the detection signal by turning off. If this happens, use the **/NoSerialMice** switch in the BOOT.INI file to prevent the system from sending this signal to the COM port to which your UPS unit is connected. For more information about BOOT.INI switches, see "Obtaining Debugging Information" earlier in this chapter.

Poor Performance at Start of Business Day

If performance slows noticeably while many users are logging on, you probably need to add backup domain controllers (BDCs) to help process logon requests. Any Windows NT Server can be used as a BDC.

In some instances, for example if browsing the network is slow, you might also want to divide the network into more domains. For a discussion of strategies to use in organizing your network into domains, see "Knowing the Domain Models" in Chapter 3, "How Network Security Works" of the *Windows NT Server Concepts and Planning Guide*.

The User Cannot Access Resources

Whenever a user account is created, Windows NT assigns a unique security identifier (SID) to that account, which the operating system uses to identify the account. If an accidentally deleted account is recreated, the SID will be different even though every visible detail is the same. Consequently, when the user tries to access resources, he or she will have only the permissions granted to the USERS group. To restore the privileges the old account had, the new account must be added to the groups that the old account was a member of, and any resources that granted special privileges to the individual account must be explicitly set to grant those privileges to the replacement account.

Netlogon Service Does Not Start

If the primary domain controller (PDC) is not available, and you configure a new PDC rather than promoting an existing backup domain controller, a new security identifier (SID) will be created for the domain. If the old PDC is then brought back on-line, it will not be able to process logon requests because it does not know the domain SID. To use both servers on the domain, you will need to reinstall Windows NT on one of them, while the other is available as a PDC. For more information see "How Domains Are Identified Internally" in Chapter 3, "How Network Security Works" of the *Windows NT Server Concepts and Planning Guide*.

After Upgrading, Mail Does Not Start

Certain add-on enhancements to Microsoft Mail for Windows for Workgroups prevent Windows NT Mail from starting. To avoid this problem, do not migrate applications designed for use with Windows for Workgroups to Windows NT. For more information, see the Knowledge Base article included with this resource kit.

Common Printing Problems

Paper is not Feeding from the Correct Tray

If the printer is not drawing paper from the tray you expect it to, make sure you have correctly matched your form with a source in Print Manager. For information on how to perform this task, search for "Forms, assigning to a printer" in Print Manager Help.

Print Jobs are Incomplete or Missing

Even if there is enough memory on a printer, print jobs can fail if only a small amount of memory is visible to the system. When you first install a printer driver, the default value, which may be as low as 300K, is assumed. Often, additional memory is needed to meet the demands your organization places on the printer, and has been installed. For this additional memory to be used, it must be specified as a property of the printer, using Print Manager.

The number specified as "printer memory" in the printer properties refers not to the total memory on the printer, but only to the portion available for PostScript Virtual Memory. If you specify the total amount of memory on the printer in this text box, Print Manager might in some cases use so much memory for downloaded data such as fonts that not enough is left for the printer to operate.

To find out what number should be entered in the Printer Memory text box, copy the file PS.TXT, included with this resource kit, to the printer. The output is a page that tells you what values to use.

PART VII

Appendixes

Part Seven includes appendixes with information on additional resources, advanced user rights, international issues, and a hardware compatibility list. A glossary of terms used in the *Resource Guide* and *Networking Guide* follows.

APPENDIX A

Windows NT Resource Directory

This appendix describes how to get answers to your technical questions. It also contains a list of resources to support learning and using Windows NT.

With Windows accepted as a standard for PC computing, many companies are making products and services available to enhance the Windows and Windows for Workgroups environment. Microsoft also offers a wide array of support services.

Getting Answers to Your Technical Questions

For answers to your questions and help with technical problems regarding Windows NT:

- First, check online Help (press the F1 key), the printed documentation set, and the information in the README.WRI files.

- Check the Messages database, available on the floppy disks that accompany *Microsoft Windows NT Resource Kit Volume 3: Windows NT Messages*.

- For fast answers to common questions and a library of technical notes delivered by recording or fax, call Microsoft FastTips for Windows NT at (800) 936-4400 (available seven days a week, 24 hours a day, including holidays). Microsoft FastTips is an automated system, accessible by touch-tone phone.

- Use CompuServe to interact with other users and Microsoft support engineers, or access the Microsoft Knowledge Base of product information. CompuServe members can type, at any ! prompt, **GO MICROSOFT** to access the Microsoft forums or **GO MSKB** to access the Microsoft Knowledge Base. For an introductory CompuServe membership kit, call (800) 848-8199 and ask for operator 524.

- Use the Microsoft Download Service (MSDL) via modem to access the latest technical notes on common support issues for Windows NT and to access the Windows NT Driver Library, which provides the most current Windows NT–compatible device drivers for printers, displays, networks, and other devices not included in the retail package for Windows NT. All drivers are tested by Microsoft for compatibility with the Windows NT operating system. The MSDL is at (206) 936-6735 in the United States and (905) 507-3022 in Canada (available seven days a week, 24 hours a day, including holidays). You can use either a 1200-, 2400-, or 9600-baud modem; no parity, 8 data bits, 1 stop bit.

- Use the Internet to access the Windows NT Driver Library and the Microsoft Knowledge Base for information on Windows NT. The Microsoft Internet FTP archive host, ftp.microsoft.com, supports anonymous login. When logging in as anonymous, use your complete electronic mail name as your password.

- Contact a Microsoft Solution Provider for installation services and follow-up product support. These companies have individuals who have been certified as Microsoft Certified Professionals on Windows NT. To be referred to a Microsoft Solution Provider in your area, please call Microsoft at (800) SOLPROV in the United States and Canada.

- Get technical support from a Microsoft engineer. Microsoft offers pay-as-you-go telephone support for Windows NT from a Microsoft engineer (available seven days a week, 24 hours a day, except holidays). Please have the Product ID number ready when you call. This number can be found on either the inside back cover of your *Installation Guide* or on your registration card. Choose from these options:

  - In the United States, dial (900) 555-2100. There is a service charge of $150.00 (U.S.) per incident. Charges appear on your telephone bill.

  - In the United States, dial (800) 936-5900. There is a service charge of $150.00 (U.S.) per incident. Charges billed to your Visa card, MasterCard, or American Express card.

  - In Canada, dial (800) 668-7975 for more information.

  - Annual and multiple incident support plans: For information on Microsoft support options in the United States, contact the Microsoft Support Network Sales and Information group at (800) 936-3500, from 6:00 A.M. until 6:00 P.M. Pacific time, Monday through Friday, excluding holidays. In Canada, call (800) 668-7975, from 8:00 A.M. until 8:00 P.M. Eastern time, Monday through Friday, excluding holidays.

  - Microsoft Text Telephone (TT/TDD) services are available for customers who are deaf or hard of hearing. In the United States, using a special TT/TDD modem, dial (206) 635-4948, from 6:00 A.M. until 6:00 P.M. Pacific time, Monday through Friday, excluding holidays. In Canada, dial (905) 568-9641, from 8:00 A.M. until 8:00 P.M. Eastern time, Monday through Friday, excluding holidays.

The following sections provide more information about support and services provided by Microsoft and Microsoft partners for Windows NT.

TechNet

Microsoft TechNet is the front-line resource for fast, complete answers to technical questions on Microsoft products and technologies. Subscribers to Microsoft TechNet receive 12 monthly TechNet CDs and 12 monthly TechNet Supplemental (Drivers & Patches) CDs, in addition to a dedicated CompuServe forum, a Windows-based application for accessing CompuServe, a $20 usage credit on CompuServe, and a discount on Microsoft Press books. Microsoft TechNet costs $295 annually for a single-user license, or $695 annually for a single-server license for unlimited users. Both types of licenses come with a 90-day guarantee.

For more information about Microsoft TechNet, in the United States and Canada, call (800) 344-2121, dept. 3013, from 7:00 A.M. until 7:00 P.M. Central time, Monday through Friday, excluding holidays.

The Microsoft TechNet CD is packed with valuable and accessible technical information, and monthly editions are cumulative, adding fresh information. This worldwide CD includes:

- The Microsoft Knowledge Base, which gives you answers to support questions by providing you easy access to the same extensive library of technical support information used by Microsoft Product Support Specialists every day. No need to call, no need to wait, which saves you time and money.

- Resource kits packed with technical references, troubleshooting information, utilities, and accessories to aid in installing and supporting Microsoft products.

- Technical information including application and technical notes and white papers that tell you how to get the most use out of products. The TechNet CD gives you the "tips and tricks" you need to increase your productivity.

- Migration information that helps you move people in an organization from one product to another or from one environment to another. What are the issues involved in migrating from a mainframe based electronic-mail system to one that is LAN based? TechNet helps you.

- Product facts and features to assist you in evaluating Microsoft products. You can compare versions of products to better understand the advantages of upgrading.

- Educational materials such as tutorials, training guides and training session slides with notes. Windows NT training materials are included.

- Customer solution profiles that detail how your colleagues solve real information technology problems. See how the Orlando Health Care Group developed a central database repository for access by 1800 personal computers using a client-server architecture. Or, read how the insurance and legal industries are creating state-of-the-art solutions.

- Strategic information to keep you up-to-date on the direction Microsoft and its products are taking now and in the future. If you wonder about the overall direction that Microsoft is taking, or need more information on such topics as multimedia, ODBC, MAPI, or WOSA, TechNet brings you the information. Press releases are included.

- Conference session notes from key Microsoft conferences. As part of our effort to provide timely up-to-date information, the TechNet CD delivers technical information not found in a book or a magazine, but rather, straight from the technical professionals themselves. This allows you to stay one step ahead.

- The Software Library, which gives you drivers, utilities, macros, and patches.

- The Microsoft Services Directory, a "one-stop shop" technical services directory for those who develop, implement, and support Microsoft-based solutions in the United States.

Microsoft Developer Network

The Microsoft Developer Network is the comprehensive source of development toolkits (SDKs and DDKs), operating systems, and development-related technical, strategic, and resource information for developers who write applications for the Microsoft Windows or Windows NT operating systems, or use Microsoft products for development purposes.

Developer Network Membership Benefits

The Developer Network is offered as an annual membership program to ensure that developers are kept up-to-date on the latest toolkits and information. Two levels of membership are offered in the Developer Network: Level 1 and Level 2.

Level 1 Membership

Level 1 membership in the Developer Network provides a base level of benefits (including the Development Library and the *Developer Network News*) designed to connect Windows developers to all the development information available from Microsoft. The Developer Network also gives developers the opportunity to provide feedback to Microsoft via CompuServe, Internet, fax, and mail.

Level 1 members receive the following benefits:

- Four quarterly updates to the Development Library
- Six bimonthly issues of the *Developer Network News*
- A $20 one-time credit on CompuServe connect charges
- A 20% discount on Microsoft Press books
- Invitations to Developer Network special events at shows
- A membership kit explaining how to maximize your benefits

Level 2 Membership

Level 2 membership delivers all the Level 1 membership benefits, plus four quarterly updates to the Development Platform and accompanying support. Level 2 provides developers not only with the information needed to develop Windows applications, but also provides all the SDKs, DDKs, and operating systems from Microsoft.

The Development Library

The Development Library is the comprehensive reference on programming for the Microsoft Windows and Windows NT operating systems. Because the Library is updated every three months, developers can be sure they have access to the most current product documentation and technology information.

This growing CD-ROM reference of over 125,000 pages of programming information already includes all documentation for development products such as the Win32 SDK; Visual C++ (both 16 and 32-bit editions); C/C++ 7.0; MASM 6.1; Windows 3.1 SDK, DDK, and MDK (Multimedia Development Kit); Visual Basic; Office Developer's Kit; Microsoft Excel SDK; Word for Windows Macro Development Kit; Microsoft Access; and Microsoft FoxPro for Windows.

The Development Library also includes the following:

- Over 1,600 sample applications, fully documented and tested, written in Visual Basic, C, and Visual C++™ that demonstrate development techniques.

- More than 200 previously unpublished technical articles written exclusively for the Development Library. These technical articles discuss complex Windows programming topics in great detail, helping developers solve complex programming problems.

- The latest specs, covering technologies such as Plug and Play, Extended Capabilities Port, and True Type.

- Microsoft Press books, such as Richter's *Advanced Windows NT*, Petzold's *Programming Windows 3.1*, and Kraig Brockschmidt's *Inside OLE 2*.

- Complete issues of the *Microsoft Systems Journal* with source code, plus selected articles on Visual Basic from the Cobb Group and the *Visual Basic Programmer's Journal*.

- The complete Developer Knowledge Base, containing over 13,000 articles, with bug reports and work arounds on all Microsoft development products.

- Tools and utilities such as the Windows Help Authoring Tools.

- Self-paced courses on topics such as DIBs (device-independent bitmaps), MDI (multiple document interface), palette manipulation, printing, and common dialog boxes.

- Papers, presentations, and sample code from conferences, such as Tech*Ed '94.

The Development Library is easy to browse, annotate, and search. The intuitive Windows interface lets you view formatted text and graphics, print topics, and easily import source code into your application. A Contents list displays the Library's content hierarchically by type of information (for example, Product Documentation, Technical Articles, and Sample Code), making it easy to browse all the information on the Library. A full-text, Boolean search engine makes it easy to query the entire Library for specific information.

The powerful Keywords list is the fastest way to look up information on Windows APIs and language functions. With it, you can instantaneously retrieve definitions of all the Windows 3.1 and Win32 APIs, window messages and structures, and C/C++, Visual Basic, MASM, Access, and FoxPro® functions from a scrollable, alphabetical list.

Every one of the hundreds of sample applications on the Library is preceded by a short abstract; all are clearly listed in the source index. You can also jump to relevant samples from the technical articles and *Microsoft Systems Journal* articles that refer to them. You can execute the sample code via the Library, and you can easily view and copy the source code to your own hard drive. These sample applications eliminate the need to write code for commonly used routines and save you the trouble of keying in and debugging the code. They also provide excellent examples of various programming techniques. Because you never have to leave your computer to check reference materials, you can stay focused on your project and save development time. You can also place bookmarks to identify topics that you read frequently in the Development Library.

The Development Platform

The Development Platform delivers the latest released versions of Microsoft software development kits, device driver kits, and operating systems, both domestic and international versions, all on CD. They're updated at least once each quarter, so you can always be confident you're working with current software.

The October '94 version of the Development Platform contains the following toolkits and platforms.

Operating Systems

- MS-DOS 6.22
- MS-DOS 6.2/V
- Windows for Workgroups 3.11 (Arabic, Danish, Dutch, English-Arabic, Finnish, France [complies with France's encryption regulations], French, French-Arabic, German, Hebrew, Italian, Norwegian, Portuguese, Spanish, Swedish, Thai, U.S.)
- Windows 3.11 (Dutch, French, German, Italian, Portuguese, Spanish, Swedish, Thai, U.S.)
- Windows 3.1 (Arabic, Catalan, Central and Eastern European, Chinese Simplified, Chinese Traditional, Czech, Danish, French-Arabic, Finnish, Greek, Hebrew, Hungarian, Korean, Japanese [NEC® 9800 and Intel®], Norwegian, Polish, Russian, Thai, Turkish)
- Win32s® 1.2 extension for Windows 3.1
- Windows NT 3.5 Workstation on Intel, Digital Alpha AXP, and MIPS (U.S. final release and Japanese Beta 1)

- Windows NT 3.1 Workstation on Intel, Digital Alpha AXP, and MIPS (French, German, Italian, Portuguese, Spanish, U.S.); on Intel and MIPS only (Danish, Dutch, Finnish, Norwegian, Swedish)
- Windows NT 3.1 Service Pack 2

Development Kits and Tools

- Common Messaging Calls SDK
- Embedded SQL for C Toolkit
- Mail Format File API (FFAPI) SDK 3.0 for Gateways and Applications
- Microsoft MediaView Development Toolkit
- Open Database Connectivity (ODBC) SDK 2.0
- OLE 2.01 SDK
- Schedule+ Libraries Version 1.0a
- Simple MAPI SDK
- SNA Server 2.1 SDK
- Video for Windows 1.1a Development Kit, Run-Time Extension, and samples
- Windows for Workgroups SDK, Network Device Development Kit (NDDK), and Remote Access Service API (RASAPI) kit
- Windows Help Compiler 3.10.505
- Windows 3.1 SDK and DDK
- Windows 3.1 DDK (Chinese Extension, Japanese Extension, Korean)
- Windows 3.1 SDK (Arabic Supplement, Chinese Extension, Hangeul, Hebrew Supplement, Japanese, Thai)
- Windows 3.1 Driver Library
- Windows NT Driver Library
- Windows NT 3.5 DDK for Intel, MIPS, and Digital Alpha AXP (U.S.)
- Windows Telephony API (TAPI) 1.0 SDK
- WinG SDK
- Win32 SDK 3.5 for Intel, MIPS, Digital Alpha AXP (U.S. and Japanese Beta 1)

The Developer Network News

The *Developer Network News*, our bimonthly newspaper, delivers up-to-the-minute information about Microsoft's systems strategy and development products. Recent issues have delivered detailed news stories on OLE Custom Controls, Windows95 (Windows "Chicago"), and Access 2.0—all topics on the cutting edge of programming. In the *Developer Network News*, you'll find out about the evolution of the Windows operating system, new development products, updates to current products (and how to get them), programming tips, and key phone numbers for Microsoft development information, services, and support.

The Developer Network CompuServe Forum

The Developer Network forum on CompuServe (type **GO MSDN** at any ! prompt-) provides you with all the latest technical articles and sample cod that can be easily downloaded. In addition, you can send us feedback on the Developer Network using CompuServe's messaging capabilities. The Development Library includes WinCIM, an easy-to-use, Windows-based front-end application for accessing CompuServe forums. WinCIM simplifies logging on, viewing, and downloading information. This version of WinCIM was customized by the Developer Network to facilitate your access to all of Microsoft's developer services available on CompuServe.

How To Enroll

The Microsoft Developer Network Level 1 annual membership fee is $195 U.S. ($275 Canadian) plus shipping and tax. The Level 2 annual membership fee is $495 U.S. ($695 Canadian) plus shipping and tax. If you are already a member of the Developer Network Level 1, you can upgrade to Level 2 for $395 U.S. ($555 Canadian). Upgrading ends your Level 1 membership and starts a one-year Level 2 membership, so you'll receive four quarterly updates to the Development Platform and the Development Library.

To join in the U.S. or Canada, call (800) 759-5474 (24 hours a day, seven days a week). Outside North America, please call (303) 684-0914 or contact your local Microsoft subsidiary directly.

Licensing Options

Level 1 membership includes a single-user license for the Development Library. In the U.S. and Canada, you can purchase licenses to share a single CD over a network for $40 ($55 Canadian) per additional user. Each additional license allows one designated user to install the Development Library Viewer software on a single workstation to access the CD's contents.

For large workgroups, Level 1 memberships with concurrent-user licenses are available in two configurations: a five-user license is $595 U.S. ($835 Canadian), and a 25-user license is $2495 U.S. ($3495 Canadian). Concurrent-user licenses permit the members of a large group to install the Development Library Viewer software on their workstations, but allow no more than five (or 25) users to run the application at a given time. The number of developers supported by a concurrent-user license depends primarily on their usage patterns and network performance. Developers who expect to make heavy use of the Development Library should consider individual memberships. Call (800) 759-5474 for more information on licensing.

Level 2 membership includes a single-user license for both the Development Library and the Development Platform. Additional licenses are not available for Level 2 memberships.

Microsoft Certified Professional Program

The Microsoft Certified Professional program offers you an excellent way to show employers and clients that you have proven knowledge and skills to help them build, implement, and support effective solutions, and that you have the validated expertise to help them get the most out of their technology investment. As a Microsoft Certified Professional, you are recognized and promoted by Microsoft as an expert with the technical skills and knowledge to implement and support solutions with Microsoft products.

To become a Microsoft Certified Professional, you must pass a series of rigorous standardized certification exams. Once you become a Microsoft Certified Professional, you will receive benefits including access to technical information, use of the Microsoft Certified Professional logo, and special invitations to Microsoft conferences and technical events.

For more information on Microsoft's Certified Professional Program, call Microsoft at (800) 636-7544 in the United States and Canada. In other countries, contact your local Microsoft office. Ask for the Microsoft Education and Certification Roadmap, an online guide to Microsoft Education and Certification. Or, see E&CMAP.ZIP from Library 5 of the Solution Provider forum on CompuServe (by typing **GO MSEDCERT** at any ! prompt).

Microsoft Official Curriculum

Microsoft Official Curriculum courses provide computer professionals with the knowledge required to expertly install and support Microsoft solutions. Courses are developed straight from the source—by the Microsoft product and technical support groups. They include in-depth, accurate information and hands-on labs based on real-world experience. Microsoft Official Curriculum courses are designed to help you prepare effectively for Microsoft Certified Professional exams.

Microsoft Official Curriculum is developed in two forms:

- *Instructor-led classes* are delivered by Microsoft Certified Trainers at Microsoft Solution Provider Authorized Technical Education Centers.

  As members of the Solution Provider program, the Authorized Technical Education Centers are independent businesses that have been evaluated as qualified to deliver Microsoft Official Curriculum.

- *Self-paced curriculum materials* that enable you to learn at your convenience are developed by Microsoft. Hands-on lab exercises are included.

Microsoft has developed instructor-led training for the Microsoft Windows NT version 3.5 product family. They include the following:

Support Fundamentals for Microsoft Windows NT 3.5	3-day course
Supporting Microsoft Windows NT Workstation 3.5	2-day course
Supporting Microsoft Windows NT Server 3.5	5-day course

For full course descriptions and a referral to a Microsoft Solution Provider Authorized Technical Education Center, call (800) SOLPROV in the United States and Canada. In other countries, contact your local Microsoft office. Ask for the Microsoft Education and Certification Roadmap, an online guide to Microsoft Education and Certification. Or, see E&CMAP.ZIP from Library 5 of the Solution Provider forum on CompuServe (by typing **GO MSEDCERT** at any ! prompt).

Microsoft Consulting Services

Microsoft Consulting Services (MCS) consultants are system architects with experience and expertise in Microsoft technology, methodologies, and tools, chartered to help organizations capitalize on the benefits of the most powerful platform for client-server computing—the Microsoft Windows NT Server network operating system. MCS consultants focus on transferring knowledge and skills to corporations, government organizations, and third-party Microsoft Solution Providers worldwide. MCS, in conjunction with third-party solution providers, offers organizations a number of services customized to their unique information technology environment, including planning, design, development, integration, and implementation. For more information about Microsoft Consulting Services, in the United States, call (800) 426-9400. In Canada, call (800) 563-9048.

Other Microsoft Press Books

Choose from a diverse range of timely books on both technical and nontechnical topics for users of Microsoft Windows NT at every level. Titles include *Inside Windows NT*, *MS® Windows NT Workstation Step by Step*, *Running Windows NT*, and *Advanced Win32® Programming*. Microsoft Press books are available wherever high-quality computer books are sold or direct from Microsoft Press. To order, in the United States, call (800) MSPRESS. In Canada, call (800) 667-1115. Microsoft Press books can also be ordered through CompuServe (by typing **GO MSP** at any ! prompt).

APPENDIX B

Windows NT User Rights

This appendix describes the advanced user rights defined by Windows NT. The descriptions shown in the Policy column appear in the User Rights Policy dialog box of User Manager. The description column also identifies which users are granted this user right by default.

User Right	Policy	Description
SeTcbPrivilege	Act as part of the operating system	The user can use to perform as a secure, trusted part of the operating system. Some subsystems are granted this privilege. Granted by default: None
SeChangeNotifyPrivilege	Bypass traverse checking	The user can traverse directory trees. Deny access to users using POSIX applications. Granted by default: Everyone
SeCreatePagefilePrivilege	Create a pagefile	The user can create a page file (not available in this version of Windows NT). Security is determined by a users access to the **..\CurrentControlSet\ Control\Session Management** key. Granted by default: None
SeCreateTokenPrivilege	Create a token object	Required to create access tokens. Only the Local Security Authority can do this. Granted by default: None
SeCreatePermanentPrivilege	Create permanent shared objects	Required to create special permanent objects, such as \\Device, which are used within Windows NT. Granted by default: None
SeDebugPrivilege	Debug programs	The user can debug various low-level objects such as threads. Granted by default: Administrators

User Right *(continued)*	Policy *(continued)*	Description *(continued)*
SeAuditPrivilege	Generate security audits	Required to generate security audit log entries. Granted by default: None
SeIncreaseQuotaPrivilege	Increase quotas	Required to increase object quotas (not available in this version of Windows NT). Granted by default: None
SeIncreaseBasePriorityPrivilege	Increase scheduling priority	The user can boost the priority of a process. Granted by default: Administrators and Power Users
SeLoadDriverPrivilege	Load and unload device drivers	The user can load an unload device drivers. Granted by default: Administrators
SeLockMemoryPrivilege	Lock pages in memory	The user can lock pages in memory so they cannot be paged out to a backing store such as PAGEFILE.SYS. As physical memory is a limited resource, locking pages can lead to greater disk thrashing as essentially the amount of physical pages available to other applications is reduced. Granted by default: None
No Name	Log on as a batch job	The user can log on using a batch queue facility (not available in this version of Windows NT). Granted by default: None
No Name	Log on as a service	The user can perform security services. Granted by default: None
SeSystemEnvironmentPrivilege	Modify Firmware environment variables	The user can modify system environment variables (not user environment variables). Granted by default: Administrators
SeProfileSingleProcessPrivilege	Profile single process	The user can use the profiling (performance sampling) capabilities of Windows NT on a process. Granted by default: Administrators and Power Users
SeSystemProfilePrivilege	Profile system performance	The user can use the profiling capabilities of Windows NT on the system. (This can slow the system down.) Granted by default: Administrators
SeAssignPrimaryTokenPrivilege	Replace a process level token	Required to modify a process's security access token. This is a powerful privilege used only by the system. Granted by default: None

APPENDIX C

International Considerations

This appendix includes information about using Windows NT international features, including code pages and local keyboards.

Specifying International Preferences

Users can specify preferences related to the user's country and language. This list of preferences is known as the *locale* for that user.

You can specify these preferences by double-clicking the International icon in Control Panel. You can specify your preference for the following:

Country	List separator
Language	Date and time formats
Keyboard layout	Number and currency formats
Measurement	

When you change the setting for COUNTRY, you may notice that some of the other settings change automatically. For example, the Currency Format is changed to reflect the currency used in the country you have chosen, and the date format changes to conform to the language and conventions of that country. When you change the setting for Language, code pages and fonts may change (certain letters and marks are used in some languages but not in others). Generally, if you set both Country and Language, you will have the entire set of international settings that you need.

Note   The Country and Language settings determine how alphabetical lists will be sorted. For example, in English D is followed by E. In Icelandic, an eth (ð) comes between D and E. Spanish CH sorts as a unique character between C and D; Danish AE is a unique letter after Z and before Ø. Swedish Å looks like A, but it is a unique letter that sorts after Z and before Ä (another unique letter in Swedish). In French, the ordering of basic diacritics is:

```
acute < grave < circumflex < diaeresis
```

For more information about specific fields in the International dialog box, see online Help.

Windows NT supports the following locales:

Table C.1   Code Pages

Language	Code page
Bulgarian	855, 866
Croation	852
Czech	852
Danish	850, 865
Dutch (Belgian)	850, 437
Dutch (Standard)	850, 437

Table C.1   Code Pages *(continued)*

Language	Code page
English (U.S.)	437, 850
English (Australian)	850, 437
English (British)	850, 437
English (Canadian)	863, 850
English (Irish)	850, 437
English (New Zealand)	850, 437
Finnish	850, 437
French (Belgian)	850, 437
French (Canadian)	850, 863
French (Standard)	850, 437
French (Swiss)	850, 437
German (Austrian)	850, 437
German (Standard)	850, 437
Greek	869
German (Swiss)	850, 437
Hungarian	852
Icelandic	850, 861
Italian (Standard)	850, 437
Italian (Swiss)	850, 437
Norwegian (Bokmal)	850, 865
Norwegian (Nynorsk)	850, 865
Polish	852
Portuguese (Brazilian)	850, 860
Portuguese (Standard)	850, 860
Romanian	852
Russian	866, 855
Slovak	852
Slovenian	852
Spanish (Mexican)	850, 437
Spanish (modern sort)	850, 437
Spanish (traditional sort)	850, 437
Swedish	850, 865
Turkish	857, 852

Code Pages and Unicode

A *code page* is an ordering or encoding of a standard set of characters within a specific locale. This encoding provides a consistent way for computer devices to exchange and process data. Each code page includes a common set of core characters (the first 128 characters of the code page). Windows NT supports several code pages, including ANSI and OEM code pages. ANSI code pages are supported for Windows 3.1 compatibility; OEM code pages are supported for MS-DOS and OS/2 compatibility. Other code pages are available, based on the installed locale, for use in data translation. These include secondary OEM code pages, MAC code pages, and EBCDIC code pages.

The following table shows the various code pages supported in Windows NT.

Table C.2   Windows NT Code Pages

Code page name	Number	Type
Windows 3.1 Eastern European	1250	ANSI
Windows 3.1 Cyrillic	1251	ANSI
Windows 3.1 US (ANSI)	1252	ANSI
Windows 3.1 Greek	1253	ANSI
Windows 3.1 Turkish	1254	ANSI
MS-DOS U.S.	437	OEM
MS-DOS Greek	737	OEM
MS-DOS Multilingual (Latin I)	850	OEM
MS-DOS Slavic (Latin II)	852	OEM
IBM Cyrillic (primarily Russian)	855	OEM
IBM Turkish	857	OEM
MS-DOS Portuguese	860	OEM
MS-DOS Icelandic	861	OEM
MS-DOS Canadian-French	863	OEM
MS-DOS Nordic	865	OEM
MS-DOS Russian (former USSR)	866	OEM

Table C.2   Windows NT Code Pages *(continued)*

Code page name	Number	Type
IBM Modern Greek	869	OEM
Macintosh Roman	10000	
Macintosh Greek I	10006	
Macintosh Cyrillic	10007	
Macintosh Latin II	10029	
Macintosh Icelandic	10079	
Macintosh Turkish	10081	
EBCDIC	037	
EBCDIC "500V1"	500	
EBCDIC	1026	
EBCDIC	875	

Windows NT uses Unicode (the BMP region of ISO specification 10646) for all internal text processing. *Unicode* is a 16-bit, fixed-width character encoding standard, with sufficient encoding space to accommodate most of the world's modern characters. All character sets and code pages supported by Windows NT can be mapped to Unicode.

By using Unicode-enabled applications, users can benefit from multilingual processing and a rich selection of characters.

For more information, see *The Unicode Standard* (version 1.0); The Unicode Consortium, Addison-Wesley Publishing Company, Inc.; 1991

Note   Most code pages have a core set of characters in common (ASCII characters–the first 128 characters in the code page). In addition, each code page includes some unique "extended" characters not available on other code pages. Be sure not to use these extended characters in server names, computer names, and share names. Also, don't use these extended characters with applications used across the network. The FAT and HPFS file systems, which use the OEM code page, must translate the characters they don't recognize in the filename to a best-fit character, no character, or some non-recognized character.

Common Code Pages

Two of the most commonly-used code pages are shown on the following pages.

#		#		#		#		#		#		#		#	
0		32		64	@	96	`	128	Ç	160	á	192	└	224	α
1	☺	33	!	65	A	97	a	129	ü	161	í	193	┴	225	ß
2	☻	34	"	66	B	98	b	130	é	162	ó	194	┬	226	Γ
3	♥	35	#	67	C	99	c	131	â	163	ú	195	├	227	π
4	♦	36	$	68	D	100	d	132	ä	164	ñ	196	─	228	Σ
5	♣	37	%	69	E	101	e	133	à	165	Ñ	197	┼	229	σ
6	♠	38	&	70	F	102	f	134	å	166	ª	198	╞	230	µ
7	•	39	'	71	G	103	g	135	ç	167	º	199	╟	231	τ
8	◘	40	(	72	H	104	h	136	ê	168	¿	200	╚	232	Φ
9	○	41	)	73	I	105	i	137	ë	169	⌐	201	╔	233	Θ
10	◙	42	*	74	J	106	j	138	è	170	¬	202	╩	234	Ω
11	♂	43	+	75	K	107	k	139	ï	171	½	203	╦	235	δ
12	♀	44	,	76	L	108	l	140	î	172	¼	204	╠	236	∞
13	♪	45	-	77	M	109	m	141	ì	173	¡	205	═	237	φ
14	♫	46	.	78	N	110	n	142	Ä	174	«	206	╬	238	ε
15	☼	47	/	79	O	111	o	143	Å	175	»	207	╧	239	∩
16	►	48	0	80	P	112	p	144	É	176	░	208	╨	240	≡
17	◄	49	1	81	Q	113	q	145	æ	177	▒	209	╤	241	±
18	↕	50	2	82	R	114	r	146	Æ	178	▓	210	╥	242	≥
19	‼	51	3	83	S	115	s	147	ô	179	│	211	╙	243	≤
20	¶	52	4	84	T	116	t	148	ö	180	┤	212	╘	244	⌠
21	§	53	5	85	U	117	u	149	ò	181	╡	213	╒	245	⌡
22	▬	54	6	86	V	118	v	150	û	182	╢	214	╓	246	÷
23	↨	55	7	87	W	119	w	151	ù	183	╖	215	╫	247	≈
24	↑	56	8	88	X	120	x	152	ÿ	184	╕	216	╪	248	°
25	↓	57	9	89	Y	121	y	153	Ö	185	╣	217	┘	249	·
26	→	58	:	90	Z	122	z	154	Ü	186	║	218	┌	250	·
27	←	59	;	91	[	123	{	155	¢	187	╗	219	█	251	√
28	∟	60	<	92	\	124			156	£	188	╝	220	▄	252	ⁿ
29	↔	61	=	93	]	125	}	157	¥	189	╜	221	▌	253	²
30	▲	62	>	94	^	126	~	158	₧	190	╛	222	▐	254	■
31	▼	63	?	95	_	127	⌂	159	ƒ	191	┐	223	▀	255	

437　United States

#		#		#		#		#		#		#		#	
0		32		64	@	96	`	128	Ç	160	á	192	└	224	Ó
1	☺	33	!	65	A	97	a	129	ü	161	í	193	┴	225	ß
2	☻	34	"	66	B	98	b	130	é	162	ó	194	┬	226	Ô
3	♥	35	#	67	C	99	c	131	â	163	ú	195	├	227	Ò
4	♦	36	$	68	D	100	d	132	ä	164	ñ	196	─	228	õ
5	♣	37	%	69	E	101	e	133	à	165	Ñ	197	┼	229	Õ
6	♠	38	&	70	F	102	f	134	å	166	ª	198	ã	230	µ
7	•	39	'	71	G	103	g	135	ç	167	º	199	Ã	231	þ
8	◘	40	(	72	H	104	h	136	ê	168	¿	200	╚	232	Þ
9	◊	41	)	73	I	105	i	137	ë	169	®	201	╔	233	Ú
10	◙	42	*	74	J	106	j	138	è	170	¬	202	╩	234	Û
11	♂	43	+	75	K	107	k	139	ï	171	½	203	╦	235	Ù
12	♀	44	,	76	L	108	l	140	î	172	¼	204	╠	236	ý
13	♪	45	-	77	M	109	m	141	ì	173	¡	205	═	237	Ý
14	♫	46	.	78	N	110	n	142	Ä	174	«	206	╬	238	¯
15	☼	47	/	79	O	111	o	143	Å	175	»	207	¤	239	´
16	►	48	0	80	P	112	p	144	É	176	░	208	ð	240	
17	◄	49	1	81	Q	113	q	145	æ	177	▒	209	Ð	241	±
18	↕	50	2	82	R	114	r	146	Æ	178	▓	210	Ê	242	‗
19	‼	51	3	83	S	115	s	147	ô	179	│	211	Ë	243	¾
20	¶	52	4	84	T	116	t	148	ö	180	┤	212	È	244	¶
21	§	53	5	85	U	117	u	149	ò	181	Á	213	ı	245	§
22	▬	54	6	86	V	118	v	150	û	182	Â	214	Í	246	÷
23	↨	55	7	87	W	119	w	151	ù	183	À	215	Î	247	¸
24	↑	56	8	88	X	120	x	152	ÿ	184	©	216	Ï	248	°
25	↓	57	9	89	Y	121	y	153	Ö	185	╣	217	┘	249	¨
26	→	58	:	90	Z	122	z	154	Ü	186	║	218	┌	250	·
27	←	59	;	91	[	123	{	155	ø	187	╗	219	█	251	¹
28	∟	60	<	92	\	124	¦	156	£	188	╝	220	▄	252	³
29	↔	61	=	93	]	125	}	157	Ø	189	¢	221	¦	253	²
30	▲	62	>	94	^	126	~	158	×	190	¥	222	Ì	254	■
31	▼	63	?	95	_	127	⌂	159	ƒ	191	┐	223	▀	255	

850   Multilingual (Latin I)

MS-DOS National Language Support Information

Windows NT supports the following MS-DOS 5.0 National Language Support (NLS) commands. (Note that printer device code page commands are not supported.)

Table C.3   MS-DOS 5.0 National Language Support Commands

Command	Used to
chcp	Show or change the code page used by the system. If you change the code page with the **chcp** command, it is recommended that you use the Lucida Console font as the console font to avoid incorrect glyphs on the screen.
mode	Display standard information about the active code pages in the system.
keyb	Specify the keyboard layout used.

Windows NT maintains its configuration information in the Registry. However, when the CONFIG.SYS file changes, the system automatically changes entries in the Registry, which take effect when the system is restarted. These commands in the CONFIG.SYS file are related to NLS. Changes to them will cause changes in the Windows NT Registry:

- **install=c:\dos\keyb.com** *xx,nnn,***filename**
- **device=c:\dos\display.sys**...
- **device=c:\dos\printer.sys**...
- **country=***xxx,***nnn,filename**
- **install=c:\dos\nlsfunc.exe**

NLS Information in the OS/2 Subsystem

The OS/2 subsystem typically inherits the NLS parameters (such as language, country code, and code page) from the parent process. If any of the NLS commands from OS/2 CONFIG.SYS exist, these values will supersede the Windows NT values.

▶ **To create or edit an OS/2 version 1.0 CONFIG.SYS file**

1. Use an OS/2 editor to make any changes to the file.

2. Save the file.

3. Exit the editor program. The edits you make cause the Registry to be automatically updated.

The following OS/2 NLS commands are supported by Windows NT:

Table C.4   OS/2 NLS Commands

Command	Used to
codepage	Specify one or two code pages that the OS/2 subsystem has set up for use as its primary and secondary code pages.
country	Specify the country code.
devinfo	Identify the keyboard layout selection. This defines the keyboard layout table for translating keystrokes into characters encoded according to a code page based on ASCII.

If no COUNTRY entry is found in the Registry, the OS/2 subsystem takes the current locale country code for each OS/2 application, inherited from the application's parent process.

If the Registry includes a COUNTRY entry but no CODEPAGE entry, the subsystem uses the default code page for the current country. If neither line is present, the subsystem uses the Windows NT primary OEM code page.

If no DEVINFO entry is found, the subsystem uses the default keyboard layout for the country.

APPENDIX D

Hardware Compatibility List

The following computers and peripherals have been tested and have passed compatibility testing with Windows NT 3.5 as of October, 1994. Some computers may be sold with peripherals that are not yet supported by the Windows NT operating system, or that require a device driver supplied by the manufacturer. We have not tested every computer and/or device in all possible configurations. Please refer to the SETUP.TXT file on the install media for additional compatibility information when installing Windows NT 3.5.

Attached as an addendum, is the September 1994 update of the Windows NT 3.1 x86 Architecture Uniprocessor Computers Hardware Compatibility List. All computer systems listed on the addendum are expected to run with the Windows NT 3.5 Product. If you encounter problems while running Windows NT 3.5, please file a bug report by filling out 'PROBREP.TXT' located in the \i386 directory on Windows NT 3.5 CD-ROM or floppy disk #2 of the Windows NT 3.5 installation disks and submit it as instructed in PROBREP.TXT.

Items listed with footnote number [1] require one of the device drivers available in the \DRVLIB directory on the Windows NT 3.5 CD-ROM.

Items listed with footnote number[2] are supported with device drivers available in the Windows NT Driver Library. Please see the section at the end of this document for information on accessing this library.

Updates to these lists will appear in Library 1 of the WINNT (GO WINNT) forum or Library 17 of the MSWIN32 forum (GO MSWIN32) on CompuServe® Information Services.

x86 Architecture Uniprocessor Computers

The following systems have been tested.

Absolute Computer 486/66 EISA CD SERVER
ACD OPTIMA 486 DX 33 VL
ACD Optima VLB 486SX-33
ACER 17000 SMP AA17853N
ACER AcerAltos 6031 (486DX2-66, ID3P)
ACER AcerAltos 6031 (486DX2-66, IDAB)
ACER AcerAltos 6031 (Pentium™ / 60, ID3P)
ACER AcerAltos 6031 (Pentium / 60, IDAB)

ACER AcerAltos 6031 (Pentium / 90, ID3P)
ACER AcerAltos 6031 (Pentium / 90, IDAB)
ACER AcerAltos 700/i® (486DX2-66, ID3P)
ACER AcerAltos 700/i (DX2-66, IDAB)
ACER AcerAltos 700/i (Pentium / 60, ID3P)
ACER AcerAltos 700/i (Pentium / 60, IDAB)
ACER AcerAltos 700/i (Pentium / 90, ID3P)
ACER AcerAltos 700/i (Pentium / 90, IDAB)
ACER AcerAltos 7000 (DX2-66)

ACER AcerAltos 7000 (Pentium 60)
ACER AcerAltos 7000 (Pentium 90)
ACER AcerAltos 7000/F590TU
ACER AcerAltos 7000/FT00TU
ACER AcerAltos 7000/FT66TU
ACER AcerAltos 800 Model AA868C
ACER AcerAltos 900 (486DX2-66, ID3P)
ACER AcerAltos 900 (486DX2-66, IDAB)
ACER AcerAltos 900 (Pentium / 60, ID3P)

ACER AcerAltos 900
(Pentium / 60, IDAB)
ACER AcerAltos 900
(Pentium / 90, ID3P)
ACER AcerAltos 900
(Pentium / 90, IDAB)
ACER AcerFrame 1000
(Model 1750)
ACER AcerMate 433 sp
(486SX-33)
ACER AcerMate 466 dp
(486DX2-66)
ACER AcerPower
400de/PT100E
ACER AcerPower 433 sp
(486SX-33)
ACER AcerPower 466 dp
(486DX2-66)
ACER AcerPower 466de
(DX2-66)
ACER AcerPower 486/33
ACER AcerPower 486vp
(DX2/66)
ACER AcerPower 486vp
(DX4/100)
ACER AcerPower 500h
(Pentium 100, Minitower)
ACER AcerPower 500p
(Pentium / 100)
ACER AcerPower 560e
(Pentium 60)
ACER AcerPower 560p
(Pentium 60)
ACER AcerPower
560pt/P560M
ACER AcerPower
560tu/P560TU
ACER AcerPower 566e
(Pentium 66)
ACER AcerPower 566p
(Pentium 66)
ACER AcerPower
566pt/P560M
ACER AcerPower
566tu/P560TU
ACER AcerPower 575h
(Pentium 75, Minitower)
ACER AcerPower 575p
(Pentium / 75)
ACER AcerPower 590E/P590E
ACER AcerPower 590h
(Pentium 90, Minitower)
ACER AcerPower 590p
(Pentium / 90)
ACER AcerPower 9000 Series
Model 9813N

ACER AcerPower 9000/P560E
ACER AcerPower 9000/P566E
ACER AcerPower 9000/P590E
ACER AcerPower
9000/PT100E
ACER AcerPower 9000/PT66E
ACMA P66
ACMA P90
Actech ACTion 486-33 PCI
Actech ACTion 486DX-33
GREEN VLB
Actech ACTion 486DX-50
GREEN VLB
Actech ACTion 486DX-50 PCI
Actech ACTion 486DX/2-66
GREEN VLB
Actech ACTion 486DX/2-66
PCI
Actech ACTion 486DX/4-100
GREEN VLB
Actech ACTion EISA
486DX-50
Actech ACTion EISA
486DX2-66
Actech ACTion P60
Pentium PCI
Actech ACTion Systems
P90 Pentium
ADD-X ZEPHYR
ADS INTEGRATION SERIES
486 VESA®
ADS PRO 586 EV PENTIUM
ADS PRO 586 PENTIUM
ADS PRO SERIES 486 VESA
ADS PRO SERIES 590
Advance Interface
EXPRESS^SM MICRO
PENTIUM 66
Advance Interface EXPRESS
MICRO PENTIUM 90
Alfa DELTACOM
PCI/VLB 486
ALR® BusinessVEISA 4/33D
ALR Classic Xe (1p)
ALR Evolution IV 4/33s
ALR Evolution IV 4/66d
ALR Evolution IV 4E/33s
ALR Evolution IV 4E/66d
ALR Evolution IV ST 4/33s
ALR Evolution IV ST 4/66d
ALR Evolution IV ST 4/DX4
ALR Evolution V ST/60 VL
ALR Evolution V ST/66 PCI
ALR Evolution V ST/66 VL
ALR Evolution V ST/90
ALR Evolution V STe

ALR Evolution V STP/60
ALR Evolution V X/66 PCI
ALR Evolution V X/90
ALR Evolution V-Q/60
ALR Evolution V-Q/66
ALR Evolution V/60
ALR Evolution V/66
ALR Evolution VQ-90
ALR Evolution X 4/33s
ALR Evolution X 4/66d
ALR Evolution X 4/DX4
ALR Flyer SD32 4/66d
ALR POWERPRO SMP 4/33
ALR POWERPRO/MC
SMP 4/50D
ALR PROVEISA LT 4/66d
ALR PROVEISA LT 4/DX4
ALR PROVEISA SMP 4/66D
ALR Revolution MP P/60
ALR Revolution MP P/66
ALR Revolution MP P/90 (1p)
ALR Revolution Q-SMP
P/100 (1p)
ALR Revolution Q-SMP
P/90 (1p)
Amax Engineering P6
PowerStation™
Amax Engineering P9
PowerStation
Ambra 486DX/50
Ambra D466E/VL
Ambra DP60/PCI
Ambra DP60E/VL ³
Ambra DP66E/VL
Ambra TP60E/VL ³
American Multisystems
InfoGOLD P60NT
AMI® ATLAS PCI
AMI ATLAS VIP
AMI Enterprise III
AMI Enterprise IV
AMI Excalibur PCI
AMI Excalibur PCI/EISA
AMI Excalibur VLB
AMI Super Voyager PCI
AMI Super Voyager VLB II
AMI Super Voyager VLB III
AmPAQ DaVinci PCI466S
AmPAQ DaVinci Pentium
PCI60S
AmPAQ DaVinci VLB433D
AmPAQ DaVinci VLB466D
AOX mcmaster 486250
Apricot® FT//ex Pentium 90
Apricot FTe 486DX2/66
Apricot LS-Pro 486DX4/100

Apricot XEN-PC 560
Apricot XEN-PC 590
Area Electronics AES-
  560GPIP Pentium 60
  ISA/PCI
Area Electronics AES-590DP,
  Pentium 90 EISA/PCI
Area Electronics AES-
  590GPIP Pentium 90
  ISA/PCI
Ares 486-33 VLB
Ariel 486DX2-66EVS
Asem PROSERVER 5/60
ASPECT 486DX-33 PCI
ASPECT 486DX-33 VL
ASPECT 486DX-40 VL
ASPECT 486DX4-100 VL
ASPECT 486SX-33 PCI
ASPECT PENTIUM 60 PCI
ASPECT PENTIUM 60
  PCI/EISA
Aspect SMART WEAPONS
  486 DX2-66 VL
Aspect SMART WEAPONS
  486DX2 PCI 66
Aspect SMART WEAPONS
  486DX2 PCI/EISA 66
Aspect SMART WEAPONS
  486SX VL 33
Aspect SMART WEAPONS
  PENTIUM PCI 66
Aspect SMART WEAPONS
  PENTIUM PCI/VL90
AST® Bravo LC 4/100t [4]
AST Manhattan V Series
  5090 (1p)
AST Premium II 386/33
  Model 213V
AST Premium II 486/33
AST Premium SE 4/33
  Model 333
AST Premmia 4/66d [5]
AT&T® 3372
AT&T 3372-C
AT&T 3374
AT&T 3406
AT&T 3416
AT&T Globalyst 510
  (3228) 486 ISA
AT&T Globalyst 515
  (3232) 486 ISA
AT&T Globalyst 550
  (3246) 486 ISA/PCI
AT&T Globalyst 575
  (3347) 486 ISA/PCI

AT&T Globalyst 590
  (3346) Pentium ISA/PCI
AT&T Globalyst 600
  (3356) Pentium ISA/PCI
Athena SERVER
  486DX2/66 HQ
Austin 486/50 EISA Tower
  PATRIOT
Austin Business Audio DX4
  100 Color Notebook
Austin Business Audio DX4
  100 TFT Notebook
Austin Business Audio DX4 75
  Color Notebook
Austin Business Audio DX4 75
  TFT Notebook
Axik Ace Power 486DX2-
  66VG2/Green
BAJTEX S.A.
  i486DX2/66MHz
BB Data AB Grizzly 266
  Alfredo
BB Data AB Grizzly P66
  Batman
BB Data AB Grizzly S33
  Alfredo
Beyond 2000 Systems
  STRATUS NT 90
Black Cat 486/66 VL
BROTHER® BCR4486DL
BROTHER BCR4486DX2
BROTHER BCR4486DX2/PCI
BROTHER BCR4585
BROTHER BCR4586/PCI
BROTHER BCR5486DX2
BROTHER BCR5486DX2/PCI
BROTHER BCR5585
BROTHER BCR5586/PCI
BROTHER BCR7486DX2
BROTHER BCR7586/PCI
BROTHER BCR8486DX2
BROTHER BCR8486DX2/PCI
BROTHER BCR8585
BROTHER BCR8586/PCI
Burgoyne Rocket 60
C&S Computer AMICS EISA
  VLB IV (486DX2-66)
C&S Computer AMICS P5
  Pentium VLB 60
C&S Computer AMICS
  Pentium EISA PCI 60
Caliber SMART WEAPONS
  486 DX2-66 VL
Caliber SMART WEAPONS
  486DX-33 PCI

Caliber SMART WEAPONS
  486DX-33 VL
Caliber SMART WEAPONS
  486DX-40 VL
Caliber SMART WEAPONS
  486DX2 PCI 66
Caliber SMART WEAPONS
  486DX4-100 ISA/VESA
Caliber SMART WEAPONS
  486SX VL 33
Caliber SMART WEAPONS
  486SX-33 PCI
Caliber SMART WEAPONS
  PENTIUM 60 PCI
Caliber SMART WEAPONS
  PENTIUM 60 PCI/EISA
Caliber SMART WEAPONS
  PENTIUM PCI 66
Caliber SMART WEAPONS
  PENTIUM PCI/EISA 66
Caliber SMART WEAPONS
  PENTIUM PCI/VL90
Cascade VLB-66
Cascade-PCI-Pentium-60
CELEM 486DX/33 C (ISA)
CELEM 486DX/33 VL
  (VESA)
CELEM 486DX2/66 DC
  (EISA+VESA)
CELEM 586/60 (PCI+ISA)
CELEM 586/66 (PCI+EISA)
CELEM 586/90 (PCI+EISA)
CELEM DX4/100 (VL+ISA)
CENSUS 4D266AGVL DT
  (incl. MT, IT, FT Models)
CENSUS 4D266DGVL DT
  (incl. MT, IT, FT Models)
CENSUS 4D4100AGVL DT
  (incl. MT, IT, FT Models)
CENSUS P90AGPCI DT (incl.
  MT, IT, FT Models)
Centis PowerTech model
  P60-G3
Centis Profi model 466-G5
Centis ProfiLite 466-G3
Cincinnati Milicron Acramatic
  2100 CNC
Cinet ET-100
Cinet FSE-100
Cinet HI-100
Cinet LS-100
Cinet MP-100
Cinet PPI-100
Cinet VL-100
Comark Pentium-60/VL
COMPAQ Deskpro® 386/25e

COMPAQ Deskpro 386/33®
COMPAQ® Deskpro
   386™/33L
COMPAQ Deskpro® 4/66i
COMPAQ Deskpro 486/33i
COMPAQ Deskpro 486/33L
COMPAQ Deskpro 486/33M
COMPAQ Deskpro 66M
COMPAQ Deskpro XL 466
COMPAQ Deskpro XL 566
COMPAQ LTE®
   ELITE 4/50CX
COMPAQ LTE Lite 4/25C
COMPAQ Presario 660
COMPAQ Presario CDS 633
COMPAQ ProLiant 1000
   486DX2/66
COMPAQ ProLiant 1000
   Model 5/60
COMPAQ ProLiant 1000R
   Model 486DX2/66
COMPAQ ProLinea 3/25s
COMPAQ ProLinea 4/50
COMPAQ ProLinea 4/66
COMPAQ ProLinea MT 4/66
COMPAQ ProSignia
   486DX/33
COMPAQ ProSignia
   486DX2/66
COMPAQ ProSignia 5/60
COMPAQ ProSignia VS
   486DX/33
COMPAQ ProSignia VS
   486DX2/66
COMPAQ ProSignia VS
   486SX/33
COMPAQ Systempro®/LT
   486DX2/50
COMPAQ Systempro/LT™
   486DX2/66
COMPAQ Systempro®/LT
   486DX33
COMPAQ Systempro/LT
   486SX/25
CompuAdd® 466/DX2
CompuAdd 466E DX2
CompuAdd 486-33DLC
COMPUCON 486DX/50 EV
COMPUCON 486DX2/66 EV
COMPUCON
   486DX2/66 GX4
COMPUCON 486DX2/66VG
COMPUCON 486DX33 EV
COMPUCON 486DX33 P
COMPUCON 486DX33 VG
COMPUCON 486DX4/100VG

COMPUCON 486DX50 VG
COMPUCON 486SX/33 P
COMPUCON 486SX25 EV
COMPUCON 486SX25 P
COMPUCON 486SX25 VG
COMPUCON 486SX33 EV
COMPUCON 486SX33 VG
COMPUCON DX266P
COMPUCON DX266VB
COMPUCON DX33G
COMPUCON PCI/IP-60
COMPUCON Pentium-60 P
COMPUCON Pentium-60 PE
COMPUCON Pentium-66 P
COMPUCON Pentium-66 PE
COMPUCON Pentium-90 PE
Computer Resources
   PRECISION 486/40 VL
Computer Resources
   PRECISION PENTIUM
Computer Sales Prof.
   486DX2/66
Computer Systems Resouces
   486DX-50 16M WS
Computer Systems Resources
   486DX2-66 16M WS
Computrade Express
   486-50/VLB
Computrend PREMIO
   486DX2-66
Computrend PREMIO Pentium
Computrend PREMIO Pentium
   PCI 90
Comtrade EISA GigaByte
   Ultima 486DX2-66
Comtrade VESA/PCI WIN-
   Station P90
CSS Labs MaxFrame 2000-
   462OPTIVL
CSS Labs MaxFrame 3000-
   462OPTIVL
CSS Labs MaxSys 462MTEVL
   Minitower
CSS Labs MaxSys 462REVL
   Rackmount
CSS Labs MaxSys 462TEVL
   Tower
CSS Labs Preferred
   462GAVLESP (Inc. Full,
   Mid and Tower models)
CSS Labs Preferred
   462MGEVLESP (Inc. Full,
   Mid and Tower Models)
CTM Fontek 486DX-33 VL
CTM Fontek 486DX2-50 VL
CTM Fontek 486DX2-66 VL

CTM Polaris 486DX-33 VESA
CTM Polaris 486DX2-50
   VESA
CTM Polaris 486DX2-66
   VESA
CTM Pronic 486DX-33 VESA
CTM Pronic 486DX2-50
   VESA
CTM Pronic 486DX2-66
   VESA
Cube 466 ATX Local Bus
Cybermax AMD486DX2-66
Cybermax P5/66
Cybermax P5/90
Daewoo VESA PENTIUM(60)
Daewoo Winpro 486 Vesa
   Green/2900G(DX2-50)
Daewoo Winpro 486DLC-40
Daewoo Winpro 486DX250
   Green Deskop
Daewoo Winpro 486DX250
   Vesa
Daewoo Winpro 486DX266
   Vesa Green System/2800
Dakota Computer PCI
   486DX4/100MHz
Danjen 486-50VL(Inc. Lunch
   Box, Mini, Mid,and Full
   Tower)
Data General® P60/TE2
   Pentium Tower
Data General P90/TE2
Data General P90MT
Data Stor 486-66DX2E
   Desktop/Tower
DATAFILEN PROFF
   486DX2-66
Debis Deskside 5/60
Debis Desktop 486DX2/66
DELL® 325 NC Notebook
DELL 433/DE
DELL 433/M
DELL 450/M
DELL 450/ME
DELL 450DE
DELL 4560/XE
DELL 466/ME
DELL 466/T
DELL 466DE
DELL Dimension 433SV
DELL Dimension XPS P60
DELL Dimension XPS P90
DELL OmniPlex 450
DELL OmniPlex 466
DELL OmniPlex 560
DELL OmniPlex 566

DELL OmniPlex 590
DELL PowerLine System 433E
DELL PowerLine
    System 433SE
DELL PowerLine System
    450DE/2 DGX
DELL PowerLine
    System 450SE
DELL PowerLine System
    486D/50
Delphi Comet 466NT
    model 400
Delta Micro Systems Gold
    Line 4D33V
DELTACOM EISA/VLB 486
DELTACOM Pentium PCI
DELTACOM Super Server
DELTACOM VL Bus 486
DFI CCV 486DX2-66
DFI D486CCI-33C
DFI D486CCI-40A
DFI D486ICP-66
DFI D486ICP-66 (with
    AMD486DX2/66)
DFI D486P-PRO-x50-AMD
DFI D486V-PRO
DFI DP5-Pro-66 Intel®
DFI DP5-PRO90
DFI DP586-PRO90
DFI E586IPE-60I
DFI G466EVA
DFI G466EVAx50I
DFI G486EVA-33I
DFI G486EVA-40AMD
DFI G486EVA-50AMD
DFI G486EVA-66AMD
DFI G486EVA/E-AIO-66I
DFI P486-PRO 486DX-33
Diamond DT 486DX Versa
    (AMD DX/40)
Diamond DT 486DX Versa
    (DX2/66)
Digital Equipment Corp.
    Celebris 4100
Digital Equipment Corp.
    Celebris 466
Digital Equipment Corp.
    Celebris 560
Digital Equipment Corp.
    Celebris 590
Digital Equipment Corp.
    Celebris FP 590
Digital Equipment Corp.
    DECpc 433dx DT
Digital Equipment Corp.
    DECpc 433dx MTE

Digital Equipment Corp.
    DECpc 433T
Digital Equipment Corp.
    DECpc 466d2 DT
Digital Equipment Corp.
    DECpc 466d2 MTE
Digital Equipment Corp.
    DECpc LPv+ 4100
Digital Equipment Corp.
    DECpc LPv+ 433dx
Digital Equipment Corp.
    DECpc LPv+ 433sx
Digital Equipment Corp.
    DECpc LPv+ 450d2
Digital Equipment Corp.
    DECpc LPv+ 466d2
Digital Equipment Corp.
    DECpc LPx 560
Digital Equipment Corp.
    DECpc LPx 566
Digital Equipment Corp.
    DECpc LPx+ 4100
Digital Equipment Corp.
    DECpc LPx+ 433dx
Digital Equipment Corp.
    DECpc LPx+ 433sx
Digital Equipment Corp.
    DECpc LPx+ 450d2
Digital Equipment Corp.
    DECpc LPx+ 450sx
Digital Equipment Corp.
    DECpc LPx+ 466d2
Digital Equipment Corp.
    DECpc MTE 4100
Digital Equipment Corp.
    DECpc XL 4100
Digital Equipment Corp.
    DECpc XL 433
Digital Equipment Corp.
    DECpc XL 466d2
Digital Equipment Corp.
    DECpc XL 560
Digital Equipment Corp.
    DECpc XL 566
Digital Equipment Corp.
    DECpc XL 590
Digital Equipment Corp.
    DECpc XL Server 590
Digital Equipment Corp.
    DECpc XL Server 4100
Digital Equipment Corp.
    DECpc XL Server 466d2
Digital Equipment Corp.
    DECpc XL Server 560
Digital Equipment Corp.
    DECpc XL Server 566

Digital Equipment Corp.
    DECstation® 425c
DTK FEAT39-D/M/T
Duracom 486/66DX2-CCV
Duracom DESKSAVER
    DX2/66
Dyna Micro GEMLIGHT
    VL486G/DX4
Dyna Micro SUPER
    P54VLPCI
Dynamic Decisions
    EXECUTIVE 486-33
    ISA/PCI
Dynamic Decisions
    EXECUTIVE 486-33
    VL/EISA
Dynamic Decisions
    EXECUTIVE 486-33
    VL/ISA
Dynamic Decisions
    EXECUTIVE 486-66
    DX2 PCI
Dynamic Decisions
    EXECUTIVE 486-66
    VL/EISA
Dynamic Decisions
    EXECUTIVE ISA-486-33
    SX GREEN VL
Dynamic Decisions
    EXECUTIVE ISA-486-
    50 SV2
Dynamic Decisions
    EXECUTIVE ISA-486-
    50 VL
Dynamic Decisions
    EXECUTIVE ISA-486-66
    DX2 GREEN VL
Dynamic Decisions
    EXECUTIVE ISA-486-
    66D2 SV2
Dynamic Decisions ISA-486-
    33 PCI GREEN
Dynamic Decisions
    PROFESSIONAL 486-33
    GREEN VL ISA
Dynamic Decisions
    PROFESSIONAL 486-33DX
    VL/EISA E3
Dynamic Decisions
    PROFESSIONAL 486-50DX
    VL/EISA E4
Dynamic Decisions
    PROFESSIONAL 486-66
    VL/ISA
ECE DATA i486™/VLB-
    GREEN

Edge Technology
   EDGE-PCI P60
Elonex PC-466/R
Elonex PC-466/VL
Eltech Model 4660VB
Eltech P54C-90P
Epson® ActionPC 2000
Epson ActionPC 5000
Epson Endeavor P60
Epson Endeavor WG 4DX2/50
Epson Equity 4DX/33
Epson Equity 4SX/25
Epson PowerSpan 486DX2/66
Epson Progression 4DX2/50
Ergo PowerBrick 100
Ergo PowerBrick 33
Ergo PowerBrick 66
ERIDAN Onyx DE433
ERIDAN Onyx DE466
Everex™ Step 486/33 ISA
Everex Tempo 486/33
Everex Tempo 486/33E
Evesham Micros Premier PCI
   486DX2-66 /340
Expo-Tech 410M
Expo-Tech 433M
Expo-Tech 450M
Expo-Tech 486DX-33 ELP
Expo-Tech 486DX-33 Mini
Expo-Tech 486DX-33
   Mini 72P
Expo-Tech 486DX-33 Tower
Expo-Tech 486DX2-50 ELP
Expo-Tech 486DX2-50 Mini
Expo-Tech 486DX2-50
   Mini 72P
Expo-Tech 486DX2-50 Tower
Expo-Tech 486DX2-66 ELP
Expo-Tech 486DX2-66 Mini
Expo-Tech 486DX2-66
   Mini 72P
Expo-Tech 486DX2-66 Tower
Expo-Tech 486DX4-100 Mini
Expo-Tech 486SX-25 ELP
Expo-Tech 486SX-33 ELP
Expo-Tech 486SX-33 Mini
Expo-Tech 486SX-33
   Mini 72P
Expo-Tech 486SX-33 Tower
Expo-Tech Cx486DX-33 Mini
Expo-Tech Cx486DX2-50
   Mini
Expo-Tech Pentium 566M
Expo-Tech SMP DX2-50
Expo-Tech SMP DX2-66
Fast 486DY66S520

First 486-GACV-2
First 486-GAV
First 486-GIO-VP
First 486GAC-2
First 486VIP-IO
First FIC PM-900
First LEO 486-GIO-VT2
First LEO 486-GVT2
First LEO 486-VIP
Forte Company DELTA
   486/33M
Forte Company DELTA
   486DX2/66
Forte Company GAMMA DX
   386DX/40
Fountain Technology
   486DX2/66
Fountain Technology
   486DX4-100
Fountain Technology P5/66
Fountain Technology P5/90
Free F38X-486VESA
Free F39X-486VESA
Fujitech 486DX2/66-EVL
Fujitech 486DX2/66-VL
Fujitech 486DX4/100-VL
Fujitech 486DX4/100-VL2
Fujitech i486DX2/66-VLG
Fujitsu® S-3000
Fujitsu S-500
Fujitsu S-5000MP
Fujitsu S-510
FutureTech 486DX2-66 VLB
Gateway 2000® 486/33C
Gateway 2000 486DX2/50E
Gateway 2000 486DX2/50V
Gateway 2000 486DX2/66V
   Desktop
Gateway 2000 486DX2/66V
   Tower
Gateway 2000 4DX-33V
Gateway 2000 4DX/33
Gateway 2000 4DX2-66P
Gateway 2000 4DX2/66E
Gateway 2000 4SX/25
Gateway 2000 P5-60
Gateway 2000 P5-66
Gateway 2000 P5-90
GCH AEGIS 466
GCH AEGIS 466D2V
GCH Aegis 466ES
GCH EasyData GD600
GCH EasyDate 466HI VL
GCH EiSYS Ei600 Series
Genitech Capricorn HF60
   E/PCI P5

Getek PCI PENTIUM
GMX EISAMB 486DX2/66
GoldStar GS450DT
GoldStar GS466DT
GoldStar GS486ID50L
GoldStar GS486ID66L
GRiD® 486ei-25 SVR
GRiD 486ei-33
H.D.Microsystèmes AX7
   486 DX-33
H.D.Microsystèmes AX7
   486 DX-50
H.D.Microsystèmes AX7
   486 DX2-50
H.D.Microsystèmes AX7
   486 DX2-66
H.D.Microsystèmes AX7
   Pentium 60 PCI
Hancke & Peter 486 DX4-100
   VL/ISA Professional
Hancke & Peter 486-66
   EISA/VL Professional
Hancke & Peter 486-66 PCI
   Professional
Hancke & Peter 486-66 VLG
   Professional
Hancke & Peter Pentium/90
   PCI Professional
Hancke & Peter Pentium/66
   EISA/PCI Professional
HARPO 4DX FIRMA
HARPO NT 486DX2
Harris 486DX2/66 VESA
Harris Pentium/66 PCI
Hewlett-Packard® NetServer
   4/100 LC
Hewlett-Packard NetServer
   4/100 LF
Hewlett-Packard NetServer
   4/66 LC
Hewlett-Packard NetServer
   4/66 LF
Hewlett-Packard NetServer
   4d/66 LE
Hewlett-Packard NetServer
   4d/66 LM
Hewlett-Packard NetServer
   5/100 LM
Hewlett-Packard NetServer
   5/60 LM
Hewlett-Packard NetServer
   5/66 LC
Hewlett-Packard NetServer
   5/66 LF
Hewlett-Packard NetServer
   5/66 LM

Hewlett-Packard NetServer
5/90 LM
Hewlett-Packard Vectra®
486/33N
Hewlett-Packard Vectra
486/33T
Hewlett-Packard Vectra
486/50U
Hewlett-Packard Vectra
486/66ST
Hewlett-Packard Vectra
486/66U
Hewlett-Packard Vectra
486S/20
Hi-Tech USA 486DX4-
100/256K VLB
Hi-Tech USA PENTIUM-
90/256K PCI-VLB
High Tech USA 486DX266
VLB SYSTEM
High Tech USA 486DX33
VLB SYSTEM
High Tech USA 486DX4-
100/256K VLB
High Tech USA PENTIUM
P5-66/256KVLB
High Tech USA PENTIUM-
90/256K PCI-VLB
HiQuality Systems HIQ
D66 SVL
HiQuality Systems HIQ
P66 PCI
HiQuality Systems HIQ
P90 PCI
HM Systems Minstrel
XPentium P90
HM Systems Minstrel
XPentium Server P90
HYPERTEC SYSTEMS
CIARA Discovery
Hyundai 425s
Hyundai 466d2
IBM® PC Server 486DX2/66
8640-0N*
IBM PC Server Pentium/60
8640-0P*
IBM PS/1 2155-xxx 486DX/33
IBM PS/1 2155-xxx
486DX2/50
IBM PS/1 2168-xxx 486DX/33
IBM PS/1 2168-xxx
486DX2/50
IBM PS/2® Model 50/50Z
System Board Upgrade
486SLC2/50

IBM PS/2 Model 53 9553-xxx
486SLC2/50 [6]
IBM PS/2 Model 56 9556-xxx
486SLC2/50
IBM PS/2 Model 57 9557-xxx
486SLC2/50
IBM PS/2 Model 70 8570-xxx
386DX/25
IBM PS/2 Model 70 8570-xxx
486DX/25
IBM PS/2 Model 76 9576-xxx
486DX2/66
IBM PS/2 Model 76 9576-xxx
486SX/33
IBM PS/2 Model 76i 9576-xxx
486DX2/50 [6]
IBM PS/2 Model 76i 9576-xxx
486DX2/66 [6]
IBM PS/2 Model 76s 9576-xxx
486DX2/50 [6]
IBM PS/2 Model 76s 9576-xxx
486DX2/66 [6]
IBM PS/2 Model 77 9577-xxx
486DX2/66
IBM PS/2 Model 77 9577-xxx
486SX/33
IBM PS/2 Model 77i 9577-xxx
486DX2/50 [6]
IBM PS/2 Model 77i 9577-xxx
486DX2/66 [6]
IBM PS/2 Model 77s 9577-xxx
486DX2/50 [6]
IBM PS/2 Model 77s 9577-xxx
486DX2/66 [6]
IBM PS/2 Model 80 8580-xxx
386DX/25
IBM PS/2 Model 90 XP 486
8590-0J* 486DX/25
IBM PS/2 Model 90XP 486
8590-OL* 486DX2/50
IBM PS/2 Model 95 XP 486
8595-0J* 486DX/25
IBM PS/2 Model 95 XP 486
8595-0M* 486DX/50
IBM PS/2 Model 95 XP 486
8595-xxx with 486DX2/66
processor upgrade
IBM PS/2 Model 95 XP 486
8595-xxx with Enhanced
486DX/50 processor
upgrade
IBM PS/2 Model 95 XP 486
8595-xxx with Enhanced
486DX2/66 processor
upgrade

IBM PS/2 Model 95 XP 486
8595-xxx with processor
upgrade with Pentium
Technology
IBM PS/2 Model 95 XP 486
9595-0M* 486DX/50
IBM PS/2 Model 95 XP 486
9595-xxx with 486DX2/66
processor upgrade
IBM PS/2 Model 95 XP 486
9595-xxx with Enhanced
486DX/50 processor
upgrade
IBM PS/2 Model 95 XP 486
9595-xxx with Enhanced
486DX2/66 processor
upgrade
IBM PS/2 Model 95 XP 486
9595-xxx with processor
upgrade with Pentium
Technology
IBM PS/2 Model P75 8573-
xxx 486DX/33
IBM PS/2 Server 85 433
9585-0K*
IBM PS/2 Server 85 466
9585-0N*
IBM PS/2 Server 85 9585-0X*
with 486DX2/66 processor
upgrade
IBM PS/2 Server 95 566
9595-0QT
IBM PS/2 Server 95 Array 466
9595-3N* [7]
IBM PS/2 Server 95 Array 560
9595-3P* [7]
IBM PS/2 Server 95 Array 566
9595-3Q* [7]
IBM PS/2 Ultimedia™ DV
M57 9557-xxx 486SLC2/50
IBM PS/2 Ultimedia M57
9557-xxx 486SLC2/50
IBM PS/2 Ultimedia M77
9577-xxx 486DX2/66
IBM PS/2 Ultimedia M77
9577-xxx 486SX/33
IBM PS/ValuePoint 433DX/S
6472-xxx
IBM PS/ValuePoint 433SX/D
6384-Kxx
IBM PS/ValuePoint 433SX/S
6382-Kxx
IBM PS/ValuePoint 466DX2/D
6384-Wxx
IBM PS/ValuePoint 466DX2/T
6387-Wxx

IBM PS/ValuePoint P60/D
IBM ThinkPad® 360CS [8]
IBM ThinkPad 720 [9,8]
IBM ThinkPad 720C [9,8]
IBM ThinkPad 750 [8]
IBM ThinkPad 750c [8]
IBM ThinkPad 755
   486DX2/50 [8]
IBM ThinkPad 755
   486DX4/75 [8]
ICL ErgoPRO D4/33d
ICL ErgoPRO D4/50 V
ICL ErgoPRO D4/50de P
ICL ErgoPRO D4/66d
ICL ErgoPRO D4/66d P
ICL ErgoPRO D4/66d XGi
ICL ErgoPRO D5/60
ICL ErgoPRO D5/60 P
ICL ErgoPRO D5/90 P
ICL ErgoPRO E5/60
ICL System Platform
   FX486/33
ICL TEAMSERVER E180i
ICL TEAMSERVER E380i
ICL TEAMSERVER E430i
ICL TEAMSERVER H180i
ICL TEAMSERVER H430i
ICL ValuePlus DL/100d i
ICL ValuePlus DL/66d i
ICL ValuePlus MD/66
ICL ValuePlus MD/P60
Image® 486DX/50 EISA
ImAtrex Predator Series
   ProV 90
Innovax Aurora 486DX/33
Insight 60MHz-PCI
Intel Classic / PCI LP
Intel Classic-R
Intel Classic-R Plus
Intel Classic/PCI Expandable
   Desktop
Intel L486-Series/Professional
   GX
Intel L486-Series/Professional
   Workstation
Intel Premiere 60/PCI Baby AT
   OEM Platform
Intel Premiere 66/PCI
   Baby-AT
Intel Premiere/PCI 66 LPX
Intel Premiere/PCI Baby AT
Intel Premiere/PCI II Baby-AT
Intel Premiere/PCI II LX Low
   Profile™ Desktop
Intel Premiere/PCI LPX
Intel X486/50E

Intel Xpress Deskside/MX
   Pentium 90Mhz Pentium
   Processor
Intel Xpress LXS/ 60Mhz
   Pentium Processor
Intel Xpress/MX 486/33
Intel Xpress/MX 486/50
Intel Xpress/MX 486DX2/66
Intel Xpress/MX 66Mhz
   Pentium Pentium
Intelicom 486DX/33 EISA
Intelicom 486DX/33 ISA
Intelicom 486DX/33
   VESA EISA
Intelicom 486DX/33 VLB
Intelicom 486DX/50 EISA
Intelicom 486DX/50 ISA
Intelicom 486DX/50
   VESA EISA
Intelicom 486DX/50 VLB
Intelicom 486DX2/50 EISA
Intelicom 486DX2/50 ISA
Intelicom 486DX2/50
   VESA EISA
Intelicom 486DX2/50 VLB
Intelicom 486DX2/66 EISA
Intelicom 486DX2/66 ISA
Intelicom 486DX2/66
   VESA EISA
Intelicom 486DX2/66 VLB
Intelicom 486DX4/100 VESA
Intelicom PENTIUM/60 PCI
Intelicom PENTIUM/66 PCI
INTERCOMP Digit 486DX/33
   VLB
INTERCOMP Digit
   486DX2/66
INTERCOMP Digit
   486DX2/66 VLB
INTERCOMP Entry DX-33
INTERCOMP Entry SX-25
INTERCOMP IDAS8000
INTERCOMP IDAS8000/H
INTERCOMP IDAS8000/P 60
INTERCOMP Master EISA
   DX/33
INTERCOMP Master EISA
   DX2/66
INTERCOMP Master
   PENTIUM/66
INTERCOMP Target EN
   DX/33
INTERCOMP Target EN
   DX/33 VLB
INTERCOMP Target EN
   DX2/66

INTERCOMP Target EN
   DX2/66 VLB
Interface Electronic System X
   EISA
Intergraph® PC 433
Intergraph PC 466
Intergraph TD 1
Intergraph TD 2 Personal
   Workstation
Intergraph TD 3 Personal
   Workstation
International Instrumentation
   BLUE MAX 486 DX66 PCI
International Instrumentation
   BLUE MAX P-60 PCI
International Instrumentation
   Business Partner P-90
Investronica INVES
   BS-486 VL
Investronica INVES
   BS-486 VS
Investronica INVES BS-
   486VT+
Investronica INVES IFS-1000
Investronica INVES IFS-900
Investronica INVES MP-900
   XM UniProcessor
Investronica INVES WS-1000
Investronica INVES WS-900
   EVL
INWAR S.A. AS5PCI
INWAR S.A. WS4VL
IPC DYNASTY HE (GREEN)
   486DX-33
IPC DYNASTY HE (GREEN)
   486DX2-50
IPC DYNASTY HE (GREEN)
   486SX-25
IPC DYNASTY HE (GREEN)
   486SX-33
IPC DYNASTY SE
   486DX-33C
IPC DYNASTY SE
   486DX2-66C PCI
IPC DYNASTY SE P5-60C
IPC DYNASTY SE P5-90C
IPC DYNASTY SEL
   486DX-33C
IPC DYNASTY SEL
   486DX2-66C
IPC DYNASTY SEL P5-60C
IPC DYNASTY SEL P5-66C
IPC DYNASTY SEL P5-90C
IPC VALUEMAGIC
   486DX-33

IPC VALUEMAGIC
  486DX2-66
IPC VALUEMAGIC P5-90C
Ipex 486DX2-66 Centra 1000
  ISA/VESA
Ipex 486DX2-66 Centra 2000
  ISA/VESA
Ipex 486DX2-66 Centra 5000
  ISA/VESA
Ipex 486DX2-66 Green Desk
  Top ISA/VESA
Ipex 486DX2-66 Green Mini
  Tower ISA/VESA
Ipex 486DX2-66 Green Ulti-
  mate ISA/VESA
Ipex 486DX2-66 Slimline
  ISA/VESA
ITG NT 486DX-50
ITG NT Pentium/60
JAI PC 845-66-32VL
JAI PC 852/PENTIUM-66/64
  BR
LANIX BRAIN 486DX2-66
LANIX BRAIN PENTIUM 60
LANIX MART 486DX2-50
LANIX MART 486DX2-66
LANIX MART 486SX-25
LASER 410M
LASER 433M
LASER 450M
LASER 486DX-33 ELP
LASER 486DX-33 Mini
LASER 486DX-33 Mini 72P
LASER 486DX-33 Tower
LASER 486DX2-50 ELP
LASER 486DX2-50 Mini
LASER 486DX2-50 Mini 72P
LASER 486DX2-50 Tower
LASER 486DX2-66 ELP
LASER 486DX2-66 Mini
LASER 486DX2-66 Mini 72P
LASER 486DX2-66 Tower
LASER 486DX4-100 Mini
LASER 486SX-25 ELP
LASER 486SX-33 ELP
LASER 486SX-33 Mini
LASER 486SX-33 Mini 72P
LASER 486SX-33 Tower
LASER Cx486DX-33 Mini
LASER Cx486DX2-50 Mini
LASER Pentium 566M
LASER SMP DX2-50
LASER SMP DX2-66
Leading Edge® DT4000
  DX-33

Leading Edge DT4000
  DX2-50
Leading Edge DT4000
  DX2-66
Leading Edge DT4000 SX-33
Leading Edge DT4000 SX-33
Leading Edge MT4000 Cyrix
  DX2-50
Leading Edge MT4000 DX-33
Leading Edge MT4000
  DX2-66
Leading Edge SL4000 DX-33
Leading Edge SL4000 DX2-50
Leading Edge SL4000 DX2-66
Leading Edge SL4000 SX-33
Leading Edge WinPro
  486e/DX-33
Leading Edge WinPro
  486e/DX2-50
Leading Edge WinPro
  486e/DX2-66
Leading Edge WinPro
  486e/SX-25
Leading Edge WinPro D
  DLC/40
Leading Edge WinTower 486
  DX-33
Leading Edge WinTower 486
  DX2-50
Leading Edge WinTower 486
  DX2-66
Leading Edge WinTower 486
  SX-25
Leading Edge WinTower Cyrix
  DX2-50
Liuski G-MD266D-34-8
Liuski G-MP60F-34-8
Master PENTIUM/60 PCI
Maximus 486-50MHz
  Maxi-CAD
Maximus P5-90 PCI/ISA
Mega Computer ECO Series
  486 DX2/66 VLB
Metro Computers Pentium 60
Micro Express ME 486DX2/66
Microbits EISA/PCI Pentium
Microbits Me5PI-s
Microbits VESA/ISA PT586V
  Pentium
Micron 4100 PCI Magnum
Micron 4100 VL Magnum
Micron 486PCI WINSTATION
  CD
Micron P5PCI Platinum® CD
Micron P5PCI PowerStation
  CD

Micron P66PCI PowerServer™
Micron P90PCI PowerStation
Microniche MIS Computer
  Systems M466EV
Microniche MIS Computer
  Systems M466VL
Microniche MIS Computer
  Systems M560P
Microniche MIS Computer
  Systems M560PE
Micronics Mpro 486DX/50
Midwest Micro 486DX2/50
  Vesa/ISA
Midwest Micro Elite
  Cx486DX2-50
MIND 486DX/33 EISA
MIND 486DX/33 VLB
MIND 486DX/40 EISA
MIND 486DX/40 VLB
MIND 486DX2/50 VLB
MIND 486DX2/66 EISA
MIND 486DX2/66 VLB
MIND 486DX2/66 VLB ALI
MIND 486DX4/100
MIND Pentium 60 PCI/EISA
MIND Pentium 60 VLB
MIND Pentium 66 PCI/EISA
Minitronics MINTEC
  486DX2-66 VL/16
MiTAC 4021GC/T
MiTAC 4022GC
MiTAC 5080i
MiTAC DM4077C
MiTAC DM4500A
MiTAC DM5500C
MiTAC DV4077C
MiTAC DV4077D
Mitsuba M-South Series 560
  Model AP5MP3-5A
Mitsuba M-South Series 566
  Model 5A
Mitsuba M-South Series 590
  Model 5A
Mitsuba M-South Series 590
  Model 5B
Modular Server Module 450
Modular Server Module 466
Modular Server Module
  Pentium
Monydata Modula 300 / 90
Monydata Station 486 / 90
Mustek MECER3486-VL
Mustek MECER486DL
Mustek MECER7486-VIP
Mustek MECER7486-VL
Mustek MECER7586

Mustek MECER8586/PCI

National Microcomputers
Power System DX2-66

NCR® StarStation

NCR System 3000 Model 3314

NCR System 3000 Model 3335

NCR System 3000 Model 3350

NCR System 3000 Model 3355

NCR System 3000 Model 3410

NCR System 3000 Model 3431

NCR System 3000 Model 3445

NCR System 3000 Model 3525

NEC® Express 4100ST

NEC Express/II 466 ST

NEC Express/II P601 LT

NEC Express/II P60ST

NEC Image 4100es

NEC Image 466

NEC Image P60

NEC PowerMate 466D

NEC PowerMate 466es

NEC PowerMate 486/33e

NEC Ready 466D

NEC Ready 466es

NEC Versa E

NETiS 486 DX2/50

NETiS 486DX/33 VL

NETiS 486DX/50 VL

NETiS 486DX2/50 PCI

NETiS 486DX2/66 PCI

NETiS 486DX2/66 VL

NETiS 486DX33 PCI

NETiS AMD 486 DX 40 VL

NETiS AMD 486 DX2/50

NETiS AMD 486DX2/50 PCI

NETiS Pentium 66 PCI

NETiS Pentium 90

Network Connection
Triumph® M2

Network Connection
Triumph M2V

Network Connection
Triumph T3000

Network Connection
Triumph T4000

Network Connection
Triumph TNX

Northgate® Elegance 333

Northgate Elegance 433i

Northgate Elegance SP 433

OKI if 486VX550D

OKI if Server 466/SL

OKI if Server 566/SL

OKI if Station 425/DL

OKI if Station 433/DE

OKI if Station 466/DE

OKI if Station 560/DE

Olidata MDS-P60/A

Olidata MDS-P90/A

Olivetti® LSX5010

Olivetti LSX5015

Olivetti LSX5025

Olivetti LSX5025 E

Olivetti M4-40

Olivetti M4-452

Olivetti M4-464

Olivetti M4-60

Olivetti M4-82

Olivetti M400-60

Olivetti M6-440

Olivetti M6-460

Olivetti M6-540

Olivetti M6-620

Olivetti M6-640

Olivetti M6-770

Olivetti M6-880

Olivetti SNX 140 Systema

Olivetti SNX 160 Systema

Olympia Olystar 400D-66
EISA

Omni Tech 5100

Omni Tech 5300

Omni Tech 8600 486DX2-66

Optima OCT 486DX/33 VL
Green Desktop

Optima OCT 486DX/4 100
PCI Local Bus

Optima OCT 486DX/4 100
Vesa Local Bus

Optima OCT 486DX2/50 VL
Desktop Green

Optima OCT 486DX2/50 VL
Mini Tower Green

Optima OCT 486DX2/50 VL
Slimeline WorkStation
Green

Optima OCT 486DX2/50 VL
Tower Green

Optima OCT 486DX2/66 PCI
Desktop

Optima OCT 486DX2/66 PCI
Mini Tower

Optima OCT 486DX2/66 PCI
Slimline WorkStation

Optima OCT 486DX2/66 PCI
Tower

Optima OCT 486DX2/66 VL

Optima OCT 486DX2/66 VL
Green Desktop

Optima OCT 486DX2/66 VL
Mini Tower Green

Optima OCT 486DX2/66 VL
Slimline WorkStation Green

Optima OCT 486DX2/66 VL
Tower Green

Optima OCT 486DX33 PCI
Desktop

Optima OCT 486DX33 PCI
Mini Tower

Optima OCT 486DX33 PCI
Slimline WorkStation

Optima OCT 486DX33 PCI
Tower

Optima OCT 486DX33 VL
Mini Tower Green

Optima OCT 486DX33 VL
Slimline WorkStation Green

Optima OCT 486DX33 VL
Tower Green

Optima OCT 486DX4/100 VL
Desktop

Optima OCT 486SX33 PCI
Bus Desktop

Optima OCT 486SX33 PCI
Mini Tower

Optima OCT 486SX33 PCI
Slimline WorkStation

Optima OCT 486SX33 PCI
Tower

Optima OCT 486SX33 VL

Optima OCT DX4/100 VL
Mini Tower Green

Optima OCT DX4/100 VL
Slimline WorkStation Green

Optima OCT DX4/100 VL
Tower Green

Optima OCT PENTIUM 60
PCI Desktop

Optima OCT PENTIUM 60
PCI Tower

Optima OCT PENTIUM 66
PCI Desktop

Optima OCT PENTIUM 66
PCI MXpress

Optima OCT PENTIUM 66
PCI Tower

Optima OCT PENTIUM 90
PCI Tower

Optima Pentium 90 PCI
Desktop

Optima Sprinter 486DX2/50
VL Desktop Green

Optima Sprinter 486DX2/50
VL Mini Tower Green

Optima Sprinter 486DX2/50
VL Slimline WorkStation
Green

Optima Sprinter 486DX2/50
VL Tower Green
Optima Sprinter 486DX2/66
PCI Desktop
Optima Sprinter 486DX2/66
PCI Mini Tower
Optima Sprinter 486DX2/66
PCI Slimline WorkStation
Optima Sprinter 486DX2/66
PCI Tower
Optima Sprinter 486DX2/66
VL
Optima Sprinter 486DX2/66
VL Desktop Green
Optima Sprinter 486DX2/66
VL Mini Tower Green
Optima Sprinter 486DX2/66
VL Slimline WorkStation
Green
Optima Sprinter 486DX2/66
VL Tower Green
Optima Sprinter 486DX33 PCI
Desktop
Optima Sprinter 486DX33 PCI
Mini Tower
Optima Sprinter 486DX33 PCI
Slimline WorkStation
Optima Sprinter 486DX33 PCI
Tower
Optima Sprinter 486DX33 VL
Desktop Green
Optima Sprinter 486DX33 VL
Mini Tower Green
Optima Sprinter 486DX33 VL
Slimline WorkStation Green
Optima Sprinter 486DX33 VL
Tower Green
Optima Sprinter 486SX33 PCI
Desktop
Optima Sprinter 486SX33 PCI
Mini Tower
Optima Sprinter 486SX33 PCI
Slimline WorkStation
Optima Sprinter 486SX33 PCI
Tower
Optima Sprinter 486SX33
Vesa Local Bus
Optima Sprinter DX4/100 VL
Desktop Green
Optima Sprinter DX4/100 VL
Mini Tower Green
Optima Sprinter DX4/100 VL
Slimline WorkStation Green
Optima Sprinter DX4/100 VL
Tower Green
Optima Sprinter P560 PCI

Optima Sprinter P566 PCI ISA
Optima Sprinter PENTIUM 60
PCI Desktop
Optima Sprinter PENTIUM 60
PCI Tower
Optima Sprinter PENTIUM 66
PCI Desktop
Optima Sprinter PENTIUM 66
PCI MXpress
Optima Sprinter PENTIUM 66
PCI Tower
Optima Xpress/ MX
PENTIUM 60 EISA
Optima Xpress/ MX
PENTIUM 66 EISA
Osborne DX4-100
Osborne LP4D-33
Osborne LP4D-50
Osborne LP4D-50A
Osborne LP4D-66
Osborne LP4D-66A
Osborne LP4S-33
Osborne LP4S-50
Osborne MT4D-66E
Osborne MT5D-60P
Osborne MT5D-66P
Osborne Pentium 90
Packard Bell AX 120CD
Packard Bell AX 121CD
Packard Bell AX 122CDT
Packard Bell AX 46CD
Packard Bell AX 47CD
Packard Bell AX 48CD
Packard Bell AX 49CDT
Packard Bell AX 51CDT
Packard Bell AX533H
Packard Bell AX533J
Packard Bell Axcel 205
Packard Bell Axcel 230
Packard Bell Axcel 630
Minitower
Packard Bell DMM 70
Packard Bell F 101CD
Packard Bell F 102CD
Packard Bell F 103CD
Packard Bell F 111CDT
Packard Bell F 15
Packard Bell F 54CD
Packard Bell F 55CDT Plus
Packard Bell F 56CD
Packard Bell F 57CD
Packard Bell F 57CDT
Packard Bell F 58CD
Packard Bell F 59CDT
Packard Bell F486DX/DH
Packard Bell F486DX/DJ

Packard Bell F486DX/DJ-W
Packard Bell Force 200
Packard Bell Force 250
Packard Bell Force 386
Packard Bell Force 715
Minitower
Packard Bell Legend 207
Packard Bell Legend 233
Packard Bell Legend 234 Elite
Packard Bell Legend 245
Packard Bell Legend 747
Minitower
Packard Bell Legend 780
Supreme
Packard Bell Legend 840
Minitower
Packard Bell Legend 845
Minitower
Packard Bell Legend 848
Minitower
Packard Bell LG 100CD
Packard Bell LG 105CD
Packard Bell LG 110CDT
Packard Bell LG 200CD
Packard Bell LG 205CD
Packard Bell LG 20CD
Packard Bell LG 210CDT
Packard Bell LG 21CD
Packard Bell LG 22CD
Packard Bell LG 23CD
Packard Bell LG 24CD
Packard Bell LG 25CDT
Packard Bell LG 26CDT
Packard Bell LG 27CDT
Packard Bell LG 28CDT
Packard Bell LG 29TV
Packard Bell LG 35CD SUP
Packard Bell LG 38CD SUP
Packard Bell LG 42CD
Packard Bell LG 5
Packard Bell LG 61CD
Packard Bell LG 62CDT
Packard Bell LG 63CDT
Packard Bell LG 64TV
Packard Bell LG 9CD
Packard Bell LG635J
Packard Bell LG660H
Packard Bell LG760 Supreme
Packard Bell PackMate
733 C MT
Packard Bell PB 1120
Packard Bell PB 20CD
Packard Bell PB 20CD+
Packard Bell PB 28CDT
Packard Bell PB2555CD
Packard Bell PB410SX/33

Packard Bell PB420SX/33
Packard Bell PB43028DX/25
Packard Bell PB43028DX2/66
Packard Bell PB450DX2/66
Packard Bell PB450SX/25
Packard Bell PB520R
Packard Bell PB527-60
Packard Bell PB550
Packard Bell PM 27
Packard Bell PM 66CD
Packard Bell PM 74CD
Packard Bell PM486DX33X
Packard Bell PM486DX33Y
Patch Computers Supra 3600
    PENTIUM 60 NOTEBOOK
Patch Computers Supra
    PENTIUM 90 PCI/EISA
PC Expanders VANGUARD
    486DX ISA/VESA 33Mhz
PC Expanders VANGUARD
    PENTIUM VESA/PCI
    90Mhz
PC Tech 486DX2/66
    (AMD) VL
PC Tech 486DX33 (AMD) VL
PC Tech 486VL33
PC Tech VLB 486DX-4/100
PC Tech VLB 486DX2/66
Peacock Server Modell
    SSE 8364
Pionex 486DX2-66
Pionex 486DX4-100
Pionex P5/66
Pionex P5/90
Poly 486-50E
Poly 486SX-25Y
Poly 586EP2
POWER DESK 486/33
POWER DESK
    EISA/ISA/VESA
POWER DESK GREEN
POWER DESK PCI Pentium
Powerland Power2
    486dx-2/66 VLB
Precision 486/66 VL-Bus
Precision Pentium Eisa-Vesa
Professional Concepts Beeker
    4-33/VL2
Professional Concepts Beeker
    4-66/VL2
Professional Concepts Beeker
    6900
Professional Concepts Quinn
    4-33/VLE
Professional Concepts Quinn
    4-66/VLE

Professional Concepts Saavij
    4-33/VL3
Professional Concepts Saavij
    4-33/VL3 Model E
Professional Concepts Saavij
    4-50/VL3
Professional Concepts Saavij
    4-66/VL3
Professional Concepts Saavij
    4-66/VL3 Model E
Professional Concepts Saavij
    4-66/VL3 Model S
Protech 486-66Mhz ISA/VL
Protech Pentium PCI/ISA
QTech 486 DX2/66
Quantex 486DX2/66
Quantex 486DX4-100
Quantex P5/66
Quantex P5/90
Quattro® Prompt486/66 VL
Quattro Prompt586
Radisys EPC-7
Radisys EPC-8
RDIpc Systeme Pentium-90
Reason Technology 4 LX Plus
    486DX2/66
Reason Technology Square
    4LX W32i Mitsumi FX001D
Reason Technology Square
    4LX/AIO
Reason Technology Square
    5VL
Repco Data Pentium/I
Repco Data R33VLB486
Repco Data R50VLB486
Repco Data R66VLB486
Reply PS/2 Model 50/50SX
    Power Board Upgrade
    486DX4/100
Reply PS/2 Model 50/50SX
    System Board Upgrade
    486SLC2/50
Reply PS/2 Model 55/55SX
    Power Board Upgrade
    486DX
Reply PS/2 Model 56/57
    PowerBoard Upgrade
    486DX4-100
Reply PS/2 Model 60/80
    System Board Upgrade
    486DX2/66
Reply PS/2 Model 70
    PowerBoard Upgrade
    486DX4/100
Reply PS/2 Model 70 System
    Board Upgrade 486DX2/66

Research Machines RM D
    Series PC-466
Research Machines
    SYSTEMBASE
Robotech Cobra RS
    486DX2-66
Rolta STATION 486/66
    ENGG.
Samsung P5 Workstation
Samsung SPC5800N
Samsung SPC7600P VW234L
Samsung SPC7600P VW242H
Sanyo MBC-20CV
SCA Professional EISA 486
SCA Professional Pentium 66
    EISA-PCI
Seanix ASI 9000 EFAR
    486DX2-66
Seanix ASI 9000 P5PCI-VL
Seanix ASI 9000 PREMIERE
    PENTIUM PCI-60
Seanix ASI 9000 YUKON
    486DX-33
Seanix ASI 9000 YUKON
    486DX2-66
Seanix ASI 9000 YUKON
    486DX4-100
Seanix ASI 9000 YUKON
    S801 486DX2-50
Serius Systems Technology
    486/66 EISA
Shuttle HOT-407
    EISA/VESA/DX2-66
Shuttle HOT-409
    VLB/DX2-50
Shuttle HOT-409
    VLB/DX2-66
Shuttle HOT-419 DX4-100
Shuttle HOT-419
    VLB/DX2-66
Shuttle HOT-503
    PENTIUM/60
Shuttle HOT-503
    PENTIUM/66
Shuttle HOT-523
    PCI/PENTIUM/60
Shuttle HOT-523
    PCI/PENTIUM/66
Shuttle HOT-528 EISA/PCI
    PENTIUM/60
Shuttle HOT-543
    VESA/ISA/PCI/P90
Siemens-Nixdorf PCD-4H
Siemens-Nixdorf PCD-4H PCI
Siemens-Nixdorf PCD-4H VL
Siemens-Nixdorf PCD-4L

Siemens-Nixdorf PCD-4L VL
Siemens-Nixdorf PCD-4ND
Siemens-Nixdorf PCD-4T
Siemens-Nixdorf PCD-5H
Siemens-Nixdorf PCD-5T /
  PCI 60E
Siemens-Nixdorf PCD-5T 90 E
Siemens-Nixdorf PCE-5S/60
Siemens-Nixdorf SCENIC 4H
Siemens-Nixdorf SCENIC 4T
Siemens-Nixdorf SCENIC
  4T VL
Siemens-Nixdorf SCENIC 5H
Siemens-Nixdorf SCENIC
  5T PCI
SKAI AXIOM 486DX-33
SKAI AXIOM 486DX2-66
SKAI PCI 486DX2-66
SKAI SPECTRUM 486SX-33
SPC TRADING AB SPC P-90
  Ergoline
SRC Systems 486 VL
SRC Systems 486 VL Plus
SRC Systems Pentium 90
SRC Systems Pentium 90S
SRC Systems Pentium PCI
STS Tecom Gmbh STS-
  486DX/PCIG
STS Tecom Gmbh STS-
  486SL/40
STS Tecom Gmbh STS-
  P5/66IS
STS Tecom Gmbh STS-
  P54/90IS
SUPERCOM 3/486
Supra 486DX-33 VESA/ISA
Supra 486DX2-66 VESA/ISA
Supra 486DX4-100 VESA/ISA
Supra 486SX-33 VESA/ISA
Supra 9200 i486DX2-66
  NOTEBOOK
Supra PENTIUM 60 PCI/ISA
Svensk LAPLINE 3600
Swan 486DX2/66 EISA-DB
Syncomp Microstar 486DX2
  /VLB
Syncomp Microstar 486SX
  /VLB PC
Syncomp Mini 486DX2
  /EISA PC
Syncomp Mini 486DX2
  /PCI PC
Syncomp Mini 486DX2 /VLB
Syncomp Mini 486SX
  /EISA PC
Syncomp Mini 486SX /PCI PC

Syncomp Mini 486SX
  /VLB PC
Syncomp Mini PENTIUM
  /PCI PC
T-DATA LIN 486-40 DX
T-DATA LIN 486-50 DX2
T-DATA LIN 486-66 DX2
T-DATA LIN Pentium
Tandy® 4100 MT
Tandy MMPC
Tangent Just N' Case Dual
  SMP Server
Tangent Just N' Case Dual
  SMP Server 250
Tangent P590 PCI EISA Dual
  SMP /M
Tangent P590 PCI EISA Dual
  SMP /T
Tangent P590 PCI EISA Dual
  SMP PowerStation
Tangent P590 PCI EISA Dual
  SMP Server
Tangent VL433 Server
Tangent VL433sd
Tangent VL433sm
Tangent VL433st
Tangent VL450 Server
Tangent VL450d
Tangent VL450m
Tangent VL450t
Tatung TCS-5600 PCI/EISA
Tatung TCS-9130 VIP
Tatung TCS-9345
Tatung TCS-9510 VL ISA
Tatung TCS-9545
Tatung TCS-9546
Tatung TCS-9730 VIP
Techway Endeavour E62VL
Techway Endeavour E62VL-D
  SX33 Green
Techway Endeavour
  E62VL-GX4
Techway Endeavour E62VL-M
  SX33 Green
Techway Endeavour E62VL-T
  SX33 Green
Techway Endeavour E77VL
Techway Endeavour E77VL-D
  DX2/66 Green
Techway Endeavour E77VL-D
  DX33 Green
Techway Endeavour E77VL-D
  DX4/100 Green
Techway Endeavour
  E77VL-GX4

Techway Endeavour E77VL-M
  DX2/66 Green
Techway Endeavour E77VL-M
  DX33 Green
Techway Endeavour E77VL-M
  DX4/100 Green
Techway Endeavour E77VL-T
  DX2/66 Green
Techway Endeavour E77VL-T
  DX33 Green
Techway Endeavour E77VL-T
  DX4/100 Green
Techway Endeavour E84VL
Techway Endeavour
  E84VL-GX4
Techway Endeavour
  E84VL100-GX4
TELEMECANIQUE
  FTX507-8C
Texas Instruments®
  TravelMate™ 4000
  WinDX2 [10]
Texas Instruments TravelMate
  4000E in TravelMate
  DeskTop
Texas Instruments TravelMate
  TM4000E TFT
Texas Instruments TravelMate
  TM4000M TFT
Toshiba® T1910CS/200
Toshiba T1950CT/320
Toshiba T2400CS/250
Toshiba T2400CT/320
Toshiba T3600CT/250 [11]
Toshiba T4400SX
Toshiba T4400SXC
Toshiba T4600C/200]
Toshiba T4700CT/320
Toshiba T4800CT/500
Tri-Star Tri-CAD Ultimate
  464V PCI P60
TriGem 486/66VC
TriGem 486G/T10(incl. 486H+
  T10G model)
TriGem 486G/T15(incl. 486G+
  T15 model)
TriGem 486G/T20
TriGem 486G/T25(incl. 486G+
  T25 model)
TriGem 486G/T40(incl. 486H+
  T40G,T43G models)
TriGem 486G/T45(incl. 486G+
  T45 model)
TriGem 486G/T50
TriGem 486G/T55(incl. 486G+
  T55 model)

TriGem 486GP T15
TriGem 486GP T25
TriGem 486GP T45
TriGem 486GP T55
TriGem P5/PT
TriGem P5/T
Tulip® DT 4/50
Tulip Vision Line DE 4/100
Tulip Vision Line DE 4/33S
Tulip Vision Line DE 4/50
Tulip Vision Line DE 4/50S
Tulip Vision Line DE 5/60
Tulip Vision Line DE 5/90
Tulip Vision Line DS 4/100
Tulip Vision Line DS 5/60
Tulip Vision Line DS 5/90
Tulip Vision Line DT 4/100
Tulip Vision Line DT 4/33S
Tulip Vision Line DT 4/50S
Tulip Vision Line DT 5/60
Tulip Vision Line DT 5/90
Tulip Vision Line WS 4/33S
U.S. Micro Jet 386DX-33
U.S. Micro Jet 386DX-40
U.S. Micro Jet 486DLC-33
U.S. Micro Jet 486DLC-40
U.S. Micro Jet 486DX-33
U.S. Micro Jet 486DX-40
U.S. Micro Jet 486DX-50
U.S. Micro Jet 486DX2-50
U.S. Micro Jet 486DX2-66
U.S. Micro Jet 486SX-25
U.S. Micro Jet P5-60 PCI/EISA
U.S. Micro Jet P5-60 PCI/ISA
U.S. Micro Jet P5-66 PCI/EISA
U.S. Micro Jet P5-66 PCI/ISA
U.S. Micro Jet P5-90 PCI/ISA
U.S. Micro Jet PCI 486DX-33
U.S. Micro Jet PCI 486DX2-50
U.S. Micro Jet PCI 486DX2-66
U.S. Micro Jet PCI 486SX-25
U.S. Micro Jet VL 486BL-75
U.S. Micro Jet VL 486DX-33
U.S. Micro Jet VL 486DX-40
U.S. Micro Jet VL 486DX-50
U.S. Micro Jet VL 486DX2-50
U.S. Micro Jet VL 486DX2-66
U.S. Micro Jet VL
    486DX4-100
U.S. Micro Jet VL 486DX4-75
U.S. Micro Jet VL
    486SLC2-50
U.S. Micro Jet VL
    486SLC2-66
U.S. Micro Jet VL 486SX-25

U.S. Micro Jet VL/EISA
    486DX-33
U.S. Micro Jet VL/EISA
    486DX-40
U.S. Micro Jet VL/EISA
    486DX-50
U.S. Micro Jet VL/EISA
    486DX2-50
U.S. Micro Jet VL/EISA
    486DX2-66
U.S. Micro Jet VL/EISA
    486SX-25
U.S. Micro Jet VL/PCI
    486DX-33
U.S. Micro Jet VL/PCI
    486DX2-50
U.S. Micro Jet VL/PCI
    486DX2-66
U.S. Micro Jet VL/PCI
    486DX4-100
U.S. Micro Jet VL/PCI
    486DX4-75
U.S. Micro Jet VL/PCI
    486SX-25
Ultra Technologies UL P5 60
Ultra Technologies
    UL486DX 50
Ultra Technologies
    UL486DX/2 66
Ultra-Comp 486DX24913
Unique Computers, Ltd.
    Pentium 60
Unisys® Pathway Series 5669
Unisys Pathway Series
    PS243-331
Unisys Pathway Series
    PS243-661
Unisys Pathway Series
    PS246-331
Unisys Pathway Series
    PS246-661
Unisys Pathway Series
    PS255-601
Unisys Pathway Series
    PSA445-661
Unisys Pathway Series
    PSA458-601
Unisys PW2 Advantage 3256
Unisys PW2 Advantage 3336
Unisys PW2 Advantage Plus
    4668
Unisys SVE56691-FDD
UNITEK Power Vesa 486DX2
Vektron PCI Power Station
    P66

Vextrec Technologies VTI-
    486D66SG
Viglen Eisa Express Single
    Processor.
Viglen Genie 4DX33
Viglen PCI Pentium 60MHz
Vtech 410M
Vtech 433M
Vtech 450M
Vtech 466M
Vtech 486DX-33
Vtech 486DX-33 ELP
Vtech 486DX-33 Mini
Vtech 486DX-33 Mini 72P
Vtech 486DX-33 Tower
Vtech 486DX2-50 ELP
Vtech 486DX2-50 Mini
Vtech 486DX2-50 Mini 72P
Vtech 486DX2-50 Tower
Vtech 486DX2-66 ELP
Vtech 486DX2-66 Mini
Vtech 486DX2-66 Mini 72P
Vtech 486DX2-66 Tower
Vtech 486DX4-100 Mini
Vtech 486SX-25 ELP
Vtech 486SX-33 ELP
Vtech 486SX-33 Mini
Vtech 486SX-33 Mini 72P
Vtech 486SX-33 Tower
Vtech 560M
Vtech 566M
Vtech Cx486DX-33 Mini 72P
Vtech Cx486DX2-50 Mini 72P
Vtech LT432 Notebook
Vtech LT433C Color
    Notebook
Vtech LT433C Notebook
Vtech Platinum SMP DX-50
Vtech Platinum SMP DX2-66
Wang® Microsystems PC
    350/40C
Western 486V-100 DX4 EISA
Western 486V-100 DX4 VESA
Western 486V-33 DX EISA
Western 486V-33 DX VESA
Western 486V-33 SX VESA
Western 486V-50 DX EISA
Western 486V-50 DX VESA
Western 486V-66 DX2 EISA
Western 486V-66 DX2 VESA
Western 586G 60 EISA/PCI
Western 586G 66 EISA/PCI
WIPRO Fusion 510
WIPRO LANDMARK E
    SQUARE - MODEL 200
Wyse® Decision 486se-66DX2

Wyse Decision 486si-66DX2
Wyse Forte` GSV
Wyse Series 6000i, Model 665
Zenith® Data Systems
   Desktop/Tower P5-60
Zenith Data Systems Z-
   386/33E
Zenith Data Systems Z-
   486/33E
Zenith Data Systems Z-
   486/33ET
Zenith Data Systems Z-
   486SX/25E
Zenith Data Systems Z-
   SERVER LT 466XE Model
   500 (incl. Model 1000)
Zenith Data Systems
   ZNOTEFLEX
Zenon Z-OPTIMUS PCI,SCSI-
   II, Pentium/60
ZEOS® 486DX/33ISA
ZEOS 486DX/50
ZEOS Pantera P66

x86 Architecture Multiprocessor Computers

The following x86 architecture multiprocessor systems have been tested.

ACER AcerAltos
   17000 / 3255 (2p)
ACER AcerAltos
   7000/F560TU
ACER AcerAltos
   7000/F566TU
ACER AcerFrame 3000MP 50
   (Model 3257) [9]
ALR PROVEISA DMP 4/66D
ALR Revolution MP P/90 (2p)
ALR Revolution Q-SMP
   P/100 (2p)
ALR Revolution Q-SMP
   P/100 (3p)
ALR Revolution Q-SMP
   P/100 (4p)
ALR Revolution Q-SMP
   P/90 (2p)
ALR Revolution Q-SMP
   P/90 (3p)
ALR Revolution Q-SMP
   P/90 (4p)
Ambra TP66E2/VL

AST Manhattan SMP
   486/50 (4p)
AST Manhattan SMP P60 (4p)
AST Premmia GX P90
COMPAQ ProLiant 2000
   Model 486/50
COMPAQ ProLiant 2000
   Model 5/66
COMPAQ ProLiant 2000
   Model 5/90
COMPAQ ProLiant 2000R
   Model 486DX/50
COMPAQ ProLiant 2000R
   Model 5/66
COMPAQ ProLiant 4000
   Model 486/50
COMPAQ ProLiant 4000
   Model 5/66
COMPAQ ProLiant 4000R
   Model 5/66
COMPAQ Systempro Dual
   486/33
COMPAQ Systempro Dual
   486DX2/66
COMPAQ Systempro XL
   486/50
COMPAQ Systempro XL 5/66
Corollary Extended C-bus
   486DX2/66
Hewlett-Packard NetServer
   5/66 LM2 [12]
Hewlett-Packard Vectra XU
   590/C
Intel Xpress Deskside/MX
   66Mhz Dual Pentium
   Processor
Intergraph ISMP22 InterServe
Intergraph TD 4 Personal
   Workstation
Intergraph TD 5 Personal
   Workstation
Modular Server Module Dual
   Pentium DAC
NCR System 3000 Model 3360
   Panther
NCR System 3000 Model 3430
NCR System 3000 Model
   3450[13]
NCR System 3000 Model 3455
NCR System 3000 Model
   3550[13,14]
NCR System 3000 Model
   3555[13,14]
Olivetti LSX5030
Olivetti LSX5040
Sequent® WinServer 3000[14]

Sequent WinServer 500
Siemens-Nixdorf PCD-5T
   90 DE
Wyse Series 7000i Model
   740MP/33
Wyse Series 7000i model
   740MP/66

MIPS® RISC Architecture Computers

The following MIPS RISC architecture systems have been tested.

ACER ARC1
AcerFormula
Carerra R4000™
DESKStation Technology
   Evolution E4400 RISC PC
DESKStation Technology
   Evolution R4000 RISC PC
DESKStation Technology
   Tyne v4633x
   RISC PC
MIPS ArcSystem Magnum PC-
   50
MIPS Millenium PC-50
NEC Image RISCstation
NeTpower NeTserver 1000
NeTpower NeTstation 100
NeTpower NeTstation 200
NeTpower NeTstation 300
Olivetti PWS4000
Progen R4400-50/100
Shuttle RiscPC 4475
UniMicro RISCStation
   4400NT

MIPS RISC Multiprocessor Architecture Computers

The following MIPS RISC multiprocessor architecture systems have been tested.

NEC Express RISCserver
NEC RISCstation 2000
NeTpower Server 2000

Digital Alpha AXP™ RISC Architecture Computers

The following Digital Alpha AXP RISC systems have been tested.

Actech ACTion Alpha
  AXP 150
Aspen Systems Inc. Alpine
  166 RS[14]
Aspen Systems Inc. Alpine
  233 XS[14]
Digital Equipment Corp.
  AlphaServer 1000 4/200
Digital Equipment Corp.
  AlphaStation 200 4/166
Digital Equipment Corp.
  AlphaStation 200 4/233
Digital Equipment Corp.
  AlphaStation 400 4/233
Digital Equipment Corp.
  DECpc 2000-300 AXP
  Server
Digital Equipment Corp.
  DECpc 2000-500 AXP
  Server
Digital Equipment Corp.
  DECpc AXP 150
Digital Equipment Corp.
  DECpc AXP 150 Universal
  Platform
Digital Equipment Corp.
  DECpc XL AXP 233

Digital Alpha AXP RISC Multiprocessor Architecture Computers

The following Digital Alpha AXP RISC multiprocessor systems have been tested.

Digital Equipment Corp.
  AlphaServer 2000 4/200
Digital Equipment Corp.
  AlphaServer 2100 4/200
Digital Equipment Corp. 2100
  Server model A500MP

Processor Upgrade Products

The following Processor Upgrade Products have been tested with Windows NT. Please consult the manufacturer for information on compatibility with specific models of computers.

Cyrix CX486DRx2-20/40
Cyrix CX486DRx2-25/50
Digital Equipment Corp.
  DECpc XL AXP 233
  Upgrade
Intel OverDrive™ 486DX-33
  (66Mhz)

SCSI Host Adapters

The following SCSI adapters have been tested on the indicated platforms with the following scanner, CD-ROM, tape, fixed and removable drives (except as noted): ArchiveST 4000 DAT, CD-Technologies CD Porta-Drive™ T-3401, Hewlett-Packard ScanJet® IIc NEC Intersect CDR-74, Micropolis 1924, Peripheral Land Infinity 88, Procom Technology MCD-DS, Syquest® 5110, Toshiba TXM-3401E, WangTek 5150es.

SCSI Host Adapter	BUS	x86	MIPS	ALPHA
Adaptec™ AHA-1510 [15]	ISA-16	X		X
Adaptec AHA-1520 [15]	ISA-16	X		X
Adaptec AHA-1522 [15]	ISA-16	X		X
Adaptec AHA-1542A [16]	ISA-16	X	X	X
Adaptec AHA-1540B [17]	ISA-16	X	X	X
Adaptec AHA-1542B [17]	ISA-16	X	X	X
Adaptec AHA-1540C [18]	ISA-16	X	X	X
Adaptec AHA-1542C [18]	ISA-16	X	X	X
Adaptec AHA-1542CF [19]	ISA-16	X	X	X
Adaptec AHA-1640	MCA	X		
Adaptec AHA-1740 [20]	EISA	X	X	X
Adaptec AHA-1742 [20]	EISA	X	X	X
Adaptec AHA-1740A [21]	EISA	X	X	X
Adaptec AHA-1742A [21]	EISA	X	X	X
Adaptec AHA-2740	EISA	X	X	X
Adaptec AHA-2742	EISA	X	X	X
Adaptec AHA-2740A	EISA	X	X	X
Adaptec AHA-2742A	EISA	X	X	X
Adaptec AHA-2742AT	EISA	X	X	X
Adaptec AHA-2840	VLB	X		
Adaptec AHA-2940	PCI	X		X
Adaptec AIC-6260	EMBEDDED	X[22]		
Adaptec AIC-7770 [23]	EMBEDDED	X[24]		
Advanced System Products ABP-842 [1]	VLB	X		
Always IN-2000	ISA-16	X		
AMIscsi Series 441 [25]	EISA	X		
AMIscsi Series 48 [1]	EISA	X		
AMIscsi Series 48 (with cache) [0]	EISA	X		
AMD PC-NET SCSI [1]	EMBEDDED	X[26]		
BusLogic BT-445S	VLB	X		
BusLogic BT-542B	ISA-16	X	X	X
BusLogic BT-545C	ISA-16	X	X	
BusLogic BT-545S	ISA-16	X	X	X
BusLogic BT-640A	MCA	X		
BusLogic BT-646S [27]	MCA	X		
BusLogic BT-742A	EISA	X		X
BusLogic BT-747S	EISA	X	X	X

SCSI Host Adapter	BUS	x86	MIPS	ALPHA
CMD Tech CSA-6000/F [1]	EISA	X		
COMPAQ Fast SCSI-2 Controller	EISA	X		
COMPAQ 6260 SCSI-2 Controller	ISA-16	X		X
DPT PM2011b	ISA-16	X	X	X
DPT PM2011b (with cache) [25]	ISA-16	X		
DPT PM2012b	EISA	X	X	X
DPT PM2012b (with cache) [25]	EISA	X		X
DPT PM2021	ISA-16	X		
DPT PM2021 (with Cache) [25]	ISA-16	X		
DPT PM2022	EISA	X		
DPT PM2022 (with Cache) [25]	EISA	X		
DPT PM2122	EISA	X		
DPT PM2122 (with Cache) [25]	EISA	X		
Data Technology Corp. 3290	EISA	X		X
Digital Equipment KZESC (SWXCR) EISA Raid Controller	EISA	X		X
Digital Equipment KZPAA (KZPSC) NCR 53C810-S PCI SCSI Adapter	PCI	X		X
Future Domain® MCS-600	MCA	X		
Future Domain MCS-700	MCA	X		
Future Domain TMC-845 [28,29]	ISA-8	X	X	X
Future Domain TMC-850 [28,29]	ISA-8	X	X	X
Future Domain TMC-850M(ER) [29]	ISA-8	X	X	X
Future Domain TMC-860 [28,29]	ISA-8	X	X	X
Future Domain TMC-860M [29]	ISA-8	X	X	X
Future Domain TMC-885 [28,29]	ISA-16	X	X	X
Future Domain TMC-885M [29]	ISA-16	X	X	X
Future Domain TMC-1610	ISA-16	X	X	X
Future Domain TMC-1610mex	ISA-16	X	X	X
Future Domain TMC-1610mer	ISA-16	X	X	X
Future Domain TMC-1650	ISA-16	X	X	X
Future Domain TMC-1660	ISA-16	X	X	X
Future Domain TMC-1670	ISA-16	X	X	X
Future Domain TMC-1680	ISA-16	X	X	X
Future Domain TMC-3260	PCI	X		
Future Domain TMC-7000EX	EISA	X	X	X
IBM PS/2 Microchannel SCSI Host Adapter	MCA	X[30]		
IBM PS/2 Microchannel SCSI Host Adapter (with cache)	MCA	X[30]		
Maynard 16-bit SCSI Adapter [27,31]	ISA-16	X		
MediaVision Pro Audio Spectrum-16 [32]	ISA-16	X		
Mylex DAC960	EISA	X	X	X
NCR 53C700 SCSI Adapter	MCA	X		
NCR 53C710 SCSI Adapter	MCA	X		
NCR 53C810 SCSI Controller	EMBEDDED	X[33]		X[34]
NCR 53C90 SCSI Controller	EMBEDDED	X[35]		
NCR 53C94 SCSI Controller	EMBEDDED	X[36]	X	
NCR 8150S PCI Host Adapter Board [2]	PCI	X		
NCR 8100S PCI Host Adapter Board [2]	PCI	X		
Olivetti ESC-1	EISA	X		

SCSI Host Adapter	BUS	x86	MIPS	ALPHA
Olivetti ESC-2	EISA	X		
Procom Tech Xelerator - ISA [1,37]	ISA-16	X		
QLogic Fast!SCSI ISA FL [1]	ISA-16	X		
QLogic Fast!SCSI EISA FL [1]	EISA	X		
QLogic Fast!SCSI IQ PCI [1]	PCI	X		
QLogic Fast!SCSI VESA Local FL [1]	VLB	X		
Rancho Technology RT1600-5 [1,27]	ISA-16	X		
Trantor T-128 [28,38,16]	ISA-8	X		
Trantor T-130B [28,38]	ISA-8	X		
UltraStor 14f [39]	ISA-16	X	X	X
UltraStor 24f [40]	EISA	X	X	X
UltraStor 24fa	EISA	X	X	X
UltraStor 34f	VLB	X		

SCSI CD-ROM Drives

The following SCSI CD-ROM drives have been tested with the following adapters: Adaptec AHA-1510, AHA-1542C, AHA-1640 and AHA-1742A; Future Domain TMC-1670 and MCS-600; IBM PS/2 Microchannel SCSI Host Adapter (with cache); Ultrastor 24fa, and are supported on X86, MIPS and Alpha AXP platforms except as noted. Drives have been tested for data access as well as for the audio capabilities indicated.

Standard (CD) Audio	MultiMedia Audio	SCSI CD-ROM Drives
X	X	CD-Technology CD Porta-Drive T-3301
X	X	CD-Technology CD Porta-Drive T-3401
X		Chinon® CDS-435
X		Chinon CDX-435
X	X	Chinon CDS-535
X	X	Chinon CDX-535
X	X	COMPAQ DualSpeed CD-ROM Drive
X	X	Digital Equipment RRD42
X	X	Digital Equipment RRD43
X	X	Digital Equipment RRD44
X		Hitachi® CDR-1750S
X	X	Hitachi CDR-1950s
X	X	Hitachi CDR-3750
X	X	Hitachi CDR-6750
X	X	IBM Enhanced Internal CDROM II Drive 32G2958
X	X	IBM Enhanced External CDROM II Drive 3510005
X	X	IBM PS/2 CDROM II Drive
X		Laser Magnetic Storage CM-215 [41]
X	X	NEC CDR-500 (3Xi) [42,43]
X	X	NEC CDR-600 (3Xe) [42,43]
X	X	NEC Intersect CDR-73M [44]
X	X	NEC Intersect CDR-83M [44]
X	X	NEC Intersect CDR-74
X	X	NEC Intersect CDR-84

Standard (CD) Audio	MultiMedia Audio	SCSI CD-ROM Drives
X	X	NEC Intersect CDR-74-1
X	X	NEC Intersect CDR-84-1
		Panasonic® CR-501
X	X	Panasonic CR-503
X	X	Pioneer® DRM-600 [45,46]
X	X	Procom Technology MCD-DS
X	X	Sony® CDU-541
X	X	Sony CDU-561
X	X	Sony CDU-6211
X	X	Sony CDU-7211
X	X	Sony CDU-7811
X	X	Sony CDU-55S
		Texel DM-5021
X	X	Texel DM-5024 [47]
X	X	Texel DM-5028
		Toshiba TXM-3201
X	X	Toshiba TXM-3301E
X	X	Toshiba XM-3301B
X	X	Toshiba TXM-3401E
X	X	Toshiba XM-3401B
X	X	Toshiba XM-4101B

Non-SCSI CD-ROM Drives

The following CD-ROM drives with non-SCSI interfaces have been tested. Please see SETUP.TXT on the Windows NT 3.5 CDROM for additional information on these drives and the adapters that they are supported on.

Standard (CD) Audio	Multi-Media Audio	Selection in Setup	Interface	Non-SCSI CD-ROM Drives
X	X	Panasonic CD-ROM	Panasonic LMEP0084B	Creative Labs Sound Blaster Pro™ CDROM [48]
X	X	Panasonic CD-ROM	Sound Blaster™ Pro	Creative Labs Sound Blaster Pro CDROM [48]
X	X	Panasonic CD-ROM	Sound Blaster 16	Creative Labs Sound Blaster Pro CDROM [48]
X	X	Panasonic CD-ROM	Sound Blaster 16 MultiCD	Creative Labs Sound Blaster Pro CDROM [48]
X	X	Mitsumi CD-ROM	Mitsumi 74-1881A	Mitsumi CRMC-FX001D
X	X	Mitsumi CD-ROM	Sound Blaster 16 MultiCD	Mitsumi CRMC-FX001D
X	X	Panasonic CD-ROM	Panasonic LMEP0084B	Panasonic CR-521
X	X	Panasonic CD-ROM	Sound Blaster Pro	Panasonic CR-521
X	X	Panasonic CD-ROM	Sound Blaster 16	Panasonic CR-521

Standard (CD) Audio	Multi-Media Audio	Selection in Setup	Interface	Non-SCSI CD-ROM Drives
X	X	Panasonic CD-ROM	Sound Blaster 16 MultiCD	Panasonic CR-521
X	X	Panasonic CD-ROM	Panasonic LMEP0084B	Panasonic CR-523
X	X	Panasonic CD-ROM	Sound Blaster Pro	Panasonic CR-523
X	X	Panasonic CD-ROM	Sound Blaster 16	Panasonic CR-523
X	X	Panasonic CD-ROM	Sound Blaster 16 MultiCD	Panasonic CR-523
X	X	Panasonic CD-ROM	Panasonic LMEP0084B	Panasonic CR-562
X	X	Panasonic CD-ROM	Sound Blaster Pro	Panasonic CR-562
X	X	Panasonic CD-ROM	Sound Blaster 16	Panasonic CR-562
X	X	Panasonic CD-ROM	Sound Blaster 16 MultiCD	Panasonic CR-562
X	X	Panasonic CD-ROM	Panasonic LMEP0084B	Panasonic CR-563
X	X	Panasonic CD-ROM	Sound Blaster Pro	Panasonic CR-563
X	X	Panasonic CD-ROM	Sound Blaster 16	Panasonic CR-563
X	X	Panasonic CD-ROM	Sound Blaster 16 MultiCD	Panasonic CR-563
X	X	Sony CD-ROM	Sony CDB-334	Sony CDU 31a
X	X	Sony CD-ROM	Sound Blaster 16 MultiCD	Sony CDU 31a
X	X	Sony CD-ROM	Sony CDB-334	Sony CDU 33a
X	X	Sony CD-ROM	Sound Blaster 16 MultiCD	Sony CDU 33a
X	X	IDE CD-ROM (ATAPI 1.2)	IDE Interface	Sony CDU55E

SCSI Tape Drives

The following SCSI tape drives have been tested with the following adapters using the Windows NT Backup program: Adaptec AHA-1510, AHA-1542C, AHA-1640 and AHA-1742A; Future Domain TMC-1670 and MCS-600; IBM PS/2 Microchannel SCSI Host Adapter (with cache); Ultrastor 24fa, and are supported on X86, MIPS and Alpha AXP platforms except as noted. Drives are listed under their appropriate Tape entry in SETUP.

4 Millimeter DAT

Archive® 4326NP
Archive 4326RP
Archive 4356XP
ArchiveST 2000DAT (4520NT)
ArchiveST 2000DAT (EAX4350) [49]
ArchiveST 4000DAT (4324NP)
ArchiveST 4000DAT (4352XP)
Compaq 4/16 Gigabyte TurboDAT
Compaq TurboDAT Autoloader[50]
Conner 4326NP
Conner 4326RP
Conner 4356XP
Digital Equipment TLZ06[51]
Digital Equipment TLZ07
Exabyte 4200
Exabyte 4200c[52]
Hewlett-Packard JetStore 2000
Hewlett-Packard JetStore 2000e
Hewlett-Packard JetStore 2000i
Hewlett-Packard JetStore 5000
Hewlett-Packard JetStore 5000e
Hewlett-Packard JetStore 5000i

Hewlett-Packard JetStore 6000e
Hewlett-Packard JetStore 6000i
Hewlett-Packard 35470a
Hewlett-Packard 35480a
Hewlett-Packard C1503a
Hewlett-Packard C1504a
Hewlett-Packard C1533a
Hewlett-Packard C2224c
Hewlett-Packard C2225b
IBM 2.0Gb 4mm Tape Drive Option (part number 55F9428)
IBM 2.0Gb 4mm DAT 3440 001
IBM 4/10GB 4mm DAT Drive[53]
Maynard Maynstream 1300DAT[49]
Maynard 2000 DAT[49]
Tecmar® DATaVault 2000
Tecmar DATaVault 4000
WangDAT Model 1300XL
WangDAT Model 3100
WangDAT Model 3200
WangDAT Model 3400DX

4 Millimeter Sony

Sony SDT 2000[54,55,56]
Sony SDT 4000[54,55,56]
Sony SDT 5000[54,55,56]
Sony SDT 5200[54,55,56]

Archive 2150S, 2525S, 2750

Archive 2150/2250[57]
Archive 2525
Archive 2750
Archive 2800
Maynard 525Q
Maynard 1350Q

Digital TZ86 and DLT2000

Digital Equipment DLT2000[58]
Digital Equipment TZ86 [59]
Digital Equipment TZ87 [58]
Digital Equipment TLZ875 [50,60]
Digital Equipment TZ8877[50,61]

Exabyte 2501 miniqic drive

Exabyte 2501

Exabyte 8200 Series (SCSI-1)

Exabyte EXB-8200
Exabyte EXB-8200ST
Exabyte EXB-8205[54]
Exabyte EXB-8205ST[54]
IBM 3532-023 8mm Tape Drive

Exabyte 8500 Series (SCSI-2)

Exabyte EXB-8500
Exabyte EXB-8500ST
Exabyte EXB-8500c
Exabyte EXB-8500cST
Exabyte EXB-8505
Exabyte EXB-8505ST
IBM 5.0Gb 8mm Tape Drive Option
IBM 3445 Model 001 5.0Gb 8mm Tape
Drive

Tandberg 3660, 3820, 4120, 4220

Digital Equipment TZK10
Digital Equipment TZK11
Digital Equipment TZK12
IBM 3450 1.2Gb Tape Drive Model 001
Tandberg 3660
Tandberg 3820
Tandberg 4120
Tandberg 4220
Tecmar QICVault 4000ex

Wangtek 525, 250

Tecmar QICVault 720ex
Tecmar QICVault 2400ex
Tecmar QT-525ES
Wangtek 5150ES
Wangtek 5525ES
Wangtek 51000ES

Other Tape Drives

The following tape drives have been tested using the Windows NT Backup program on X86 computers.

QIC-40/QIC-80 Floppy Tape Drive [62]

Archive 51250Q
  (SuperHornet)
Archive 5540
Archive 5580
Colorado Jumbo 120
Colorado Jumbo 250
Iomega® Tape 250
Mountain Filesafe 8000
WangTek 3040
WangTek 3080

SCSI Removable Media

The following SCSI removable media (cartridge) drives have been tested with the following adapters: Adaptec AHA-1510, AHA-1542C, AHA-1640 and AHA-1742A; Future Domain TMC-1670 and MCS-600; IBM PS/2 Microchannel SCSI Host Adapter (with cache); Ultrastor 24fa, and are supported on X86, MIPS and Alpha AXP platforms except as noted.

Hewlett-Packard Series 6300
  650/C
Hewlett-Packard 1300T
  Rewritable Optical drive
IBM 0632 Model C2*
IBM 3 1/2-Inch 127mb
  Rewritable Optical Disk
  Drive MTA-3127
Insite 21mb Floptical
Iomega 21mb Floptical
Iomega Bernoulli
  Transportable 90 Pro
Iomega Bernoulli
  Transportable 150
Maxoptix TMT 2m MO drive
Maxoptix T3-1300
Panasonic LF-7304

Peripheral Land Infinity 40
  Turbo
Peripheral Land Infinity 88
Pinnacle Micro PMO-650 [54]
Pinnacle Micro Sierra 1.3
Quantum Passport XL 85
Quantum Passport XL 127
Sony SMO-S511A-11
Sony RMO-S350
Syquest 555 44mb cartridge
Syquest 5110 88mb cartridge

SCSI Scanners

The following SCSI scanners have been tested with the following adapters: Adaptec AHA-1510, AHA-1542c, AHA-1640 and AHA-1742A; Future Domain TMC-1670 and MCS-600; IBM PS/2 Microchannel SCSI Host Adapter (with cache); Ultrastor 24fa. Scanners are supported on the x86 platform only.

HP® ScanJet IIc
HP ScanJet IIcx
HP ScanJet IIp

Disk Controllers

The following disk controllers have been tested.

COMPAQ Intelligent Drive
  Array Controller[9]
COMPAQ Intelligent Drive
  Array Controller-2[9]
COMPAQ SMART Array
  Controller[9]
DELL Drive Array Controller[9]
DELL SCSI Array
  Controller[9,63]
IBM MODEL 95 RAID
  Controller[1]
Olivetti EFP-2[64]
UltraStor 124f EISA Disk
  Array Controller
Western Digital™ 1003
  (ESDI, IDE)

Hard Drives

The following hard drives have been tested. SCSI hard drives have been tested with the following SCSI adapters: Adaptec AHA-1510, AHA-1542C, AHA-1640 and AHA-1742A; Future Domain TMC-1670 and MCS-600; IBM PS/2 Microchannel SCSI Host Adapter (with cache); Ultrastor 24fa. and are supported on X86, MIPS and Alpha AXP platforms except as noted.

SCSI Hard Drives

Conner CFA540S
Conner CFP1060S
Conner CFP2105S
Conner CR1-1000D
Hewlett Packard C3323A
Maxtor 7120SR
Maxtor 7213SR
Maxtor 7245SR
Maxtor 7345SR
Maxtor LXT340SY
Maxtor MXT1240S
Micropolis 1924
Storage Solutions SSI-2000M

IDE Hard Drives

Conner CFA540A
Conner CFA810A
Conner CFA1080A
Conner CFS210A
Conner CFS420A
Maxtor LXT340A
Maxtor 7120AT
Maxtor 7131AT
Maxtor 7171AT
Maxtor 7213AT
Maxtor 7245AT
Maxtor 7273AT
Maxtor 7345AT
Maxtor 7546AT
Maxtor MXT-540AL

Storage Cabinets

The following peripheral storage cabinets have been tested, and are supported on X86, MIPS and Alpha AXP platforms.

Hewlett-Packard Storage
  System with HP EISA HBA
Hewlett-Packard Storage
  System with HP MCA HBA
IBM 3510 SCSI Storage
  Enclosure
Professional Concepts SCSI
  Storage Cabinet
Professional Concepts SCSI
  Storage Cabinet+
Digital Equipment
  StorageWorks BA-350
  Deskside Expansion Unit
Digital Equipment
  StorageWorks BA-353
  "Pizza Box" Desktop
  Expansion Unit

RAID Systems

The following RAID storage systems have been tested with the following SCSI adapters: Adaptec AHA-1510, AHA-1542C, AHA-1640 and AHA-1742A; Future Domain TMC-1670 and MCS-600; IBM PS/2 Microchannel SCSI Host Adapter (with cache); Ultrastor 24fa, and are supported on X86, MIPS and Alpha AXP platforms except as noted.

Conner CR6-RAID
Micropolis RAIDION LT
  2100[65,66]
Micropolis MICRODISK
  LT2100 [65,66]
Professional Concepts SCSI
  iRAID Cabinet+
Storage Solutions, Inc.
  RACa-ray Model 10
Storage Solutions, Inc.
  RACa-ray Model 20
Storage Solutions, Inc.
  RACa-ray Model 30

Video Display Support

The following display adapters have been tested on X86 systems. Most common scan frequencies are supported. Your video monitor should support the same resolutions and scan frequencies as your display adapter. Please refer to README.WRI for more information on display support.

Display Adapters	DRIVER	640x480	800x600	1024x768	1280x1024	OTHER
#9 GXE 64 PCI	S3	256, 65k, TRUE	256, 65k, TRUE	256, 65k	256	D, E
#9 GXE 64 PRO PCI	S3	256, 65k, TRUE	256, 65k, TRUE	256, 65k, TRUE	256, 65k	D, E, F, J, K
#9 GXE LEVEL 12 ISA (3mb) [67]	S3	256, 65k, TRUE	256, 65k, TRUE	256, 65k	256	
#9 GXE LEVEL 12 VLB (1mb) [67]	S3	256, 65k	256	256		
ACTIX GRAPHICS ENGINE	S3	256	256	256		
ACTIX GRAPHICS ENGINE 32 PLUS	S3	256, 65k	256, 65k	256		
ACTIX GRAPHICS ENGINE 32 VLB	S3	256, 65k	256, 65k	256, 65k	256	
ACTIX PROSTAR VLB	CIRRUS	16, 256, 65k	16, 256	16, 256	16	
ARTIST GRAPHICS WINSPRINT 1000i [1]	ART	256	256	256	256	J
ARTIST GRAPHICS XJ1000 [1]	ART	256	256	256	256	
ATI 8514 ULTRA	8514A	256	256	256		

Display Adapters	DRIVER	640x480	800x600	1024x768	1280x1024	OTHER
ATI GRAPHICS PRO TURBO PCI	ATI	256, 65k, 16.7m, TRUE	256, 65k, 16.7m, TRUE	256, 65k, 16.7m, TRUE	256, 65k, 16.7m	
ATI GRAPHICS PRO TURBO VLB	ATI	256, 65k, 16.7m, TRUE	256, 65k, 16.7m, TRUE	256, 65k, 16.7m, TRUE	256, 65k, 16.7m	
ATI GRAPHICS ULTRA	ATI	256	256	256		
ATI GRAPHICS ULTRA PLUS [68]	ATI	256, 65k, 16.7m	256, 65k, 16.7m	256, 65k	256	
ATI GRAPHICS ULTRA PRO ISA [68]	ATI	256, 65k, 16.7m	256, 65k, 16.7m	256, 65k	256	
ATI GRAPHICS ULTRA PRO EISA [68]	ATI	256, 65k, 16.7m	256, 65k, 16.7m	256, 65k	256	
ATI GRAPHICS ULTRA PRO PCI [69]	ATI	256, 65k, 16.7m	256, 65k, 16.7m	256, 65k	256	
ATI GRAPHICS ULTRA PRO VLB [68]	ATI	256, 65k, 16.7m	256, 65k, 16.7m	256, 65k	256	
ATI GRAPHICS VANTAGE	ATI	256	256	256		
ATI GRAPHICS WONDER ISA [68]	ATI	256, 65k, 16.7m	256	256		
ATI GRAPHICS WONDER VLB [68]	ATI	256, 65k, 16.7m	256, 65k	256		
ATI GRAPHICS XPRESSION PCI	ATI	16, 256, 65k, 16.7m, TRUE	16, 256, 65k, 16.7m, TRUE	16, 256, 65k	16, 256	
ATI GRAPHICS XPRESSION VLB	ATI	16, 256, 65k, 16.7m, TRUE	16, 256, 65k, 16.7m, TRUE	16, 256, 65k	16, 256	
ATI VGA Wonder XL24 [1]	ATIVGA	16, 256	16, 256	16, 256		
CARDEX VLB	CIRRUS	16, 256, 65k	16, 256	16, 256	16	
COMPAQ AVGA [70]	AVGA[1]	16, 256	16			
COMPAQ QVISION 1024/I	QV	16, 256	256	256		
COMPAQ QVISION 1024/E	QV	16, 256	256	256		
COMPAQ QVISION 1024/I (ENHANCED)	QV	16, 256	256	256		
COMPAQ QVISION 1024/E (ENHANCED)	QV	16, 256	256	256		
COMPAQ QVISION 1280/I	QV	16, 256	256	256	256	
COMPAQ QVISION 1280/E	QV	16, 256	256	256	256	
COMPAQ QVISION 2000 PCI	MGA[1]	256, 65k, 16.7m	256, 65k, 16.7m	256, 65k	256	G, H

Display Adapters	DRIVER	640x480	800x600	1024x768	1280x1024	OTHER
DIAMOND SPEEDSTAR	ET4000	16, 256, 65k	16, 256	16, 256		
DIAMOND SPEEDSTAR 24X	WD	16, 256	16, 256	16, 256		
DIAMOND SPEEDSTAR PRO	CIRRUS	16, 256, 65k	16, 256	16, 256	16	
DIAMOND SPEEDSTAR PRO VLB	CIRRUS	16, 256, 65k	16, 256	16, 256	16	
DIAMOND SPEEDSTAR 64 ISA	CIRRUS	16, 256, 65k	16, 256, 65k	16, 256, 65k	16, 256	
DIAMOND SPEEDSTAR 64 PCI	CIRRUS	16, 256, 65k	16, 256, 65k	16, 256, 65k	16, 256	
DIAMOND STEALTH 24	S3	256, 65k	256, 65k	256		
DIAMOND STEALTH 24 VLB	S3	256, 65k	256, 65k	256		
DIAMOND STEALTH 32 PCI	ET4000	16, 256, 65k	16, 256	16, 256		
DIAMOND STEALTH 64 DRAM PCI	S3	256, 65k, TRUE	256, 65k, TRUE	256, 65k	256	D, E, J
DIAMOND STEALTH 64 DRAM VLB	S3	256, 65k, TRUE	256, 65k, TRUE	256, 65k	256	D, E, J
DIAMOND STEALTH 64 PCI	S3	256, 65k, TRUE	256, 65k, TRUE	256, 65k, TRUE	256, 65k	D, E, F, J, K
DIAMOND STEALTH 64 VLB	S3	256, 65k, TRUE	256, 65k, TRUE	256, 65k, TRUE	256, 65k	D, E, F, J, K
DIAMOND STEALTH PRO	S3	256, 65k	256, 65k	256, 65k	256	
DIAMOND STEALTH PRO VLB	S3	256, 65k	256, 65k	256, 65k	256	
DIAMOND STEALTH VRAM	S3	256	256	256		
DIAMOND VIPER PCI [9]	WEITEKP 9	256, 65k, TRUE	256, 65k, TRUE	256, 65k	256	J
DIAMOND VIPER VLB [71]	WEITEKP 9	256, 65k, TRUE	256, 65k, TRUE	256, 65k	256	J
DIGITAL PCXAG-AL S3-864 PCI	S3	256, 65k, TRUE	256, 65k, TRUE	256, 65k, TRUE	256, 65k	D, J, K
ELSA WINNER 1000	S3	256, 65k	256, 65k	256		
GENOA PHANTOM 32I 8900 VLB	ET4000	16, 256, 65k	16, 256	16, 256		
IBM XGA	XGA®	256		256		
IBM XGA-2	XGA	256	256	256		A, B, C
MATROX ULTIMA PCI	MGA[1]	256, 65k, 16.7m	256, 65k, 16.7m	256, 65k	256	G, H
MATROX ULTIMA + PCI	MGA[1]	256, 65k, 16.7m	256, 65k, 16.7m	256, 65k, 16.7m	256, 65k	G, H, I, J, K
MEDIAVISION THUNDER & LIGHTNING	CIRRUS	16, 256, 65k	16, 256	16, 256		

Display Adapters	DRIVER	640x480	800x600	1024x768	1280x1024	OTHER
METHEUS PREMIER 928	S3	256, 65k	256, 65k	256, 65k	256, 65k	
MICRONICS VL-BUS	S3	256, 65k	256, 65k	256		
MIRO CRYSTAL 20sd VLB	S3	256, 65k, TRUE	256, 65k, TRUE	256, 65k	256	
NCR 32BLT VLB	NCR77C22	16, 256	16, 256	16, 256	256	
NCR 77C22	NCR77C22	16, 256	16, 256	16		
NCR 77C22E	NCR77C22	16, 256	16, 256	16, 256		
ORCHID FAHRENHEIT 1280	S3	256	256	256		
ORCHID FAHRENHEIT 1280 PLUS ISA	S3	256, 65k	256, 65k	256		
ORCHID FAHRENHEIT 1280 PLUS VLB	S3	256, 65k	256, 65k	256, 65k	256	
ORCHID FAHRENHEIT VA	S3	256, 65k	256, 65k	256		
ORCHID FAHRENHEIT VA/VLB	S3	256, 65k	256, 65k	256, 65k	256	
ORCHID PRODESIGNER 2	ET4000	16, 256	16, 256	16, 256		
ORCHID PRODESIGNER IIS EISA	ET4000	16, 256, 65k	16, 256	16, 256		
ORCHID PRODESIGNER IIS ISA	ET4000	16, 256, 65k	16, 256	16, 256		
PARADISE WINDOWS GRAPHICS ACCELERATOR	WD	16, 256	16, 256	16, 256		
TRIDENT 8900C	TRIDENT	16, 256	16, 256	16, 256		
TRIDENT 9000	TRIDENT	16, 256	16	16		
VIDEO SEVEN™ VRAM	VIDEO7	16, 256	16	16		
VIDEO SEVEN VRAM II	VIDEO7	16, 256	16, 256	16, 256		
VIDEO SEVEN VRAM II ERGO	VIDEO7	16, 256	16, 256	16, 256		
WIZARD 9000VL	WEITEKP9	256, 65k, TRUE	256, 65k, TRUE	256, 65k	256	J

The following display adapters have been tested on Digital Equipment Alpha AXP systems. Most common scan frequencies are supported. Your video monitor should support the same resolutions and scan frequencies as your display adapter. Please refer to README.WRI for more information on display support.

Display Adapters	DRIVER	640x480	800x600	1024x768	1280x1024	OTHER
#9 GXE 64 PCI	S3	256, 65k, TRUE	256, 65k, TRUE	256, 65k	256	D, E
#9 GXE 64 PRO PCI	S3	256, 65k, TRUE	256, 65k, TRUE	256, 65k, TRUE	256, 65k	D, E, F, J, K
#9 GXE LEVEL 12 ISA (3mb) [67]	S3	256, 65k, TRUE	256, 65k, TRUE	256, 65k	256	
ACTIX GRAPHICS ENGINE	S3	256	256	256		
ACTIX GRAPHICS ENGINE 32 PLUS	S3	256, 65k	256, 65k	256		
COMPAQ QVISION 1024/E	QV	16, 256	256	256		
COMPAQ QVISION 1024/E (ENHANCED)	QV	16, 256	256	256		
COMPAQ QVISION 1280/E	QV	16, 256	256	256		
DIAMOND STEALTH 24	S3	256, 65k	256, 65k	256		
DIAMOND STEALTH 64 DRAM PCI	S3	256, 65k, TRUE	256, 65k, TRUE	256, 65k	256	D, E, J
DIAMOND STEALTH 64 PCI	S3	256, 65k, TRUE	256, 65k, TRUE	256, 65k, TRUE	256, 65k	D, E, F, J, K
DIAMOND STEALTH PRO	S3	256, 65k	256, 65k	256, 65k	256	
DIAMOND STEALTH VRAM	S3	256	256	256		
DIGITAL PCXAG-AL S3-864 PCI	S3	256, 65k, TRUE	256, 65k, TRUE	256, 65k, TRUE	256, 65k	D, J, K
ELSA WINNER 1000	S3	256, 65k	256, 65k	256		
METHEUS PREMIER 928	S3	256, 65k	256, 65k	256, 65k	256, 65k	
ORCHID FAHRENHEIT 1280	S3	256	256	256		
ORCHID FAHRENHEIT 1280 PLUS ISA	S3	256, 65k	256, 65k	256		

	Color Depths
16	16 colors
256	256 colors
32k	32,768 colors
65k	65,536 colors
16.7m	16.7 million colors (24 bits\pixel)
TRUE	True Color(16.7m accelerated)

Display modes in the 'Other' Column	
A	640x400x256
B	1040x768x256
C	1104x828x256
D	1152x864x256
E	1152x864x65k
F	1152x864xTRUE
G	1182x882x256
H	1182x882x65k
I	1182x882x16.7m
J	1600x1200x256
K	1600x1200x65k

Display adapters not listed above are expected to work on X86 systems if they use the following supported chip sets. Install first as Standard VGA, then select the corresponding driver from the Display Applet in the Control Panel.

Manufacturer	Chip Set	Driver	Color Depths	Max Res.
IBM	8514/a	8514A	256	1024x768
	XGA	XGA	256	1104x828
ATI	8514 Ultra	8514A	256	1024x768
	MACH 8	ATI	256	1024x768
	MACH 32	ATI	256, 65K, 16.7M	1280x1024
	MACH 64	ATI	16, 256, 65K, 16.7M, TRUE	1280x1024
Compaq	AVGA	AVGA	16, 256	800x600
	QVision 1024	QV	16, 256	1024x768
	QVision 1280	QV	16, 256	1280x1024
	QVision 2000	MGA[1]	256, 65K, 16.7M	1280x1024
Cirrus Logic	5422, 5424[72]	CIRRUS	16, 256, 65k	1280x1024
	5426, 5428[72]	CIRRUS	16, 256, 65k	1280x1024
	5434	CIRRUS	16, 256, 65k	1280x1024
Tseng Labs	ET4000	ET4000	16, 256, 65k	1024x768
	ET4000-W32i	ET4000	16, 256, 65k	1024x768
	ET4000-W32p	ET4000	16, 256, 65k	1024x768
Matrox	MGA (ATLAS)	MGA[1]	256, 65K, 16.7M	1600x1200
NCR	NCR77C22	NCR77C22	16, 256	1024x768
	NCR77C22E	NCR77C22	16, 256	1024x768
	NCR BLT 32	NCR77C22	16, 256	1280x1024
S3	911, 911a, 924	S3	256	1024x768
	801[73]	S3	256, 32k/65k	1024x768
	805[73]	S3	256, 32k/65k	1280x1024
	928[73,74]	S3	256, 32k/65k, TRUE	1280x1024
	864	S3	256, 65k, TRUE	1280x1024
	964[75]	S3	256, 65k, TRUE	1600x1200

Manufacturer	Chip Set	Driver	Color Depths	Max Res.
Trident	9000	TRIDENT	16, 256	1024x768
	8900c	TRIDENT	16, 256	1024x768
Headlands	Video 7	V7VRAM	16, 256	1024x768
Western Digital	WD90C30[76]	WDVGA	16, 256	1024x768
	WD90C31[76]	WDVGA	16, 256	1024x768
	WD90C33[76]	WDVGA	16, 256	1024x768
Weitek	P9000[75]	WEITEKP9	256, 65K, TRUE	1600x1200

The following table shows the maximum display and color resolutions available with each video driver using different amounts of video RAM. Most display adapters can use the standard VGA driver for 16-color modes.

Drivers	Video RAM	Colors				
		16	256	32k/65k	16m	True Color
8514/a	1MB		1024x768			
ART[2]	2MB		1600x1280			
ATI[77]	512Kb		640x480			
	1Mb	1280x1024	1024x768	800x600	640x480	
	2Mb	1280x1024	1280x1024	1024x768	800x600	800x600
	4Mb	1280x1024	1280x1024	1280x1024	1280x1024	1024x768
ATIVGA[2]	1MB		1024x768			
AVGA	512Kb	800x600	640x480			
Cirrus[78]	512Kb	1024x768	640x480			
	1Mb	1280x1024	1024x768	640x480		
	2Mb	1280x1024	1280x1024	1024x768		
DGX	2Mb		1280x1024	1152x900		
ET4000	512Kb	1024x768	640x480			
	1Mb	1024x768	1024x768	640x480		
MGA[1]	2Mb		1280x1024	1182x882	800x600	
	4Mb		1600x1200	1600x1200	1182x882	
NCR 77C22	1Mb	1024x768	1024x768			
	2Mb	1024x768	1280x1024			
QV	512KB	640x480				
	1Mb	640x480	1024x768			
	2Mb	640x480	1280x1024			
S3	512		800x600			
	1Mb		1152x864	800x600		
	2Mb		1600x1200	1152x864		800x600
	4MB		1600x1200	1600x1200		1152x864

Drivers	Video RAM	Colors				
		16	**256**	**32k/65k**	**16m**	**True Color**
Trident	512Kb	1024x768	640x480			
	1Mb	1024x768	1024x768			
Video7	512Kb	1024x768	640x480			
	1Mb	1024x768	1024x768			
VGA	256Kb	640x480				
	512Kb	800x600				
WD	512Kb	1024x768	640x480			
	1Mb	1024x768	1024x768			
WEITEKP9	2Mb		1600x1280	1024x768		800x600
XGA	1Mb		1104x828			

Network Adapters
The following network adapters have been tested on the indicated platforms.

x86	MIPS	ALPHA	Network Adapter
X	X	X	3Com® 3C503 EtherLink II® (Coax & TP) [79]
X	X	X	3Com 3C503/16 EtherLink® II/16 (Coax & TP) [79]
X	X		3Com 3C507 EtherLink 16 (Coax & TP) [79]
X	X	X	3Com 3C509 EtherLink III Parallel Tasking Adapter - ISA (Coax, TP and Combo) [79]
X			3Com 3C523 EtherLink/MC (Coax & TP) [79]
X			3Com 3C527 EtherLink/MC 32 Bus Mastering Adapter [2]
X			3Com 3C529 EtherLink III Parallel Tasking Adapter - MCA (Coax & TP) [79]
X	X	X	3Com 3C579 EtherLink III Parallel Tasking Adapter - EISA (Coax & TP) [79]
X			3Com 3C770 FDDILink-F for Optical, UTP & STP [79,1,80]
X			Advanced Micro Devices Am1500T Ethernet Adapter
X			Advanced Micro Devices Am2100 Ethernet Adapter
X			Advanced Micro Devices PCnet® Family Adapters [1]
X			Andrew ISA IIA Adapter [1]
X			Cabletron E21XX Ethernet DNI [1]
X			Cabletron T20XX 16/4 Token Ring DNI [1]
X			Cabletron F30XX FDDI Adapter [1,80]
X			Cabletron F70XX FDDI Adapter [1,80]
X			Cisco C321T-PC Turbo EISA FDDI Adapter/PC [1]
X			Cogent eMASTER + 960 PCI Ethernet Adapter [1]
X	X	X	COMPAQ 32-Bit Dualspeed Token Ring Controller
X	X	X	COMPAQ 32-Bit Netflex Controller
X	X	X	COMPAQ 32-Bit Netflex Controller with Token Ring Module
X	X	X	COMPAQ Ethernet 16TP Controller
X	X	X	COMPAQ NetFlex-2 ENET-TR Controller [79]
X	X	X	COMPAQ NetFlex-2 TR Controller [79]
X	X	X	COMPAQ NetFlex-2 DualPort TR Controller
X	X	X	COMPAQ NetFlex-2 DualPort ENET Controller [79]
X			COPS LTI ISA

x86	MIPS	ALPHA	Network Adapter
X			Crescendo C321M-PC EISA FDDI ADAPTER/PC [1,80]
X			DayStar Digital LocalTalk® Adapter
X			DCA® IRMAtrac 16/4 Convertible Token Ring Adapter [1]
X	X	X	DEC® DE100 EtherWORKS LC
X	X	X	DEC DE101 EtherWORKS LC/TP
X	X	X	DEC DE200 EtherWORKS Turbo
X	X	X	DEC DE201 EtherWORKS Turbo/TP [79]
X	X	X	DEC DE202 EtherWORKS Turbo TP/BNC
X	X	X	DEC DE422 EtherWORKS EISA TP/BNC
X		X	DEC DE435 PCI Ethernet Adapter [1]
X		X	DEC DC21040 PCI Ethernet Controller [1]
X			Hewlett-Packard HP J2573A 10/100VG ISA LAN Adapter [1]
X			Hewlett-Packard HP J2577A 10/100VG EISA LAN Adapter [1]
X			Hewlett-Packard HP 27245A PC LAN Adapter/8 TP [1]
X			Hewlett-Packard HP 27246A MC LAN Adapter/16 TP [1]
X			Hewlett-Packard HP 27247A PC LAN Adapter/16 TP [1]
X			Hewlett-Packard HP 27247B PC LAN Adapter/16 TP Plus [1]
X			Hewlett-Packard HP 27250 PC LAN Adapter/8 TL [1]
X			Hewlett-Packard HP 27252A PC LAN Adapter/16 TL Plus [1]
X	X	X	IBM Token Ring Adapter 16/4
X			IBM Token Ring Adapter 16/4 /A
X	X	X	IBM 16/4 Token Ring ISA-16 Adapter
X	X	X	IBM 16/4 Token Ring II ISA Adapter
X			IBM LANStreamer™ MC 32 Adapter [1]
X			ICL EtherTeam16i Combo Adapter [1]
X			ICL EtherTeam16i Duo Adapter [1]
X			ICL EtherTeam16i TP Adapter [1]
X			ICL EtherTeam32 EISA Adapter [1]
X			Intel 82595 Ethernet Adapter [2]
X	X	X	Intel EtherExpress™ 16 PCLA8110
X	X	X	Intel EtherExpress 16C PCLA8100
X	X	X	Intel EtherExpress 16TP PCLA8120
X			Intel EtherExpress Flash 32 Ethernet Adapter [2]
X	X	X	Intel EtherExpress FlashC PCLA8105
X			Intel TokenExpress™ ISA/16S [1]
X			Intel TokenExpress MCA 16/4 [1]
X			Intel TokenExpress EISA 16/4 [1]
X			Intel TokenExpress EISA/32 [1]
X			Intel EtherExpress PRO (i82595) [1]
X			Madge Smart 16/4 AT Ringnode [1]
X			Madge Smart 16/4 AT Plus Ringnode [1]
X			Madge Smart 16/4 EISA Ringnode [79.1]
X			Madge Smart 16/4 ISA Client Plus [1]
X			Madge Smart 16/4 MC Ringnode [1]
X			Madge Smart 16/4 MC32 Ringnode [1]

x86	MIPS	ALPHA	Network Adapter
	X		National Semiconductor DP83932 (SONIC) Motherboard Ethernet Controller on MIPS ARC/R4000 systems [79]
X			NCR WaveLAN/AT [1]
X			NCR WaveLAN/MC [1]
X	X	X	Network Peripherals NP-EISA/S FDDI
X			Network Peripherals NP-MCA/S FDDI
X			Novell®/Eagle Technology NE1000
X	X	X	Novell/Eagle Technology NE2000 [79]
X	X	X	Novell/Eagle Technology NE3200 [79]
X			Olicom Token-Ring,PowerMAC MCA WS,OC-3129 [1]
X			Olicom Token-Ring,PowerMAC EISA WS,OC-3133 [1]
X			Olicom Token-Ring,PowerMAC ISA WS,OC-3117 [1]
X			Olicom Token-Ring,PowerMAC EISA SRV,OC-3135 [1]
X	X	X	Proteon ProNET-4/16 p1390 Token Ring Adapter
X	X	X	Proteon ProNET 4/16 p1392 Token Ring Adapter
X	X	X	Proteon ProNET 4/16 p1392plus Token Ring Adapter
X			Proteon ProNET 4/16 p1892 Token Ring Adapter
X	X	X	Proteon ProNET 4/16 p1990 Token Ring Adapter
X	X	X	Proteon ProNET 4/16 p1990plus Token Ring Adapter
X	X	X	Standard Microsystems 8003EP EtherCard™ PLUS
X	X	X	Standard Microsystems 8013EBT EtherCard PLUS16
X	X	X	Standard Microsystems 8013EP EtherCard PLUS Elite16
X			Standard Microsystems 8013EP/A EtherCard PLUS Elite/A
X	X	X	Standard Microsystems 8013EPC EtherCard PLUS Elite16
X	X	X	Standard Microsystems 8013EW EtherCard PLUS EliteCombo
X	X	X	Standard Microsystems 8013EWC EtherCard PLUS EliteCombo
X	X	X	Standard Microsystems 8013W EtherCard PLUS Elite16T
X	X	X	Standard Microsystems 8013WB EtherCard PLUS
X	X	X	Standard Microsystems 8013WC EtherCard PLUS Elite16T
X			Standard Microsystems 8013WP/A EtherCard PLUS Elite10T/A
X			Standard Microsystems 8216C EtherCard Elite Ultra [1]
X			Standard Microsystems 8232 EtherCard Elite 32 Ultra [1]
X			Standard Microsystems 8416 Ultra PnP [1]
X			Standard Microsystems 8432 PCI Ethernet Adapter [1]
X			Thomas-Conrad TC4045 ISA Token Ring Adapter [1]
X			Thomas-Conrad TC4046 MCA Token Ring Adapter [1,79]
X	X	X	Thomas-Conrad Arcnet® (Generic Driver)
X	X	X	Ungermann-Bass® NIUpc
X	X	X	Ungermann-Bass NIUpc/EOTP
X			Ungermann-Bass NIUps/EOTP [79]
X			Xircom Corporate Series CreditCard Ethernet Adapter [1,79]
X			Xircom Pocket Ethernet II Adapter [1,81,82]
X			Xircom Pocket Ethernet III Adapter [1,81,79,82]

Uninterruptible Power Supplies

The following Uninterruptible Power Supplies have been tested, and are supported on X86, MIPS and Alpha AXP platforms except as noted.

Manufacturer's Cable Part #	Power Failure Signal	Low Battery Signal	Remote UPS Shutdown	Uninterruptible Power Supplies
AP940-0020B	Positive	Positive	Positive	American Power Conversion Back-UPS 400
AP940-0020B	Positive	Positive	Positive	American Power Conversion Back-UPS 450
AP940-0020B	Positive	Positive	Positive	American Power Conversion Back-UPS 600
AP940-0020B	Positive	Positive	Positive	American Power Conversion Back-UPS 900
AP940-0020B	Positive	Positive	Positive	American Power Conversion Back-UPS 1250
AP940-0020B	Positive	Positive	Positive	American Power Conversion Matrix®-UPS 3000
AP940-0020B	Positive	Positive	Positive	American Power Conversion Matrix-UPS 5000
AP940-0020B	Positive	Positive	Positive	American Power Conversion Smart-UPS 250
AP940-0020B	Positive	Positive	Positive	American Power Conversion Smart-UPS 400
AP940-0020B	Positive	Positive	Positive	American Power Conversion Smart-UPS 600
AP940-0020B	Positive	Positive	Positive	American Power Conversion Smart-UPS 600RM
AP940-0020B	Positive	Positive	Positive	American Power Conversion Smart-UPS 600XL
AP940-0020B	Positive	Positive	Positive	American Power Conversion Smart-UPS 900
AP940-0020B	Positive	Positive	Positive	American Power Conversion Smart-UPS 900XL
AP940-0020B	Positive	Positive	Positive	American Power Conversion Smart-UPS 1250
AP940-0020B	Positive	Positive	Positive	American Power Conversion Smart-UPS 1250RM
AP940-0020B	Positive	Positive	Positive	American Power Conversion Smart-UPS 2000
AP940-0020B	Positive	Positive	Positive	American Power Conversion Smart-UPS 2000RM
BIK008L, BAA-0162	Positive	Positive	Positive	Best Power Technology FERRUPS FE500VA
BIK008L, BAA-0162	Positive	Positive	Positive	Best Power Technology FERRUPS FE700VA

Manufacturer's Cable Part #	Power Failure Signal	Low Battery Signal	Remote UPS Shutdown	Uninterruptible Power Supplies
BIK008L, BAA-0162	Positive	Positive	Positive	Best Power Technology FERRUPS FE850VA
BIK008L, BAA-0162	Positive	Positive	Positive	Best Power Technology FERRUPS FE1.15KVA
BIK008L, BAA-0162	Positive	Positive	Positive	Best Power Technology FERRUPS FE1.4KVA
BIK008L, BAA-0162	Positive	Positive	Positive	Best Power Technology FERRUPS FE1.8KVA
BIK008L, BAA-0162	Positive	Positive	Positive	Best Power Technology FERRUPS FE2.1KVA
BIK008L, BAA-0162	Positive	Positive	Positive	Best Power Technology FERRUPS FE3.1KVA
BIK008L, BAA-0162	Positive	Positive	Positive	Best Power Technology FERRUPS FE4.3KVA
BIK008L, BAA-0162	Positive	Positive	Positive	Best Power Technology FERRUPS FE5.3KVA
BIK008L, BAA-0162	Positive	Positive	Positive	Best Power Technology FERRUPS FE7KVA
BIK008L, BAA-0162	Positive	Positive	Positive	Best Power Technology FERRUPS FE10KVA
BIK008L, BAA-0162	Positive	Positive	Positive	Best Power Technology FERRUPS FE12.5KVA
BIK008L, BAA-0162	Positive	Positive	Positive	Best Power Technology FERRUPS FE18KVA
BIK009L, INT-0023	Positive	Positive	Positive	Best Power Technology Fortress LI 360B/D
BIK009L, INT-0023	Positive	Positive	Positive	Best Power Technology Fortress LI 460B/D
BIK009L, INT-0023	Positive	Positive	Positive	Best Power Technology Fortress LI 660B/D
BIK009L, INT-0023	Positive	Positive	Positive	Best Power Technology Fortress LI 950B/D
BIK009L, INT-0023	Positive	Positive	Positive	Best Power Technology Fortress LI 1.3KB/D
BIK009L, INT-0023	Positive	Positive	Positive	Best Power Technology Fortress LI 1.7KF/FX™
BIK009L, INT-0023	Positive	Positive	Positive	Best Power Technology Fortress LI 1.7KG/GX
BIK009L, INT-0023	Positive	Positive	Positive	Best Power Technology Fortress LI 1.7KJX
BIK009L, INT-0023	Positive	Positive	Positive	Best Power Technology Fortress LI 2KF/G/H/J
BIK009L, INT-0023	Positive	Positive	Positive	Best Power Technology Fortress LI 2.5KP/PX
BIK009L, INT-0023	Positive	Positive	Positive	Best Power Technology Fortress LI 3KL/LX
BIK009L, INT-0023	Positive	Positive	Positive	Best Power Technology Fortress LI 3KN/NX

Manufacturer's Cable Part #	Power Failure Signal	Low Battery Signal	Remote UPS Shutdown	Uninterruptible Power Supplies
BIK009L, INT-0023	Positive	Positive	Positive	Best Power Technology Fortress LI 3KQ/QX
BIK009L, INT-0023	Positive	Positive	Positive	Best Power Technology Fortress LI 3KR/RX
BIK009L, INT-0023	Positive	Positive	Positive	Best Power Technology Fortress LI 3KS/SX
BIK009L, INT-0023	Positive	Positive	Positive	Best Power Technology Fortress LI 3KS
73-0665	Positive	Positive	Positive	Tripp Lite BC400LAN
73-0665	Positive	Positive	Positive	Tripp Lite BC500LAN
73-0665	Positive	Positive	Positive	Tripp Lite BC600LAN
73-0665	Positive	Positive	Positive	Tripp Lite BC750LAN
73-0665	Positive	Positive	Positive	Tripp Lite BC800LAN
73-0665	Positive	Positive	Positive	Tripp Lite BC900LAN
73-0665	Positive	Positive	Positive	Tripp Lite BC1250LAN
73-0665	Positive	Positive	Positive	Tripp Lite OMNI500LAN
73-0665	Positive	Positive	Positive	Tripp Lite OMNI600LAN
73-0665	Positive	Positive	Positive	Tripp Lite OMNI750LAN
73-0665	Positive	Positive	Positive	Tripp Lite OMNI900LAN
73-0665	Positive	Positive	Positive	Tripp Lite OMNI1250LAN
73-0665	Positive	Positive	Positive	Tripp Lite OMNI2000LAN
73-0665	Positive	Positive	Positive	Tripp Lite SMART200
73-0665	Positive	Positive	Positive	Tripp Lite SMART400
73-0665	Positive	Positive	Positive	Tripp Lite SMART500
73-0665	Positive	Positive	Positive	Tripp Lite SMART600
73-0665	Positive	Positive	Positive	Tripp Lite SMART750
73-0665	Positive	Positive	Positive	Tripp Lite SMART900
73-0665	Positive	Positive	Positive	Tripp Lite SMART1250
73-0665	Positive	Positive	Positive	Tripp Lite Unison PS4.5
73-0665	Positive	Positive	Positive	Tripp Lite Unison PS6.0
73-0665	Positive	Positive	Positive	Tripp Lite Unison PS9.0

Multimedia Audio Adapters

The following multimedia audio adapters have been tested, and are supported on X86, MIPS and Alpha AXP platforms except as noted.

x86	MIPS	ALPHA	Multimedia Audio Adapter
X			COMPAQ Business Audio
X	X	X	Creative Labs Sound Blaster 1.x
X	X	X	Creative Labs Sound Blaster Pro [83]
X	X	X	Media Vision™ Pro AudioSpectrum-16 [84]
X	X	X	Media Vision Pro AudioStudio [84]
X	X	X	Media Vision Thunder Board [83]
X	X	X	Microsoft Windows Sound System
	X		Built-in audio adapter on MIPS ARC/R4000 systems

Modems

The following modems are supported for use with Remote Access Service, and are supported on X86, MIPS and Alpha AXP platforms except as noted.

3X
3X 396D
3X 514D
3X WYSIWYF 496D
3X WYSIWYF 496DB
3X WYSIWYF 514D
3X WYSIWYF 514DB
3X WYSIWYF 514DBX
3X WYSIWYF 514DP
3X WYSIWYF 514DPX
3X WYSIWYF 514DS
3X WYSIWYF 514DSX
AJ 1445/1446
AJ 2423
AJ 9636
Andest Rocket
Angia DataStart for
   CompaqLTE
ARN DX
ARN Generique
AT&T 2224 CEO
AT&T 4024
AT&T Comsphere 3810
AT&T Comsphere 3811
AT&T Comsphere 3820
AT&T Comsphere 3830
AT&T Dataport
ATI 2400 etc/e
ATI 9600 etc/e
ATTEL MX 144_14400bps
ATTEL MX 144_9600bps
ATTEL MX 96xxx
Avtek CD900
Avtek CD930
Banksia MX-6 V.32bis
Banksia XM124/R
   FAXMODEM
Boca Modem V.Fast Class
Bocamodem M1440 Alt
Cardinal 14400
Cardinal 14400 Internal
Cardinal 2400e
Cardinal 9600
CDC 6436

CDC 6438
Codex 2264
Codex 3220
Codex 3220 Plus
Codex 3260
Codex 3260 Fast
Codex 3261
Codex 3261 Fast
Codex 3262
Codex 3262 Fast
Codex 3263
Codex 3263 Fast
Codex 3265
Codex 3265 Fast
Codex 326x
Codex 326x FAST
Codex V.34R
COM1 MC215
COM1 MC216
COM1 MV214
COM1 MV215
COM1 MV216
COM1 MV219
ComCom Spirit II
ComCom Spirit TERBO
Compaq SpeedPAQ 144
Compaq SpeedPAQ 144
Creatix LC144VF
Creatix LC288FC
CTK SHORTY 144 SL
CXR Telcom 1445
DATACONSYST DAC124
Dataflex Rapier+ V32Bis
DataRace RediModem
   V.32bis[94]
Datatrek 2424AMH
Datatrek Elite 624D[95]
Datatrek V.32[96]
Digicom Scout
Digicom Scout Plus
DIGICOM SNM28
Dr Neuhaus Fury 14400 TI®
Dr Neuhaus Fury 19200 TI
Dr Neuhaus Fury 2403 TI
Dr Neuhaus Fury Card 144
Dr Neuhaus Fury Card 24
Dr Neuhaus Niccy 3000 TI
Dr Neuhaus Smarty 144 TI
Dr Neuhaus SMARTY 19200
Dr Neuhaus Smarty 24 TI
DSI 9624E
DSI 9624LE Plus
DYNALINK

EEH Elink 29-3 analog
EEH Elink 29-3 ISDN
EEH Elink 301
EEH Elink 310
EEH Elink 32
EEH Elink 32-3 analog
EEH Elink 32-3 ISDN
ELISA 144
ELSA MicroLink 14.4 PC
ELSA MicroLink 14.4 T
ELSA MicroLink 14.4 TL
ELSA MicroLink 14.4 TM
ELSA MicroLink 14.4MC
ELSA MicroLink 2440T
ELSA MicroLink 2440TR
ELSA MicroLink 2460MC
ELSA MicroLink 2460PC
ELSA MicroLink 2460TL
ELSA MicroLink 288ooTL
ELSA MicroLink ISDN/TL
ELSA ZIFF 144
ETech UFOMATE P1496MX
Evercom 24
Evercom 24E
Evercom 24E+
Gateway 2000 Internal
Gateway 2000 Internal Alt
Gateway 2000 Nomad 14400
GENER - Generique 14400
GENER GE925
GENFAX 14400
GVC FM14400
GVC FM14400
GVC SM2400
GVC SM2400
GVC SM96
GVC SM96
Hayes® Accura 14400
Hayes Accura 28800
Hayes Compatible 1200
Hayes Compatible 14400
Hayes Compatible 2400
Hayes Compatible 9600
Hayes Optima 14400
Hayes Optima 14400
Hayes Optima 28800
Hayes Optima 9600
Hayes Optima 9600
Hayes Pocket Modem® 2400
Hayes Smartmodem™ 2400
Hayes Smartmodem 9600
Hayes Ultra 14400
Hayes Ultra 14400

Hayes Ultra 14400
Hayes Ultra 9600
Hayes Ultra 9600
Hayes V Series Smartmodem 9600
Hidem 14400/FAX
Hidem 2442P/FAX
Holmes 14.4 all models
Infotel 1414VQE External
Intel 14400EX
Intel 9600EX
Intel SatisFaxtion®
Intel SatisFaxtion 100
Intel SatisFaxtion 400e
ke WorldBlazer
KORTEX KXPOCKET 9600
KORTEX KXPRO 2400
KORTEX KXPRO 144 BOX
KORTEX KXPRO 144 CARTES
KORTEX KXPRO 144 POCKET
KORTEX KXPRO 9600
KORTEX NFX 144 CARTES
KORTEX NFX 144 POCKET
LASAT Unique 144
LCE 126P
LCE 132P
LIGHTFAX 1440LC
LOGEM 914
LOGEM 928
M. Bullet 100E V.34
M. Bullet E1414MX
M. Bullet ModemMan
M. Bullet ModemMan V.terbo
M. Bullet PC1414MX
M. Bullet PC192MX V.terbo
M. Bullet PCMCIA 1414M
M. CashCom
M. SpiderMan
Macronix Maxlite Fax 9696
Macronix VOMAX 2000
Maestro 144FMEI
Maestro RC224FMI
Megahertz Alternative
Megahertz C5144 for Compaq LTE
Megahertz C596FM for CompaqLTE
Megahertz P2144 AA Batteries
Megahertz P2144 Pkt Faxmodem
Megahertz P296FMV AA Batteries

Megahertz T3144 for Toshiba
Megahertz T396FM for Toshiba
Megahertz Z3144 for Zenith
Megahertz Z396FM for Zenith
Metricom Wireless 9600
MicroCom® DeskPorte FAST
MicroCom DeskPorte FAST ES28.8
MicroCom QX 4232bis [95]
MicroComQX 4232HS
MicroGate MG144 [94]
MicroGate MG96 [94]
MicroPorte 1042
MultiTech MT932
MultiTech MultiModem 224 [97]
MultiTech MultiModem MT2834
MultiTech MultiModem MT932
NEC 9635E Plus
Netcomm Pocket M/F 2400
Netcomm Pocket Rocket PA
Netcomm Smartmodem E7F
Octocom 8324 [94]
Octocom 8396
PDI-1000 [96]
PIAL FAXMOD PC
PNB AMAZONE 2400
PNB Baby RIO 14400
Practical Peripherals 14400FX
Practical Peripherals 14400SA
Practical Peripherals 2400MNP[95]
Practical Peripherals 2400SA[96]
Practical Peripherals 9600FX
Practical Peripherals 9600SA
Practical Peripherals PC288MT
Practical Peripherals PC288SA
Practical Peripherals PM288PKT
Practical Peripherals2400 Pkt
Psion Dacom PDM 50F
QUATERNAIRE V32.BIS
Racal ALM 3226
Racal RMD 2412
Racal RMD 2412/2[98]
Racal RMD 2422
Racal RMD 3221
Racal RMD 3222
Racal RMD 3223
Racal RMD 3226
Racal RMD 9632PA
Racal RMD 9642PA

SAT 14402
SBN 2314C
SEMAFOR 1496A
SEMAFOR 2324C
Smartlink Pocket 2400
Smartlink V32Bis/Fax
Supra Fax Modem 288
Supra Fax Modem 288 internal
Supra Fax Modem 9624 Internal
Supra Fax Modem Plus
Supra Fax Modem V32
Supra Fax Modem V32bis
SupraModem 2400
SYSNET SMF-04
SYSNET SMF-36
Telebit® QBlazer
Telebit T1000
Telebit T1500[96]
Telebit T1600[95]
Telebit T2000
Telebit T2500
Telebit T3000
Telebit TrailBlazer® Plus
Telebit WorldBlazer
Telebit WorldBlazer-Rackmount
Telejet 14400
Telelink IMS08
Tornado 2400
Tornado 96
Tornado FM14400
TOSHIBA SLIM ASYNC
TOSHIBA SLIM FAX / 2400
TOSHIBA SLIM SYNC
UCOM FASTLINK 144
UCOM TRAVELLER 144
UDS Motorola® CELLect 144
UDS Motorola FasTalk II
UDS Motorola FasTalk V.32/42b[99]
UDS Motorola FasTalk V32
UDS Motorola V.3225[95]
UDS Motorola V.3227[99]
UDS Motorola V.3229
UDS Motorola V.3400
UFOMATE P1496MX
US Robotics Courier Dual
US Robotics Courier HST
US Robotics Courier V.32bis
US Robotics Sportster 14400
US Robotics Sportster 2400
US Robotics Sportster 28800 VFC

US Robotics Sportster 9600
US Robotics V32bis Quad
  Digital
US Robotics Worldport 14400
USR Courier V.32bis
USR Sportster 14400
USR Worldport 14400
USR Worldport 14400
Ven-Tel 14400 Fax
Ven-Tel 14400 Fax Internal
Ven-Tel 9600 Plus II[100]
Ven-Tel ECV 32bis II
Ven-Tel Pocket 24 V.42bis
  FAX
ViVa 144 Fax
Western Datacom Worldcom[96]
Zoom AFX
Zoom FX 9624V
Zoom VFP 28.8 internal
Zoom VFX V.32bis
ZyXel U-1496
ZyXEL U-1496 Plus
ZyXEL U-1496A Plus
ZyXEL U-1496B
ZyXEL U-1496B Plus
ZyXel U-1496E
ZyXEL U-1496E Plus
ZyXEL U-1496EA
ZyXEL U-1496EA Plus
ZyXEL U-1496EG
ZyXEL U-1496EG Plus
ZyXEL U-1496G Plus
ZyXEL U-1496P
ZyXEL U-1496R
ZyXEL U-1496R Plus
ZyXEL U-1496RN
ZyXEL U-1496RN Plus
ZyXEL U-1496SN Plus

Hardware Security Hosts

*The following hardware
security hosts have been tested
for use with Remote Access
Service, and are supported on
X86, MIPS and Alpha AXP
platforms except as noted.*

Digital Pathways Defender
  1000D
Racal Gaurdata GSM
Security Dynamics ACM400

ISDN Adapters

*The following ISDN adapters
have been tested for use with
Remote Access Service, and
are supported on X86, MIPS
and Alpha AXP platforms
except as noted.*

DigiBoard PCIMAC ISA
  Adapter
DigiBoard PCIMAC/4 Adapter

Multi-port Serial Adapters

*The following multi-port serial
adapters have been tested for
use with Remote Access
Service, and are supported on
X86, MIPS and Alpha AXP
platforms except as noted.*

Comtrol Hostess 550[85]
Consensys ChiliPORTS /4
  RAS Adapter[1]
Consensys ChiliPORTS /8
  RAS Adapter[1]
Consensys ChiliPORTS/16
  RAS Adapter[1]
Consensys ChiliPORTS MC/4
  RAS Adapter[1]
Consensys ChiliPORTS MC/8
  RAS Adapter[1]
Consensys ChiliPORTS MC/16
  RAS Adapter[1]
DigiBoard 2Port
DigiBoard 4Port
DigiBoard 8Port
DigiBoard CX Adapter
DigiBoard DigiCHANNEL
  PC/X Host Adapter for ISA
  bus[85]
DigiBoard PC/2e (8K) Adapter
DigiBoard PC/4e Adapter
DigiBoard PC/4e (8K) Adapter
DigiBoard PC/8e Adapter
DigiBoard PC/8e (8K) Adapter
DigiBoard PC/8i Adapter
DigiBoard PC/16e Adapter
DigiBoard PC/16i Adapter
DigiBoard PC/Xem Adapter

GlobTek Dual RS-232
  Asynchronous Adapter
  I1001
Sealevel System COMM+8[86]
Sealevel System COMM+232
  /EX[86]
Sealevel System VESA
  COMM+4[86]
Star Gate Technologies Plus
  8[85]
Star Gate Technologies
  ACL[1,87]
Star Gate Technologies
  ACL II+[1,87]
Star Gate Technologies
  ACL IIR+[1,87]
Star Gate Technologies
  Avanstar 100i[1,87]
Star Gate Technologies
  Avanstar 100e[1,87]
Star Gate Technologies
  Avanstar 100m[1,87]

X.25 Adapters

*The following X.25 adapters
have been tested for use with
RemoteAccess Service, and are
supported on the X86 single
processor platform.*

EiconCard EC/PC 1 Meg
EiconCard EC/MC 1 Meg
EiconCard HSI/PC 1 Meg
EiconCard HSI/MC 1 Meg
EiconCard IMC/PC (UK
  version only)
EiconCard IMC/MC (UK
  version only)
Eicon Dual-Port Network-
  Adapter (DPNA) 2 Meg
Eicon Multi-Port Network-
  Adapter (MPNA) 2 Meg

Third Party Remote Access Servers

The following third party remote access servers have been tested for use with Remote Access Service on the Windows NT 3.5 Workstation. See Remote Access readme file (rasread.txt) for details on third party product versions supported.

Shiva® LAN Rover
Telebit NetBlazer
Cisco
3Com/Centrum AccessBuilder

Keyboards

Any keyboard 100% compatible with those listed below.

101/102-key
IBM AT (84-key)]

Pointing Devices

The following pointing devices have been tested. The MIPS and Alpha platforms support mouseport and serial pointing devices.

Acer M-SG14
AT&T 320 Mouse CA-93-6MD
CompuAdd Serial Mouse
Digital Equipment PCXAS-AA
Digital Equipment PC7XS-AA
Hewlett-Packard C1413A
Honeywell 2HW53-3E
IBM 33G3835
IBM 33G5430
IBM 6450350
IBM 96F9275
IBM TrackPoint II™
ICL M-SF14-6MD
Logitech™ Mouseman, Bus
Logitech Mouseman, Cordless
Logitech Series 9 mice
Logitech Series M mice

Logitech Trackman Portable Mouse
Logitech Trackman Stationary Mouse
Microsoft Bus Mouse (Original - Green Buttons)
Microsoft Mouse, BallPoint
Microsoft Mouse, Inport
Microsoft Mouse, PS/2 Compatible
Microsoft Mouse, Serial
Microsoft Mouse, Serial / PS/2
Microsoft Mouse 2.0, BallPoint
Microsoft Mouse 2.0, Bus
Microsoft Mouse 2.0, MousePort
Microsoft Mouse 2.0, Serial
Microsoft Mouse 2.0, Serial-MousePort
MotorMouse
Olivetti M-SE9-6MD

Printers

Drivers are included for the following printers, and are supported on X86, MIPS and Alpha AXP platforms except as noted.

Agfa Compugraphic 400PS
Agfa Compugraphic Genics
Agfa Matrix® ChromaScript v51.8
Agfa TabScript C500 PostScript® Printer v50®.3
Agfa-Compugraphic 9400P v49.3
Apple® LaserWriter® II NT v47.0
Apple LaserWriter II NTX v47.0
Apple LaserWriter II NTX v51.8
Apple LaserWriter II NTX-J v50.5
Apple LaserWriter IIf v2010.113
Apple LaserWriter IIg v2010.113
Apple LaserWriter Plus v38.0
Apple LaserWriter Plus v42.2
Apple LaserWriter Pro 600
Apple LaserWriter Pro 630

Apple LaserWriter Pro 810
Apple LaserWriter v23.0
Apple Personal LaserWriter NTR v2010.129
Apricot Laser
APS-PS PIP with APS-6-108 v49.3 or 52.2
APS-PS PIP with APS-6-80 v49.3 or 52.2
APS-PS PIP with LZR 1200 v49.3 or 52.2
APS-PS PIP with LZR 2600 v49.3 or 52.2
AST TurboLaser-PS v47.0
AT&T 470/475
AT&T 473/478
Brother HJ-100
Brother HJ-100i
Brother HJ-770
Brother HL-10DV
Brother HL-10h
Brother HL-10V
Brother HL-4
Brother HL-4V
Brother HL-4Ve
Brother HL-6V
Brother HL-8
Brother HL-8D
Brother HL-8e
Brother HL-8V
Brother M-1309
Brother M-1324
Brother M-1809
Brother M-1818
Brother M-1824L
Brother M-1909
Brother M-1918
Brother M-1924L
Bull Compuprint PageMaster 1025
Bull Compuprint PageMaster 413
Bull Compuprint PageMaster 815
Bull Compuprint PageMaster 825
Bull Compuprint PM 201
C-Itoh 8510
Canon® Bubble-Jet BJ-10e
Canon Bubble-Jet BJ-10ex
Canon Bubble-Jet BJ-10sx
Canon Bubble-Jet BJ-130
Canon Bubble-Jet BJ-130e
Canon Bubble-Jet BJ-20
Canon Bubble-Jet BJ-200

Canon Bubble-Jet BJ-200e
Canon Bubble-Jet BJ-230
Canon Bubble-Jet BJ-300
Canon Bubble-Jet BJ-330
Canon Bubble-Jet BJC-600
Canon Bubble-Jet BJC-800
Canon LBP-4
Canon LBP-4 Lite
Canon LBP-4 Plus
Canon LBP-4 PS-2 v51.4
Canon LBP-430
Canon LBP-4i
Canon LBP-4sx
Canon LBP-4U
Canon LBP-8 II
Canon LBP-8 III
Canon LBP-8 III Plus
Canon LBP-8 IIIR
Canon LBP-8 IIIT
Canon LBP-8 IIR
Canon LBP-8 IIT
Canon LBP-8 IV
Canon LBP-860
Canon LBP-8III PS-1 v51.4
Canon LBP-8IIIR PS-1 v51.4
Canon LBP-8IIIT PS-1 v51.4
Canon LBP-8sx
Canon PS-IPU Color Laser
  Copier v52.3
Canon PS-IPU Kanji Color
  Laser Copier v52.3
Citizen 120D
Citizen 120D+
Citizen 124D
Citizen 180D
Citizen 200GX
Citizen 200GX/15
Citizen 224
Citizen ABC ESC/P 2
Citizen GSX 240 Scalable Font
Citizen GSX-130
Citizen GSX-140
Citizen GSX-140+
Citizen GSX-145
Citizen GSX-220 ESC/P 2
Citizen GSX-230
Citizen GSX-240 ESC/P 2
Citizen HSP-500
Citizen HSP-550
Citizen PN48
Citizen Prodot 24
Citizen Prodot 9
Citizen Prodot 9x
Citizen PROjet
Citizen ProLaser 6000

Citizen Swift 200
Citizen Swift 24
Citizen Swift 240 ESC/P 2
Citizen Swift 240 Scalable
  Font
Citizen Swift 24e
Citizen Swift 24x
Citizen Swift 9
Citizen Swift 9x
ColorAge ColorQ
Colormate PS v51.9
COMPAQ PAGEMARQ 15
COMPAQ PAGEMARQ 15
  v2012.015
COMPAQ PAGEMARQ 20
COMPAQ PAGEMARQ 20
  v2012.015
Dataproducts LZR 1260 v47.0
Dataproducts LZR 1560
  v2010.127
Dataproducts LZR 960
  v2010.106
Dataproducts LZR-2665 v46.2
Diconix 150 Plus
Digital Colormate PS v51.9
Digital DECcolorwriter 1000
  17
Digital DECcolorwriter 1000
  39
Digital DEClaser 1100 (LJ)
Digital DEClaser 1100
Digital DEClaser 1150 v51.4
Digital DEClaser 1152 17 fonts
Digital DEClaser 1152 43 fonts
Digital DEClaser 2100
Digital DEClaser 2100plus
  (LJ)
Digital DEClaser 2150 plus
  v51.4
Digital DEClaser 2150 v51.4
Digital DEClaser 2200
Digital DEClaser 2200plus
  (LJ)
Digital DEClaser 2250 plus
  v51.4
Digital DEClaser 2250 v51.4
Digital DEClaser 3200 (LJ)
Digital DEClaser 3200
Digital DEClaser 3250 v47
Digital DEClaser 5100
Digital DECmultiJET 1000
Digital DECmultiJET 2000
Digital DECwriter 95
Digital LA310
Digital LA324

Digital LA424
Digital LA70
Digital LA75 Plus
Digital LA75
Digital LN03R ScriptPrinter
Digital PrintServer 17/600
Digital PrintServer 17
  12mb/L2
Digital PrintServer 17 v48.3
Digital PrintServer 20 v48.3
Digital PrintServer 32 Kanji
  v48.3
Digital PrintServer 32 v48.3
Digital PrintServer 40 Plus
  Kanji v48.3
Digital PrintServer 40 Plus
  v48.3
Digital turbo PrintServer 20
Digital turbo PrintServer 20
  Kanji v48.3
Epson ActionLaser 1500
Epson ActionLaser 1600
Epson ActionLaser II
Epson AP-3250 ESC/P 2
Epson AP-3250 Scalable Font
Epson AP-3260 ESC/P 2
Epson AP-5000 ESC/P 2
Epson AP-5000 Scalable Font
Epson AP-5000+ ESC/P 2
Epson AP-5500 ESC/P 2
Epson AP-5500 Scalable Font
Epson AP-5500+ ESC/P 2
Epson Compatible 24 Pin
Epson Compatible 9 Pin
Epson DFX-5000
Epson DLQ-2000
Epson EPL-4000
Epson EPL-4200
Epson EPL-4300
Epson EPL-5200
Epson EPL-5600
Epson EPL-6000
Epson EPL-7000
Epson EPL-7500 v52.3
Epson EPL-8000
Epson EPL-8100
Epson EX-1000
Epson EX-800
Epson FX-100
Epson FX-100+
Epson FX-1000
Epson FX-105
Epson FX-1050
Epson FX-185
Epson FX-286

Epson FX-286e
Epson FX-80
Epson FX-80+
Epson FX-800
Epson FX-85
Epson FX-850
Epson FX-86e
Epson GQ-3500
Epson JX-80
Epson L-1000
Epson L-750
Epson LP-3000PS F2 v52.3
Epson LP-3000PS F5 v52.3
Epson LQ-100 ESC/P 2
Epson LQ-100 Scalable Font
Epson LQ-1000
Epson LQ-1010
Epson LQ-1050
Epson LQ-1060
Epson LQ-1070 ESC/P 2
Epson LQ-1070 Scalable Font
Epson LQ-1070+ ESC/P 2
Epson LQ-1170 ESC/P 2
Epson LQ-1170 Scalable Font
Epson LQ-150 ESC/P 2
Epson LQ-1500
Epson LQ-200
Epson LQ-2500
Epson LQ-2550
Epson LQ-400
Epson LQ-450
Epson LQ-500
Epson LQ-510
Epson LQ-550
Epson LQ-570 ESC/P 2
Epson LQ-570 Scalable Font
Epson LQ-570+ ESC/P 2
Epson LQ-800
Epson LQ-850
Epson LQ-850+
Epson LQ-860
Epson LQ-870 ESC/P 2
Epson LQ-870 Scalable Font
Epson LQ-950
Epson LX-1050
Epson LX-400
Epson LX-80
Epson LX-800
Epson LX-810
Epson LX-850
Epson LX-850+
Epson LX-86
Epson MX-100
Epson MX-80 F/T
Epson MX-80

Epson PostScript CARD v52.5
Epson RX-100
Epson RX-100+
Epson RX-80
Epson RX-80 F/T
Epson RX-80 F/T+
Epson SQ-1170 ESC/P 2
Epson SQ-1170 Scalable Font
Epson SQ-2000
Epson SQ-2500
Epson SQ-2550
Epson SQ-850
Epson SQ-870 ESC/P 2
Epson SQ-870 Scalable Font
Epson Stylus 1000 ESC/P 2
Epson Stylus 300 ESC/P 2
Epson Stylus 800 ESC/P 2
Epson T-1000
Epson T-750
Fujitsu Breeze 100
Fujitsu Breeze 200
Fujitsu DL 1100 Colour
Fujitsu DL 1100
Fujitsu DL 1150
Fujitsu DL 1200
Fujitsu DL 1250
Fujitsu DL 2400
Fujitsu DL 2600
Fujitsu DL 3300
Fujitsu DL 3350
Fujitsu DL 3400
Fujitsu DL 3450
Fujitsu DL 3600
Fujitsu DL 4400
Fujitsu DL 4600
Fujitsu DL 5600
Fujitsu DL 900
Fujitsu DX 2100
Fujitsu DX 2200
Fujitsu DX 2300
Fujitsu DX 2400
Fujitsu RX7100PS v50.3
GCC BLP Elite v52.3
GCC BLP II v52.3
GCC BLP IIS v52.3
GCC Business LaserPrinter
  v49.2
GCC Business LaserPrinter
  v51.4
Generic IBM Graphics 9pin
  wide
Generic IBM Graphics 9pin
Gestetner GLP800-Scout v52.3
Hermes H 606 PS (13 Fonts)
Hermes H 606 PS (35 fonts)

Hermes H 606
Hewlett-Packard HP-GL®/2
  Plotter
HP 7550 Plus
HP DesignJet 200 (C3180A)
HP DesignJet 200 (C3181A)
HP DesignJet 600 (C2847A)
HP DesignJet 600 (C2848A)
HP DesignJet 650C (C2858A)
HP DesignJet 650C (C2858B)
HP DesignJet 650C (C2859A)
HP DesignJet 650C (C2859B)
HP DesignJet 650C v2013.109
HP DesignJet (C3180A)
HP DeskJet® 1200C
HP DeskJet 1200C/PS
HP DeskJet 310 (Color)
HP DeskJet 310
  (Monochrome)
HP DeskJet 500
HP DeskJet 500C (Color)
HP DeskJet 500C
  (Monochrome)
HP DeskJet 510
HP DeskJet 520
HP DeskJet 550C
HP DeskJet 560C
HP DeskJet Plus
HP DeskJet Portable
HP DeskJet
HP DraftMaster RX/MX
HP DraftMaster SX
HP DraftPro® Plus (C3170A)
HP DraftPro Plus (C3171A)
HP LaserJet 2000
HP LaserJet 4
HP LaserJet 4 Plus
HP LaserJet 4/4M PS
HP LaserJet 4/4M PS (300 dpi)
HP LaserJet 4L
HP LaserJet 4L/4ML
  PostScript
HP LaserJet 4M Plus
HP LaserJet 4ML
HP LaserJet 4MP
HP LaserJet 4P
HP LaserJet 4P/4MP PS
HP LaserJet 4P/4MP PS (300
  dpi)
HP LaserJet 4Si
HP LaserJet 4Si/4Si MX PS
HP LaserJet 4Si/4Si MX PS
  (300 dpi)
HP LaserJet 500+

HP LaserJet IID PostScript
   Cartridge v52.2
HP LaserJet IID
HP LaserJet III PostScript
   Cartridge v52.2
HP LaserJet III PostScript Plus
   v2010.118
HP LaserJet III
HP LaserJet IIID PostScript
   Cartridge v52.2
HP LaserJet IIID PostScript
   Plus v2010.118
HP LaserJet IIID
HP LaserJet IIIP PostScript
   Cartridge v52.2
HP LaserJet IIIP PostScript
   Plus v2010.118
HP LaserJet IIIP
HP LaserJet IIISi PostScript
   v52.3
HP LaserJet IIISi
HP LaserJet IIP
HP LaserJet IIP Plus
HP LaserJet IIP PostScript
   Cartridge v52.2
HP LaserJet Plus
HP LaserJet Series II
HP LaserJet
HP PaintJet® XL 300
HP PaintJet XL
HP PaintJet XL300 v2011.112
HP PaintJet
HP QuietJet® Plus
HP QuietJet
HP ThinkJet® (2225 C-D)
IBM 4019 LaserPrinter
IBM 4019 LaserPrinter PS17
IBM 4019 LaserPrinter PS39
IBM 4029 LaserPrinter
IBM 4029 LaserPrinter PS17
IBM 4029 LaserPrinter PS39
IBM 4037 5E
IBM 4039 LaserPrinter
IBM 4039 LaserPrinter PS
IBM 4039 LaserPrinter Plus
IBM 4039 LaserPrinter plus PS
IBM 4070 IJ
IBM 4079 Color Jetprinter PS
IBM 4216-020 v47.0
IBM 4216-030 v50.5
IBM ExecJet® 4072
IBM ExecJet 4076 II
IBM Graphics
IBM Personal Page Printer II-
   31

IBM Personal Printer II 2380
IBM Personal Printer II 2381
IBM Personal Printer II 2390
IBM Personal Printer II 2391
IBM Portable 5183
IBM Proprinter® II
IBM Proprinter III
IBM Proprinter X24
IBM Proprinter X24e
IBM Proprinter XL II
IBM Proprinter XL III
IBM Proprinter XL
IBM Proprinter XL24
IBM Proprinter XL24e
IBM Proprinter
IBM PS/1 2205
IBM QuickWriter® 5204
IBM QuietWriter® III
Kodak® ColorEase PS Printer
Kodak EktaPlus 7016
Kyocera® F-1000
Kyocera F-1000A
Kyocera F-1010
Kyocera F-1200S
Kyocera F-1500T
Kyocera F-1800
Kyocera F-1800A
Kyocera F-2000A
Kyocera F-2010
Kyocera F-2200
Kyocera F-2200S
Kyocera F-3000
Kyocera F-3000A
Kyocera F-3010
Kyocera F-3300
Kyocera F-5000
Kyocera F-800
Kyocera F-800A
Kyocera F-820
Kyocera FS-400 / FS-400A
Kyocera FS-1500 / FS-1500A
Kyocera FS-2600 / FS-2600A
Kyocera FS-3500 / FS-3500A
Kyocera FS-5500 / FS-5500A
Kyocera FS-850 / FS-850A
LaserWriter Personal NT v51.8
Linotronic™ 100 v42.5
Linotronic 200 v47.1
Linotronic 200 v49.3
Linotronic 200/230
Linotronic 300 v47.1
Linotronic 300 v49.3
Linotronic 330 v52.3
Linotronic 330-RIP 30 v52.3
Linotronic 500 v49.3

Linotronic 530 v52.3
Linotronic 530-RIP 30 v52.3
Linotronic 630 v52.3
Linotronic 830 v52.3
Linotronic 930 v52.3
Linotronic Pr60 v52.3
Mannesmann Tally® MT
   130/24
Mannesmann Tally MT 131/24
Mannesmann Tally MT 150/24
Mannesmann Tally MT 151/24
Mannesmann Tally MT 230/24
Mannesmann Tally MT 330
Mannesmann Tally MT 350
Mannesmann Tally MT 360
Mannesmann Tally MT
   730/735
Mannesmann Tally MT 82
Mannesmann Tally MT 90
Mannesmann Tally MT 904
   Plus
Mannesmann Tally MT 908
Mannesmann Tally MT 91
Mannesmann Tally MT 92
Mannesmann Tally MT 92C
Mannesmann Tally MT 93
Mannesmann Tally MT 94
Mannesmann Tally MT 98/99
Mannesmann Tally T9017
Microtek TrueLaser
Minolta SP 3000
Minolta SP 3500
Monotype® ImageMaster 1200
   v52.3
Monotype Imagesetter v52.2
NEC Colormate PS/40 v51.9
NEC Colormate PS/80 v51.9
NEC Jetmate 400
NEC Jetmate 800
NEC Pinwriter CP6
NEC Pinwriter CP7
NEC Pinwriter P20
NEC Pinwriter P2200
NEC Pinwriter P2plus
NEC Pinwriter P30
NEC Pinwriter P3200
NEC Pinwriter P3300
NEC Pinwriter P5200
NEC Pinwriter P5300
NEC Pinwriter P5XL
NEC Pinwriter P6
NEC Pinwriter P60
NEC Pinwriter P6200
NEC Pinwriter P6300
NEC Pinwriter P6plus

NEC Pinwriter P7
NEC Pinwriter P70
NEC Pinwriter P7plus
NEC Pinwriter P90
NEC Pinwriter P9300
NEC Pinwriter P9XL
NEC SilentWriter® 95
  v2010.119
NEC Silentwriter 95
  v2011.111
NEC Silentwriter 97
  v2011.111
NEC Silentwriter LC 860 Plus
NEC Silentwriter LC 860
NEC Silentwriter LC890 v47.0
NEC Silentwriter LC890XL
  v50.5
NEC Silentwriter S102
NEC Silentwriter2 290 v52.0
NEC Silentwriter2 90 v52.2
NEC Silentwriter2 990 v52.3
OceColor G5241 PS
OceColor G5242 PostScript
  Printer v50.3
OKI MICROLINE 801PS+F
  v52.3
Oki ML 182 Elite (IBM)
Oki ML 192 Elite (IBM)
Oki ML 193 Elite (IBM)
Oki ML 280 Elite (IBM)
Oki ML 320 Elite (IBM)
Oki ML 321 Elite (IBM)
Oki ML 3410 Elite (IBM)
Oki ML 380 Elite
Oki ML 390 Elite
Oki ML 391 Elite
Oki ML 393 Elite
Oki ML 393C Elite
Oki ML 590
Oki ML 591
OKI OL-400
Oki OL-410
OKI OL-800/840
Oki OL-810
Oki OL-870
Oki OL830-PS v52.5
Oki OL840-PS v51.8
Oki OL850-PS v52.5
Oki OL870-PS v2013.108
Okidata® LaserLine 6
Okidata ML 192 Plus
Okidata ML 192
Okidata ML 192-IBM
Okidata ML 193 Plus
Okidata ML 193

Okidata ML 193-IBM
Okidata ML 292-IBM
Okidata ML 293-IBM
Okidata ML 320
Okidata ML 320-IBM
Okidata ML 321
Okidata ML 321-IBM
Okidata ML 380
Okidata ML 390 Plus
Okidata ML 390
Okidata ML 391 Plus
Okidata ML 391
Okidata ML 393 Plus
Okidata ML 393
Okidata ML 393C Plus
Okidata ML 393C
Okidata ML 92-IBM
Okidata ML 93-IBM
Okidata OL-400
Okidata OL-410
Okidata OL-800
Okidata OL-810
Olivetti DM 109
Olivetti DM 124 C
Olivetti DM 124 L
Olivetti DM 124
Olivetti DM 309 L
Olivetti DM 309 S
Olivetti DM 309 SL
Olivetti DM 309
Olivetti DM 324 L
Olivetti DM 324 S
Olivetti DM 324 SL
Olivetti DM 324
Olivetti DM 600 S
Olivetti DM 600
Olivetti DM 624
Olivetti ETV 5000
Olivetti JP 150
Olivetti JP 350
Olivetti JP 350S
Olivetti PG 108
Olivetti PG 208 M2
Olivetti PG 306 PS (13 Fonts)
Olivetti PG 306 PS (35 Fonts)
Olivetti PG 306
Olivetti PG 308 HS PostScript
Olivetti PG 308 HS
Olivetti PG 308
Olivetti PG 404
Olivetti PG 408
Panasonic KX-P1081
Panasonic KX-P1123
Panasonic KX-P1124
Panasonic KX-P1124i

Panasonic KX-P1180
Panasonic KX-P1624
Panasonic KX-P1695
Panasonic KX-P2123
Panasonic KX-P2124
Panasonic KX-P2180
Panasonic KX-P2624
Panasonic KX-P3134
Panasonic KX-P3634
Panasonic KX-P4410
Panasonic KX-P4420
Panasonic KX-P4430
Panasonic KX-P4440
Panasonic KX-P4450
Panasonic KX-P4450i
Panasonic KX-P4451
Panasonic KX-P4455 v51.4
Panasonic KX-P5400
  v2013.112
Panasonic KX-P5410
  v2013.110
QMS® 1060 Print System
QMS 1660 Print System
QMS 1725 Print System
QMS 2025 Print System
QMS 3225 Print System
QMS 420 Print System
  v2011.22 r15
QMS 4525 Level 2
QMS 4525 Print System
QMS 860 Print System
  v2011.22 r15
QMS 860+ Level 2
QMS ColorScript 100 Mod
  30si
QMS ColorScript 100 Model
  10 v50.3
QMS ColorScript 100 Model
  20 v50.3
QMS ColorScript 100 Model
  30 v50.3
QMS ColorScript 100 v49.4
QMS ColorScript 1000 Level 1
QMS ColorScript 1000 Level 2
QMS ColorScript 210
  v2011.22
QMS ColorScript 230
  v2011.22
QMS PS Jet Plus v46.1
QMS PS Jet v46.1
QMS-PS® 1700 v52.4
QMS-PS 2000 v52.4
QMS-PS 2200 v51.0 or 52.3
QMS-PS 2210 v51.0 or 52.3
QMS-PS 2220 v51.0 or 52.3

QMS-PS 410 v52.4
QMS-PS 800 Plus v46.1
QMS-PS 800 v46.1
QMS-PS 810 Turbo v. 51.7
QMS-PS 810 v47.0
QMS-PS 815 MR v52.4
QMS-PS 815 v52.4
QMS-PS 820 Turbo v51.7
QMS-PS 820 v51.7
QMS-PS 825 MR v52.4
QMS-PS 825 v52.4
QuadLaser I
Qume ScripTEN v47.0
Ricoh LP-1200
Ricoh PC Laser 6000-PS v50.5
Royal CJP 450
Scantext 2030-51 v49.3 or 52.2
Schlumberger 5232 Color
    PostScript Printer v50.3
Seiko ColorPoint PS Model 04
Seiko ColorPoint PS Model 14
Seiko Professional ColorPoint
    8BPP
Seikosha LT-20
Seikosha SL-80 IP
Seikosha SL-92 Plus
Seikosha SL-92
Seikosha SP-1900
Seikosha SP-1900+
Seikosha SP-2000
Seikosha SP-2400
Seikosha SP-2415
Sharp JX-9300
Sharp JX-9460
Sharp JX-9460 PS
Sharp JX-9500
Sharp JX-9500 PS
Sharp JX-9500E
Sharp JX-9500H
Sharp JX-9600
Sharp JX-9600 PS
Sharp JX-9660
Sharp JX-9660 PS
Sharp JX-9700
Sharp JX-9700E
Sharp JX-9700E PS
Shinko Color CHC-746PSJ
    PostScript Printer v52.2
Star FR-10
Star FR-15
Star LaserPrinter 4 III
Star LaserPrinter 4
Star LaserPrinter 5 EX
Star LaserPrinter 5
Star LaserPrinter 8 DB

Star LaserPrinter 8 DX
Star LaserPrinter 8 II
Star LaserPrinter 8 III
Star LaserPrinter 8
Star LC-10
Star LC-10 Colour
Star LC-100 Colour
Star LC-15
Star LC-20
Star LC-200
Star LC24-10
Star LC24-100
Star LC24-15
Star LC24-20
Star LC24-200
Star LC24-200 Colour
Star NB24-10
Star NB24-15
Star NL-10
Star NX-1000 Rainbow
Star NX-1000
Star NX-1001
Star NX-1020 Rainbow
Star NX-1500
Star NX-2400
Star NX-2410
Star NX-2415
Star NX-2420 Rainbow
Star NX-2420
Star NX-2430
Star SJ-48
Star XB-2410
Star XB-2415
Star XB-2420
Star XB-2425
Star XB24-10
Star XB24-15
Star XB24-200
Star XB24-250
Star XR-1000
Star XR-1020
Star XR-1500
Star XR-1520
Star ZA-200
Star ZA-250
Tandy LP-1000
Tegra Genesis
Tektronix® Phaser™ 200e with
    17 fonts v2011.108(3)
Tektronix Phaser 200e with 39
    fonts v2011.108(3)
Tektronix Phaser 200i
    v2011.108(3)
Tektronix Phaser 200J

Tektronix Phaser 220e with 17
    fonts
Tektronix Phaser 220e with 39
    fonts
Tektronix Phaser 220i
Tektronix Phaser 220J
Tektronix Phaser 300i
Tektronix Phaser 300J
Tektronix Phaser 480
Tektronix Phaser 480J
Tektronix Phaser II PX
Tektronix Phaser II PXe
    v2010.128 with 17 fonts
Tektronix Phaser II PXe
    v2010.128 with 39 fonts
Tektronix Phaser II PXi
    v2010.116
Tektronix Phaser II PXi
    v2011.108
Tektronix Phaser II PXiJ
    v2011.108
Tektronix Phaser III PXi
    v2010.116
Tektronix Phaser III PXi
    v2011.108
Tektronix Phaser III PXiJ
    v2011.108
Tektronix Phaser IISD
    v2011.108
Tektronix Phaser IISDJ
Tektronix Phaser IISDX
Tektronix Phaser PX
Tektronix Phaser PXi
TI 2115 13 fonts v47.0
TI 2115 35 fonts v47.0
TI 850/855
TI microLaser 600
TI microLaser PS17 v.52.1
TI microLaser PS35 v.52.1
TI microLaser XL PS17 v.52.1
TI microLaser XL PS35 v.52.1
TI microLaser16 Turbo
    v2010.119
TI microLaser6 Turbo
    v2010.119
TI microLaser9 Turbo
    v2010.119
TI OmniLaser™ 2108 v45.0
TI OmniLaser 2115 v47.0
Toshiba GX-400
Toshiba PageLaser12
Triumph Adler SDR 7706
    PS13
Triumph Adler SDR 7706
    PS35

Triumph Adler SDR 7706
UNISYS AP9210 17 Fonts
v52.1
UNISYS AP9210 39 Fonts
v52.1
UNISYS AP9210
UNISYS AP9415 v47.0
Varityper 4000-L300 v52.3
Varityper 4000-L330 v52.3
Varityper 4000-L500 v52.3
Varityper 4000-L530 v52.3
Varityper 4200B-P v49.3 or
52.2
Varityper 4300P v49.3 or 52.2
Varityper Series 4000-5300
v49.3 or 52.2
Varityper Series 4000-5330
v49.3 or 52.2
Varityper Series 4000-5500
v52.2
Varityper VT-600P v48.0
Varityper VT-600P
Varityper VT-600W v48.0
Varityper VT4990 v52.3
Varityper VT4_510A v52.3
VT4_530A v52.3
VT4_530B v52.3
VT4_530C v52.3
VT4_533B v52.3
VT4_533C v52.3
VT4_53EA v52.3
VT4_53EB v52.3
VT4_550A v52.3
VT4_550B v52.3
VT4_550C v52.3
VT4_551A v52.3
VT4_563A v52.3
VT4_563B v52.3
Wang LCS15 FontPlus
Wang LCS15
Wang LDP8
Xerox® DocuTech 135
v2010.130
Xerox DocuTech 85
v2010.130
Xerox DocuTech 90
v2010.130

Windows NT 3.1 x86 Architecture Uniprocessor Computers

The following systems have been tested as of September 1994 with Windows NT 3.1. They are considered compatible with the Windows NT 3.5 product.

Absolute Computer 486/66
VL/EISA
ACD OPTIMA 486 DX 33 VL
ACD OPTIMA 486 DX 50 VL
ACD OPTIMA 486 DX2 66
VL
ACER 17000 SMP AA17853N
ACER AcerAcros 486DX2/66
(Model PT66DB)
ACER AcerAltos 700 Model
AA768C
ACER AcerAltos 7000 (DX2-
66)
ACER AcerAltos 7000
(Pentium 90)
ACER AcerAltos
7000/F433TU
ACER AcerAltos
7000/FT66TU
ACER AcerAltos 800 Model
AA868C
ACER AcerFrame 1000
(Model 1733)
ACER AcerFrame 1000
(Model 1766)
ACER AcerFrame 300 (Model
F433T)
ACER AcerFrame 500 (Model
F433TE)
ACER AcerFrame 500 (Model
FT50TE)
ACER AcerFrame 500 (Model
FT66TE)
ACER AcerFrame 700
ACER AcerMate 433 sp
(486SX-33)
ACER AcerMate 466d (Model
MT66D3)
ACER AcerPower 425s
ACER AcerPower 433 sp
(486SX-33)
ACER AcerPower 433e/P433E
ACER AcerPower 433s

ACER AcerPower 433v
ACER AcerPower 450d
ACER AcerPower
450de/PT50E
ACER AcerPower 466d
ACER AcerPower 466de
(DX2-66)
ACER AcerPower 466dv
ACER AcerPower 486/33
ACER AcerPower 560e
(Pentium 60)
ACER AcerPower 566e
(Pentium 66)
ACER AcerPower 9000 Series
Model 9813N
ACER AcerPower 9000/P560E
ACER AcerPower 9000/P566E
ACER AcerPower 9000/PT66E
ACMA 486/33 TI-VLB
ACMA 486/50 TS-E
ACMA 486/50-2 TI-VLB
ACMA 486/66-2 TI-VLB
ACMA 486/66-2 TS-E
ACMA 486/66-2 TS-VLB
ACS Meritel 486-50SF
ACS Meritel 486-66SF
Actech ACTion EISA 486DX-
50
Actech ACTion EISA
486DX2-66
Actech ACTion ISA 486DX-
33
Actech ACTion ISA 486DX-
50
Actech ACTion ISA 486DX/2-
50
Actech ACTion ISA 486DX/2-
66
Actech ACTion ISA 486SX-25
Actech ACTion VLB 486DX-
33
Actech ACTion VLB 486DX-
50
Actech ACTion VLB
486DX/2-50
Actech ACTion VLB
486DX/2-66
Actech ACTion VLB 486SX-
25
Adaptive Data System Pro
3/486-40
Adaptive Data System Pro
486/33 VESA

Adaptive Data System Pro
   486/33DX
Adaptive Data System Pro
   Series 486/50
Adaptive Data System TAI
   386DX/40CF System
Adaptive Data System TAI
   486DX/50CS System
ADD-X 486 All In One 33
   MHz
ADD-X Systemes 486/33Mhz
   ISA bus
ADPS 486 Power Notebook
   486DX2-50Mhz
ADPS 486 Power Notebook
   Color 486-33Mhz
ADPS Ambassador
ADPS Bat Computer-33MHz
ADPS Bat Computer-50MHz
ADPS Local Bus 33
ADPS Medallion
ADPS Multimedia Power
   House
ADPS Power Notebook 486-
   33Mhz
ADPS System 3000
ADPS System 4000
ADPS System 5000
ADPS System 6000 EISA
ADPS System 6000 Plus
ADPS System 6000 Plus EISA
ADS 486 EISA+VESA
   UPGRADEABLE
ADS 486VL UPGRADEABLE
ADS ADA 466 EV
ADS ADA 466 ISA/VESA
ADS ADA 466E
ADS ADA-560-P
ADS LDI-466 ISA/VESA
ADS UPGRADEABLE 3/486
Advance Interface EISA VESA
   486DX-50
Advance Interface EISA VESA
   486DX2-66
Advance Interface VL-BUS
   486DX-50
Advance Interface VL-BUS
   486DX2-66
Advanced Computer SPIRAL
   386DX/40
Advanced Computer SPIRAL
   486/33
Advanced Computer SPIRAL
   486DX2/50
AIC STM 386DX-33Mhz

AIC STM 486DX-33Mhz
AIC STM 486DX2-66Mhz
AIC STM 486DX2-66Mhz
   Local Bus
Alcotini AmiTech 386DX-40
   STD
Alcotini AmiTech 486DX-33
   STD
Alcotini AmiTech 486DX2-50
   STD
Alcotini AmiTech 486DX2-66
   STD
Alcotini AmiTech 486SX-25
   STD
Alcotini Weston 486DX-66
   TFT
AllWare 466-EV
ALR BusinessVEISA 3/33
ALR BusinessVEISA 4/33D
ALR BusinessVEISA 4/66D
ALR Evolution IV 4/25s
ALR Evolution IV 4/33
ALR Evolution IV 4/33s
ALR Evolution IV 4/66d
ALR Evolution IV 4E/25s
ALR Evolution IV 4E/33
ALR Evolution IV 4E/33s
ALR Evolution IV 4E/66d
ALR Evolution V STP/60
ALR Evolution V-Q/60
ALR Evolution V-Q/66
ALR Evolution V/60
ALR Evolution V/66
ALR Flyer 32LCT 4/50D
ALR Flyer 32LCT 4/66D
ALR Flyer 32LCT 4DX/33
ALR Flyer SD32 4/33
ALR Flyer SD32 4/66d
ALR Flyer VL 4/33d
ALR Flyer VL 4/66d
ALR Modular Processor
   System 486DX2/66
ALR PowerCache 4 33e
ALR POWERPRO/MC SMP
   4/50D
ALR PROVEISA V/66
ALR RANGER M4/25
ALR RANGER MC4/25S
ALR RANGER MC4DX/25
ALR RANGER MCT4/25
AMAX 486/2-50 VESAmax
   Power Station
AMAX 486/33 VESAmax
   Power Station

AMAX 486/50 EISAmax
   Power Station
AMAX 486/66 EISAmax
   Power Station
AMAX 486/66 VESAmax
   Power Station
Ambra 486DX/50
Ambra D4100BL
Ambra D466E/VL
Ambra DP60/PCI
Ambra DP66E/VL
Ambra T4100BL
Ambra T466E/VL
American Multisystems
   InfoGOLD EISA VLB Line
   (DX2/66)
American Multisystems
   InfoGOLD P60NT
AMI Enterprise III
AMI Enterprise IV
AMI Excalibur PCI
AMI Excalibur VLB
AMI Omni Business Partner
AMI Super Voyager LC
AMI Super Voyager PCI
AMI Super Voyager VLB
AMI Super Voyager VLB II
AmPAQ Ultimate 466 VLB/S2
AMS TravelPro 5300
AMSYS UPG VLbus DX2-50
   DT
Annabelle Bits ASI 486/33
   Vesa Local Bus
AOX PS/2 80-081 w/Aox
   McMASTER48633
Applied Computer ACT
   486/33 DX
Applied Computer ACT
   PENTIUM TOWER
Apricot FTe 486DX2/66
Apricot FTs 486DX2/66
Apricot XEN-LS II
Aquiline NT 466c System
Ares 486-33 VLB
Ariel 486DX2-66EVS
Ariel 486DX2-66VLS2
Asem DP 486/66 II
Asem DS 486/33 II
Asem ECO-PC 4/33
Asem ECO-PC 4/66
Asem MID-SERVER 4/33
Asem PROSERVER 5/60
ASL 433
Aspect 3/486 386DX-40 ISA
Aspect 3/486DX-33 ISA

Aspect 3/486DX-50 ISA
Aspect 3/486DX2-66 ISA
Aspect 486DX2-66 PCI
Aspect EISA 486DX-33
Aspect EISA 486DX-50
Aspect EISA 486DX2-66
Aspect ISA 486DX-33
Aspect ISA 486DX-50
Aspect ISA 486DX2-66
Aspect ISA 486SX-33
Aspect Pentium PCI 60
Aspect VESA 486DX-33
Aspect VESA 486DX-33F
Aspect VESA 486DX-50
Aspect VESA 486DX-50F
Aspect VESA 486DX2-66
Aspect VESA 486DX2-66F
Aspect VESA 486SX-33
Aspect VESA 486SX-33F
AST Advantage 486sx/33
AST Advantage!™ Plus
    486DX/33
AST Advantage! Pro
    486SX/25 Model 173
AST Advantage+ 4/50d
AST Bravo 3/25s Model 3V
AST Bravo LC 4/25s
AST Bravo LC 4/33
AST Bravo LC 4/33s
AST Bravo LC 4/50d
AST Bravo LC 4/66 SL
AST Bravo LC 4/66d
AST Bravo LP 4/25s
AST Bravo LP 4/33
AST Bravo LP 4/66d
AST Bravo MT 4/33
AST Bravo MT 4/66d
AST Bravo MT P60
AST Manhattan SMP P60 (1p)]
AST Power Premium 4/33
    EISA
AST Power Premium 4/50d
AST PowerExec 4/25SL
AST Premiere MTE P/60
AST Premium 386/33T
AST Premium II 386/33 Model
    213V
AST Premium II 486/33
AST Premium SE 4/33 Model
    333
AST Premium SE 4/50
AST Premium SE 4/50d
AST Premium SE 4/66d
AST Premium SE 486/33
AST Premium SE P/60

AST Premmia 4/33
AST Premmia 4/33SX
AST Premmia 4/66d
AST Premmia MTE 4/66d
AST Premmia SE 4/33
AST Premmia SE 4/66d
AST Premmia SE P60
AT&T 3372
AT&T 3372-C
AT&T 3374
AT&T 3406
AT&T 3416
AT&T Globalyst 200
    486/50MHz
Athena ALM 486 DX 33
Athena ALM 486 DX 50
Athena ALM 486 DX 66
Athena HQ / ISA 486DLC 40
Athena HQ / ISA 486DX 33
Athena HQ / ISA 486DX 50
Athena HQ / ISA 486DX2 66
Athena HQ / VESA 486DX 33
Athena HQ / VESA 486DX2
    50
Athena HQ / VESA 486DX2
    66
Austin 486/50 EISA Tower
    PATRIOT
Austin 486/50 VESA-LB
    PATRIOT
Austin 486/50 VESA-LB
    PATRIOT PLUS
Austin 486DLC
Austin 486DX/33 EISA Tower
    PATRIOT
Austin 486DX/33 VESA-LB
    PATRIOT
Austin 486DX/33 VESA-LB
    PATRIOT PLUS
Austin 486DX2/50 EISA
    Tower PATRIOT
Austin 486DX2/66 EISA
    Tower PATRIOT
Austin 486DX2/66 VESA-LB
    PATRIOT PLUS
Austin Winstation 486DX2/66
Axik Ace Cache 486DX-33V
Axik Ace Cache 486DX-33VG
Axik Ace Cache 486DX2-
    50VG
Axik Ace Cache 486DX2-66V
Axik Ace Cache 486DX2-
    66VG
Axik Ace Cache 486SX-33VG

Aztech TRACER SERIES
    386DX/40
Aztech TRACER SERIES
    486DX/33
Aztech TRACER SERIES
    486DX2/66
Bear 486/50 Desktop
Brett ExecEISA
Brett Executive
Brett Executive PCI Pentium
Brett Pro PCI
Brett Pro VLB
Brett Station NTe EISA
BROTHER BCR4486DX2
BROTHER BCR5486DX2
BROTHER BCR7486DX2
BROTHER BCR8486DX2
C&S Computer E III 486/VLB
C. THIIM 486DX33
CAF CT-02 L737/486DX-33
Caliber 3/486 386DX-40 ISA
Caliber 3/486DX-33 ISA
Caliber 3/486DX-50 ISA
Caliber 3/486DX2-66 ISA
Caliber 486DX2-66 PCI
Caliber EISA 486DX-33
Caliber EISA 486DX-50
Caliber EISA 486DX2-66
Caliber ISA 486DX-33
Caliber ISA 486DX-50
Caliber ISA 486DX2-66
Caliber ISA 486SX-33
Caliber Pentium 60 PCI
Caliber VESA 486DX-33
Caliber VESA 486DX-33F
Caliber VESA 486DX-50
Caliber VESA 486DX-50F
Caliber VESA 486DX2-66
Caliber VESA 486DX2-66F
Caliber VESA 486SX-33
Caliber VESA 486SX-33F
CELEM 486DX/33 C (ISA)
CELEM 486DX/33 VL
    (VESA)
CELEM 486DX/50 VL
    (VESA)
CELEM 486DX/50 MC (EISA)
CELEM 486DX2/66 DC
    (EISA+VESA)
CELEM 586/60 (PCI+ISA)
CENSUS 4D266S DT (incl.
    MT, IT, FT Models)
CENSUS 4D33S DT (incl. MT,
    IT, FT Models)

CENSUS 4D40S DT (incl. MT, IT, FT Models)
CENSUS 4D50S DT (incl. MT, IT, FT Models)
CENSUS 4S25S DT (incl. MT, IT, FT Models)
CENSUS 4S33S DT (incl. MT, IT, FT Models)
Centis Profi 433-1G
Centis Profi Lite 433-G25
Chaplet HALIKAN NBD-486T/25M
Chicony Electronics 486 33P
Chicony Electronics Subnote 486SX/25
Cinet ET-100
Cinet EVL Series 486DX2/66
Cinet FSE-100
Cinet HI Series 486DX2/66
Cinet HI-100
Cinet LS-100
Cinet MP-100
Cinet PPI-100
Cinet VL Series 486DX2/66
Cinet VL-100
Cinet VLG-100
Clone 9433
Colfax P1-486 EISA/VLB
Comark CAT486-33/VL
Comark CAT486-66/VL
Comark flex 486
Comark Pentium VL60 - SCSI
Comark Pentium-60/VL
Comark Pentium-VL-60 Rackmount
Comark PENTIUM-VL66-SCSI
Commodore® 486DX-33C
Commodore 486SLC-25
Commodore 486SX-25
Commodore DT 486SX-20
Commodore LB 486DX-33C
Commodore LB 486DX2-66C
Commodore LB 486SX-33C
Commodore LB T486DX2-66C
Commodore T486DX-50C
COMPAQ Concerto 4/25
COMPAQ Contura 4/25C
COMPAQ Deskpro 386/25®
COMPAQ Deskpro 386/25e
COMPAQ Deskpro 386/33
COMPAQ Deskpro 386/33L
COMPAQ Deskpro 4/66i
COMPAQ Deskpro 486/25

COMPAQ Deskpro 486/25i
COMPAQ Deskpro 486/33i
COMPAQ Deskpro 486/33L
COMPAQ Deskpro 486/33M
COMPAQ Deskpro 486/50L
COMPAQ Deskpro 486/50M
COMPAQ Deskpro 5/60M
COMPAQ Deskpro 5/66M
COMPAQ Deskpro 66M
COMPAQ Deskpro XE 4/50
COMPAQ Deskpro XE 4/66
COMPAQ Deskpro XE 4100
COMPAQ Deskpro XE 433s
COMPAQ Deskpro XE 560
COMPAQ Deskpro XL 566 [14]
COMPAQ LTE Elite 4/75CX
COMPAQ LTE Lite 4/25
COMPAQ LTE Lite 4/25C
COMPAQ LTE Lite 4/33C
COMPAQ Portable 486c
COMPAQ Portable 486C/66
COMPAQ Presario 425
COMPAQ Presario CDS 520
COMPAQ Presario CDS 633
COMPAQ ProLiant 1000 486DX2/66
COMPAQ ProLiant 1000 Model 5/60
COMPAQ ProLiant 1000R Model 486DX2/66
COMPAQ ProLinea 3/25s
COMPAQ ProLinea 4/50
COMPAQ ProLinea 4/66
COMPAQ ProLinea CDS 200
COMPAQ ProLinea MT 4/33s
COMPAQ ProSignia 486DX/33
COMPAQ ProSignia 486DX2/66
COMPAQ ProSignia 5/60
COMPAQ ProSignia VS 486DX/33
COMPAQ ProSignia VS 486DX2/66
COMPAQ ProSignia VS 486SX/33
COMPAQ Systempro/LT 386/25
COMPAQ Systempro/LT 486DX2/50
COMPAQ Systempro/LT 486DX2/66
COMPAQ Systempro/LT 486DX33

COMPAQ Systempro/LT 486SX/25
COMPAQ Systempro/LT 486SX33
Comper DC486-662V
CompuAdd 420s
CompuAdd 433
CompuAdd 433 ELB
CompuAdd 433 LB
CompuAdd 433 LP
CompuAdd 433DLC LP
CompuAdd 433E
CompuAdd 450
CompuAdd 450DX2 LP
CompuAdd 466/DX2
CompuAdd 466DX2 LB
CompuAdd 466DX2E LB
CompuAdd 486-33DLC
COMPUCON 386DX/40
COMPUCON 486DX/33
COMPUCON 486DX/33 ISA/VL
COMPUCON 486DX/50
COMPUCON 486DX/50 EV
COMPUCON 486DX/50 VL
COMPUCON 486DX2-66
COMPUCON 486DX2/66 EV
COMPUCON PCI/I486SP3
COMPUCON PCI/IP-60
Compudyne 4DX2/50 EISA16340 DESKTOP (incl. MINITOWER and SERVERTOWER)
Compudyne 4DX2/50 VLB16340 DESKTOP (incl. MINITOWER and SERVERTOWER)
Compudyne 4DX2/66 EISA16245 DESKTOP (incl. MINITOWER and SERVERTOWER)
Compudyne 4DX2/66 Slimnote
Compudyne 4DX2/66 VLB16245 DESKTOP (incl. MINITOWER and SERVERTOWER)
Compudyne 4DX33 EISA16245 DESKTOP (incl. MINITOWER and SERVERTOWER)
Compudyne 4DX33 VLB16245 DESKTOP (incl. MINITOWER and SERVERTOWER)

Compudyne 4DX50
EISA16340 DESKTOP (incl.
MINITOWER and
SERVERTOWER)

Compudyne 4DX50
VLB16340 DESKTOP (incl.
MINITOWER and
SERVERTOWER)

Compudyne UM486V AIO
DX2/50 2VLB DIP
DESKTOP (incl.
MINITOWER and
SERVERTOWER)

Compudyne UM486V AIO
DX2/50 2VLB SMT
DESKTOP (incl.
MINITOWER and
SERVERTOWER)

Compudyne UM486V AIO
DX2/66 2VLB DIP
DESKTOP (incl.
MINITOWER and
SERVERTOWER)

Compudyne UM486V AIO
DX2/66 2VLB SMT
DESKTOP (incl.
MINITOWER and
SERVERTOWER)

Compudyne UM486V AIO
DX33 2VLB DIP DESKTOP
(incl. MINITOWER and
SERVERTOWER)

Compudyne UM486V AIO
DX33 2VLB SMT
DESKTOP (incl.
MINITOWER and
SERVERTOWER)

Compudyne UM486V AIO
DX50 2VLB DIP DESKTOP
(incl. MINITOWER and
SERVERTOWER)

Compudyne UM486V AIO
DX50 2VLB SMT
DESKTOP (incl.
MINITOWER and
SERVERTOWER)

Compudyne UM486V AIO
SX25 2VLB DIP DESKTOP
(incl. MINITOWER and
SERVERTOWER)

Compudyne UM486V AIO
SX25 2VLB SMT
DESKTOP (incl.
MINITOWER and
SERVERTOWER)

Compudyne UM486V AIO
SX33 2VLB DIP DESKTOP
(incl. MINITOWER and
SERVERTOWER)

Compudyne UM486V AIO
SX33 2VLB SMT
DESKTOP (incl.
MINITOWER and
SERVERTOWER)

CompuPartner 4D250

CompuPartner 4D33

CompuPartner 4DV266

Computer Extension CESI 486
66

Computer Resources
486DX266 ISA

Computer Resources 486DX33
FULL TOWER

Computer Resources 486DX33
LOCAL BUS

Computer Resources 486DX50
EISA

Computer Sales Prof.
486DX/33 VL

Computer Sales Prof.
486DX2/50 VL

Computer Sales Prof.
486DX2/66 EISA/VL

Computer Sales Prof.
486DX2/66 VL

Computer Sales Prof.
486SX/25 VL

Computer Sonics CSI
EISA/VL 486

Computer Sonics CSI ISA
486/33

Computer Sonics CSI VL/ISA
486

Computer Systems Resources
P5/60MHZ PCI

Computrend PREMIO 486DX-
33

Computrend PREMIO 486DX-
50

Computrend PREMIO
486DX2-66

Comtrade EISA GigaByte
Ultima 486DX2-66

Cornell Computer Systems
HOME OFFICE PAK
486/33 VLB

Cornell Computer Systems
Opti 486/66 VLB

Cornell Computer Systems
Tyan 486/33 EISA-VLB

Cornell Computer Systems
Tyan 66/EISA

Cornell Computer Systems
VALUE PAK 486/33 VLB

Cornell Computer Systems
VALUE PAK 486/66 VLB

Cornell Computer Systems
Vega™ 33/VLB

Cornell Computer Systems
Win NT Pak

CPU Sir Henry NT

Crescent 486-33VL

Crescent 486-66VL

CSS Labs MaxSys 433MTA

CSS Labs MaxSys
433MTMGE

CSS Labs MaxSys 433TA

CSS Labs MaxSys 433TMGE

CSS Labs MaxSys
450MTMGE

CSS Labs MaxSys 450TMGE

CSS Labs MaxSys
452MTMGE

CSS Labs MaxSys 452TMGE

CSS Labs MaxSys 462MTA

CSS Labs MaxSys 462MTE

CSS Labs MaxSys
462MTMGE

CSS Labs MaxSys 462TA

CSS Labs MaxSys 462TE

CSS Labs MaxSys 462TMGE

CSS Labs Preferred 433GA

CSS Labs Preferred 433GE

CSS Labs Preferred 433MGE

CSS Labs Preferred 450MGE

CSS Labs Preferred 452MGE

CSS Labs Preferred 462GA

CSS Labs Preferred 462GE

CSS Labs Preferred 462MGE

CTM Fontek 486DX-33 VL

CTM Fontek 486DX2-50 VL

CTM Fontek 486DX2-66 VL

CTM Polaris 486DX-33 VESA

CTM Polaris 486DX2-50
VESA

CTM Polaris 486DX2-66
VESA

CTM Pronic 486DX-33 VESA

CTM Pronic 486DX2-50
VESA

CTM Pronic 486DX2-66
VESA

Cube 340 ATX

Cube 433 ATX

Cube 450 ATX

Cube 466 ATX
Cube 466 ATX Local Bus
Cube 486/40
CyberStar Alliance DX2/50
CyberStar FilePro 1000
CyberStar FilePro 2000
CyberStar FilePro 2000 5/60
Cyclone NT SERVER
Daewoo 486 PCI SYSTEM
   (DX2-66)
Daewoo 486 VESA GREEN
   SYSTEM
   (DX2-50)
Daewoo 486 VESA GREEN
   SYSTEM
   (SX-25)
Daewoo 486 VESA GREEN
   SYSTEM
   (SX-33)
Daewoo 486 VESA
   System/2700(33)
Daewoo 486 VESA
   System/2900(33)
Daewoo Modular
   Desktop/2300
Daewoo Modular Mini
   Tower/2400
Daewoo VESA PENTIUM(60)
DAN for Windows 25
DAN for Windows 33
DAN for Windows 50
DAN for Windows 66
DAN Vantage/25
DAN Vantage/33
DAN Vantage/50
DAN Vantage/66
Danjen 486DLC 33 MHz
Danjen 486DX 33 MHz Local
   Bus
Danjen 486DX 50 MHz EISA
Danjen 486DX 50 MHz ISA
Dassault AT CUSTOMER
   ACTIVATED TERMINAL
   D633
Data General P60/TE2 Pentium
   Tower
Data Stor 386-33DX
   Desktop/Tower
Data Stor 386-33SX
   Desktop/Tower
Data Stor 486-25SX
   Desktop/Tower [88]
Data Stor 486-33 PCI
Data Stor 486-33DX
   Desktop/Tower [88]

Data Stor 486-33SX
   Desktop/Tower [88]
Data Stor 486-50DX
   Desktop/Tower [88]
Data Stor 486-66DX2
   Desktop/Tower [88]
Data Stor 486-66DX2E
   Desktop/Tower
Data Stor Pentium VL-60
Data Stor Pentium-60 PCI
DataExpert Model 486DX/2i-
   PCI
DataExpert Model 486DX/2i-
   VL
DataExpert Model 486DXe-
   VL66
DataExpert Model 486DXi-
   VL33
DATAFILEN PROFF 386DX-
   40
DATAFILEN PROFF 486DX-
   33 VL
DATAFILEN PROFF
   486DX2-66 VL
Datavarehuset BRICK 486DX-
   33 EISA
Datavarehuset BRICK
   486DX2-50 Local Bus
Datavarehuset BRICK
   486DX2-66 Local Bus
Datavarehuset BRICK 9003
   486DX-33
Datavarehuset BRICK 9003
   486DX2-50
Datavarehuset BRICK 9003
   4DXV
DDK Soft DDK-4066/2LV
Debis DCS Minitower 486
   EISA
Debis DCS Tower 486 MC
Debis DCS Tower 486 MP
   EISA
Deico 486DLC
Deico Predator III
DELL 325 N Notebook
DELL 325 NC Notebook
DELL 4033/XE
DELL 4050/XE
DELL 4066/XE
DELL 425s/L
DELL 433/L
DELL 433/M
DELL 433/ME
DELL 433/T
DELL 450/M

DELL 450s/L
DELL 4560/XE
DELL 466/M
DELL 466/ME
DELL Dimension 466/T
DELL Dimension 486DX/33
DELL Dimension 486DX/50
DELL Dimension 486DX2/50s
DELL Dimension 486SX/25
DELL Dimension XPS P60
DELL OmniPlex 560
DELL OmniPlex 566
DELL OptiPlex 425s/MXV
DELL OptiPlex 433/MXV
DELL OptiPlex 433s/MXV
DELL OptiPlex 450/MXV
DELL OptiPlex 466/MXV
DELL PowerLine 466DE
DELL PowerLine 466SE
DELL PowerLine System 325
DELL PowerLine System
   433DE
DELL PowerLine System 433E
DELL PowerLine System
   433SE
DELL PowerLine System
   450/T
DELL PowerLine System
   450DE
DELL PowerLine System
   450DE/2 DGX
DELL PowerLine System
   450SE
DELL PowerLine System
   486D/33
DELL PowerLine System
   486D/50
DELL PowerLine System
   486P/25
DELL PowerLine System
   486P/33
Delphi Olympus
Delta Micro Systems Gold
   Line 4D33V
Delta Micro Systems Gold
   Line 4D50C
DELTACOM 486-33
DELTACOM 486-50
DELTACOM 486SX-25
DELTACOM EISA 486-50
DELTACOM VESA 486DX2-
   66
Destiny Blitz 486SLC 33
DFI CCV 486DX-33
DFI CCV 486DX2-50

DFI CCV 486DX2-66
DFI CCV 486SX-25
DFI D486P-PRO
DFI P9800T [89]
DFI TN 486DX-33
DFI TN 486DX2-50
DFI TN 486DX2-66
DFI TN 486SX-25
DFI UCE 486DX-33
DFI UCE 486DX-50
DFI UCE 486DX2-50
DFI UCE 486DX2-66
DFI UCE 486SX-25
DFI UCF 486DX-33
DFI UCF 486DX-50
DFI UCF 486DX2-50
DFI UCF 486DX2-66
DFI UCF 486SX-25
Diamond DT 486DX Versa
    (AMD DX/40)
Diamond DT 486DX Versa
    (DX2/66)
Digital Equipment Corp.
    application DEC 400xP
Digital Equipment Corp.
    Celebris 4100
Digital Equipment Corp.
    Celebris 466
Digital Equipment Corp.
    Celebris 560
Digital Equipment Corp.
    Celebris 590
Digital Equipment Corp.
    Celebris FP 590
Digital Equipment Corp.
    DECpc 333
Digital Equipment Corp.
    DECpc 425
Digital Equipment Corp.
    DECpc 425 SE Notebook
Digital Equipment Corp.
    DECpc 425 ST
Digital Equipment Corp.
    DECpc 425i
Digital Equipment Corp.
    DECpc 425i DX2
Digital Equipment Corp.
    DECpc 433
Digital Equipment Corp.
    DECpc 433 SE
Digital Equipment Corp.
    DECpc 433 ST
Digital Equipment Corp.
    DECpc 433 Workstation

Digital Equipment Corp.
    DECpc 433dx DT
Digital Equipment Corp.
    DECpc 433dx LP
Digital Equipment Corp.
    DECpc 433dx MT
Digital Equipment Corp.
    DECpc 433dx MTE
Digital Equipment Corp.
    DECpc 433sx DT
Digital Equipment Corp.
    DECpc 433T
Digital Equipment Corp.
    DECpc 450 ST
Digital Equipment Corp.
    DECpc 450d2 LP
Digital Equipment Corp.
    DECpc 450d2 MT
Digital Equipment Corp.
    DECpc 452 ST
Digital Equipment Corp.
    DECpc 466 ST
Digital Equipment Corp.
    DECpc 466d2 DT
Digital Equipment Corp.
    DECpc 466d2 LP
Digital Equipment Corp.
    DECpc 466d2 LPx
Digital Equipment Corp.
    DECpc 466d2 MT
Digital Equipment Corp.
    DECpc 466d2 MTE
Digital Equipment Corp.
    DECpc 560 ST
Digital Equipment Corp.
    DECpc LPv 425sx
Digital Equipment Corp.
    DECpc LPv 433dx
Digital Equipment Corp.
    DECpc LPv 433sx
Digital Equipment Corp.
    DECpc LPv 450d2
Digital Equipment Corp.
    DECpc LPv 466d2
Digital Equipment Corp.
    DECpc LPv+ 4100
Digital Equipment Corp.
    DECpc LPv+ 433dx
Digital Equipment Corp.
    DECpc LPv+ 433sx
Digital Equipment Corp.
    DECpc LPv+ 450d2
Digital Equipment Corp.
    DECpc LPv+ 450s2

Digital Equipment Corp.
    DECpc LPv+ 466d2
Digital Equipment Corp.
    DECpc LPx 433dx
Digital Equipment Corp.
    DECpc LPx 433sx
Digital Equipment Corp.
    DECpc LPx 450d2
Digital Equipment Corp.
    DECpc LPx 560
Digital Equipment Corp.
    DECpc LPx 566
Digital Equipment Corp.
    DECpc LPx+ 433dx
Digital Equipment Corp.
    DECpc LPx+ 433sx
Digital Equipment Corp.
    DECpc LPx+ 450d2
Digital Equipment Corp.
    DECpc LPx+ 466d2
Digital Equipment Corp.
    DECpc MTE 4100
Digital Equipment Corp.
    DECpc XL 4100
Digital Equipment Corp.
    DECpc XL 433
Digital Equipment Corp.
    DECpc XL 466d2
Digital Equipment Corp.
    DECpc XL 560
Digital Equipment Corp.
    DECpc XL 566
Digital Equipment Corp.
    DECpc XL 590
Digital Equipment Corp.
    DECpc XL Server 466d2
Digital Equipment Corp.
    DECpc XL Server 560
Digital Equipment Corp.
    DECpc XL Server 566
Digital Equipment Corp.
    DECstation 425c
Dolch C.P.A.C. 486-33C
Dolch C.P.A.C. 486-33E
Dolch C.P.A.C. 486-50 EISA
Dolch C.P.A.C. 486-66C
Dolch C.P.A.C. 486-66E
Dolch M.A.C.H. 486-33
Dolch M.A.C.H. 486-66
Dolch V.P.A.C. 486-33C
Dolch V.P.A.C. 486-33E
Dolch V.P.A.C. 486-66C
Dolch V.P.A.C. 486-66E
DTK 486VL

DTK FEAT03-D33
DTK FEAT03-D40
DTK FEAT03-D50
DTK FEAT03-T66
DTK FEAT04-D33
DTK FEAT33-D33
DTK FEAT33-D40
DTK FEAT33-D50
DTK FEAT33-T66
DTK FEAT34-D33
DTK FEAT34-D40
DTK FEAT34-D50
DTK FEAT34-T66
DTK FEAT35-D33
DTK FEAT36-D33
DTK FEAT5030-D33
DTK FEAT5030-D50
DTK FEAT5030-T66
DTK FEAT5031-D33
DTK FEAT5031-D50
DTK FEAT5031-T66
DTK FEAT62-D33
DTK FEAT62-T66
DTK Grafika 4A
DTK Grafika 4C
DTK Grafika 4D
DTK Grafika 4E
DTK Grafika 4F
DTK Grafika 4G
DTK Grafika 4I
DTK Grafika 4J
DTK Grafika 4V2D-D3
DTK Grafika 4V2D-T6
DTK Grafika 4V2T-D3
DTK Grafika 4V2T-T6
DTK Grafika 5V1T-60
DTK Grafika 5VID-60
DTK PENT-01 (incl. -31, -32
   Models)
DTK SPAN0030
DTK SPAN01-D33
DTK SPAN01-D50
DTK SPAN01-T66
DTK SPAN3330
DTK SPAN5030
Duracom 486/25SX-CCV
Duracom 486/25SX-TN
Duracom 486/25SX-UCF
Duracom 486/33-CCV
Duracom 486/33-TN
Duracom 486/33-UCF
Duracom 486/50DX-UCF
Duracom 486/50DX2-CCV
Duracom 486/50DX2-TN

Duracom 486/50DX2-UCF
Duracom 486/66DX2-CCV
Duracom 486/66DX2-TN
Duracom 486/66DX2-UCF
Dyna Micro ASUS 486DX/33
   PCI/ISA
Dynamic Decisions DYNEX
   EXEC-50 EISA
Dynamic Decisions DYNEX
   EXECUTIVE ISA-486-33
   SV2G
Dynamic Decisions
   EXECUTIVE 486-33 ISA
Dynamic Decisions
   EXECUTIVE 486-33
   ISA/PCI
Dynamic Decisions
   EXECUTIVE 486-33
   VL/EISA
Dynamic Decisions
   EXECUTIVE 486-33
   VL/ISA
Dynamic Decisions
   EXECUTIVE 486-33SX
Dynamic Decisions
   EXECUTIVE 486-50
   VL/EISA
Dynamic Decisions
   EXECUTIVE 486-66 DX2
   VL/ISA
Dynamic Decisions
   EXECUTIVE 486-66
   VL/EISA
Dynamic Decisions
   EXECUTIVE ISA-486-33
   SV2
Dynamic Decisions
   EXECUTIVE ISA-486-50
   SV2
Dynamic Decisions
   EXECUTIVE ISA-486-
   66D2 SV2
Dynamic Decisions
   EXECUTIVE P5-60
   PENTIUM-PCI/ISA
Dynamic Decisions
   PROFESSIONAL 486-33
   VL/ISA
Dynamic Decisions
   PROFESSIONAL 486-33DX
   VL/EISA E3
Dynamic Decisions
   PROFESSIONAL 486-33DX
   VL/EISA E4

Dynamic Decisions
   PROFESSIONAL 486-50DX
   VL/EISA E4
Dynamic Decisions
   PROFESSIONAL 486DX66
   EISA VLB E
ECE DATA i486/VLB
ECG Unitron 340
ECG Unitron 425
ECG Unitron 433
ECG Unitron 450
ECG Unitron 450 DX/2
ECG Unitron 466 DX/2
ECG Unitron 466 DX/2 EISA
Elite Industries MB-1433AEA-
   V 486/33
Elite Industries MB-1433AEA-
   V 486/50
Elite Industries MB-1433AEA-
   V 486DX2/66
Elitegroup UC4917-G
Elitegroup UM4910
Elitegroup VL486
Elonex PC-400 Series
   Computer
Eltech Model 4660VB
Epson Action PC 1500
Epson ActionDesk 4000
   (4DX2/66-LB)
Epson ActionDesk 4000+
Epson ActionPC 1500
Epson ActionPC 2000
Epson ActionPower 5000
Epson EL 486UC+
Epson EL 4S/33+
Epson Endeavor 486L
Epson Endeavor P60
Epson Endeavor VL66
Epson Endeavor WG 4DX2/50
Epson Endeavor WG 4DX2/66
Epson Endeavor WG 4SX33
Epson Equity 4DX/33
Epson Equity 4DX2/50
Epson Equity 4SX/25
Epson PowerSpan 486DX2/66
Epson Progression 486DX/33
Epson Progression 486DX2/66
Epson Progression 486SX/25
Epson Progression 4DX2/50
Epson Progression 4SX/33
Ergo Ultra Moby Brick 486/66
ERIDAN Onyx DE433
Erre 486DX2-66 VLB
EverCom ISA 486SR/33

EverCom VL 486SV2/66
Everex Cube DX/33
Everex Step 486/33 ISA
Everex Step DP
Everex Step Plus DX 33
Everex Step Plus DX/2 50
Everex Step Plus DX/2 66
Everex Step UP-60
Everex Step VL EISA
    486DX2/50
Everex Step VL EISA
    486DX2/66
Everex Step VL ISA
    486DX2/50
Everex Step VL ISA
    486DX2/66
Everex Tempo 486/33
Everex Tempo 486/33E
Everex Tempo 486DX2/50
Everex Tempo 486SX/25
Everex Tempo VL EISA DX/2
    50
Everex Tempo VL EISA DX/2
    66
Everex Tempo VL EISA
    DX/33
Everex Tempo VL ISA DX/2
    50
Everex Tempo VL ISA DX/2
    66
Everex Tempo VL ISA DX/33
Evergreen Systems CAPcard
    425e
Evesham Micros VALE™
    PREMIER + 486DX2-66
Evesham Micros VALE
    PREMIER 486DX2-66
Evesham Micros VALE
    PRESTIGE® 486DX2-66
Expo-Tech 386 Ultra Slim
Expo-Tech 486DX/3 Desktop
Expo-Tech 486DX/3 Desktop
    (w/LBVGA)
Expo-Tech 486DX/3 Desktop
    (w/VLBUS)
Expo-Tech 486DX/3 Mini
    (w/VLBUS)
Expo-Tech 486DX/3 Tower
Expo-Tech 486DX/3 Tower
    (w/VLBUS)
Expo-Tech 486DX2/4 Desktop
Expo-Tech 486DX2/4 Desktop
    (w/LBVGA)
Expo-Tech 486DX2/4 Desktop
    (w/VLBUS)

Expo-Tech 486DX2/4 Tower
Expo-Tech 486DX2/4 Tower
    (w/VLBUS)
Expo-Tech 486DX2/6 Desktop
Expo-Tech 486DX2/6 Desktop
    (w/LBVGA)
Expo-Tech 486DX2/6 Desktop
    (w/VLBUS)
Expo-Tech 486DX2/6 Mini
    (w/VLBUS)
Expo-Tech 486DX2/6 Tower
Expo-Tech 486DX2/6 Tower
    (w/VLBUS)
Expo-Tech 486SX/3 Desktop
Expo-Tech 486SX/3 Desktop
    (w/LBVGA)
Expo-Tech 486SX/3 Tower
Expo-Tech 486SX/3 Ultra Slim
Expo-Tech 486SX/3 Ultra Slim
    (w/LBVGA)
Expo-Tech 486SX/4 Desktop
Expo-Tech 486SX/4 Desktop
    (w/LBVGA)
Expo-Tech 486SX/4 Desktop
    (w/VLBUS)
Expo-Tech 486SX/4 Mini
    (w/VLBUS)
Expo-Tech 486SX/4 Tower
Expo-Tech 486SX/4 Ultra Slim
Expo-Tech 486SX/4 Ultra Slim
    (w/LBVGA)
Expo-Tech LT322 Notebook
Expo-Tech LT421 Notebook
Expo-Tech SMP DX2-66
Express Micro EISA VESA
    486DX-50
Express Micro EISA VESA
    486DX2-66
Express Micro VL-BUS
    486DX-50
Express Micro VL-BUS
    486DX2-66
Fast 486DY66S520
Federal Technologies
    Guardian^SM WinMaster
    486/33SX
First Jupiter 486DX66 All In
    One ISA Bus
First Krypton 486DX50 VL-
    Bus
First LEO 4386VCV DX33
First LEO 486DX66-VL
First LEO 486VC DX/50
First LEO 486VC DX2/66
First LEO DESKTOP 486/33

First LEO DESKTOP 486/50
First LEO DESKTOP 486/66
First LEO MINITOWER
    486/33
First LEO MINITOWER
    486/50
First LEO MINITOWER
    486/66
First President Pak 486DX2/66
    VLB
First Venus 486DX2/66 EISA
    and VL-Bus
First Venus 486DX2/66 VL-
    Bus
Fountain Technology
    486DX/33 VL
Fountain Technology
    486DX2/50 VL
Fountain Technology
    486DX2/66 EISA/VL
Fountain Technology
    486DX2/66 VL
Fountain Technology
    486SX/25 VL
Free 586F34X-PCI
Free VESA23X50
Fujitech 486DX/50 E
Fujitech 486DX2/50-VL
Fujitsu S-400
Fujitsu S-466
Fujitsu S-500
Fujitsu S-5000MP
FUTURE COMPUTERS 486
    Eisa/Vesa NTPC
FutureTech 486DX2-66 VLB
Gain TITON WORKSTATION
Gateway 2000 386/33
Gateway 2000 486/33C
Gateway 2000 486/33E
Gateway 2000 486DX2/50
Gateway 2000 486DX2/50E
Gateway 2000 486DX2/50V
Gateway 2000 486DX2/66V
    Desktop
Gateway 2000 4DX/33
Gateway 2000 4DX2-66P
Gateway 2000 4DX2/66E
Gateway 2000 4SX/25
Gateway 2000 4SX/33V
Gateway 2000 Color Book
Gateway 2000 Nomad
    425DXL [9]
Gateway 2000 Nomad
    450DXL [9]
Gateway 2000 P5-60

GCH AEGIS 433
GCH AEGIS 466
GCH EasyData 433HI
GCH EasyData 466HI
GCH EasyDate 466HI VL
GCH EiSYS Ei433DX
GCH EiSYS Ei466DX
GCH EiSYS Ei600 Series
Genitech Capricorn JF/33
Genitech Capricorn JF2/66
Genitech Capricorn KF33 PCI
GES DATAMINI MF 486DX-
  33
GES DATAMINI MF
  486DX2-66
GES DATAMINI MF 486SX-
  25
Getek 486 DX 50 LOCAL
  BUS
GMX EISAMB 486DX2/66
GoldStar 425SXE
GoldStar GS425SX
GoldStar GS466DX
GoldStar GS466DXE
GRiD 486ei-25 SVR
GRiD 486ei-33
GRiD APT/425se
GRiD APT/450e
GRiD MFP 425s+
GRiD MFP 433+
GRiD MFP 433s+
GRiD MFP 450+
GRiD MFP 466+
GRiD MFP/420s
GRiD MFP/425s
GRiD MFP/450
GRiD MFP/540
GVH 486DX2 66 Vesa Bus
H.D.Microsystèmes AX7 486
  DX-33
H.D.Microsystèmes AX7 486
  DX-50
H.D.Microsystèmes AX7 486
  DX2-50
H.D.Microsystèmes AX7 486
  DX2-66
H.D.Microsystèmes AX7
  Pentium 60 PCI
Hancke & Peter 386w
  Professional
Hancke & Peter 486/33w
  Professional
Hancke & Peter 486/50w
  Professional

Hancke & Peter 486/66w
  Professional
Hancke & Peter 486w EISA
  Professional
Harris Epoch 486/33 VESA
Harris Epoch 486/50 EISA
Harris Epoch 486/50 ISA
Hauppauge 4860 EISA DX2-
  66
Hauppauge 486M Local Bus
  DX2-66
Hertz 486/D50e
Hertz 486/D50Ee
Hertz 486/D66X2e
Hertz 486/D66X2Ee
Hewitt Rand 486DX-33 3VL
Hewitt Rand HR486DX-33Ce
  VESA
Hewitt Rand PENTIUM/60
Hewlett-Packard NetServer
  4/100 LC
Hewlett-Packard NetServer
  4/100 LF
Hewlett-Packard NetServer
  4/33 LE
Hewlett-Packard NetServer
  4/33 LM
Hewlett-Packard NetServer
  4/66 LC
Hewlett-Packard NetServer
  4/66 LF
Hewlett-Packard NetServer
  4d/66 LE
Hewlett-Packard NetServer
  4d/66 LM
Hewlett-Packard NetServer
  4s/33 LE
Hewlett-Packard NetServer
  5/100 LM
Hewlett-Packard NetServer
  5/60 LM
Hewlett-Packard NetServer
  5/66 LC
Hewlett-Packard NetServer
  5/66 LF
Hewlett-Packard NetServer
  5/66 LM
Hewlett-Packard NetServer
  5/90 LM
Hewlett-Packard Vectra 386/25
Hewlett-Packard Vectra
  386/33N
Hewlett-Packard Vectra
  386/33NI

Hewlett-Packard Vectra
  486/25M
Hewlett-Packard Vectra
  486/25N
Hewlett-Packard Vectra
  486/25NI
Hewlett-Packard Vectra
  486/25T
Hewlett-Packard Vectra
  486/25U
Hewlett-Packard Vectra
  486/33M
Hewlett-Packard Vectra
  486/33N
Hewlett-Packard Vectra
  486/33NI
Hewlett-Packard Vectra
  486/33ST
Hewlett-Packard Vectra
  486/33T
Hewlett-Packard Vectra
  486/33U
Hewlett-Packard Vectra
  486/33XM
Hewlett-Packard Vectra
  486/50U
Hewlett-Packard Vectra
  486/50XM
Hewlett-Packard Vectra 486/66
  XM
Hewlett-Packard Vectra
  486/66N
Hewlett-Packard Vectra
  486/66ST
Hewlett-Packard Vectra
  486/66U
Hewlett-Packard Vectra
  486S/20
Hewlett-Packard Vectra
  486s/25 MI
Hewlett-Packard Vectra
  486s/33M
Hewlett-Packard Vectra
  486s/33N
Hewlett-Packard Vectra
  486s/33NI
Hewlett-Packard Vectra
  486s/33XM
Hewlett-Packard Vectra
  RS/25C
Hewlett-Packard Vectra XP/60
  PC
High Tech USA 486DX266
  VLB SYSTEM

High Tech USA 486DX33
VLB SYSTEM
HM Systems Minstrel
XPentium
HM Systems Minstrel
XPentium Server
HM Systems Minstrel Xpresso
486
HM Systems Minstrel Xpresso
XL
Hyundai 425s
Hyundai 433DDV
Hyundai 466d2
Hyundai Prestige 433d
IBM Eduquest™ Model 50
486DX/33 (9605-040)
IBM PC Server 486DX2/66
8640-0N*
IBM PC Server Pentium/60
8640-0P*
IBM PS/1 2133-XXX
486SX2/33MHz
IBM PS/1 2133-xxx 486SX/25
IBM PS/1 2133-xxx 486SX/33
IBM PS/1 2133A-xxx
486DX/33 [90]
IBM PS/1 2133A-xxx
486DX2/66 [90]
IBM PS/1 2133A-xxx
486SX/25 [90]
IBM PS/1 2133A-xxx
486SX/33 [90]
IBM PS/1 2155-87C (SL-B)
IBM PS/1 2155-xxx 486DX/33
IBM PS/1 2155-xxx
486DX2/50
IBM PS/1 2155-xxx
486DX2/66
IBM PS/1 2155-xxx 486SX/25
IBM PS/1 2155-xxx 486SX/33
IBM PS/1 2155A-xxx
486DX2/66 [90]
IBM PS/1 2155A-xxx
486SX/25 [90]
IBM PS/1 2155A-xxx
486SX/33 [90]
IBM PS/1 2155C-XX
IBM PS/1 2168-xxx 486DX/33
IBM PS/1 2168-xxx
486DX2/50
IBM PS/1 2168-xxx
486DX2/66
IBM PS/1 2168-XXX
486DX2/66MHz

IBM PS/1 2168-xxx 486SX/25
IBM PS/1 2168-xxx 486SX/33
IBM PS/1 2168A-xxx
486DX2/66 [90]
IBM PS/1 2168A-xxx
486SX/25 [90]
IBM PS/1 2168A-xxx
486SX/33 [90]
IBM PS/1 486DX33 - 2133-
XX
IBM PS/1 Consultant
486SX/25 2133B-xxx
IBM PS/1 Consultant
486SX/33 2133B-xxx
IBM PS/1 Consultant
486SX/33 2155B-xxx
IBM PS/2 56 486SLC3-xxx
IBM PS/2 56LS 486SLC3-xxx
IBM PS/2 57 486SLC3-xxx
IBM PS/2 M57 486SLC3-xxx
IBM PS/2 Model 50/50Z
System Board Upgrade
486SLC2/50 [91]
IBM PS/2 Model 53 9553-xxx
486SLC2/50]
IBM PS/2 Model 55/55SX
System Board Upgrade
486SX/25 [91]
IBM PS/2 Model 56 8556-xxx
486SLC/20
IBM PS/2 Model 56 9556-xxx
486SLC2/50
IBM PS/2 Model 57 8557-xxx
486SLC/20
IBM PS/2 Model 57 9557-xxx
486SLC2/50
IBM PS/2 Model 60/80 System
Board Upgrade 486DX/33 [91]
IBM PS/2 Model 70 8570-xxx
386DX/25
IBM PS/2 Model 70 8570-xxx
486DX/25
IBM PS/2 Model 70 System
Board Upgrade 486DX/33 [91]
IBM PS/2 Model 76 9576-xxx
486DX2/66
IBM PS/2 Model 76 9576-xxx
486SX/33
IBM PS/2 Model 76i 9576-xxx
486DX2/50]
IBM PS/2 Model 76s 9576-xxx
486DX2/50]
IBM PS/2 Model 77 9577-xxx
486DX2/66

IBM PS/2 Model 77 9577-xxx
486SX/33
IBM PS/2 Model 77i 9577-xxx
486DX2/50]
IBM PS/2 Model 77s 9577-xxx
486DX2/50]
IBM PS/2 Model 80 8580-xxx
386DX/25
IBM PS/2 Model 90 XP 486
8590-0H* 486SX/25
IBM PS/2 Model 90 XP 486
8590-0J* 486DX/25
IBM PS/2 Model 90 XP 486
8590-0K* 486DX/33
IBM PS/2 Model 90 XP 486
8590-0L* 486DX2/50
IBM PS/2 Model 90 XP 486
8590-xxx with 486DX2/66
processor upgrade
IBM PS/2 Model 90 XP 486
8590-xxx with Enhanced
486DX/50 processor
upgrade
IBM PS/2 Model 90 XP 486
8590-xxx with Enhanced
486DX2/66 processor
upgrade
IBM PS/2 Model 90 XP 486
8590-xxx with processor
upgrade with Pentium
Technology
IBM PS/2 Model 90 XP 486
9590-0L* 486DX2/50
IBM PS/2 Model 90 XP 486
9590-xxx with 486DX2/66
processor upgrade
IBM PS/2 Model 90 XP 486
9590-xxx with Enhanced
486DX/50 processor
upgrade
IBM PS/2 Model 90 XP 486
9590-xxx with Enhanced
486DX2/66 processor
upgrade
IBM PS/2 Model 90 XP 486
9590-xxx with processor
upgrade with Pentium
Technology
IBM PS/2 Model 95 XP 486
8595-0H* 486SX/25
IBM PS/2 Model 95 XP 486
8595-0J* 486DX/25
IBM PS/2 Model 95 XP 486
8595-0K* 486DX/33

IBM PS/2 Model 95 XP 486
8595-0L* 486DX2/50
IBM PS/2 Model 95 XP 486
8595-0M* 486DX/50
IBM PS/2 Model 95 XP 486
8595-xxx with 486DX2/66
processor upgrade
IBM PS/2 Model 95 XP 486
8595-xxx with Enhanced
486DX/50 processor
upgrade
IBM PS/2 Model 95 XP 486
8595-xxx with Enhanced
486DX2/66 processor
upgrade
IBM PS/2 Model 95 XP 486
8595-xxx with processor
upgrade with Pentium
Technology
IBM PS/2 Model 95 XP 486
9595-0L* 486DX2/50
IBM PS/2 Model 95 XP 486
9595-0M* 486DX/50
IBM PS/2 Model 95 XP 486
9595-xxx with 486DX2/66
processor upgrade
IBM PS/2 Model 95 XP 486
9595-xxx with Enhanced
486DX/50 processor
upgrade
IBM PS/2 Model 95 XP 486
9595-xxx with Enhanced
486DX2/66 processor
upgrade
IBM PS/2 Model 95 XP 486
9595-xxx with processor
upgrade with Pentium
Technology
IBM PS/2 Model P75 8573-
xxx 486DX/33
IBM PS/2 Server 85 433 9585-
0K*
IBM PS/2 Server 85 466 9585-
0N*
IBM PS/2 Server 85 9585-0X*
486SX/33
IBM PS/2 Server 85 9585-0X*
with 486DX2/66 processor
upgrade
IBM PS/2 Server 95 466 9595-
1N*
IBM PS/2 Server 95 560 9595-
0PT
IBM PS/2 Server 95 566 9595-
0QT

IBM PS/2 Server 95 Array 466
9595-3N*
IBM PS/2 Server 95 Array 560
9595-3P*
IBM PS/2 Server 95 Array 566
9595-3Q*
IBM PS/2 Ultimedia DV M57
9557-xxx 486SLC2/50
IBM PS/2 Ultimedia M57
8557-xxx 486SLC/20
IBM PS/2 Ultimedia M57
9557-xxx 486SLC2/50
IBM PS/2 Ultimedia M77
9577-xxx 486DX2/66
IBM PS/2 Ultimedia M77
9577-xxx 486SX/33
IBM PS/ValuePoint 425SX/D
6384-Fxx
IBM PS/ValuePoint 425SX/S
6382-Fxx
IBM PS/ValuePoint 433DX/D
6384-Mxx
IBM PS/ValuePoint 433DX/S
6382-Mxx
IBM PS/ValuePoint 433DX/T
6387-Mxx
IBM PS/ValuePoint 433SX/D
6384-Kxx
IBM PS/ValuePoint 433SX/S
6382-Kxx
IBM PS/ValuePoint 466DX2/D
6384-Wxx
IBM PS/ValuePoint 466DX2/T
6387-Wxx
IBM ThinkPad 300]
IBM ThinkPad 360CS
IBM ThinkPad 700C [9,7]
IBM ThinkPad 720 [9,7]
IBM ThinkPad 720C [9,7]
IBM ThinkPad 750 [92,7]
IBM ThinkPad 750c [92,7]
IBM ThinkPad 755
486DX2/50 [92,7]
ICL ErgoPRO C4/33
ICL ErgoPRO D4/25
ICL ErgoPRO D4/33d
ICL ErgoPRO D4/66d XG
ICL ErgoPRO D5/60
ICL ErgoPRO E4/66d
ICL System Platform
CXe486/66
ICL System Platform CXe486i
ICL System Platform CXe486s
ICL System Platform
FX486/33

ICL System Platform
FX486/50
ICL System Platform
FX486/66
ICL ValuePlus D4i
ICL ValuePlus M4e
ICL ValuePlus M4i
ICL ValuePlus MD/33
ICL ValuePlus MD/50
ICL ValuePlus MD/66
Image 486DX/50 EISA
Image 486DX2/66 VESA
Index INDEXPORT 486 OVD
66 LOCAL BUS CACHE
Index INDEXPORT 486/33
Index INDEXPORT 486/33
VL VESA CACHE
Index INDEXPORT 486/50 I
CACHE
Index INDEXPORT 486/50
VL VESA CACHE
Inelco INTEL XPRESS
50MHZ
Innovax Aurora 486DX/33
Insight 66 MHz EISA/VESA
486DX2
Insight 66 MHz ISA/VESA
486DX2
Intel Classic R-Series
Intel Classic/PCI Expandable
Desktop
Intel Entrada OEM Platform
Intel L486-Series/Professional
GX
Intel L486-Series/Professional
Workstation
Intel Ninja DX2-66 OEM
Platform
Intel Premiere/PCI 66 LPX
Intel Premiere/PCI Baby AT
Intel Premiere/PCI LPX
Intel X486/50E
Intel Xpress/MX 486/33
Intel Xpress/MX 66Mhz
Pentium Pentium
Intelicom 486DX/33 EISA
Intelicom 486DX/33 ISA
Intelicom 486DX/33 VESA
EISA
Intelicom 486DX/33 VLB
Intelicom 486DX/50 EISA
Intelicom 486DX/50 ISA
Intelicom 486DX/50 VESA
EISA
Intelicom 486DX/50 VLB

Intelicom 486DX2/50 EISA
Intelicom 486DX2/50 ISA
Intelicom 486DX2/50 VESA
EISA
Intelicom 486DX2/50 VLB
Intelicom 486DX2/66 EISA
Intelicom 486DX2/66 ISA
Intelicom 486DX2/66 VESA
EISA
Intelicom 486DX2/66 VLB
Intelicom 486SX/25 ISA
Intelicom 486SX/25 VLB
Intelicom 486SX/33 ISA
INTERCOMP Digit
486SLC/25
INTERCOMP Entry 486/33
INTERCOMP Master
486DX/50
INTERCOMP Planet 486/50
EISA
INTERCOMP Planet
486DX2/66 EISA
INTERCOMP Planet LC
486/33 EISA
INTERCOMP Target 486/33
INTERCOMP Target 486/50
VLB
INTERCOMP Target
486DX/50
Interface Electronic
486DX2/66
Intergraph PC 433
Intergraph PC 466
Intergraph TD 2 Personal
Workstation
Intergraph TD 3 Personal
Workstation
Intergraph Technical Desktop
1220
International Data DGI
486DX-66
International Data DGI ISA
O/D 20
International Instrumentation
BLUE MAX 486 DX2 66
International Instrumentation
BLUE MAX 486 DX33
International Instrumentation
BLUE MAX 486 DX66 PCI
International Instrumentation
BLUE MAX P-60 PCI
International Instrumentation
BLUE MAX PENTIUM P5-
60

Investronica INVES BS-486
Investronica INVES BS-486
VL
Investronica INVES IFS-486
Investronica INVES IFS-900
Investronica INVES MP-900
XM UniProcessor
Investronica INVES WS-900
EVL
Investronica INVES WS-900
VL
IPC DYNASTY G-PC 486DX-
33CV
IPC DYNASTY G-PC
486DX2-50CV
IPC DYNASTY G-PC
486DX2-66CV
IPC DYNASTY G-PC 486SX-
25CV
IPC DYNASTY HE (GREEN)
486DX-33
IPC DYNASTY HE (GREEN)
486DX2-50
IPC DYNASTY HE (GREEN)
486DX2-66
IPC DYNASTY HE (GREEN)
486SX-25
IPC DYNASTY HE (GREEN)
486SX-33
IPC DYNASTY HE 486DX-33
IPC DYNASTY HE 486DX-
33C
IPC DYNASTY HE 486DX2-
50
IPC DYNASTY HE 486DX2-
50C
IPC DYNASTY HE 486DX2-
66
IPC DYNASTY HE 486DX2-
66C
IPC DYNASTY HE 486SX-25
IPC DYNASTY HE 486SX-
25C
IPC DYNASTY HE 486SX-33
IPC DYNASTY LE 486DX-33
(incl. 33C)
IPC DYNASTY LE 486DX2-
50 (incl. 50C)
IPC DYNASTY LE 486DX2-
66 (incl. 66C)
IPC DYNASTY LE 486SX-25
(incl. 25C)
IPC DYNASTY S-PC 586DX-
60CV

IPC DYNASTY SE 486DX-
33C
IPC DYNASTY SE 486DX2-
50C
IPC DYNASTY SE 486DX2-
66C
IPC DYNASTY SE 486SX-
25C
IPC DYNASTY SE
PENTIUM-60
IPC DYNASTY SEL
PENTIUM-60
IPC VALUEMAGIC 486DX-
33
IPC VALUEMAGIC 486DX2-
50
IPC VALUEMAGIC 486DX2-
66
IPC VALUEMAGIC 486SX-
25
IPC VALUEMAGIC 486SX-
33
Ipex 486DX-33 Green Desk
Top ISA/VESA
Ipex 486DX2-66 Centra 1000
Ipex 486DX2-66 Centra 1000
EISA
Ipex 486DX2-66 Centra 1000
EISA (Entry Level)
Ipex 486DX2-66 Centra 1000
EISA/VL-BUS
Ipex 486DX2-66 Centra 1000
ISA/VESA
Ipex 486DX2-66 Centra 1000
VESA
Ipex 486DX2-66 Centra 2000
Ipex 486DX2-66 Centra 2000
EISA
Ipex 486DX2-66 Centra 2000
EISA (Entry Level)
Ipex 486DX2-66 Centra 2000
EISA/VL-BUS
Ipex 486DX2-66 Centra 2000
ISA/VESA
Ipex 486DX2-66 Centra 2000
VESA
Ipex 486DX2-66 Centra 5000
ISA/VESA
Ipex 486DX2-66 Desktop
Ipex 486DX2-66 Desktop
(EISA)
Ipex 486DX2-66 Desktop
EISA (Entry Level)
Ipex 486DX2-66 Desktop
EISA/VL-BUS

Ipex 486DX2-66 Desktop VESA

Ipex 486DX2-66 Green Desk Top ISA/VESA

Ipex 486DX2-66 Green Mini Tower ISA/VESA

Ipex 486DX2-66 Green Ultimate ISA/VESA

Ipex 486DX2-66 Mini Tower

Ipex 486DX2-66 Mini Tower EISA

Ipex 486DX2-66 Mini Tower EISA (Entry Level)

Ipex 486DX2-66 Mini Tower EISA/VL-BUS

Ipex 486DX2-66 Mini Tower VESA

Ipex 486DX2-66 Slimline

Ipex 486DX2-66 Slimline (WD Form Factor)

Ipex 486DX2-66 Slimline ISA/VESA

Ipex 486DX33 Centra 1000

Ipex 486DX33 Centra 1000 EISA

Ipex 486DX33 Centra 1000 EISA (Entry Level)

Ipex 486DX33 Centra 1000 EISA/VL-BUS

Ipex 486DX33 Centra 1000 VESA

Ipex 486DX33 Centra 2000

Ipex 486DX33 Centra 2000 EISA

Ipex 486DX33 Centra 2000 EISA (Entry Level)

Ipex 486DX33 Centra 2000 EISA/VL-BUS

Ipex 486DX33 Centra 2000 VESA

Ipex 486DX33 Desktop

Ipex 486DX33 Desktop EISA

Ipex 486DX33 Desktop EISA (Entry Level)

Ipex 486DX33 Desktop EISA/VL-BUS

Ipex 486DX33 Desktop VESA

Ipex 486DX33 Green Centra 1000 ISA/VESA

Ipex 486DX33 Green Centra 2000 ISA/VESA

Ipex 486DX33 Green Centra 5000 ISA/VESA

Ipex 486DX33 Green Mini Tower ISA/VESA

Ipex 486DX33 Green Slimline ISA/VESA

Ipex 486DX33 Green Ultimate ISA/VESA

Ipex 486DX33 Mini Tower

Ipex 486DX33 Mini Tower EISA

Ipex 486DX33 Mini Tower EISA (Entry Level)

Ipex 486DX33 Mini Tower EISA/VL-BUS

Ipex 486DX33 Mini Tower VESA

Ipex 486DX33 Slimline

Ipex 486DX33 Slimline (WD Form Factor)

Ipex 486DX50 Centra 1000

Ipex 486DX50 Centra 1000 EISA

Ipex 486DX50 Centra 1000 EISA (Entry Level)

Ipex 486DX50 Centra 1000 EISA/VL-BUS

Ipex 486DX50 Centra 1000 VESA

Ipex 486DX50 Centra 2000

Ipex 486DX50 Centra 2000 EISA

Ipex 486DX50 Centra 2000 EISA (Entry Level)

Ipex 486DX50 Centra 2000 EISA/VL-BUS

Ipex 486DX50 Centra 2000 VESA

Ipex 486DX50 Desktop

Ipex 486DX50 Desktop EISA

Ipex 486DX50 Desktop EISA (Entry Level)

Ipex 486DX50 Desktop EISA/VL-BUS

Ipex 486DX50 Desktop VESA

Ipex 486DX50 Mini Tower

Ipex 486DX50 Mini Tower EISA

Ipex 486DX50 Mini Tower EISA (Entry Level)

Ipex 486DX50 Mini Tower EISA/VL-BUS

Ipex 486DX50 Mini Tower VESA

Ipex 486DX50 Slimline

Ipex 486DX50 Slimline (WD Form Factor)

Ipex 486SX25 Centra 1000

Ipex 486SX25 Centra 1000 EISA

Ipex 486SX25 Centra 1000 EISA (Entry Level)

Ipex 486SX25 Centra 1000 EISA/VL-BUS

Ipex 486SX25 Centra 1000 VESA

Ipex 486SX25 Centra 2000

Ipex 486SX25 Centra 2000 EISA

Ipex 486SX25 Centra 2000 EISA (Entry Level)

Ipex 486SX25 Centra 2000 EISA/VL-BUS

Ipex 486SX25 Centra 2000 VESA

Ipex 486SX25 Desktop

Ipex 486SX25 Desktop EISA

Ipex 486SX25 Desktop EISA (Entry Level)

Ipex 486SX25 Desktop EISA/VL-BUS

Ipex 486SX25 Desktop VESA

Ipex 486SX25 Mini Tower

Ipex 486SX25 Mini Tower (EISA)

Ipex 486SX25 Mini Tower EISA (Entry Level)

Ipex 486SX25 Mini Tower EISA/VL-BUS

Ipex 486SX25 Mini Tower VESA

Ipex 486SX25 Slimline

Ipex 486SX25 Slimline (WD Form Factor)

Ipex 486SX33 Centra 1000 EISA

Ipex 486SX33 Centra 1000 EISA (Entry Level)

Ipex 486SX33 Centra 1000 EISA/VL-BUS

Ipex 486SX33 Centra 1000 ISA

Ipex 486SX33 Centra 1000 VESA

Ipex 486SX33 Centra 2000 EISA

Ipex 486SX33 Centra 2000 EISA (Entry Level)

Ipex 486SX33 Centra 2000 EISA/VL-BUS

Ipex 486SX33 Centra 2000 ISA

Ipex 486SX33 Centra 2000
VESA
Ipex 486SX33 Desktop
Ipex 486SX33 Desktop EISA
Ipex 486SX33 Desktop EISA
(Entry Level)
Ipex 486SX33 Desktop
EISA/VL-BUS
Ipex 486SX33 Desktop VESA
Ipex 486SX33 Mini Tower
EISA
Ipex 486SX33 Mini Tower
EISA (Entry Level)
Ipex 486SX33 Mini Tower
EISA/VL-BUS
Ipex 486SX33 Mini Tower ISA
Ipex 486SX33 Mini Tower
VESA
Ipex 486SX33 Slimline
Ipex 486SX33 Slimline (WD
Form Factor)
Ipex Pentium/60 Centra 1000
EISA/PCI
Ipex Pentium/60 Centra 1000
ISA/PCI
Ipex Pentium/60 Centra 1000
ISA/VESA
Ipex Pentium/60 Centra 2000
EISA/PCI
Ipex Pentium/60 Centra 2000
ISA/PCI
Ipex Pentium/60 Centra 2000
ISA/VESA
Ipex Pentium/60 Centra 5000
EISA/PCI
Ipex Pentium/60 Centra 5000
ISA/PCI
Ipex Pentium/60 Centra 5000
ISA/VESA
Ipex Pentium/60 Desk Top
EISA/PCI
Ipex Pentium/60 Desk Top
ISA/PCI
Ipex Pentium/60 Desk Top
ISA/VESA
Ipex Pentium/60 Mini Tower
EISA/PCI
Ipex Pentium/60 Mini Tower
ISA/PCI
Ipex Pentium/60 Mini Tower
ISA/VESA
Ipex Pentium/60 Slimline 1000
EISA/PCI
Ipex Pentium/60 Slimline
ISA/PCI

Ipex Pentium/60 Slimline
ISA/VESA
Ipex Pentium/60 Ulti-mate
EISA/PCI
Ipex Pentium/60 Ulti-mate
ISA/PCI
Ipex Pentium/60 Ulti-mate
ISA/VESA
Ipex Pentium/66 Centra 1000
EISA/PCI
Ipex Pentium/66 Centra 1000
ISA/PCI
Ipex Pentium/66 Centra 1000
ISA/VESA
Ipex Pentium/66 Centra 2000
EISA/PCI
Ipex Pentium/66 Centra 2000
ISA/PCI
Ipex Pentium/66 Centra 2000
ISA/VESA
Ipex Pentium/66 Centra 5000
EISA/PCI
Ipex Pentium/66 Centra 5000
ISA/PCI
Ipex Pentium/66 Centra 5000
ISA/VESA
Ipex Pentium/66 Desk Top
EISA/PCI
Ipex Pentium/66 Desk Top
ISA/PCI
Ipex Pentium/66 Desk Top
ISA/VESA
Ipex Pentium/66 Mini Tower
EISA/PCI
Ipex Pentium/66 Mini Tower
ISA/PCI
Ipex Pentium/66 Mini Tower
ISA/VESA
Ipex Pentium/66 Slimline
EISA/PCI
Ipex Pentium/66 Slimline
ISA/PCI
Ipex Pentium/66 Slimline
ISA/VESA
Ipex Pentium/66 Ulti-mate
EISA/PCI
Ipex Pentium/66 Ulti-mate
ISA/PCI
Ipex Pentium/66 Ulti-mate
ISA/VESA
ITG NT 486DX-50
ITOS KT 486/33
ITOS MT 386DX/40
JAI PC 845-66-32VL
JDR C486-50

JDR V486-33
JDR V486-66
JDR V486SX-33
KT Technology KT386DX-33
KT Technology KT386DX-40
KT Technology KT486DX-33
KT Technology KT486DX-50
KT Technology KT486DX2-
50 VESA
KT Technology KT486DX2-
66 VESA LB
L.E.M. Technologies
Sys38640/M
LABTAM 486/66-2 VLB
LANIX BRAIN 486DX2-66
LANIX LIM 486SLC2-66
LANIX MART 486DLC-40
LANIX MART 486DX-33
LANIX MART 486DX2-66
LASER 386 Ultra Slim
LASER 486DX/3 Desktop
LASER 486DX/3 Desktop
(w/LBVGA)
LASER 486DX/3 Desktop
(w/VLBUS)
LASER 486DX/3 Mini
(w/VLBUS)
LASER 486DX/3 Tower
LASER 486DX/3 Tower
(w/VLBUS)
LASER 486DX2/4 Desktop
LASER 486DX2/4 Desktop
(w/LBVGA)
LASER 486DX2/4 Desktop
(w/VLBUS)
LASER 486DX2/4 Tower
LASER 486DX2/4 Tower
(w/VLBUS)
LASER 486DX2/6 Desktop
LASER 486DX2/6 Desktop
(w/LBVGA)
LASER 486DX2/6 Desktop
(w/VLBUS)
LASER 486DX2/6 Mini
(w/VLBUS)
LASER 486DX2/6 Tower
LASER 486DX2/6 Tower
(w/VLBUS)
LASER 486SX/3 Desktop
LASER 486SX/3 Desktop
(w/LBVGA)
LASER 486SX/3 Desktop
w/VLBUS
LASER 486SX/3 Tower
LASER 486SX/3 Ultra Slim

LASER 486SX/3 Ultra Slim (w/LBVGA)
LASER 486SX/4 Desktop
LASER 486SX/4 Desktop (w/LBVGA)
LASER 486SX/4 Desktop (w/VLBUS)
LASER 486SX/4 Mini (w/VLBUS)
LASER 486SX/4 Tower
LASER 486SX/4 Ultra Slim
LASER 486SX/4 Ultra Slim (w/LBVGA)
LASER LT322 Notebook
LASER LT421 Notebook
LASER SMP DX2-66
Leading Edge D4/DX-33 Plus DeskTop
Leading Edge D4/DX-50 Plus DeskTop
Leading Edge D4/DX2-50 Plus DeskTop
Leading Edge D4/MTDX-33 MiniTower
Leading Edge D4/MTDX-50 MiniTower
Leading Edge D4/MTDX2-50 MiniTower
Leading Edge D4/MTDX2-66 MiniTower
Leading Edge D4/MTSX-25 MiniTower
Leading Edge D4/MTSX-33 MiniTower
Leading Edge D4/SX-25 Plus DeskTop
Leading Edge D4/SX-33 Plus DeskTop
Leading Edge WinPro 486/SLC33
Leading Edge WinPro 486/SX-25
Leading Edge WinPro 486e/DX-33
Leading Edge WinPro 486e/DX-33(VL)
Leading Edge WinPro 486e/DX-50
Leading Edge WinPro 486e/DX2-50
Leading Edge WinPro 486e/DX2-50(VL)
Leading Edge WinPro 486e/DX2-66

Leading Edge WinPro 486e/DX2-66(VL)
Leading Edge WinPro 486e/SX-25
Leading Edge WinPro 486e/SX-25(VL)
Leading Edge WinPro 486e/SX-33
Leading Edge WinPro 486e/SX-33(VL)
Leading Edge WinTower 486 DX-33
Leading Edge WinTower 486 DX2-50
Leading Edge WinTower 486 DX2-66
Leading Edge WinTower 486 SX-25
Leading Edge WinTower SX-33
Legacy 486DLC-33 SYSTEM
Legacy VLB 486DX-33
Lightning Power EISA
Lightning VLB Pak
Lucky Star System w/ Cyrix 486S-33
Lundin 400 Series 486 EISA w/ 486DX/50
Lundin 400 Series 486 ISA w/ 486DX/33
Lundin 400 Series 486 VESA w/ 486DX/33
Magitronic G-MD433L-170-4M
Magitronic G-MD440G-130-4M
Magitronic G-MD466L-210-4M
Magitronic G-MS466L-10-16M
Master Cascade 386-40 Small Desktop
Master Cascade 486-33 Mini-Tower
Maximus 486-50MHz Maxi-CAD
Maximus Cyrix 486/40 VESA Local Bus
MetaTech 486DX/33 ISA
MetaTech 486DX/33 VESA
MetaTech 486DX/50 EISA
Metro Computers 486Dx - 33
Metro Computers 486SX - 33 mhz

Metro Computers AMD 486DX - 40 mhz
Metro Computers Pentium 60
Micro Arts EISA Pro
Micro Arts Power Pro Stealth
Micro Arts Power Pro Vesa
Micro Assistance Group MAG NT 4000
Micro Express ME 486DX2/66
Microbyte Lyrebird Model 451
Microbyte Lyrebird Model 455
Microbyte Lyrebird Model 457
Micron 4100 VL Magnum
Micron 486PCI WINSTATION CD
Micron 486VL Magnum 433 DX
Micron 486VL Magnum 433 SX
Micron 486VL Magnum 450 DX2
Micron 486VL Magnum 466 DX2
Micron 486VL MagServer 433 DX
Micron 486VL MagServer 450 DX2
Micron 486VL MagServer 466 DX2
Micron 486VL PowerStation 433 DX
Micron 486VL PowerStation 433 SX
Micron 486VL PowerStation 450 DX2
Micron 486VL PowerStation 466 DX2
Micron 486VL ValueLine 466 DX2
Micron 486VL WinServer 433 DX
Micron 486VL WinServer 450 DX2
Micron 486VL WinServer 466 DX2
Micron 486VL WinStation 433 DX
Micron 486VL WinStation 433 SX
Micron 486VL WinStation 450 DX2
Micron 486VL WinStation 466 DX2
Micron P5PCI Platinum CD

Micron P5PCI PowerStation CD

Microniche MIS Computer Systems M466EV

Microniche MIS Computer Systems M466VL

Microtec MF486 EISA/66MHz

Microtech MTECH GX4-D250

Microtech MTECH GX4-D266

Microtech MTECH GX4-D33

Microtech MTECH GX4-S33

Microtech MTECH VI7-P560

Midgards Micro ISA 486DX-33

Midgards Micro VESA 486DX-33

Midwest Micro 486DX2/50 Vesa/ISA

MIKROLOG OY Osborne MT4D-33CLB

MIKROLOG OY Osborne MT4D-33N

MIKROLOG OY Osborne MT4D-50CLB

MIKROLOG OY Osborne MT4D-50N

MIKROLOG OY Osborne MT4D-66CLB

MIKROLOG OY Osborne MT4D-66N

MIKROLOG OY Osborne MT4S-25N

MIKROLOG OY Osborne MT4S-33CLB

MIKROLOG OY Osborne MT4S-33N

MIND 386DX/33 ISA

MIND 486DX/33 EISA

MIND 486DX/33 ISA

MIND 486DX/33 VLB

MIND 486DX/50 EISA

MIND 486DX/50 ISA

MIND 486DX2/50 EISA

MIND 486DX2/50 ISA

MIND 486DX2/50 VLB

MIND 486DX2/66 EISA

MIND 486DX2/66 ISA

MIND 486DX2/66 VLB

MIND 486SX/25 EISA

MIND 486SX/25 ISA

MIND 486SX/33 EISA

MIND 486SX/33 ISA

MIND 486SX/33 VLB

MIND Pentium 60 VLB

Minitronics MINTEC 486DX-33

MiTAC DM4066

Modular MST/200

Modular Server Module 450

Modular Server Module 466

Modular Server Module Pentium

Modular Server Tower/32

Monydata Entry 486 / 33

Monydata Modula 200 / 80

Monydata Station 486 / 80

Multitech ProSpec 486DX-50 PS450DE-ST

Mustek MECER3486-VL

Mustek MECER7486-VL

MYNIX MYCOMP 486/66VLG

National Instruments™ VXIpc-486 Model 200

National Instruments VXIpc-486 Model 500

National Microcomputers Power System DX2-66

NCR StarStation

NCR System 3000 Model 3230

NCR System 3000 Model 3314

NCR System 3000 Model 3330

NCR System 3000 Model 3333

NCR System 3000 Model 3335

NCR System 3000 Model 3345

NCR System 3000 Model 3350

NCR System 3000 Model 3355

NCR System 3000 Model 3410

NCR System 3000 Model 3445

NCR System 3000 Model 3447

NEC Express II

NEC Express/II 433 ST

NEC Express/II 466 ST

NEC Express/II P601 LT

NEC Image 425

NEC Image 433

NEC Image 433ES

NEC Image 466

NEC Image 466es

NEC Image P60

NEC PowerMate 386/25S

NEC PowerMate 425

NEC PowerMate 425es

NEC PowerMate 433

NEC PowerMate 433es

NEC PowerMate 466

NEC PowerMate 466es

NEC PowerMate 486/33e

NEC PowerMate 486/33i

NEC PowerMate 486/50e

NEC PowerMate 486/50i

NEC PowerMate 486sx/25e

NEC PowerMate DX2/66e

NEC UltraLite™ Versa

NETiS 386DX/40 ISA

NETiS 486DX/33 ISA

NETiS 486DX/33 VL

NETiS 486DX/33 VL EISA

NETiS 486DX/50 VL

NETiS 486DX/50 VL EISA

NETiS 486DX2/50 VL EISA

NETiS 486DX2/66 ISA

NETiS 486DX2/66 VL

NETiS 486DX2/66 VL EISA

NETiS 486SX/33 VL

NETiS Ultra 486DX/33 ISA

NETiS Ultra 486DX/50 ISA

NETiS Ultra 486DX2/66 ISA

NETiS Ultra 486DX2/66 VL

NETiS Ultra 486SX/25 ISA

NETiS Ultra N433VL

NETiS Ultra N450VL

Network Connection M2

Network Connection T-3000

Network Connection T-4000

Network Connection TNX

Network Connection Triumph T.R.A.C.

Network Connection Triumph T.S.C.V

Nimrod 486 DESKTOP VESA

Nimrod 486 LC-DESKTOP VESA

Nimrod 486 MINI-TOWER VESA

Nimrod 486 TOWER VESA

Nimrod DESKTOP 486DX/33 VESA VL

Nimrod DESKTOP 486DX2/66 ISA

Nimrod LC-DESKTOP 486DX/33 VESA VL

Nimrod LC-DESKTOP 486DX2/66 ISA

Nimrod MINI-TOWER 486DX/33 VESA VL

Nimrod MINI-TOWER 486DX2/66 ISA

Nimrod TOWER 486DX/33 VESA VL

Nimrod TOWER 486DX2/66 ISA

Nix PCs 486DX2/66 Vesa
NORTH-EAST NE Micro
  433LV
NORTH-EAST NE Micro
  450LV
NORTH-EAST NE Micro
  466LV
Northern Micro NM486/66VL
Northgate 486/33
Northgate 486/33 Slimline
  ZXP
Northgate 486/33 VESA ISA
Northgate 486/33e Baby AT
Northgate Elegance 333
Northgate Elegance 425i
Northgate Elegance 433e
Northgate Elegance 433i
Northgate Elegance SP 386/33
Northgate Elegance SP 433
Northgate Elegance ZXP
Northwest Micro Signature I
  4/33
Northwest Micro Signature II
  4/33 VLB
OKI if 486VX550D
OKI if Server 466/SL
OKI if Station 425/DL
OKI if Station 433/DE
Olidata P/60
Olivetti LSX5010
Olivetti LSX5015
Olivetti LSX5020
Olivetti LSX5025
Olivetti LSX5025 E
Olivetti M300-28
Olivetti M300-30
Olivetti M300-30P
Olivetti M380-40
Olivetti M4-40
Olivetti M4-46
Olivetti M4-60
Olivetti M4-62
Olivetti M4-64
Olivetti M4-65
Olivetti M4-66
Olivetti M4-82
Olivetti M400-10
Olivetti M400-40
Olivetti M400-60
Olivetti M480-10
Olivetti M480-20
Olivetti M480-40
Olivetti M6-400
Olivetti M6-420
Olivetti M6-440

Olivetti M6-450
Olivetti M6-460
Olivetti M6-520
Olivetti M6-540
Olivetti M6-560
Olivetti M6-620
Olivetti M6-850
Olivetti M6-860
Olivetti M6-880
Olivetti SNX 140 Systema
Olympia Olystar 300D-33
Olympia Olystar 400D-33
Olympia Olystar 400D-33
  EISA
Olympia Olystar 400D-50
Olympia Olystar 400D-66
Olympia Olystar 400D-66
  EISA
Olympia Olystar 400S-25
Olympia Olystar 400S-33SL
Omni Tech 8600 486DX2-66
Omni Tech 9600 486DX2-66
Optima OCT 486DX2/66 VL
Optima OCT 486DX250 EISA
Optima OCT 486DX266 EISA
Optima OCT 486DX33 EISA
Optima OCT 486DX33 VL
Optima OCT 486DX50 EISA
Optima OCT 486DX50 VL
Optima OCT 486SX25 EISA
Optima OCT 486SX25 VL
Optima OCT DX2-50 VL
Optima Sprinter 486DX250
  EISA
Optima Sprinter 486SX25
  EISA
Optimus 486DX/50 EISA
Optimus 486DX/50 LocalBus
Optimus 486DX2-50 VLB
Optimus 486DX2-66 EISA
Optimus 486DX2-66 VLB
Optimus 486DX2/66
Optimus 486SX/25 VL
Optimus Lan Server LX
OPUS Pentium/60Mhz
OPUS Premier 4D-50
Osborne 4280G-66
Osborne EISA 486DX50
  Fileserver
Osborne IX5-60E
Osborne LP4D-33
Osborne LP4D-33CLB
Osborne LP4D-33N
Osborne LP4D-50
Osborne LP4D-50C

Osborne LP4D-50CLB
Osborne LP4D-50N
Osborne LP4D-66
Osborne LP4D-66CLB
Osborne LP4D-66N
Osborne LP4S-25
Osborne LP4S-25N
Osborne LP4S-33CLB
Osborne LP4S-33N
Osborne Mpower 486DX2-66
Osborne Mpower3 486DX33
Osborne Mpower3 486SX33
Osborne Mpower4 486DX33
Osborne Mpower4 486SX33
Osborne Pentium 60
Osborne VESA 486DX2-66
Osicom 4133L 486/DX266
  VESA LB
Osicom 4133L 486/DX33
  VESA LB
Packard Bell 1110
Packard Bell 1120
Packard Bell 1150
Packard Bell 2050
Packard Bell 400T
Packard Bell 470
Packard Bell 485
Packard Bell 486CDM
Packard Bell 486DX/33
Packard Bell 486SX/25
Packard Bell 495
Packard Bell 515E
Packard Bell 525E
Packard Bell 545E
Packard Bell 550
Packard Bell 560
Packard Bell 565E
Packard Bell AXCEL 1033
Packard Bell AXCEL 105
Packard Bell AXCEL 1066
Packard Bell AXCEL 130
Packard Bell AXCEL 2005
Packard Bell AXCEL 2015
Packard Bell AXCEL 2033
Packard Bell AXCEL 205
Packard Bell AXCEL 2066
  MINITOWER
Packard Bell AXCEL 230
Packard Bell AXCEL 405
  (incl. H model)
Packard Bell AXCEL 410
Packard Bell AXCEL 410E
  (incl. H, F and W G models)
Packard Bell AXCEL 420

Packard Bell AXCEL 450G
(incl. H, J and TJ models)
Packard Bell AXCEL 460
Packard Bell AXCEL 460H
(incl. TJ model)
Packard Bell AXCEL 486/33
Packard Bell AXCEL 486A66
Packard Bell AXCEL 486SX
Packard Bell AXCEL 530
Packard Bell AXCEL 533H
(incl. J and TJ models)
Packard Bell AXCEL 533STJ
Packard Bell AXCEL 550
Packard Bell AXCEL 550MT/J
Packard Bell AXCEL 570
Packard Bell AXCEL 630
MINITOWER
Packard Bell AXCEL 666J
(incl. TJ and TL models)
Packard Bell AXCEL 850
Packard Bell EXECUTIVE
486/33 (incl. ELITE model)
Packard Bell EXECUTIVE
486/33 G (incl. J model)
Packard Bell EXECUTIVE
486DX2/JW (incl. TY
model)
Packard Bell EXECUTIVE
486SX (incl. -2F and -G
models)
Packard Bell EXECUTIVE
486SX ELITE (incl. SERIES
SI model)
Packard Bell EXECUTIVE
486SX-EC
Packard Bell EXECUTIVE
486SX/FW (incl. /HW
model)
Packard Bell EXECUTIVE
486SX250
Packard Bell EXECUTIVE
486XE (incl. C and S
models)
Packard Bell EXECUTIVE
Elite Series 486SXCC
Packard Bell FORCE 1066
Packard Bell FORCE 107
Packard Bell FORCE 110
Packard Bell FORCE 1135
Packard Bell FORCE 1137
Packard Bell FORCE 117
Packard Bell FORCE 200
Packard Bell FORCE 2010
Packard Bell FORCE 2020

Packard Bell FORCE 2040
MINITOWER
Packard Bell FORCE 2233
MINITOWER
Packard Bell FORCE 2376
(incl. F model)
Packard Bell FORCE 2386
MINITOWER
Packard Bell FORCE 250
Packard Bell FORCE 405
Packard Bell FORCE 425
Packard Bell FORCE 486 SX
(incl. E, -M1, and -M130
models)
Packard Bell FORCE 486/25
Packard Bell FORCE 486/33
(incl. +, E, -M1, and -M210
models)
Packard Bell FORCE 486/33G
(incl. J, JW, and PLUS
models)
Packard Bell FORCE 48625
(incl. EX model)
Packard Bell FORCE
486CDM-1/TV
Packard Bell FORCE
486DX/DJ-W (incl. G-W, H,
H2, J and JT-W models)
Packard Bell FORCE 486DX2
-WG
Packard Bell FORCE
486DX2/EJT (incl. W
model)
Packard Bell FORCE
486DX2/F JT (incl. JT-W, J-
W and LT-W models)
Packard Bell FORCE
486DX2/G-W
Packard Bell FORCE
486MT50J
Packard Bell FORCE 486SX
(incl. /20, /20G, E, M1, and
M130 models)
Packard Bell FORCE 486SX-
WG
Packard Bell FORCE
486SX/25 (incl. G and W
models)
Packard Bell FORCE
486SX/BE (incl. FW, FW-2,
M, MM and H2 models)
Packard Bell FORCE
486SX/OH-W
Packard Bell FORCE 515

Packard Bell FORCE 515S
(incl. PLUS model)
Packard Bell FORCE 525 (incl.
B and S models)
Packard Bell FORCE 545 (incl.
B and S models)
Packard Bell FORCE 565 (incl.
S model)
Packard Bell FORCE 600 (incl.
B and S models)
Packard Bell FORCE 715
MINITOWER
Packard Bell FORCE T66
Packard Bell LEGEND 102H
(incl. ELITE model)
Packard Bell LEGEND 1066
WG ELITE
Packard Bell LEGEND 1133
Packard Bell LEGEND 1134
ELITE
Packard Bell LEGEND 1135
Packard Bell LEGEND 1136
Packard Bell LEGEND 115
Packard Bell LEGEND 1166
Packard Bell LEGEND 1176
Packard Bell LEGEND 120
Packard Bell LEGEND 125
Packard Bell LEGEND 126
ELITE
Packard Bell LEGEND 127
Packard Bell LEGEND 128
Packard Bell LEGEND 135
(incl. H model)
Packard Bell LEGEND 140
Packard Bell LEGEND 1900
Packard Bell LEGEND 1910
Packard Bell LEGEND 2000
Packard Bell LEGEND 2001
Packard Bell LEGEND 2002
ELITE
Packard Bell LEGEND 2011
SUPREME
Packard Bell LEGEND 2025
Packard Bell LEGEND 207
Packard Bell LEGEND 2133
MINITOWER
Packard Bell LEGEND 2135
MINITOWER
Packard Bell LEGEND 2176
ELITE MT
Packard Bell LEGEND 2266
MINITOWER
Packard Bell LEGEND 2270
MINITOWER

Packard Bell LEGEND 2276
MINITOWER
Packard Bell LEGEND 2300
MINITOWER
Packard Bell LEGEND 233
Packard Bell LEGEND 234
ELITE
Packard Bell LEGEND 245
Packard Bell LEGEND 33T
SUPREME
Packard Bell LEGEND 33T
SUPREME MINITOWER
Packard Bell LEGEND 430 G
(incl. WG and F models)
Packard Bell LEGEND 430
WG ELITE
Packard Bell LEGEND 430E
(incl. E2 and EL models)
Packard Bell LEGEND 435E
ELITE (incl. 2 ELITE
model)
Packard Bell LEGEND 440G
Packard Bell LEGEND 445 G
ELITE (incl. G 2 ELITE
model)
Packard Bell LEGEND
486CDM-1/TV
Packard Bell LEGEND
486T/50
Packard Bell LEGEND 510H
Packard Bell LEGEND 605H
ELITE
Packard Bell LEGEND 625
Packard Bell LEGEND 635J
Packard Bell LEGEND 635TJ
ELITE
Packard Bell LEGEND 660
(incl. H and ELITE models)
Packard Bell LEGEND 660H
Packard Bell LEGEND 660TJ
(incl. H model)
Packard Bell LEGEND 66D
SUPREME
Packard Bell LEGEND 66T
SUPREME
Packard Bell LEGEND 670
Packard Bell LEGEND 695
SUPREME
Packard Bell LEGEND 700
(incl. ELITE model)
Packard Bell LEGEND 740
Packard Bell LEGEND 747
MINITOWER

Packard Bell LEGEND 750
SUPREME
Packard Bell LEGEND 760
SUPREME
Packard Bell LEGEND 770
(incl. ELITE model)
Packard Bell LEGEND 780
Packard Bell LEGEND 780
SUPREME
Packard Bell LEGEND 790
Packard Bell LEGEND 800
SUPREME (incl. 800+)
Packard Bell LEGEND 800
SUPREME/50
Packard Bell LEGEND 840
MINITOWER
Packard Bell LEGEND 845
MINITOWER
Packard Bell LEGEND 848
MINITOWER
Packard Bell LEGEND 900 F
(incl. F-ELITE, and G
models)
Packard Bell LEGEND 920SX
SUPREME
Packard Bell LEGEND 925 G
(incl. G ELITE and J model)
Packard Bell LEGEND 933 G
(incl. G ELITE, J, J ELITE
and J+)
Packard Bell LEGEND 950
ELITE (incl. J and J ELITE
models)
Packard Bell LEGEND 960TJ
Packard Bell LEGEND 966J
(incl. ELITE model)
Packard Bell LEGEND 966TJ
(incl. TJ ELITE, TJ2 ELITE,
TJ-W ELITE, WG and TZ
models)
Packard Bell LEGEND M950
Packard Bell LEGEND MT950
(incl. J model)
Packard Bell LEGEND T66
Packard Bell PACKMATE
486/33G (incl. J model)
Packard Bell PACKMATE
486/E
Packard Bell PACKMATE
48625
Packard Bell PACKMATE
486DX/33 Y (incl. Y-W and
X models)

Packard Bell PACKMATE
486DX2/50TY (incl. TY-W
model)
Packard Bell PACKMATE
486DX2/T Z -W (incl. Y
model)
Packard Bell PACKMATE
486DX33/T Y (incl. /TY-W
model)
Packard Bell PACKMATE
486SX
Packard Bell PACKMATE
486SX/20 E (incl. F, and G
models)
Packard Bell PACKMATE
486SX/25G
Packard Bell PACKMATE
486SX/25W (incl. TG
model)
Packard Bell PACKMATE
486SX/33X (incl. X2 and
TM models)
Packard Bell PACKMATE
486SX25U (incl. U2 and X
models)
Packard Bell PACKMATE 733
C MT
Packard Bell PACKMATE
X225
Packard Bell PACKMATE
X230
Packard Bell PACKMATE
X233
Packard Bell PACKMATE
X240
Packard Bell PACKMATE
X250 (incl. Y model)
Packard Bell PACKMATE
XT266
Packard Bell PB430_5428
Packard Bell PB430SX25
Packard Bell PB530_5428
PC Direct 486ep
PC Expanders VANGUARD
PENTIUM 60MHZ VLB
PC House Micro Q 486dx2-66
PC Tech Zeos Upgradable
PC-Brand Leader 486dx/33
Cache
PC-Brand Leader 486dx2/66
Cache
PC-Brand NB 486slc
Peacock 486DX 50

Pionex 486DX/33 VL
Pionex 486DX2/50 VL
Pionex 486DX2/66 EISA/VL
Pionex 486DX2/66 VL
Pionex 486SX/25 VL
Poly 486-33VZ
Poly 486-50E
Poly 486-66E
Poly 486-66EV
Poly 486-66VI
Poly 486-66VL
Poly 486-66VR3
Poly 486SX-25Y
Poly 486SX-33VL
Poly 586-60VLB
Positive by Tandon 486dx/33
Positive by Tandon 486dx2/66
Precision 486/50 EISA
Precision 486/50F
Precision 486/66 EISA VL-Bus
Precision 486/66 VL-Bus
Precision 486/66E
Primax 425SVI
Primax 433VI
Primax 450VE
Primax 450VI
Primax 466VI
Primax 486/33E
Primax 486/66E
Procomp TW 9300
Professional Concepts Beeker
    4-33/VL2
Professional Concepts Beeker
    4-50/VL2
Professional Concepts Beeker
    4-66/VL2
Professional Concepts Beeker
    6900
Professional Concepts Quinn
    4-33/VLE
Professional Concepts Quinn
    4-50/VLE
Professional Concepts Quinn
    4-66/VLE
Professional Concepts Saavij
    4-33/VL3
Professional Concepts Saavij
    4-50/VL3
Professional Concepts Saavij
    4-66/VL3
Progen 466
Protech 486-66Mhz EISA
Protech 486-66Mhz EISA/VL
Protech 486-66Mhz ISA

Protech 486-66Mhz ISA/VL
QNIX OMNI486DX2/66
Quadrant 486DX/33 VESA
    LOCAL BUS
Quadrant 486DX/50 VESA
    LOCAL BUS
Quadrant 486DX2/66 VESA
    LOCAL BUS
Quadrant 486SX/25 VESA
    LOCAL BUS
Quadrant 486SX/33 VESA
    LOCAL BUS
Quantex 486DX/33 VL
Quantex 486DX2/50 VL
Quantex 486DX2/66 EISA/VL
Quantex 486DX2/66 VL
Quantex 486SX/25 VL
Quattro Prompt4
Radisys EPC-23
Radisys EPC-4
Radisys EPC-5
Radisys EPC-7
Rask REC 486-50F
RDIpc i486DX2/66c Eisa
RDIpc i486DX2/66c Isa
RDIpc i486DX2/66c VL Bus
Reason Technology Square
    4LX-C 486DX/2-66
Reason Technology Square
    4LX/DX2-66
Repco Data R33B486
Repco Data Turbo APM-420
    DX
Repco Data Turbo APM-425
    DX
Repco Data Turbo APM-433
Reply Model 32
Reply PS/2 Model 50/50SX
    System Board Upgrade
    486SLC2/50 [91]
Reply PS/2 Model 55/55SX
    System Board Upgrade
    486/25 [91]
Reply PS/2 Model 60/80
    System Board Upgrade
    486/33 [91]
Reply PS/2 Model 70 System
    Board Upgrade 486/33 [91]
Research Machines RM E
    Series QE-486/33
Research Machines RM S
    Series PC-486/25SX
Research Machines RM
    SystemBase 486/33

Research Machines RM V
    Series V466
Rolta ROLTASTATION 433E
Rose Computer Cidex 386DX-
    40 ISA(AMD)
Rose Computer Cidex 486DX-
    40 ISA
Samsung DeskMaster 486/33P
Samsung DeskMaster
    486D2/66E
Samsung DeskMaster
    486S/25N
Sanyo MBC-19te
SCA Professional 3486DX2/66
    VLB
SCA Professional 486DX 50
    VLB
SCA Professional 486DX2/66
    VLB
SCHADT SCT Proline
    486DX2-66 VLB
Seanix ASI 9000 EFAR
    486DX2-66
Seanix ASI 9000 PREMIERE
    PENTIUM PCI-60
Seanix ASI 948633VM
Seanix ASI 948650VM
Seanix ASI 9DX266VM
Sequent WinServer 1000up [14]
Sequent WinServer 1500up [14]
Sequent WinServer 3000up [14]
Shuttle 486VL 50
Shuttle HOT-407
    EISA/VESA/DX-33
Shuttle HOT-407
    EISA/VESA/DX-40
Shuttle HOT-407
    EISA/VESA/DX-50
Shuttle HOT-407
    EISA/VESA/DX2-50
Shuttle HOT-407
    EISA/VESA/DX2-66
Shuttle HOT-409 VLB/DX-33
Shuttle HOT-409 VLB/DX-40
Shuttle HOT-409 VLB/DX-50
Shuttle HOT-409 VLB/DX2-
    50
Shuttle HOT-409 VLB/DX2-
    66
Shuttle HOT-413 VLB/DX-33
Shuttle HOT-413 VLB/DX-40
Shuttle HOT-413 VLB/DX-50
Shuttle HOT-413 VLB/DX2-
    66

Shuttle HOT-426 PCI/DX-33
Shuttle HOT-503
    PENTIUM/60
Shuttle HOT-503
    PENTIUM/66
Sidus Formula 486/33i
Sidus Formula 486/50e
Siemens-Nixdorf PCD-3M/25
Siemens-Nixdorf PCD-3T/33
Siemens-Nixdorf PCD-4G/33
Siemens-Nixdorf PCD-4G/66
Siemens-Nixdorf PCD-
    4GSX/25
Siemens-Nixdorf PCD-4H
Siemens-Nixdorf PCD-4H VL
Siemens-Nixdorf PCD-4HSX
Siemens-Nixdorf PCD-4LSL
Siemens-Nixdorf PCD-4LSX
Siemens-Nixdorf PCD-4T
Siemens-Nixdorf PCD-4T/66
Siemens-Nixdorf PCD-5H
Siemens-Nixdorf PCD-5T /
    PCI 60E
Siemens-Nixdorf PCE-4C/66-1
Siemens-Nixdorf PCE-
    4C/DX2-66
Siemens-Nixdorf PCE-
    4C/SX25
Siemens-Nixdorf PCE-4R/33
Siemens-Nixdorf PCE-
    4RSX/25
Siemens-Nixdorf PCE-4T/66
Siemens-Nixdorf PCE-5S/60
Siemens-Nixdorf PCE-5S/66
Silicon Star AV4 486DX2/66
Silicon Star AV4 486DX33
Silicon Star AV4 50MHz
Sirex Eaton 486DX-33
    EISA/LocalBus
Sirex PowerMaster 486DX-33
    EISA/VLB
Sirex PowerMaster 486DX2-
    50 EISA/VLB
Sirex PowerMaster 486DX2-
    66 EISA/VLB
Sirex SpeedMaster 486DX-33
    ISA
Sirex SpeedMaster 486DX-33
    LocalBus
Sirex SpeedMaster 486DX-50
    ISA
Sirex SpeedMaster 486DX2-50
    ISA
Sirex SpeedMaster 486DX2-50
    LocalBus

Sirex SpeedMaster 486DX2-66
    ISA
Sirex SpeedMaster 486DX2-66
    LocalBus
Sirex SpeedMaster 486SX-33
    LocalBus
SKAI 486DX/50VL
SKAI 486DX2/66EVL
Softlet Standard 486DX-40
Softlet Standard 486DX-50
Softlet Standard 486DX2-50
    VL
Softlet Standard 486DX2-66
Softworks Citus MDC 386-33
Softworks Citus MDC 486DX-
    33
Softworks Citus MDC 486DX-
    50
Softworks Citus MDC
    486DX2-50
Softworks Citus MDC
    486DX2-66
Softworks Citus MDC X 486
    50
SRC Systems 486 VL
SRC Systems
    GRAPHICSTATION
SRC Systems High
    Performance SCSI 66MHz
SRC Systems Pentium PCI
Standard Computronics
    HIPPO-VL 486DX2-66
    VESA LOCAL BUS
Standard Computronics
    HIPPO-VL+ 486DX2-66
    DCA SYSTEM
STD 4D250
STD 4D33
STD 4DV266
STD 4DX250B
STD 4DX266B
STD 4DX33B
SuperCom Touch TI433
SuperCom Touch TI450
SuperCom Touch TI466
Supra 486DX-33 VESA/ISA
Supra 486SX-33 VESA/ISA
Svensk LAPLINE DeskTop
    462 (incl. MiniTower Model)
Swan 486/33DB
Swan 486/33V
Swan 486/50ES
Swan 486/66ES
Swan 486DX/33 EISA-DB
Swan 486DX2/50DB

Swan 486DX2/66 EISA-DB
Swan 486DX2/66DB
Swan 486SX/25DB
Swan 486SX/25V
Syncomp Mega+386i 40 PC
Syncomp Mega+486DX2/50e
    PC
Syncomp Mega+486DX2/50i
    PC
Syncomp Mega+486DX2/66e
    PC
Syncomp Mega+486DX2/66i
    PC
Syncomp Mega+486e-33 PC
Syncomp Mega+486e-50 PC
Syncomp Mega+486i-33 PC
Syncomp Mega+486i-50 PC
Syncomp Mega+486SXe-25
    PC
Syncomp Mega+486SXi 33 PC
Syncomp Mega+486SXi-25
    PC
Syncomp Micro 386i 40 PC
Syncomp Micro 486DX2/50i
    PC
Syncomp Micro 486i-33 PC
Syncomp Micro 486i-50 PC
Syncomp Micro 486SXi-25 PC
Syncomp Mini 386i-40PC
Syncomp Mini 486-50i PC
Syncomp Mini 486DX2/50e
    PC
Syncomp Mini 486DX2/50i PC
Syncomp Mini 486DX2/66e
    PC
Syncomp Mini 486DX2/66i PC
Syncomp Mini 486e-33 PC
Syncomp Mini 486e-50 PC
Syncomp Mini 486i-33 PC
Syncomp Mini 486SXe-25 PC
Syncomp Mini 486SXi-25 PC
Syncomp Mini 486SXi-33 PC
Syncomp Mini+386i 40 PC
Syncomp Mini+486DX2/50e
    PC
Syncomp Mini+486DX2/50i
    PC
Syncomp Mini+486DX2/66e
    PC
Syncomp Mini+486DX2/66i
    PC
Syncomp Mini+486e-33 PC
Syncomp Mini+486e-50 PC
Syncomp Mini+486i-33 PC
Syncomp Mini+486i-50 PC

Syncomp Mini+486SXe-25 PC
Syncomp Mini+486SXi-25 PC
Syncomp Mini+486SXi-33 PC
Sys Technology ST486DX-
33VM
T-DATA LIN 486-33 DX
T-DATA LIN 486-50 DX
Tagram Computers 486DX-33
Tandon 486dx/33
Tandon 486dx2/66
Tandon MCSII 486dx/33
Tandon MCSII 486dx/33c
Tandon MCSII 486dx2/66c
Tandon NII 486dx/33
Tandon PACII plus 486dx2/66
Tandon PCAII 486dx2/66
Tandon PCAII 486sx/25
Tandon Profile 486dx/33
Tandon TargetII 486dx2/66
Tandon TargetII 486sx/25
Tandon Tower 486dx2/66e
Tandon TowerII 486dx2/66
Tandy 3100
Tandy 425 SX
Tandy 433 DX
Tandy 433 SX
Tandy 450 DX2
Tandy 466 DX2
Tandy 4825 SX
Tandy 4833 LX/T
Tandy 4850 EP
Tandy 4866 LX/T
Tandy Omni Profile II 425 SX
Tandy Omni Profile II 433 DX
Tandy Omni Profile II 433 SX
Tandy Omni Profile II 450
DX2
Tandy Omni Profile II 466
DX2
Tandy Onmi II MT 425 SX
Tandy Onmi II MT 433 DX
Tandy Onmi II MT 433 SX
Tandy Onmi II MT 450 DX2
Tandy Onmi II MT 466 DX2
Tangent 486DX/33 EISA
Tangent 486DX/33 ISA
Tangent EISA /VL 466 Server
Tangent EISA /VL 466d
Tangent EISA /VL 466m
Tangent EISA /VL 466t
Tangent P560 Server
Tangent P560d
Tangent P560m
Tangent P560t
Tangent P566 Server

Tangent P566d
Tangent P566m
Tangent P566t
Tangent VL450 Server
Tangent VL450d
Tangent VL450m
Tangent VL450t
Tangent VL450x Server
Tangent VL450xd
Tangent VL450xm
Tangent VL450xt
Tatung TCS-8460S 386SX/25
Tatung TCS-9300T
486DX2/66
Tatung TCS-9360T 486DX/33
Tatung TCS-9370T
486DX2/66
Tatung TCS-9510 486DX/33
Tatung TCS-9540 486DX/33
Tatung TCS-9620E
486DX2/66
Tatung TCS-9650E
486DX2/66
Tatung TCS-9700 486DLC/40
Tatung TCS-9910S 486SLC/33
Techway Endeavour E62
Techway Endeavour E62VL
Techway Endeavour E77
Techway Endeavour E77VL
Techway Endeavour E84
Techway Endeavour E84VL
TELEMECANIQUE FTX507-
6B
TELEMECANIQUE FTX507-
8C
Texas Instruments TravelMate
4000 Color Series [9]
Texas Instruments TravelMate
4000 Series [9]
Texas Instruments TravelMate
4000
WinDX2 [9]
Texas Instruments TravelMate
4000E in TravelMate
DeskTop
TFE Atlantic 486 DX 50Mhz
Tiki-Data PC UNIVERSAL
Toshiba Satellite T1900C
Toshiba T1910CS/200
Toshiba T1950CT/320
Toshiba T1960CS/250
Toshiba T1960CT/320
Toshiba T2400CS/250
Toshiba T2400CT/320
Toshiba T3400CT/250

Toshiba T3600CT/250
Toshiba T4400SXC
Toshiba T4500
Toshiba T4600C/200
Toshiba T4600C/320
Toshiba T4700CS/200
Toshiba T4700CT/320
Toshiba T4800CT/500
Toshiba T6400SX
Toshiba T6600C Multimedia
Computer [93]
Tri-Star Tri-Win Station
Tri-Star TriCAD 486/66
TriGem 486/33MM (incl. 486
/P (Type 30) model)
TriGem 486/50F
TriGem 486/66F
TriGem 486/66VC
TriGem 486DX2/50MM (incl.
486 /P (Type 40) model)
TriGem 486DX2/66MM (incl.
486 /P (Type 50) model)
TriGem 486G/T20
TriGem 486G/T40
TriGem 486H/T12G
TriGem 486P/T15V
TriGem 486P/T25V
TriGem 486P/T35V
TriGem 486P/T45V
TriGem 486P/T55V
TriGem 486VC
TriGem 4DX/33ME
TriGem 4DX/33ML
TriGem 4DX2/50
TriGem 4DX2/50ME
TriGem 4DX2/66 ML
TriGem 4DX2/66ME
TriGem 4SX/25ME
TriGem 4SX/25ML
TriGem 4SX/33ME
TriGem 4SX/33ML
TriGem 586T
TriGem SX486/25C
TriGem SX486/25MM (incl.
486 /P (Type 10 and 12)
models)
TriGem SX486/33MM (incl.
486 /P (Type 20) model)
Trinity Technology Genesis
Viper
Tulip Vision Line DE 4/66
Tulip Vision Line DS 4/66
Tulip Vision Line DS 486
dx/50i

Tulip Vision Line DS 486
SX/33i
Tulip Vision Line DS 586
DX/60
Tulip Vision Line DS/DE 486
dx/33i
Tulip Vision Line DT 4/66
Tulip Vision Line DT/DC 486
DX/33i
Tulip Vision Line DT/DC 486
DX/50i
Tulip Vision Line DT/DC 486
DX/66i
Tulip Vision Line series
486DX-33i
Tulip Vision Line series
486DX-50i
Tulip Vision Line series
486DX-66e
Tulip Vision Line Series
486DX-66i
Tulip Vision Line TR 586
DX/60
Tulip WS 4/66
TWINHEAD Superset 700
U.S. Micro Jet 386DX-33
U.S. Micro Jet 386DX-40
U.S. Micro Jet 486DLC-33
U.S. Micro Jet 486DX-33
U.S. Micro Jet 486DX-50
U.S. Micro Jet 486DX2-50
U.S. Micro Jet 486DX2-66
U.S. Micro Jet 486SX-25
U.S. Micro Jet EISA 486-33
U.S. Micro Jet EISA 486-50
U.S. Micro Jet EISA 486DX2-
50
U.S. Micro Jet EISA 486DX2-
66
U.S. Micro Jet EISA 486SX-25
U.S. Micro Jet VL 486DX-33
U.S. Micro Jet VL 486DX-50
U.S. Micro Jet VL 486DX2-50
U.S. Micro Jet VL 486DX2-66
U.S. Micro Jet VL 486SX-25
Ultra Technologies UL P5 60
Ultra Technologies UL486DX
33
Ultra Technologies UL486DX
50
Ultra Technologies
UL486DX/2 66
Ultra-Comp 486DX-33
Ultra-Comp 486DX-33 EISA
VLB

Ultra-Comp 486DX-33 VLB
Ultra-Comp 486DX-50
Ultra-Comp 486DX-50 EISA
VLB
Ultra-Comp 486DX-50 VLB
Ultra-Comp 486DX2-66
Ultra-Comp 486DX2-66 EISA
VLB
Ultra-Comp 486DX2-66 VLB
Unidata 486 66 Mhz ISA
Unique Computers, Ltd.
UNIQUE 486DX50-VL
Unisys Pathway Series PS243-
331
Unisys Pathway Series PS243-
661
Unisys Pathway Series PS246-
331
Unisys Pathway Series PS246-
661
Unisys Pathway Series PS445-
661
Unisys Pathway Series
PSA456-601
Unisys Pathway Series
PSA458-601
Unisys PW2 3336
Unisys PW2 Advantage 3256
Unisys PW2 Advantage 3336
Unisys PW2 Advantage 4163
Unisys PW2 Advantage 4253
Unisys PW2 Advantage 4256
Unisys PW2 Advantage 4336
Unisys PW2 Advantage 4506
Unisys PW2 Advantage 46662
Unisys PW2 Advantage
Partner 43334
Unisys PW2 Advantage Plus
4668
Unisys PW2 Advantage Plus
5606
Unisys PW2 Advantage Plus
5608
Unisys SVE56691-FDD
Unisys SVI 59071
US Logic Falcon II Single
Board Computer
Vektron VL 486DX/33
Vektron VL 486DX2/50
Business Multimedia
Vektron VL 486DX2/66
Professional Multimedia
Victor 400 DX/50
Victor 400 SX/25
Victor 486 DX/33

Victor 486 DX/66
Victor DX/50
Victor V486DSX/25
Viglen Contender 4DX33
Viglen EX-Series 4DX50
Viglen Genie 4DX66
Vobis 4386 VIO SX25
Vobis 486 VC-HD 33
Vobis 486 VC-HD 50
Vobis 486 VIO 66
Vtech 386 Ultra Slim
Vtech 466M
Vtech 486DX/3 Desktop
Vtech 486DX/3 Desktop
(w/LBVGA)
Vtech 486DX/3 Desktop
(w/VLBUS)
Vtech 486DX/3 Mini
(w/VLBUS)
Vtech 486DX/3 Tower
Vtech 486DX/3 Tower
(w/VLBUS)
Vtech 486DX2/4 Desktop
Vtech 486DX2/4 Desktop
(w/LBVGA)
Vtech 486DX2/4 Desktop
(w/VLBUS)
Vtech 486DX2/4 Tower
Vtech 486DX2/4 Tower
(w/VLBUS)
Vtech 486DX2/6 Desktop
Vtech 486DX2/6 Desktop
(w/LBVGA)
Vtech 486DX2/6 Desktop
(w/VLBUS)
Vtech 486DX2/6 Mini
(w/VLBUS)
Vtech 486DX2/6 Tower
Vtech 486DX2/6 Tower
(w/VLBUS)
Vtech 486SX/3 Desktop
Vtech 486SX/3 Desktop
(w/LBVGA)
Vtech 486SX/3 Desktop
w/VLBUS
Vtech 486SX/3 Tower
Vtech 486SX/3 Ultra Slim
Vtech 486SX/3 Ultra Slim
(w/LBVGA)
Vtech 486SX/4 Desktop
Vtech 486SX/4 Desktop
(w/LBVGA)
Vtech 486SX/4 Desktop
(w/VLBUS)

Vtech 486SX/4 Mini
(w/VLBUS)
Vtech 486SX/4 Tower
Vtech 486SX/4 Ultra Slim
Vtech 486SX/4 Ultra Slim
(w/LBVGA)
Vtech 560M
Vtech LT322 Notebook
Vtech LT421 Notebook
Vtech LT432 Notebook
Vtech LT433C Color
Notebook
Vtech LT433C Notebook
Vtech Platinum SMP DX2-66
WANG DT250S
WANG DT266
WANG DT33S
Wang Microsystems ASI-CPU-
E266
Wang Microsystems DTE-33
Wang Microsystems PC
350/40C
Western 486V25 SX VESA
LOCAL BUS
Western 486V33 DX EISA
Western 486V33 DX ISA
Western 486V50 DX EISA
Western 486V50 DX ISA
Western 486V50 DX2 ISA
Western 486V66 DX2 EISA
Western 486V66 DX2 ISA
WIPRO Fusion 510
WIPRO LANDMARK E
WIPRO LANDMARK E
SQUARE MODEL - 560
WIPRO Super Genius 386DX
WIPRO Super Genius 386SX
WIPRO Super Genius 486DX
WIPRO Super Genius 486SX
Wyle Laboratories Intel Xpress
Deskside w/486DX-50MHz
Wyle Laboratories Intel Xpress
DeskTop w/486DX2-66MHz
Wyle Laboratories Intel Xpress
DeskTop w/486DX-50MHz
Wyse Decision 386/25
Wyse Decision 386/40
Wyse Decision 386SX/25C
Wyse Decision 486/25
Wyse Decision 486/33
Wyse Decision 486/33E
Wyse Decision 486/33T
Wyse Decision 486DX2/50
Wyse Decision 486GSI

Wyse Decision 486se-25SX
Wyse Decision 486se-33DX
Wyse Decision 486se-33SX
Wyse Decision 486se-50DX2
Wyse Decision 486se-66DX2
Wyse Decision 486si-25SX
Wyse Decision 486si-33DX
Wyse Decision 486si-33SX
Wyse Decision 486si-50DX2
Wyse Decision 486si-66DX2
Wyse Forte` GSV
Wyse Series 6000i Model 640
Wyse Series 6000i Model 645
Wyse Series 7000i Model 740
Xycom XVME-674
Zenith Data Systems Z-
386/33E
Zenith Data Systems Z-425/SX
Zenith Data Systems Z-425S+
Zenith Data Systems Z-
433/DX
Zenith Data Systems Z-450X+
Zenith Data Systems Z-
486/33ET
Zenith Data Systems Z-
486SX/20
Zenith Data Systems Z-
486SX/25E
Zenith Data Systems Z-Note
425Ln
Zenith Data Systems Z-
SELECT 100 DX2/50
Zenith Data Systems Z-
SELECT 100 DX2/66
Zenith Data Systems Z-
SELECT 100 DX33
Zenith Data Systems Z-
SELECT 100 SX25
Zenith Data Systems Z-
SELECT 100 SX33
Zenith Data Systems Z-
SERVER 425SE
Zenith Data Systems Z-
SERVER 433DE
Zenith Data Systems Z-
SERVER 450DE
Zenith Data Systems Z-
SERVER EX 433DE Model
1000A (incl. Model 2000A)
Zenith Data Systems Z-
SERVER EX 433DE Model
500 (incl. Model 1000)
Zenith Data Systems Z-
SERVER EX 450DE Model
1000A (incl. Model 2000A)

Zenith Data Systems Z-
SERVER EX 450DE Model
500 (incl. Model 1000)
Zenith Data Systems Z-
SERVER EX 90E Model
2000
Zenith Data Systems Z-
SERVER EX P60E Model
1000A (incl. Model 2000A)
Zenith Data Systems Z-
SERVER EX P60E Model
500 (incl. Model 1000)
Zenith Data Systems Z-
SERVER EX P90E MODEL
1000
Zenith Data Systems Z-
SERVER LT 433DE Model
245 (incl. Model 1000)
Zenith Data Systems Z-
SERVER LT 466XE Model
500 (incl. Model 1000)
Zenith Data Systems Z-
SERVER LT P60E Model
1000A (incl. Model 2000A)
Zenith Data Systems Z-
SERVER LT P60E Model
500 (incl. Model 1000)
Zenith Data Systems Z-Station
420SEh
Zenith Data Systems Z-Station
420SEn
Zenith Data Systems Z-Station
420Sh
Zenith Data Systems Z-Station
420Sn
Zenith Data Systems Z-Station
425Sh
Zenith Data Systems Z-Station
425Sn
Zenith Data Systems Z-Station
433DEh
Zenith Data Systems Z-Station
433DEn
Zenith Data Systems Z-Station
433Dh
Zenith Data Systems Z-Station
433SEh
Zenith Data Systems Z-Station
450XEh
Zenith Data Systems Z-Station
450Xh
Zenith Data Systems Z-Station
450Xn
Zenith Data Systems Z-
STATION 500 Model 433

Zenith Data Systems Z-
STATION 500 Model 466X
Zenith/INTEQ TEMPEST 486
WORKSTATION / SERVER
Zenon Z-Dream IIII
EISA/VESA 486DX/66
Zenon Z-OPTIMUS PCI,SCSI-
II, Pentium/60

ZEOS 486DX/33CDT
ZEOS 486DX/33EISA
ZEOS 486DX/33ISA
ZEOS 486DX/50
ZEOS 486SX/20DT
ZEOS Freestyle™ 386SL 25
ZEOS Pantera 60

ZEOS Upgradable 486 DX/33
Cache
ZEOS Upgradable 486 DX2/66
Cache
ZEOS Upgradable 486 SX/33
Cache
ZEOS Upgradable Local Bus
DX2/66

Technical Notes

The Windows NT Driver Library is provided on the Windows NT CD-ROM in the \DRVLIB directory, as well as several locations for electronic transmission. Please see the section at the end of this document for instructions on downloading and accessing Windows NT Driver Library drivers.

1. This device requires a driver from the \DRVLIB directory on the Windows NT CD-ROM, or the Windows NT Driver Library.

2. This device requires a driver from the Windows NT driver Library. See the following section on accessing these drivers.

3. External Cache must be disabled to run Windows NT 3.5

4. Requires AST BIOS Rev. 1.02 to install and run Windows NT 3.5.

5. Requires AST BIOS Rev. 2.03 to install and run Windows NT 3.5.

6. Must copy ABIOS.SYS and *.BIO from reference diskette to root directory of boot drive to install Windows NT on this system.

7. Requires the IBM RAID Controller v2.0 driver located in Windows NT Driver Library.

8. This system only supports 640x480x16 video resolution.

9. Refer to SETUP.TXT on the Windows NT 3.5 CDROM for information on configuring this machine/device before installation.

10. To Install Windows NT 3.5 on this system SCSI detection must be skipped during setup.

11. Refer to setup.txt to properly configure this system for printing in Windows NT 3.5.

12. Requires AMD Bios Revision 0.02.18 to function as a multiprocessor system.

13. Only the NCR 53c710 SCSI Host Adapter is supported in this machine.

14. Contact the manufacturer for information on running Windows NT on this machine.

15. For best performance, this adapter should be configured to IRQ-11.

16. Tape drives are not supported with this adapter.

17. Tested with firmware revisions 3.10 and 3.20.

18. This adapter requires an active terminator for proper performance.

19. The floppy controller on this adapter is not supported.

20. This adapter must be configured for 5 MB/second asynchronous I/O to work with listed CD-ROM drives from NEC.

21. This adapter must be configured for 5 MB/second asynchronous I/O to work with listed CD-ROM drives from Chinon, Hitachi, and NEC.

22. Tested with the Unisys PW2 Advantage 3256 (Flemington).

23. IC-7770c and AIC-7770e are supported.

24. Tested with the Unisys PW2 Advantage Plus MPE 4668.

25. Removable media drives are not supported with cache module installed.

26. Tested with Compaq Deskpro XL 466 and HP Vectra XU 5/90c.

27. Scanners are not supported with this adapter.

28. To use this adapter, at least one device on the bus must provide termination power.

29. Refer to SETUP.TXT for information on configuring this adapter.

30. SCSI BIOS dated before 1991 requires PS/2 Reference Diskette version 1.12 or later.

31. This adapter cannot be used for CD Setup. To install Windows NT with this adapter, use the WINNT.EXE Setup method.

32. The driver for this adapter defaults to IRQ-15.

33. Tested with Dell Omniplex 560 and Digital Equipment Corp. AlphaServer 2100 4/200 (Digital Equipment Corp. 2100 Server model A500MP).

34. Tested with Digital Equipment Corp. AlphaServer 2100 4/200 (Digital Equipment Corp. 2100 Server model A500MP).

35. Tested with COMPAQ Portable 486c.

36. Tested with NCR System 3000 Model 3360.

37. This driver is not supported on Multi-Processor computers.

38. This adapter is only supported on IRQ-5.

39. Tested with firmware revision 005.

40. Tested with firmware revision 008.

41. This drive is not supported for use with the Future Domain TMC-850M and TMC-1670 adapters.

42. Users may encounter problems with CD-R (recordable) discs.

43. May require a Firmware upgrade for proper operation, please contact NEC Technical support (800-388-8888) for assistance

44. This drive requires double-termination when used with the Adaptec AHA-1742A.

45. The Ultrastor 24f supports only a single disk when used with this drive.

46. Only supported with access to 1 CD at a time.

47. Requires firmware revision 1.10C to function properly with Windows NT.

48. Supported with CD-ROM drives based on Panasonic CR-52x and CR-56x models only.

49. This drive is not supported with the Adaptec AHA-1640 adapter.

50. NTBackup does not support autoloaders. This drive is supported in single-tape operation only.

51. Requires firmware version 484 or later for proper operation.

52. This drive is not supported with the Future Domain TMC-850M(ER).

53. Tested with firmware rev. ARCHIVE IBM4326NP/RP !D04AP

54. This drive is not supported with the IBM PS/2 Microchannel SCSI Host Adapter (with cache).

55. This drive is not supported with the Adaptec AHA-1510 adapter.

56. The Future Domain TMC-1670 with bios version 3.0 requires that the bios be disabled when used with this drive.

57. This drive is not supported with the UltraStor 24fa adapter.

58. Requires firmware rev.DEC9314

59. Tested with firmware rev. DEC4318

60. Tested with firmware rev. DEC930A

61. Tested with firmware rev. DEC9514

62. For use with floppy controllers. Separate interface controllers for these types of drives are not supported.

63. The Adaptec emulation mode on the Dell Drive Array(DDA) must be disabled for compatibility with the hardware's Windows NT Driver.

64. This adapter is currently supported in its ESC-1/ESC-2 compatibility mode only.

65. Not supported with the Future Domain TMC-850m.

66. Tested with firmware revision HQ30.

67. Requires firmware version 1.15.15s for proper performance.

68. Versions of this board based on the 688LX or 68003 chip require more than 1mb of video memory to support 800x600x65k.

69. Some revisions of this board are not supported under Windows NT. Please see the Release Notes on how to identify these boards.

70. The AVGA will occasionally present "snow" on the screen at 800x600.

71. Requires Rev E. Bios 3.09 for proper performance.

72. Video boards based on the Cirrus 542x family of chips are not supported in Pentium computers.

73. 65k colors are supported with a 565 DAC, 32k colors with a 555 DAC.

74. Some older 928 chips do not support 800x600xTRUE with 2Mb of RAM.

75. Not all video board/monitor combinations are able to properly display 1600x1200.

76. Some video boards based on Western Digital chips have experienced misplaced pixels when running in Pentium based computers.

77. ATI Mach 32 based boards with rev. 003 of the Mach 32 chip will not support 800x600 with only 1Mb of RAM.

78. 2MB Video Memory only supported on Cirrus 543x series of chips.

79. This adapter has been verified to work with Network Monitor

80. FDDI tested only.

81. Not compatible with IBM Thinkpad 700.

82. Non-bi-directional parallel ported machines may suffer performance degradation when the driver for this adapter is installed.

83. Supported in Sound Blaster 1.x compatibility mode.

84. Not supported in Sound Blaster 1.x compatibility mode.

85. Tested as standard serial ports only.

86. Shared interrupt configuration is not recommended when running RAS, use one interrupt for each port.

87. Supported on x86 only.

88. If this model was purchased prior to March 1993, contact Data Storage Marketing for compatibility verification.

89. To install Windows NT on this system, SCSI detection must be skipped during setup.

90. Windows NT does not currently support Advanced Power Management (APM).

91. This system requires an ABIOS.SYS driver dated after 11/1/93 to support IDE drives. Call Microsoft Product Support Services to obtain this update.

92. Patch required for the IBM Thinkpad 750 series to install Windows NT 3.1. Available on CompuServe in the WINNT forum in library 2 and also in the same locations as the Windows NT Driver Library.

93. IDE drives greater than 500MB are only supported with BIOS Version 1.23 or later, with BIOS setting for IDE in standard mode.

94. Error control and flow control forced on.

95. Advanced features disabled.

96. Supported as a client modem only

97. Flow control forced on

98. Maximum DTE speed set to 2400

99. Maximum DTE speed set to 9600

100. Modem compression forced on

How To Find New Drivers in the Windows NT Driver Library (WNTDL)

COMPUSERVE

A. If you are using WinCIM℠:

1. From the Services menu, select GO.

2. Type MSL in the GO dialog box.

3. Select 2 to scan.

4. Search for WNTDL to view the whole WNTDL list or another key word to view specific files.

B. If you are not using WinCIM, log onto CompuServe, type GO MSL, then follow instructions 3 and 4 above.

ONLINE

A. Log onto OnLine.

1. From the Database menu, select the option to Select DB.

2. Choose the Software Library option.

3. From the Software Library option, select the option Host Items.

4. In the Query box, type WNTDL to review the whole WNTDL list or another key word to view a specific file.

B. To get more information on a specific file, highlight the file with the cursor and press <Enter>. This brings up more details about the file.

GENie™

Log onto Genie.

1. From the main menu, select option 5 - Computing Services.

2. From the Computing Services menu, select option 6 - IBM PC/TANDY Roundtables.

3. From the IBM PC/TANDY Roundtables menu, select option 3 - Software Libraries.

4. From the Software Libraries menu, select option 3 - Search File Directory.

5. Type WNTDL as the search string to view the WNTDL list or any other key word to view a specific file.

MICROSOFT DOWN LOAD SERVICES

Log onto MSDL by calling (206) 936-6735.

1. Enter name and location.

2. From the main menu, press F for File index.

3. Select L to list the whole WNTDL list or E to examine a specific file.

IF YOU DO NOT HAVE A MODEM

You can obtain an individual driver from the WNTDL on a disk by calling
Microsoft Product Support Services at (206) 637-7098.

While we have endeavored to supply as complete and accurate a list as possible,
MICROSOFT MAKES NO WARRANTIES, EXPRESS OR IMPLIED, AS TO
THE COMPLETENESS AND ACCURACY OF THIS LIST. This list does not
constitute an endorsement of any particular manufacturer.

Microsoft and BallPoint are registered trademarks and Windows and Windows NT
are trademarks of Microsoft Corporation.

Glossary

A

access control entry (ACE) An entry in an access control list (ACL). The entry contains a security ID (SID) and a set of access rights. A process with a matching security ID is either allowed access rights, denied rights, or allowed rights with auditing. See also *access control list.*

access control list (ACL) The part of a security descriptor that enumerates the protections applied to an object. The owner of an object has discretionary access control of the object and can change the object's ACL to allow or disallow others access to the object. ACLs are made up of *access control entries* (ACEs).

access mask In an ACE, defines all possible actions for a particular object type. Permissions are granted or denied based on this access mask.

access right The permission granted to a process to manipulate a particular object in a particular way (for example, by calling a service). Different object types support different access rights, which are stored in an object's *access control list* (ACL).

account See *user account.*

ACE See *access control entry.*

ACK An acknowledgment signal.

ACL See *access control list.*

address resolution protocol (ARP) An IP maintenance protocol that supports the IP framework.

administrative alerts Relate to server and resource use; warn about problems in areas such as security and access, user sessions, server shutdown because of power loss (when UPS is available), directory replication, and printing. When a computer generates an administrative alert, a message is sent to a predefined list of users and computers. See also *Alerter service.*

Alerter service A Windows NT Server service that notifies selected users and computers of administrative alerts that occur on a computer. Used by the Server and other services. Requires the Messenger service. See also *administrative alerts.*

API See *application programming interface.*

application programming interface (API) A set of routines that an application program uses to request and carry out lower-level services performed by the operating system.

ARC computer See *RISC-based computer.*

ARP A TCP/IP command that allows a user to view and modify the ARP (*address resolution protocol*) table entries on the local computer.

asynchronous I/O A method many of the processes in Windows NT use to optimize their performance. When an application initiates an I/O operation, the I/O Manager accepts the request but doesn't block the application's execution while the I/O operation is being performed. Instead, the application is allowed to continue doing work. Most I/O devices are very slow in comparison to a computer's processor, so an application can do a lot of work while waiting for an I/O operation to complete. See also *synchronous I/O.*

audit policy   Defines the type of security events that are logged for a domain or for an individual computer; determines what Windows NT will do when the security log becomes full.

auditing   The ability to detect and record security-related events, particularly any attempt to create, access, or delete objects. Windows NT uses *security IDs* (SIDs) to record which process performed the action.

authentication   A security step performed by the Remote Access server, before logon validation, to verify that the user had permission for remote access. See also *validation*.

B

banding   A process in printing whereby the document is replayed several times to generate the full image.

batch program   An ASCII file (unformatted text file) that contains one or more Windows NT commands. A batch program's filename has a .BAT or .CMD extension. When you type the filename at the command prompt, the commands are processed sequentially.

binding   A process that establishes the initial communication channel between the protocol driver and the network adapter card driver.

Boot Loader   The operating system loader, provided by NTOSKRNL in Windows NT. Defines the information needed for system startup, such as the location for the operating system's files. Windows NT automatically creates the correct configuration and checks this information whenever you start your system.

boot partition   The volume, formatted for either an NTFS, FAT, or HPFS file system, that contains the Windows NT operating system and its support files. The boot partition can be (but does not have to be) the same as the *system partition*.

bound application   An application that can run under both OS/2 and MS-DOS.

browser service   See *Computer Browser service*.

B-tree   A tree structure with a root and several nodes. It contains data organized in some logical way so that the whole structure can be quickly traversed.

buffer   A reserved portion of memory in which data is temporarily held pending an opportunity to complete its transfer to or from a storage device or another location in memory.

buffering   The process of using buffers to hold data that is being transferred, particularly to or from I/O devices such as disk drives and serial ports.

C

character mode   A mode of operation in which all information is displayed as text characters. This is the mode in which MS-DOS–based and OS/2 version 1.2 applications are displayed in windows under Windows NT. Also called alphanumeric mode or text mode.

client   A computer that accesses shared network resources provided by another computer (called a server). See also *server*.

Computer Browser service   Maintains an up-to-date list of computers and provides the list to applications when requested, for example, in the Select Computer and Select Domain dialog boxes. When a user attempts to connect to a resource in the domain, the domain's browser is contacted to provide a list of resources available. The active browser for the domain is elected dynamically through a network election process.

computername A unique name of up to 15 uppercase characters that identifies a computer to the network. The name cannot be the same as any other computer or domain name in the network, and it cannot contain spaces.

Configuration Registry See *Registry*.

connected user A user accessing a computer or a resource across the network.

console A character-mode window managed by the Win32 subsystem in Windows NT. Environment subsystems direct the output of character-mode applications to consoles.

container object An object that logically contains other objects. For example, a directory is a container object that logically contains files and other directories. Files are noncontainer objects.

control set A complete set of parameters for devices and services in the HKEY_LOCAL_MACHINE\SYSTEM key in the Registry.

CPU cycles The smallest unit of time recognized by the central processing unit—typically a few hundred-millionths of a second; it is also used to refer to the time required for the CPU to perform the simplest instruction. Also called a clock tick.

D

data frame Logical, structured packets in which data can be placed. The Data Link layer packages raw bits from the Physical layer into data frames. The exact format of the frame used by the network depends on the topology.

Data Link Control (DLC) A protocol interface device driver in Windows NT, traditionally used to provide connectivity to IBM mainframes and also used to provide connectivity to local-area network printers directly attached to the network.

data type The second of three components that make up a value entry in the Registry. Five data types can be edited in Registry Editor: *REG_BINARY, REG_DWORD, REG_EXPAND_SZ, REG_MULTI_SZ,* and *REG_SZ.*

datagram A packet of information and associated delivery information, such as the destination address, that is routed through a packet-switching network.

DDE See *dynamic data exchange*.

default profile See *system default profile, user default profile*.

default printer The printer that is used if you choose the Print command without first specifying which printer you want to use with an application.

demand paging Refers to a method by which data is moved in pages from physical memory to a temporary paging file on disk. As the data is needed by a process, it is paged back into physical memory.

dependent service A service that requires the support of another service. For example, the Alerter service is dependent on the Messenger service.

device A generic term for a computer subsystem such as a printer, serial port, or disk drive. A device frequently requires its own controlling software called a *device driver*.

device contention The way Windows NT allocates access to peripheral devices, such as a modem or a printer, when more than one application is trying to use the same device.

device driver   A software component that allows the computer to transmit and receive information to and from a specific device. For example, a printer driver translates computer data into a form understood by a particular printer. Although a device may be installed on your system, Windows NT cannot recognize the device until you have installed and configured the appropriate driver.

directory replication   The copying of a master set of directories from a server (called an export server) to specified servers or workstations (called import computers) in the same or other domains. Replication simplifies the task of maintaining identical sets of directories and files on multiple computers, because only a single master copy of the data must be maintained. Files are replicated when they are added to an exported directory and every time a change is saved to the file. See also *Directory Replicator service.*

Directory Replicator service   Replicates directories, and the files in those directories, between computers. See also *directory replication.*

disk caching   A method used by a file system to improve performance. Instead of reading and writing directly to the disk, frequently used files are temporarily stored in a cache in memory, and reads and writes to those files are performed in memory. Reading and writing to memory is much faster than reading and writing to disk.

disk duplexing   Establishing a mirrored copy on a disk with a different controller.

disk mirroring   Maintaining a fully redundant copy of a partition on another disk.

disk striping   Writing data in stripes across a volume that has been created from areas of free space on from 2 to 32 disks.

distributed application   An application that has two parts—a front-end to run on the client computer and a back-end to run on the server. In distributed computing, the goal is to divide the computing task into two sections. The front-end requires minimal resources and runs on the client's workstation. The back-end requires large amounts of data, number crunching, or specialized hardware and runs on the server.

DLC   See *Data Link Control.*

DLL   See dynamic-link library.

DMA channel   A channel for direct memory access that does not involve the microprocessor, providing data transfer directly between memory and a disk drive.

domain   For Windows NT Server, a networked set of workstations and servers that share a Security Accounts Manager (SAM) database and that can be administered as a group. A user with an account in a particular network domain can log onto and access his or her account from any system in the domain. See also *SAM database*; *workgroup.*

domain controller   For a Windows NT Server domain, the server that authenticates domain logons and maintains the security policy and the master database for a domain. Both servers and domain controllers are capable of validating a user's logon; however, password changes must be made by contacting the domain controller. See also *server.*

domain database   See *SAM database.*

domain master browser   The domain controller responsible for keeping in sync all the master browsers for its domain in the internet.

domain name   The name by which a domain is known to the network.

Domain Name System (DNS) A hierarchical name service for TCP/IP hosts (sometimes referred to as the BIND service in BSD UNIX). The network administrator configures the DNS with a list of *hostnames* and IP addresses, allowing users of workstations configured to query the DNS to specify remote systems by *hostnames* rather than IP addresses. DNS domains should not be confused with Windows NT networking *domains*.

domain synchronization See *synchronize*.

downloaded fonts Fonts that you send to a printer either before or during the printing of a document. When you send a font to a printer, it is stored in printer memory until it is needed.

dynamic data exchange (DDE) A form of interprocess communication (IPC) implemented in the Microsoft Windows family of operating systems. Two or more programs that support dynamic data exchange (DDE) can exchange information and commands.

dynamic-link library (DLL) An application programming interface (API) routine that user-mode applications access through ordinary procedure calls. The code for the API routine is not included in the user's executable image. Instead, the operating system automatically modifies the executable image to point to DLL procedures at run time.

E

environment subsystems User-mode protected servers that run and support programs from different operating systems environments. Examples of these subsystems are the Win32™ subsystem and the OS/2 subsystem. Contrast *integral subsystem*.

environment variable A string consisting of environment information, such as a drive, path, or filename, associated with a symbolic name that can be used by Windows NT. You use the System option in Control Panel or the **set** command from the Windows NT command prompt to define environment variables.

event Any significant occurrence in the system or in an application that requires users to be notified or an entry to be added to a log.

Event Log service Records events in the system, security, and application logs.

Executive module The Kernel-mode module that provides basic operating system services to the environment subsystems. It includes several components; each manages a particular set of system services. One component, the Security Reference Monitor, works together with the protected subsystems to provide a pervasive security model for the system.

export server In directory replication, a server from which a master set of directories is exported to specified servers or workstations (called import computers) in the same or other domains. See also *directory replication.*

extended partition Created from free space on a hard disk, it can be subpartitioned into zero or more logical drives. Only one of the four partitions allowed per physical disk can be an extended partition, and no primary partition needs to be present to create an extended partition.

extensibility Indicates the modular design of Windows NT, which provides for the flexibility of adding future modules at several levels within the operating system.

external command A command that is stored in its own file and loaded from disk when you use the command.

F

FAT file system A file system based on a file allocation table maintained by the operating system to keep track of the status of various segments of disk space used for file storage.

fault tolerance The ability of a computer and an operating system to respond gracefully to catastrophic events such as power outage or hardware failure. Usually, fault tolerance implies the ability to either continue the system's operation without loss of data or to shut the system down and restart it, recovering all processing that was in progress when the fault occurred.

file control block (FCB) A small block of memory temporarily assigned by the operating system to hold information about a file that has been opened for use. An FCB typically contains information such as the file's ID, its location on disk, and a pointer that marks the user's current (or last) position in the file.

File Replication service The Windows NT file replication service allows specified file(s) to be replicated to remote systems ensuring that copies on each system are kept in synchronization. The system that maintains the master copy is called the *exporter*; the systems that receive updates are known as *importers*.

file sharing The ability for Windows NT Workstation or Windows NT Server to share parts (or all) of its local file system(s) with remote computers. An administrator creates *shares (or sharepoints)* by using either the File Manager or by using the **net share** command from the command line.

file system In an operating system, the overall structure in which files are named, stored, and organized.

Finger A TCP/IP application that allows the user to retrieve system information on remote systems supporting TCP/IP and a Finger service.

Fnodes Each directory points to Fnodes for files contained in that directory. An Fnode is 512 bytes in length and contains a header, the filename (truncated to 15 characters), the file length, extended attributes (EA) and access control list (ACL) information, and the location of the file's data.

font set A collection of font sizes for one font, customized for a particular display and printer. Font sets determine what text looks like on screen and on paper.

frame See *data frame*.

free space An unused and unformatted portion of a hard disk that can be partitioned or subpartitioned. Free space within an extended partition is available for the creation of logical drives. Free space that is not within an extended partition is available for the creation of a partition, with a maximum of four partitions allowed.

FTP service File transfer protocol service, which offers file transfer services to remote systems supporting this protocol. FTP supports a host of commands allowing bidirectional transfer of binary and ASCII files between systems.

Ftpsvc service The FTP Server services, which provides an FTP server for Windows NT. This service is not installed by default but can be installed by choosing the Network icon in Control Panel.

Fully Qualified Domain Name (or FQDN)
In TCP/IP, *hostnames* with their *domain names* appended to them. For example, a host with hostname *rhino* and domain name *microsoft.com* has a FQDN of *rhino.microsoft.com.*

G

global account   For Windows NT Server, a normal user account in a user's home domain. If there are multiple domains in the network, it is best if each user in the network has only one user account, in only one domain, and each user's access to other domains is accomplished through the establishment of domain trust relationships. See also *local account.*

global group   For Windows NT Server, a group that can be used in its own domain, servers and workstations of the domain, and trusting domains. In all these places it can be granted rights and permissions and can become a member of local groups. However, it can contain only user accounts from its own domain. Global groups provide a way to create handy sets of users from inside the domain, available for use both in and out of the domain.

Global groups cannot be created or maintained on Window NT Workstation. However, for Windows NT Workstation computers that participate in a domain, domain global groups can be granted rights and permissions at those workstations and can become members of local groups at those workstations. See also *group, local group.*

graphics engine   GDI32.DLL, which is the print component that provides WYSIWYG support across devices. This component sits between the GDI and the DDI, and communicates through the GDI to the application and through the DDI to the printer driver.

group   In User Manager, an account containing other accounts called members. The permissions and rights granted to a group are also provided to its members, making groups a convenient way to grant common capabilities to collections of user accounts. For Windows NT, groups are managed with User Manager. For Windows NT Server, groups are managed with User Manager for Domains. See also *global group, local group, user account.*

group memberships   The groups to which a user account belongs. Permissions and rights granted to a group are also provided to its members. In most cases, the actions a user can perform in Windows NT are determined by the group memberships of the user account the user is logged on to. See also *group.*

H

handle   See *object handle.*

hard links   POSIX applications need certain file-system functionality, such as support for case-sensitive filenames and support for files with multiple names, called *hard links*. The Windows NT file system, NTFS, supports these POSIX requirements.

Hardware Abstraction Layer (HAL)
Virtualizes hardware interfaces, making the hardware dependencies transparent to the rest of the operating system. This allows Windows NT to be portable from one hardware platform to another.

hive A discrete body of keys, subkeys, and values that is rooted at the top of the Registry hierarchy. A hive is backed by a single file and a .LOG file. For example, the hive HKEY_USERS\.DEFAULT maps to the physical file *SystemRoot*\SYSTEM32\CONFIG \DEFAULT. Hives were named by a Windows NT developer as an analogy for the cellular structure of a bee hive.

HKEY_CLASSES_ROOT A predefined Registry handle that defines object linking and embedding (OLE) and file-class association data. This key is a symbolic link to a subkey of HKEY_LOCAL_ MACHINE\SOFTWARE.

HKEY_CURRENT_USER A predefined Registry handle that defines the current user's preferences, including environment variables, personal program groups, desktop settings, network connections, printers, and application preferences. This key maps to a subkey of HKEY_USERS.

HKEY_LOCAL_MACHINE A predefined Registry handle that defines the hardware and operating system characteristics such as bus type, system memory, installed device drives, and boot control data.

HKEY_USERS A predefined Registry handle that defines the default user configuration for users on the local computer and configuration data from user profiles stored on the local computer.

home directory A directory that is accessible to the user and contains files and programs for that user. A home directory can be assigned to an individual user or can be shared by many users.

host table The HOSTS or LMHOST file that contains lists of known IP addresses.

hostname A TCP/IP command that returns the local workstation's *hostname* used for authentication by TCP/IP utilities. This value is the workstation's *computername* by default, but it can be changed by using the Network icon in Control Panel.

hot-fixing A technique HPFS uses to handle write errors.

HPFS The high-performance file system designed for OS/2 version 1.2.

I

impersonation A technique by which Windows NT allows one process to take on the security attributes of another.

import computers In directory replication, the servers or workstations that receive copies of the master set of directories from an export server. See also *directory replication*.

import path In directory replication, the path to which imported subdirectories, and the files in those subdirectories, will be stored on an import computer. See also *directory replication*.

.INI files Initialization files used by Windows-based applications to store per-user information that controls application startup. In Windows NT, such information is stored in the Registry, and the correlation between Registry entries and .INI entries is defined under HKEY_LOCAL_ MACHINE\SOFTWARE\Microsoft\Windows NT \CurrentVersion\IniFileMapping.

integral subsystem A subsystem such as the Security subsystem that affects the entire Windows NT operating system. Contrast *environment subsystems*.

interactive logon The user must type information at the keyboard in response to a dialog box the operating system displays on the screen. Windows NT grants or denies access based upon the information provided by the user. Contrast *remote logon*.

internal command Commands that are stored in the file CMD.EXE and that reside in memory at all times.

internet control message protocol (ICMP) An IP maintenance protocol that supports the IP framework.

interrupt An asynchronous operating condition that disrupts normal execution and transfers control to an interrupt handler. Interrupts are usually initiated by I/O devices requiring service from the processor.

interrupt request lines (IRQ) Hardware lines over which devices can send signals to get the attention of the processor when the device is ready to accept or send information. Typically, each device connected to the computer uses a separate IRQ.

I/O device An input/output device, which is a piece of hardware used for providing information to and receiving information from the computer, for example, a disk drive, which transfers information in one of two directions, depending on the situation. Some input devices such as keyboards can be used only for input, and some output devices such as a printer or a monitor can be used only for output. Most of these devices required installation of device drivers.

I/O request packet (IRP) Data structures that drivers use to communicate with each other.

IP router Describes a system connected to multiple physical TCP/IP networks, capable of routing or delivering IP packets between them. Also called a *gateway*.

IRP See *I/O request packet.*

IRQ See *interrupt request lines.*

K

kernel The portion of Windows NT that manages the processor.

kernel driver A driver that accesses hardware.

Kernel module The core of the Windows NT layered architecture that manages the most basic operations of Windows NT. The Kernel is responsible for thread dispatching, multiprocessor synchronization, hardware exception handling, and the implementation of low-level, hardware-dependent functions.

kernel objects Two types of objects used only by the Kernel: Dispatcher objects, which include events, mutants, mutexes, semaphores, threads, and timers. Dispatcher objects have a signal state (signaled or nonsignaled) and control the dispatching and synchronization of system operations; and Control objects, which include asynchronous procedure calls, interrupts, power notifies, power statuses, processes, and profiles. Control objects are used to control the operation of the Kernel but do not affect dispatching or synchronization.

L

LastKnownGood The control set that is a clean copy of the last control set that actually worked while starting the computer.

lazy commit Similar to *lazy write*. Instead of immediately marking a transaction as successfully completed, the committed information is cached and later written to the file system log as a background process.

lazy write   The ability to record changes in the file structure cache, which is quicker than recording them on disk; later, when demand on the computer's CPU is low, the Cache Manager writes the changes to the disk. See also *lazy commit.*

link   A connection at the LLC layer that is uniquely defined by the adapter's address and the destination service access point (DSAP).

LLC   Logical link control, in the Data Link layer of the networking model.

local account   For Windows NT Server, a user account provided in a domain for a user whose global account is not in a trusted domain. Not required where trust relationships exist between domains. See also *global account, user account.*

local group   1. For Windows NT Workstation, a group that can be granted permissions and rights only for its own workstation. 2. For Windows NT Server, a group that can be granted permissions and rights only for the servers of its own domain. See also *global group, group.*

local printer   A printer that is directly connected to one of the ports on your computer.

Local Security Authority (LSA)   Creates a security access token for each user accessing the system.

locale   The national and cultural environment in which a system or program is running. The locale determines the language used for messages and menus, the sorting order of strings, the keyboard layout, and data and time formatting conventions.

logical drive   A subpartition of an extended partition on a hard disk.

logon authentication   Refers to the validation of a user either locally or in a domain. At logon time, the user specifies his or her name, password, and the intended logon domain. The workstation then contacts the *domain controllers* for the domain, which verify the user's logon credentials.

LSA   See *Local Security Authority.*

M

MAC   Media access control. A layer in the network architecture.

management information base (MIB)
The entire set of objects that any service or protocol uses in SNMP. Because different network-management services are used for different types of devices or for different network-management protocols, each service has its own set of objects.

mandatory user profile   For Windows NT Server, a user profile created by an administrator and assigned to one or more users. A mandatory user profile cannot be changed by the user and remains the same from one logon session to the next. See also *personal user profile, user profile.*

map   To translate one value into another.

MAPI   See *Messaging Application Program Interface.*

Messaging Application Program Interface (MAPI)
A set of calls used to add mail-enabled features to other Windows-based applications.

Messenger service   Sends and receives messages sent by administrators or by the Alerter service. Examples of the Messenger service include print job notification or a message from an administrator that a server will be going down for service shortly.

MIB See *management information base.*

MS-DOS–based application An application that is designed to run with MS-DOS and which therefore may not be able to take full advantage of all Windows NT features.

multihomed workstation A system that has multiple network adapters.

N

named pipe An interprocess communication mechanism that allows one process to send data to another local or remote process.

NBF transport protocol NetBEUI Frame protocol. A descendant of the NetBEUI protocol, which is a Transport layer protocol, not the programming interface NetBIOS.

NDIS See *Network driver interface specification.*

NetBEUI transport NetBIOS (Network Basic Input/Output System) Extended User Interface. The primary local area network transport protocol in Windows NT. See also *NetBIOS interface.*

NetBIOS interface A programming interface that allows I/O requests to be sent to and received from a remote computer. It hides networking hardware from applications.

Netlogon service For Windows NT Server, performs authentication of domain logons and keeps the domain's database synchronized between the domain controller and the other Windows NT Servers of the domain.

Network DDE service The Network DDE (dynamic data exchange) service provides a network transport and security for DDE conversations. The Network DDE DSDM (DDE share database manager) service manages shared DDE conversations.

network device driver Software that coordinates communication between the network adapter card and the computer's hardware and other software, controlling the physical function of the network adapter cards.

network directory See *shared directory.*

network driver interface specification (NDIS) A Windows NT interface for network card drivers that provides transport independence, because all transport drivers call the NDIS interface to access network cards.

network-interface printers Printers with built-in network cards. Network-interface printers need not be adjacent to a print server since they are directly connected to the network.

non-Windows NT application Refers to an application that is designed to run with Windows 3.*x*, MS-DOS, OS/2, or POSIX, but not specifically with Windows NT and that may not be able to take full advantage of all Windows NT features (such as memory management).

nonpaged pool The portion of system memory that cannot be paged to disk. Compare *paged pool.*

NTDETECT.COM The Windows NT Hardware Recognizer program for *x*86-based computers.

NTFS The Windows NT file system.

NTFS (Windows NT file system) An advanced file system designed for use specifically with the Windows NT operating system. NTFS supports file system recovery and extremely large storage media, in addition to other advantages. It also supports object-oriented applications by treating all files as objects with user-defined and system-defined attributes.

O

object 1. A single run-time instance of a Windows NT object type that contains data that can be manipulated only by using a set of services provided for objects of its type. 2. Any piece of information, created by using a Windows-based application with object linking and embedding capabilities, that can be linked or embedded into another document.

object handle Includes access control information and a pointer to the object itself. Before a process can manipulate a Windows NT object, it must first acquire a handle to the object through Object Manager.

object linking and embedding (OLE)
A way to transfer and share information between applications.

object type Includes a system-defined data type, a list of operations that can be performed upon it (such as wait, create, or cancel), and a set of object attributes. Object Manager is the part of the Windows NT Executive that provides uniform rules for retention, naming, and security of objects.

OLE See *object linking and embedding*.

orphan A member of a mirror set or a stripe set with parity that has failed in a severe manner, such as a loss of power or a complete head crash.

P

packet A unit of information transmitted as a whole from one device to another on a network.

page 1. In ClipBook, one complete entry that has been pasted in. 2. In memory, a fixed-size block.

paged pool The portion of system memory that can be paged to disk. Compare *nonpaged pool*.

paging file A system file that contains the contents of virtual pages that have been paged out of memory by the Virtual Memory Manager. Sometimes called a *swap file*.

partition A portion of a physical disk that functions as though it were a physically separate unit. See also *system partition*.

password A unique string of characters that must be provided before a logon or an access is authorized as a security measure used to restrict logons to user accounts and access to computer systems and resources.

permission A rule associated with an object (usually a directory, file, or printer) in order to regulate which users can have access to the object and in what manner. See also *right*.

personal user profile For Windows NT Server, a user profile created by an administrator and assigned to one user. A personal user profile retains changes the user makes to the per-user settings of the Windows NT environment and reimplements the newest settings each time that user logs on at any Windows NT Workstation. See also *mandatory user profile, user profile*.

port A connection or socket used to connect a device to a computer, such as a printer, monitor, or modem. Information is sent from the computer to the device through a cable.

portability Windows NT runs on both CISC and RISC processors. CISC includes computers running with Intel 80386 or higher processors. RISC includes computers with MIPS R4000 or DEC Alpha processors.

POSIX   Portable Operating System Interface for Computing Environments. A set of standards being drafted by the Institute of Electrical and Electronic Engineers (IEEE) that define various aspects of an operating system, including topics such as programming interface, security, networking, and graphical interface.

postoffice   A temporary message store, holding the message until the recipient's workstation retrieves it. The postoffice exists as a directory structure on a server and has no programmatic components.

primary partition   A portion of a physical disk that can be marked for use by an operating system. There can be up to four primary partitions (or up to three, if there is an extended partition) per physical disk. A primary partition cannot be subpartitioned.

print device   Refers to the actual hardware device that produces printed output. See also *printer.*

printer   In Windows NT, refers to the software interface between the application and print device. See also *print device.*

printer driver   A program that controls how your computer and printer interact.

printer fonts   Fonts that are built into your printer. These fonts are usually located in the printer's read-only memory (ROM).

print monitor   Keeps track of printers and print devices. It is the component that receives information from the printer driver via the spooler and sends it on to the printer or destination file. The print monitor tracks physical devices so the spooler doesn't have to.

print processor   A dynamic link library that interprets data types. It receives information from the spooler and sends the interpreted information to the graphics engine.

print provider   A software component that allows the client to print to the print server's device.

protocol   A set of rules and conventions by which two computers pass messages across a network. Networking software usually implements multiple levels of protocols layered one on top of another. Windows NT includes NBT, TCP/IP, DLC, and NWLink protocols. Windows NT Server also includes AppleTalk.

provider   The component that allows a Windows NT computer to communicate with the network. Windows NT includes a provider for the Windows NT network; other provider DLLs are supplied by the alternate networks' vendors.

R

redirector   Networking software that accepts I/O requests for remote files, named pipes, or mailslots and then sends (*redirects*) them to a network service on another computer. Redirectors are implemented as file system drivers in Windows NT.

REG_BINARY   A data type for Registry value entries that designates binary data.

REG_DWORD   A data type for Registry value entries that designates data represented by a number that is 4 bytes long.

REG_EXPAND_SZ   A data type for Registry value entries that designates an expandable string. For example, in the entry *%SystemRoot%\file*.**exe**, the string *%SystemRoot%* will be replaced by the actual location of the directory containing Windows NT system files.

REG_MULTI_SZ   A data type for Registry value entries that designates a multiple string.

REG_SZ   A data type for Registry value entries that designates a data string that usually represents human readable text.

Registry In Windows NT, the database repository for information about the computer's configuration, including the hardware, installed software, environment settings, and other information.

Registry Editor An application provided with Windows NT that allows users to view and edit entries in the Registry.

remote administration Administration of one computer by an administrator located at another computer and connected to the first computer across the network.

remote logon When a user establishes a connection from a remote computer, the access validation performed by a server on which no security access token currently exists for the user. (Security access tokens are otherwise created during interactive logon.) Contrast *interactive logon*.

A process invisible to the user where The user must type information at the keyboard in response to a dialog box the operating system displays on the screen. Windows NT grants or denies access based upon the information provided by the user. Contrast *remote logon*.

Remote Procedure Call (RPC) A message-passing facility that allows a distributed application to call services available on various computers in a network. Used during remote administration of computers. RPC provides a procedural view, rather than a transport-centered view, of networked operations. The RPC subsystem includes the endpoint mapper and other miscellaneous RPC services. See also *RPC Locator Service*.

replication See *directory replication*.

Replicator service See *Directory Replicator service*.

resource Any part of a computer system or a network, such as a disk drive, printer, or memory, that can be allotted to a program or a process while it is running.

right Authorizes a user to perform certain actions on the system. Rights apply to the system as a whole and are different from *permissions*, which apply to specific objects. (Sometimes called a *privilege*.)

RISC-based computer A computer based on a RISC (reduced instruction set) microprocessor, such as a Digital Alpha AXP, MIPS R4000 or Atlas computer. Compare with the *x86-based computer*.

router 1. The printing model component that locates the requested printer and sends information from the workstation spooler to the print server's spooler. 2. TCP/IP gateways—computers with two or more network adapters that are running some type of IP routing software; each adapter is connected to a different physical network.

RPC Remote procedure call. For TCP/IP, RPC provides a mechanism to copy files between two systems unidirectionally.

RPC Locator service The Remote Procedure Call Locator service allows distributed applications to use the RPC Name service. The RPC Locator service manages the RPC Name service database.

The server side of a distributed application registers its availability with the RPC Locator service. The client side of a distributed application queries the RPC Locator service to find available compatible server applications.

RPC transport provider interface A DLL that acts as an interface between the RPC facility and network transport software, allowing RPCs to be sent over various transports.

rules Printable rectangles extracted from the bitmap and sent to the printer as a separate command as supported by Hewlett-Packard LaserJet and compatible printers.

S

SAM See *Security Accounts Manager.*

SAM database The database of security information that includes user account names and passwords and the settings of the security policies. For Windows NT Workstation, it is managed with User Manager. For a Windows NT Server domain, it is managed with User Manager For Domains.

scalability Windows NT is not bound to single-processor architectures but takes full advantage of symmetric multiprocessing hardware.

Schedule service Supports and is required for use of the **at** command, which can schedule commands and programs to run on a computer at a specified time and date.

screen fonts Fonts displayed on your screen. Soft-font manufacturers often provide screen fonts that closely match the soft fonts for your printer. This ensures that your documents look the same on the screen as they do when printed.

security access token Includes a security ID for the user, other security IDs for the groups to which the user belongs, plus other information such as the user's name and the groups to which that user belongs. In addition, every process that runs on behalf of this user will have a copy of his or her access token.

Security Accounts Manager (SAM)
A Windows NT protected subsystem that maintains the SAM database and provokes an API for accessing the database.

security context Controls what access the *subject* has to *objects* or system services. When a program or process runs on the user's behalf, it is said to be running in the security context of that user.

security database See *SAM database.*

security descriptor The security attributes for an object, which include an owner *security ID*, a group security ID, a discretionary *access control list* (ACL), and a system ACL.

security ID (SID) A unique name that identifies a logged-on user to the Windows NT security system. A security ID can identify either an individual user or a group of users.

send window The number of frames that the sender is allowed to send before it must wait for an ACK.

server 1. For a LAN, a computer running administrative software that controls access to all or part of the network and its resources. A computer acting as a server makes resources available to computers acting as workstations on the network. 2. For Windows NT Workstation, refers to a computer that provides shared resources to network users. See also *client.* 3. For Windows NT Server domains, refers to a computer that receives a copy of the domain's security policy and domain database, and authenticates network logons. See also *domain controller.*

Server service A Windows NT service that supplies an API for managing the Windows NT network software. Provides RPC (remote procedure call) support, and file, print, and named pipe sharing.

service A process that performs a specific system function and often provides an application programming interface (API) for other processes to call. Windows NT services are RPC-enabled, meaning that their API routines can be called from remote computers.

service controller The networking component that loads and starts Windows NT services and also loads and unloads many drivers, including device drivers and network transport drivers.

session A connection that two applications on different computers establish, use, and end. The Session layer performs name recognition and the functions needed to allow two applications to communicate over the network.

share To make resources, such as directories, printers, and ClipBook pages, available to network users.

share name The name of a shared resource.

shared directory A directory that network users can connect to.

shared resource Any device, data, or program that is used by more than one other device or program. For Windows NT, shared resources refer to any resource that is made available to network users, such as directories, files, printers, and named pipes.

SID See *Security ID*.

SMB Server message block.

socket Provides an end point to a connection; two sockets form a complete path. A socket works as a bidirectional pipe for incoming and outgoing data between networked computers. The Windows Sockets API is a networking API tailored for use by programmers using the Microsoft Windows family of products.

source directory The directory that contains the file or files you intend to copy or move.

spooler A scheduler for the printing process. It coordinates activity among other components of the print model and schedules all print jobs arriving at the print server.

string A data structure composed of a sequence of characters, usually representing human-readable text.

stubs Nonexecutable placeholders used by calls from the server environment.

subject The combination of the user's access token plus the program acting on the user's behalf. Windows NT uses subjects to track and manage permissions for the programs each user runs. A *simple subject* is a process that was assigned a security context when the corresponding user logged on. A *server subject* is a process implemented as a protected server (such as the Win32 subsystem) and does have other subjects as clients.

Subnet masks Under TCP/IP, 32-bit values that allow the recipient of IP packets to distinguish the network ID portion of the IP address from the host ID.

swap file See *paging file*.

synchronize To replicate the domain database from the domain controller to one server of the domain or to all the servers of a domain. This is usually performed automatically by the system, but can also be invoked manually by an administrator.

synchronous I/O The simplest way to perform I/O, by synchronizing the execution of applications with completion of the I/O operations that they request. When an application performs an I/O operation, the application's processing is blocked. When the I/O operation is complete, the application is allowed to continue processing. See also *asynchronous I/O*.

syntax The order in which you must type a command and the elements that follow the command. Windows NT commands have up to four elements: command name, parameters, switches, and values.

system default profile
For Windows NT Server, the user profile that is loaded when Windows NT is running and no user is logged on. When the Welcome dialog box is visible, the system default profile is loaded. See also *user default profile, user profile*.

system partition The volume that contains the hardware-specific files needed to load Windows NT. See also *partition*.

T

TCP/IP transport Transmission Control Protocol/Internet Protocol. The primary wide area network (WAN) transport protocol used by Windows NT to communicate with systems on TCP/IP networks and to participate in UNIX-based bulletin boards and electronic mail services.

TDI See *Transport Driver Interface*.

Telnet service The service that provides basic terminal emulation to remote systems supporting the Telnet protocol over TCP/IP.

text file A file containing only letters, numbers, and symbols. A text file contains no formatting information, except possibly linefeeds and carriage returns. A text file is an ASCII file.

thread An executable entity that belongs to a single process, comprising a program counter, a user-mode stack, a kernel-mode stack, and a set of register values. All threads in a process have equal access to the processor's address space, object handles, and other resources. In Windows NT, threads are implemented as objects.

thunking The transformation between 16-bit and 32-bit formats, which is carried out by a separate layer in the VDM.

Ti The inactivity timer in a transport protocol.

time-out If a device is not performing a task, the amount of time the computer should wait before detecting it as an error.

time slice The amount of processor time allocated to an application, usually measured in milliseconds.

Transport Driver Interface (TDI) In the networking model, a common interface for network components that communicate at the Session layer.

transport protocol Defines how data should be presented to the next receiving layer in the networking model and packages the data accordingly. It passes data to the network adapter card driver through the *NDIS* Interface, and to the *redirector* through the *Transport Driver Interface*.

trust relationship Trust relationships are links between domains that enable pass-through authentication, in which a user has only one user account in one domain, yet can access the entire network. A trusting domain honors the logon authentications of a trusted domain.

U

UDP See *user datagram protocol*.

UI frames Used by the NBF protocol to establish connections and for connectionless services such as datagrams.

UNC See *uniform naming convention names*.

Unicode A fixed-width, 16-bit character encoding standard capable of representing all of the world's scripts.

uniform naming convention (UNC) names
Filenames or other resource names that begin with the string \\, indicating that they exist on a remote computer.

user account Consists of all the information that defines a user to Windows NT. This includes the user name and password required for the user to log on, the groups in which the user account has membership, and the rights and permissions the user has for using the system and accessing its resources. See also *group*.

user datagram protocol (UDP) A TCP complement that offers a connectionless datagram service that guarantees neither delivery nor correct sequencing of delivered packets (much like IP).

user default profile For Windows NT Server, the user profile that is loaded by a server when a user's assigned profile cannot be accessed for any reason, when a user without an assigned profile logs on to the computer for the first time, or when a user logs on to the Guest account. See also *system default profile, user profile*.

user mode A nonprivileged processor mode in which application code runs.

user profile Configuration information retained on a user-by-user basis. The information includes all the per-user settings of the Windows NT environment, such as the desktop arrangement, personal program groups and the program items in those groups, screen colors, screen savers, network connections, printer connections, mouse settings, window size and position, and more. When a user logs on, the user's profile is loaded, and the user's Windows NT environment is configured according to that profile.

user right See *right*.

username A unique name identifying a user account to Windows NT. An account's username cannot be identical to any other group name or username of its own domain or workstation. See also *user account*.

V

validation Authorization check of a user's logon information. When a user logs on to an account on a Windows NT Workstation computer, the authentication is performed by that workstation. When a user logs on to an account on a Windows NT Server domain, that authentication may be erformed by any server of that domain. See also *trust relationship*.

value entry A parameter under a key or subkey in the Registry. A value entry appears as a string with three components: a name, a type, and the value.

value name The first of three components that make up a Registry value entry.

VDM See *virtual DOS machine*.

virtual DOS machine (VDM) A Windows NT-protected subsystem that supplies a complete MS-DOS environment and a console in which to run an MS-DOS–based application or Windows 16-bit applications. A VDM is a Win32 application that establishes a complete virtual *x*86 (that is, 80386 or higher) computer running MS-DOS. Any number of VDMs can run simultaneously. See also *console.*

virtual memory Space on a hard disk that Windows NT uses as if it were actually memory. Windows NT does this through the use of paging files. The benefit of using virtual memory is that you can run more applications at one time than your system's physical memory would otherwise allow. The drawbacks are the disk space required for the virtual-memory paging file and the decreased execution speed when swapping is required.

virtual printer memory In a PostScript printer, a part of memory that stores font information. The memory in PostScript printers is divided into banded memory and virtual memory. The banded memory contains graphics and page-layout information needed to print your documents. The virtual memory contains any font information that is sent to your printer either when you print a document or when you download fonts.

volume A partition or collection of partitions that have been formatted for use by a file system.

W

wildcard A character that represents one or more characters. The question mark (?) wildcard can be used to represent any single character, and the asterisk (*) wildcard can be used to represent any character or group of characters that might match that position in other filenames.

Win32 API A 32-bit application programming interface for both Windows for MS-DOS and Windows NT. It updates earlier versions of the Windows API with sophisticated operating system capabilities, security, and API routines for displaying text-based applications in a window.

Windows NT The portable, secure, 32-bit, preemptive multitasking member of the Microsoft Windows operating system family.

Windows NT Server A superset of Windows NT, Windows NT Server provides centralized management and security, advanced fault tolerance, and additional connectivity.

Windows on Win32 (WOW) A Windows NT-protected subsystem that runs within a virtual DOS machine (VDM) process. It provides a 16-bit Windows environment capable of running any number of 16-bit Windows applications under Windows NT.

workgroup For Windows NT, a workgroup is a collection of computers running Windows NT and/or Windows for Workgroups that are grouped for browsing and sharing purposes. Each workgroup is identified by a unique name. User accounts maintained on workgroup servers are local to the servers themselves, that is, each server maintains all accounts for users wanting to share its resources. See also *domain.*

workstation In general, a powerful computer having considerable calculating and graphics capability. For Windows NT, computers running the Windows NT Workstation operating system are called workstations, as distinguished from computers running Windows NT Server, which are called servers. See also *server, domain controller.*

Workstation service A Windows NT service that supplies user-mode API routines to manage the Windows NT redirector. Provides network connections and communications.

WOW The subsystem for running Windows for MS-DOS under Windows NT; sometimes also called Win16 on Win32.

x86-based computer A computer using a microprocessor equivalent to an Intel® 80386 or higher chip. Compare with a *RISC-based computer*.

Index

C

D

continued from page ii

NTFS

An inside look at the advanced features not found in any other mainstream file system

INSIDE THE
Windows NT
File System

Microsoft

Helen Custer
AUTHOR OF INSIDE WINDOWS NT

ISBN 1-55615-660-X
104 pages
$9.95 ($12.95 Canada)

NTFS sets a new standard for reliability and speed in PC, workstation, and server file systems. This detailed new book by Helen Custer, critcally acclaimed author of *Inside Windows NT,* includes the first discussion of data compression in Windows NT, describes the file system's internal structure, and explains in detail how NTFS recovers a volume and reconstructs itself after a system failure. Along with clear explanations of how NTFS works, Custer provides detailed information about:

- The NTFS design
- File system recoverability
- Fault-tolerant disk volumes

INSIDE THE WINDOWS NT FILE SYSTEM is a must-read for anyone installing or developing for Microsoft's advanced operating system for workstations and servers.

Microsoft Press® books are available wherever quality books are sold and through CompuServe's Electronic Mall—**GO MSP**. Call **1-800-MSPRESS** for more information or to place a credit card order.* Please refer to **BBK** when placing your order. Prices subject to change.
*In Canada, contact Macmillan Canada, Attn: Microsoft Press Dept., 164 Commander Blvd., Agincourt, Ontario, Canada M1S 3C7, or call 1-800-667-1115. Outside the U.S. and Canada, write to International Coordinator, Microsoft Press, One Microsoft Way, Redmond, WA 98052-6399 or fax +(206) 936-7329.

Your Guide to
Applying the
Security and Audit
Capabilities of
Windows NT™ 3.5

ISBN 1-55615-814-9
304 pages
$49.95 ($67.95 Canada)

**A joint research
project by Citibank
N.A., Coopers & Lybrand,
The Institute of Internal Auditors,
and Microsoft Corporation**

The technology of interconnecting personal workstations, servers, and multiple wide-area networks, although young in comparison with more traditional information systems, is affecting every sector of society. This explosion in technology is not without risks. As organizations and individuals become increasingly reliant on networked information systems, adequate levels of security and control over these systems have become critical concerns. Mission-critical business applications placed on networks need to provide internal controls, security, and auditing capabilities.

This book is designed to help managers, network security specialists, auditors, and users understand the control, security, and audit implications of the Microsoft® Windows NT Server Operating System.

IMPORTANT—READ CAREFULLY BEFORE OPENING SOFTWARE PACKET(S). By opening the sealed packet(s) containing the software, you indicate your acceptance of the following Microsoft License Agreement.

MICROSOFT LICENSE AGREEMENT

(Resource Kit Companion Disks)

This is a legal agreement between you (either an individual or an entity) and Microsoft Corporation. By opening the sealed software packet(s) you are agreeing to be bound by the terms of this agreement. If you do not agree to the terms of this agreement, promptly return the unopened software packet(s) and any accompanying written materials to the place you obtained them for a full refund.

MICROSOFT SOFTWARE LICENSE

1. GRANT OF LICENSE. Microsoft grants to you the right to use copies of the Microsoft software program included with this book (the "SOFTWARE") for your internal use. The SOFTWARE is in "use" on a computer when it is loaded into the temporary memory (i.e., RAM) or installed into the permanent memory (e.g., hard disk, CD-ROM, or other storage device) of that computer.

2. COPYRIGHT. The SOFTWARE is owned by Microsoft or its suppliers and is protected by United States copyright laws and international treaty provisions. Therefore, you must treat the SOFTWARE like any other copyrighted material (e.g., a book or musical recording). You may not copy the written materials accompanying the SOFTWARE.

3. OTHER RESTRICTIONS. You may not rent or lease the SOFTWARE, but you may transfer the SOFTWARE and accompanying written materials on a permanent basis provided you retain no copies and the recipient agrees to the terms of this Agreement. You may not reverse engineer, decompile, or disassemble the SOFTWARE. If the SOFTWARE is an update or has been updated, any transfer must include the most recent update and all prior versions.

DISCLAIMER OF WARRANTY

The SOFTWARE (including instructions for its use) is provided "AS IS" WITHOUT WARRANTY OF ANY KIND. MICROSOFT FURTHER DISCLAIMS ALL IMPLIED WARRANTIES INCLUDING WITHOUT LIMITATION ANY IMPLIED WARRANTIES OF MERCHANTABILITY OR OF FITNESS FOR A PARTICULAR PURPOSE OR AGAINST INFRINGEMENT. THE ENTIRE RISK ARISING OUT OF THE USE OR PERFORMANCE OF THE SOFTWARE AND DOCUMENTATION REMAINS WITH YOU.

IN NO EVENT SHALL MICROSOFT, ITS AUTHORS, OR ANYONE ELSE INVOLVED IN THE CREATION, PRODUCTION, OR DELIVERY OF THE SOFTWARE BE LIABLE FOR ANY DAMAGES WHATSOEVER (INCLUDING, WITHOUT LIMITATION, DAMAGES FOR LOSS OF BUSINESS PROFITS, BUSINESS INTERRUPTION, LOSS OF BUSINESS INFORMATION, OR OTHER PECUNIARY LOSS) ARISING OUT OF THE USE OF OR INABILITY TO USE THE SOFTWARE OR DOCUMENTATION, EVEN IF MICROSOFT HAS BEEN ADVISED OF THE POSSIBILITY OF SUCH DAMAGES. BECAUSE SOME STATES/COUNTRIES DO NOT ALLOW THE EXCLUSION OR LIMITATION OF LIABILITY FOR CONSEQUENTIAL OR INCIDENTAL DAMAGES, THE ABOVE LIMITATION MAY NOT APPLY TO YOU.

U.S. GOVERNMENT RESTRICTED RIGHTS

The SOFTWARE and documentation are provided with RESTRICTED RIGHTS. Use, duplication, or disclosure by the Government is subject to restrictions as set forth in subparagraph (c)(1)(ii) of The Rights in Technical Data and Computer Software clause at DFARS 252.227-7013 or subparagraphs (c)(1) and (2) of the Commercial Computer Software — Restricted Rights 48 CFR 52.227-19, as applicable. Manufacturer is Microsoft Corporation, One Microsoft Way, Redmond, WA 98052-6399.

If you acquired this product in the United States, this Agreement is governed by the laws of the State of Washington.

Should you have any questions concerning this Agreement, or if you desire to contact Microsoft Press for any reason, please write: Microsoft Press, One Microsoft Way, Redmond, WA 98052-6399.